# CHARITIES LEGISLATION & COMMENTARY
## 2006 EDITION
### (FORMERLY CHARITIES LAW)

Maria Elena Hoffstein
Terrance S. Carter
Adam Parachin

Imagine Canada
Give. Volunteer. Engage.
Donner. S'engager. Agir.

LexisNexis®
Butterworths

**2006 Charities Legislation & Commentary**
© LexisNexis Canada Inc. 2005
October 2005

## Members of the LexisNexis Group worldwide

| | |
|---|---|
| **Canada** | LexisNexis Canada Inc, 123 Commerce Valley Dr. E., MARKHAM, Ontario |
| **Argentina** | Abeledo Perrot, Jurisprudencia Argentina and Depalma, BUENOS AIRES |
| **Australia** | Butterworths, a Division of Reed International Books Australia Pty Ltd, CHATSWOOD, New South Wales |
| **Austria** | ARD Betriebsdienst and Verlag Orac, VIENNA |
| **Chile** | Publitecsa and Conosur Ltda, SANTIAGO DE CHILE |
| **Czech Republic** | Orac sro, PRAGUE |
| **France** | Éditions du Juris-Classeur SA, PARIS |
| **Hong Kong** | Butterworths Asia (Hong Kong), HONG KONG |
| **Hungary** | Hvg Orac, BUDAPEST |
| **India** | Butterworths India, NEW DELHI |
| **Ireland** | Butterworths (Ireland) Ltd, DUBLIN |
| **Italy** | Giuffré, MILAN |
| **Malaysia** | Malayan Law Journal Sdn Bhd, KUALA LUMPUR |
| **New Zealand** | Butterworths of New Zealand, WELLINGTON |
| **Poland** | Wydawnictwa Prawnicze PWN, WARSAW |
| **Singapore** | Butterworths Asia, SINGAPORE |
| **South Africa** | Butterworth Publishers (Pty) Ltd, DURBAN |
| **Switzerland** | Stämpfli Verlag AG, BERNE |
| **United Kingdom** | Butterworths Tolley, a Division of Reed Elsevier (UK), LONDON, WC2A |
| **USA** | LexisNexis, DAYTON, Ohio |

**Library and Archives Canada Cataloguing in Publication**

Hoffstein, M. Elena

Charities legislation & commentary / Maria Elena Hoffstein, Terrance S. Carter, Adam Parachin. — 2006 ed.

Originally publ. under title: Charities law.
Includes index.
ISBN 0-433-45154-8

1. Charity laws and legislation—Canada. 2. Nonprofit organizations—Law and legislation —Canada. I. Carter, Terrance S. II. Parachin, Adam III. Title. IV. Title: Charities legislation and commentary.

KE1373.H64 2005          346.71'064'0263          C2005-905855-2
KF1388.H64 2005

Printed and bound in Canada.

# ABOUT THE AUTHORS

Elena Hoffstein, B.A., M.A., LL.B., is a partner of the Toronto law firm Fasken Martineau DuMoulin LLP. Her practice focuses on personal tax and estate planning, family business succession planning, estate administration and estate litigation and charities, including public organizations, private family foundations, hospitals and hospital related organizations and non-profit entities. Elena has been ranked by Lexpert as one of the most frequently recommended Toronto private client practitioners and as one of the leading experts in the area of charity and not for profit law in Canada and as one of the top 500 lawyers in Canada. Ms. Hoffstein is an active member of a variety of professional and community organizations, as well as a frequent speaker and an author of an extensive list of conference articles.

Terrance S. Carter, B.A., LL.B., is a partner of Carter & Associates Professional Corporation, practising in the area of charity and not-for-profit law and is counsel to and affiliated with Fasken Martineau DuMoulin LLP. Mr. Carter is a member of Canada Revenue Agency's Charity Advisory Committee and Technical Issues Committee, past Chair of the National Charity and Not-for-Profit Section of the Canadian Bar Association, a past member of the Uniform Law Conference of Canada Task Force on Uniform Fundraising Legislation. Recognized by Lexpert as one of the leading experts in the area of charity and not-for-profit law in Canada, Mr. Carter is also a frequent writer and speaker on legal issues relating to charities and not-for-profit organizations across Canada and internationally, as well as editor of www.charitylaw.ca.

Adam Parachin, B.A., LL.B., LL.M., is a law professor at the Faculty of Law at the University of Western Ontario. He holds law degrees from both the Osgoode Hall Law School and the University of Toronto. His principal areas of teaching and research include charities, trusts, estates and property. Prior to becoming a law professor, he was an associate in the estates, trusts and charities department of Fasken Martineau DuMoulin LLP.

# GENERAL TABLE OF CONTENTS

# DETAILED TABLE OF CONTENTS

## CANADA CORPORATIONS ACT
### R.S.C. 1970, c. C-32

### PART I
#### COMPANIES WITH SHARE CAPITAL

*Interpretation*

*Preliminaries*

*Formation of New Companies*

*General Powers and Duties of Companies*

*Change of Provisions of Letters Patent*

*Contracts, etc.*

*Head Office*

*Name of Company*

*Forfeiture of Charter*

*Surrender of Charter*

*Transfer of Shares*

*Borrowing Powers*

*Information as to Mortgages and Charges*

*Directors*

## *Meetings of Shareholders*

## *Books*

## *Accounts and Audit*

## *Evidence*

## *Procedure*

## *Offences and Penalties*

# PART III
## INSIDER TRADING

# PART IV
## PROXIES AND PROXY SOLICITATION

# PART V
## TAKE-OVER BIDS

# PART VI
## PRESCRIBED FEE

# CANADA-UNITED STATES TAX CONVENTION ACT, 1984
### S.C. 1984, c. 20

### Schedule I

# CHARITIES REGISTRATION
# (SECURITY INFORMATION) ACT
### S.C. 2001, c. 41, s. 113

### SHORT TITLE

### PURPOSE AND PRINCIPLES

### INTERPRETATION

### CERTIFICATE BASED ON INTELLIGENCE

### JUDICIAL CONSIDERATION OF CERTIFICATE

### REVIEW OF CERTIFICATE

# CIVIL MARRIAGE ACT
## S.C. 2005, C. 33
### PREAMBLE

# CRIMINAL CODE
## R.S.C. 1985, c. C-46

## PART II.1
### TERRORISM

*Interpretation*

*Financing of Terrorism*

*List of Entities*

*Freezing of Property*

*Seizure and Restraint of Property*

*Forfeiture of Property*

## PART IX
### OFFENCES AGAINST RIGHTS OF PROPERTY

# CULTURAL PROPERTY EXPORT AND IMPORT ACT
### R.S.C. 1985, c. C-51

#### SHORT TITLE

#### INTERPRETATION

#### HER MAJESTY

#### CANADIAN CULTURAL PROPERTY EXPORT CONTROL LIST

#### PERMIT OFFICERS

#### EXPERT EXAMINERS

#### EXPORT PERMITS

## GENERAL PERMITS

## REVIEW BOARD

### *Review Board Established*

### *Duties*

### *Head Office and Sittings*

### *Advisers*

### *Administration*

### *Rules and Procedure*

### *Review of Applications for Export Permits*

### *Determination Relating to Income Tax Matters*

### *Income Tax Certificate*

### *Appeals Before the Tax Court of Canada*

## CANADIAN CULTURAL PROPERTY EXPORT CONTROL LIST
### C.R.C., c. 448

# GROUP I
## OBJECTS RECOVERED FROM THE SOIL OR WATERS OF CANADA

# GROUP II
## OBJECTS OF ETHNOGRAPHIC MATERIAL CULTURE

# GROUP III
## MILITARY OBJECTS

# GROUP IV
## OBJECTS OF APPLIED AND DECORATIVE ART

# GROUP V
## OBJECTS OF FINE ART

# GROUP VI
## SCIENTIFIC OR TECHNOLOGICAL OBJECTS

# GROUP VII
## TEXTUAL RECORDS, GRAPHIC RECORDS AND SOUND RECORDINGS

### TEXTUAL RECORDS

### GRAPHIC RECORDS

## SOUND RECORDINGS

## GROUP VIII
## MUSICAL INSTRUMENTS

# CULTURAL PROPERTY EXPORT REGULATIONS
## C.R.C., c. 449

# INCOME TAX ACT
## R.S.C. 1985, c. 1 (5th Supp.)

## PART I
### INCOME TAX

### DIVISION B, SUBDIVISION C
### TAXABLE CAPITAL GAINS AND ALLOWABLE CAPITAL LOSSES

### DIVISION B, SUBDIVISION F
### RULES RELATING TO COMPUTATION OF INCOME

### DIVISION B, SUBDIVISION H
### CORPORATIONS RESIDENT IN CANADA AND THEIR SHAREHOLDERS

### DIVISION C
### COMPUTATION OF TAXABLE INCOME

### DIVISION E, SUBDIVISION A
### RULES APPLICABLE TO INDIVIDUALS

### DIVISION F
### DEFERRED AND OTHER SPECIAL INCOME ARRANGEMENTS

### DIVISION H
### EXEMPTIONS

## DIVISION I
## RETURNS, ASSESSMENTS, PAYMENT AND APPEALS

### *Returns*

## REVOCATION OF REGISTRATION OF
## CERTAIN ORGANIZATIONS AND ASSOCIATIONS

## DIVISION J
## APPEALS TO THE TAX COURT OF CANADA AND THE FEDERAL COURT

## PART I.3
### TAX ON LARGE CORPORATIONS

## PART V
### TAX IN RESPECT OF REGISTERED CHARITIES

## PART XI.2
### TAX IN RESPECT OF DISPOSITIONS OF CERTAIN PROPERTIES

## PART XII.2
### TAX ON DESGNATED INCOME OF CERTAIN TRUSTS

# PART XIII
## TAX ON INCOME FROM CANADA OF NON-RESIDENT PERSONS

# PART XIV
## ADDITIONAL TAX ON NON-RESIDENT CORPORATIONS

# PART XV
## ADMINISTRATION AND ENFORCEMENT

### *General*

### *Offences and Punishment*

# PART XVII
## INTERPRETATION

# INCOME TAX REGULATIONS
## C.R.C., c. 945

# PART II
## INFORMATION RETURNS

# PART XXXV
## RECEIPTS FOR DONATIONS AND GIFTS

# PART XXXVII
## CHARITABLE FOUNDATIONS

# GENERAL
## O. Reg. 282/98

### PART IV — EXEMPT CONSERVATION LAND

### PART VII — DISPUTES RELATING TO CONSERVATION LAND

# CHARITABLE GIFTS ACT
## R.S.O. 1990, c. C.8

# CHARITIES ACCOUNTING ACT
## R.S.O. 1990, c. C.10

## APPROVED ACTS OF EXECUTORS AND TRUSTEES
### O. Reg. 4/01

## CORPORATIONS ACT
### R.S.O. 1990, c. C.38

## PART I
### CORPORATIONS, INCORPORATION AND NAME

## PART II
### COMPANIES

## PART III
### CORPORATIONS WITHOUT SHARE CAPITAL

## PART VI
### WINDING UP

# PART VII
## CORPORATIONS, GENERAL

# GENERAL
## R.R.O. Reg. 181

# CORPORATIONS TAX ACT
## R.S.O. 1990, c. C.40

## PART I
### GENERAL

*Liability for Taxes*

## PART II
### INCOME TAX

### DIVISION C — COMPUTATION OF TAXABLE INCOME

### DIVISION F — SPECIAL RULES APPLICABLE IN CERTAIN CIRCUMSTANCES

### DIVISION G — EXEMPTIONS

## PART II.1
### CORPORATE MINIMUM TAX

### DIVISION D — COMPUTATION OF CAPITAL TAX PAYABLE

## PART V
### RETURNS, PAYMENTS, ASSESSMENTS AND APPEALS

### DIVISION A — RETURNS

# SMALL BUSINESS INVESTMENT TAX CREDIT FOR BANKS
### O. Reg. 318/97

## PART II
### INVESTMENTS THROUGH A SMALL BUSINESS INVESTMENT FUND

# DONATION OF FOOD ACT, 1994
### S.O. 1994, CHAPTER 19

# EDUCATION ACT
### R.S.O. 1990, C. E.2

## PART IX — FINANCE
### DIVISION A — GENERAL

# TAX RELIEF IN UNORGANIZED TERRITORY FOR 2001 AND SUBSEQUENT YEARS
### O. Reg. 3/02

## PART I — INTERPRETATION

## PART IV — REBATES TO CHARITIES — COMMERCIAL AND INDUSTRIAL PROPERTY CLASSES

## PART V — GROSS LEASES

# ESTATES ACT
**R.S.O. 1990, c. E. 21**

# HOSPITALS AND CHARITABLE INSTITUTIONS INQUIRIES ACT
**R.S.O. 1990, c. H.15**

# INCOME TAX ACT
**R.S.O. 1990, c. I.2**

## PART I — INTERPRETATION

## PART II — INCOME TAX
### DIVISION A — LIABILITY FOR TAX

### DIVISION B   COMPUTATION OF TAX

### DIVISION C.1 — TAX OVERPAYMENTS

### DIVISION D — RETURNS, ASSESSMENTS, PAYMENT AND APPEALS

# LAND TRANSFER TAX ACT
**R.S.O. 1990, c. L.6**

## EXEMPTION(S) — FOR CERTAIN LIFE LEASE INTERESTS
### O. Reg. 88/04

## EXEMPTION — HOSPITAL RESTRUCTURING
### O. Reg. 676/98

## MINISTRY OF COMMUNITY AND SOCIAL SERVICES ACT
### R.S.O. 1990, c. M.20

## CONTROL OF ORGANIZATION BY MINISTER
### O. Reg. 191/04

## MUNICIPAL ACT, 2001
### S.O. 2001, c. 25

## PERPETUITIES ACT, 2001
### R.S.O. 1990, c. P.9

## PROVINCIAL LAND TAX ACT
### R.S.O. 1990, c. P.32

*Liability to Tax, Exemptions*

*Pipe Lines*

*Regulations*

## PUBLIC GUARDIAN AND TRUSTEE ACT
### R.S.O. 1990, c. P.51

## RELIGIOUS ORGANIZATIONS' LANDS ACT
### R.S.O. 1990, c. R.23

## RETAIL SALES TAX ACT
### R.S.O. 1990, c. r.31

### DEFINITIONS, EXEMPTIONS AND REBATES
### R.R.O. 1990, Reg. 1012

### GENERAL
### R.R.O. 1990, Reg. 1013

# SUBSTITUTE DECISIONS ACT, 1992
## S.O. 1992, c. 30

## PART 1 – PROPERTY
*Property Management*

# TRUSTEE ACT
## R.S.O. 1990, c. T.23

### RETIREMENT OF TRUSTEES

### APPOINTMENT OF NEW TRUSTEES

### VESTING INSTRUMENTS

### VESTING ORDERS, ORDERS RELEASING CONTINGENT RIGHTS, ETC.

### TRUSTEES FOR CHARITIES

### WHO MAY APPLY

## CERTAIN POWERS AND RIGHTS OF TRUSTEES

## POWER TO AUTHORIZE RECEIPT OF MONEY

## INVESTMENTS

## TECHNICAL BREACHES OF TRUST

## PAYMENT INTO COURT

## PERSONAL REPRESENTATIVES AND DEVISEES IN TRUST

## RIGHTS AND LIABILITIES OF PERSONAL REPRESENTATIVES
### Actions for torts

# UNIVERSITY FOUNDATIONS ACT, 1992
## S.O. 1992, c. 22

# GENERAL
## O. Reg. 731/93

# PENDING LEGISLATIVE CHANGES

**Note:** The legislation reproduced in this consolidation is current to the *Canada Gazette* Part I, Vol. 139, No. 38, (September 17, 2005), the *Canada Gazette* Part II, Vol. 139, No. 19, (September 21, 2005), and the *Ontario Gazette*, Vol. 138, No. 38, (September 17, 2005). However, some changes to legislation were pending as this consolidation went to print and are summarized below.

## BILL S-37

### An Act to amend the Criminal Code and the Cultural Property Export and Import Act

(Passed by the Senate July 18, 2005)

CULTURAL PROPERTY EXPORT AND IMPORT ACT

**4. The Cultural Property Export and Import Act is amended by adding the following after section 36:**

CONVENTION FOR THE PROTECTION OF CULTURAL
PROPERTY IN THE EVENT OF ARMED CONFLICT
AND ITS PROTOCOLS

**36.1** (1) **Definitions** — The following definitions apply in this section.

"Convention" means the Convention for the Protection of Cultural Property in the Event of Armed Conflict, done at The Hague on May 14, 1954. Article 1 of the Convention is set out in the schedule.

"First Protocol" means the first protocol, done at The Hague on May 14, 1954, to the Convention.

"Second Protocol" means the second protocol, done at The Hague on March 26, 1999, to the Convention.

"State Party" means a state that is a party to the Convention and the First or Second Protocol.

(2) **Export or removal of cultural property** — No person shall knowingly export or otherwise remove cultural property as defined in subparagraph (a) of Article 1 of the Convention from an occupied territory of a State Party to the Second Protocol, unless the export or removal conforms with the applicable laws of that territory or is necessary for the property's protection or preservation.

(3) **Offence outside Canada deemed in Canada** — Despite anything in this Act or any other Act, a person who commits an act or omission outside Canada that if committed in Canada would constitute an offence under subsection (2), or a conspiracy or an attempt to commit such an offence, or being an accessory after

the fact or counselling in relation to such an offence, is deemed to have committed that act or omission in Canada if the person

(a) is a Canadian citizen;

(b) is not a citizen of any state and ordinarily resides in Canada; or

(c) is a permanent resident within the meaning of subsection 2(1) of the Immigration and Refugee Protection Act and is, after the commission of the act or omission, present in Canada.

(4) **Action for recovery of cultural property** — If the government of a State Party submits a request in writing to the Minister for the recovery and return of any cultural property that has been exported from an occupied territory of that State Party and that is in Canada in the possession of or under the control of any person, institution or public authority, the Attorney General of Canada may institute an action in the Federal Court or in a superior court of a province for the recovery of the property by the State Party.

(5) **Notice** — Notice of the commencement of an action under this section on behalf of a State Party shall be served by the Attorney General of Canada on such persons and given in such manner as is provided by the rules of the court in which the action is taken, or, if the rules do not so provide, served on such persons and given in such manner as is directed by a judge of the court.

(6) **Order for recovery of cultural property** — The court in which an action has been taken under this section may, after affording all persons that it considers to have an interest in the action a reasonable opportunity to be heard, make an order for the recovery of the property in respect of which the action has been taken or any other order sufficient to ensure the return of the property to the State Party, if the court is satisfied that the property was exported in contravention of the applicable laws of the occupied territory of the State Party or was imported into Canada for its protection or preservation and that the amount fixed under subsection (7), if any, has been paid.

(7) **Compensation** — The court in which an action has been taken under this section may fix any amount that it considers just in the circumstances to be paid as compensation by the State Party to a person, institution or public authority that establishes to the satisfaction of the court that the person, institution or public authority is a bona fide purchaser for value or has a valid title to the property in respect of which the action has been taken and had no knowledge at the time the property was purchased or the title to the property was acquired that the property

(a) had been exported in contravention of the applicable laws of the occupied territory of the State Party; or

(b) had been imported into Canada for its protection or preservation.

(8) **Safe-keeping** — The court may, at any time in the course of an action under this section, order that the property in respect of which the action has been taken be turned over to the Minister for safe-keeping and conservation pending final disposition of the action.

(9) **Permit to export** — The Minister shall, on receipt of a copy of a court order made under subsection (6), issue a permit authorizing any person authorized

by the State Party on behalf of which the action was taken to export the property in respect of which the order was made to that State.

(10) **Limitations inapplicable** — Section 39 of the Federal Courts Act does not apply in respect of any action taken under this section.

**5. The portion of subsection 45(1) of the Act before paragraph (a) is replaced by the following:**

45. (1) **Offences and punishment** — Every person who contravenes any of the provisions of subsection 36.1(2) and sections 40 to 44 is guilty of an offence and liable

**6. The Act is amended by adding, after section 52, the schedule set out in the schedule to this Act.**

SCHEDULE
(Section 6)


SCHEDULE
(Subsection 36.1(1))


ARTICLE 1 OF THE CONVENTION FOR THE PROTECTION
OF CULTURAL PROPERTY IN THE EVENT OF ARMED
CONFLICT DONE AT THE HAGUE ON MAY 14, 1954


ARTICLE 1


DEFINITION OF CULTURAL PROPERTY

For the purposes of the present Convention, the term "cultural property" shall cover, irrespective of origin or ownership:

(a)  movable or immovable property of great importance to the cultural heritage of every people, such as monuments of architecture, art or history, whether religious or secular; archaeological sites; groups of buildings which, as a whole, are of historical or artistic interest; works of art; manuscripts, books and other objects of artistic, historical or archaeological interest; as well as scientific collections and important collections of books or archives or of reproductions of the property defined above;

(b)  buildings whose main and effective purpose is to preserve or exhibit the movable cultural property defined in subparagraph (a) such as museums, large libraries and depositories of archives, and refuges intended to shelter, in the event of armed conflict, the movable cultural property defined in subparagraph (a);

(c)  centres containing a large amount of cultural property as defined in subparagraphs (a) and (b), to be known as "centres containing monuments".

# COMMENTARY

The purpose of this consolidation is to assist those undertaking research in the area of charity law. Anyone who has undertaken research in this field can attest to the fact that the statutory regime governing charities consists of numerous, complex and, in some cases, unexpected legislative requirements. There is no single statute that sets out all of the legislative requirements applicable to charities. The statutory provisions applicable to charities are instead set out in multiple federal and provincial statutes. To further complicate matters, the statutory rules governing charities have in recent years proven susceptible to ongoing revision. Indeed, since the time of the first edition of this consolidation, the legislative provisions applicable to charities have undergone significant change. The consequence is that an applicable statute or legislative amendment can all too easily be overlooked.

Having regard to this complicated legislative context, this consolidation aims to facilitate charity law research by setting out excerpts from or the entire text of the key Federal and Ontario statutes that apply to charities. A brief description of the statutes included in this consolidation is set out below. Before proceeding, though, we offer the following observations.

Not *every* statutory provision applicable to charities is included in this consolidation. We have excluded statutes that deal with highly specialized subject matters, those that are only tangentially related to charities or those that are otherwise unlikely to arise with recurrence in charity law research. A brief description of some of the statutes that have been omitted appears below.

At the time of writing, the law of charity, is in some key respects, in a state of transition. Since the time of the first edition of this consolidation, a number of relevant legislative amendments have been proposed and enacted into law. Other amendments have been proposed, but at the time of writing have yet to be enacted into law.[1] Still other amendments, namely, proposed amendments to the Income Tax Act (Canada), have yet to be enacted into law, but nevertheless are being administered by government regulators as though they were enacted into law.[2] This consolidation includes all of these amendments. To avoid confusion, we note in the description below and in the body of the text the status of relevant legislative amendments.

## Federal Statutes:

### *Income Tax Act*, R.S.C. 1985, c. 1 (5th Supplement), as amended.

There are two key tax advantages under the *Income Tax Act (Canada)* for an institution to obtain the status of a "registered charity". First, registered charities are generally exempt from tax under the *Income Tax Act (Canada)*. Second, registered

---

[1]  Bill C-21, *Canada Not-For-Profit Corporations Act.*
[2]  Legislative Proposals Relating to Income Tax, July 2005. See Technical News No. 26 published by the Canada Revenue Agency.

charities are allowed to issue to donors official donation receipts, which entitle donors to tax relief under the *Income Tax Act (Canada)*. The excerpts from the *Income Tax Act (Canada)* included in this consolidation generally relate to these two issues. In particular, these excerpts set out the various requirements that must be complied with in order for charities to both obtain and maintain registered status and also set out the rules applicable to the tax consequences of charitable donations. The excerpts can be generally categorized as follows:

| **Select Provisions of the *Income Tax Act (Canada)*** | **General Description** |
|---|---|
| **Tax Exemptions for Registered Charities** | |
| Paragraph 149(1)(f) <br><br> Paragraph 181.1(3)(c) <br><br> Paragraph 210.1(c)[3] <br><br> Subsection 212(14) <br><br> Paragraph 219(2)(c) | Paragraph 149(1)(f) exempts registered charities from Part 1 tax. Paragraph 181.1(3)(c) exempts registered charities from Part I.3 tax. Paragraph 210.1(c) exempts registered charities from Part XII.2 tax. Subsection 212(14) allows for the issuance of certificates of exemption to non-resident charities, which exempts from Part XIII tax interest income described in paragraph 212(1)(b)(iv). Paragraph 219(2)(c) exempts registered charities from Part XIV tax. Due to either practical or technical considerations, registered charities are also generally exempt from tax levied under those Parts of the Act that do not contain an express exempting provision. |
| **General Requirements for Charitable Registration** | |
| Section 149.1 <br><br> Regulations 3500 – 3502 <br><br> Regulations 3700 – 3702 | Section 149.1 sets out the key rules applicable to charitable registration. These include rules applicable to the: <br><br> • designation of registered charities as charitable organizations, public foundations and private foundations; <br><br> • disbursement quota requirements of registered charities; |

---

[3]  Proposed amendments to the *Income Tax Act (Canada)* released July, 2005 provide for the repeal of para. 210.1(c) and the re-enactment of this paragraph in proposed new para. 210(2)(c).

| **General Requirements for Charitable Registration** | |
|---|---|
| | • permissible expenditures of registered charities; <br><br> • restrictions on activities such as political activities and business activities; and <br><br> • grounds for revocation of charitable registration. <br><br> Regulations 3500-3502 set out rules applicable to proper gift receipting practices of registered charities. <br><br> Regulations 3700-3702 provide for rules relevant to calculating the disbursement quota obligations of charitable foundations. |
| **Loss or Denial of Charitable Registration** | |
| Subsections 149.1(2), (3), (4) & (4.1) <br><br> Section 168 <br><br> Section 172 | The grounds for revocation of charitable registration are set out in subsections 149.1(2), (3), (4) and (4.1). Sections 168 and 172 establish the procedural rules in this regard. In particular, section 168 establishes the procedure by which charitable registration may be revoked and section 172 establishes the procedure by which the revocation or denial of registered charity status may be appealed. |
| **Special Taxes and Penalties in Respect of Registered Charities** | |
| Section 163.2 <br><br> Part V (Sections 187.7, 188, 188.1, 188.2 & 189)[4] <br><br> Part XI.2 (Sections 207.3, 207.31 & 207.4) | These sections establish special taxes and penalties in respect of registered charities. Section 163.2 provides for penalties that could apply in relation to certain charitable fundraising schemes. Subsections 188(1)-(2.1) provide for a revocation tax applicable where a charity's registration is revoked. Subsections 188(3)-(5) provide for a |

---

[4] Sections 188.1 and 188.2 derive from the proposed amendments to the *Income Tax Act (Canada)* released in July, 2005, which, at the time of writing, have yet to be enacted into law.

## Special Taxes and Penalties in Respect of Registered Charities

|  | transfer of property tax applicable to certain inter-charity transfers. Subsections 188.1(1)-(2) provide for a penalty for carrying on an impermissible business. Subsection 188.1(3) provides for a penalty where a charitable foun-dation acquires control of a corporation. Subsections 188.1(4)-(5) provide for a penalty for conferring an "undue benefit". Subsection 188.1(6) provides for a penalty for failure to file a return as required under paragraph 149.1(14). Paragraphs 188.1(7)-(10) provide for a penalty where a charity issues an improper gift receipt. Subsection 188.1(11) provides for a penalty for participating in a gifting scheme to delay expenditures of amounts on charitable activities. Section 188.2 provides for the suspension of receipting privileges where certain penalties under section 188.1 apply. Subsections 189(1)-(5) provide for a tax regarding non-qualified investments of private foundations. Subsections 189(6.2)-(6.3) indicate how charities are to satisfy, respectively, revocation tax liability / penalties. Sections 207.3 and 207.31 provide for a tax applicable in certain circumstances where a charity disposes of, respectively, a culturally significant object or an ecological gift. Section 207.4 provides for a filing obligation applicable where sections 207.3 or 207.31 apply. |
|---|---|

## Obtaining Information Relating to Registered Charities

| Subsections 241(1), (3.2) & (4)(f.1) | These provisions allow government regulators to release certain information relating to registered charities to certain persons. |
|---|---|

| Miscellaneous Provisions Applicable to Registered Charities | |
|---|---|
| Paragraph 150(1.1)(a)<br>Regulation 204(3)(c)<br>Subsection 230(2)<br>Subsection 248(1) | Paragraph 150(1.1)(a) exempts charitable corporations from the obligation of corporations to file returns pursuant to paragraph 150(1)(a). Regulation 204(3)(c) exempts charities from the requirement to file returns as provided for in Regulation 204(1). Subsection 230(2) sets out the requirement for registered charities to keep certain records. Subsection 248(1) provides definitions for "private foundation", "public foundation", "qualified donee" and "registered charity". |
| **Capital Gains Arising from Charitable Donations** | |
| Subsections 38(a),(a.1) & (a.2)<br>Regulation 6210<br>Subparagraph 39(1)(a)(i.1)<br>Subsection 46(5)<br>Subsection 69(1)<br>Subsection 40(1.01) & Paragraph 72(1)(c) | Subsections 38(a) and 69(1) provide the basic rules regarding capital gains arising from charitable donations. Subsections 38(a.1) and (a.2) modify the basic rules for, respectively, donations of certain types of securities (see Regulation 6210) and donations of ecological property to charity. Subparagraph 39(1)(a)(i.1) and subsection 46(5) provide special rules for, respectively, donations of culturally significant objects and arrangements such as "art flips". Subsection 40(1.01) and paragraph 72(1)(c) provide special rules re capital gains arising from the donation of "non-qualifying securities" |
| **General Provisions Regarding Charitable Donations** | |
| Section 110.1<br>Section 118.1<br>Subsections 248(30)-(38)[5]<br>Regulation 3503<br>Schedule VIII of Regulations | These provisions provide the tax advantages for charitable donations. Section 110.1 provides for a charitable tax deduction for corporations and section 118.1 provides for a charitable tax credit for individuals. Subsections 248(30)-(38) set out the rules for calculating the "eligible amount" of a donation — the amount for which a |

[5] These subsections derive from the proposed amendments to the *Income Tax Act (Canada)* released in July, 2005, which at the time of writing, have yet to be enacted into law.

| **General Provisions Regarding Charitable Donations** | |
|---|---|
| | receipt may be issued. Regulation 3503 and Schedule VIII to the Regulations enumerate the foreign universities to which receiptable charitable donations may be made. |

| **Special Provisions Regarding Charitable Donations** | |
|---|---|
| Subsection 43(2) | These provisions provide special rules applicable to certain charitable donations. Subsection 43(2) applies to ecological gifts. Also, subsections 169(1.1) & 171(1.1) are relevant to the valuation of gifts of ecological property. Section 43.1 applies to gifts of remainder interests in real estate. Paragraphs 87(2)(m.1) and 88(1)(e.2) apply to gifts of "non-qualifying securities" in the context of, respectively, an amalgamation and winding-up. Paragraph 67.1(2)(b) provides for a special rule regarding the deductibility of meal expenses incurred for a charitable fund-raising event. Paragraph 87(2)(v) applies to a gift to charity by a corporation that subsequently amalgamates. Paragraphs 88(1)(e.6) & 88(1)(e.61) apply to gifts made by a corporation that subsequently winds up. Paragraph 110(1)(d.01) applies to gifts of stock options to charity. Subsection 110(2.1) provides for special rules for the donation of the proceeds of disposition of stock options. Subsection 110(2) provides special rules for donations made to religious orders by members of such orders who have taken vows of perpetual poverty. Section 143 provides special rules for donations made by "congregations". Paragraph 152(6)(c) allows for the amendment of a tax return to reflect charitable donations. Section 217 enables a non-resident person to elect to pay tax under Part I instead of Part XIII and to thereby utilize the tax benefits of |
| Subsections 169(1.1) & 171(1.1) | |
| Section 43.1 | |
| Paragraphs 87(2)(m.1) & 88(1)(e.2) | |
| Paragraph 67.1(2)(b) | |
| Paragraphs 87(2)(v), 88(1)(e.6) & 88(1)(e.61) | |
| Paragraph 110(1)(d.01) | |
| Subsections 110(2) & (2.1) | |
| Section 143 | |
| Section 143.2 | |
| Paragraph 152(6)(c) | |
| Section 217 | |
| Section 237.1 / 237.2 | |

| Special Provisions Regarding Charitable Donations | |
|---|---|
| | donations to registered charities. Sections 143.2, 237.1 and 237.2 provide for special rules for gifting arrangements that constitute "tax shelters". |

The reader is encouraged to also consult the various interpretation bulletins, information circulars, advance tax rulings, technical interpretations and guides that elaborate on these provisions. Certain of these documents are available at the charities page of the Canada Revenue Agency web site <http://www.cra-arc.gc.ca/tax/charities/menu-e.html>.

The reader should be aware that on December 20, 2002 a number of proposed amendments to the provisions of the *Income Tax Act (Canada)* that are relevant to registered charities were released. These amendments were revised and re-released in July, 2005. As of the date of writing, these proposed amendments have not been enacted into law. Nevertheless, certain of these amendments are presently being applied by the Canada Revenue Agency.[6] In this regard, the reader is encouraged to consult Technical News No. 26, published by the Canada Revenue Agency, for an explanation of the current administrative practices in relation to the proposed amendments.

By way of summary, there are four key respects in which the proposed amendments impact registered charities.

First, amendments pertaining to the circumstances in which a donor will be entitled to a charitable gift receipt have been proposed. Previously, a donor was not entitled to a charitable gift receipt if the donor received any consideration for the "gift". Also, it was previously the case that charitable gift receipts were required to be issued for the full fair market value of the donated property or not at all. The proposed amendments allow for a practice known as "split-receipting". In particular, under the proposed amendments, a donor is entitled to a charitable gift receipt even if an "advantage" is received as a result of making a gift to charity. The amount of the gift receipt is the "eligible amount", *i.e.*, the fair market value of the property donated minus the value of the "advantage". A number of technical amendments are required to give effect to this proposed amendment.

Second, amendments to the definitions of "charitable organization" and "public foundation" in subsection 149.1(1) have been proposed. There has historically been a limit on the amount of a charity's capital that may have been contributed by one person or a group of persons not dealing at arm's length with one another in order for it to qualify as either a "charitable organization" or a "public foundation". The limit for a "charitable organization" has been 50 per cent and for a "public foundation" it has been either 50 per cent or 75 per cent depending upon

---

[6] See *Richert v. Stewards' Charitable Foundation*, [2005] B.C.J. No. 279 (S.C.) for a judicial acknowledgement of this administrative practice.

when the foundation was registered.[7] Under the proposed amendments, large capital contributions from a single person or group of persons not dealing at arm's length with one another will not preclude an entity from qualifying as a "charitable organization" or a "public foundation", provided that such person or persons do not control the charity.

Third, the creation of an additional basis upon which charitable registration may be revoked under subsections 149.1(2) to (4) has been proposed. Under the proposed amendments, charitable registration may be revoked where a registered charity transfers property to a person or entity other than a "qualified donee", except where the transfer is in the course of the charity carrying on charitable activities. We understand that this proposed amendment is intended, at least in part, to remedy ambiguity under the *Income Tax Act (Canada)* regarding whether a charitable foundation may disburse property to an entity that, although charitable at common law, does not constitute a "qualified donee". If enacted this proposed amendment will bring the wording of the *Income Tax Act (Canada)* into conformity with the administrative position of the Canada Revenue Agency to the effect that such transfers are not permitted.[8]

Fourth, the proposed amendments alter the scope of the "gifting arrangements" that are caught by the definition of "tax shelter" set out in subsection 237.1(1). Upon this proposed amendment being enacted, taxpayers who donate to registered charities via such charitable gifting arrangements could have the value of the resultant charitable gift receipt significantly reduced.

*Canada-United States Tax Convention Act, 1984 — Article XXI*, S.C. 1984, c. 20.

Article XXI of the *Canada-United States Tax Convention Act, 1984* deals with a variety of cross-border tax issues applicable to donations to charities in Canada and the U.S. In particular, Article XXI sets out the circumstances in which the U.S. source income of a Canadian charity will be exempt from tax in the U.S. and vice versa. Article XXI also provides rules regarding the extent to which a U.S. donor will be entitled to tax relief in respect of donations to a Canadian charity and vice versa.

*Canada Corporations Act*, R.S.C. 1970, c. C-32.

A charity may take on a variety of legal forms, such as, for example, a corporation, an unincorporated association or a trust. A charity organized as a corporation may be incorporated under the federal or a provincial incorporating statute. The *Canada Corporations Act* is the federal incorporating statute. The *Canada Corporations Act* establishes the basic corporate framework for a federally incorporated charity. Since most incorporated charities are structured as non-share capital corporations, the excerpts from the *Canada Corporations Act* included in this consolidation are those relevant to this corporate structure. The reader is encouraged to also consider the Not for Profit Policy Summary published by Industry Canada

---

[7]   See the current definitions of "charitable organization" and "public foundation" in subs. 149.1(1).

[8]   See *Registered Charities Newsletter* (CCRA: Newsletter No. 9, Spring 2000).

for a practical discussion of certain of the requirements for a federally incorporated charity. A link to this policy summary is available from the Industry Canada homepage at <http://strategis.ic.gc.ca/engdoc/main.html>.

The federal government has proposed successor legislation to the *Canada Corporations Act*. At the time of writing, the successor legislation, Bill C-21, the *Canada Not-For-Profit Corporations Act*, is in draft form. Given that it is currently in the early legislative stages, we have not included the proposed, successor legislation in this consolidation. We nevertheless make the following observations regarding the current draft of the proposed new legislation with a view to giving the reader a general sense of the direction that the law may take in the near future.

### Transitional Provisions

If Bill C-21 is passed, all corporations that are currently governed by Part II of the *Canada Corporations Act* will be required to apply for a certificate of continuance under the new legislative regime. If an existing corporation fails to take this step within three years after the coming into force of Bill C-21, it may be subject to dissolution.

### Incorporation:

Bill C-21 proposes the replacement of the current system of federal incorporation — the discretionary "letters patent" system — with the faster and more efficient system of incorporation "as of right". In addition, it is proposed that three individuals will no longer be required to establish a new incorporation. Instead, one or more individuals or corporations will be able to incorporate a corporation by sending signed articles of incorporation and other specified documents to the "Director", a new position created by Bill C-21 the scope of which is to exercise regulatory powers under the new legislation and to act as a public registrar of corporations.

### Capacity and Powers of the Corporation:

Bill C-21 provides not-for-profit corporations with the capacity, rights, powers and privileges of natural persons. It does not require the passage of by-laws in order to confer any power on a corporation or its directors. Corporations will still be precluded, though, from carrying on activities or exercising powers in a manner contrary to their mission as articulated in their articles.

### Financial Accountability and Disclosure:

Bill C-21 imposes additional financial disclosure obligations on corporations by requiring that they make financial statements available to members on request. Incorporated charities that constitute "soliciting corporations", which generally will include charities that engage in fundraising activities, will also be required to file their financial statements with the Director who will make them available to the public. Different levels of financial accountability will be imposed on different corporations depending upon variables such as annual revenue.

Administrative Obligations:

Bill C-21 requires all corporations to file annual returns, keep registered offices and maintain corporate records for specified periods of time. The required records will include registers of directors, officers and members, debt obligations, minutes of members meetings, accounting records and corporate documents such as articles and by-laws.

Directors:

Bill C-21 introduces a number of important changes in relation to the directors of not-for-profit corporations. These changes bring the duties and responsibilities of such directors more in line with those of their for-profit counterparts. The proposed changes include the following.

There will be greater flexibility in the composition of boards and in the meetings of directors. Soliciting corporations will be required to have at least three directors whereas non-soliciting corporations need only have one director. There is also provision for directors' written resolutions in lieu of holding meetings, a flexible and rotating board and a maximum term of three years.

With respect to the duties of directors, under the current legislative regime, the standard of care to which directors are subject is determined by a fluctuating common law. By contrast, Bill C-21 specifically sets out express duties. These include the duty to act honestly and in good faith with a view to the best interests of the corporation, the duty to exercise the care, diligence and skill that a reasonably prudent person would exercise in comparable circumstances, the duty to comply with the new legislation and any governing corporate documents; the duty to manage or supervise the management of the activities and affairs of the corporation; and the duty to disclose all conflicts of interest.

With respect to defences available to directors, the current legislative regime does not explicitly provide directors facing liability claims with any defences. Bill C-21, though, specifically provides a due diligence defence available to directors who have exercised the care, diligence and skill that a reasonably prudent person would have demonstrated in comparable circumstances. Under Bill C-21, due diligence includes reliance in good faith on the reports of professionals and on financial statements. Bill C-21 also allows corporations in some circumstances to indemnify directors and to maintain insurance for the benefit of directors.

With respect to statutory liabilities, Bill C-21 provides that directors can be liable to employees of the corporation for up to six months' wages. In addition, directors may be liable where they have authorized, permitted or acquiesced to an offence committed by the corporation.

Members:

Bill C-21 expands the rights of members. For example, unlike the current legislative regime, members are given the right to requisition directors to call members meetings. In addition, Bill C-21 explicitly addresses matters relating to members meetings such as the conduct of electronic meetings, voting in absentia and the replacement of meetings by written resolution of members.

With respect to the issues dealt with at members meetings, Bill C-21 provides that members are able to submit notice of a proposal that they wish to raise at members meetings and the corporation, subject to certain exceptions, will be required to include the proposal in the notice of the meeting.

With respect to the control of members over the affairs of the corporation, Bill C-21 provides for "unanimous member agreements". This mechanism allows members in limited circumstances to restrict the powers of the directors to manage or supervise the management of the corporation.

With respect to member remedies, Bill C-21 makes available to members derivative actions and the oppression remedy. In short, the derivative action can be used by members to commence actions in the name of the corporation and the oppression remedy allows members to bring claims seeking relief from the oppression of their rights. Courts are given wide latitude to order remedies when satisfied of the merits of a derivative or oppression action. A faith-based defence, though, is made available for religious non-profit organizations.

### Changes to the Corporation:

Bill C-21 outlines specific circumstances in which special resolutions of members — two-thirds vote — are required to make "fundamental changes" to the corporation. This includes altering the conditions and rights of membership, the number of required directors and/or the distribution of assets upon dissolution. There are also detailed provisions dealing with circumstances in which a corporation wishes to amalgamate with one or more other corporations, liquidate, dissolve or be continued under the laws of another jurisdiction.

In short, Bill C-21 introduces profound changes to the federal law pertaining to not-for-profit corporations. The reader is encouraged to monitor the status of Bill C-21 so as to ensure compliance with its provisions if and when it is enacted into law.

*Civil Marriage Act*, S.C. 2005, c. 33.

The *Civil Marriage Act* extended the institution of marriage to include same-sex relationships. The statute contains provisions that were intended to put to rest concerns that charities whose activities and purposes reflect the traditional view of marriage would be considered discriminatory at law and possibly thus non-charitable. The statute declares that no benefit shall be deprived from any person or organization under any law of the Parliament of Canada due to the exercise or expression of the view that marriage is restricted to heterosexual relationships. In addition, the statute enacted an amendment to the *Income Tax Act (Canada)* — new subsection 149.1(6.21) — that expressly provides that the charitable registration of institutions organized for the advancement of religion shall not be revoked due solely to the exercise of freedom of conscience in relation to this issue.

*Criminal Code*, R.S.C. 1985, c. C-46.

As is true of other entities, charities are required to conduct their affairs within the bounds of criminal law. The *Criminal Code* is therefore of general application to charities. There are, however, specific *Criminal Code* provisions of which charities should be aware. Section 336, for example, provides that it is a criminal breach of trust for the trustee of a charitable purpose trust to convert, with the intent to defraud, the property of the trust to a use not authorized under the trust. The maximum penalty for this offence is 14 years in prison.

Also, the *Criminal Code* contains provisions dealing with gambling that are fundamental to the regime of statutes and regulations that regulate charitable gaming. These provisions, while not included in this consolidation, are discussed below.

In addition, in response to the events of September 11, 2001, Parliament enacted a variety of legislative measures to combat terrorism, including the *Anti-Terrorism Act*, S.C. 2001, c. 41. Many aspects of the *Anti-Terrorism Act* impact charities. Among these is the creation of Part II.1 of the *Criminal Code*.

In short, Part II.1 of the *Criminal Code* criminalizes the direct or indirect participation in and facilitation of terrorist activities and terrorist groups. While the provisions of Part II.1 of the *Criminal Code* have not been drafted to apply exclusively to charities, the potential application of these provisions should nevertheless be of concern to charities. This is especially true for charities that fund activities overseas. The wording of Part II.1 of the *Criminal Code* is very broad and the consequences of running afoul of these provisions are severe, including the forfeiture of charitable property and the loss of charitable registration under the *Charities Registration (Security Information) Act* (discussed below). It is therefore important for charities to be advised of the potential effect of Part II.1 of the *Criminal Code* so that appropriate due diligence measures may be established.

*Charities Registration (Security Information) Act*, S.C. 2001, c. 41.

The new *Charities Registration (Security Information) Act* was created by the *Anti-Terrorism Act*. The *Charities Registration (Security Information) Act* is intended to provide a means to ensure that charities do not directly or indirectly fund terrorist activities. In particular, the *Charities Registration (Security Information) Act* provides a two-step process whereby a registered charity or an applicant for registered charity status may, respectively, be de-registered or denied charitable registration for supporting terrorist activities.

The first step of the process is for the Solicitor General of Canada or the Minister of National Revenue to sign a certificate stating that there are reasonable grounds to believe that the registered charity or applicant for registered charity status has made or will make resources available for terrorist activities. The second step is for the certificate to be referred to the Federal Court for a determination of whether the certificate is reasonable. A determination by the Federal Court that the certificate is reasonable is deemed to be conclusive proof that the registered charity has ceased to comply with the requirements for registered charity status or that the applicant is ineligible for such status. A notable aspect of the *Charities Registration (Security Information) Act* is that the registered charity or applicant in respect of whom a certificate has been issued may not be entitled to examine copies of the intelligence reports on which the certificate is based and may not be entitled to be present during the entire hearing before the Federal Court.

*Cultural Property Export and Import Act*, R.S.C. 1985, Chap. C-51.

The *Cultural Property Export and Import Act*, as it relates to charities, must be read in conjunction with certain provisions of the *Income Tax Act (Canada)*. There are provisions in the *Income Tax Act (Canada)* that are intended to encourage the donation of culturally significant objects to designated institutions. In particular, the *Income Tax Act (Canada)* provides that the donation of culturally significant objects to designated institutions will not result in the donor realizing a capital gain in respect of such objects (see sub-paragraph 39(1)(a)(i.1) of the *Income Tax Act (Canada)*) and further provides for a donation limit of 100 per cent of the donors' income with a five year carry-forward in respect of such donations (see paragraph (c) of the definition of "total gifts" in sub-paragraph 118.1(1) for individual donors and sub-paragraph 110.1(1) for corporate donors). The *Cultural Property Export and Import Act* establishes the procedure by which an institution, such as, for example, a charity, may be designated as a designated institution, an object may be designated a culturally significant object and the fair market value of such an object may be determined.

## Ontario Statutes:

*Accumulations Act*, R.S.O. 1990, c. A.5.

The *Accumulations Act* provides that no disposition of any property (real or personal) may direct the accumulation of income derived from such property for any longer than the applicable accumulations period. There are six possible accumulations periods enumerated in subsection 1(1). The statute should be consulted any time property is held in trust on terms that provide for the capitalization of income derived from the property. Where the terms of a trust provide for the accumulation of income beyond the applicable accumulations period, subsection 1(6) of the *Accumulations Act* directs how such income is to be distributed.

*Assessment Act*, R.S.O. 1990, c. A.31.

Although the key tax benefits associated with charitable status relate to income tax, there are additional tax benefits. The *Assessment Act*, for example, provides for a limited exemption from real property tax. Two key observations may be made in relation to excerpts from the *Assessment Act* included in this consolidation. First, the default rule under the *Assessment Act* is that all real property in Ontario is subject to real property tax.[9] Thus, although the *Assessment Act* sets out exemptions from real

---

[9]     Subsection 3(1). Note, though, that the *Assessment Act* does not establish a complete regime for the taxation of all real property situate in Ontario. For real property situate in territories of Ontario without municipal organization, resort must be had to the *Provincial Land Tax Act*, R.S.O. 1990, c. P. 32 (discussed below).

property tax, the bias of the statute is towards its application.[10] Second, the *Assessment Act* does not contain a blanket exemption from real property tax for lands held or occupied by charities. Instead, the *Assessment Act* enumerates specific examples of charities that are exempt from real property tax. This marks a critical divergence from the approach adopted in the provincial income tax statutes, which generally rely upon the conferral of charitable status under the *Income Tax Act (Canada)* as a means of identifying the institutions that should be similarly benefited under provincial income tax law. The result is that an institution may qualify as "charitable" at common law and under federal and provincial income tax law, but nevertheless fail to qualify for exemption from real property tax under the *Assessment Act*. The excerpts and regulations that have been included relate generally to identifying when and to what extent an exemption from real property tax under the *Assessment Act* will apply.

*Charities Accounting Act*, R.S.O. 1990, c. C. 10.

The *Charities Accounting Act* serves two main purposes. First, the *Charities Accounting Act* vests in the Ontario Public Guardian and Trustee (the "PGT") a supervisory jurisdiction over charities in Ontario. Second, the *Charities Accounting Act* establishes certain legal requirements applicable to charities in Ontario.

With respect to the supervisory jurisdiction of the PGT, the *Charities Accounting Act* vests in the PGT a variety of powers in relation to charities. By way of example, this includes the power to investigate certain complaints brought against charities, to consent to certain matters that would otherwise require the consent of a court, to require a passing of accounts and to advise the Attorney General to enact regulations under the *Charities Accounting Act*. The web site for the PGT may be found at <http://www.attorneygeneral.jus.gov.on.ca/english/family/pgt/>.

With respect to establishing legal requirements applicable to charities, notable provisions of the *Charities Accounting Act* include the restriction on the ability of charities to hold land for any purpose other than the actual use of the land for charitable purposes, the express recognition that the prudent investor provisions of the *Trustee Act* (discussed below) apply to incorporated charities and certain notice requirements where property is being held by an executor or trustee for charitable purposes.

*Charitable Gifts Act*, R.S.O. 1990, c. C. 8.

The *Charitable Gifts Act* places restrictions on the business and investment activities of charities. In particular, the *Charitable Gifts Act* prohibits most charities in Ontario from owning more than a ten per cent interest in any business. A charity with an interest in a business in excess of ten per cent is required to dispose of the excess portion of the interest within seven years, or such longer period as may be determined by a court, of having acquired the interest. Upon the disposition of

---

[10] The general rule set out in subsection 3(1) of the *Assessment Act* is that, subject to specifically enumerated exemptions, "[a]ll real property in Ontario is liable to assessment and taxation".

such an interest in a business, a charity may invest the proceeds of disposition only in investments authorized by the *Insurance Act*, R.S.O. 1990, c. I.8.

During the permissible "hold period", a charity holding more than a 50% interest in a business is required to determine jointly with the business and the PGT the profits of the business. The charity's share of these profits are required under the *Charitable Gifts Act* to be paid to the charity rather than retained in the business.

The penalty for contravening the *Charitable Gifts Act* is a $10,000 fine and/or imprisonment for up to one year.

*Corporations Act*, R.S.O. 1990, c. C. 38.

The *Corporations Act* is the provincial analogue to the *Canada Corporations Act*. As such, the *Corporations Act* establishes the basic corporate framework for charities incorporated under Ontario law. Since most incorporated charities are structured as non-share capital corporations, the excerpts from the *Corporations Act* included in this consolidation are those relevant to this corporate structure. The reader is encouraged to also consider the *Not-For-Profit Incorporator's Handbook* (Toronto: Queen's Printer for Ontario) prepared jointly by the Companies Branch of the Ministry of Consumer and Commercial Relations and the PGT.

*Corporations Tax Act*, R.S.O. 1990, c. C.40.

The *Corporations Tax Act* provides the legislative framework for the taxation of corporations in Ontario. The statute extends under Ontario corporate tax law important charitable tax benefits afforded to corporations under the *Income Tax Act (Canada)*. In particular, section 57, paragraph 57.11(a) and paragraph 71(1)1 of the Ontario *Corporations Tax Act* exempt incorporated registered charities under the *Income Tax Act (Canada)* from, respectively, income tax, corporate minimum tax and capital tax in Ontario. Also, section 34 of the *Corporations Tax Act* contains provisions allowing corporations to deduct for Ontario corporate tax purposes charitable gifts for which receipts have been issued as contemplated by section 110.1 of the *Income Tax Act (Canada)*. The provisions of the Ontario *Corporations Tax Act* that have been included in this consolidation generally relate to these two issues.

*Donation of Food Act, 1994*, S.O. 1994, c. 19.

The *Donation of Food Act, 1994* protects donors of food and distributors of donated food from liability resulting from injuries or death caused by the consumption of donated food. The exclusion of liability generally applies except where the donated or distributed food was unfit for human consumption and the donor or distributor acted with reckless disregard or with the intent to injure or cause death. The *Donation of Food Act, 1994* does not protect persons who distribute donated food on a for profit basis.

*Education Act*, R.S.O. 1990, c. E.2.

Section 257.2.1 of the *Education Act* authorizes the Minister of Finance to enact regulations providing in certain circumstances for a rebate of property taxes relating to school purposes. The section applies only in relation to land situate in territories without municipal organization.[11] Regulation 3/02 enacted pursuant to the *Education Act* provides for the circumstances in which such a tax rebate will be available to charities.[12]

*Estates Act*, R.S.O. 1990, c. E.21.

Subsection 49(8) of the *Estates Act* provides that every executor, administrator or trustee shall provide notice to the Public Trustee where the executor, administrator or trustee receives under a will or other written instrument property to be applied for a charitable purpose.

*Hospitals and Charitable Institutions Inquiries Act*, R.S.O. 1990, c. H. 15.

The *Hospitals and Charitable Institutions Inquiries Act* grants the Lieutenant Governor in Council the broad discretion to cause an inquiry to be made in any matter affecting a hospital, sanatorium, charitable institution or other organization granted public aid by the Ontario Legislature.

*Income Tax Act*, R.S.O. 1990, c. I.2.

The Ontario *Income Tax Act* is restricted in its application to "individuals", which is defined in subsection 1(1) to generally mean natural persons and certain trusts. The statute extends under Ontario income tax law important charitable tax benefits afforded to "individuals" under the *Income Tax Act (Canada)*. In particular, section 6 of the Ontario *Income Tax Act* provides that individuals exempt from federal income tax by virtue of subsection 149(1) of the *Income Tax Act (Canada)* are also exempt from provincial income tax under the Ontario *Income Tax Act*. In effect, this section exempts unincorporated registered charities from provincial income tax.[13] In addition, subsection 4(3.1) of the Ontario *Income Tax Act* entitles individuals, subject to certain limitations, to deduct the charitable tax credit provided for in subsection 118.1(3) of the *Income Tax Act (Canada)* from the income tax otherwise payable under provincial income tax law. The provisions of the Ontario *Income Tax Act* that have been included in this consolidation generally relate to these two issues.

*Land Transfer Tax Act*, R.S.O. 1990, c. L. 6.

The *Land Transfer Tax Act* provides for a tax that is triggered by a conveyance of land. Charities do not enjoy a blanket exemption from land transfer tax. Section 1.1 of the *Land Transfer Tax Act* explicitly states that exempt status under any other statute does not automatically result in an exemption from land transfer tax. Nevertheless, a charity will in some circumstances be able to avail itself of an

---

[11] See the discussion below of the *Municipal Act, 2001*, S.O. 2001, c. 25, for similar provisions relating to property situate in territories with municipal organization.
[12] Section 8 of Regulation 509/98, which we have omitted, contains similar provisions that are restricted in their application to taxation years 1998, 1999 and 2000.
[13] Note that para. 149(1)(f) of the *Income Tax Act (Canada)* exempts "registered charities" from tax payable under Part 1 of the *Income Tax Act (Canada)*.

exemption. Subsection 2(1) of the *Land Transfer Tax Act*, for example, provides that land transfer tax is calculated on the basis of the "value of the consideration for the conveyance". Therefore, no land transfer tax is payable where land is transferred to a charity for no consideration. Also, regulations passed pursuant to the *Land Transfer Tax Act* exempt from land transfer tax the conveyances of "life lease interests" to charities[14] and conveyances taking place in the course of the restructuring of certain hospitals.[15]

*Ministry of Community and Social Services Act*, R.S.O. 1990, c. M.20.

The *Ministry of Community and Social Services Act* authorizes in subsection 13(1) the Lieutenant Governor in Council to make regulations designating a charity to be subject to the control and management of the Minister of Community and Social Services. The circumstances in which such regulations may be enacted include circumstances in which those persons managing the charity so request and circumstances in which the Lieutenant Governor in Council determines that doing so is necessary to ensure the proper application of publicly donated funds or is within the best interests of those relying upon the charity's services.

*Municipal Act, 2001*, S.O. 2001, c. 25.

Section 361 of the *Municipal Act, 2001* requires every municipality to have a real property tax rebate program for registered charities that occupy properties situate in territories with municipal organization that are designated in the "commercial" or "industrial" class. The excerpts included elaborate on the program requirements and the extent of the tax rebate available.

*Perpetuities Act*, R.S.O. 1990, c. P.9.

The *Perpetuities Act* sets out various statutory rules pertaining to the doctrine of law known as the "rule against perpetuities". This doctrine can be especially difficult to apply,[16] but the essence of the rule may be stated simply enough. The rule against perpetuities has been said to consist of two key elements.[17] The first is a prohibition against perpetual trusts.[18] The second is a requirement that "contingent interests"[19] must "vest" within a period of time known as the "perpetuities period", which is the period terminating on the 21st anniversary of the date of death of a

---

[14]    O. Reg. 88/04. See also Tax Bulletin LTT 1-2004, "Exemption for Certain Transfers of Life Lease Interests under the *Land Transfer Tax Act*" (April 2004).

[15]    O. Reg. 676/98.

[16]    By way of illustration, a U.S. decision, *Lucas v. Hamm*, 364 P.2d 685 (Cal.S.C. 1961), held that a lawyer was not professionally negligent for misunderstanding the doctrine.

[17]    See, for example, D. Waters, M. Gillen and L. Smith, *Waters' Law of Trusts in Canada*, 3rd ed. (Carswell: Toronto, 2005) at pp. 645 to 656.

[18]    This aspect of the rule has been described as the "rule against inalienability". See *ibid* at p. 646.

[19]    An interest in property will be contingent if it has yet to vest in a person. This could be for any number of reasons. The person may, for example, have yet to satisfy a condition precedent in respect of the property. Alternatively, the identity of the person may as yet be unknown.

life "in being".[20] Charities are exempt from the first aspect of the rule. There are, however, circumstances in which the second aspect of the rule may apply to charities, although the precise scope of such circumstances appears to be as yet unresolved.

Although the rule against perpetuities originated as a judge made rule, it has been legislatively codified, albeit in a modified form, in several jurisdictions of Canada, including in Ontario via the *Perpetuities Act*. A critical change effected by the enactment of the *Perpetuities Act* was the adoption of the "wait and see" approach to applying the rule against remoteness of vesting. Initially, a contingent interest was held to be invalid if there was a possibility, however remote, that it might vest beyond the perpetuity period. In contrast, subsection 4(1) of the *Perpetuities Act* now provides that the mere possibility of vesting beyond the perpetuities period will not invalidate a contingent interest in property. In effect, we "wait and see" whether the interest will vest within the perpetuities period. Another critical reform was the adoption under the *Perpetuities Act* of an attenuated perpetuities period for interests subject to "conditions subsequent" and "determinable limitations". Subsection 15(3) of the statute provides that the perpetuities period for such interests cannot exceed 40 years. The potential application of the statute should be considered whenever a charity holds a contingent interest in property.

*Provincial Land Tax Act*, R.S.O. 1990, c. P. 32.

The *Provincial Land Tax Act* should be read together with the *Assessment Act*, since both statutes provide for the taxation of real property situate in Ontario. The *Provincial Land Tax Act* is the relevant statute for land situate in territories of Ontario without municipal organization. It contains a limited exemption from real property tax that is similar (although not identical) to that provided under the *Assessment Act*. In short, the *Provincial Land Tax Act* provides a limited exemption from real property tax for specifically enumerated charities rather than a blanket exemption for all land held or occupied by charities. As with the *Assessment Act*, it is therefore possible for an institution to qualify as "charitable" at law, but nevertheless fail to qualify for exemption from real property tax under the *Provincial Land Tax Act*. The excerpts that have been included relate generally to identifying when and to what extent an exemption from real property tax under the *Provincial Land Tax Act* will apply.[21]

*Public Guardian and Trustee Act*, R.S.O. 1990, c. P.51.

Section 12 of the *Public Guardian and Trustee Act* specifically authorizes the Public Guardian and Trustee to administer charitable trusts.

---

[20] This aspect of the rule has been described as the "rule against remoteness of vesting". See D. Waters, M. Gillen and L. Smith, *Waters' Law of Trusts in Canada*, 3rd ed. (Carswell: Toronto, 2005) at p. 645.

[21] Paragraph 38(1)(b) of the *Provincial Land Tax Act* authorizes the Lieutenant Governor in Council to make regulations declaring classes of land to be exempt from real property tax. At the date of writing, there are no such regulations of specific relevance to charities.

*Religious Organizations' Lands Act*, R.S.O. 1990, c. R. 23.

The *Religious Organizations' Lands Act* serves two broad purposes. First, the Act provides a mechanism by which an unincorporated "religious organization" may own land. In particular, the Act provides that land can be held by a religious organization through "trustees" appointed by the religious organization for that purpose. The Act vests in the trustees a variety of powers that are coincident to the ownership of land, such as, for example, the power to conduct actions with respect to, mortgage, purchase and alienate land. The trustees may exercise the powers granted to them under the statute, however, only where they are so authorized by a resolution of the religious organization.

Second, the Act provides a limited exception to the restrictions set out in the *Charities Accounting Act*, discussed above, on holding land. In particular, the Act provides that an unincorporated religious organization that holds land that it is not using for a religious purpose may lease out such land for up to a forty year period. Otherwise, the land must be used for a religious purpose, as defined in the Act, or must be sold.

*Retail Sales Tax Act*, R.S.O. 1990, c. R. 31.

The *Retail Sales Tax Act* provides for a tax applicable where a "purchaser" acquires certain property or services. The tax is generally calculated as a percentage of the "fair value" of the property or service acquired. There is no blanket exemption for charities. Section 1.1 of the *Retail Sales Tax Act* explicitly states that exempt status under any other statute does not automatically result in an exemption from retail sales tax. Nevertheless, a charity will in some circumstances be able to avail itself of an exemption or rebate. The excerpts and regulations that have been included relate generally to identifying when and to what extent an exemption or rebate will apply.

*Substitute Decisions Act, 1992*, S.O. 1992, c. 30.

The *Substitute Decisions Act, 1992* provides a statutory regime to regulate substitute decision making in Ontario. Of particular interest to charities is the fact that section 37 of the *Substitute Decisions Act, 1992* explicitly empowers a substitute decision maker to make charitable gifts out of the property of an incapable person subject to the various requirements enumerated therein.

*Trustee Act*, R.S.O. 1990, c. T.23.

The *Trustee Act* is a statute of general application to trustees. It contains provisions that deal with issues such as the retirement and appointment of trustees, the powers and rights of trustees and the investments of trust property made by trustees.

While there is no doubt that the *Trustee Act* applies to charities, the law is presently not clear regarding the extent to which this is the case. In this regard, it is useful to note that a charity may take on a variety of legal forms, such as, for example, a charitable trust and a charitable corporation. Charitable trusts are, not surprisingly, generally subject to the *Trustee Act*. Charitable corporations, however, are not *per se* subject to the *Trustee Act* in all circumstances.

Determining whether a charitable corporation is subject to the *Trustee Act* in any given circumstance is a complicated issue. It will suffice for the purposes of this consolidation to note the following with respect to this issue.

First, the issue of whether the *Trustee Act* applies to a charitable corporation will often times reflect the particular activity of the charity that is in question. For example, recent amendments to the *Charities Accounting Act* (discussed above) have made it clear that a charitable corporation constitutes a trustee for the purposes of the investment provisions of the *Trustee Act*. Sections 27 to 31 of the *Trustee Act* therefore apply to the investment activities of charitable corporations. In this regard, the reader should be aware that the *Trustee Act* allows trustees to invest in any form of property in which a prudent investor may invest and specifically authorizes trustees to invest in mutual funds.[22] The *Trustee Act* also allows trustees to delegate investment responsibilities to an agent in limited circumstances.

Second, the issue of whether the *Trustee Act* applies to a charitable corporation may also reflect the particular asset of the charity that is in question. In this regard, it is necessary to delineate between the assets of a charitable corporation that are held for specific charitable purposes and those that are held generally for the charitable objects of the corporation.[23] It is in relation to the first category of assets that a charitable corporation may in some circumstances be considered to be a "trustee".

Third, even though it may not be said without qualification that directors of charitable corporations are for all purposes "trustees", it is clear that they are subject to trustee-like duties. Therefore, to the extent that the *Trustee Act* illuminates the general nature of these duties, it is of relevance to charitable corporations.

*University Foundations Act, 1992*, S.O. 1992, c. 22.

The *University Foundations Act, 1992* establishes a parallel foundation for each of the major post-secondary institutions in Ontario. The Act provides for the basic structure of each foundation, including the legal form (i.e., non-share capital corporation), objects, board composition, quorum requirements, fiscal year, indemnification of directors, etc. Of particular interest is the fact that the Minister of Colleges and Universities is given the power under the Act to issue "policy directives" in respect of a particular foundation. The board of a foundation in respect of which any such policy directives have been issued is required to implement them "promptly".

---

[22] Prior to the *Trustee Act* being amended to allow for investments by trustees in mutual funds, such investments were considered to constitute an impermissible delegation to mutual fund managers of trustees' investment responsibilities. See *Haslam v. Haslam* (1994), 3 E.T.R. (2d) 206 (Ont. Gen. Div.).

[23] See *Christian Brothers of Ireland in Canada (Re)*, [1998] O.J. No. 823, 37 O.R. (3d) 367 (Gen. Div.), varied [2000] O.J. No. 1117, 47 O.R. (3d) 674 (C.A.); leave to appeal dismissed [2000] S.C.C.A. No. 277 (S.C.C.).

## Omitted Statutes:

The statutes included in this consolidation generally include the main statutes that are applicable to charities. Not every statute that may be applicable to charities has been included. The statutes that have been omitted include the following:

*Athletics Control Act*, R.S.O. 1990, c. A. 34.

Subsection 5(1) of the *Athletics Control Act* provides that every person conducting a professional boxing or wrestling contest or exhibition must pay a tax calculated as a percentage (between 1 per cent and 5 per cent) of the gross receipts derived therefrom. Subsection 5(3) of the statute affords the Minister discretion to alter the amount payable where he or she is satisfied that the entire proceeds of the contest or exhibition will be applied for charitable purposes.

*Cemeteries Act (Revised)*, R.S.O. 1990, c. C.4.

A cemetery may in some circumstances qualify as charitable at law. Such a cemetery must comply not only with the various requirements of general application to charities but also those of special application to cemeteries. In Ontario, the latter statutory requirements are set out in the *Cemeteries Act (Revised)*, which provides a detailed regime for the licensing and operating of a cemetery or crematorium.

*Competition Act*, R.S.C. 1985, c. C-34.

The *Competition Act* is a federal statute, the purpose of which is to encourage competition and to prohibit unfair business practices. The *Competition Act* was recently amended so that the term "business" is now defined to include the "raising of funds for charitable or other non-profit purposes". The *Competition Act* therefore currently provides for a variety of rules that regulate the fundraising activities of charities. This includes rules that regulate telemarketing, promotional contests, lotteries and the making of representations to the public. In addition, any charity carrying on a business activity will be required to comply with the *Competition Act* regarding the manner in which the business activity is carried out. For more information regarding the *Competition Act*, including the Bulletins and Guidelines published by the Competition Bureau, the reader is encouraged to visit <http://www.competitionbureau.gc.ca>.

*Conservation Land Act*, R.S.O. 1990, c. C.28.

The *Conservation Land Act* contains various provisions that enhance the capacity of "conservation bodies" to encourage and support responsible, environmental stewardship. The statute is of interest to charities inasmuch as subsection 3(1) defines "conservation body" to include registered charities designated as charitable foundations under the *Income Tax Act (Canada)*.[24]

---

[24]    See also s. 1 of the *Conservation Land Act*, O.R. 293/03, which prescribes all registered charities created by statute to be conservation bodies.

*Crown Foundations Act, 1996*, S.O. 1996, c. 22.

The *Crown Foundations Act, 1996* allows the Lieutenant Governor in Council to establish by order foundations for the purpose of benefiting one or more "institutions". The statute defines institutions to include certain categories of charities, including public hospitals, the Royal Ontario Museum and various other cultural organizations. The statute provides for the objects, powers and various other matters pertaining to the governance of such foundations.

*Employer Health Tax Act*, R.S.O. 1990, c. E.11.

Every "employer" in Ontario is subject to employer health tax pursuant to the *Employer Health Tax Act*. The tax is calculated as a percentage of the "total Ontario remuneration" paid by an employer. There is no blanket exemption for charities. Subsection 2(4) of the *Employer Health Tax Act* explicitly states that exempt status under any other statute does not automatically result in an exemption from employer health tax. Nevertheless, a charity will in some circumstances be able to avail itself of a reduction of employer health tax. Section 5 of Regulation 319 passed pursuant to the *Employer Health Tax Act* provides for relief from employer health tax for employers who are registered charities under the *Income Tax Act (Canada)* and who employ persons who work outside of Canada for a continuous period of at least 183 days.

*Excise Tax Act*, R.S.C. 1985, c. E-15.

Part IX of the *Excise Tax Act* (Canada) (the "ETA") contains the rules relating to the application of the goods and services tax ("GST"). The GST applies to charities in a very different manner than it applies to most other organizations. Accordingly, there are numerous special rules and exemptions that apply to charities.

One of the main differences between charities and other organizations is that most of the goods and services supplied by charities are exempt from the application of GST. Therefore, as a general rule, charities do not need to charge and collect GST on property or services they provide. Further, charities are generally not required to register under the ETA for GST purposes. Unlike commercial entities, however, charities generally are not entitled to recover the GST that they pay on their expenses. A charity's ability to recover the GST that it incurs is instead limited to special rebates that range from 50 to 83 percent, depending upon the charity and its activities.

However, not all goods and services supplied by charities are necessarily exempt from GST. For example, any charity making GST taxable supplies is generally required to register for GST purposes if its GST taxable revenues exceed $50,000.

As well, charities that have registered for GST (whether voluntarily or otherwise) are required to account for it in a different manner than other organizations. Charities are required to use a special calculation known as the "Net Tax Calculation for Charities" when making the required calculations to complete their tax returns.

Finally, the ETA distinguishes between charities that are hospital authorities, school authorities, public colleges, universities and local municipal authorities and those charities that are none of the foregoing. The former group is referred to as "public institutions" for GST purposes and follow their own unique rules for GST purposes.

*French Language Services Act*, R.S.O. 1990, c. F. 32.

The *French Language Services Act* provides in subsection 5(1) that a person has the right to receive a "service" in French from a "government agency". Section 1 defines "government agency" broadly enough to include certain charities, namely, those designated as a "public service agency" under the regulations.[25]

*Highway Traffic Act*, R.S.O. 1990, c. H. 8.

The *Highway Traffic Act* requires in subsection 11.1(1) that every person who sells or transfers a used motor vehicle shall provide to the purchaser or transferee a "used vehicle information package". In turn, subsection 11.1(3) of the statute provides that the purchaser or transferee of a used motor vehicle must provide a copy of the used vehicle information package to the Ministry of Transportation before obtaining a permit for the vehicle. Sections 2 and 3 of Regulation 601/93 passed pursuant to the *Highway Traffic Act* provide an exemption from these requirements where a used vehicle is transferred to a charity for no consideration.

*Human Rights Code*, R.S.O. 1990, c. H. 19.

Membership and participation in charitable institutions is sometimes restricted on grounds that could be said to be discriminatory at law. A religious charity may, for example, restrict membership to adherents to a specific religion or a denomination thereof. The Ontario *Human Rights Code* contains provisions (see, for example, section 18) that expressly allow for such practices.

*Liquor Licence Act*, R.S.O. 1990, c. L. 19.

Section 19 of the *Liquor Licence Act* allows for the issuance of a permit — a special occasion permit — authorizing the holder thereof to sell or serve liquor on a prescribed special occasion. Section 3 of Regulation 389/91 describes the circumstances that qualify for purposes of section 19 of the statute as special occasions. Fundraising events and auctions conducted by registered charities under the *Income Tax Act (Canada)* are specifically enumerated. In turn, subsection 3(6) of Regulation 720 authorizes a manufacturer of liquor to give liquor to a registered charity holding a special occasion permit.

*Mining Tax Act*, R.S.O. 1990, c. M. 15.

The *Mining Tax Act* provides for a special tax payable by the "operator" of a mine. The tax is levied as a percentage of the operator's profit as determined under the

---

[25]    See O. Reg. 398/93 for a complete list of these institutions.

statute. Paragraph 3(5)(f) of the statute allows for the deduction of certain charitable donations for the purposes of calculating the operator's profit.

*Ontario Energy Board Act, 1998*, S.O. 1998, c. 15, Sched. B.

The *Ontario Energy Board Act, 1998* provides for unique treatment for certain charities. Subsection 79.1(14), for example, provides that a "distributor" shall make a payment of sorts to each "designated consumer" who held an account with the distributor on November 25, 2002. "Designated consumer" is defined in section 56 to include registered charities.

*Personal Health Information Protection Act, 2004*, S.O. 2004, c. 3, Schedule A.

The *Personal Health Information Protection Act, 2004* establishes a statutory regime for the protection of "personal health information". Section 32 of the statute provides that personal health information may be used for the purpose of fundraising activities so long as certain requirements are complied with. Section 10 of Regulation 329/04 passed pursuant to the statute elaborates on these requirements.

*Personal Information Protection and* Electronic *Documents Act*, S.C. 2000, c. 5.

The *Personal Information Protection and Electronic Documents Act* ("PIPEDA") applies to any organization that collects, uses or discloses personal information in the course of commercial activities. Charities that engage in commercial activities should therefore consider the implications of PIPEDA. It will be a question of fact as to whether a particular activity of a charity constitutes a commercial activity within the meaning of PIPEDA. In this regard, however, it is important to note that the definition of "commercial activity" set out in PIPEDA specifically includes in the definition the "selling, bartering or leasing of donor, membership or other fundraising lists". It therefore appears certain that the transfer of a donor list by a charity will trigger the application of PIPEDA.

Where it does apply to an organization, PIPEDA requires that certain measures be implemented by the organization to ensure that personal information is protected and secured. In particular, PIPEDA specifically provides that every organization subject to its provisions is, subject to certain exceptions, required to comply with Schedule 1 to PIPEDA. This schedule incorporates the privacy standards that are based on those established by the Canadian Standards Association International in its *Model Code for the Protection of Personal Information*.

*Proceeds of Crime (Money Laundering) and Terrorist Financing Act*, S.C. 2000, c. 17.

The *Proceeds of Crime (Money Laundering) and Terrorist Financing Act* imposes an obligation to file various reports with respect to certain types of financial transactions. The reporting obligations are applicable mainly, although not exclusively, to financial entities. The intent of the statute is to provide a mechanism by which money laundering and terrorist financing offences may be detected. It may be viewed as a companion statute to Part II.1 of the *Criminal Code* (discussed above) and the *Charities Registration (Security Information) Act* (discussed above) as reports filed under the *Proceeds of Crime (Money Laundering) and Terrorist Financing Act* could conceivably contribute to the creation of an evidentiary basis to support a criminal prosecution or the revocation of charitable registration under those statutes.

*Securities Act*, R.S.O. 1990, c. S.5.

Under the *Securities Act*, anyone who "trades" in "securities" is required to comply with various requirements, including a registration requirement. There is a limited exception from the registration requirement set out in paragraph 35(2)7 for securities issued by corporations organized exclusively for educational, benevolent, fraternal, charitable, religious or recreational purposes. This exception may have application to charities that have been incorporated as share capital corporations rather than as member based or non-share capital corporations.

*Statutes Authorizing the Gifting of Lost, Abandoned or Confiscated Property to Charity.*

The latin maxim "*nemo dat qui non habet*" articulates a foundational rule of property law: he who hath not cannot give. There are, however, a number of statutory exceptions to the *nemo dat* rule that are of interest to charities. Several statutes in Ontario authorize a non-owner to transfer ownership to a charity in limited circumstances. These circumstances include instances where an article has been lost, abandoned or confiscated or where it has been retained in the possession of a lien claimant for over twelve months. See, for example, section 24 of the *Niagara Parks Act*, R.S.O. 1990, c. N.3, section 15 of the *Provincial Parks Act*, R.S.O. 1990, c. P. 34, section 27.1 of the *Public Lands Act*, R.S.O. 1990, c. P.43, section 17 of the *St. Lawrence Parks Commission Act*, R.S.O. 1990, c. S. 24, sections 11 and 27 of the *Ministry of Correctional Services Act*, R.S.O. 1990, c. M. 22, section 63 of the *Municipal Act, 2001*, S.O. 2001, c. 25 and sections 19 and 20 of the *Repair and Storage Liens Act*, R.S.O. 1990, c. R. 25.

*Statutory Regime Applicable to Charitable Gaming.*

Societal attitudes regarding gambling have in recent years become more permissive. One of the manifestations of this phenomenon is that charitable gaming has grown in popularity as a fundraising mechanism for many charities.

The regime of laws and regulations regulating the charitable gaming industry is highly complicated and technical. This regime may be briefly described as follows.

> The starting point for the analysis of charitable gaming is the *Criminal Code*. Subject to certain exceptions, gambling is an offence under the *Criminal Code*. One of the exceptions to this general rule is set out in paragraph 207(1)(b) of the *Criminal Code*, which provides that a charitable or religious organization may conduct a lottery scheme if authorized to do so by a licence issued by a province.

In Ontario, the issuance of licences to conduct lottery schemes is governed by Order-in-Council 2688/93. This Order-in-Council sets out in very broad terms the basic framework within which licences to conduct lottery schemes may be granted or revoked. The framework established by Order-in-Council 2688/93 is explained in great detail in the *Lottery Licensing Policy Manual* (Toronto: Entertainment Standards Branch, 1993). The *Lottery Licensing Policy Manual* also sets out the eligibility criteria for lottery licences and the terms and conditions that may be attached to their issuance.

Once a charity has been issued a licence, it will need access to gaming premises, gaming assistants and gaming equipment in order to conduct a lottery scheme. The supply of this equipment and these services by third parties is regulated under the *Gaming Control Act, 1992*, S.O. 1992, c. 24. As per the *Alcohol and Gaming Regulation and Public Protection Act, 1996*, S.O. 1996, c. 26, Sched., the administration of the *Gaming Control Act, 1992* and the regulations passed thereunder is the responsibility of the Alcohol and Gaming Commission of Ontario. Certain gambling activities are also provided by the Ontario Lottery and Gaming Corporation, which is created by and subject to the *Ontario Lottery and Gaming Corporation Act, 1999*, S.O. 1999, c. 12, Sched. L.

For an in-depth commentary on the law of charitable gaming, the reader is referred to Donald J. Bourgeois, *The Law of Charitable and Casino Gaming* (Toronto: Butterworths, 1999).

*Statutory Regime Applicable to Hospitals and Other Health Care Facilities.*

The promotion of health has long since been recognized as being charitable at common law. Hospitals and other health care facilities are therefore very often subject to the various statutes and rules of common law applicable to charities. These entities, however, are also subject to the unique requirements of the various statutes that regulate hospitals and other health care facilities. An incomplete list of such statutes includes the *Public Hospitals Act*, R.S.O. 1990, c. P. 40, the *Private Hospitals Act*, R.S.O. 1990, c. P. 24, the *Charitable Institutions Act*, R.S.O. 1990, c. C.9., the *Nursing Homes Act*, R.S.O. 1990, c. N. 7, the *Independent Health Facilities Act*, R.S.O. 1990, c. I.3, the *Homes for the Aged and Rest Homes Act*, R.S.O. 1990, c. H. 13, the *Community Psychiatric Hospitals Act*, R.S.O. 1990, c. C. 21, the *Homes for Special Care Act*, R.S.O. 1990, c. H. 12, the *Long-Term Care Act, 1994*, S.O. 1994, c. 26, the *Elderly Persons Centres Act*, R.S.O. 1990, c. E.4, the *Medical Radiation Technology Act, 1991*, S.O. 1991, c. 29 and the *Mental Health Act*, R.S.O. 1990, c. M.7

*Statutory Regime Relating to Means Tested Public Assistance.*

Provincial statutes providing for means tested public assistance contain provisions that outline in detail how eligibility for such public assistance is to be determined. These provisions include formulas for calculating the income of applicants. It will be of interest for many charities to know that several statutes exclude (in whole or in part) from an applicant's income donations received by him or her from a charity. The result is that the receipt by an applicant of assistance from a charity may not disqualify him or her from public assistance. See, for example, section 43 of the *Ontario Disability Support Program Act, 1997*, O. Reg. 222/98, section 54 of the *Ontario Works Act, 1997*, O. Reg. 134/98 and section 50 of the *Social Housing Reform Act, 2000*, O. Reg. 298/01.[26]

*Statutory Regime Applicable to Provincial Parks.*

The statutes regulating provincial parks in Ontario contain various provisions that provide charities with privileged access to such parks. Regulations enacted pursuant to section 7.1 of the *Provincial Parks Act*, R.S.O. 1990, c. P. 34, for example, allow certain charities to enter provincial parks for either no fee or for a reduced fee.[27] Similarly, regulations passed pursuant to the *Public Lands Act*, R.S.O. 1990, c. P. 43 relax the rules relating to camping on Crown land as they apply to charities.[28]

*Tax Court of Canada Act*, R.S.C. 1985, c. T-2.

Subsection 12(5) of the *Tax Court of Canada Act* provides that the Tax Court of Canada has exclusive jurisdiction to hear and determine applications relating to subsection 188.2(4) of the *Income Tax Act (Canada)*. In effect, this affords the Tax Court of Canada exclusive jurisdiction to resolve disputes pertaining to the suspension of a registered charity's receipting privileges.

*Tourism Act*, R.S.O. 1990, c. T. 16.

The *Tourism Act* establishes various statutory rules applicable to every "tourist establishment", defined broadly in section 1 to include premises providing sleeping accommodations for the traveling public or for use of the public engaging in recreational activities. In order to exempt certain charities that would otherwise be subject to the *Tourism Act*, the definition of "tourist establishment" explicitly excludes certain charitable camps and not-for-profit clubs.

---

[26] See also s. 4 of the *Ontario Guaranteed Annual Income Act*, R.R.O. 1990, Reg. 874, which provides that absences from Ontario by a person for the purposes of his or her employment with an international charitable organization will not interrupt that person's residence in Ontario for purposes of determining eligibility for benefits under the *Ontario Guaranteed Annual Income Act*, R.S.O. 1990, c. O.17.

[27] See ss. 34 and 36 of the *Provincial Parks Act*, R.R.O. 1990, Reg. 952.

[28] See subs. 2(1) of the *Public Lands Act*, O. Reg. 326/94. See also subs. 8(3) of the *Conservation Authorities Act*, R.R.O. 1990, Reg. 136.

# CANADA CORPORATIONS ACT

## (R.S.C. 1970, c. C-32)

**Amended by:** R.S., 1970, c. 10 (1st Supp.), ss. 2, 3, 11, 12, 21-23, 25, 26; 1972, c. 17, s. 2; 1978-79, c. 11, s. 10; 1985, c. 26, ss. 36, 87; 1986, c. 26, ss. 51-53; 1986, c. 35, s. 14; 1995, c. 1, s. 32; 1999, c. 3, s. 17.

[Note: Only sections pertaining to non-share capital charitable corporations are reproduced]

## PART I

## COMPANIES WITH SHARE CAPITAL

. . .

### *Interpretation*

**3.** (1) **Definitions** — In this Part and in all letters patent and supplementary letters patent issued under it

"accounts receivable" includes existing or future book debts, accounts, claims, moneys and choses in action or any class or part thereof and all contracts, securities, bills, notes, books, instruments and other documents securing, evidencing or in any way relating to the same or any of them, but shall not include uncalled share capital of the company or calls made but not paid;

"court" means

    (a)   in Ontario, Nova Scotia, British Columbia and Newfoundland, the Supreme Court,

    (a.1) in Prince Edward Island, the Trial Division of the Supreme Court,

    (b)   in Quebec, the Superior Court,

    (c)   in Manitoba, Saskatchewan, Alberta and New Brunswick, the Court of Queen's Bench, and

    (d)   in Yukon, the Supreme Court of Yukon, in the Northwest Territories, the Supreme Court of the Northwest Territories, and in Nunavut, the Nunavut Court of Justice;

"debenture" includes bonds, debenture stock, and any other securities of a company that constitute or are entitled to the benefit of a charge on the assets of the company;

"Department" means the Department of Consumer and Corporate Affairs;

"director" includes any person occupying the position of director by whatever name he is called;

"document" includes notice, order, certificate, register, summons or other legal process;

"equity share" means any share of any class of shares of a company carrying voting rights under all circumstances and any share of any class of shares carrying voting rights by reason of the occurrence of any contingency that has occurred and is continuing;

"judge" means in the said respective Provinces and Territories a judge of the said courts respectively;

"Minister" means the Minister of Industry

"mortgage" includes charge and hypothec;

"officer" means the chairman or vice-chairman of the board of directors, the president, vice-president, secretary, treasurer, comptroller, general manager, managing director or any other individual who performs functions for the company similar to those normally performed by an individual occupying any such office;

"private company" means a company as to which by letters patent or supplementary letters patent;

    (a)   the right to transfer its shares is restricted,

    (b)   the number of its shareholders is limited to fifty,

not including persons who are in the employment of the company and persons, who, having been formerly in the employment of the company, were, while in that employment, and have continued after the termination of that employment to be shareholders of the company, two or more persons holding one or more shares jointly being counted as a single shareholder, and

    (c)   any invitation to the public to subscribe for any shares or debentures of the company is prohibited;

"public company" means a company that is not a private company;

"real estate" or "land" includes messuages, lands, tenements, and hereditaments of any tenure, and all immovable property of any kind;

"securities" means any shares of a company or any debenture or other obligations of a company, whether secured or unsecured;

"shareholder" means every subscriber for or holder of a share in the capital stock of the company and includes the personal representatives of a deceased shareholder and every person who agrees with the company to become a shareholder;

"the company" or "a company" means any company to which this Part applies and "another company" or "any company" means any company wherever or however incorporated;

"undertaking" means the business of every kind which the company is authorized to carry on.

(2) **Special resolution** — A by-law mentioned in section 20, subsection 29(1), section 51 or 52 may be referred to as a "special resolution".

[R.S., 1970, c. 10 (1st Supp.), s. 2; 1972, c. 17, s. 2; 1978-79, c. 11, s. 10; 1986, c. 35, s. 14; 1995, c. 1, s. 32; 1999, c. 3, s. 17; 2002, c. 7, s. 89.]

*Preliminaries*

**4. Provisions directory only** — The provisions of this Part relating to matters preliminary to the issue of the letters patent or supplementary letters patent are directory only, and no letters patent or supplementary letters patent issued under this Part shall be held void or voidable on account of any irregularity or insufficiency in respect of any matter preliminary to the issue of the letters patent or supplementary letters patent.

*Formation of New Companies*

. . .

**5.6.** (1) **Grounds for winding-up company** — Where a company

(a)  carries on a business that is not within the scope of the objects set forth in its letters patent or supplementary letters patent,

(b)  exercises or professes to exercise any powers that are not truly ancillary or reasonably incidental to the objects set forth in its letters patent or supplementary letters patent,

(c)  exercises or professes to exercise any powers expressly excluded by its letters patent or supplementary letters patent,

the company is liable to be wound up and dissolved under the *Winding-up Act* upon the application of the Attorney General of Canada to a court of competent jurisdiction for an order that the company be wound up under the Act, which application may be made upon receipt by the Attorney General of Canada of a certificate of the Minister setting forth his opinion that any of the circumstances described in paragraphs (a) to (c) apply to that company.

(2) **Costs of winding-up** — In any application to the court under subsection (1) the court shall determine whether the costs of the winding-up shall be borne by the company or personally by any or all of the directors of the company who participated or acquiesced in the carrying on of any business or the exercise or the professing of the exercise of any powers described in subsection (1).

[R.S., 1970, c. 10 (1st Supp.), s. 3.]

. . .

**6. Seal of Office** — The Governor in Council may, from time to time, designate the seal of office to be used by the Minister as the seal under which letters patent may be granted under this Act.

. . .

**9.** (1) **Establishing conditions precedent to the issue of letters patent** — Before the letters patent are issued the applicants shall establish to the satisfaction of the Minister

(a)    the sufficiency of the application and the truth and sufficiency of the facts therein set forth, and

(b)    that the proposed name is not the same or similar to the name under which any other company, society, association or firm, in existence, is carrying on business in Canada or is incorporated under the laws of Canada or any province thereof or so nearly resembles the same as to be calculated to deceive and is not otherwise on public grounds objectionable, or that such existing company, society, association or firm is in the course of being dissolved or changing its name and has signified its consent to the use of the said name.

(2) **Evidence may be taken** — The Minister or any officer to whom the application may be referred may take any requisite evidence in writing by oath or affirmation or by statutory declaration and the Minister shall keep of record any such evidence so taken.

(3) **Averments to be recited** — The letters patent shall recite such of the established averments in the application as to the Minister seems expedient.

(4) **Name of company** — The Minister, after giving reasonable notice to the applicants, or to their authorized representative or agent, may give to the company a corporate name different from that proposed by the applicants in any case in which the proposed name is deemed by the Minister to be objectionable.

(5) **Alterations in application for letters patent** — The Minister after giving notice to the applicants or to their authorized representative or agent may, with the consent of such applicants or their authorized representative or agent, make such alterations in the application as may be deemed expedient by the Minister.

**10. Notice to be published** — Notice of the granting of letters patent or supplementary letters patent shall be forthwith given by the Minister by one insertion in the *Canada Gazette*.

**11.** (1) **Corrections** — When the letters patent or supplementary letters patent contain any misnomer, misdescription, clerical error or other defect, the Minister may direct the letters patent or supplementary letters patent to be corrected.

(2) **Notice of correction** — Notice of the correction of the letters patent or supplementary letters patent shall be forthwith given by the Minister in the *Canada Gazette* if the correction made causes them to depart materially from the text of the original notice given pursuant to section 10.

**12. Date of existence** — A company comes into existence on the date of the letters patent incorporating it.

. . .

*General Powers and Duties of Companies*

**15. Powers given subject to this Act** — All powers given to a company by letters patent or supplementary letters patent shall be exercised subject to the provisions and restrictions contained in this Part.

**16.** (1) **Incidental and ancillary powers** — A company may, as ancillary and incidental to the objects set out in its letters patent or supplementary letters patent, exercise any or all of the following powers, namely the power:

(a)    to carry on any other business that may seem to the company capable of being conveniently carried on in connection with its business or calculated directly or indirectly to enhance the value of or render profitable any of the company's property or rights;

(a.1)  to purchase or otherwise acquire and undertake all or any of the assets, business, property, privileges, contracts, rights, obligations and liabilities of any other company or any society, firm or person carrying on any business that the company is authorized to carry on, or possessed of property suitable for the purposes of the company;

(b)    to apply for, purchase or otherwise acquire any patents, patent rights, copyrights, trade marks, formulae, licences, concessions and the like, conferring any exclusive or non-exclusive or limited right to use, or any secret or other information as to any invention that may seem capable of being used for any of the purposes of the company, or the acquisition of which may seem calculated directly or indirectly to benefit the company, and to use, exercise, develop or grant licenses in respect of, or otherwise turn to account, the property, rights or information so acquired;

(b.1)  to amalgamate or enter into partnership or into any arrangement for sharing of profits, union of interests, cooperation, joint adventure, reciprocal concession or otherwise, with any other company or any society, firm or person, carrying on or engaged in or about to carry on or engage in any business or transaction that the company is authorized to carry on or engage in, or any business or transaction capable of being conducted so as directly or indirectly to benefit the company; and to lend money to, guarantee the contracts of, or otherwise assist any such company, society, firm or person, and to take or otherwise acquire shares and securities of any such company, and to sell, hold or otherwise deal with the same;

(c)    to take, or otherwise acquire and hold, shares, debentures or other securities of any other company having objects altogether or in part similar to those of the company, or carrying on any business capable of being conducted so as, directly or indirectly, to benefit the company, and to sell or otherwise deal with the same;

(d)    to enter into any arrangements with any government or authority, municipal, local or otherwise, that may seem conducive to the company's objects, or any of them, and to obtain from any such government or authority any rights, privileges and concessions that the company may think it desirable to obtain, and to carry out, exercise and comply with any such arrangements, rights, privileges and concessions;

(e)    to establish and support or aid in the establishment and support of associations, institutions, funds, trusts and conveniences calculated to benefit employees or ex-employees of the company or of its predecessors in business, or the dependants or connections of such persons, and to grant pensions and allowances, and to make payments toward insurance, and to subscribe or guarantee money for charitable or benevolent objects, or for any exhibition or for any public, general or useful object;

(f) to promote any other company or companies for the purpose of acquiring or taking over all or any of the property and liabilities of the company, or for any other purpose that may seem directly or indirectly calculated to benefit the company;

(g) to purchase, take on lease or in exchange, hire, and otherwise acquire and hold, sell or otherwise deal with any real and personal property and any rights or privileges that the company may think necessary or convenient for the purposes of its business and in particular any land, buildings, easements, machinery, plant and stock-in-trade;

(h) to construct, improve, maintain, work, manage, carry out or control any roads, ways, branches or sidings, bridges, reservoirs, watercourses, wharfs, manufactories, warehouses, electric works, shops, stores and other works and conveniences that may seem calculated directly or indirectly to advance the company's interests, and to contribute to, subsidize or otherwise assist or take part in the construction, improvement, maintenance, working, management, carrying out or control thereof;

(i) to lend money to any other company, or any society, firm or person, having dealings with the company or with whom the company proposes to have dealings or to any other company any of whose shares are held by the company;

(j) to draw, make, accept, endorse, discount, execute and issue promissory notes, bills of exchange, bills of lading, warrants and other negotiable or transferable instruments;

(k) to sell or dispose of the undertaking of the company or any part thereof for such consideration as the company may think fit, and in particular for shares, debentures or securities of any other company that has objects altogether or in part similar to those of the company;

(l) to apply for, secure, acquire by grant, legislative enactment, assignment, transfer, purchase or otherwise, and to exercise, carry out and enjoy any charter, licence, power, authority, franchise, concession, right or privilege, that any government or authority or any corporation or other public body may be empowered to grant, and to pay for, aid in and contribute toward carrying the same into effect, and to appropriate any of the company's shares, debentures, or other securities and assets to defray the necessary costs, charges and expenses thereof;

(m) to procure the company to be registered and recognized in any foreign country or place, and to designate persons therein according to the laws of such foreign country or place to represent the company and to accept service for and on behalf of the company of any process or suit;

(n) to remunerate any other company, or any society, firm or person for services rendered, or to be rendered, in placing or assisting to place or guaranteeing the placing of any of the shares in the company's capital or any debentures or other securities of the company, or in or about the organization, formation or promotion of the company or the conduct of its business;

(o)    to raise and assist in raising money for, and to aid by way of bonus, loan, promise, endorsement, guarantee or otherwise, any other company with which the company may have business relations or any of whose shares, debentures or other obligations are held by the company and to guarantee the performance or fulfilment of any contracts or obligations of any such company or of any person with whom the company may have business relations, and in particular to guarantee the payment of the principal of and interest on debentures or other securities, mortgages and liabilities of any such company;

(p)    to adopt such means of making known the products of the company as may seem expedient, and in particular by advertising in the press, by circulars, by purchase and exhibition of works of art or interest, by publication of books and periodicals and by granting prizes, rewards and donations;

(q)    to sell, improve, manage, develop, exchange, lease, dispose of, turn to account or otherwise deal with all or any part of the property and rights of the company;

. . .

(s)    to distribute among the shareholders of the company in kind, specie or otherwise, any property or assets of the company including any proceeds of the sale or disposal of any property of the company and in particular any shares, debentures, or other securities of or in any other company belonging to the company, or of which it may have power to dispose, if either such distribution is made for the purpose of enabling the company to surrender its charter under the provisions of this Act, or such distribution, apart from the provisions of this paragraph, would have been lawful if made in cash;

(t)    to pay out of the funds of the company all or any of the expenses of or incidental to the formation and organization thereof, or which the company may consider to be preliminary;

(u)    to establish agencies and branches;

(v)    to invest and deal with the moneys of the company not immediately required in such manner as may from time to time be determined;

(w)    to apply for, promote and obtain any statute, ordinance, order, regulation or other authorization or enactment that may seem calculated directly or indirectly to benefit the company; and to oppose any proceedings or application that may seem calculated directly or indirectly to prejudice the company's interests;

(x)    to take or hold mortgages, hypothecs, liens and charges to secure payment of the purchase price, or for any unpaid balance of the purchase price of any part of the company's property of whatsoever kind sold by the company, or any money due to the company from purchasers and others and to sell or otherwise dispose of said mortgages, hypothecs, liens and charges;

(y)    to carry out all or any of the objects of the company and do all or any of the things set out in this subsection as principal, agent, contractor, or otherwise, and either alone or in conjunction with others; and

(z)    to do all such other things as are incidental or conducive to the attainment of the objects and the exercise of the powers of the company.

(2) **Property and rights** — The company shall from the date of its letters patent become and be vested with all property and rights, real and personal, theretofore held for it under any trust created with a view to its incorporation.

(3) **Other powers** — Nothing in this section prevents the inclusion in the letters patent or supplementary letters patent of a company of other powers in addition to or in modification of the powers mentioned in subsection (1).

(4) **Withholding or limiting powers** — Any of the powers set out in subsection (1) may be withheld or limited by the letters patent or supplementary letters patent of the company.

. . .

### Change of Provisions of Letters Patent

**20.** (1) **Application to extend or reduce powers** — Subject to any special rights attaching to shares of any class or classes as set forth in the letters patent or supplementary letters patent, a company may from time to time, when authorized by by-law sanctioned by two-thirds of the votes cast at a special general meeting of shareholders called for the purpose, apply for supplementary letters patent, as provided in such by-law,

(a)    extending the objects of the company to such further or other objects for which a company may be incorporated under this Part, or

(b)    reducing, limiting, amending or varying the objects or the powers of the company or any of the provisions of the letters patent or supplementary letters patent issued to the company; but no such extension, reduction, limitation, amendment or variation may have the effect of altering or permitting the alteration of the authorized capital of the company in any manner other than pursuant to the issue of supplementary letters patent under sections 51 to 60 or section 134, as the circumstances of the case may require.

. . .

(3) **Limitation** — An application under subsection (1) or (2) may be made only within six months after the by-law therein mentioned has been sanctioned by the shareholders.

(4) **Evidence of by-law** — Before such supplementary letters patent are issued, the company shall establish to the satisfaction of the Minister the due passage and sanction of the by-law authorizing the application, and for that purpose

the Minister may take any requisite evidence in writing, by oath or affirmation, or by statutory declaration and shall keep a record of any such evidence so taken.

(5) **Supplementary letters patent** — Upon the due sanctioning of a by-law pursuant to subsection (1) or (2), as the case may be, being so established, the Minister may grant supplementary letters patent

    (a)   extending the objects of the company;

    (b)   reducing, limiting, amending or varying the objects or the powers of the company or any of the provisions of the letters patent or supplementary letters patent of the company; or

    (c)   converting the company into a public or private company, as the case may be, and as provided in such by-law; and notice thereof shall be forthwith given by the Minister in the Canada Gazette and the supplementary letters patent take effect from their date.

*Contracts, etc.*

**21.** (1) **Contracts of agent binding on company** — Every contract, agreement, engagement or bargain made, and every bill of exchange drawn, accepted or endorsed, and every promissory note and cheque made, drawn or endorsed on behalf of the company, by any agent, officer or servant of the company within the apparent scope of his authority as such agent, officer or servant, is binding upon the company.

(2) **Cases where seal not necessary** — In no case is it necessary to have the seal of the company affixed to any such contract, agreement, engagement, bargain, bill of exchange, promissory note or cheque, or to prove that the same was made, drawn, accepted or endorsed, as the case may be, in pursuance of any by-law or special vote or order.

(3) **No individual liability** — No person so acting as such agent, officer or servant of the company is thereby subjected individually to any liability whatever to any third person.

**22. Acts of attorney binding** — Every deed that any person, lawfully empowered in that behalf by the company as its attorney, signs on behalf of the company and seals with his seal is binding on the company and has the same effect as if it were under the seal of the company.

**23.** (1) **Official seal, facsimile of corporate seal** — A company if authorized by its by-laws may have for use in any province, not being the province in which the head office of the company is situated, or for use in any territory, district or place outside Canada, an official seal, which shall be a facsimile of the corporate seal, with the addition on its face of the name of the province, territory, district or place where it is to be used.

(2) **Authorization to affix seal** — A company having such an official seal may by writing under its corporate seal authorize any person appointed for the purpose to affix the same to any deed or other document to which the company is party in any capacity in such province, territory, district or place.

(3) **Agent's authority** — The authority of any such agent shall, as between the company and any person dealing with the agent, continue during the period, if any, mentioned in the instrument conferring the authority, or if no period is therein mentioned, then until notice of the revocation or determination of the agent's authority has been given to the person dealing with him.

(4) **Date and place certified** — The person affixing any such official seal shall, by writing under his hand, on the deed or other document to which the official seal is affixed, certify the date and place of affixing the same, but failure to do so does not invalidate the deed or other document.

(5) **Deed to bind the company** — A deed or other document to which an official seal is duly affixed binds the company as if it had been sealed with the corporate seal.

## Head Office

**24.** (1) **Head office** — The company shall at all times have a head office in the place within Canada where the head office is to be situated in accordance with the letters patent or the provisions of this Part, which head office is the domicile of the company in Canada; and the company may establish such other offices and agencies elsewhere within or outside Canada, as it deems expedient.

(2) **Change of head office by by-law** — The company may, by by-law, change the place where the head office of the company is to be situated.

(3) **Change to be sanctioned** — No by-law for the purpose of changing the place where the head office is to be situated is valid or shall be acted upon until it is sanctioned by at least two-thirds of the votes cast at a special general meeting of the shareholders duly called for considering the by-law.

(4) **Filing by-law** — A copy of the by-law certified under the seal of the company shall be forthwith filed with the Minister and shall be available for inspection at the office thereof during normal business hours.

(5) **Notice of by-law** — A notice of the by-law shall be forthwith published in the *Canada Gazette*.

## Name of Company

**25.** (2) **Use of French or English form of name** — If the company has a name consisting of a separated or combined French and English form, it may from time to time use, and it may be legally designated by, either the French or English form of its name or both forms.

(3) **Publishing name of company** — A company shall

. . .

(b)  keep its name engraved in legible characters on its seal and, if the company has a name consisting of a French and English form, whether separated or combined, the company shall show on its seal both the French and English forms of its name or shall have two seals, each of which shall be equally valid, one showing the French and the other the English form of its name; and

. . .

**27. Authorizing seal where name not engraven properly** — Every director, manager or officer of a company, and every person on its behalf, who

(a)    uses or authorizes the use of any seal purporting to be a seal of the company, whereon its name is not engraven in legible characters,

(b)    issues or authorizes the issue of any notice, advertisement, or other official publication of such company,

(c)    signs or authorizes to be signed on behalf of the company, any bill of exchange, promissory note, endorsement, cheque, order for money or goods, or

(d)    issues or authorizes to be issued any bill of parcels, invoice or receipt of the company, wherein its name is not mentioned in legible characters, is liable to a penalty of two hundred dollars, and is also personally liable to the holder of any such bill of exchange, promissory note, cheque, or order for money or goods, for the amount thereof, unless the same is duly paid by the company.

**28.** (1) **Not to have identical name** — A company shall not be incorporated

(a)    with a name that is the same or similar to the name under which any other company, society, association or firm, in existence, is carrying on business in Canada or is incorporated under the laws of Canada or any province thereof, or that so nearly resembles that name as to be calculated to deceive, except where the existing company, society, association or firm is in the course of being dissolved or of changing its name and signifies its consent in such manner as the Minister requires, or

(b)    with a name that is otherwise on public grounds objectionable.

(2) **Minister may change name by supplementary letters** — Where a company, through inadvertence or otherwise, is without the consent mentioned in subsection (1) incorporated with a name that is the same or similar to the name under which any other company, society, association or firm in existence has been previously carrying on business in Canada or has been previously incorporated under the laws of Canada or any province thereof, or with a name that so nearly resembles that name as to be calculated to deceive, or that is otherwise on public grounds objectionable, the Minister, after he has given notice to the company of intention so to do, may direct the issue of supplementary letters patent changing the name of the company to some other name, which shall be set forth in the supplementary letters patent.

(3) **Notice** — Notice of the issue of such supplementary letters patent shall be published in the *Canada Gazette*.

**29.** (1) **Company may obtain change in name** — When a company desires to adopt another name it may, subject to confirmation by supplementary letters patent, change its corporate name by by-law sanctioned by at least two-thirds of the votes cast at a special general meeting of shareholders called for the purpose.

(2) **Supplementary letters patent** — The Minister, upon application of the company and upon being satisfied that the change desired is not objectionable, may direct the issue of supplementary letters patent, changing the name of the company to some other name which shall be set forth in the supplementary letters patent.

(3) **Notice** — Notice of the issue of such supplementary letters patent shall be published in the *Canada Gazette*.

**30. Change not to affect rights or obligations** — No alteration of name under sections 28 and 29 affects the rights or obligations of the company; and all proceedings may be continued or commenced by or against the company under its new name that might have been continued or commenced by or against the company under its former name.

## *Forfeiture of Charter*

**31. (1) Forfeiture of charter for non-user** — Where a company does not go into actual bona fide operation within three years after incorporation or for three consecutive years does not use its corporate powers its charter shall be and become forfeited.

(2) **Proof of user** — In any action or proceeding where such non-user is alleged, proof of user lies upon the company.

(3) **Revival of charter** — The Minister may upon application of any person interested revive any charter so forfeited upon compliance with such conditions as he may prescribes.

## *Surrender of Charter*

**32. (1) Surrender of charter** — The charter of a company may be surrendered if the company proves to the satisfaction of the Minister

  (a)    that the company has no assets and that, if it had any assets immediately prior to the application for leave to surrender its charter, such assets have been divided ratably among its shareholders or members, and either,

    (i)    that it has no debts, liabilities or other obligations, or

    (ii)    that the debts, liabilities or other obligations of the company have been duly provided for or protected or that the creditors of the company or other persons having interests in such debts, liabilities or other obligations consent; and

  (b)    that the company has given notice of the application for leave to surrender by publishing the same once in the *Canada Gazette* and once in a newspaper published at or as near as may be to the place where the company has its head office.

(2) **Application by inoperative company** — Where an application to surrender a charter is made by a company that has not gone into bona fide operation or that has been inoperative for three or more consecutive years, if the circumstances mentioned in paragraph (1)(a) are proved to the satisfaction of the Minister, the Minister shall publish a notice of such application in the *Canada Gazette* and, unless an objection to the surrender is received by him within one year after such publication of the notice, he may accept the application for the surrender of the charter.

(3) **Acceptance of surrender** — Where the Minister has accepted the surrender of a charter upon due compliance with subsection (1) or subsection (2), as the case may be, the Minister may direct the cancellation of the charter of the company and fix a date upon and from which the company shall be dissolved, and the company is thereby and thereupon dissolved accordingly.

(4) **No fee payable by inoperative company** — No fee shall be charged in respect of a surrender under this section of the charter of a company described in subsection (2).

**33. Liability of shareholders after dissolution of company** — Notwithstanding the dissolution of a company under section 32, the shareholders of the company among whom its assets have been divided remain, to the amount received by them respectively upon such division, jointly and severally liable to the creditors of the company; and an action may be brought in any court of competent jurisdiction to enforce such liability, but the action shall be commenced within and not after one year from the date of such dissolution of the company.

. . .

### Transfer of Shares

**43. Transfer of shares of a deceased shareholder** — A transfer of the shares or other interest of a deceased shareholder, made by his personal representative, is, notwithstanding that the personal representative is not himself a shareholder, of the same validity as if he had been a shareholder at the time of his execution of the instrument of transfer.

. . .

### Borrowing Powers

**65. (1) Borrowing powers** — When authorized by by-law, duly passed by the directors and sanctioned by at least two-thirds of the votes cast at a special general meeting of the shareholders duly called for considering the by-law, the directors of a company may from time to time

(a)   borrow money upon the credit of the company;
(b)   limit or increase the amount to be borrowed;

(c)    issue debentures or other securities of the company;

(d)    pledge or sell such debentures or other securities for such sums and at such prices as may be deemed expedient; and

(e)    secure any such debentures, or other securities, or any other present or future borrowing or liability of the company, by mortgage, hypothec, charge or pledge of all or any currently owned or subsequently acquired real and personal, movable and immovable, property of the company, and the undertaking and rights of the company.

(2) **Delegation of powers** — Any such by-law may provide for the delegation of such powers by the directors to such officers or directors of the company to such extent and in such manner as may be set out in the by-law.

(3) **Limitation as to bills and notes** — Nothing in this section limits or restricts the borrowing of money by the company on bills of exchange or promissory notes made, drawn, accepted or endorsed by or on behalf of the company.

**66. Perpetual debenture** — A condition contained in any debentures or in any deed for securing any debentures is not invalid by reason only that the debentures are thereby made irredeemable or redeemable only on the happening of a contingency, however remote, or on the expiration of a period, however long, any rule of equity to the contrary notwithstanding.

**67. (1) Power to reissue debentures in certain cases** — Where either before or after the 1st day of October 1934, a company has redeemed any debentures previously issued, then

(a)    unless any provision to the contrary, whether express or implied, is contained in the debentures or in any contract entered into by the company; or

(b)    unless the company has, by resolution of its shareholders or by some other act, manifested its intention that the debentures shall be cancelled,

the company shall have power to reissue the debentures, either by reissuing the same debentures or by issuing other debentures in their place, but the reissue of a debenture or the issue of another debenture in its place, under the power by this section given to a company, shall not be treated as the issue of a new debenture for the purposes of any provision limiting the amount or number of debentures to be issued.

(2) **Priorities on reissue** — On a reissue of redeemed debentures, the person entitled to the debentures has the same rights and priorities as if the debentures had never been redeemed.

(3) **Particulars in balance sheet** — here a company has power to reissue debentures that have been redeemed, particulars with respect to the debentures that can be so reissued shall be included in every balance sheet of the company.

(4) **Debentures deposited to secure advances** — Where a company has deposited any of its debentures to secure advances from time to time on current account or otherwise, the debentures shall not be deemed to have been redeemed by reason only of the account of the company having ceased to be in debit while the debentures remained so deposited.

(5) **Right saved** — Nothing in this section prejudices any power to issue debentures in the place of any debentures, paid off or otherwise satisfied or extinguished, reserved to a company by its debentures or by any deed securing payment of the same.

*Information as to Mortgages and Charges*

**68.** (1) **Delivery of prescribed particulars** — In respect of every mortgage or charge created by a company after the 1st day of October 1934, being either

(a)   a mortgage or charge for the purpose of securing any issue of debentures,

(b)   a mortgage or charge on uncalled share capital of the company,

(c)   a floating charge on the undertaking or property of the company,

(d)   a mortgage or charge on calls made but not paid, or

(e)   a mortgage or charge on goodwill, on any patent or licence under a patent, on any trade mark or on any copyright or licence under a copyright, the company shall deliver to the Minister the prescribed particulars of the mortgage or charge, and a copy of the instrument, if any, by which the mortgage or charge is created or evidenced, certified by the secretary of the company, or, in the Province of Quebec, a notarial copy of such instrument within thirty days after the date of its creation.

(2) **Exception** — Subsection (1) does not apply to the giving by a company of any warehouse receipt or bill of lading or any security under the provisions of the *Bank Act* as collateral security for the payment of any debt or liability of the company, nor to a floating charge created by a company on its accounts receivable or any of them after the 1st day of October 1934.

(3) **Idem** — In the case of a mortgage or charge created out of Canada comprising solely property situated outside Canada, it is sufficient if the prescribed particulars and the certified copy of the instrument by which the mortgage or charge is created or evidenced are delivered to the Minister within ninety days after the date on which the instrument or copy could in due course of post and if dispatched with due diligence have been received in Canada.

(4) **Property acquired subject to mortgage or charge** — Where after the 1st day of October 1934 a company acquires any property that is subject to a mortgage or charge of any such kind that, if it had been created by the company after the acquisition of the property, particulars thereof would have been required to be delivered to the Minister under subsection (1), the company shall deliver to the Minister the prescribed particulars of the mortgage or charge and a copy of the instrument, if any, by which the mortgage or charge is created or evidenced, certified by the secretary of the company, or, in the Province of Quebec, a notarial copy of such instrument, within ninety days after the date on which the acquisition is completed.

(5) **Register to be kept by Minister** — The Minister shall keep with respect to each company a register in the prescribed form in which shall be entered with respect to every mortgage or charge a copy of which has been delivered to the Minister the date of the mortgage or charge, the amount secured by it, short par-

ticulars of the property mortgaged or charged and the names of the mortgagees or persons entitled to the charge or the particulars required to be delivered to the Minister under subsection (6) as the case may be.

(6) **Particulars** — Where a series of debentures containing or giving by reference to any other instrument any charge to the benefit of which the debenture holders of that series are entitled *pari passu* is created by a company, it is sufficient if there are delivered to the Minister within thirty days after the execution of the deed containing the charge or if there is no such deed after the execution of any debentures of the series, the following particulars:

(a)  the total amount secured by the whole series;

(b)  the date of the covering deed, if any, by which the security is created or defined or if there is no such deed the date of the issuance of the first debenture of the series;

(c)  a general description of the property charged; and

(d)  the names of the trustees, if any, for the debenture holders;

together with a copy of the covering deed, if any, certified by the secretary of the company under the corporate seal or in the Province of Quebec a notarial copy thereof, or if there is no such deed a copy of one of the debentures of the series certified by the secretary of the company under its corporate seal; and the Minister shall on payment of the prescribed fee enter those particulars in the register.

(7) **Rate of commission** — Where any commission, allowance, or discount has been paid or made either directly or indirectly by the company to any person in consideration of his subscribing or agreeing to subscribe, whether absolutely or conditionally, for any debentures of the company, or procuring or agreeing to procure subscriptions, whether absolute or conditional, for any such debentures, the particulars required to be delivered for registration under this section shall include particulars as to the amount or rate per cent of the commission, discount, or allowance so paid or made.

(8) **Debentures as security** — The deposit of any debentures as security for any debt of the company shall not, for the purposes of subsection (7), be treated as the issue of the debentures at a discount.

(9) **Failure to comply** — Failure to comply with this section does not affect the validity of the mortgage or charge or of the debentures issued, but every director or officer knowingly and wilfully authorizing or permitting such default and the company are liable on summary conviction to a fine not exceeding twenty dollars for every day during which the default continues.

(10) **Register to be open to inspection** — The register kept in pursuance of this section shall be open to inspection by any person on payment of the prescribed fee.

(11) **Copies of instruments to be kept at head office** — very company shall cause a copy of every instrument creating any mortgage or charge particulars of which are required to be delivered to the Minister under this section to be kept at the head office of the company.

**69.** (1) **Notice of order appointing receiver** — Where any person obtains an order for the appointment of a receiver or receiver and manager of the property of a company, or appoints such receiver or receiver and manager under any powers contained in any instrument, he shall, within fourteen days from the date of the order or of the appointment under the powers contained in the instrument, give notice of the fact to the Minister who shall on payment of the prescribed fee enter the fact in the register.

(2) **Penalty** — Where any person wilfully makes default in complying with the requirements of this section he is liable on summary conviction to a fine not exceeding twenty dollars for every day during which the default continues.

**70. Entry of satisfaction** — The Minister, on evidence being given to his satisfaction that the debt, for which any mortgage or charge was created and entered on the register kept by him, has been paid or satisfied, may order that a memorandum of satisfaction be entered on such register, and shall if required furnish the company with a copy thereof.

**71.** (1) **Company's register of mortgages** — Every company shall keep a register of mortgages and enter therein all mortgages and charges particulars of which are required to be delivered to the Minister and of all other mortgages and charges specifically affecting property of the company, not being mortgages or charges to which subsection 68(1) does not apply, giving in each case a short description of the property mortgaged or charged, the amount of the mortgage or charge, and, except in the case of securities to bearer, the names and addresses, if known, of the mortgagees or persons entitled thereto unless such names and addresses, if known, are entered in a register of holders of debentures kept by or on behalf of the company.

(2) **Omission of entries** — Where any director, manager, or other officer of the company wilfully authorizes or permits the omission of any entry required to be made in pursuance of this section, he is liable on summary conviction to a fine not exceeding two hundred dollars.

**72.** (1) **Right to inspect copies of instruments** — The copies of instruments creating any mortgage or charge that, under this Act, are required to be delivered to the Minister, and the register of mortgages kept in pursuance of section 71, shall be open at all reasonable times to the inspection of any creditor or shareholder of the company without fee, and the register of mortgages shall also be open to the inspection of any other person on payment of such fee, not exceeding twenty-five cents for each inspection, as the company may prescribe.

(2) **Where inspection refused** — Where inspection of the said copies or register is refused, any officer of the company wrongfully refusing inspection, and every director or officer of the company wilfully authorizing or permitting such refusal, is liable on summary conviction to a fine not exceeding twenty dollars, and a further fine not exceeding ten dollars for every day during which the wrongful refusal continues.

**73.** (1) **Right of debenture holders to inspect register** — Every register of holders of debentures of a company shall, except when closed in accordance with the by-laws of the company or the provisions of the debentures or the covering deed, if any, during such period or periods, not exceeding in the whole thirty days in any year, as may be specified in the said by-laws or provisions, be open to the inspection of the registered holder of any such debentures, and of any share-holder, but subject to such reasonable restrictions as the company may impose, so that at least two hours in each day are appointed for inspection, and every such holder may require a copy of the register or any part thereof on payment of ten cents for every hundred words required to be copied.

(2) **Copy of trust deed to be forwarded** — A copy of any trust deed for securing payment of any issue of debentures shall be forwarded to every holder of any such debentures at his request, on payment in the case of a printed trust deed of the sum of twenty-five cents, or such less sum as may be prescribed by by-law of the company, or, where the trust deed has not been printed, on payment of ten cents for every hundred words required to be copied.

(3) **Where inspection refused** — Where inspection is wrongfully refused, or a copy is wrongfully refused or not forwarded, the company is liable on summary conviction to a fine not exceeding twenty dollars, and to a further fine not exceeding ten dollars for every day during which the refusal or neglect to forward a copy continues, and every director, manager, secretary, or other officer of the company who wilfully authorizes or permits such refusal shall incur the like penalty.

. . .

*Directors*

**93. Director indemnified in suits respecting execution of his office** — Every director of the company, and his heirs, executors and administrators, and estate and effects, respectively, may, with the consent of the company, given at any meeting of the shareholders thereof, from time to time and at all times, be indemnified and saved harmless out of the funds of the company, from and against,

(a) all costs, charges and expenses whatever that such director sustains or incurs in or about any action, suit or proceeding that is brought, commenced or prosecuted against him, for or in respect of any act, deed, matter or thing whatever, made, done or permitted by him, in or about the execution of the duties of his office, and

(b) all other costs, charges and expenses that he sustains, or incurs, in or about or in relation to the affairs thereof, except such costs, charges or expenses as are occasioned by his own wilful neglect or default.

. . .

**98.** (1) **Director interested in a contract with the company** — Subject to this section, it is the duty of a director of a company who is in any way, whether directly or indirectly, interested in a contract or proposed contract with the company to declare his interest at a meeting of directors of the company.

(2) **At what meeting declaration to be made** — In the case of a proposed contract the declaration required by this section to be made by a director shall be made at the meeting of directors at which the question of entering into the contract is first taken into consideration, or, if the director is not at the date of that meeting interested in the proposed contract, at the next meeting of the directors held after he becomes so interested, and, in a case where the director becomes interested in a contract after it is made, the declaration shall be made at the first meeting of directors held after the director becomes so interested.

(3) **What is deemed sufficient declaration** — For the purposes of this section, a general notice given to the directors of a company by a director to the effect that he is a shareholder of or otherwise interested in any other company or is a member of a specified firm and is to be regarded as interested in any contract made with such other company or firm shall be deemed to be a sufficient declaration of interest in relation to any contract so made.

(4) **Director not to vote if interested** — o director shall vote in respect of any contract or proposed contract in which he is so interested as aforesaid and if he does so vote his vote shall not be counted, but this prohibition does not apply

(a)    in the case of any contract by or on behalf of the company to give to the directors or any of them security for advances or by way of indemnity,

(b)    in the case of a private company, where there is no quorum of directors in office who are not so interested, or

(c)    in the case of any contract between the company and any other company where the interest of the director in the last-mentioned company consists solely in his being a director or officer of such last-mentioned company, and the holder of not more than the number of shares in such last-mentioned company requisite to qualify him as a director.

(5) **When director not accountable** — A director who has made a declaration of his interest in a contract or proposed contract in compliance with this section and has not voted in respect of such contract contrary to the prohibition contained in subsection (4), if such prohibition applies, is not accountable to the company or any of its shareholders or creditors by reason only of such director holding that office or of the fiduciary relationship thereby established for any profit realized by such contract.

(6) **"Contract" and "meeting of directors"** — For the purposes of this section "contract" includes "arrangement" and "meeting of directors" includes a meeting of an executive committee elected in accordance with section 96.

(7) **No liability when contract confirmed** — Nothing in this section imposes any liability upon a director in respect of the profit realized by any contract that has been confirmed by the vote of shareholders of the company at a special general meeting called for that purpose.

**99.** (1) **Liability of directors for wages unsatisfied** — The directors of the company are jointly and severally liable to the clerks, labourers, servants and apprentices thereof, for all debts not exceeding six months wages due for services performed for the company while they are such directors respectively.

(2) **When not liable** — A director is not liable under subsection (1) unless

(a)    the company has been sued for the debt within six months after it has become due and execution has been returned unsatisfied in whole or in part, or

(b)    the company has within that period gone into liquidation or has been ordered to be wound up under the *Winding-up and Restructuring Act*, or has made an authorized assignment under the *Bankruptcy and Insolvency Act* or a bankruptcy order under the *Bankruptcy and Insolvency Act* has been made against it and a claim for such debt has been duly filed and proved,

nor unless he is sued for such debt while a director or within one year after he has ceased to be a director.

(3) **Amount recoverable** — Where execution has so issued the amount recoverable against the director shall be the amount remaining unsatisfied on the execution.

(4) **Directors' preference** — Where the claim for such debt has been proved in liquidation or winding-up proceedings or under the *Winding-up Act* or the *Bankruptcy Act* a director, upon payment of the debt, is entitled to any preference that the creditor paid would have been entitled to, and where a judgment has been recovered he is entitled to an assignment of the judgment.

[2004, c. 25, s. 189.]

. . .

### *Meetings of Shareholders*

**102.** (1) **Annual meeting** — An annual meeting of the shareholders of the company shall be held at some date not later than eighteen months after the incorporation of the company and subsequently once at least in every calendar year and not more than fifteen months after the holding of the last preceding annual meeting.

(2) **In case of default** — Where default is made in holding any annual meeting as provided under subsection (1), the court in the province in which the head office of the company is situated may, on the application of any shareholder of the company, call or direct the calling of an annual meeting of the shareholders.

. . .

**106. Power of court to order meeting to be called** — Where for any reason it is impracticable to call a meeting of shareholders of the company in any manner in which meetings of shareholders may be called, or to conduct the meeting in manner prescribed by the letters patent, supplementary letters patent, the by-laws or this Part, the court in the province in which the head office of the company is situated, may, either of its own motion, or on the application of any director or any shareholder who would be entitled to vote at the meeting, order a meeting to be called, held and conducted in such manner as the court thinks fit and, where any such order is made, may give such ancillary or consequential directions as it thinks expedient; and any meeting called, held and conducted in accordance with any such order shall for all purposes be deemed to be a meeting of shareholders of the company duly called, held and conducted.

. . .

*Books*

**109.** (1) **Contents of books** — The company shall cause a book or books to be kept by the secretary, or some other officer specially charged with that duty, wherein shall be kept recorded

(a)  a copy of the letters patent, all by-laws of the company and any supplementary letters patent issued to the company and a copy of the memorandum of agreement of the company, if any;

(b)  the names, alphabetically arranged of all persons who are and have been shareholders of the company;

(c)  the address and calling of every such person, while such shareholder, as far as can be ascertained;

(d)  the names, addresses and callings of all persons who are or have been directors of the company, with the several dates at which each became or ceased to be such director;

. . .

**111.1.** (1) **List of shareholders** — Any person, upon payment of the costs thereof and upon filing with the company or its transfer agent such declaration as may be prescribed by regulation, is entitled to obtain from a company, other than a private company, or its transfer agent within ten days from the filing of such declaration a list setting out the names of all persons who are shareholders of the company, the number of shares owned by each such person and the address of each such person as shown on the books of the company made up to a date not more than ten days prior to the date of filing the declaration.

(2) **Declaration of company** — Where the applicant is a corporation, the prescribed declaration shall be made by the president or other officer authorized by resolution of the board of directors thereof.

(3) **Offence and punishment** — Every person who, for the purpose of communicating to any shareholders any information relating to any goods, services, publications or securities except securities of the company, and except securities of any other company offered in exchange for the securities of the company pursuant to a take-over bid made pursuant to sections 135.1 to 135.93 or on an amalgamation pursuant to section 137, uses a list of shareholders obtained under this section is guilty of an offence and is liable on summary conviction to a fine not exceeding one thousand dollars or to imprisonment for a term not exceeding six months or to both and where that person is a corporation, every director or officer

of the corporation who knowingly authorized, permitted or acquiesced in the offence is also guilty of an offence and is liable on summary conviction to a like penalty.

(4) **Idem** — Every company or transfer agent that fails to furnish a list in accordance with subsection (1) when so required is guilty of an offence and is liable on summary conviction to a fine not exceeding one thousand dollars and every director or officer of such company or transfer agent who knowingly authorized, permitted or acquiesced in the offence is also guilty of an offence and is liable on summary conviction to a like fine, or to imprisonment for a term not exceeding six months or to both.

(5) **Idem** — Every person who offers for sale, sells, purchases or otherwise traffics in a list or a copy of a list of all or any of the shareholders of a company is guilty of an offence and is liable on summary conviction to a fine not exceeding one thousand dollars or to imprisonment for a term not exceeding six months or to both, and where that person is a corporation, every director or officer of the corporation who knowingly authorized, permitted or acquiesced in the offence is also guilty of an offence and is liable on summary conviction to a like penalty.

[R.S., 1970, c. 10 (1st Supp.), s. 11.]

**112.** (1) **Minutes or proceedings** — Every company shall cause minutes of all proceedings at meetings of the shareholders and of the directors and of any executive committee to be entered in books kept for that purpose.

(2) **Minutes to be evidence** — Any such minutes if purporting to be signed by the chairman of the meeting at which the proceedings were had, or by the chairman of the next succeeding meeting are evidence of the proceedings.

(3) **Meeting deemed duly called, etc.**— Where minutes, in accordance with this section, have been made of the proceedings of any meeting of the shareholders or of the directors or executive committee, then, until the contrary is proved, the meeting shall be deemed to have been duly called and held and all proceedings had thereat to have been duly had and all appointments of directors, managers or other officers shall be deemed to have been duly made.

**113. Neglect to keep books** — Every company that neglects to keep any book or books required by this Part to be kept by the company, is guilty of an offence and liable on summary conviction to a penalty not exceeding twenty dollars for each day that such neglect continues.

. . .

**114.1** (1) **Investigating ownership of securities** — Where it appears to the Minister that, for the purposes of sections 100 to 100.6, and sections 135.1 to 135.93, there is reason to inquire into the ownership of any securities of a company, the Minister or his authorized representative may require any person whom the Minister has reasonable cause to believe

(a)    is interested or has been interested in those securities, or
(b)    is acting or has acted in relation to those securities as the agent or financial or investment adviser of someone interested therein,

to give him any information that such person has or can reasonably be expected to obtain as to the present and past interests in those securities and the names and addresses of the persons interested and of any persons who act or have acted on their behalf in relation to the securities.

(2) **Presumption of interest** — For the purposes of subsection (1), a person shall be deemed to have an interest in any securities if he has any right to acquire or dispose of them, or any interest therein, or to vote in respect thereof, or if his consent is necessary for the exercise of any of the rights of other persons interested therein, or if other persons interested therein can be required or are accustomed to exercise their rights in accordance with his instructions.

(3) **Publication or report** — The Minister may

(a) forward to such person or persons as he thinks fit a copy of such part of any report made to him that relates to the ownership of any securities of a company and may cause any such report or any part thereof to be published;

(b) divulge as he thinks fit any information relating to the ownership of any securities of a company obtained by him as a result of his investigation and may cause any such information to be published; and

(c) cause to be published monthly in the periodical referred to in section 100.2, such part of such report as relates to the ownership of any securities of the company.

(4) Any person who wilfully fails to give any information required of him under this section, or who in giving any such information knowingly makes any statement that is false in a material particular is guilty of an offence and is liable on summary conviction to a fine not exceeding one thousand dollars or to imprisonment for a term not exceeding six months or to both.

[R.S., 1970, c. 10 (1st Supp.), s. 12.]

**114.2** (1) **Where default occurs** — Where pursuant to this Act a company or any officer thereof is required to file or deposit with the Department of Consumer and Corporate Affairs any report, return, record, bylaw, statement or other document, or any copy thereof, and the company or officer defaults in doing so, the Minister may

(a) cause an inspection to be made of the affairs and management of the company by a person authorized by him in that behalf to determine the reasons for such default, and to report thereon to the Minister, or

(b) by notice require any company or any director thereof to make a return upon any subject connected with its default within the time specified in the notice.

(2) **Inspections** — Subject to subsection (2.1), any person (in this section called an "inspector") authorized pursuant to subsection (1) to carry out an inspection pursuant to this section may at any reasonable time enter the premises of any company in respect of whose affairs and management an inspection has been authorized pursuant to subsection (1) and may examine any thing on the premises and may, for further examination, copy, or have a copy made of, any book or

paper, or other document or record that in the opinion of the inspector is relevant to his inspection.

(2.1) **Authority to issue warrant** — Where on ex parte application a justice of the peace is satisfied by information on oath that there are reasonable grounds to believe that there is in any premises referred to in subsection (2) any evidence relevant to the matters being investigated under this section, he may issue a warrant under his hand authorizing the inspector named therein to enter those premises and to exercise any of the other powers referred to in subsection (2), subject to such conditions as may be specified in the warrant.

(2.2) **Use of force** — In executing a warrant issued under subsection (2.1), an inspector shall not use force unless he is accompanied by a peace officer and the use of force has been specifically authorized in the warrant.

(2.3) **Where warrant not necessary** — An inspector may exercise any of the powers referred to in subsection (2) without a warrant issued under subsection (2.1) if the conditions for obtaining the warrant exist but by reason of exigent circumstances it would not be practical to obtain the warrant.

(2.4) **Exigent circumstances** — For the purposes of subsection (2.3), exigent circumstances include circumstances in which the delay necessary to obtain a warrant under subsection (2.1) would result in danger to human life or safety or the loss or destruction of evidence.

(2.5) **Duty to give assistance** — The person in charge of any premises entered pursuant to this section and all directors, officers, agents and employees of any company investigated pursuant to this section shall give all reasonable assistance to enable an inspector to carry out his inspection.

(3) **Producing authority** — On entering any premises pursuant to this section, an inspector shall, if so requested, produce the authorization of the Minister to the person in charge thereof.

(4) **Offence and punishment** — A person who

(a)    fails to permit an inspector to enter upon any premises or to make any inspection in pursuance of his duties under this section, or

(b)    in any manner obstructs an inspector in the execution of his duties under this section,

is guilty of an offence and is liable on summary conviction to a fine not exceeding one thousand dollars or to imprisonment for a term not exceeding six months or to both.

(5) **Idem** — Every director and officer of the company who knowingly authorizes or permits a default in making a return required under paragraph (1)(b) is guilty of an offence and is liable on summary conviction to a fine not exceeding fifty dollars for every day during which the default continues.

[R.S., 1970, c. 10 (1st Supp.), s. 12; 1985, c. 26, s. 36 (in force October 15, 1985).]

**114.3** (1) **Compelling evidence** — No person shall be excused from attending and giving evidence and producing books, papers, documents or records in accordance with section 114.2 on the grounds that the oral evidence or documents required of him may tend to criminate him or subject him to any proceeding or penalty, but no such oral evidence so required shall be used or is receivable against him in any criminal proceedings thereafter instituted against him, other than a prosecution for perjury in giving the evidence.

(2) **Solicitor's communications** — Nothing in section 114.2 or this section compels the production by a solicitor of a document containing a privileged communication made by or to him in that capacity or authorizes the taking of possession of any document in his possession without the consent of his client or an order of a court.

[R.S., 1970, c. 10 (1st Supp.), s. 12; 1986, c. 26, s. 52 (in force June 19, 1986).]

**114.4** (1) **Expenses of investigations** — The expenses of, and incidental to, an investigation, inquiry or inspection under section 114, 114.1 or 114.2 shall be defrayed out of moneys provided by Parliament therefor, but the following persons are, to the extent mentioned, liable to pay those expenses as a debt owing to Her Majesty in right of Canada:

(a)   a person who is convicted on a prosecution arising out of facts disclosed by an investigation under section 114 or who is ordered to restore property or pay damages or compensation in proceedings brought under subsection 114(27) may in the same proceeding be ordered to pay to the Receiver General such expenses to such extent as may be specified in the order;

(b)   a company in whose name proceedings are brought under subsection 114(27) is liable to Her Majesty in right of Canada for the amount or value of any sums or property recovered by it as a result of those proceedings, and the expenses are a first charge on such sums or property.

(2) **Idem** — For the purposes of this section, any costs or expenses incurred by the Minister in connection with proceedings brought under subsection 114(27) shall be treated as expenses of the investigation giving rise to the proceedings.

(3) **Security for costs** — Upon the recommendation of the Minister, the Commission may require any or all shareholders applying for an investigation to give such security as the Commission deems appropriate for the payment of the costs of the investigation and any resulting inquiry and inspection.

(4) **Order to pay costs** — Upon the termination of the investigation, the Commission may order that any security given pursuant to subsection (3) be returned to the applicant but if the Commission holds that the application was vexatious or malicious it may

(a)   order the applicant to pay to the Receiver General any or all of the costs of such investigation and any resulting inquiry or inspection,

(b)   order the applicant to pay to the company any or all of the costs that it has incurred in connection with the investigation and any resulting inquiry or inspection, and

(c)   order that any security given pursuant to subsection (3) be applied toward the payment of the costs referred to in paragraphs (a) and (b), in that order, and that the residue, if any, of such security not so applied, be returned to the applicant.

**(5) Debt to Her Majesty** — Any costs ordered by the Commission to be paid to the Receiver General pursuant to subsection (4) shall be a debt owing to Her Majesty in right of Canada.

[R.S., 1970, c. 10 (1st Supp.), s. 12; 1986, c. 26, s. 53 (in force June 19, 1986).]

**115. (1) Power to appoint inspectors** — A company may by resolution of its shareholders at any annual or special general meeting called for that purpose appoint inspectors to investigate its affairs.

**(2) Powers and duties of inspectors** — Inspectors so appointed have the same powers and duties as inspectors appointed by the Minister, except that, instead of reporting to the Minister, they shall report in such manner and to such persons as the shareholders by resolution may direct.

**(3) Refusing to produce books or answer questions** — Officers and agents of the company shall incur the like penalties in ease of refusal to produce any book or document required to be produced to inspectors so appointed, or to answer any question, as they would have incurred if the inspectors had been appointed by the Minister.

**116. Report of inspectors to be evidence** — A copy of the report of any inspectors appointed under this Act, authenticated by the seal of the company whose affairs they have investigated or by the seal of the Minister, is admissible in any legal proceeding as evidence of the opinion of the inspectors in relation to any matter contained in the report.

*Accounts and Audit*

**117. (1) Books of account and accounting records** — Every company shall cause to be kept proper accounting records with respect to all financial and other transactions of the company, and, without limiting the generality of the foregoing, shall cause records to be kept of

(a) all sums of money received and disbursed by the company and the matters in respect of which receipt and disbursement take place;
(b) all sales and purchases by the company;
(c) all assets and liability of the company; and
(d) all other transactions affecting the financial position of the company.

**(2) Records to be kept at head office** — The accounting records shall be kept at the head office of the company or at such other place in Canada as the directors think fit, and shall at all times be open to inspection by the directors.

**(3) Keeping records at other offices** — In case the operating accounts of the company are kept at some place outside Canada, there shall be kept at the head office of the company such comprehensive records as will enable the directors to ascertain with reasonable accuracy the financial position of the company at the end of each three months period.

. . .

**130.** (1) **Appointment of auditor at first general meeting** — The shareholders of a company at their first general meeting shall appoint one or more auditors to hold office until the close of the next annual meeting, and, if the shareholders fail to do so, the directors shall forthwith make such appointment or appointments.

(2) **Annual appointment of auditor** — The shareholders of a company at each annual meeting shall appoint one or more auditors to hold office until the close of the next annual meeting, and, if an appointment is not so made, the auditor in office continues in office until a successor is appointed.

(3) **Notice of intention to nominate auditor** — A person, other than a retiring auditor, is not capable of being appointed auditor at an annual meeting unless notice in writing of an intention to nominate that person to the office of auditor has been given by a shareholder of the company not less than fourteen days before the annual meeting; and the company shall send a copy of any such notice to the retiring auditor and to the person it is intended to nominate, and shall give notice thereof to the shareholders, either by advertisement or in any other mode provided by the by-laws of the company, not less than seven days before the annual meeting.

(4) **Vacancy** — The directors may fill any casual vacancy in the office of auditor, but while the vacancy continues the surviving or continuing auditor, if any, may act.

(5) **Removal of auditor** — The shareholders, by a resolution passed by at least two-thirds of the votes cast at a general meeting of which notice specifying the intention to pass such resolution was given, may remove any auditor before the expiration of his term of office, and shall by a majority of the votes cast at that meeting appoint another auditor in his stead for the remainder of his term.

(6) **Remuneration** — The remuneration of an auditor appointed by the shareholders shall be fixed by the shareholders or by the directors, if they are authorized to do so by the shareholders, and the remuneration of an auditor appointed by the directors shall be fixed by the directors.

(7) **Appointment by Minister** — Where for any reason no auditor is appointed, the Minister may, on the application of any shareholder, appoint one or more auditors to hold office until the close of the next annual meeting and fix the remuneration to be paid by the company for his or their services.

(8) **Notice of appointment** — When an auditor is appointed under this section, the company shall give him notice thereof forthwith in writing unless he held that office immediately prior to his appointment.

**131.** (1) **Disqualification for appointment** — Except as provided in subsection (2), no person shall be appointed as auditor of a company who is a director, officer or employee of that company or an affiliated company or who is a partner, employer or employee of any such director, officer or employee.

(2) **Private company exception** — Upon the unanimous vote of the shareholders of a private company, present or represented at the meeting at which the auditor is appointed, a director, officer or employee of that company or an affiliated company, or a partner, employer or employee of that director, officer or employee may be appointed as auditor of that company.

(2.1) **Non-application of subsection (2)** — Subsection (2) does not apply if the company is a company to which paragraph 128(1)(b) applies, or if the company is a subsidiary of a company incorporated in any jurisdiction in Canada that is not a private company within the meaning of this Act.

(3) **Statement of auditor's position** — A person appointed as auditor under subsection (2) shall indicate in his report to the shareholders on the annual financial statement of the company that he is a director, officer or employee of the company or an affiliated company or a partner, employer or employee of the director, officer or employee.

[R.S., 1970, c. 10 (1st Supp.), s. 21.]

**132.** (1) **Annual audit** — The auditor shall make such examination as will enable him to report to the shareholders as required under subsection (2).

(2) **Auditor's report** — The auditor shall make a report to the shareholders on the financial statement, other than the part thereof that relates to the period referred to in subparagraph 118(1)(a)(ii), to be laid before the company at any annual meeting during his term of office and shall state in his report whether in his opinion the financial statement referred to therein presents fairly the financial position of the company and the results of its operations for the period under review in accordance with generally accepted accounting principle applied on a basis consistent with that of the preceding period.

(3) **Where statement required** — The auditor in his report shall make such statements as he considers necessary in any case where

(a)  the financial statement of the company is not in agreement with the accounting records;

(b)  the financial statement of the company is not in accordance with the requirements of this Act;

(c)  he has not received all the information and explanation that he has required; or

(d)  proper accounting records have not been kept, so far as appears from his examination.

(4) **Right of access to records** — The auditor of a company shall have access at all times to all records, documents, books, accounts and vouchers of the company, and is entitled to require from the directors and officers of the company

(a)  such information and explanations,

(b)  such access to all records, documents, books, accounts and vouchers of any subsidiary company, and

(c)  such information and explanations from the directors and officers of any subsidiary company,

as in his opinion may be necessary to enable him to report as required by subsection (2).

(5) **Right to attend meetings** — The auditor of a company is entitled to attend any meeting of shareholders of the company and to receive all notices and other communications relating to any such meeting that any shareholder is entitled to

receive, unless waived by such auditor, and to be heard at any such meeting that he attends on any part of the business of the meeting that concerns him as auditor.

(6) **Required attendance of auditor** — A company, upon receipt, not less than seven days before a meeting of shareholders, of a written application of shareholders holding not less than ten per cent of the issued shares of the company that the auditor of the company be requested to attend the meeting, shall forthwith in writing request the auditor to attend that meeting of shareholders, and the auditor or his representative shall so attend.

[R.S., 1970, c. 10 (1st Supp.), s. 22.]

**133.** (1) **Annual returns** — Every company shall, on or before the 1st day of June in every year, make a summary as of the 31st day of March preceding, specifying the following particulars:

(a)  the corporate name of the company;
(b)  the manner in which the company is incorporated and the date of incorporation;
(c)  the complete postal address of the head office of the company;
(d)  the date upon which and the place where the last annual meeting of the shareholders of the company was held;
(e)  the names and complete postal addresses of the persons who at the date of the return are the directors of the company; and
(f)  the name and complete postal address of the auditor of the company.

(2) **Summary to be filed, signed and certified** — The summary mentioned in subsection (1) shall be completed and filed in duplicate in the Department on or before the 1st day of June aforesaid, and each of the duplicates shall be signed and certified by a director or an officer of the company.

(3) **Defaults** — A company that makes default in complying with any requirement of this section is guilty of an offence and is liable on summary conviction to a fine of not less than twenty dollars and not more than one hundred dollars for each day during which the default continues; and every director or officer who knowingly authorized, permitted or acquiesced in any such default is guilty of an offence and is liable on summary conviction to a like fine.

(4) **Duplicate of summary** — The Minister, or an official of the Department designated for that purpose, shall endorse upon one duplicate of the above summary the date of the receipt thereof at the Department and shall return the duplicate summary to the company and it shall be retained at the head office of the company available for perusal of, and for the purpose of making copies thereof or extracts therefrom by, any shareholder or creditor of the company.

(5) **Proof of endorsement** —The duplicate of the said summary endorsed as required under subsection (4) is evidence that the summary was filed in the Department pursuant to this section on any prosecution under this section and the written or stamped signature of an official of the Department to the endorsement of the said duplicate shall be deemed *prima facie* proof that the said official has been designated to affix his signature thereto.

(6) **Proof of failure to file summary** — A certificate under the hand and seal of office of the Minister that the aforesaid summary in duplicate was not filed in the Department by a company pursuant to this section is evidence on a prosecution under this section that such summary was not filed in the Department.

(7) **Companies exempt** — Companies incorporated after the 1st day of March in any year are not subject to the provisions of this section until the 31st day of March of the following year.

(8) **Where default exists** — Where a summary in respect of an earlier year has not been filed with the Department or where the annual fees are in default, the summary required under subsection (1) may not be filed until the summary in respect of the earlier year has been filed or until the annual fee has been paid, as the case may be.

(9) **Failure to file for two consecutive years** — Where a company has for two consecutive years failed to file in the Department the summary required under subsection (1), the Minister may, notwithstanding paragraph 150(1)(c), give notice to the company that an order dissolving the company will be issued unless within one year after the publication of the notice in the *Canada Gazette* the company files a summary in respect of those two years.

(10) **Publication of notice** — The notice under subsection (9) shall be given by registered mail to the company or by publication of the notice in the *Canada Gazette*.

(11) **Dissolution of company** — One year after the publication of notice in the *Canada Gazette*, if the company has not filed a summary for the two years in respect of which it was in default, the Minister may, by order published in the *Canada Gazette*, declare the company dissolved, and thereupon the company is dissolved, and section 33 applies mutatis mutandis thereto.

(11.1) **"Winding-up"** — For the purpose of distributing the assets of a company dissolved by order under subsection (11) among shareholders or creditors, the affairs of the company may be wound up under the *Winding-up Act*, upon an application to a court of competent jurisdiction, by a director, shareholder or creditor of the company or the Attorney General of Canada, for an order winding up the company under that Act, as a company described in paragraph 10(a) of that Act.

(12) **Notice of winding-up or bankruptcy** — Where a company is being wound up or where a company is being administered by a trustee in bankruptcy, the liquidator or trustee, as the case may be, shall annually, without fee therefor, give notice of the winding-up or bankruptcy to the Department in lieu of the summary required under subsection (1).

[R.S., 1970, c. 10 (1st Supp.), s. 23.]

. . .

*Evidence*

**138.** (1) **Books to be evidence** — All books required by this Part to be kept by the company are, in any action, suit or proceeding against the company or against any shareholder, evidence of all facts purporting to be thereby stated.

(2) **Section 112 not affected** — Nothing in this section limits the meaning or effect of section 112.

**139. Proof of service by letter** — Proof that any letter properly addressed containing any notice or other document permitted by this Part to be served by post was properly addressed and was put into a post office with postage prepaid, and of the time when it was so put in, and of the time requisite for its delivery in the ordinary course of post, is sufficient evidence of the fact and time of service.

**140. Evidence of by-laws** — A copy of any by-law of the company under its seal and purporting to be signed by any officer of the company shall, as against any shareholder of the company, be received in evidence as *prima facie* proof of such by-law in all courts in Canada.

**141. Proof of incorporation** — In any action or other legal proceeding, the notice in the *Canada Gazette* of the issue of letters patent or supplementary letters patent under this Part is *prima facie* proof of all things therein contained, and on production of such letters patent or supplementary letters patent or of any exemplification or copy thereof certified by the Registrar General of Canada, the fact of such notice and publication shall be presumed.

**142. Proof of matters set forth in letters patent** — Except in any proceeding by *scire facias* or otherwise for the purpose of rescinding or annulling letters patent or supplementary letters patent issued under this Part, such letters patent or supplementary letters patent, or any exemplification or copy thereof certified by the Registrar General of Canada, are conclusive proof of every matter and thing therein set forth.

**143. Proof by declaration or affidavit** — Proof of any matter that is necessary to be made under this Part may be made by oath or affirmation or by statutory declaration before any justice of the peace, or any commissioner for taking affidavits, to be used in any of the courts in any of the provinces of Canada, or any notary public, each of whom is hereby authorized and empowered to administer oaths and receive affidavits and declarations for that purpose.

*Procedure*

**144. Cases where use of seal not necessary** — Any summons, notice, order, document or proceeding requiring authentication by the company may be signed by any director, manager or other authorized officer of the company, and need not be under the seal of the company.

**145. Service of notices on shareholders** — In the absence of any other provision in this Part or in the by-laws, notices to be served by the company upon its shareholders may be served either personally or by sending them through the post, by registered mail, addressed to the shareholders at their places of abode as they appear on the books of the company.

**146. Time from which service reckoned** — A notice or other document served by post by the company on a shareholder shall be deemed to be served at the time when the registered letter containing it would be delivered in the ordinary course of post.

**147. Action between company and shareholders** — Any description of action may be prosecuted and maintained between the company and any shareholder thereof.

**148. Setting forth incorporation in legal proceedings** — In any action or other legal proceeding, it shall not be requisite to set forth the mode of incorporation of the company, otherwise than by mention of it under its corporate name as incorporated by virtue of letters patent, or of letters patent and supplementary letters patent, as the case may be.

## Offences and Penalties

**149. Penalties not otherwise provided for** — Every one who, being a director, manager or officer of a company, or acting on its behalf, commits any act contrary to the provisions of this Part, or fails or neglects to comply with any such provision, is, if no penalty for such act, failure or neglect is expressly provided by this Part, liable, on summary conviction, to a fine of not more than one thousand dollars, or to imprisonment for not more than one year, or to both, but no proceeding shall be taken under this section without the consent in writing of the Minister.

**150. (1) Grounds for winding up company** — Notwithstanding any other provisions in this Act where a company

(a) fails for two or more consecutive years to hold an annual meeting of its shareholders,

(b) fails to comply with the requirements of section 128, or

(c) defaults in complying for six months or more with any requirement of section 133, the company is liable to be wound up and dissolved under the *Winding-up Act* upon the application of the Attorney General of Canada to a court of competent jurisdiction for an order that the company be wound up under that Act, which application may be made upon receipt by the Attorney General of Canada of a certificate of the Minister setting forth his opinion that any of the circumstances described in paragraphs (a) to (c) apply to that company.

**(2) Costs of winding-up** — In any application to the court under subsection (1), the court shall determine whether the costs of the winding-up shall be borne by the company or personally by any or all of the directors of the company who were knowingly responsible for the company's failure or default as described in subsection (1).

[R.S., 1970, c. 10 (1st Supp.), s. 25.]

*Fees and Regulations*

**151. (1) Tariff by Governor in Council** — The Governor in Council may establish, alter and regulate the tariff of fees to be paid on application for any letters patent or supplementary letters patent under this Part, on filing any document, on any certificate issued under this Act, on making any return under this Act and on the making of any search of the files of the Department respecting a company.

(2) **Amount may be varied** — The amount of any fee may be varied according to the nature of the company, the amount of the capital stock of the company, or other particulars, as the Governor in Council deems fit.

(3) **Fees to be paid** — No steps shall be taken in the Department toward the issue of any letters patent or supplementary letters patent under this Part, and no by-law, return, prospectus or other document may be filed or deposited in the Department and no certificate may issue therefrom under this Part, until after all fees therefor are duly paid.

**152. Forms and regulations** — The Governor in Council may, from time to time, prescribe forms and make, vary or repeal regulations for carrying out the purposes of this Part.

# PART II

## CORPORATIONS WITHOUT SHARE CAPITAL

**153. Application of Part** — This Part applies to all corporations incorporated under it and to all corporations incorporated under section 7A of the *Companies Act Amending Act, 1917*, or to which supplementary letters patent have been issued under subsection (5) of that section and all corporations incorporated under section 8 of the *Companies Act*, chapter 27 of the Revised Statutes of Canada, 1927, or to which supplementary letters patent have been issued under subsection (5) of that section of that Act.

**154. (1) Application without objects of gain** — The Minister may by letters patent under his seal of office grant a charter to any number of persons, not being fewer than three, who apply therefor, constituting the applicants and any other persons who thereafter become members of the corporation thereby created, a body corporate and politic, without share capital, for the purpose of carrying on, without pecuniary gain to its members, objects, to which the legislative authority of the Parliament of Canada extends, of a national, patriotic, religious, philanthropic, charitable, scientific, artistic, social, professional or sporting character, or the like objects.

(2) **No power to issue paper money or for banking** — Nothing in this Part shall be construed to authorize the corporation to issue any note payable to the bearer thereof or any promissory note intended to be circulated as money or as the note of a bank, or to engage in the business of banking or insurance.

**155.** (1) **Application to be filed** — The applicants for such letters patent, who shall be of the full age of eighteen years and have power under law to contract, shall file in the Department an application signed by each of the applicants and setting forth the following particulars:

(a) the proposed name of the corporation;

(b) the purposes for which its incorporation is sought;

(c) the place within Canada where the head office of the corporation is to be situated;

(d) the names in full and the address and calling of each of the applicants; and

(e) the names of the applicants, not less than three, who are to be the first directors of the corporation.

(2) **By-laws to accompany application** — The application shall be accompanied by the by-laws, in duplicate, of the proposed corporation, which by-laws shall include provisions upon the following matters:

(a) conditions of membership, including societies or companies becoming members of the corporation;

(b) mode of holding meetings, provision for quorum, rights of voting and of enacting by-laws;

(c) mode of repealing or amending by-laws with special provision that the repeal or amendment of by-laws not embodied in the letters patent shall not be enforced or acted upon until the approval of the Minister has been obtained;

(d) appointment and removal of directors, trustees, committees and officers, and their respective powers and remuneration;

(e) audit of accounts and appointment of auditors;

(f) whether or how members may withdraw from the corporation; and

(g) custody of the corporate seal and certifying of documents issued by the corporation.

(3) **By-laws may be embodied in letters patent** — The applicants may ask to have embodied in the letters patent any provision which could under this Part be contained in any by-law of the corporation.

[1985, c. 26, s. 87 (in force October 15, 1985).]

**156. Letters patent to existing corporation** — Any existing corporation without share capital created by or under any Act of the Parliament of Canada, for any of the purposes or objects set forth in section 154, may apply for the issue of letters patent creating it a corporation under this Part, and upon the issue of such letters patent the provisions of this Part and those provisions of Part I, enumerated in section 157, apply to the corporation created thereby.

**157.** (1) **Sections of Part I applicable** — The following provisions of Part I apply to corporations to which this Part applies, namely:

(a) sections 3 and 4, section 5.6, section 6, sections 9 to 12 and section 15;

(b) section 16 (except paragraph (1)(r) thereof) and subsections 20(1), (3), (4) and (5);

(c) sections 21 to 24, subsection 25(2), paragraph 25(3)(b), sections 27 to 33, section 43, sections 65 to 73, sections 93, 98, 99, 102 and 106;

(d) paragraphs 109(1)(a) to (d); and

(e) sections 111.1, 112 to 117, sections 130 to 133 and sections 138 to 152.

(2) [Repealed, R.S., 1970, c. 10 (1st Supp.), s. 26]

(3) **Interpretation** — In construing the sections of Part I made applicable to corporations under this Part,

"shareholder" means a member of such corporation;

"the company" or "a company" means a corporation to which this Part applies.

[R.S., 1970, c. 10 (1st Supp.), s. 26.]

**157.1 (1) Sections of *Canada Business Corporations Act* applicable** — Sections 222 to 227, 229 to 233 and 235 of the *Canada Business Corporations Act* apply, with such modifications as the circumstances require, in respect of corporations to which this Part applies.

(2) **Interpretation** — In construing the sections of the *Canada Business Corporations Act* made applicable to corporations under this Part, "security holder", or "registered holder or beneficial owner" in relation to a security, means a member of a corporation to which this Part applies.

(3) **Powers of Director** — A Director or Deputy Director appointed under section 253 of the *Canada Business Corporations Act* may, for the purpose of giving effect to this section with respect to the application of sections 222 to 227, 229 to 233 and 235 of that Act, exercise the powers and perform the functions and duties of the Director under those sections.

[S.C. 1986, c. 26, s. 54.]

. . .

# PART VI

## PROVISIONS OF GENERAL APPLICATION

**217. Definitions** — In this Part

"company" means any company incorporated by or under the authority of any Act of the Parliament of Canada or of the Legislature of the former Province of Canada;

"corporation" means a corporation to which Part II applies.

**218. (1) Registration and transfer offices within and outside Canada** — Every company has, and always has had, the capacity to maintain offices for the registration and transfer of shares of its capital stock and of the bonds, debentures, debenture stock and other securities issued by the company at any place within or beyond the limits of Canada.

(2) **Books for entry of particulars of registrations and transfers** — Unless the books for the registration and transfer of the shares of the capital stock and of the bonds, debentures, debenture stock and other securities of the company are kept at the chief place of business or head office of the company in Canada, a book or books shall be kept at such chief place of business or head office or at the place in Canada where one of its branch registration and transfer offices is maintained, in which shall be recorded particulars of every registration and transfer of shares of its capital stock and of the bonds, debentures, debenture stock and other securities issued by the company; but entry of the transfer of any share, bond, debenture, debenture stock or other security in a register of transfers or a branch register of transfers, whether kept at the chief place of business or head office of the company or elsewhere, is, for all purposes, a complete and valid transfer.

(3) **Part I companies** — In the case of a company to which Part I applies, subsection (2) does not apply to the register of transfers, branch registers of transfers and books mentioned in section 110.

(4) **Rectification of books** — The court, as defined in subsection 3(1), of the province in which the head office or chief place of business of the company is situated, has jurisdiction, on the application of any person interested, to order that any entry in the books for the registration and transfer of shares of the capital stock of a company be struck out or otherwise rectified on the ground that at the date of such application the entry as it appears in any such book does not accurately express or define the existing rights of the person appearing to be the registered owner of any shares of the capital stock of the company; and the court, in deciding such application, may make such order as to costs as the court may deem proper.

(5) **Application for rectification** — An application for the rectification of any such entry under subsection (4) may be made either by filing with the proper officer of the court a petition or an originating summons or notice of motion; and the court may direct the trial of any issue arising out of such application.

(6) **Saving of jurisdiction** — Subsections (4) and (5) do not deprive the court of any jurisdiction it may otherwise have.

**219.** (1) **Persons to whom this section applies** — The persons to whom this section applies are: directors of a company or corporation; managers of a company or corporation; officers of a company or corporation; persons employed by a company or corporation as auditors, whether they are or are not of the company or corporation.

(2) **Power of court to grant relief in certain cases** — Where in any proceeding for breach of or non-compliance with this Act or breach of or non-compliance with the letters patent, supplementary letters patent, Special Act, or by-laws of a company or corporation, against a person to whom this section applies, it appears to the court hearing the case that that person is or may be liable in respect of such breach or non-compliance, but that he has acted honestly and reasonably, and that, having regard to all the circumstances of the case, including those connected with his appointment, he ought fairly to be excused for such breach or non-compliance,

that court may relieve him, either wholly or partly, from his liability on such terms as the court may think fit.

(3) **Application for relief** — Where any person to whom this section applies has reason to apprehend that any claim will or might be made against him in respect of any such breach or non-compliance, he may apply to the court, as defined in subsection 3(1), of the province in which the head office or the principal place of business of the company or corporation is situated, for relief, and the court on such application has the same power to relieve him as under this section it would have had if it had been a court before which proceedings against that person for such breach or non-compliance had been brought.

(4) **Case may be withdrawn from jury** — Where any case to which subsection (2) applies is being tried by a judge with a jury, the judge, after hearing the evidence, may, if he is satisfied that the defendant ought in pursuance of that subsection to be relieved either in whole or in part from the liability sought to be enforced against him, withdraw the case in whole or in part from the jury and forthwith direct judgment to be entered for the defendant on such terms as to costs or otherwise as the judge may think proper.

**220. Certain sections not applicable** — The following provisions of *The Companies Act Amendment Act, 1935*, namely, sections 2, 3, 6, 7, 13 and 16, do not apply to any company to which Part I is made applicable by paragraph 2(b), (c), (d) or (e), nor to any company incorporated prior to the 15th day of September 1935, and every such company is subject to this Act as if the foregoing sections of *The Companies Act Amendment Act, 1935*, had not been enacted, but each of the other provisions of *The Companies Act Amendment Act, 1935*, pursuant to its terms, applies to all companies, irrespective of the date of their incorporation, to which Part I applies.

# CANADA CORPORATIONS REGULATIONS

(C.R.C., c. 424)

*Short Title*

**1.** These Regulations may be cited as the Canada Corporations Regulations.

*Interpretation*

**2.** In these Regulations,

"Act" means the *Canada Corporations Act*;

"associate" has the same meaning as in subsection 100(1) of the Act;

"body corporate" means any company wherever or however incorporated;

"control" has the meaning assigned by subsection 125(4) of the Act;

"corporation" means a company to which the Act applies;

"document" means a document required to be sent to or filed with the Department or the Minister under the Act;

"recognized stock exchange" means

    (a)   a stock exchange recognized pursuant to the securities act of a province, or

    (b)   a stock exchange outside Canada on which shares of a corporation are listed for trading.

[SOR/78-46, s. 1.]

# PART I

## GENERAL

*Forms*

**3.** The periodical referred to in subsection 100.2(3) of the Act shall set out any administrative forms, procedures and policy guidelines established by the Minister from time to time, for the better administration of the Act, particularly any declaration delegating the exercise of the powers and duties conferred upon the Minister by the Act.

**4.** The summary referred to in subsection 133(1) of the Act shall be on Form 3 of Schedule I furnished by the Department.

**4.1** The declaration referred to in subsection 111.1(1) of the Act shall be on Form 6.

[SOR/78-46, s. 2.]

*Format of Documents*

**5.** All applications sent to or filed with the Department or the Minister shall be

(a)    on good quality white paper approximately 8 1/2 by 11 inches in size;

(b)    printed or typewritten; and

(c)    legible and suitable for microfilming and photocopying.

**6.** Where possible, each individual item in a document shall be set out in one or more contiguous, sequentially numbered paragraphs and each such item shall be preceded by an appropriate heading.

**7.** (1) Numbers in a document shall be in numerals and not in words.

(2) Information in a document shall, where practical, be set out in tabular form.

**8.** Abbreviations in documents shall,

(a)    if formed by the truncation of a word, be followed by a period; and

(b)    if formed by deletion of alphabetic characters from the middle of a word, not be followed by a period, but a corporate name may contain alphabetic characters that are not followed by a period.

**9.** (1) If an item of information required to be disclosed in a form does not apply, it shall be so indicated by the phrase "not applicable", by the abbreviation "N/A" or by a brief explanatory statement.

(2) If information is set out in response to one item in a document, it may be referred to in response to any other item in that document by a cross reference. SOR/78-46, s. 3.

**10.** (1) Where

(a)    any provision required to be set out in a form furnished by the Director is too long to be set out in the space provided in the form, or

(b)    an agreement or other document is to be incorporated by reference in and to be part of the form,

the person completing the form may, subject to subsection (2), incorporate the provision, agreement or other document in the form by setting out in the space provided in the form the following sentence: "The annexed Schedule 1 (or as the case may be) is incorporated in this form." and by annexing the provision, agreement or other documents to the form as that schedule.

(2) A separate schedule is required in respect of each item that is incorporated in a form by reference pursuant to subsection (1).

# PART II

## CORPORATE NAMES

### *Interpretation*

**11.** For the purposes of subsection 29(2) of the Act, the proposed name of a corporation shall be considered objectionable when the name is prohibited or deceptively misdescriptive.

**12.** In this Part,

"confusing", in relation to a corporate name, means a corporate name the use of which causes confusion with a trade mark or trade name in the manner described in section 13;

"distinctive", in relation to a trade name, means a trade name that actually distinguishes the business in association with which it is used by its owner from the business of others or that is adapted so as to distinguish them;

"secondary meaning", in relation to a trade name, means a trade name that has been used in Canada or elsewhere by any applicant or his predecessors so as to have become distinctive in Canada as at the date of filing an application for a corporate name;

"trade mark" means a trade mark as defined by the *Trade Marks Act*;

"trade name" means the name under which any business is carried on, whether it is the name of a body corporate, a trust, a partnership, a proprietorship or an individual;

"use" means actual use by a person that carries on business in Canada or elsewhere.

### *Confusion of Names*

**13.** A corporate name is confusing with

(a) a trade mark if the use of both the corporate name and the trade mark is likely to lead to the inference that the business carried on or intended to be carried on under the corporate name and the business connected with the trade mark are one business, whether or not the nature of the business of each is generally the same; or

(b) a trade name if the use of both names is likely to lead to the inference that the business carried on or intended to be carried on under the corporate name and the business carried on under the trade name are one business, whether or not the nature of the business of each is generally the same.

### *Consideration of Whole Name*

**14.** Subject to section 19, when determining whether a trade name is distinctive, the name as a whole and not only its separate elements shall be considered.

*Reservation of Name*

**15.** A request to search and reserve a corporate name may be in Form 5 of Schedule I or may be made by telephone.

*Prohibited Names*

**16.** For the purposes of section 11, a corporate name is prohibited where the name contains any of the following:

(a)    "Air Canada";

(b)    "Trans Canada Airlines" or "Lignes aériennes Trans Canada";

(c)    "Canada Standard" or "CS";

(d)    "Cooperative", "Coopérative", "co-op" or "pool" when it connotes a co-operative venture;

(e)    "Parliament Hill" or "Colline du Parlement";

(f)    "Royal Canadian Mounted Police", "Gendarmerie Royale du Canada", "RCMP" or "GRC"; or

(g)    "United Nations", "Nations Unies", "UN" or "ONU".

**17.** For the purposes of section 11, a corporate name is prohibited where the name connotes that the corporation

(a)    carries on business under royal, vice-regal or governmental patronage, approval or authority, unless the appropriate government department or agency requests the name in writing;

(b)    is sponsored or controlled by or is affiliated with the Government of Canada, the government of a province, the government of a country other than Canada or a political subdivision or agency of any such government, unless the appropriate government, political subdivision or agency consents in writing to the use of the name;

(c)    is sponsored or controlled by or is affiliated with a university or an association of accountants, architects, engineers, lawyers, physicians, surgeons or any other professional association recognized by the laws of Canada or a province unless the appropriate university or professional association consents in writing to the use of the name; or

(d)    carries on the business of a bank, loan company, insurance company, trust company, other financial intermediary or a stock exchange that is regulated by a law of Canada or a province unless the appropriate government department or agency consents in writing to the use of the name.

**18.** For the purposes of section 11, a corporate name is prohibited where the name contains a word or phrase that is obscene or connotes a business that is scandalous, obscene or immoral.

**19.** For the purposes of section 11, a name is prohibited where the name is not distinctive because

(a)    it is too general,

(b) it is only descriptive in any language of the quality, function or other characteristic of the goods or services in which the corporation deals or intends to deal,

(c) it is primarily or only the name or surname used alone of an individual who is living or has died within 30 years preceding the date of the request for that name, or

(d) it is primarily or only a geographic name used alone,

unless the person requesting the name establishes that it has, through use, acquired and continues to have secondary meaning at the time of the request.

**20.** For the purposes of section 11, a corporate name is prohibited where the name is confusing having regard to all the circumstances, including

(a) the inherent distinctiveness of the whole or any element of any trade mark or trade name and the extent to which it has become known;

(b) the length of time the trade mark or trade name has been in use;

(c) the nature of the goods or services associated with a trade mark or the nature of the business carried on under or associated with a trade name, including the likelihood of any competition among businesses using such a trade mark or trade name;

(d) the nature of the trade with which a trade mark or trade name is associated, including the nature of the products or services and the means by which they are offered or distributed;

(e) the degree of resemblance between the proposed corporate name and any trade mark or trade name in appearance or sound or in the ideas suggested by them; and

(f) the territorial area in Canada in which the proposed corporate name or an existing trade name is likely to be used.

**21.** For the purposes of section 11, a corporate name is prohibited where an element of the name is the family name of an individual, whether or not preceded by his given name or initials, unless the individual or his heir or legal representative consents in writing to the use of his name and the individual has or had a material interest in the corporation.

**22.** For the purposes of section 11,

(a) a corporate name is prohibited where its use is likely to lead to the inference that the business carried on or intended to be carried on under it and the business of a body corporate that is dissolved are one business, whether or not the nature of their businesses is generally the same; and

(b) the name of a revived corporation is prohibited where it is confusing with a name acquired by another corporation between the date of dissolution and revival of the revived corporation.

*Deceptively Misdescriptive Names*

**23.** For the purposes of section 11, a corporate name is deceptively misdescriptive if it misdescribes in any language

(a) the business, goods or services in association with which it is proposed to be used;

(b) the conditions under which the goods or services will be produced or supplied or the persons to be employed in the production or supply of those goods or services; or

(c) the place of origin of those goods or services.

### Certain Names Not Prohibited

**24.** A corporate name is not prohibited only because it contains alphabetic or numeric characters, initials, punctuation marks or any combination thereof.

**25.** A corporate name that is confusing with the name of a body corporate that has not carried on business in the two years immediately preceding the date of a request for that corporate name shall not for that reason alone be prohibited if the body corporate that has that name

(a) consents in writing to the use of the name; and

(b) undertakes in writing to dissolve forthwith or to change its name before the corporation proposing to use the name commences to use it.

**26.** A corporate name containing a word that is the same as or similar to the distinctive element of an existing trade mark or trade name shall not for that reason alone be prohibited if

(a) the person who has the trade mark or trade name consents in writing to the use of the corporate name; and

(b) the corporate name is not confusing.

**27.** (1) A corporate name that is confusing with the name of a body corporate shall not for that reason alone be prohibited if

(a) the request for that corporate name relates to a proposed corporation that is the successor to the business of the body corporate and the body corporate has ceased or will cease to carry on business;

(b) the body corporate undertakes in writing to dissolve forthwith or to change its name before the corporation proposing to use the name commences to carry on business; and

(c) subject to subsection (2), the corporate name sets out in numerals the year of incorporation in parentheses immediately before the word "limited", "limitée" or the abbreviation thereof.

(2) A corporate name referred to in paragraph (1)(c) after two years of use may be changed to delete the reference to the year of incorporation if the corporate name so changed is not confusing. SOR/78-46, s. 4.

**28.** (1) When two or more corporations amalgamate, the name of the amalgamated corporations shall not be prohibited if

(a) it is the same as one of the amalgamating corporations;

(b) it is a distinctive combination of the names of the amalgamating corporations and is not otherwise confusing or prohibited; or

(c)   it is a distinctive new name that is not confusing.

(2) Where a corporation acquires all or substantially all the property of an affiliated body corporate, the use by the corporation of the name of the affiliated body corporate will not be prohibited if the body corporate undertakes in writing to dissolve forthwith or to change its name before the corporation adopts the name.

# PART III

## INSIDER TRADING

### *First Insider Report*

**29.** A report required to be sent to the Department by subsections 100.1(2) and (3) of the Act shall be in Form 1 of Schedule I.

### *Subsequent Insider Report*

**30.** A report required to be sent to the Department by subsection 100.1(4) of the Act shall be in Form 2 of Schedule I.

### *Deemed Insider Report*

**31.** A report required to be sent to the Department by subsection 100.1(5) of the Act shall be in Form 1 or Form 2 of Schedule I, as applicable.

# PART IV

## PROXIES AND PROXY SOLICITATION

### *Interpretation*

**32.** In this Part,

"dissident's proxy circular" means an explanatory memorandum referred to in paragraph 108.4(1)(b) of the Act;

"management proxy circular" means an information circular referred to in paragraph 108.4(1)(a) of the Act.

### *Contents of Management Proxy Circular*

**33.** A management proxy circular shall contain the following information:

(a)   a statement of the right of a shareholder to revoke a proxy under subsection 108.2(5) of the Act and the method by which he may exercise it;

(b)    a statement, in bold faced type, to the effect that solicitation is made by or on behalf of the management of the corporation;

(c)    the name of any director of the corporation who has informed the management in writing that he intends to oppose any action intended to be taken by the management and the action that he intends to oppose;

(d)    the method of solicitation, if otherwise than by mail, and if the solicitation is to be made by specially engaged employees or agents, the material features of any contract or arrangement for the solicitation, the parties to the contract or arrangement and the cost or anticipated cost thereof;

(e)    the name of the person by whom the cost of the solicitation has been or will be borne, directly or indirectly;

(f)    the number of shares of each class of shares of the corporation entitled to be voted at the meeting and the number of votes to which each share of each such class is entitled;

(g)    if the corporation has amended its letters patent under section 41.1 of the Act to constrain the issue or transfer of its voting shares, the general nature of the constrained-share provisions;

(h)    if the proceeds of an issue of securities were used for a purpose other than that stated in the document under which the securities were issued, the date of the document, the amount and designation of the securities so issued and details of the use made during the financial period of the proceeds;

(i)    if insurance is purchased for the benefit of directors or officers against any liability incurred by them in their capacity as director or officer of the corporation,

    (i)    the amount or, where there is a comprehensive liability policy, the approximate amount of premium paid by the corporation in respect of directors as a group and officers as a group,

    (ii)    the aggregate amount of premium, if any, paid by the individuals in each such group,

    (iii)   the total amount of insurance purchased for each such group, and

    (iv)   a summary of any deductibility or co-insurance clause or other provision in the insurance contract that exposes the corporation to liability in addition to the payment of the premiums;

(j)    details of any action by a shareholder on behalf of the corporation;

(k)    the name of each person who, to the knowledge of the directors or officers of the corporation, beneficially owns or exercises control or direction over shares carrying more than 10 per cent of the votes attached to shares of the corporation, the approximate number of the shares so owned, controlled or directed by each such person, and the percentage of voting shares of the corporation represented by the number of shares so owned, controlled or directed;

(l)    if a change in the effective control of the corporation has occurred since the beginning of its last financial year, the name of the person who, to the knowledge of the directors or officers of the corporation, acquired control, the date and a description of the transaction in which control was acquired and the percentage of shares entitled to be voted now owned, controlled or directed by the person;

(m)  the percentage of votes required for the approval of any matter that is to be submitted to a vote of shareholders at the meeting other than the election of directors or the appointment of an auditor;

(n)  if a new auditor is proposed to be appointed, the name of the proposed auditor, or the name of each auditor appointed within the preceding five years, and the date on which each auditor was first appointed;

(o)  if directors are to be elected, a statement of the right of any class of shareholders to elect a specified number of directors or to cumulate their votes and of any conditions precedent to the exercise thereof;

(p)  if directors are to be elected, the following information in tabular form, so far as practicable, with respect to each person proposed to be nominated by management for election as a director and each director whose term of office will continue after the meeting:

   (i)   the name of each person, the time when his term of office or the term of office for which he is a proposed nominee will expire and all other major positions and offices with the corporation or any of its significant affiliates presently held by him, indicating which of the persons are proposed nominees for election as directors at the meeting,

   (ii)  the present principal occupation or employment of each such person, giving the name and principal business of any body corporate or other organization in which the occupation or employment is carried on and similar information as to all principal occupations or employments of each such person within the five preceding years, unless he is now a director and was elected to his present term of office by a vote of shareholders at a meeting the notice of which was accompanied by a proxy circular containing that information,

   (iii) if any such person is or has been a director of the corporation, the period or periods during which he has so served,

   (iv)  the approximate number of shares of each class of shares of the corporation and of its holding body corporate beneficially owned or over which control or direction is exercised by each such person, and

   (v)   if more than 10 per cent of the votes attached to shares of any class of the corporation or of its holding body corporate are beneficially owned or subject to control or direction by any such person and his associates, the approximate number of each class of shares so owned, controlled or directed by the associates and the name of each associate;

(q)  the details of any contract, arrangement or understanding between any proposed management nominee and any other person, except the directors and officers of the corporation acting solely in their capacity as such, pursuant to which the nominee is to be elected, including the name of the other person;

(r)    if action is to be taken with respect to

     (i)     the election of directors,

     (ii)    any bonus, profit sharing or other plan of remuneration, contract or arrangement in which any director or officer of the corporation will participate,

     (iii)   any pension or retirement plan of the corporation in which any director or officer of the corporation will participate, or

     (iv)   the granting to any director or officer of the corporation of any option or right to purchase any securities other than rights issued rateably to all shareholders or to all shareholders resident in Canada,

a statement

     (v)     in Form 4 of the aggregate remuneration paid or payable by the corporation and by each of its subsidiaries in respect of the corporation's last completed financial year,

         (A)   to the directors of the corporation in their capacity as directors of the corporation and any of its subsidiaries, and

         (B)   separately, to the officers of the corporation who received in their capacity as officers or employees of the corporation and any of its subsidiaries aggregate remuneration in excess of $40,000 in that year,

excluding any remuneration paid or payable to a partnership in which any person in receipt of such remuneration was a partner,

     (vi)   where practicable, of the estimated aggregate cost to the corporation and its subsidiaries in the last completed financial year of all benefits proposed to be paid under any pension or retirement plan upon retirement at normal retirement age to the persons referred to in subparagraph (v) as a group, and

     (vii)   where practicable, of the aggregate of all remuneration payments other than those referred to in subparagraphs (v) and (vi) made during the corporation's last completed financial year and, as a separate amount, proposed to be made in the future by the corporation or any of its subsidiaries pursuant to an existing plan to the persons referred to in subparagraph (v), and for the purposes of this subparagraph,

         (A)   "plan" includes all plans, contracts, authorizations or arrangements, whether or not contained in any formal document or authorized by a resolution of the directors of the corporation or any of its subsidiaries but does not include the Canada Pension Plan or a similar government plan,

         (B)   "remuneration payments" include deferred compensation benefits, retirement benefits or other benefits, except those paid or to be paid under a pension or retirement plan of the corporation and any of its subsidiaries, and

    (C)  if it is impracticable to state the amount of proposed remuneration payments, the aggregate amount accrued to date in respect of such payments may be stated, with an explanation of the basis of future payments,

but information need not be included as to payments to be made for or benefits to be received from group life or accident insurance, group hospitalization or similar group benefits or payments;

(s)  if action is to be taken with respect to any of the matters referred to in subparagraphs (r)(i) to (iv), a statement containing, in respect of options to purchase securities of the corporation or any of its subsidiaries that, since the commencement of the corporation's last financial year, were granted to or exercised by the persons referred to in subparagraph (r)(v) as a group:

    (i)  where options were granted,

        (A)  the description and number of optioned securities of each class,

        (B)  the dates on which and the prices at which the options were granted, the expiry dates and other material provisions,

        (C)  the consideration received for the granting of the options, and

        (D)  where reasonably ascertainable, a summary showing the price range of the optioned securities in the 30 days preceding the date on which the options were granted or, if not reasonably ascertainable, a statement to that effect, and

    (ii)  where options were exercised,

        (A)  the description and number of securities of each class purchased,

        (B)  the purchase price, and

        (C)  where reasonably ascertainable, a summary showing the price range of the securities in the 30 days preceding the date of purchase or, if not reasonably ascertainable, a statement to that effect,

and for the purposes of this paragraph,

    (iii)  "options" includes rights other than rights issued rateably to all shareholders of the same class or to all shareholders of the same class resident in Canada, and

    (iv)  information on the option price of securities may be given

        (A)  in the form of price ranges for each calendar quarter during which options were granted or exercised, or

        (B)  if the price of the optioned securities is not fixed, by setting out the formula by which the price of the optioned securities will be fixed;

(t)  if action is to be taken with respect to any of the matters referred to in subparagraphs (r)(i) to (iv), a statement in respect of

    (i)  each director and officer of the corporation,

  (ii) each proposed management nominee for election as a director of the corporation, and

  (iii) each associate of any director, officer or proposed management nominee

who is or has been indebted to the corporation or any of its subsidiaries at any time during the last completed financial year, of the largest aggregate amount of debt outstanding at any time since the beginning of the corporation's last completed financial year, the nature of the debt, details of the transaction in which it was incurred, the amount presently outstanding and the rate of interest paid or charged thereon, but

  (iv) an amount owing for purchases subject to usual trade terms, for ordinary travel and expense advances and for other transactions in the ordinary course of business may be omitted in determining the amount of debt, and

  (v) information need not be furnished in respect of a person whose aggregate debt did not exceed $10,000 at any time during the period;

(u) the details including, where practicable, the approximate amount of any material interest of

  (i) a director or officer of the corporation,

  (ii) a proposed management nominee for election as a director of the corporation,

  (iii) a shareholder required to be named by paragraph (k), and

  (iv) an associate or affiliate of any of the foregoing persons

in any transaction since the beginning of the corporation's last completed financial year or in any proposed transaction that has materially affected or will materially affect the corporation or any of its affiliates, but

  (v) an interest arising from the ownership of securities of the corporation may be omitted unless the security holder receives a benefit or advantage not shared rateably by all holders of the same class of security or all holders of the same class of security who are resident in Canada,

  (vi) any transaction or interest may be omitted where

    (A) the rate or charges involved in the transaction are fixed by law or determined by competitive bids,

    (B) the interest of the person in the transaction is solely that of a director of another body corporate that is a party to the transaction,

    (C) the transaction involves services as a bank or other depository of funds, transfer agent, registrar, trustee under a trust indenture or other similar services, or

    (D) the transaction does not involve remuneration for services, and

      (I) the interest of the person results from the beneficial ownership of less than 10 per cent of any class of shares of another body corporate that is a party to the transaction,

> > > (II)    the transaction is in the ordinary course of business of the corporation or any of its affiliates, and
> > > (III)   the amount of the transaction or series of transactions is less than 10 per cent of the total sales or purchases, as the case may be, of the corporation and its affiliates for the last completed financial year, and

> > (vii)    details of transactions not omitted under subparagraphs (v) and (vi) that involve remuneration paid, directly or indirectly, to any of the persons referred to in this paragraph for services in any capacity shall be included, unless the interest of the person arises solely from the beneficial ownership of less than 10 per cent of any class of shares of another body corporate furnishing the services to the corporation or its affiliates;

(v)    details of each transaction referred to in paragraph (u), the name and address of each person whose interest in the transaction is disclosed and the nature of the relationship by reason of which the interest is required to be disclosed;

(w)    where a transaction referred to in paragraph (u) involves the purchase or sale of assets by the corporation or any affiliate otherwise than in the ordinary course of business, the cost of the assets to the purchaser and the cost of the assets to the seller if acquired by the seller within two years prior to the transaction;

(x)    details of a material underwriting discount or commission with respect to the sale of securities by the corporation where any person referred to in paragraph (u) has contracted or will contract with the corporation in respect of an underwriting or is an associate or affiliate of a person that has so contracted or will so contract;

(y)    details of any material interest of

> (i)     each person who was a director or officer of the corporation at any time since the beginning of its last completed financial year,
> (ii)    each proposed management nominee for election as a director of the corporation, and
> (iii)   each associate of any of the foregoing persons

in any matter to be acted upon at the meeting other than the election of directors or the appointment of an auditor;

(z)    if action is to be taken with respect to the authorization or issue of securities, except to exchange the securities for other securities of the corporation,

> (i)     the designation and number or amount of securities to be authorized or issued,
> (ii)    a description of the securities, but
> > (A)    if the terms of securities to be authorized cannot be stated because no issue thereof is contemplated in the immediate future and if no further authorization by shareholders for their issue

is to be obtained, a statement that the terms of the securities to be authorized, including dividend or interest rates, conversion prices, voting rights, redemption prices, maturity dates and other matters will be determined by the directors, and

    (B)  if the securities are shares of an existing class, the description required except for a statement of any preemptive rights may be omitted,

(iii)  details of the transaction in which the securities are to be issued including the nature and approximate amount of the consideration received or to be received by the corporation, and the purpose for which the consideration has been or is to be used,

(iv)  if it is impracticable to furnish the details required under subparagraph (iii), a statement of the reason why it is impracticable, the purpose of the authorization and whether shareholders' approval for the issue of the securities will be sought, and

(v)  if the securities are to be issued other than in a general public offering for money or other than rateably to all holders of the same class of securities or all holders of the same class of securities who are resident in Canada, the reasons for the proposed authorization or issue and its effect on the rights of present security holders;

(aa)  if action is to be taken under sections 41.1, 51 or 52 of the Act to modify the rights, privileges, restrictions or conditions attached to any class of securities of the corporation or to authorize or issue securities in order to exchange them for other securities of the corporation,

(i)  the designation and number or amount of outstanding securities that are to be modified, and, if securities are to be issued in exchange, the designation and number or amount of securities to be exchanged and the basis of the exchange,

(ii)  details of material differences between the outstanding securities and the modified or new securities,

(iii)  the reasons for the proposed modification or exchange and the general effect on the rights of existing security holders,

(iv)  a brief statement of arrears in dividends or of defaults in principal or interest in respect of the outstanding securities that are to be modified or exchanged, and

(v)  all other information material to the proposed modification or exchange;

(bb)  if action is to be taken with respect to any plan for

(i)  an amalgamation with another corporation other than a wholly-owned subsidiary,

(ii)  a sale, lease or exchange of all or substantially all of the property of the corporation,

(iii)  the liquidation or dissolution of the corporation,

the material features of the plan including the reasons for it and its general effect on the rights of existing security holders;

(cc) if action is to be taken with respect to a plan referred to in subparagraph (bb)(i), a statement containing, with respect to the corporation and the other body corporate,

    (i)    a brief description of the business,

    (ii)   the location and general character of the plants and other important physical properties,

    (iii)  a brief description of arrears in dividends or defaults in principal or interest in respect of securities of the corporation or body corporate and of the effect of the plan,

    (iv)  the existing and pro forma capitalization in tabular form,

    (v)   an historical summary of earnings in tabular form for each of the last five fiscal years including per share amounts of net earnings, dividends declared for each year and book value per share at the end of the most recent period,

    (vi)  a combined pro forma summary of earnings in tabular form for each of the last five fiscal years, indicating the aggregate and per share earnings for each such year and the pro forma book value per share at the end of the most recent period, but if the transaction will establish a new basis of accounting for the assets of the corporation or body corporate, the pro forma summary of earnings may be furnished only for the most recent fiscal year and interim period and shall reflect appropriate pro forma adjustments resulting from the new basis of accounting,

    (vii) the high and low sale prices for each quarterly period within the previous two years for each class of securities of the corporation and of the other body corporate that is traded on a stock exchange and that will be materially affected by the plan, and

    (viii) an introductory summary, not exceeding six pages in length, of the contents of the proxy circular that highlights the salient features of the transaction including a summary of the financial information, with appropriate cross-references to the more detailed information in the circular;

(dd) if action is to be taken with respect to a matter referred to in paragraph (bb), such financial statements of the corporation as would be required to be included in a prospectus under the laws of one of the jurisdictions referred to in paragraph 43(a);

(ee) if action is to be taken with respect to a matter referred to in paragraph (cc), such financial statements of the other body corporate as would be required to be included in a prospectus under the laws of one of the jurisdictions referred to in paragraph 43(a);

(ff) if action is to be taken with respect to any matter other than the approval of financial statements, the substance of each such matter or group of related matters, to the extent it has not been described pursuant to paragraph (a) to (ee), in sufficient detail to permit shareholders to form a reasoned judgment concerning the matter, and if any such matter is not required to be submitted to a vote of the shareholders, the reasons for so submitting it and the action intended to be taken by management in the event of a negative vote by the shareholders; and

(gg) a statement, signed by a director or officer of the corporation, that the contents and the sending of the circular have been approved by the directors.

[SOR/78-46, s. 5; SOR/79-318, s. 1.]

**34.** A management proxy circular that is sent to the Department shall be accompanied by a statement signed by a director or officer that a copy of the circular has been sent to each director, each shareholder entitled to notice of the meeting to which the circular relates and to the auditor of the corporation.

## *Dissident's Proxy Circular*

**35.** For the purposes of section 36, "dissident" means any person, other than the management of the corporation or its affiliates and associates, by or on behalf of whom a solicitation is made, and includes a committee or group that solicits proxies, any member of the committee or group, and any person whether or not named as a member who, acting alone or with one or more other persons, directly or indirectly engages in organizing, directing or financing any such committee or group, except

(a) a person who contributes not more than $250 and who does not otherwise participate in the solicitation;

(b) a bank or other lending institution or a broker or dealer that, in the ordinary course of business, lends money or executes orders for the purchase or sale of shares and that does not otherwise participate in the solicitation;

(c) a person who is employed to solicit and whose activities are limited to the performance of his duties in the course of such employment;

(d) a person who only sends soliciting material or performs other ministerial or clerical duties;

(e) a person employed in the capacity of lawyer, accountant, advertiser, public relations or financial adviser, and whose activities are limited to the performance of his duties in the course of such employment; and

(f) an officer or director of, or a person employed by, a person by or on behalf of whom a solicitation is made if he does not directly participate in the solicitation.

## *Contents of Dissident's Proxy Circular*

**36.** A dissident's proxy circular shall contain the following information:

(a) the name and address of the corporation to which the solicitation relates;

(b) the information required by paragraphs 33(a), (d) and (e);

(c) details of the identity and background of each dissident, including

  (i) his name and business address,

  (ii) his present principal occupation or employment and the name, principal business and address of any body corporate or other person in which the occupation or employment is carried on,

    (iii)  all material occupations, offices or employments during the preceding five years, with starting and ending dates of each and the name, principal business and address of the body corporate or other business organization in which each such occupation, office or employment was carried on,

    (iv)  whether he is or has been a dissident within the preceding 10 years and, if so, the body corporate involved, the principals and his relationship to them, the subject matter and the outcome of the solicitation, and

    (v)  convictions in criminal proceedings during the preceding 10 years for which a pardon has not been granted, other than in respect of violations for which the maximum penalty is a fine of not more than $5,000 or imprisonment for not more than six months, or both, and the date and nature of the conviction, the name and location of the court and the sentence imposed;

(d)  the circumstances under which each dissident became involved in the solicitation and the nature and extent of his activities as a dissident;

(e)  the information required by paragraphs 33(k), (l) and (m), if known to a dissident;

(f)  details of the interest of each dissident in the securities of the corporation to which the solicitation relates, including

    (i)  the number of each class of shares of the corporation that he owns beneficially or over which he exercises control or direction,

    (ii)  the dates on which securities of the corporation were purchased or sold during the preceding two years, the amount purchased or sold on each date, and the price at which they were purchased or sold,

    (iii)  if any part of the purchase price or market value of any of the securities specified in subparagraph (ii) is represented by funds borrowed or otherwise obtained for the purpose of acquiring or holding the securities, the amount of the indebtedness as of the latest practicable date and a brief description of the transaction including the names of the parties, other than a bank, broker or dealer acting in the transaction in the ordinary course of business,

    (iv)  whether he is or was within the preceding year a party to a contract, arrangement or understanding with any person in respect of securities of the corporation, including joint ventures, loan or option arrangements, puts or calls, guarantees against loss or guarantees of profit, division of losses or profits or the giving or withholding of proxies and, if so, the names of the parties to, and the details of the contract, arrangement or understanding,

    (v)  the number of each class of shares of an affiliate of the corporation that he owns beneficially or over which he exercises control or direction, and

    (vi)  the number of each class of shares of the corporation that each associate of the dissident beneficially owns or exercises control or direction over and the name and address of each such associate;

(g)    if directors are to be elected, information required by paragraphs 33(p), (q), (u) and (y) in respect of each proposed nominee for election as a director and his associates;

(h)    the information required by paragraphs 33(u) and (y) in respect of each dissident and his associates; and

(i)    details of any contract, arrangement or understanding, including the names of the parties, between a dissident or his associates and any person with respect to

     (i)    future employment by the corporation or any of its affiliates, or

     (ii)    future transactions to which the corporation or any of its affiliates will or may be a party.

[SOR/78-46, s. 6; SOR/82-250, s. 1.]

**37.** If a dissident is a partnership, body corporate, association or other organization, the information required by paragraphs 36(c), (d), (f), (h) and (i) to be included in a dissident's proxy circular shall be given in respect of each partner, officer and director of and each person who controls the dissident and who is himself not a dissident.

**38.** Information that is not known to a dissident and that cannot be reasonably ascertained by him may be omitted from a dissident's proxy circular, but the circumstances that render the information unavailable shall be disclosed therein.

**39.** (1) A dissident's proxy circular shall contain a statement, signed by a dissident or a person authorized by him, that the contents and the sending of the circular have been approved by the dissident.

(2) A dissident's proxy circular that is sent to the Department pursuant to subsection 108.4(3) of the Act shall be accompanied by a statement signed by a dissident or a person authorized by him to the effect that

(a)    the circular complies with these Regulations; and

(b)    a copy of the circular has been sent to each director, each shareholder and to the auditor of the corporation.

### Date of Proxy Circular Information

**40.** A proxy circular shall be dated as of a date not more than 30 days before the date on which it is first sent to a shareholder of the corporation and the information, other than financial statements, required to be contained in it shall be given as of the date of the circular.

### Financial Statements in Proxy Circular

**41.** (1) Where financial statements accompany or form part of a management proxy circular, the statements shall be prepared in accordance with the recommendations of the Canadian Institute of Chartered Accountants set out in the C.I.C.A. Handbook.

(2) The financial statements referred to in subsection (1), if not reported upon by the auditor of the corporation, shall be accompanied by a report of the chief financial officer of the corporation stating that the financial statements have not been audited but have been prepared in accordance with subsection (1).

# PART V

## TAKE-OVER BIDS

*Take-Over Bid Circular under Subsection 135.6(2) of the Act*

**42.** A take-over bid circular referred to in subsection 135.6(2) of the Act shall contain the following information:

(a)   the identity and business background of the offeror;

(b)   a statement of the withdrawal rights of the offerees under paragraph 135.2(c) of the Act and the date before which offerees who deposit their shares may exercise those rights;

(c)   the date on which any other time period mentioned in the circular begins or ends;

(d)   the details of the method and time of payment of the money or other consideration to be paid for the shares of the offeree corporation;

(e)   where the obligation of the offeror to take up and pay for shares under a take-over bid is conditional upon a minimum number of shares being deposited, the details of the condition;

(f)   he number, without duplication, and designation of any securities of the offeree corporation beneficially owned or over which control or direction is exercised by

    (i)   the offeror,

    (ii)   an associate or affiliate of the offeror,

    (iii)   each director and each officer of the offeror and their respective associates, and

    (iv)   any person known to the directors or officers of the offeror who beneficially owns or exercises control or direction over shares of the offeror carrying more than 10 per cent of the votes attached to shares of the offeror, or, if none are so owned, controlled or directed, a statement to that effect;

(g)   where known to the offeror or the directors or officers of the offeror, the number and designation of any shares of the offeree corporation traded by a person referred to in paragraph (f) during the six months preceding the date of the take-over bid, including the purchase or sale price and the date of each transaction;

(h)   details of any contract, arrangement or understanding, formal or informal, between the offeror and

    (i)   any shareholder of the offeree corporation with respect to the take-over bid, and

    (ii)    any person with respect to any shares of the offeree corporation in relation to the bid;

(i)    where the shares of the offeree corporation are to be paid for wholly or partly in money, details of any arrangements that have been made by the offeror to ensure that the required funds are available to take up and pay for the shares of the offeree corporation deposited pursuant to the take-over bid;

(j)    details of any contract or arrangement made or proposed to be made between the offeror and any of the directors or officers of the offeree corporation, including details of any payment of other benefit proposed to be made or given by way of compensation in respect of loss of office or in respect of their remaining in or retiring from office if the take-over bid is successful;

(k)    details of any business relationship between the offeror and the offeree corporation that is material to either of them;

(l)    if a purpose of the take-over bid is to acquire effective control of the business of the offeree corporation, any plans or proposals that the offeror has to liquidate the offeree corporation, to sell, lease or exchange all or substantially all its assets or to amalgamate it with any other body corporate, or to make any other major change in its business, corporate structure, management or personnel;

(m)    if the offeror intends to purchase shares of the offeree corporation other than pursuant to the take-over bid, a statement of his intention to do so;

(n)    if the offeror intends to invoke the right referred to in section 136 of the Act to acquire the shares of offerees who do not accept the take-over bid, a statement of that intention;

(o)    where reasonably ascertainable, a summary showing, in reasonable detail for the six months preceding the date of the take-over bid, the volume of trading and price range of the shares sought to be acquired pursuant to the take-over bid;

(p)    particulars of any information known to the offeror that indicates any material change in the financial position or prospects of the offeree corporation since the date of the most recent publicly filed interim or annual financial statements of the offeree corporation; and

(q)    all other material facts known to the offeror.

### Take-Over Bid Circular under Section 135.92 of the Act

**43.** Where a take-over bid states that the consideration for the shares of the offeree corporation is to be, in whole or in part, securities of the offeror or any other body corporate, the take-over bid circular shall contain, in addition to the information required by section 42,

(a)    the information required to be included in the take-over bid circular under the laws of

    (i)    Alberta,

    (ii)   British Columbia,
    (iii)  Manitoba,
    (iv)  Ontario,
    (v)   Quebec,
    (vi)  Saskatchewan, or
    (vii) the United States if the bid is made in the United States;

(b)  the financial statements of the offeror on a *pro forma* basis as of the date of the offeror's financial statements giving effect to the take-over bid based on the information in the most recent publicly filed financial statements of the offeree corporation;

(c)  a description of the financial statements of the offeree corporation relied upon and of the basis of preparation of the *pro forma* financial statements; and

(d)  basic and fully diluted earnings per share figures based upon the *pro forma* financial statements.

**44.** A take-over bid circular referred to in section 43 shall contain an introductory summary of its contents, not exceeding six pages in length, that highlights the salient features of the take-over bid, including a summary of the financial information, with appropriate cross-references to the more detailed information in the circular.

### *Where Offeror Has Effective Control*

**45.** (1) If an offeror exercises effective control over the offeree corporation when a take-over bid is made, the take-over bid circular, in addition to the information required by sections 42 to 44 may contain

(a)  the information required to be included in a directors' circular under section 50 that has not already been set out in that take-over bid circular; and

(b)  a statement indicating whether the remuneration of the directors of the offeror and of the offeree corporation will be affected if the take-over bid is successful and, if so, details of the effect.

(2) A take-over bid circular that complies with the requirements of subsection (1) is the directors' circular required by subsection 135.7(1) of the Act.

### *Statement of Directors' Approval*

**46.** Where the offeror is a body corporate, a take-over bid circular shall contain a statement, signed by one or more directors, that the contents and the sending of the circular have been approved by the directors of the offeror.

### *Experts' Consent*

**47.** Where a report, opinion or statement of a person referred to in section 135.8 of the Act is included in a take-over bid circular, his consent in writing shall be reproduced in the circular.

## Certificate Required

**48.** A copy of a take-over bid circular sent to the Department pursuant to subsection 135.3(1) of the Act shall be accompanied by a certificate signed by the offeror or, if the offeror is a body corporate, by a certificate signed by a director, officer or agent of the offeror, certifying that a copy of the circular has been sent to each director and to each shareholder of the offeree corporation resident in Canada.

## Amendment to Take-Over Bid

**49.** (1) Sections 42 to 48 apply to an amendment of the terms of a take-over bid circular but it is not necessary to repeat in an amendment to a take-over bid circular any information contained in the circular that continues to be accurate.

(2) An amendment to a take-over bid circular shall correct any material statement in the take-over bid circular that is discovered to be misleading or that has become misleading by reason of events subsequent to the date of the circular.

## Contents of Directors' Circular

**50.** A directors' circular referred to in subsection 135.7(1) of the Act shall contain the following information:

(a)  the number, without duplication and designation of any securities of the offeree corporation beneficially owned or over which control or direction is exercised

  (i)  by each director and each officer of the offeree corporation and their associates, and

  (ii)  where known to the directors or officers, by each person who beneficially owns or exercises control or direction over shares of the offeree corporation carrying more than 10 per cent of the votes attached to shares of the offeree corporation,

or, if none are so owned, controlled or directed, a statement to that effect;

(b)  where the offeror is a body corporate the number, without duplication, and designation of any securities of the offeror beneficially owned or over which control or direction is exercised

  (i)  by each director and each officer of the offeree corporation and their associates, and

  (ii)  where known to the directors or officers, by each person who beneficially owns or exercises control or direction over shares of the offeree corporation carrying more than 10 per cent of the votes attached to shares of the offeree corporation,

or, if none are so owned, controlled or directed, a statement to that effect;

(c)  where known to the directors or officers of the offeree corporation, the number and designation of any shares of the offeree corporation or of the offeror traded by a person referred to in paragraphs (a) or (b) during the six months preceding the date of the take-over bid, including the purchase or sale price and the date of each transaction;

(d) where the offeror is a body corporate, the number and designation of any securities of the offeror beneficially owned or over which control or direction is exercised by the offeree corporation;

(e) the number and designation of any shares of the offeree corporation or of the offeror traded by the offeree corporation during the six months preceding the date of the take-over bid, including the purchase or sale price, the date and the purpose of each such transaction;

(f) if the directors make a recommendation in relation to the take-over bid, a statement of the recommendation and the reasons therefor;

(g) whether

    (i) a director or officer of the offeree corporation or an associate of such director or officer, or

    (ii) where known to the directors or officers, any person who beneficially owns or exercises control or direction over shares of the offeree corporation carrying more than 10 per cent of the votes attached to shares of the offeree corporation,

has accepted or intends to accept the offer in respect of any shares of the offeree corporation;

(h) whether

    (i) a director or officer of the offeree corporation or an associate of a director or officer, or

    (ii) where known to the directors or officers, any person who beneficially owns or exercises control or direction over shares of the offeree corporation carrying more than 10 per cent of the votes attached to shares of the offeree corporation,

has any interest in any material contract to which the offeror is a party and, if so, details of the nature and extent of the interest;

(i) details of all service contracts of directors and officers of the offeree corporation or any of its affiliates with more than a 12-month period remaining or, if there are no such contracts, a statement of that fact;

(j) if a contract referred to in paragraph (i) has been entered into or amended within the six months preceding the date of the take-over bid, the details of the contract replaced or amended;

(k) details of any contract or arrangement made or proposed to be made between the offeror and any of the directors or officers of the offeree corporation, including details of any payment or other benefit proposed to be made or given by way of compensation in respect of loss of office or in respect of their remaining in or retiring from office if the take-over bid is successful;

(l) where known to the directors or officers of the offeree corporation, the details of any special contract, arrangement or understanding, formal or informal, made or proposed to be made between the offeror and any shareholder of the offeree corporation with respect to the take-over bid;

(m)  where reasonably ascertainable, a summary showing, in reasonable detail for the six months preceding the date of the take-over bid, the volume of trading and the price range of the shares sought to be acquired pursuant to the take-over bid if such information is not disclosed in the take-over bid circular or if, in the opinion of the directors of the offeree corporation, such information is not adequately disclosed therein;

(n)  financial statements of the offeree corporation prepared for public filing subsequent to the date of its most recent publicly filed financial statements and not previously sent to shareholders;

(o)  where the information contained in the most recent financial statements of the offeree corporation is materially misleading because of events subsequent to its preparation, a statement of the material events necessary to correct any such misleading representations;

(p)  details of any information known to any director or officer of the offeree corporation concerning any material change in the prospects of the offeree corporation since the date of the last financial statements of the offeree corporation;

(q)  where a director or officer of the offeree corporation intends to purchase shares of the offeree corporation during the take-over bid or where he knows of the existence of such an intention on the part of any person, a statement of the intention and the purpose of such purchases, or if no such intention is known to exist, a statement to that effect;

(r)  where a director of the offeree corporation disagrees with any statement in the directors' circular and submits a statement indicating his opinion or disagreement and the reasons therefor, the statement submitted by the director;

(s)  all other material facts known to the directors or officers of the offeree corporation.

### *Notice of Directors' Circular*

**51.** (1) It is not necessary to repeat in an amendment to a directors' circular any information contained in the directors' circular.

(2) An amendment to a directors' circular shall correct any material statement in the directors' circular that is discovered to be misleading or that has become misleading by reason of events subsequent to the date of the directors' circular.

### *Report to Accompany Financial Statements*

**52.** (1) Where financial statements accompany or form part of a directors' circular, the statements shall be prepared in accordance with the recommendation of the Canadian Institute of Chartered Accountants set out in the C.I.C.A. Handbook.

(2) The financial statements referred to in subsection (1), if not reported upon by the auditor of the corporation, shall be accompanied by a report of the chief

financial officer of the corporation stating that the financial statements have not been audited but have been prepared in accordance with subsection (1).

### Statement of Directors' Approval

**53.** A directors' circular and a notice under subsection 51(1) shall contain a statement, signed by one or more directors, that the contents and the sending of the circular have been approved by the directors of the offeree corporation.

### Experts' Consent

**54.** Where a report, opinion or statement of a person referred to in section 135.8 of the Act is included in a directors' circular, his consent in writing shall be reproduced in the circular.

### Certificate Required

**55.** A copy of a directors' circular sent to the Department pursuant to subsection 135.7(2) of the Act shall be accompanied by a certificate signed by the directors of the offeree corporation certifying that a copy of the circular has been sent to the offeror, to each director, and to each shareholder of the offeree corporation resident in Canada.

# PART VI

## PRESCRIBED FEE

**56.** (1) The fee payable in respect of an application for letters patent or supplementary letters patent, filing a document, issuing a certificate, making a return under the Act, or searching a file as permitted by the Act shall be the fee set out in Schedule II.

(2) No fee is payable

(a)  on an application for supplementary letters patent issued under section 29 if the purpose of the change of name is to add an English or French version to a corporation's name;

(b)  on an application for the surrender of a charter under section 32.

(3) No fee is payable by a department or agency of the Government of Canada or the government of a province for a service described in items 3, 4, 5, 6, 8 and 10 of Schedule II.

[SOR/78-46, s. 7.]

# SCHEDULE I

## (ss. 4, 4.1, 15, 29, 30, 31 and 33)

SCHEDULE I

(ss. 4, 15, 29, 30, 31 and 33)
CANADA CORPORATIONS ACT
FORM 1
INITIAL REPORT OF INSIDER INTEREST IN
THE SECURITIES OF A COMPANY (s. 100.1 (1),
(2), (3) AND (5))

INSTRUCTIONS FOR THE PROPER COMPLETION OF THIS FORM:

1. FILE TWO SIGNED COPIES OF THE REPORT WITH THE DEPARTMENT OF CONSUMER AND CORPORATE AFFAIRS AS AND WHEN REQUIRED BY SUBSECTIONS (1), (2), (3) AND (5) OF SECTION 100.1 OF THE ACT.

   AN INSIDER WHO HAS NO INSIDER INTEREST IN THE SECURITIES OF THE COMPANY IS NOT REQUIRED TO FILE A NIL REPORT.

2. FILE A SEPARATE REPORT WITH RESPECT TO EACH COMPANY OF WHICH YOU ARE AN INSIDER.

3. INDICATE IN WHAT CAPACITY YOU QUALIFY AS AN INSIDER, FOR EXAMPLE:

   (A) A DIRECTOR OF A PUBLIC COMPANY,

   (B) AN OFFICER OF A PUBLIC COMPANY, OR

   (C) A PERSON WHO BENEFICIALLY OWNS DIRECTLY OR INDIRECTLY, OR WHO MAY EXERCISE CONTROL OR DIRECTION OVER, EQUITY SHARES OF A PUBLIC COMPANY CARRYING MORE THAN 10 PER CENT OF THE VOTING RIGHTS ATTACHED TO ALL EQUITY SHARES OF THE COMPANY FOR THE TIME BEING OUTSTANDING.

   IF YOU QUALIFY AS AN INSIDER IN MORE THAN ONE CAPACITY, STATE EACH CAPACITY.

4. STATE SEPARATELY YOUR BENEFICIAL OWNERSHIP OF SECURITIES OF THE COMPANY AS OF THE DATE REFERRED TO IN EITHER SUBSECTION (1), (2), (3) AND (5) OF SECTION 100.1 OF THE ACT AS MAY BE APPLICABLE, AND STATE THE CAPACITY IN WHICH CONTROL OR DIRECTION OVER EQUITY SHARES MAY BE EXERCISED.

5. UNDER "DESIGNATION OF SECURITIES AND EQUITY SHARES", IDENTIFY EACH CLASS OF SECURITIES BENEFICIALLY OWNED AND EACH CLASS OF EQUITY SHARES OVER WHICH CONTROL OR DIRECTION MAY BE EXERCISED, FOR EXAMPLE: "COMMON SHARES", "FIRST PREFERENCE SHARES", "FIVE PER CENT DEBENTURES DUE 1995", ETC.

6. IN REPORTING THE AMOUNT OR NUMBER OF SECURITIES BENEFICIALLY OWNED OR EQUITY SHARES OVER WHICH CONTROL OR DIRECTION MAY BE EXERCISED, IN THE CASE OF DEBT SECURITIES GIVE THE PRINCIPAL AMOUNTS THEREOF, AND IN THE CASE OF SHARES GIVE THE NUMBER THEREOF.

7. UNDER "NATURE OF OWNERSHIP, CONTROL OR DIRECTION".

   (A) STATE WHETHER AND TO WHAT EXTENT YOUR BENEFICIAL OWNERSHIP OF SECURITIES IS DIRECT OR INDIRECT. TO THE EXTENT YOUR OWNERSHIP IS INDIRECT INDICATE IN A FOOTNOTE OR SOME OTHER APPROPRIATE MANNER THE NAME OR IDENTITY OF THE MEDIUM THROUGH WHICH THE SECURITIES ARE INDIRECTLY OWNED AND STATE THE AMOUNT OR NUMBER OF SECURITIES SO OWNED BY EACH SUCH MEDIUM.

   (B) REPORT SECURITIES OWNED INDIRECTLY ON SEPARATE LINES FROM SECURITIES OWNED DIRECTLY.

   (C) STATE WHETHER YOU MAY EXERCISE CONTROL OR DIRECTION OVER EQUITY SHARES AND REPORT THE AMOUNT OR NUMBER ON A SEPARATE LINE. TO THE EXTENT THAT YOU MAY EXERCISE CONTROL OR DIRECTION OVER EQUITY SHARES INDICATE THE MEANS BY WHICH THE CONTROL OR DIRECTION IS EXERCISED AND STATE THE AMOUNT OR NUMBER OF THE EQUITY SHARES.

8. YOU MAY INCLUDE ANY ADDITIONAL INFORMATION OR EXPLANATION THAT YOU DEEM RELEVANT.

9. IF THE REPORT IS FILED ON BEHALF OF A COMPANY, PARTNERSHIP, TRUST OR OTHER ENTITY, THE NAME OF THE COMPANY OR OTHER ENTITY MUST APPEAR OVER THE SIGNATURE OF THE OFFICER OR OTHER PERSON AUTHORIZED TO SIGN THE REPORT. IF THE REPORT IS FILED BY AN INDIVIDUAL, IT MUST BE SIGNED BY HIM OR SPECIFICALLY ON HIS BEHALF BY A PERSON AUTHORIZED TO SIGN FOR HIM.

10. IF SPACE PROVIDED FOR ANY ITEM IS INSUFFICIENT, ADDITIONAL SHEETS MAY BE USED BUT MUST BE CROSS REFERRED TO THE ITEM AND PROPERLY IDENTIFIED.

ANNEXE I

(art. 4, 15, 29, 30, 31 et 33)
LOI SUR LES CORPORATIONS CANADIENNES
FORMULE I
PREMIER RAPPORT SUR LES DROITS DE DIRECTION
EN CE QUI CONCERNE LES VALEURS D'UNE COMPAGNIE
(ART. 100.1 (1), (2), (3) ET (5))

INSTRUCTIONS À SUIVRE EN REMPLISSANT CETTE FORMULE:

1. FAIRE PARVENIR DEUX COPIES SIGNÉES DU RAPPORT AU MINISTÈRE DE LA CONSOMMATION ET DES CORPORATIONS DE LA FAÇON ET AU MOMENT PRESCRITS AUX PARAGRAPHES (1), (2), (3) ET (5) DE L'ARTICLE 100.1 DE LA LOI.

   UN DIRIGEANT QUI N'A PAS DE DROIT DE DIRECTION EN CE QUI CONCERNE LES VALEURS DE LA COMPAGNIE N'A PAS À PRÉSENTER DE RAPPORT.

2. FOURNIR UN RAPPORT DISTINCT EN CE QUI A TRAIT À CHAQUE COMPAGNIE DONT VOUS ÊTES UN DIRIGEANT.

3. INDIQUER EN VERTU DE QUELLE FONCTION VOUS AVEZ DROIT AU TITRE DE DIRIGEANT, PAR EXEMPLE.

   (A) ADMINISTRATEUR D'UNE COMPAGNIE PUBLIQUE.

   (B) FONCTIONNAIRE D'UNE COMPAGNIE PUBLIQUE, OU

   (C) UNE PERSONNE QUI EST DIRECTEMENT OU INDIRECTEMENT PROPRIÉTAIRE D'ACTIONS D'UNE COMPAGNIE PUBLIQUE QUI DONNENT PLUS DE 10 POUR CENT DES DROITS DE VOTE AFFÉRENTS AUX ACTIONS OU SONT EN CIRCULATION À L'ÉPOQUE CONSIDÉRÉE, OU QUI PEUT EXERCER UN CONTRÔLE OU UNE DIRECTION SUR CES ACTIONS.

   SI VOUS AVEZ DROIT AU TITRE DE DIRIGEANT EN VERTU DE PLUS D'UNE FONCTION, VEUILLEZ INDIQUER CHAQUE FONCTION.

4. ÉNONCER SÉPARÉMENT VOTRE DROIT DE PROPRIÉTÉ SUR LES VALEURS DE LA COMPAGNIE À LA DATE PRÉVUE À L'UN OU L'AUTRE DES PARAGRAPHES (1), (2), (3) ET (5) DE L'ARTICLE 100.1 DE LA LOI POUVANT S'APPLIQUER, ET ÉNONCER LA FONCTION EN VERTU DE LAQUELLE VOUS POUVEZ EXERCER UN CONTRÔLE OU UNE DIRECTION SUR LES ACTIONS DONNANT DROIT DE VOTE.

5. SOUS «DÉSIGNATION DES VALEURS ET DES ACTIONS DONNANT DROIT DE VOTE», DÉTERMINER CHAQUE CATÉGORIE DE VALEURS À L'ÉGARD DESQUELLES VOUS AVEZ UN DROIT DE PROPRIÉTÉ ET CHAQUE CATÉGORIE D'ACTIONS DONNANT DROIT DE VOTE SUR LESQUELLES VOUS POUVEZ EXERCER UN CONTRÔLE OU UNE DIRECTION, PAR EXEMPLE «ACTIONS ORDINAIRES», «ACTIONS PRIVILÉGIÉES DE PREMIER RANG», «DÉBENTURES À CINQ POUR CENT À ÉCHOIR EN 1955», ETC.

6. EN FAISANT RAPPORT DU MONTANT OU DU NOMBRE DES VALEURS À L'ÉGARD DESQUELLES VOUS AVEZ UN DROIT DE PROPRIÉTÉ OU DES ACTIONS DONNANT DROIT DE VOTE SUR LESQUELLES VOUS POUVEZ EXERCER UN CONTRÔLE OU UNE DIRECTION, DANS LE CAS DE GARANTIES DE CRÉANCES DÉTERMINER LES MONTANTS PRINCIPAUX, ET DANS LE CAS DES ACTIONS EN DONNER LE NOMBRE.

7. SOUS «NATURE DU DROIT DE PROPRIÉTÉ DU CONTRÔLE OU DE LA DIRECTION».

   (A) INDIQUER SI VOTRE DROIT DE PROPRIÉTÉ DE VALEURS EST DIRECT OU INDIRECT ET DANS QUELLE MESURE. SI VOTRE DROIT DE PROPRIÉTÉ EST INDIRECT, INDIQUER DANS UNE NOTE AU BAS DE LA PAGE OU D'UNE AUTRE FAÇON APPROPRIÉE LE NOM OU L'IDENTITÉ DE L'AGENT, PAR L'ENTREMISE DUQUEL LES VALEURS SONT INDIRECTEMENT POSSÉDÉES ET MENTIONNER LE MONTANT OU LE NOMBRE DE CES VALEURS DONT IL EST LE PROPRIÉTAIRE.

   (B) INSCRIRE LES VALEURS INDIRECTEMENT POSSÉDÉES SUR DES LIGNES DISTINCTES DE CELLES DES VALEURS DIRECTEMENT POSSÉDÉES.

   (C) INDIQUER SI VOUS POUVEZ EXERCER UN CONTRÔLE OU UNE DIRECTION SUR DES ACTIONS DONNANT DROIT DE VOTE ET INSCRIRE LE MONTANT OU LE NOMBRE SUR UNE LIGNE DISTINCTE DANS LA MESURE OÙ VOUS POUVEZ EXERCER UN CONTRÔLE OU UNE DIRECTION SUR DES ACTIONS DONNANT DROIT DE VOTE, INDIQUER LES MOYENS D'EXERCICE DU CONTRÔLE OU DE LA DIRECTION ET INDIQUER LE MONTANT OU LE NOMBRE DES ACTIONS DONNANT DROIT DE VOTE.

8. VOUS POUVEZ INCLURE DES RENSEIGNEMENTS OU EXPLICATIONS COMPLÉMENTAIRES.

9. SI LE RAPPORT EST FOURNI POUR LE COMPTE D'UNE COMPAGNIE, SOCIÉTÉ, FIDUCIE OU AUTRE ENTITÉ, LE NOM DE LA COMPAGNIE OU DE L'AUTRE ENTITÉ DOIT PARAÎTRE AU-DESSUS DE LA SIGNATURE DU FONCTIONNAIRE AUTORISÉ. SI LE RAPPORT EST FOURNI PAR UN PARTICULIER, IL DOIT ÊTRE SIGNÉ PAR LUI OU PAR SON MANDATAIRE.

10. SI L'ESPACE PRÉVU À UN NUMÉRO QUELCONQUE EST INSUFFISANT, UTILISER DES FEUILLES SUPPLÉMENTAIRES EN PRENANT SOIN D'Y INSCRIRE UN RENVOI AU NUMÉRO ET DE LES DÉSIGNER CORRECTEMENT.

SEE OVER
AU VERSO

FURTHER DIRECTIONS

1. DEPARTMENT EMPLOYEES ARE NOT PERMITTED TO VARY A REPORT, THEREFORE ALL ITEMS MUST BE COMPLETED STATE "N/A" IF AN ITEM IS NOT APPLICABLE.

2. CHECK TO ENSURE THAT THE REPORT IS CONSISTENT WITH PREVIOUS REPORTS THE DATA IN THE REPORTS MUST RECONCILE.

3. WHERE ATTACHMENTS ARE USED TO RECORD DETAILED TRANSACTIONS THESE SHOULD BE TOTALLED AND THE TOTALS CARRIED FORWARD TO ITEM 5.

4. IF REPORTING AN INDIRECT HOLDING ALWAYS REFER TO EACH COMPANY OR TRUST INVOLVED BY ITS FULL LEGAL NAME.

5. PURCHASE WARRANTS, PUT, CALL OR OTHER TRANSFERABLE OPTIONS ARE EQUITY SECURITIES THAT MUST BE REPORTED.

IF FURTHER INFORMATION IS REQUIRED, WRITE TO THE CORPORATIONS BRANCH, DEPARTMENT OF CONSUMER AND CORPORATE AFFAIRS, OTTAWA 4, CANADA.

AUTRES RENSEIGNEMENTS

1. LES EMPLOYÉS DU MINISTÈRE NE SONT PAS AUTORISÉS À MODIFIER UN RAPPORT ET EN CONSÉQUENCE IL FAUT DONNER UNE RÉPONSE À TOUS LES ARTICLES SI UN ARTICLE NE S'APPLIQUE PAS INSCRIRE LA MENTION «SANS OBJET» OU «S/O».

2. ASSUREZ VOUS QUE LE RAPPORT EST CONFORME AUX RAPPORTS ANTÉRIEURS IL DOIT Y AVOIR CONCORDANCE DES DONNÉES DANS LES RAPPORTS.

3. LORSQUE DES FEUILLES SUPPLÉMENTAIRES SONT UTILISÉES POUR L'INSCRIPTION D'OPÉRATIONS EN DÉTAIL, IL FAUT ÉTABLIR LE TOTAL DE CHACUNE ET LE REPORTER AU NUMÉRO DE LA FORMULE.

4. EN FAISANT RAPPORT AU SUJET D'UNE DÉTENTION INDIRECTE, VEUILLEZ TOUJOURS FAIRE MENTION DE CHAQUE COMPAGNIE OU FIDUCIE EN CAUSE EN LUI DONNANT SON NOM JURIDIQUE INTÉGRAL.

5. LES TITRES D'ACHAT, PRIMES DIRECTES, PRIMES INDIRECTES, OU AUTRES PRIMES CESSIBLES SONT DES VALEURS DONNANT DROIT DE VOTE QUI DOIVENT ÊTRE INSCRITES DANS LE RAPPORT.

POUR TOUT RENSEIGNEMENT SUPPLÉMENTAIRE, PRIÈRE DE VOUS ADRESSER À LA DIRECTION DES CORPORATIONS, MINISTÈRE DE LA CONSOMMATION ET DES CORPORATIONS, OTTAWA 4, CANADA.

# FORM 1

CHARITIES LAW

<table>
<tr><td>

CANADA CORPORATIONS ACT<br>
FORM I<br>
INITIAL REPORT OF INSIDER INTEREST IN<br>
THE SECURITIES OF A COMPANY (s. 100.1 (1),<br>
(2), (3) AND (5))

</td><td>

LOI SUR LES CORPORATIONS CANADIENNES<br>
FORMULE I<br>
PREMIER RAPPORT SUR LES DROITS DE DIRECTION<br>
EN CE QUI CONCERNE LES VALEURS D'UNE COMPAGNIE<br>
(ART. 100.1 (1), (2), (3), ET (5))

</td></tr>
</table>

<table>
<tr><td>

PLEASE PRINT OR TYPE, AND FILE IN TWO SIGNED COPIES TO

DEPARTMENT OF CONSUMER AND CORPORATE AFFAIRS<br>
CORPORATIONS BRANCH<br>
OTTAWA, CANADA

</td><td>

REMPLIR EN LETTRES D'IMPRIMERIE OU À LA MACHINE À ÉCRIRE
ET FAIRE PARVENIR DEUX COPIES SIGNÉES AU

MINISTÈRE DE LA CONSOMMATION ET DES CORPORATIONS<br>
DIRECTION DES CORPORATIONS<br>
OTTAWA, CANADA

</td></tr>
</table>

1. NAME OF COMPANY OF WHICH THE UNDERSIGNED IS INSIDER
   NOM DE LA COMPAGNIE DONT LE SOUSSIGNÉ EST DIRIGEANT

<table>
<tr><td>

2. FULL NAME OF THE UNDERSIGNED
   NOM ET PRÉNOMS DU SOUSSIGNÉ

</td><td>

3. BUSINESS ADDRESS OF THE UNDERSIGNED
   ADRESSE PROFESSIONNELLE DU SOUSSIGNÉ

</td></tr>
</table>

4. INDICATE IN WHAT CAPACITY OR CAPACITIES THE UNDERSIGNED QUALIFIES AS AN INSIDER (SEE INSTRUCTION 3)
   INDIQUER EN VERTU DE QUELLE(S) FONCTION(S) LE SOUSSIGNÉ A DROIT AU TITRE DE DIRIGEANT (VOIR INSTRUCTION 3)

5. INSIDER INTEREST IN THE FOLLOWING SECURITIES OF THE COMPANY
   DROITS DE DIRECTION EN CE QUI CONCERNE LES VALEURS SUIVANTES DE LA COMPAGNIE

<table>
<tr><td>

(A) SECURITIES BENEFICIALLY OWNED DIRECTLY OR INDIRECTLY, BY THE
UNDERSIGNED ON (Day  Month  Year  )<br>
VALEURS DONT LE SOUSSIGNÉ EST DIRECTEMENT OU INDIRECTEMENT
PROPRIÉTAIRE BÉNÉFICIAIRE LE (jour   mois   année  )

</td><td>

(B) EQUITY SHARES OVER WHICH THE UNDERSIGNED MAY EXERCISE CON-
TROL OR DIRECTION AS OF (Day  Month  Year  )<br>
ACTIONS DONNANT DROIT DE VOTE SUR LESQUELLES LE SOUSSIGNÉ PEUT
EXERCER UN CONTRÔLE OU UNE DIRECTION EN DATE DU (jour mois année )

</td></tr>
</table>

| DESIGNATION OF SECURITIES AND EQUITY SHARES<br>DÉSIGNATION DES VALEURS ET DES ACTIONS<br>DONNANT DROIT DE VOTE<br>(SEE VOIR INSTRUCTION 5) | AMOUNT OR NUMBER<br>MONTANT OU NOMBRE<br><br>(SEE VOIR INSTRUCTION 6) | NATURE OF OWNERSHIP, CONTROL OR DIRECTION<br>NATURE DU DROIT DE PROPRIÉTÉ, DU CONTRÔLE<br>OU DE LA DIRECTION<br>(SEE VOIR INSTRUCTION 7) |
|---|---|---|
|  |  |  |
|  |  |  |
|  |  |  |
|  |  |  |

6. ADDITIONAL REMARKS   OBSERVATIONS COMPLÉMENTAIRES

<table>
<tr><td>

THE UNDERSIGNED HEREBY CERTIFIES THAT THE INFORMATION GIVEN IN
THIS REPORT IS TRUE AND COMPLETE IN EVERY RESPECT

</td><td>

LE SOUSSIGNÉ CERTIFIE PAR LES PRÉSENTES QUE LES RENSEIGNEMENTS
DONNÉS DANS LE PRÉSENT RAPPORT SONT VÉRIDIQUES ET COMPLETS À
TOUS ÉGARDS

</td></tr>
<tr><td>

DATE OF REPORT   DATE DU RAPPORT

</td><td>

SIGNATURE (SEE — VOIR INSTRUCTION 9)

</td></tr>
</table>

IT IS AN OFFENCE UNDER THE CANADA CORPORATIONS ACT TO FILE A FALSE OR MISLEADING REPORT
FOURNIR UN RAPPORT FAUX OU TROMPEUR CONSTITUE UNE INFRACTION EN VERTU DE LA LOI SUR LES CORPORATIONS CANADIENNES

| CANADA CORPORATIONS ACT | LOI SUR LES CORPORATIONS CANADIENNES |
|---|---|
| FORM 2 | FORMULE 2 |
| REPORT OF CHANGE IN INSIDER INTEREST IN THE SECURITIES OF A COMPANY (S.100.1(4) AND (5) ) | RAPPORT SUR LES CHANGEMENTS DES DROITS DE DIRECTION EN CE QUI CONCERNE LES VALEURS D'UNE COMPAGNIE (ART.100.1(4) ET (5) |

| INSTRUCTIONS FOR THE PROPER COMPLETION OF THIS FORM | INSTRUCTIONS À SUIVRE EN REMPLISSANT CETTE FORMULE |
|---|---|
| 1. FILE TWO SIGNED COPIES OF THE REPORT WITH THE DEPARTMENT OF CONSUMER AND CORPORATE AFFAIRS AS AND WHEN REQUIRED BY SUBSECTIONS (4) AND (5) OF SECTION 100.1 OF THE ACT. | 1. FAIRE PARVENIR DEUX COPIES SIGNÉES DU RAPPORT AU MINISTÈRE DE LA CONSOMMATION ET DES CORPORATIONS DE LA FAÇON ET AU MOMENT PRESCRITS AUX PARAGRAPHES (4) ET (5) DE L'ARTICLE 100.1 DE LA LOI. |
| 2. FILE A SEPARATE REPORT WITH RESPECT TO EACH COMPANY OF WHICH YOU ARE AN INSIDER. | 2. FOURNIR UN RAPPORT DISTINCT EN CE QUI A TRAIT À CHAQUE COMPAGNIE DONT VOUS ÊTES UN DIRIGEANT. |
| 3. INDICATE IN WHAT CAPACITY YOU QUALIFY AS AN INSIDER, FOR EXAMPLE. | 3. INDIQUER EN VERTU DE QUELLE FONCTION VOUS AVEZ DROIT AU TITRE DE DIRIGEANT, PAR EXEMPLE. |
| (A) A DIRECTOR OF A PUBLIC COMPANY, | (A) ADMINISTRATEUR D'UNE COMPAGNIE PUBLIQUE, |
| (B) AN OFFICER OF A PUBLIC COMPANY, OR | (B) FONCTIONNAIRE D'UNE COMPAGNIE PUBLIQUE, OU |
| (C) A PERSON WHO BENEFICIALLY OWNS DIRECTLY OR INDIRECTLY, OR WHO MAY EXERCISE CONTROL OR DIRECTION OVER, EQUITY SHARES OF A PUBLIC COMPANY CARRYING MORE THAN 10 PER CENT OF THE VOTING RIGHTS ATTACHED TO ALL EQUITY SHARES OF THE COMPANY FOR THE TIME BEING OUTSTANDING. | (C) UNE PERSONNE QUI EST DIRECTEMENT OU INDIRECTEMENT PROPRIÉTAIRE BÉNÉFICIAIRE D'ACTIONS D'UNE COMPAGNIE PUBLIQUE QUI DONNENT PLUS DE 10 POUR CENT DES DROITS DE VOTE AFFÉRENTS À TOUTES LES ACTIONS DONNANT DROIT DE VOTE DE LA COMPAGNIE ET QUI SONT EN CIRCULATION À L'ÉPOQUE CONSIDÉRÉE, OU QUI PEUT EXERCER UN CONTRÔLE OU UNE DIRECTION SUR CES ACTIONS. |
| IF YOU QUALIFY AS AN INSIDER IN MORE THAN ONE CAPACITY, STATE EACH CAPACITY. | SI VOUS AVEZ DROIT AU TITRE DE DIRIGEANT EN VERTU DE PLUS D'UNE FONCTION VEUILLEZ INDIQUER CHAQUE FONCTION. |
| 4. STATE ALL CHANGES IN YOUR BENEFICIAL OWNERSHIP OF SECURITIES AND IN YOUR CONTROL OR DIRECTION OVER EQUITY SHARES OF THE COMPANY DURING THE MONTH FOR WHICH YOU ARE REPORTING, AND STATE ALSO YOUR BENEFICIAL OWNERSHIP OF SECURITIES AND YOUR CONTROL OR DIRECTION OVER EQUITY SHARES OF THE COMPANY AS OF THE END OF THE MONTH. | 4. INDIQUER TOUTES LES DIFFÉRENCES QUANT À VOTRE DROIT DE PROPRIÉTAIRE BÉNÉFICIAIRE DE VALEURS ET À VOTRE CONTRÔLE OU DIRECTION SUR LES ACTIONS DONNANT DROIT DE VOTE DE LA COMPAGNIE AU COURS DU MOIS CIVIL À L'ÉGARD DUQUEL VOUS PRÉSENTEZ UN RAPPORT, ET INDIQUER ÉGALEMENT VOTRE DROIT DE PROPRIÉTÉ BÉNÉFICIAIRE DE VALEURS ET VOTRE CONTRÔLE OU VOTRE DIRECTION SUR LES ACTIONS DONNANT DROIT DE VOTE DE LA COMPAGNIE À LA FIN DU MOIS. |
| REPORT EVERY TRANSACTION INVOLVING A CHANGE IN YOUR BENEFICIAL OWNERSHIP OF SECURITIES OR IN YOUR CONTROL OR DIRECTION OVER EQUITY SHARES OF THE COMPANY DURING THE MONTH EVEN IF PURCHASES AND SALES OR OTHER CHANGES DURING THE MONTH ARE EQUAL OR THE CHANGE INVOLVES ONLY THE NATURE OF OWNERSHIP, FOR EXAMPLE, FROM DIRECT TO INDIRECT OWNERSHIP. | INDIQUER CHAQUE OPÉRATION COMPORTANT UNE DIFFÉRENCE QUANT À VOTRE DROIT DE PROPRIÉTÉ BÉNÉFICIAIRE DE VALEURS OU À VOTRE CONTRÔLE OU DIRECTION SUR LES ACTIONS DONNANT DROIT DE VOTE DE LA COMPAGNIE AU COURS DU MOIS, MÊME SI LES ACHATS ET LES VENTES OU AUTRES DIFFÉRENCES AU COURS DU MOIS SONT ÉQUIVALENTS OU QUE LA DIFFÉRENCE SE RAPPORTE SEULEMENT À LA NATURE DE LA PROPRIÉTÉ, PAR EXEMPLE LE CHANGEMENT DU DROIT DE PROPRIÉTÉ DIRECT AU DROIT DE PROPRIÉTÉ INDIRECT. |
| 5. UNDER "DESIGNATION OF SECURITIES AND EQUITY SHARES", IDENTIFY EACH CLASS OF SECURITIES BENEFICIALLY OWNED AND EACH CLASS OF EQUITY SHARES OVER WHICH CONTROL OR DIRECTION MAY BE EXERCISED, FOR EXAMPLE, "COMMON SHARES", "FIRST PREFERENCE SHARES", "FIVE PER CENT DEBENTURES DUE 1995", ETC. | 5. SOUS «DÉSIGNATION DES VALEURS ET DES ACTIONS DONNANT DROIT DE VOTE», DÉTERMINER CHAQUE CATÉGORIE DE VALEURS À L'ÉGARD DESQUELLES VOUS AVEZ UN DROIT DE PROPRIÉTÉ BÉNÉFICIAIRE, ET CHAQUE CATÉGORIE D'ACTIONS DONNANT DROIT DE VOTE SUR LESQUELLES VOUS POUVEZ EXERCER UN CONTRÔLE OU UNE DIRECTION, PAR EXEMPLE, «ACTIONS ORDINAIRES», «ACTIONS PRIVILÉGIÉES DE PREMIER RANG», «DÉBENTURES À CINQ POUR CENT À ÉCHOIR EN 1995» ETC. |
| 6. SHOW THE DATE (DAY, MONTH AND YEAR) OF EACH TRANSACTION INVOLVING A SALE OR PURCHASE OF A SECURITY OR EQUITY SHARE OPPOSITE THE AMOUNT OR NUMBER OF SECURITIES OR EQUITY SHARES INVOLVED IN THE TRANSACTION AND THE PRICE PER UNIT OR SHARE AT WHICH THE SECURITIES OR EQUITY SHARES WERE SOLD OR PURCHASED. | 6. INDIQUER LA DATE (JOUR, MOIS ET ANNÉE) DE CHAQUE OPÉRATION VISANT LA VENTE OU L'ACHAT D'UNE VALEUR OU D'UNE ACTION DONNANT DROIT DE VOTE EN REGARD DU MONTANT OU DU NOMBRE DES VALEURS OU DES ACTIONS DONNANT DROIT DE VOTE QUE COMPORTE L'OPÉRATION AINSI QUE LE PRIX PAR UNITÉ OU ACTION AUQUEL LES VALEURS OU LES ACTIONS DONNANT DROIT DE VOTE ONT ÉTÉ VENDUES OU ACHETÉES. |
| 7. IN REPORTING THE AMOUNT OR NUMBER OF SECURITIES ACQUIRED OR BENEFICIALLY OWNED OR EQUITY SHARES OVER WHICH CONTROL OR DIRECTION MAY BE EXERCISED, IN THE CASE OF DEBT SECURITIES GIVE THE PRINCIPAL AMOUNTS THEREOF, AND IN THE CASE OF SHARES GIVE THE NUMBER THEREOF. | 7. EN FAISANT RAPPORT DU MONTANT OU DU NOMBRE DES VALEURS ACQUISES OU À L'ÉGARD DESQUELLES VOUS AVEZ UN DROIT DE PROPRIÉTÉ BÉNÉFICIAIRE OU DES ACTIONS DONNANT DROIT DE VOTE SUR LESQUELLES VOUS POUVEZ EXERCER UN CONTRÔLE OU UNE DIRECTION, DANS LE CAS DE GARANTIES DE CRÉANCES EN INDIQUER LES MONTANTS PRINCIPAUX ET DANS LE CAS DES ACTIONS EN DONNER LE NOMBRE. |
| 8. UNDER "NATURE OF OWNERSHIP, CONTROL OR DIRECTION": | 8. SOUS «NATURE DU DROIT DE PROPRIÉTÉ, DU CONTRÔLE OU DE LA DIRECTION», |
| (A) STATE WHETHER AND TO WHAT EXTENT YOUR BENEFICIAL OWNERSHIP OF SECURITIES IS DIRECT OR INDIRECT, TO THE EXTENT YOUR OWNERSHIP IS INDIRECT INDICATE IN A FOOTNOTE OR SOME OTHER APPROPRIATE MANNER THE NAME OR IDENTITY OF THE MEDIUM THE AMOUNT OR NUMBER OF SECURITIES SO OWNED BY EACH SUCH MEDIUM. | (A) INDIQUER SI VOTRE DROIT DE PROPRIÉTÉ DE VALEUR EST DIRECT OU INDIRECT ET DANS QUELLE MESURE. DANS LA MESURE OÙ VOTRE DROIT DE PROPRIÉTÉ EST INDIRECT, INDIQUER DANS UNE NOTE AU BAS DE LA PAGE OU D'UNE AUTRE FAÇON APPROPRIÉE LE NOM OU L'IDENTITÉ DE L'AGENT PAR L'ENTREMISE DUQUEL LES VALEURS SONT DIRECTEMENT POSSÉDÉES ET MENTIONNER LE MONTANT OU LE NOMBRE DE CES VALEURS DONT CET AGENT EST AINSI PROPRIÉTAIRE. |
| (B) REPORT SECURITIES OWNED INDIRECTLY ON SEPARATE LINES FROM SECURITIES OWNED DIRECTLY. | (B) INSCRIRE LES VALEURS INDIRECTEMENT POSSÉDÉES SUR DES LIGNES DISTINCTES DE CELLES DES VALEURS DIRECTEMENT POSSÉDÉES. |
| (C) STATE WHETHER YOU MAY EXERCISE CONTROL OR DIRECTION OVER EQUITY SHARES AND REPORT THE AMOUNT OR NUMBER ON A SEPARATE LINE, TO THE EXTENT THAT YOU MAY EXERCISE CONTROL OR DIRECTION OVER EQUITY SHARES INDICATE THE MEANS BY WHICH THE CONTROL OR DIRECTION IS EXERCISED AND STATE THE AMOUNT OR NUMBER OF THE EQUITY SHARES. | (C) INDIQUER SI VOUS POUVEZ EXERCER UN CONTRÔLE OU UNE DIRECTION SUR LES ACTIONS DONNANT DROIT DE VOTE ET INSCRIRE LE MONTANT OU LE NOMBRE SUR UNE LIGNE DISTINCTE, DANS LA MESURE OÙ VOUS POUVEZ EXERCER UN CONTRÔLE OU UNE DIRECTION SUR DES ACTIONS DONNANT DROIT DE VOTE, INDIQUER LES MOYENS D'EXERCICE DU CONTRÔLE OU DE LA DIRECTION ET INDIQUER LE MONTANT OU LE NOMBRE DES ACTIONS DONNANT DROIT DE VOTE. |

9. IF YOU ACQUIRED FROM OR SOLD TO THE COMPANY OF WHICH YOU ARE AN INSIDER ANY OF ITS SECURITIES OR EQUITY SHARES, GIVE PARTICULARS OF THE ACQUISITION OR SALE.

IF THE ACQUISITION OF SECURITIES OR EQUITY SHARES WAS THROUGH THE EXERCISE OF AN OPTION, GIVE PARTICULARS OF THE ACQUISITION AND THE PRICE PER SHARE OR UNIT PAID. IF ANY PURCHASE OR SALE WAS EFFECTED OTHERWISE THAN IN THE OPEN MARKET, GIVE THE DETAILS OF THE PURCHASE OR SALE. IF THE TRANSACTION WAS NOT A PURCHASE OR SALE INDICATE ITS CHARACTER, FOR EXAMPLE, "GIFT", "STOCK DIVIDEND", ETC. (THIS INFORMATION MAY BE SET OUT IN ITEM 8 OF THIS FORM).

10. YOU MAY INCLUDE ANY ADDITIONAL INFORMATION OR EXPLANATION THAT YOU DEEM RELEVANT.

11. IF THE REPORT IS FILED ON BEHALF OF A COMPANY, PARTNERSHIP, TRUST OR OTHER ENTITY, THE NAME OF THE COMPANY OR OTHER ENTITY MUST APPEAR OVER THE SIGNATURE OF THE OFFICER OR OTHER PERSON AUTHORIZED TO SIGN THE REPORT, IF THE REPORT IS FILED BY AN INDIVIDUAL, IT MUST BE SIGNED BY HIM OR SPECIFICALLY ON HIS BEHALF BY A PERSON AUTHORIZED TO SIGN FOR HIM.

12. IF SPACE PROVIDED FOR ANY ITEM IS INSUFFICIENT, ADDITIONAL SHEETS MAY BE USED BUT MUST BE CROSS-REFERRED TO THE ITEM AND PROPERLY IDENTIFIED.

9. SI VOUS AVEZ ACHETÉ DE LA COMPAGNIE DONT VOUS ÊTES UN DIRIGEANT QUELQUES-UNES DE SES VALEURS OU DE SES ACTIONS DONNANT DROIT DE VOTE OU LUI EN AVEZ VENDU, DONNER LES DÉTAILS DE L'ACQUISITION OU DE LA VENTE SI L'ACQUISITION DES VALEURS OU DES ACTIONS DONNANT DROIT DE VOTE S'EST EFFECTUÉE AU MOYEN D'UNE OPTION, IL FAUT DONNER LES DÉTAILS DE L'ACQUISITION AINSI QUE LE PRIX PAYÉ PAR ACTION OU UNITÉ. SI LES ACHATS OU LES VENTES ONT ÉTÉ EFFECTUÉS AUTREMENT QUE SUR LE MARCHÉ LIBRE, DONNER LES DÉTAILS DES ACHATS OU DES VENTES. SI L'OPÉRATION N'ÉTAIT PAS UN ACHAT OU UNE VENTE, INDIQUER SA NATURE, PAR EXEMPLE «DON», «DIVIDENDE D'ACTIONS», ETC. (CES RENSEIGNEMENTS PEUVENT ÊTRE INDIQUÉS AU NUMÉRO 8 DE LA PRÉSENTE FORMULE).

10. VOUS POUVEZ INCLURE LES RENSEIGNEMENTS OU EXPLICATIONS COMPLÉMENTAIRES QUE VOUS JUGEZ PERTINENTS.

11. SI LE RAPPORT EST FOURNI POUR LE COMPTE D'UNE COMPAGNIE, SOCIÉTÉ, FIDUCIE OU AUTRE ENTITÉ, LE NOM DE LA COMPAGNIE OU DE L'AUTRE ENTITÉ DOIT PARAÎTRE AU-DESSUS DE LA SIGNATURE DU FONCTIONNAIRE OU D'UNE AUTRE PERSONNE AYANT L'AUTORISATION DE SIGNER LE RAPPORT. SI LE RAPPORT EST FOURNI PAR UN PARTICULIER, IL DOIT ÊTRE SIGNÉ PAR LUI OU SPÉCIFIQUEMENT POUR SON COMPTE PAR UNE PERSONNE AUTORISÉE À SIGNER POUR LUI.

12. SI L'ESPACE PRÉVU À UN NUMÉRO QUELCONQUE EST INSUFFISANT, UTILISER DES FEUILLES SUPPLÉMENTAIRES EN PRENANT SOIN D'Y INSCRIRE UN RENVOI AU NUMÉRO ET DE LES DÉSIGNER CORRECTEMENT.

---

<table>
<tr><td align="center">SEE OVER</td><td align="center">AU VERSO</td></tr>
</table>

---

<table>
<tr><td align="center">REFERENCES TO<br>SECTIONS OF THE ACT</td><td align="center">RÉFÉRENCES AUX<br>DISPOSITIONS DE LA LOI</td></tr>
</table>

1. DEFINITIONS:
"INSIDER" .................................................. S. 100
"ASSOCIATE" ............................................... S. 100
"AFFILIATE" ............................................... S. 125
"COMPANY" ................................................. S. 3
"ANY OTHER COMPANY" ....................................... S. 3
"PUBLIC COMPANY" .......................................... S. 100
"DIRECTOR" ................................................ S. 3
"OFFICER" ................................................. S. 3
"EQUITY SHARE" ............................................ S. 3
"SECURITIES" .............................................. S. 3

1. DÉFINITIONS:
«ACTION DONNANT DROIT DE
VOTE» ..................................................... ART. 3
«ADMINISTRATEUR» .......................................... ART. 3
«AFFILIÉ» ................................................. ART. 125
«ASSOCIÉ» ................................................. ART. 100
«COMPAGNIE» ............................................... ART. 3
«COMPAGNIE PUBLIQUE» ...................................... ART. 100
«DIRIGEANT» ............................................... ART. 100
                                                          ART. 100
«FONCTIONNAIRE» ........................................... ART. 3
«TOUTE AUTRE COMPAGNIE» ................................... ART. 3
«VALEURS» ................................................. ART. 3

2. DUTY TO FILE INSIDER
REPORTS ................................................... S. 100.1

2. OBLIGATION DE FOURNIR DES RAPPORTS
SUR LES DROITS DE DIRECTION ............................... ART. 100.1

3. PUBLIC INSPECTION OF
REPORTS ................................................... S. 100.2

3. INSPECTION PAR LE PUBLIC
DES RAPPORTS FOURNIS ...................................... ART. 100.2

4. OFFENCE AND PUNISHMENT .................................... S. 100.3

4. INFRACTION ET PEINE ...................................... ART. 100.3

5. CIVIL LIABILITY OF
INSIDER ................................................... S. 100.4

5. RESPONSABILITÉ CIVILE
DU DIRIGEANT .............................................. ART. 100.4

<table>
<tr><td align="center">(FOR MORE DETAILS SEE GENERALLY<br>SECTIONS 100 TO 100.6 OF THE ACT)</td><td align="center">(POUR DE PLUS AMPLES DÉTAILS VOIR<br>LES ARTICLES 100 À 100.6 DE LA LOI)</td></tr>
<tr><td align="center">FURTHER DIRECTIONS</td><td align="center">AUTRES RENSEIGNEMENTS</td></tr>
</table>

1. DEPARTMENT EMPLOYEES ARE NOT PERMITTED TO VARY A REPORT. THEREFORE ALL ITEMS MUST BE COMPLETED. STATE "N.A" IF AN ITEM IS NOT APPLICABLE.

2. CHECK TO ENSURE THAT THE REPORT IS CONSISTENT WITH PREVIOUS REPORTS. THE DATA IN THE REPORTS MUST RECONCILE.

3. WHEN REPORTING A CHANGE IN THE MANNER OF HOLDING SECURITIES, SAY, FROM "DIRECT" TO "INDIRECT", REPORT BOTH SIDES OF THE TRANSACTION: E.G. IF A TRANSFERS 100 SHARES OF COMPANY M TO COMPANY X (OF WHICH A IS THE SOLE SHAREHOLDER), THE TRANSFER SHOULD BE REPORTED AS A SALE BY A AND A PURCHASE BY COMPANY X UNDER ITEM 6 THE CHANGE IN A'S HOLDING FROM "DIRECT" TO "INDIRECT" MAYBE EXPLAINED UNDER ITEM 8.

4. A "STOCK SPLIT" CONSTITUTES A CHANGE IN SHARE HOLDINGS AND MUST BE REPORTED UNDER ITEM 6.

5. WHEN ATTACHEMENTS ARE USED TO RECORD DETAILED TRANSACTIONS THESE SHOULD BE TOTALLED AND THE TOTALS CARRIED FORWARD TO ITEM 6.

6. ALWAYS COMPLETE ITEM 7 TO SHOW A CONSOLIDATION OF ALL SECURITIES OF THE COMPANY HELD BY THE INSIDER.

7. IF REPORTING AN INDIRECT HOLDING ALWAYS REFER TO EACH COMPANY OR TRUST INVOLVED BY ITS FULL LEGAL NAME.

8. PURCHASE WARRANTS, PUT, CALL OR OTHER TRANSFERABLE OPTIONS ARE EQUITY SECURITIES THAT MUST BE REPORTED.

IF FURTHER INFORMATION IS REQUIRED, WRITE TO THE CORPORATIONS BRANCH, DEPARTMENT OF CONSUMER AND CORPORATE AFFAIRS, OTTAWA 4, CANADA.

1. LES EMPLOYÉS DU MINISTÈRE NE SONT PAS AUTORISÉS À MODIFIER UN RAPPORT ET EN CONSÉQUENCE IL FAUT DONNER UNE RÉPONSE À TOUS LES ARTICLES SI UN ARTICLE NE S'APPLIQUE PAS, INSCRIRE LA MENTION «SANS OBJET» OU «S/O».

2. ASSUREZ-VOUS QUE LE RAPPORT EST CONFORME AUX RAPPORTS ANTÉRIEURS. IL DOIT Y AVOIR CONCORDANCE DES DONNÉES DANS LES RAPPORTS.

3. EN FAISANT RAPPORT D'UN CHANGEMENT DANS LA FAÇON DE DÉTENIR DES VALEURS, DISONS DE «DIRECTEMENT» À «INDIRECTEMENT» SIGNALER LES DEUX ASPECTS DE L'OPÉRATION E.G. SI A TRANSFÈRE 100 ACTIONS DE LA COMPAGNIE M À LA COMPAGNIE X (DONT LA COMPAGNIE A EST ACTIONNAIRE UNIQUE, LE TRANSFERT DOIT ÊTRE INDIQUÉ COMME VENTE PAR A ET COMME ACHAT PAR LA COMPAGNIE X AU NUMÉRO 6. LE CHANGEMENT DANS LA DÉTENTION DE A DE «DIRECT» À «INDIRECTE» PEUT ÊTRE EXPLIQUÉ AU NUMÉRO 8.

4. UN «FRACTIONNEMENT D'ACTIONS» CONSTITUE UN CHANGEMENT DANS LA DÉTENTION D'ACTIONS ET DOIT ÊTRE SIGNALÉ AU NUMÉRO 6.

5. LORSQUE DES FEUILLES SUPPLÉMENTAIRES SONT UTILISÉES POUR L'INSCRIPTION D'OPÉRATIONS EN DÉTAILS, IL FAUT ÉTABLIR LE TOTAL DE CHACUNE ET LE REPORTER AU NUMÉRO 6.

6. IL FAUT TOUJOURS RÉPONDRE AU NUMÉRO 7 AFIN D'INDIQUER L'ENSEMBLE DE TOUTES LES VALEURS DE LA COMPAGNIE DÉTENUES PAR LE DIRIGEANT.

7. EN FAISANT RAPPORT AU SUJET D'UNE DÉTENTION INDIRECTE, VEUILLEZ TOUJOURS FAIRE MENTION DE CHAQUE COMPAGNIE OU FIDUCIE EN CAUSE EN LUI DONNANT SON NOM JURIDIQUE INTÉGRAL.

8. LES TITRES D'ACHAT, PRIMES DIRECTES, PRIMES INDIRECTES, OU AUTRES PRIMES CESSIBLES SONT DES VALEURS DONNANT DROIT DE VOTE QUI DOIVENT ÊTRE INSCRITES DANS LE RAPPORT.

POUR TOUT RENSEIGNEMENT SUPPLÉMENTAIRE, PRIÈRE DE VOUS ADRESSER À LA DIRECTION DES CORPORATIONS, MINISTÈRE DE LA CONSOMMATION ET DES CORPORATIONS, OTTAWA 4, CANADA.

| CANADA CORPORATIONS ACT | LOI SUR LES CORPORATIONS CANADIENNES |
|---|---|
| FORM 2 | FORMULE 2 |
| REPORT OF CHANGE IN INSIDER INTEREST IN | RAPPORT SUR LES CHANGEMENTS DES DROITS DE |
| THE SECURITIES OF A COMPANY | DIRECTION EN CE QUI CONCERNE LES VALEURS D'UNE COMPAGNIE |
| (S.100.1(4) AND (5)) | (ART. 100.1(4) ET (5)) |

PLEASE PRINT OR TYPE, AND FILE IN TWO SIGNED COPIES TO:

REMPLIR EN LETTTRES D'IMPRIMERIE OU À LA MACHINE À ÉCRIRE, ET FAIRE PARVENIR DEUX COPIES SIGNÉES AU

DEPARTMENT OF CONSUMER AND CORPORATE AFFAIRS
CORPORATIONS BRANCH
OTTAWA, CANADA

MINISTÈRE DE LA CONSOMMATION ET DES CORPORATIONS
DIRECTION DES CORPORATIONS
OTTAWA, CANADA

1- NAME OF COMPANY OF WHICH THE UNDERSIGNED IS INSIDER — NOM DE LA COMPAGNIE DONT LE SOUSSIGNÉ EST DIRIGEANT

2- FULL NAME OF THE UNDERSIGNED
NOM ET PRÉNOMS DU SOUSSIGNÉ

3- BUSINESS ADDRESS OF THE UNDERSIGNED
ADRESSE PROFESSIONNELLE DU SOUSSIGNÉ

4- INDICATE IN WHAT CAPACITY OR CAPACITIES THE UNDERSIGNED QUALIFIES AS INSIDER (SEE INSTRUCTION 3) — INDIQUER EN VERTU DE QUELLE(S) FONCTION(S) LE SOUSSIGNÉ A DROIT AU TITRE DE DIRIGEANT (VOIR INSTRUCTION 3)

5- INFORMATION GIVEN FOR CALENDAR MONTH OF . . . RENSEIGNEMENTS DONNÉS POUR LE MOIS CIVIL DE . . .

6- CHANGES DURING MONTH IN THE UNDERSIGNED'S INTEREST IN THE FOLLOWING SECURITIES OF THE COMPANY
(A) SECURITIES BENEFICIALLY OWNED DIRECTLY OR INDIRECTLY BY THE UNDERSIGNED, AND
(B) EQUITY SHARES OVER WHICH THE UNDERSIGNED MAY EXERCISE CONTROL OR DIRECTION (SEE INSTRUCTION 4)

DIFFÉRENCES SURVENUES AU COURS DU MOIS DANS LE DROIT DU SOUSSIGNÉ EN CE QUI CONCERNE LES VALEURS SUIVANTES DE LA COMPAGNIE
(A) VALEURS DONT LE SOUSSIGNÉ EST DIRECTEMENT OU INDIRECTEMENT PROPRIÉTAIRE BÉNÉFICIAIRE
(B) ACTIONS DONNANT DROIT DE VOTE SUR LESQUELLES LE SOUSSIGNÉ PEUT EXERCER UN CONTRÔLE OU UNE DIRECTION (VOIR INSTRUCTION 4)

| Designation of Securities and Equity Shares Désignation des valeurs et des actions donnant droit de vote (See — Voir instruction 5) | Date of Purchase or Sale Transaction Date de l'opération d'achat ou de vente (See — Voir instruction 6) | Amount or Number Purchased or otherwise acquired Montant ou nombre à l'égard d'achat ou autre acquisition (See — Voir instruction 7) | Amount or Number Sold or otherwise disposed Montant ou nombre à l'égard de vente ou autre aliénation (See — Voir instruction 7) | Price per share or unit at which sold or purchased or otherwise acquired or disposed of—Prix par action ou unité auquel la vente ou autre acquisition ou aliénation a été effectuée | Nature of Ownership Control or Direction Nature du droit de propriété du contrôle ou de la direction (See — Voir instruction 8) |
|---|---|---|---|---|---|
| | | | | | |
| | | | | | |
| | | | | | |
| | | | | | |

7- INSIDER INTEREST AT THE END OF THE MONTH IN THE FOLLOWING SECURITIES OF THE COMPANY:
(A) SECURITIES BENEFICIALLY OWNED DIRECTLY OR INDIRECTLY BY THE UNDERSIGNED, AND
(B) EQUITY SHARES OVER WHICH THE UNDERSIGNED MAY EXERCISE CONTROL OVER DIRECTION

DROIT DE DIRECTION EN CE QUI CONCERNE LES VALEURS SUIVANTES DE LA COMPAGNIE À LA FIN DU MOIS
(A) VALEURS DONT LE SOUSSIGNÉ EST DIRECTEMENT OU INDIRECTEMENT PROPRIÉTAIRE BÉNÉFICIAIRE
(B) ACTIONS DONNANT LE DROIT DE VOTE SUR LESQUELLES LE SOUSSIGNÉ PEUT EXERCER UN CONTRÔLE OU UNE DIRECTION

| DESIGNATION OF SECURITIES AND EQUITY SHARES DÉSIGNATION DES VALEURS ET DES ACTIONS DONNANT DROIT DE VOTE (SEE — VOIR INSTRUCTION 5) | AMOUNT OR NUMBER MONTANT OU NOMBRE (SEE — VOIR INSTRUCTION 7) | NATURE OF OWNERSHIP CONTROL OR DIRECTION NATURE DU DROIT DE PROPRIÉTÉ, DU CONTRÔLE OU DE LA DIRECTION (SEE — VOIR INSTRUCTION 8) |
|---|---|---|
| | | |
| | | |
| | | |
| | | |

8- ADDITIONAL REMARKS
OBSERVATIONS COMPLÉMENTAIRES

THE UNDERSIGNED HEREBY CERTIFIES THAT
LE SOUSSIGNÉ CERTIFIE PAR LES PRÉSENTES QUE:

(1) NO USE HAS BEEN MADE OF ANY SPECIFIC CONFIDENTIAL INFORMATION THAT IF GENERALLY KNOWN MIGHT REASONABLY BE EXPECTED TO AFFECT MATERIALLY THE VALUE OF THE CAPITAL SECURITIES OF THE CORPORATION.

AUCUN USAGE N'A ÉTÉ FAIT DE QUELQUE RENSEIGNEMENT PARTICULIER DONT IL EST RAISONNABLE DE PRÉVOIR QU'IL INFLUERAIT DE MANIÈRE SENSIBLE, S'IL ÉTAIT CONNU EN GÉNÉRAL, SUR LA VALEUR DES VALEURS MOBILIÈRES DE LA CORPORATION.

(2) THE INFORMATION GIVEN IN THIS REPORT IS TRUE AND COMPLETE IN EVERY RESPECT.

LES RENSEIGNEMENTS DONNÉS DANS LE PRÉSENT RAPPORT SONT VÉRIDIQUES ET COMPLETS À TOUS ÉGARDS.

| DATE OF REPORT DATE DU RAPPORT | SIGNATURE (SEE — VOIR INSTRUCTION 11) |
|---|---|

CCA-875 (10-72)

IT IS AN OFFENCE UNDER THE CANADA CORPORATIONS ACT TO FILE A FALSE OR MISLEADING REPORT
FOURNIR UN RAPPORT FAUX OU TROMPEUR CONSTITUE UNE INFRACTION EN VERTU DE LA LOI SUR LES CORPORATIONS CANADIENNES.

Canada Corporations
Act

**ANNUAL SUMMARY**

FORM 3
INSTRUCTIONS

### 1. Application

This annual summary must be filed on or before the first day of June each year by the following corporations:

(a) companies with share capital incorporated under Part I of the Canada Corporations Act;

(b) companies with share capital incorporated by Special Act of Parliament;

(c) corporations without share capital incorporated under Part II of the Canada Corporations Act; and

(d) corporations without share capital incorporated by Special Act of Parliament.

The only companies or corporations exempted are those incorporated after the 1st day of March of the current year.

### 2. Penalties

Section 133(3)

A company that makes default in complying with any requirement of this section is guilty of an offence and is liable on summary conviction to a fine of not less than twenty dollars and not more than one hundred dollars for each day during which the default continues; and every director or officer who knowingly authorized, permitted or acquiesced in any such default is guilty of an offence and is liable on summary conviction to a like fine.

### 3. Bylaws

Bylaws changing the location of the head office and the number of directors are regulated by sections 24 and 89 of the Canada Corporations Act. Such bylaws must be filed with this department.

---

Completed documents in duplicate and fees payable to the Receiver General of Canada, are to be sent to:

The Director, Corporations Branch,
🍁    Consumer and    Consommation et
      Corporate Affairs    corporations
Place du Portage,
Ottawa/Hull, Canada,
K1A 0C9.

---

Loi sur les corporations
canadiennes

**SOMMAIRE ANNUEL**

FORMULE 3
INSTRUCTIONS

### 1. Application

Ce sommaire doit être déposé le ou avant le 1er juin de chaque année par:

(a) les compagnies avec capital-actions constituées en vertu de la partie I de la Loi sur les corporations canadiennes;

(b) les compagnies avec capital-actions constituées par loi spéciale du Parlement;

(c) les corporations sans capital-actions constituées en vertu de la partie II de la Loi sur les corporations canadiennes; et

(d) les corporations sans capital-actions constituées par loi spéciale du Parlement.

Les seules compagnies ou corporations exemptées sont celles constituées après le 1er mars de l'année courante.

### 2. Sanctions

Article 133(3)

Une compagnie qui omet de se conformer aux prescriptions du présent article est coupable d'une infraction et passible, sur déclaration sommaire de culpabilité, d'une amende d'au moins vingt dollars et d'au plus cent dollars pour chaque jour que dure cette omission; et tout administrateur ou fonctionnaire qui, sciemment, a autorisé ou permis cette omission ou y a consenti est coupable d'une infraction et passible, sur déclaration sommaire de culpabilité, d'une amende semblable.

### 3. Règlements

Les règlements qui changent l'endroit du siège social ainsi que le nombre d'administrateurs sont régis par les articles 24 et 89 de la Loi sur les corporations canadiennes. Ces règlements doivent être déposés à notre ministère.

---

Les documents complétés en duplicata et les droits, payables au Receveur-Général du Canada, doivent être envoyés à:

Le Directeur, Direction des Corporations
🍁    Consommation et    Consumer and
      corporations    Corporate Affairs
Place du Portage,
Ottawa/Hull, Canada,
K1A 0C9.

---

FORM 3

FORMULE 3

Annual Summary
(Under Section 133 of the
Canada Corporations Act)

Sommaire annuel
(Article 133 de la Loi sur
les corporations canadiennes)

As of 31st March 19

Au 31 mars 19

| A NAME AND MAILING ADDRESS OF COMPANY<br>NOM ET ADRESSE POSTALE DE LA COMPAGNIE | B POSTAL ADDRESS OF HEAD OFFICE IF DIFFERENT FROM A<br>ADRESSE POSTALE DE SIÈGE SOCIAL SI DIFFÉRENTE DE A |
|---|---|

| C INCORPORATED BY<br>INCORPORÉE PAR | D. DATE OF INCORPORATION<br>DATE DE L'INCORPORATION | E. LAST ANNUAL MEETING OF SHAREHOLDERS OR MEMBERS HELD PRIOR TO APRIL 1ST   DERNIÈRE ASSEMBLÉE ANNUELLE DES ACTIONNAIRES OU MEMBRES TENUE AVANT LE 1er avril. |
|---|---|---|

☐ LETTERS PATENT
LETTRES PATENTES

☐ SPECIAL ACT — LOI SPÉCIALE

DATE          PLACE — LIEU

F  NAMES AND ADDRESSES OF THE PERSONS WHO AT THE DATE OF THE RETURN ARE THE DIRECTORS OF THE COMPANY. VARIATIONS FROM THE AUTHORIZED NUMBER OF DIRECTORS SHOULD BE EXPLAINED. — NOMS ET ADRESSES DES PERSONNES QUI, À LA DATE DU RAPPORT, SONT ADMINISTRATEURS DE LA COMPAGNIE. UN CHANGEMENT DANS LE NOMBRE D'ADMINISTRATEURS DEVRAIT ÊTRE EXPLIQUÉ.

NAMES AND COMPLETE POSTAL ADDRESSES — NOMS ET ADRESSES POSTALES COMPLÈTES

| 1 | 9 |
|---|---|
| 2 | 10 |
| 3 | 11 |
| 4 | 12 |
| 5 | G NAME AND COMPLETE POSTAL ADDRESS OF THE AUDITOR OF THE COMPANY   NOM ET ADRESSE POSTALE COMPLÈTE DU VÉRIFICATEUR DE LA COMPAGNIE |
| 6 | |
| 7 | SIGNATURE AND TITLE (OFFICER OR DIRECTOR)<br>SIGNATURE ET TITRE (FONCTIONNAIRE OU ADMINISTRATEUR) |
| 8 | TELEPHONE NO. DE TÉLÉPHONE     DATE |

RECEIVED    REÇU                          DATE

DEPARTMENTAL USE ONLY
À L'USAGE DU MINISTÈRE SEULEMENT

DATE RECEIVED    DATE DE RÉCEPTION        VALIDATION

KEY CODE—CLÉ    CHÈQUE · CHÈQUE    AMOUNT   MONTANT

# FORM 4

## STATEMENT

### DIRECTORS' AND OFFICERS' REMUNERATION
### FROM THE CORPORATION AND ITS AFFILIATES
### SUBPARAGRAPH 33(r)(v) OF THE CANADA CORPORATIONS REGULATIONS

**NATURE OF REMUNERATION EARNED**

| Directors' fees | Salaries | Bonuses | Non-accountable expense all. | Others (note 1) | Total |
|---|---|---|---|---|---|
|  |  |  |  |  |  |

**TOTALS**

**REMUNERATION OF DIRECTORS**

(A) Number of directors:

(B) *Body Corporate incurring the expense*

3036

**REMUNERATION OF OFFICERS**

(A) Number of officers:

(B) *Body Corporate incurring the expense*

Note 1: Describe in a note to this form the nature of the remuneration conferred.

## CANADA CORPORATIONS ACT
### REQUEST FOR NAME RESERVATION
### FORM 5
### INSTRUCTIONS

**Items 1, 2 and 3**

Set out the name of any legal firm, the name of the lawyer or employee responsible to process the Request and the address and phone number of the firm (indicate area code and any extension number).

**Item 4**

Set out the proposed names in the order of your preference. If more than one Request is sent to the Director a separate fee must be paid in respect of each Request. If more than 3 names are required to be searched, one or more additional Requests must be sent to the Director and a fee paid in respect of each Request.

**Item 5**

If this replaces a name previously requested indicate whether the previous name was submitted as a name reservation only or with application for letters patent or supplementary letters patent and state the previous name.

**Item 6**

State details of the nature of the business, describing the industrial sector, the actual functions and the products and services of the corporation. Indicate the industrial sector as specifically as possible by reference to the S.I.C. Code or to the Statistics Canada Standard Industrial Classification Manual.

**Item 7**

Show the derivation of the distinctive element of the name; e.g., "Q.E.D." derived from Quéneau, Edwards and Dorion.

**Items 8, 9 and 10**

Indicate proposed use of name and name of any holding body corporate of a new corporation.

**Item 11**

Set out the name of any individual, body corporate or firm required to consent to the name under sections 21, 25, or 26 of the Regulations.

**Item 12**

Give details of any similar trade names or trade marks used by the applicant body corporate.

**Other Documents**

The Request must be accompanied by any consent referred to in Item 11.

**Caution**

An indication that a name appears to be available at this time is not to be construed as an undertaking that the said name will be granted if and when a formal application is made. It is only a tentative indication that the name might be available at the time of the issue of the certificate of incorporation. If any printing or other use of the name is made in advance, it will be done entirely at the risk of the applicants.

Where applicants are to accept full responsibility for risk of confusion with other names, acceptance of such responsibility will comprise an obligation to change the name to a dissimilar one in the event that representations are made and established that confusion occurs. Errors and omissions excepted.

The use of any name granted is subject to any laws of the jurisdiction where the company carries on business.

---

Completed document in duplicate and a fee of $10 for each Request form, payable to the Receiver General of Canada, are to be sent to:

The Director, Corporations Branch,
Consommation et
Consumer and
Corporate Affairs
corporations
Place du Portage,
Ottawa/Hull, Canada,
K1A 0C9.

---

## LOI SUR LES CORPORATIONS CANADIENNES
### DEMANDE DE RÉSERVATION D'UN NOM
### FORMULE 5
### INSTRUCTIONS

**Rubriques 1, 2 et 3**

Indiquer le nom de l'étude légale, le nom de l'avocat ou de l'employé responsable de la demande de réservation du nom, et l'adresse et le numéro de téléphone de l'étude (indiquer le code régional et le numéro d'extension).

**Rubrique 4**

Indiquer les noms proposés par ordre de préférence. Si plus d'une demande est envoyée au Directeur le droit doit être payé en regard de chaque demande. Si une recherche doit être faite pour plus de trois noms, une ou plusieurs demandes additionnelles doivent être envoyées au Directeur et un droit payé à l'égard de chaque demande.

**Rubrique 5**

S'il s'agit d'une demande pour un nom précédemment demandé, indiquer si le nom précédent a été soumis lors d'une réservation de nom seulement ou avec une demande pour lettres patentes ou lettres patentes supplémentaires et donner le nom précédent.

**Rubrique 6**

Donner les détails de la nature des entreprises en décrivant le secteur industriel, les opérations actuelles et les produits et services vendus par la corporation. Indiquer le secteur industriel le plus spécifiquement possible en référant au Code S.I.C. ou au Manuel de classification des activités économiques de Statistique Canada.

**Rubrique 7**

Montrer la dérivation de l'élément distinctif du nom; par exemple, «T.C.M.» dérivé de Tanguay, Côté et Masson.

**Rubriques 8, 9 et 10**

Indiquer l'utilisation projetée du nom et le nom de toute personne morale mère de la nouvelle corporation.

**Rubrique 11**

Indiquer le nom de tout individu, personne morale ou firme dont le consentement est requis pour l'octroi du nom en vertu des articles 21, 25, ou 26 du règlement.

**Rubrique 12**

Donner les détails de tout nom commercial ou marque de commerce semblable utilisé par la personne morale demanderesse.

**Autres documents**

La demande doit être accompagnée de tout consentement mentionné à la rubrique 11.

**Attention**

Toute indication qu'un nom corporatif semble en ce moment disponible ne doit pas être considérée comme un engagement de notre part à accorder ledit nom si une demande formelle devait par la suite nous être présentée. Un tel avis ne sert qu'à établir la disponibilité probable du nom suggéré à la date de l'émission du certificat d'incorporation. Si les promoteurs de la compagnie projetée ou les requérants font des dépenses d'imprimerie ou autres avant confirmation officielle, ils le font à leur propre risque.

Quand un nom est accordé à la condition que les requérants soient prêts à assumer toute responsabilité pour risque de confusion avec les noms d'autres compagnies, cette acceptation de responsabilité comprend l'obligation de changer le nom de la compagnie en un nom différent advenant le cas où des représentations sont faites établissant qu'il y a confusion. Sauf erreurs et omissions.

L'utilisation de tout nom octroyé est sujette à toute loi de la juridiction où la corporation exploite son entreprise.

---

Les documents complétés en duplicata et un droit de $10 pour chaque formule de demande, payable au Receveur-Général du Canada, doivent être envoyés à:

Le Directeur, Direction des Corporations,
Consommation et
Consumer and
corporations
Corporate Affairs
Place du Portage,
Ottawa/Hull, Canada,
K1A 0C9.

---

| CANADA CORPORATIONS ACT | | LOI SUR LES CORPORATIONS CANADIENNES |
|---|---|---|
| FORM 5 | | FORMULE 5 |
| REQUEST FOR NAME RESERVATION | | DEMANDE DE RÉSERVATION D'UN NOM |

Name and Address of Legal Firm - Nom et adresse de l'étude légale

⌐ ☐                                      ⌐
L                                        —

---

4- Proposed name or names in order of preference
Nom(s) proposé(s) par ordre de préférence

2-

3-

---

5- In lieu of . . .  ☐ Name previously submitted
Au lieu de . . .       Nom soumis précédemment

☐ Name submitted with application
   Nom soumis avec une demande

Previous Name - Nom précédent

---

6- Nature of business (details of functions, products, services) - Nature des entreprises (détails des fonctions, produits, services)

---

7- Derivation of Name (Origin of distinctive feature in name such as initials, coined word, etc....)
Dérivation du nom (Origine de l'élément distinctif du nom tel qu'initiales, mot fabriqué, etc....)

---

| 8- ☐ New Corporation nouvelle | 9- If change of name of existing federal Corporation give present name  S'il s'agit d'une modification du nom d'une corporation fédérale existante donner le nom actuel | 10- Name and address of holding body corporate (if applicable)  Lorsqu'applicable, les nom et adresse de la personne morale mère |
|---|---|---|

---

11- Consent of other individual, body corporate or firm. Give name and address of consenting person.
Consentement d'une autre personne, personne morale ou firme. Donner les nom et adresse de la personne consentante.

---

| 12- Similar trade names and trade marks used by applicant  Noms commerciaux et marques de commerce semblables utilisés par le demandeur | Date of Registration  Date d'enregistrement | Length of time in use  Période d'utilisation |
|---|---|---|

---

| FOR DEPARTMENTAL USE ONLY | À L'USAGE DU MINISTÈRE SEULEMENT |
|---|---|
| Names reserved until...(specify date)  Noms réservés jusqu'au...(spécifier la date) | For Director - Pour le directeur |
| 1- ☐ _____   2- ☐ _____   3- ☐ _____ | |
| | See attached letter if name not reserved.  Voir lettre attachée si le nom n'est pas réservé. |
| Date received  Date de réception | Request received by  Demande reçue par |

**Caution**
Name Reservations are granted in accordance with the conditions on the reverse side hereto.

**Attention**
Les réservations de nom sont accordées conformément aux conditions énoncées au verso.

CCA-1396

## FORM 6

## STATUTORY DECLARATION

(Section 111.1)

CANADA

Province of..................

In re

(name of Company)

(List of shareholders under section 111.1 of the *Canada Corporations Act.*)

I, . . . . . . . . . . . . . . . . . . . . . . . . . . . . . . . . . . . . . . . . . . . . . . . . . . . . . . . . . .

(name) (resident address) (occupation)

having been duly sworn make oath and say that:

(If the applicant is a body corporate, indicate the office and authority of the deponent, the name and address for service of the body corporate and word the declaration accordingly.)

1. I hereby apply for a list of the shareholders of the above named company.

2. The list of shareholders and the information contained therein will not be used for any purpose prohibited by section 111.1 of the *Canada Corporations Act.*

3. The list of shareholders and the information contained therein will not be used except in connection with

(a) an effort to influence the voting of shareholders of the corporation;

(b) an offer to acquire shares of the company; or

(c) any other matter relating to the affairs of the company.

Declared, etc.

[SOR/78-46, s. 8.]

# SCHEDULE II

## (s. 56)

1. (a) Each direct request to the Minister to search one proposed corporate name, including the reservation of the name ................................................................................................ $15.00

(b) Each request for access to the database and automated name search system administered by the Minister, for the purpose of making a search of one proposed corporate name, made by a government agency or a private sector firm that offers name search services ............................................. 2.00

(b.1) [Revoked, SOR/79-318, s. 3]

(c) Each request for a name search or an analysis of the trade name database that cannot be effected by a standard computer search ............................................................................ Cost plus 20%

2. An application to the Minister for

(a) letters patent issued under sections 137*, 154 and 159 ........................ $200.00

(b) supplementary letters patent issued under sections 13, 20, 29, 60 and 135 ................................................................................................. 50.00

(c) a certificate of increase in consideration for shares without par value .................................................................................. 50.00

3. On the issuance by the Minister of any certificate ....................................... 10.00

4. On filing a summary under section 133 ......................................................... 30.00

5. For uncertified copies of or extract from documents supplied by the Minister under subsection 129(2), per document if in excess of nine (9) documents ................................................. 1.00

6. Certified copies of or extract from documents supplied by the Minister under subsection 129(2) ........................................................... 10.00

7. On registering particulars of mortgages or charges under subsection 68(6) ................................................................................ 10.00

8. On any search of the register under section 68 ............................................. 10.00

9. On registering an order for the appointment of a receiver or receiver and manager under section 69 ...................................................... 10.00

10. On the inspection of documents under sections 100.1 and 108.4 ............................................................................................................. 10.00

*Note: All references are references to numbers of provisions of the Act.

[SOR/78-46, s. 9; SOR/78-365, s. 1; SOR/79-223, s. 1; SOR/79-318, ss. 2, 3.]

# CANADA-UNITED STATES TAX CONVENTION ACT, 1984

## (S.C. 1984, C. 20)

[Note: Only Article XXI is reproduced]

# SCHEDULE I

## CONVENTION BETWEEN CANADA AND THE UNITED STATES OF AMERICA WITH RESPECT TO TAXES ON INCOME AND ON CAPITAL

### Article XXI Exempt Organizations

1. Subject to the provisions of paragraph 3, income derived by a religious, scientific, literary, educational or charitable organization shall be exempt from tax in a Contracting State if it is resident in the other Contracting State but only to the extent that such income is exempt from tax in that other State.

2. Subject to the provisions of paragraph 3, income referred to in Articles X (Dividends) and XI (Interest) derived by a trust, company or other organization constituted and operated exclusively to administer or provide benefits under one or more funds or plans established to provide pension, retirement or other employee benefits shall be exempt from tax in a Contracting State if it is resident in the other Contracting State and its income is generally exempt from tax in that other State.

3. The provisions of paragraphs 1 and 2 shall not apply with respect to the income of a trust, company or other organization from carrying on a trade or business or from a related person other than a person referred to in paragraph 1 or 2.

4. A religious, scientific, literary, educational or charitable organization which is resident in Canada and which has received substantially all of its support from persons other than citizens or residents of the United States shall be exempt in the United States from the United States excise taxes imposed with respect to private foundations.

5. For the purposes of United States taxation, contributions by a citizen or resident of the United States to an organization which is resident in Canada, which is generally exempt from Canadian tax and which could qualify in the United States to receive deductible contributions if it were resident in the United States shall be treated as charitable contributions; however, such contributions (other than such contributions to a college or university at which the citizen or resident or a member of his family is or was enrolled) shall not be deductible in any taxable

year to the extent that they exceed an amount determined by applying the percentage limitations of the laws of the United States in respect of the deductibility of charitable contributions to the income of such citizen or resident arising in Canada. The preceding sentence shall not be interpreted to allow in any taxable year deductions for charitable contributions in excess of the amount allowed under the percentage limitations of the laws of the United States in respect of the deductibility of charitable contributions.

6. For the purposes of Canadian taxation, gifts by a resident of Canada to an organization which is resident in the United States, which is generally exempt from United States tax and which could qualify in Canada to receive deductible gifts if it were created or established and resident in Canada shall be treated as gifts to a registered charity; however, such gifts (other than such gifts to a college or university at which the resident or a member of his family is or was enrolled) shall not be deductible in any taxable year to the extent that they exceed an amount determined by applying the percentage limitations of the laws of Canada in respect of the deductibility of gifts to registered charities to the income of such resident arising in the United States. The preceding sentence shall not be interpreted to allow in any taxable year deductions for gifts to registered charities in excess of the amount allowed under the percentage limitations of the laws of Canada in respect of the deductibility of gifts to registered charities.

# CHARITIES REGISTRATION
# (SECURITY INFORMATION) ACT

(S.C. 2001, c. 41, s. 113)

## SHORT TITLE

**Amended by:** S.C. 2001, c. 41, s. 125

**1. Short title** — This Act may be cited as the *Charities Registration (Security Information) Act*.

## PURPOSE AND PRINCIPLES

**2.** (1) **Purpose** — The purpose of this Act is to demonstrate Canada's commitment to participating in concerted international efforts to deny support to those who engage in terrorist activities, to protect the integrity of the registration system for charities under the *Income Tax Act* and to maintain the confidence of Canadian taxpayers that the benefits of charitable registration are made available only to organizations that operate exclusively for charitable purposes.

(2) **Principles** — This Act shall be carried out in recognition of, and in accordance with, the following principles:

(a)  maintaining the confidence of taxpayers may require reliance on information that, if disclosed, would injure national security or endanger the safety of persons; and

(b)  the process for relying on the information referred to in paragraph (a) in determining eligibility to become or remain a registered charity must be as fair and transparent as possible having regard to national security and the safety of persons.

## INTERPRETATION

**3. Definitions** — The following definitions apply in this Act.

"applicant" means a corporation, an organization or a trust that applies to the Minister of National Revenue to become a registered charity.

"information" means security or criminal intelligence information and information that is obtained in confidence from a source in Canada, from the government of a foreign state, from an international organization of states or from an institution of such a government or organization.

"judge" means the Chief Justice of the Federal Court or a judge of the Trial Division of that Court designated by the Chief Justice.

"Minister" means the Solicitor General of Canada.

"registered charity" means a registered charity as defined in subsection 248(1) of the *Income Tax Act*.

[2001, c. 41, s. 125 (in force June 28, 2002).]

## CERTIFICATE BASED ON INTELLIGENCE

**4.** (1) **Signature by Ministers** — The Minister and the Minister of National Revenue may sign a certificate stating that it is their opinion, based on information, that there are reasonable grounds to believe

(a)　that an applicant or registered charity has made, makes or will make available any resources, directly or indirectly, to an entity that is a listed entity as defined in subsection 83.01(1) of the *Criminal Code*;

(b)　that an applicant or registered charity made available any resources, directly or indirectly, to an entity as defined in subsection 83.01(1) of the *Criminal Code* and the entity was at that time, and continues to be, engaged in terrorist activities as defined in that subsection or activities in support of them; or

(c)　that an applicant or registered charity makes or will make available any resources, directly or indirectly, to an entity as defined in subsection 83.01(1) of the *Criminal Code* and the entity engages or will engage in terrorist activities as defined in that subsection or activities in support of them.

(2) **Statutory Instruments Act** — A certificate is not a statutory instrument for the purposes of the *Statutory Instruments Act*.

[2001, c. 41, s. 125 (in force June 28, 2002).]

## JUDICIAL CONSIDERATION OF CERTIFICATE

**5.** (1) **Notice** — As soon as the Minister and the Minister of National Revenue have signed a certificate, the Minister, or a person authorized by the Minister, shall cause the applicant or registered charity to be served, personally or by registered letter sent to its last known address, with a copy of the certificate and a notice informing it that the certificate will be referred to the Federal Court not earlier than seven days after service and that, if the certificate is determined to be reasonable, the applicant will be ineligible to become a registered charity or the registration of the registered charity will be revoked, as the case may be.

(2) **Restriction** — The certificate and any matters arising out of it are not subject to review or to be restrained, prohibited, removed, set aside or otherwise dealt with, except in accordance with this Act.

(3) **Non-publication or confidentiality order** — Notwithstanding subsection (2), the applicant or registered charity may apply to a judge for an order

(a)　directing that the identity of the applicant or registered charity not be published or broadcast in any way except in accordance with this Act; or

(b)　that any documents to be filed with the Federal Court in connection with the reference be treated as confidential.

(4) **No appeal** — An order on an application referred to in subsection (3) is not subject to appeal or review by any court at the instance of a party to the application.

(5) **Filing in Federal Court** — Seven days after service under subsection (1), or as soon afterwards as is practicable, the Minister or a person authorized by the Minister shall

(a)  file a copy of the certificate in the Federal Court for it to make a determination under section 7; and

(b)  cause the applicant or registered charity to be served, personally or by registered letter sent to its last known address, with a notice informing it of the filing of the certificate.

[2001, c. 41, s. 125 (in force June 28, 2002).]

**6. Judicial consideration** — The following provisions govern the determination:

(a)  the judge shall hear the matter;

(b)  the judge shall ensure the confidentiality of the information on which the certificate is based and of any other evidence that may be provided to the judge if, in the opinion of the judge, its disclosure would be injurious to national security or endanger the safety of any person;

(c)  the judge shall deal with all matters as informally and expeditiously as the circumstances and considerations of fairness and natural justice permit;

(d)  the judge shall, without delay after the matter is referred to the Federal Court, examine the information and any other evidence in private;

(e)  on each request of the Minister or the Minister of National Revenue, the judge shall hear all or part of the information or evidence in the absence of the applicant or registered charity named in the certificate and their counsel if, in the opinion of the judge, its disclosure would be injurious to national security or endanger the safety of any person;

(f)  the information or evidence described in paragraph (e) shall be returned to the Ministers and shall not be considered by the judge in determining whether the certificate is reasonable if either

(i)  the judge determines that the information or evidence is not relevant or, if it is relevant, that it should be part of the summary, or

(ii)  the matter is withdrawn;

(g)  the information or evidence described in paragraph (e) shall not be included in the summary but may be considered by the judge in determining whether the certificate is reasonable if the judge determines that the information or evidence is relevant but that its disclosure would be injurious to national security or endanger the safety of any person;

(h)  the judge shall provide the applicant or registered charity with a summary of the information or evidence that enables it to be reasonably informed of the circumstances giving rise to the certificate, but that does not include anything that in the opinion of the judge would be injurious to national security or endanger the safety of any person if disclosed;

(i)    the judge shall provide the applicant or registered charity with an opportunity to be heard; and

(j)    the judge may receive into evidence anything that, in the opinion of the judge, is reliable and appropriate, even if it is inadmissible in a court of law, and may base the decision on that evidence.

[2001, c. 41, s. 125 (in force June 28, 2002).]

**7.** (1) **Determination whether certificate is reasonable** — The judge shall determine whether the certificate is reasonable on the basis of the information and evidence available.

(2) **Certificate quashed** — The judge shall quash a certificate if the judge is of the opinion that it is not reasonable.

[2001, c. 41, s. 125 (in force June 28, 2002).]

**8.** (1) **Effect of determination** — A certificate that is determined to be reasonable under subsection 7(1) is conclusive proof that, in the case of an applicant, it is ineligible to become a registered charity or, in the case of a registered charity, that it does not comply with the requirements to continue to be a registered charity.

(2) **No appeal or review** — The determination of the judge is final and is not subject to appeal or judicial review.

(3) **Publication** — The Minister shall, without delay after a certificate is determined to be reasonable, cause the certificate to be published in the Canada Gazette.

[2001, c. 41, s. 125 (in force June 28, 2002).]

**9.** [Repealed, 2001, c. 41, s. 125.]

## REVIEW OF CERTIFICATE

**10.** (1) **Ministerial review** — An applicant or former registered charity in relation to which a certificate was determined to be reasonable under subsection 7(1) and that believes that there has been a material change in circumstances since the determination made under that subsection may apply in writing to the Minister for a review of the certificate by the Minister and the Minister of National Revenue.

(2) **Notice to Minister of National Revenue** — The Minister shall, without delay, notify the Minister of National Revenue of an application for review.

(3) **Material to be considered** — For the purpose of a review, the Ministers may consider any submission made by the applicant or former registered charity that applied for the review and any information that is made available to the Ministers.

(4) **Time for decision** — The Ministers shall make their decision on an application for review within 120 days after receipt of the application by the Minister.

(5) **Decision on review** — The Ministers may decide that, since the time the certificate was determined to be reasonable,

(a)    there has not been a material change in circumstances, in which case the Ministers shall deny the application; or

  (b)  there has been a material change in circumstances, in which case the Ministers shall determine whether there are reasonable grounds as provided in subsection 4(1) and, accordingly,

      (i)  continue the certificate in effect, or

      (ii)  cancel the certificate as of the date of the decision.

**(6) Automatic cancellation** — If no decision is made within a period of 120 days after receipt of the application, the certificate is cancelled on the expiration of that period.

**(7) Notice to applicant or charity** — As soon as a decision is made or the certificate is cancelled under subsection (6), the Minister or a person authorized by the Minister shall cause the applicant or former registered charity that applied for the review to be served, personally or by registered letter sent to its last known address, with notice of the decision or cancellation.

[2001, c. 41, s. 125 (in force June 28, 2002).]

**11.** (1) **Application for review** — An applicant or former registered charity that applied for a review under subsection 10(1) may, after giving written notice to the Minister who in turn shall notify the Minister of National Revenue, apply to the Federal Court for a review of a decision made under paragraph 10(5)(a) or subparagraph 10(5)(b)(i).

**(2) Review by Court** — The Court shall carry out the review in accordance with section 6, with any adaptations that may be required.

**(3) Referral to Ministers** — If the Court quashes a decision of the Ministers made under paragraph 10(5)(a), it shall refer the application to the Ministers for a decision under paragraph 10(5)(b).

**(4) Cancellation of certificate** — If the Court quashes a decision of the Ministers made under subparagraph 10(5)(b)(i), the certificate is cancelled as of the date the decision is quashed.

**(5) No appeal** — The determination of the Court is not subject to appeal or judicial review.

**12. Publication of spent certificate** — The Minister shall, in a manner that mentions the original publication of the certificate, cause to be published in the *Canada Gazette* notice of the cancellation of a certificate by reason of

  (a)  a decision made under subparagraph 10(5)(b)(ii);

  (b)  the operation of subsection 10(6); or

  (c)  a determination of the Federal Court referred to in subsection 11(4).

**13. Term of a certificate** — Unless it is cancelled earlier, a certificate is effective for a period of seven years beginning on the day it is first determined to be reasonable under subsection 7(1).

[2001, c. 41, s. 125 (in force June 28, 2002).]

**14. Regulations** — The Governor in Council may make any regulations that the Governor in Council considers necessary for carrying out the purposes and provisions of this Act.

# CIVIL MARRIAGE ACT

(S.C. 2005, c. 33)

## PREAMBLE

WHEREAS the Parliament of Canada is committed to upholding the Constitution of Canada, and section 15 of the *Canadian Charter of Rights and Freedoms* guarantees that every individual is equal before and under the law and has the right to equal protection and equal benefit of the law without discrimination;

WHEREAS the courts in a majority of the provinces and in one territory have recognized that the right to equality without discrimination requires that couples of the same sex and couples of the opposite sex have equal access to marriage for civil purposes;

WHEREAS the Supreme Court of Canada has recognized that many Canadian couples of the same sex have married in reliance on those court decisions;

WHEREAS only equal access to marriage for civil purposes would respect the right of couples of the same sex to equality without discrimination and civil union, as an institution other than marriage, would not offer them that equal access and would violate their human dignity, in breach of the *Canadian Charter of Rights and Freedoms*;

WHEREAS the Supreme Court of Canada has determined that the Parliament of Canada has legislative jurisdiction over marriage but does not have the jurisdiction to establish an institution other than marriage for couples of the same sex;

WHEREAS everyone has the freedom of conscience and religion under section 2 of the *Canadian Charter of Rights and Freedoms*;

WHEREAS nothing in this Act affects the guarantee of freedom of conscience and relition and, in particular, the freedom of members of religious groups to hold and declare their religious beliefs and the freedom of officials of religious groups to refuse to perform marriages that are not in accordance with their religious beliefs;

WHEREAS it is not against the public interest to hold and publicly express diverse views on marriage;

WHEREAS, in light of those considerations, the Parliament of Canada's commitment to uphold the right to equality without discrimination precludes the use of section 33 of the *Canadian Charter of Rights and Freedoms* to deny the right of couples of the same sex to equal access to marriage for civil purposes;

WHEREAS marriage is a fundamental institution in Canadian Society and the Parliament of Canada has a responsibility to support that institution because it strengthens commitment in relationships and represents the foundation of family life for many Canadians;

AND WHEREAS, in order to reflect values of tolerance, respect and equality consistent with the *Canadian Charter of Rights and Freedoms*, access to marriage for civil purposes should be extended by legislation to couples of the same sex;

NOW, THEREFORE, Her Majesty, by and with the advice and consent of the Senate and House of Commons of Canada, enacts as follows:

**1. Short title** — This Act may be cited as the *Civil Marriage Act*.

**2. Marriage — certain aspects of capacity** — Marriage, for civil purposes, is the lawful union of two persons to the exclusion of all others.

**3. Religious officials** — It is recognized that officials of religious groups are free to refuse to perform marriages that are not in accordance with their religious beliefs.

**3.1 Freedom of conscience and religion and expression of beliefs** — For greater certainty, no person or organization shall be deprived of any benefit, or be subject to any obligation or sanction, under any law of the Parliament of Canada solely by reason of their exercise, in respect of marriage between persons of the same sex, of the freedom of conscience and religion guaranteed under the *Canadian Charter of Rights and Freedoms* or the expression of their beliefs in respect of marriage as the union of a man and woman to the exclusion of all others based on that guaranteed freedom.

**4. Marriage not void or voidable** — For greater certainty, a marriage is not void or voidable by reason only that the spouses are of the same sex.

. . .

## CONSEQUENTIAL AMENDMENTS

**5 – 11.** [Consolidated into legislation]

. . .

**11.1 Section 149.1 of the *Income Tax Act* is amended by adding the following after subsection (6.2):**

(6.21) **Marriage for civil purposes** — For greater certainty, subject to subsections (6.1) and (6.2), a registered charity with stated purposes that include the advancement of religion shall not have its registration revoked or be subject to any other penalty under Part V solely because it or any of its members, officials, supporters or adherents exercises, in relation to marriage between persons of the same sex, the freedom of conscience and religion guaranteed under the *Canadian Charter of Rights and Freedoms*.

**12 – 15.** [Consolidated into legislation]

# CRIMINAL CODE

(R.S.C., 1985, c. C-46)

[Note: Only select provisions are reproduced]

## PART II.1

## TERRORISM

*Interpretation*

**83.01** (1) **Definitions** — The following definitions apply in this Part.

"Canadian" means a Canadian citizen, a permanent resident within the meaning of subsection 2(1) of the *Immigration and Refugee Protection Act* or a body corporate incorporated and continued under the laws of Canada or a province.

"entity" means a person, group, trust, partnership or fund or an unincorporated association or organization.

"listed entity" means an entity on a list established by the Governor in Council under section 83.05.

"terrorist activity" means

(a) an act or omission that is committed in or outside Canada and that, if committed in Canada, is one of the following offences:

    (i) the offences referred to in subsection 7(2) that implement the Convention for the Suppression of Unlawful Seizure of Aircraft, signed at The Hague on December 16, 1970,

    (ii) the offences referred to in subsection 7(2) that implement the Convention for the Suppression of Unlawful Acts against the Safety of Civil Aviation, signed at Montreal on September 23, 1971,

    (iii) the offences referred to in subsection 7(3) that implement the Convention on the Prevention and Punishment of Crimes against Internationally Protected Persons, including Diplomatic Agents, adopted by the General Assembly of the United Nations on December 14, 1973,

    (iv) the offences referred to in subsection 7(3.1) that implement the International Convention against the Taking of Hostages, adopted by the General Assembly of the United Nations on December 17, 1979,

    (v) the offences referred to in subsection 7(3.4) or (3.6) that implement the Convention on the Physical Protection of Nuclear Material, done at Vienna and New York on March 3, 1980,

      (vi)   the offences referred to in subsection 7(2) that implement the Protocol for the Suppression of Unlawful Acts of Violence at Airports Serving International Civil Aviation, supplementary to the Convention for the Suppression of Unlawful Acts against the Safety of Civil Aviation, signed at Montreal on February 24, 1988,

      (vii)  the offences referred to in subsection 7(2.1) that implement the Convention for the Suppression of Unlawful Acts against the Safety of Maritime Navigation, done at Rome on March 10, 1988,

      (viii) the offences referred to in subsection 7(2.1) or (2.2) that implement the Protocol for the Suppression of Unlawful Acts against the Safety of Fixed Platforms Located on the Continental Shelf, done at Rome on March 10, 1988,

      (ix)  the offences referred to in subsection 7(3.72) that implement the International Convention for the Suppression of Terrorist Bombings, adopted by the General Assembly of the United Nations on December 15, 1997, and

      (x)   the offences referred to in subsection 7(3.73) that implement the International Convention for the Suppression of the Financing of Terrorism, adopted by the General Assembly of the United Nations on December 9, 1999, or

  (b)  an act or omission, in or outside Canada,

      (i)    that is committed

          (A)  in whole or in part for a political, religious or ideological purpose, objective or cause, and

          (B)  in whole or in part with the intention of intimidating the public, or a segment of the public, with regard to its security, including its economic security, or compelling a person, a government or a domestic or an international organization to do or to refrain from doing any act, whether the public or the person, government or organization is inside or outside Canada, and

      (ii)   that intentionally

          (A)  causes death or serious bodily harm to a person by the use of violence,

          (B)  endangers a person's life,

          (C)  causes a serious risk to the health or safety of the public or any segment of the public,

          (D)  causes substantial property damage, whether to public or private property, if causing such damage is likely to result in the conduct or harm referred to in any of clauses (A) to (C), or

          (E)  causes serious interference with or serious disruption of an essential service, facility or system, whether public or private, other than as a result of advocacy, protest, dissent or stoppage of work that is not intended to result in the conduct or harm referred to in any of clauses (A) to (C), and includes a conspiracy, attempt or threat to commit any such act or omission, or being an accessory after the fact or counselling in relation to any such act or omission, but, for greater certainty, does not include an act or omission that is committed during an armed conflict and that, at the time and in the place of its commission, is in accordance with customary international law or conventional international law applicable to the conflict, or the activities undertaken by military forces of a state in the exercise of their official duties, to the extent that those activities are governed by other rules of international law.

"terrorist group" means

(a)   an entity that has as one of its purposes or activities facilitating or carrying out any terrorist activity, or

(b)   a listed entity,

and includes an association of such entities.

(1.1) **For greater certainty** — For greater certainty, the expression of a political, religious or ideological thought, belief or opinion does not come within paragraph (b) of the definition "terrorist activity" in subsection (1) unless it constitutes an act or omission that satisfies the criteria of that paragraph.

(2) **Facilitation** — For the purposes of this Part, facilitation shall be construed in accordance with subsection 83.19(2).

[2001, c. 41, ss. 4, 126 (s. 4 in force December 24, 2001; s. 126 in force June 28, 2002).]

### Financing of Terrorism

**83.02 Providing or collecting property for certain activities** — Every one who, directly or indirectly, wilfully and without lawful justification or excuse, provides or collects property intending that it be used or knowing that it will be used, in whole or in part, in order to carry out

(a)   an act or omission that constitutes an offence referred to in subparagraphs (a)(i) to (ix) of the definition of "terrorist activity" in subsection 83.01(1), or

(b)   any other act or omission intended to cause death or serious bodily harm to a civilian or to any other person not taking an active part in the hostilities in a situation of armed conflict, if the purpose of that act or omission, by its nature or context, is to intimidate the public, or to compel a government or an international organization to do or refrain from doing any act,

is guilty of an indictable offence and is liable to imprisonment for a term of not more than 10 years.

[2001, c. 41, s. 4 (in force December 24, 2001).]

**83.03 Providing, making available, etc., property or services for terrorist purposes** — Every one who, directly or indirectly, collects property, provides or invites a person to provide, or makes available property or financial or other related services

(a) intending that they be used, or knowing that they will be used, in whole or in part, for the purpose of facilitating or carrying out any terrorist activity, or for the purpose of benefiting any person who is facilitating or carrying out such an activity, or

(b) knowing that, in whole or part, they will be used by or will benefit a terrorist group,

is guilty of an indictable offence and is liable to imprisonment for a term of not more than 10 years.

[2001, c. 41, s. 4 (in force December 24, 2001).]

**83.04 Using or possessing property for terrorist purposes** — Every one who

(a) uses property, directly or indirectly, in whole or in part, for the purpose of facilitating or carrying out a terrorist activity, or

(b) possesses property intending that it be used or knowing that it will be used, directly or indirectly, in whole or in part, for the purpose of facilitating or carrying out a terrorist activity,

is guilty of an indictable offence and is liable to imprisonment for a term of not more than 10 years.

[2001, c. 41, s. 4 (in force December 24, 2001).]

*List of Entities*

**83.05** (1) **Establishment of list** — The Governor in Council may, by regulation, establish a list on which the Governor in Council may place any entity if, on the recommendation of the Minister of Public Safety and Emergency Preparedness, the Governor in Council is satisfied that there are reasonable grounds to believe that

(a) the entity has knowingly carried out, attempted to carry out, participated in or facilitated a terrorist activity; or

(b) the entity is knowingly acting on behalf of, at the direction of or in association with an entity referred to in paragraph (a).

(1.1) **Recommendation** — The Minister may make a recommendation

referred to in subsection (1) only if he or she has reasonable grounds to believe that the entity to which the recommendation relates is an entity referred to in paragraph (1)(a) or (b).

(2) **Application to Minister** — On application in writing by a listed entity, the Minister shall decide whether there are reasonable grounds to recommend to the Governor in Council that the applicant no

longer be a listed entity.

(3) **Deeming** — If the Minister does not make a decision on the application referred to in subsection (2) within 60 days after receipt of the application, he or she is deemed to have decided to recommend that the applicant remain a listed entity.

(4) **Notice of the decision to the applicant** — The Minister shall give notice without delay to the applicant of any decision taken or deemed to have been taken respecting the application referred to in subsection (2).

(5) **Judicial review** — Within 60 days after the receipt of the notice of the decision referred to in subsection (4), the applicant may apply to a judge for judicial review of the decision.

(6) **Reference** — When an application is made under subsection (5), the judge shall, without delay

(a) examine, in private, any security or criminal intelligence reports considered in listing the applicant and hear any other evidence or information that may be presented by or on behalf of the Minister and may, at his or her request, hear all or part of that evidence or information in the absence of the applicant and any counsel representing the applicant, if the judge is of the opinion that the disclosure of the information would injure national security or endanger the safety of any person;

(b) provide the applicant with a statement summarizing the information available to the judge so as to enable the applicant to be reasonably informed of the reasons for the decision, without disclosing any information the disclosure of which would, in the judge's opinion, injure national security or endanger the safety of any person;

(c) provide the applicant with a reasonable opportunity to be heard; and

(d) determine whether the decision is reasonable on the basis of the information available to the judge and, if found not to be reasonable, order that the applicant no longer be a listed entity.

(6.1) **Evidence** — The judge may receive into evidence anything that, in the opinion of the judge, is reliable and appropriate, even if it would not otherwise be admissible under Canadian law, and may base his or her decision on that evidence.

(7) **Publication** — The Minister shall cause to be published, without delay, in the Canada Gazette notice of a final order of a court that the applicant no longer be a listed entity.

(8) **New application** — A listed entity may not make another application under subsection (2), except if there has been a material change in its circumstances since the time when the entity made its last application or if the Minister has completed the review under subsection (9).

(9) **Review of list** — Two years after the establishment of the list referred to in subsection (1), and every two years after that, the Minister shall review the list to determine whether there are still reasonable grounds, as set out in subsection (1), for an entity to be a listed entity and make a recommendation to the Governor in Council as to whether the entity should remain a listed entity. The review does not affect the validity of the list.

(10) **Completion of review** — The Minister shall complete the review as soon as possible and in any event, no later than 120 days after its commencement. After completing the review, he or she shall cause to be published, without delay, in the Canada Gazette notice that the review has been completed.

**(11) Definition of "judge"** — In this section, "judge" means the Chief Justice of the Federal Court or a judge of that Court designated by the Chief Justice.

[2001, c. 41, ss. 4, 143; 2005, c. 10, s. 18]

**83.06 (1) Admission of foreign information obtained in confidence** — For the purposes of subsection 83.05(6), in private and in the absence of the applicant or any counsel representing it,

(a) the Minister of Public Safety and Emergency Preparedness may make an application to the judge for the admission of information obtained in confidence from a government, an institution or an agency of a foreign state, from an international organization of states or from an institution or an agency of an international organization of states; and

(b) the judge shall examine the information and provide counsel representing the Minister with a reasonable opportunity to be heard as to whether the information is relevant but should not be disclosed to the applicant or any counsel representing it because the disclosure would injure national security or endanger the safety of any person.

**(2) Return of information** — The information shall be returned to counsel representing the Minister and shall not be considered by the judge in making the determination under paragraph 83.05(6)(d), if

(a) the judge determines that the information is not relevant;

(b) the judge determines that the information is relevant but should be summarized in the statement to be provided under paragraph 83.05(6)(b); or

(c) the Minister withdraws the application.

**(3) Use of information** — If the judge decides that the information is relevant but that its disclosure would injure national security or endanger the safety of persons, the information shall not be disclosed in the statement mentioned in paragraph 83.05(6)(b), but the judge may base the determination under paragraph 83.05(6)(d) on it.

[2001, c. 41, s. 4 (in force December 24, 2001).]

**83.07 (1) Mistaken identity** — An entity claiming not to be a listed entity may apply to the Minister of Public Safety and Emergency Preparedness for a certificate stating that it is not a listed entity.

**(2) Issuance of certificate** — The Minister shall, within 15 days after receiving the application, issue a certificate if he or she is satisfied that the applicant is not a listed entity.

[2001, c. 41, s. 4, 2005, c. 10, s. 20]

## *Freezing of Property*

**83.08 (1) Freezing of property** — No person in Canada and no Canadian outside Canada shall knowingly

(a) deal directly or indirectly in any property that is owned or controlled by or on behalf of a terrorist group;

(b)    enter into or facilitate, directly or indirectly, any transaction in respect of property referred to in paragraph (a); or

(c)    provide any financial or other related services in respect of property referred to in paragraph (a) to, for the benefit of or at the direction of a terrorist group.

(2) **No civil liability** — A person who acts reasonably in taking, or omitting to take, measures to comply with subsection (1) shall not be liable in any civil action arising from having taken or omitted to take the measures, if the person took all reasonable steps to satisfy themself that the relevant property was owned or controlled by or on behalf of a terrorist group.

[2001, c. 41, s. 4 (in force December 24, 2001).]

**83.09** (1) **Exemptions** — The Minister of Public Safety and Emergency Preparedness, or a person designated by him or her, may authorize any person in Canada or any Canadian outside Canada to carry out a specified activity or transaction that is prohibited by section 83.08, or a class of such activities or transactions.

(2) **Ministerial authorization** —The Minister, or a person designated by him or her, may make the authorization subject to any terms and conditions that are required in their opinion and may amend, suspend, revoke or reinstate it.

(3) **Existing equities maintained** — All secured and unsecured rights and interests in the frozen property that are held by persons, other than terrorist groups or their agents, are entitled to the same ranking that they would have been entitled to had the property not been frozen.

(4) **Third party involvement** — If a person has obtained an authorization under subsection (1), any other person involved in carrying out the activity or transaction, or class of activities or transactions, to which the authorization relates is not subject to sections 83.08, 83.1 and 83.11 if the terms or conditions of the authorization that are imposed under subsection (2), if any, are met.

[2001, c. 41, s. 4, 2005, c. 10, s. 21]

**83.1** (1) **Disclosure** — Every person in Canada and every Canadian outside Canada shall disclose forthwith to the Commissioner of the Royal Canadian Mounted Police and to the Director of the Canadian Security Intelligence Service

(a)    the existence of property in their possession or control that they know is owned or controlled by or on behalf of a terrorist group; and

(b)    information about a transaction or proposed transaction in respect of property referred to in paragraph (a).

(2) **Immunity** — No criminal or civil proceedings lie against a person for disclosure made in good faith under subsection (1).

[2001, c. 41, s. 4 (in force December 24, 2001).]

**83.11** (1) **Audit** — The following entities must determine on a continuing basis whether they are in possession or control of property owned or controlled by or on behalf of a listed entity:

(a)    authorized foreign banks within the meaning of section 2 of the *Bank Act* in respect of their business in Canada, or banks to which that Act applies;

(b) cooperative credit societies, savings and credit unions and caisses populaires regulated by a provincial Act and associations regulated by the *Cooperative Credit Associations Act*;

(c) foreign companies within the meaning of subsection 2(1) of the *Insurance Companies Act* in respect of their insurance business in Canada;

(c.1) companies, provincial companies and societies within the meaning of subsection 2(1) of the *Insurance Companies Act*;

(c.2) fraternal benefit societies regulated by a provincial Act in respect of their insurance activities, and insurance companies and other entities engaged in the business of insuring risks that are regulated by a provincial Act;

(d) companies to which the *Trust and Loan Companies Act* applies;

(e) trust companies regulated by a provincial Act;

(f) loan companies regulated by a provincial Act; and

(g) entities authorized under provincial legislation to engage in the business of dealing in securities, or to provide portfolio management or investment counselling services.

(2) **Monthly report** — Subject to the regulations, every entity referred to in paragraphs (1)(a) to (g) must report, within the period specified by regulation or, if no period is specified, monthly, to the principal agency or body that supervises or regulates it under federal or provincial law either

(a) that it is not in possession or control of any property referred to in subsection (1), or

(b) that it is in possession or control of such property, in which case it must also report the number of persons, contracts or accounts involved and the total value of the property.

(3) **Immunity** — No criminal or civil proceedings lie against a person for making a report in good faith under subsection (2).

(4) **Regulations** — The Governor in Council may make regulations

(a) excluding any entity or class of entities from the requirement to make a report referred to in subsection (2), and specifying the conditions of exclusion; and

(b) specifying a period for the purposes of subsection (2).

[2001, c. 41, s. 4 (in force December 24, 2001).]

**83.12** (1) **Offences — freezing of property, disclosure or audit** — Every one who contravenes any of sections 83.08, 83.1 and 83.11 is guilty of an offence and liable

(a) on summary conviction, to a fine of not more than $100,000 or to imprisonment for a term of not more than one year, or to both; or

(b) on conviction on indictment, to imprisonment for a term of not more than 10 years.

(2) **No contravention** — No person contravenes section 83.1 if they make the disclosure referred to in that section only to the Commissioner of the Royal Canadian Mounted Police or the Director of the Canadian Security Intelligence Service.

[2001, c. 41, s. 4 (in force December 24, 2001).]

*Seizure and Restraint of Property*

**83.13** (1) **Seizure and restraint of assets** — Where a judge of the Federal Court, on an *ex parte* application by the Attorney General, after examining the application in private, is satisfied that there are reasonable grounds to believe that there is in any building, receptacle or place any property in respect of which an order of forfeiture may be made under subsection 83.14(5), the judge may issue

(a) if the property is situated in Canada, a warrant authorizing a person named therein or a peace officer to search the building, receptacle or place for that property and to seize that property and any other property in respect of which that person or peace officer believes, on reasonable grounds, that an order of forfeiture may be made under that subsection; or

(b) if the property is situated in or outside Canada, a restraint order prohibiting any person from disposing of, or otherwise dealing with any interest in, that property other than as may be specified in the order.

(1.1) **Contents of application** — An affidavit in support of an application under subsection (1) may be sworn on information and belief, and, notwithstanding the *Federal Court Rules, 1998*, no adverse inference shall be drawn from a failure to provide evidence of persons having personal knowledge of material facts.

(2) **Appointment of manager** — On an application under subsection (1), at the request of the Attorney General, if a judge is of the opinion that the circumstances so require, the judge may

(a) appoint a person to take control of, and to manage or otherwise deal with, all or part of the property in accordance with the directions of the judge; and

(b) require any person having possession of that property to give possession of the property to the person appointed under paragraph (a).

(3) **Appointment of Minister of Public Works and Government Services** — When the Attorney General of Canada so requests, a judge appointing a person under subsection (2) shall appoint the Minister of Public Works and Government Services.

(4) **Power to manage** — The power to manage or otherwise deal with property under subsection (2) includes

(a) in the case of perishable or rapidly depreciating property, the power to sell that property; and

(b) in the case of property that has little or no value, the power to destroy that property.

(5) **Application for destruction order** — Before a person appointed under subsection (2) destroys property referred to in paragraph (4)(b), he or she shall apply to a judge of the Federal Court for a destruction order.

(6) **Notice** — Before making a destruction order in relation to any property, a judge shall require notice in accordance with subsection (7) to be given to, and may hear, any person who, in the opinion of the judge, appears to have a valid interest in the property.

(7) **Manner of giving notice** — A notice under subsection (6) shall be given in the manner that the judge directs or as provided in the rules of the Federal Court.

(8) **Order** — A judge may order that property be destroyed if he or she is satisfied that the property has little or no financial or other value.

(9) **When management order ceases to have effect** — A management order ceases to have effect when the property that is the subject of the management order is returned to an applicant in accordance with the law or forfeited to Her Majesty.

(10) **Application to vary** — The Attorney General may at any time apply to a judge of the Federal Court to cancel or vary an order or warrant made under this section, other than an appointment made under subsection (3).

(11) **Procedure** — Subsections 462.32(4) and (6), sections 462.34 to 462.35 and 462.4, subsections 487(3) and (4) and section 488 apply, with such modifications as the circumstances require, to a warrant issued under paragraph (1)(a).

(12) **Procedure** — Subsections 462.33(4) and (6) to (11) and sections 462.34 to 462.35 and 462.4 apply, with such modifications as the circumstances require, to an order issued under paragraph (1)(b).

[2001, c. 41, s. 4 (in force December 24, 2001).]

## Forfeiture of Property

**83.14** (1) **Application for order of forfeiture** — The Attorney General may make an application to a judge of the Federal Court for an order of forfeiture in respect of

(a)    property owned or controlled by or on behalf of a terrorist group; or

(b)    property that has been or will be used, in whole or in part, to facilitate or carry out a terrorist activity.

(2) **Contents of application** — An affidavit in support of an application by the Attorney General under subsection (1) may be sworn on information and belief, and, notwithstanding the *Federal Court Rules, 1998*, no adverse inference shall be drawn from a failure to provide evidence of persons having personal knowledge of material facts.

(3) **Respondents** — The Attorney General is required to name as a respondent to an application under subsection (1) only those persons who are known to own or control the property that is the subject of the application.

(4) **Notice** — The Attorney General shall give notice of an application under subsection (1) to named respondents in such a manner as the judge directs or as provided in the rules of the Federal Court.

(5) **Granting of forfeiture order** — If a judge is satisfied on a balance of probabilities that property is property referred to in paragraph (1)(a) or (b), the judge shall order that the property be forfeited to Her Majesty to be disposed of as the Attorney General directs or otherwise dealt with in accordance with the law.

(5.1) **Use of proceeds** — Any proceeds that arise from the disposal of property under subsection (5) may be used to compensate victims of terrorist activities and to fund anti-terrorist initiatives in accordance with any regulations made by the Governor in Council under subsection (5.2).

(5.2) **Regulations** — The Governor in Council may make regulations for the purposes of specifying how the proceeds referred to in subsection (5.1) are to be distributed.

(6) **Order refusing forfeiture** — Where a judge refuses an application under subsection (1) in respect of any property, the judge shall make an order that describes the property and declares that it is not property referred to in that subsection.

(7) **Notice** — On an application under subsection (1), a judge may require notice to be given to any person who, in the opinion of the Court, appears to have an interest in the property, and any such person shall be entitled to be added as a respondent to the application.

(8) **Third party interests** — If a judge is satisfied that a person referred to in subsection (7) has an interest in property that is subject to an application, has exercised reasonable care to ensure that the property would not be used to facilitate or carry out a terrorist activity, and is not a member of a terrorist group, the judge shall order that the interest is not affected by the forfeiture. Such an order shall declare the nature and extent of the interest in question.

(9) **Dwelling-house** — Where all or part of property that is the subject of an application under subsection (1) is a dwelling-house, the judge shall also consider

(a)   the impact of an order of forfeiture on any member of the immediate family of the person who owns or controls the dwelling-house, if the dwelling-house was the member's principal residence at the time the dwelling-house was ordered restrained or at the time the forfeiture application was made and continues to be the member's principal residence; and

(b)   whether the member appears innocent of any complicity or collusion in the terrorist activity.

(10) **Motion to vary or set aside** — A person who claims an interest in property that was forfeited and who did not receive notice under subsection (7) may bring a motion to the Federal Court to vary or set aside an order made under subsection (5) not later than 60 days after the day on which the forfeiture order was made.

(11) **No extension of time** — The Court may not extend the period set out in subsection (10).

[2001, c. 41, s. 4 (in force December 24, 2001).]

**83.15 Disposition of property** — Subsection 462.42(6) and sections 462.43 and 462.46 apply, with such modifications as the circumstances require, to property subject to a warrant or restraint order issued under subsection 83.13(1) or ordered forfeited under subsection 83.14(5).

[2001, c. 41, s. 4 (in force December 24, 2001).]

**83.16** (1) **Interim preservation rights** — Pending any appeal of an order made under section 83.14, property restrained under an order issued under section 83.13

shall continue to be restrained, property seized under a warrant issued under that section shall continue to be detained, and any person appointed to manage, control or otherwise deal with that property under that section shall continue in that capacity.

(2) **Appeal of refusal to grant order** — Section 462.34 applies, with such modifications as the circumstances require, to an appeal taken in respect of a refusal to grant an order under subsection 83.14(5).

[2001, c. 41, s. 4 (in force December 24, 2001).]

**83.17** (1) **Other forfeiture provisions unaffected** — This Part does not affect the operation of any other provision of this or any other Act of Parliament respecting the forfeiture of property.

(2) **Priority for restitution to victims of crime** — Property is subject to forfeiture under subsection 83.14(5) only to the extent that it is not required to satisfy the operation of any other provision of this or any other Act of Parliament respecting restitution to, or compensation of, persons affected by the commission of offences.

[2001, c. 41, s. 4 (in force December 24, 2001).]

*Participating, Facilitating, Instructing and Harbouring*

**83.18** (1) **Participation in activity of terrorist group** — Every one who knowingly participates in or contributes to, directly or indirectly, any activity of a terrorist group for the purpose of enhancing the ability of any terrorist group to facilitate or carry out a terrorist activity is guilty of an indictable offence and liable to imprisonment for a term not exceeding ten years.

(2) **Prosecution** — An offence may be committed under subsection (1) whether or not

(a)  a terrorist group actually facilitates or carries out a terrorist activity;

(b)  the participation or contribution of the accused actually enhances the ability of a terrorist group to facilitate or carry out a terrorist activity; or

(c)  the accused knows the specific nature of any terrorist activity that may be facilitated or carried out by a terrorist group.

(3) **Meaning of participating or contributing** — Participating in or contributing to an activity of a terrorist group includes

(a)  providing, receiving or recruiting a person to receive training;

(b)  providing or offering to provide a skill or an expertise for the benefit of, at the direction of or in association with a terrorist group;

(c)  recruiting a person in order to facilitate or commit

(i)  a terrorism offence, or

(ii)  an act or omission outside Canada that, if committed in Canada, would be a terrorism offence;

(d)  entering or remaining in any country for the benefit of, at the direction of or in association with a terrorist group; and

(e)  making oneself, in response to instructions from any of the persons who constitute a terrorist group, available to facilitate or commit

(i)  a terrorism offence, or

(ii)  an act or omission outside Canada that, if committed in Canada, would be a terrorism offence.

(4) **Factors** — In determining whether an accused participates in or contributes to any activity of a terrorist group, the court may consider, among other factors, whether the accused

(a)  uses a name, word, symbol or other representation that identifies, or is associated with, the terrorist group;

(b)  frequently associates with any of the persons who constitute the terrorist group;

(c)  receives any benefit from the terrorist group; or

(d)  repeatedly engages in activities at the instruction of any of the persons who constitute the terrorist group.

[2001, c. 41, s. 4 (in force December 24, 2001).]

**89.19** (1) **Facilitating terrorist activity** — Every one who knowingly facilitates a terrorist activity is guilty of an indictable offence and liable to imprisonment for a term not exceeding fourteen years.

(2) **Facilitation** — For the purposes of this Part, a terrorist activity is facilitated whether or not

(a)  the facilitator knows that a particular terrorist activity is facilitated;

(b)  any particular terrorist activity was foreseen or planned at the time it was facilitated; or

(c)  any terrorist activity was actually carried out.

# PART IX

## OFFENCES AGAINST RIGHTS OF PROPERTY

### *Offences Resembling Theft*

**336. Criminal breach of trust** — Every one who, being a trustee of anything for the use or benefit, whether in whole or in part, of another person, or for a public or charitable purpose, converts, with intent to defraud and in contravention of his trust, that thing or any part of it to a use that is not authorized by the trust is guilty of an indictable offence and liable to imprisonment for a term not exceeding fourteen years.

# CULTURAL PROPERTY
# EXPORT AND IMPORT ACT

(R.S.C. 1985, c. C-51)

**Amended by:** R.S., 1985, c. 1 (2nd Supp.), s. 213; 1991, c. 49, ss. 216-219; 1994, c. 13, s. 7; 1995, c. 5, s. 25; 1995, c. 11, s. 45; 1995, c. 29, ss. 21, 22; 1995, c. 38, ss. 1, 2; 1998, c. 19, s. 261; 2000, c. 30, s. 159; 2001, c. 34, s. 38.

## SHORT TITLE

**1. Short title** — This Act may be cited as the *Cultural Property Export and Import Act*.

## INTERPRETATION

**2. Definitions** — In this Act,

"Control List" means the Canadian Cultural Property Export Control List established under section 4;

"expert examiner" means a person or institution designated as an expert examiner under section 6;

"export permit" means a permit to export issued by a permit officer under this Act;

"general permit" means a permit to export issued by the Minister under section 17;

"institution" means an institution that is publicly owned and is operated solely for the benefit of the public, that is established for educational or cultural purposes and that conserves objects and exhibits them or otherwise makes them available to the public;

"Minister" means such member of the Queen's Privy Council for Canada as is designated by the Governor in Council as the Minister for the purposes of this Act;

"permit officer" means a person designated as a permit officer under section 5;

"public authority" means Her Majesty in right of Canada or a province, an agent of Her Majesty in either such right, a municipality in Canada, a municipal or public body performing a function of government in Canada or a corporation performing a function or duty on behalf of Her Majesty in right of Canada or a province;

"resident of Canada" means, in the case of a natural person, a person who ordinarily resides in Canada and, in the case of a corporation, a corporation that has its head office in Canada or maintains one or more establishments in Canada to which employees of the corporation employed in connection with the business of the corporation ordinarily report for work;

"Review Board" means the Canadian Cultural Property Export Review Board established by section 18.

## HER MAJESTY

**3. Binding on Her Majesty** — This Act is binding on Her Majesty in right of Canada or a province.

## CANADIAN CULTURAL PROPERTY EXPORT CONTROL LIST

**4.** (1) **Establishment of Control List** — The Governor in Council, on the recommendation of the Minister made after consultation with the Minister of Foreign Affairs, may by order establish a Canadian Cultural Property Export Control List.

(2) **Inclusions** — Subject to subsection (3), the Governor in Council may include in the Control List, regardless of their places of origin, any objects or classes of objects hereinafter described in this subsection, the export of which the Governor in Council deems it necessary to control in order to preserve the national heritage in Canada:

(a) objects of any value that are of archaeological, prehistorical, historical, artistic or scientific interest and that have been recovered from the soil of Canada, the territorial sea of Canada or the inland or other internal waters of Canada;

(b) objects that were made by, or objects referred to in paragraph (d) that relate to, the aboriginal peoples of Canada and that have a fair market value in Canada of more than five hundred dollars;

(c) objects of decorative art, hereinafter described in this paragraph, that were made in the territory that is now Canada and are more than one hundred years old:

    (i) glassware, ceramics, textiles, woodenware and works in base metals that have a fair market value in Canada of more than five hundred dollars, and

    (ii) furniture, sculptured works in wood, works in precious metals and other objects of decorative art that have a fair market value in Canada of more than two thousand dollars;

(d) books, records, documents, photographic positives and negatives, sound recordings, and collections of any of those objects that have a fair market value in Canada of more than five hundred dollars;

(e) drawings, engravings, original prints and water-colours that have a fair market value in Canada of more than one thousand dollars; and

(f) any other objects that have a fair market value in Canada of more than three thousand dollars.

(3) **Exclusions** — No object shall be included in the Control List if that object is less than fifty years old or was made by a natural person who is still living.

(4) **Deeming provision** — For the purposes of this Act, an object within a class of objects included in the Control List is deemed to be an object included in the Control List.

[1995, c. 5, s. 25 (in force May 13, 1995).]

## PERMIT OFFICERS

**5. Designation of permit officers** — The Minister, with the approval of the Minister of National Revenue, may designate any persons or classes of persons employed in that portion of the Department of National Revenue under the power and authority of the Deputy Minister of National Revenue as permit officers to receive applications for export permits and to issue export permits under this Act.
[1994, c. 13, s. 7 (in force May 12, 1994).]

## EXPERT EXAMINERS

**6.** (1) **Designation of expert examiners** — The Minister may designate any resident of Canada or any institution in Canada as an expert examiner for the purposes of this Act.

(2) **Remuneration** — An expert examiner that is not an agent of Her Majesty in right of Canada or a province or is not an employee of, or an employee of an agent of, Her Majesty in right of Canada or a province shall be paid such remuneration for services performed under this Act as may be approved by the Treasury Board.

(3) **Expenses** — An expert examiner or, where an expert examiner is an institution, the person acting for the institution is entitled, within such limits as may be established by the Treasury Board, to be paid reasonable travel and living expenses incurred while absent from his ordinary place of residence in connection with services performed under this Act.

## EXPORT PERMITS

**7. Immediate issue of export permit** — A permit officer who receives from a resident of Canada an application for an export permit shall issue the permit forthwith if the person applying for the permit establishes to the satisfaction of the permit officer that the object in respect of which the application is made

(a)  was imported into Canada within the thirty-five years immediately preceding the date of the application and was not exported from Canada under a permit issued under this Act prior to that importation;

(b)  was lent to an institution or public authority in Canada by a person who was not a resident of Canada at the time the loan was made; or

(c)  is to be removed from Canada for a purpose prescribed by regulation for a period of time not exceeding such period of time as may be prescribed by regulation for the purposes of this paragraph.

**8.** (1) **Determination by permit officer** — A permit officer who receives from a resident of Canada an application for an export permit in respect of an object shall, where he does not issue an export permit under section 7, and where he is not aware of any notice of refusal sent in respect of the object under subsection 13(1) during the two years immediately preceding the date of the application, determine whether the object is included in the Control List.

(2) **Export permit where object not included in Control List** — Where a permit officer determines that an object in respect of which an application for an export permit is made is not included in the Control List, the permit officer shall forthwith issue an export permit in respect of the object.

(3) **Reference to expert examiner** — Where a permit officer determines that an object in respect of which an application for an export permit is made is or might be included in the Control List, the permit officer shall forthwith refer the application to an expert examiner for consideration.

**9. Determination by expert examiner** — Where an application for an export permit is referred to an expert examiner pursuant to subsection 8(3), the expert examiner shall forthwith determine whether the object in respect of which the application is made is included in the Control List.

**10. Where object not included in Control List** — Where an expert examiner determines that an object that is the subject of an application for an export permit that has been referred to him is not included in the Control List, the expert examiner shall forthwith in writing advise the permit officer who referred the application to issue an export permit in respect of the object and shall forthwith send a copy of that advice to the Review Board and the Minister.

**11. (1) Where object included in Control List** — Where an expert examiner determines that an object that is the subject of an application for an export permit that has been referred to him is included in the Control List, the expert examiner shall forthwith further determine

(a) whether that object is of outstanding significance by reason of its close association with Canadian history or national life, its aesthetic qualities, or its value in the study of the arts or sciences; and

(b) whether the object is of such a degree of national importance that its loss to Canada would significantly diminish the national heritage.

(2) **Export permit to be issued** — Where an expert examiner determines that an object that is the subject of an application for an export permit that has been referred to him is not of outstanding significance under paragraph (1)(a) or does not meet the degree of national importance referred to in paragraph (1)(b), the expert examiner shall forthwith in writing advise the permit officer who referred the application to issue an export permit in respect of the object and shall forthwith send a copy of that advice to the Review Board and the Minister.

(3) **Export permit not to be issued** — Where an expert examiner determines that an object that is the subject of an application for an export permit that has been referred to him is of outstanding significance under paragraph (1)(a) and meets the degree of national importance referred to in paragraph (1)(b), the expert examiner shall forthwith in writing advise the permit officer who referred the application not to issue an export permit in respect of the object and shall provide the permit officer with the reasons therefor.

**12. Issue of export permit** — Subject to sections 14 and 16, a permit officer shall issue an export permit forthwith where the permit officer is advised by an expert examiner or directed by the Review Board to do so.

**13.** (1) **Notice of refusal** — Where a permit officer is advised by an expert examiner pursuant to subsection 11(3) not to issue an export permit, the permit officer shall send a written notice of refusal to the applicant, which notice shall include the reasons given by the expert examiner for the refusal.

(2) **Copy to Review Board** — A permit officer who sends a notice of refusal under subsection (1) shall forthwith send a copy thereof to the Review Board.

**14. Deposit of copy** — No export permit shall, unless it is issued under section 7, be issued under this Act for an object within a class of objects prescribed under paragraph 39(d), where the object is included in the Control List, until a copy of that object has been deposited by the person applying for the permit in such institution as the Minister may direct.

**15. Alteration of permits by Minister and notice** — The Minister may amend, suspend, cancel or reinstate any export permit, other than an export permit issued on the direction of the Review Board, and where an export permit is amended, suspended, cancelled or reinstated, the Minister shall forthwith send a written notice to that effect to the person who applied for the permit.

**16. No export permit for two years** — No export permit shall, unless it is issued under section 7 or on the direction of the Review Board pursuant to section 29 or 30, be issued under this Act in respect of an object, where the object is included in the Control List, during a period of two years from the date on which a notice of refusal was sent in respect of that object under subsection 13(1).

## GENERAL PERMITS

**17.** (1) **General permits to export** — The Minister may issue to any resident of Canada who applies therefor a general permit to export any objects included in the Control List subject to such terms and conditions as the Minister may require and may at any time amend, suspend, cancel or reinstate any such permit.

(2) **Open general permits to export** — The Minister may, with the concurrence of the Minister of Foreign Affairs, issue generally to all persons a general permit to export objects within any class of objects that is included in the Control List and that is specified in the permit subject to such terms and conditions as the Minister may require and may, with the concurrence of the Minister of Foreign Affairs, at any time amend, suspend, cancel or reinstate any such permit.

[1995, c. 5, s. 25 (in force May 13, 1995).]

## REVIEW BOARD

### *Review Board Established*

**18.** (1) **Review Board established** — There is hereby established a board to be known as the Canadian Cultural Property Export Review Board, consisting of a Chairperson and not more than nine other members appointed by the Governor in Council on the recommendation of the Minister.

(2) **Members** — The Chairperson and one other member shall be chosen generally from among residents of Canada, and

(a)   up to four other members shall be chosen from among residents of Canada who are or have been officers, members or employees of art galleries, museums, archives, libraries or other collecting institutions in Canada; and

(b)   up to four other members shall be chosen from among residents of Canada who are or have been dealers in or collectors of art, antiques or other objects that form part of the national heritage.

(3) **Acting Chairperson** — The Review Board may authorize one of its members to act as Chairperson in the event of the absence or incapacity of the Chairperson or if the office of Chairperson is vacant.

(4) **Quorum** — Three members, at least one of whom is a person described in paragraph (2)(a) and one of whom is a person described in paragraph (2)(b), constitute a quorum of the Review Board.

[1995, c. 29, ss. 21, 22(E) (in force November 1, 1995); 2001, c. 34, s. 38 (in force December 18, 2001).]

**19.** (1) **Remuneration** — Each member of the Review Board who is not an employee of, or an employee of an agent of, Her Majesty in right of Canada or a province shall be paid such salary or other amount by way of remuneration as may be fixed by the Governor in Council.

(2) **Expenses** — Each member of the Review Board is entitled, within such limits as may be established by the Treasury Board, to be paid reasonable travel and living expenses incurred while absent from his ordinary place of residence in connection with the work of the Review Board.

## *Duties*

**20. Duties** — The Review Board shall, on request,

(a)   pursuant to section 29, review applications for export permits;

(b)   pursuant to section 30, make determinations respecting fair cash offers to purchase; and

(c)   pursuant to section 32, make determinations for the purposes of subparagraph 39(1)(a)(i.1), paragraph 110.1(1)(c), the definition "total cultural gifts" in subsection 118.1(1) and subsection 118.1(10) of the *Income Tax Act*.

[1991, c. 49, s. 216 (in force December 17, 1991).]

## *Head Office and Sittings*

**21.** (1) **Head office** — The head office of the Review Board shall be at such place in Canada as the Governor in Council may by order prescribe.

(2) **Sittings** — The Review Board may sit at such times and places in Canada as it considers necessary or desirable for the proper conduct of its business.

## Advisers

**22.** (1) **Expert advice** — The Review Board may call on any person who has professional, technical or other special knowledge to assist it in any matter in an advisory capacity.

(2) **Valuation experts** — The Minister, on the request of the Review Board, may appoint and fix the remuneration of valuation experts to assist the Review Board in making determinations pursuant to section 30 respecting fair cash offers to purchase or pursuant to section 32 respecting the fair market value of objects disposed of, or proposed to be disposed of, to institutions or public authorities.
[1991, c. 49, s. 217 (in force December 17, 1991).]

## Administration

**23. Administrative services** — The Minister shall provide administrative services to the Review Board.

## Rules and Procedure

**24. Rules** — The Review Board may make rules not inconsistent with this Act for the conduct of its proceedings and the performance of its duties and functions under this Act.

**25. Review Board may receive information** — The Review Board may receive any information presented to it orally or in writing that it considers to be relevant to any matter before it and in so doing it is not bound by any legal or technical rules of evidence.

**26. Information given to applicant** — The Review Board shall make the substance of any information received by it in respect of a matter before it known to the person who applied for an export permit in respect of the object to which the matter relates, or to the person, institution or public authority that applied for a determination under subsection 32(1), as the case may be, and, before the Review Board decides the matter, it shall give that person, institution or public authority an opportunity to make representations in respect of that information.

**27. Exclusion from hearing** — The Review Board may exclude any person not directly interested in a matter being heard before it from the hearing unless, where the matter is in respect of an object in respect of which an application for an export permit has been made, the applicant for the permit requests that the hearing be held in public, in which case it shall be so held.

**28. Review Board shall dispose of matters informally and expeditiously** — The Review Board shall dispose of any matter before it as informally and expeditiously as, in its opinion, the circumstances and considerations of fairness will permit.

*Review of Applications for Export Permits*

**29.** (1) **Request for review by Review Board** — Any person who receives a notice of refusal under section 13 or a notice under section 15 may, within thirty days after the date on which the notice was sent, by notice in writing given to the Review Board, request a review of his application for an export permit by the Review Board.

(2) **Review to be held within four months** — The Review Board shall review an application for an export permit and, unless the circumstances of a particular case require otherwise, render its decision within four months after the date a request is received under subsection (1).

(3) **Determination of the Review Board** — In reviewing an application for an export permit, the Review Board shall determine whether the object in respect of which the application was made

(a)    is included in the Control List;

(b)    is of outstanding significance for one or more of the reasons set out in paragraph 11(1)(a); and

(c)    meets the degree of national importance referred to in paragraph 11(1)(b).

(4) **Object that does not meet criteria** — Where the Review Board determines that an object fails to meet one or more of the criteria set out in subsection (3), it shall direct a permit officer to issue an export permit forthwith in respect of the object.

(5) **Object that meets criteria** — Where the Review Board determines that an object meets all of the criteria set out in subsection (3), it shall,

(a)    if it is of the opinion that a fair offer to purchase the object might be made by an institution or public authority in Canada within six months after the date of its determination, establish a delay period of not less than two months and not more than six months during which the Review Board will not direct that an export permit be issued in respect of the object; or

(b)    in any other case, direct a permit officer to issue an export permit forthwith in respect of the object.

(6) **Notification of delay period** — Where the Review Board establishes a delay period under paragraph (5)(a) in respect of an object, the Board shall give written notice of the delay period to the person who has applied for an export permit in respect of the object and to the Minister, which notice shall include the reasons for the determination of the Board that the object meets all of the criteria set out in subsection (3).

(7) **Idem** — The Minister, on receiving notice of a delay period under subsection (6), shall advise such institutions and public authorities in Canada as the Minister sees fit of the delay period and of the object in respect of which the delay period was established.

**30.** (1) **Request for determination of fair offer to purchase** — Subject to subsection (2), where the Review Board establishes a delay period under paragraph 29(5)(a) in respect of an object and an offer to purchase the object is made by an institution or a public authority in Canada within that period, either the person who applied for an export permit in respect of the object or the institution or public authority making the offer to purchase may, where the offer is not accepted, by notice in writing given to the Review Board, request the Review Board to determine the amount of a fair cash offer to purchase.

(2) **When request to be made** — No request may be made under subsection (1) less than thirty days before the end of the delay period established under paragraph 29(5)(a) in respect of the object in respect of which the request is made.

(3) **Determination of the Review Board** — Where the Review Board receives a request under subsection (1), it shall determine the amount of a fair cash offer to purchase the object in respect of which the request is made and advise the person who applied for an export permit in respect of the object and the institution or public authority that offered to purchase the object of its determination.

(4) **Direction for export permit** — Where the Review Board establishes a delay period under paragraph 29(5)(a) in respect of an object and does not receive a request under subsection (1) in respect of the object, it shall forthwith, after the expiration of the delay period and on the request of the person who requested the review under subsection 29(1), direct a permit officer to issue an export permit forthwith in respect of the object.

(5) **Idem** — Where the Review Board establishes a delay period under paragraph 29(5)(a) in respect of an object and receives a request under subsection (1) in respect of the object, it shall, after the expiration of the delay period or after it has determined the amount of a fair cash offer to purchase the object under subsection (3), whichever time is the later, and on the request of the person who requested the review under subsection 29(1), direct a permit officer to issue an export permit forthwith in respect of the object unless it is satisfied that an institution or public authority has, before the request under this subsection was made, offered to purchase the object for an amount equal to or greater than the amount of the fair cash offer to purchase determined by the Review Board.

**31. Limitation on export permits** — The Review Board shall not direct that an export permit be issued except in accordance with section 29 or 30.

*Determination Relating to Income Tax Matters*

**32.** (1) **Request for determination of Review Board** — For the purposes of subparagraph 39(1)(a)(i.1), paragraph 110.1(1)(c), the definition "total cultural gifts" in subsection 118.1(1) and subsection 118.1(10) of the *Income Tax Act*, where a person disposes of or proposes to dispose of an object to an institution or a public authority designated under subsection (2), the person, institution or public authority may request, by notice in writing given to the Review Board, a determination by the Review Board as to whether the object meets the criteria set out in paragraphs 29(3)(b) and (c) and a determination by the Review Board of the fair market value of the object.

(2) **Designated authorities and institutions** — For the purposes of subparagraph 39(1)(a)(i.1), paragraph 110.1(1)(c), the definition "total cultural gifts" in

subsection 118.1(1), subsection 118.1(10) and section 207.3 of the *Income Tax Act*, the Minister may designate any institution or public authority indefinitely or for a period of time, and generally or for a specified purpose.

(3) **Revocation of designation** — The Minister may at any time revoke a designation made under subsection (2).

(4) **Determination within four months** — The Review Board shall consider a request made under subsection (1) and, unless the circumstances of a particular case require otherwise, make a determination within four months after the date the request is received and shall give notice of the determination in writing or by electronic means to the person who has disposed of, or who proposes to dispose of, the object and, where the request was made by a designated institution or public authority, to the designated institution or public authority.

(5) **Redetermination** — Where the Review Board has, under subsection (4), determined the fair market value of an object in respect of its disposition or proposed disposition, the Review Board

(a)   shall, on request in writing by the person who has disposed of, or who proposes to dispose of, the object to a designated institution or public authority or by an agent of such a person appointed for that purpose, made within twelve months after the day on which notice was given under that subsection, redetermine the fair market value of the object; and

(b)   may, on its own initiative, at any time, redetermine the fair market value of the object.

(6) **Decision within four months and notice of redetermination** — In the case of a redetermination under paragraph (5)(a), the Review Board shall, unless the circumstances of a particular case require otherwise, make the redetermination within four months after it receives the request under that paragraph and shall give notice of the redetermination in writing or by electronic means to the person who made the request.

(7) **Notice of redetermination where no request** — In the case of a redetermination under paragraph (5)(b), the Review Board shall give notice of the redetermination in writing or by electronic means to the person who has disposed of, or who proposes to dispose of, the object and, where the request made under subsection (1) in relation to the object was made by a designated institution or public authority, to the designated institution or public authority.

(8) **Limitation** — Unless the circumstances of a particular case require otherwise, the Review Board shall not redetermine the fair market value of an object more than once.

(9) **Redetermination final and conclusive** — A redetermination under subsection (5) in respect of a proposed disposition is not subject to appeal to or review by any court.

[1991, c. 49, s. 218 (in force December 17, 1991); 1995, c. 38, s. 1 (in force July 12, 1996).]

*Income Tax Certificate*

**33.** (1) **Income tax certificate** — Where the Review Board determines or re-determines the fair market value of an object in respect of which a request was made under section 32 and determines that the object meets the criteria set out in paragraphs 29(3)(b) and (c), it shall, where the object has been irrevocably disposed of to a designated institution or public authority, issue to the person who made the disposition a certificate attesting to the fair market value and to the meeting of those criteria, in such form as the Minister of National Revenue may specify.

(1.1) **Copy to Minister of National Revenue** — The Review Board shall send a copy of a certificate referred to in subsection (1) to the Minister of National Revenue.

(1.2) **Where more than one certificate** — Where the Review Board has is-sued more than one certificate referred to in subsection (1) in relation to an object, the last certificate is deemed to be the only certificate issued by the Review Board in relation to that object.

(2) **Communication of information** — An official of the Department of Ca-nadian Heritage or a member of the Review Board may communicate to an offi-cial of the Department of National Revenue, solely for the purposes of administer-ing the *Income Tax Act*, information obtained under this Act for the purposes of administering this section and sections 32, 33.1 and 33.2.

[1991, c. 49, s. 219 (in force December 17, 1991); 1995, c. 11, s. 45 (in force July 12, 1996); 1995, c. 38, s. 2 (in force July 12, 1996).]

*Appeals Before the Tax Court of Canada*

**33.1** (1) **Appeal of redetermination of fair market value** — Any person who has irrevocably disposed of an object, the fair market value of which has been redetermined under subsection 32(5), to a designated institution or public author-ity may, within ninety days after the day on which a certificate referred to in sub-section 33(1) is issued in relation to that object, appeal the redetermination to the Tax Court of Canada.

(2) **Decision of Court** — On an appeal under subsection (1), the Tax Court of Canada may confirm or vary the fair market value and, for the purposes of the *Income Tax Act*, the value fixed by the Court is deemed to be the fair market value of the object determined by the Review Board in respect of its disposition.

[1995, c. 38, s. 2 (in force July 12, 1996).]

**33.2** (1) **Extension of time for appeal** — Where an appeal has not been insti-tuted by a person under section 33.1 within the time limited by that section, the person may make an application to the Tax Court of Canada for an order extend-ing the time within which the appeal may be instituted and the Court may make an order extending the time for appealing and may impose such terms as it con-siders just.

(2) **Contents of application** — An application made under subsection (1) shall set out the reasons why the appeal was not instituted within the time limited by section 33.1.

(3) **How application made** — An application made under subsection (1) shall be made by filing in the Registry of the Tax Court of Canada, in accordance with the provisions of the *Tax Court of Canada Act*, three copies of the application accompanied by three copies of the notice of appeal.

(4) **Copy to Deputy Attorney General** — The Tax Court of Canada shall send a copy of each application made under this section to the office of the Deputy Attorney General of Canada.

(5) **When order to be made** — No order shall be made under this section unless

(a) the application is made within one year after the expiration of the time limited by section 33.1 for appealing; and

(b) the person making the application demonstrates that

    (i) within the time limited by section 33.1 for appealing, the person

        (A) was unable to act or to instruct another to act in the person's name, or

        (B) had a *bona fide* intention to appeal,

    (ii) given the reasons set out in the application and the circumstances of the case, it would be just and equitable to grant the application,

    (iii) the application was made as soon as circumstances permitted, and

    (iv) there are reasonable grounds for the appeal.

[1995, c. 38, s. 2 (in force July 12, 1996); 2000, c. 30, s. 159 (in force October 20, 2000).]

*Report to Minister*

**34. Report to Minister** — The Chairperson of the Review Board shall, as soon as possible after March 31 in each year, submit to the Minister a report of the operations of the Review Board for the previous fiscal year and its recommendations, if any.

[1995, c. 29, s. 22(E) (in force November 1, 1995).]

## FINANCIAL

**35. Grants and loans from moneys appropriated** — The Minister may, out of moneys appropriated by Parliament for such purposes, make grants and loans to institutions and public authorities in Canada for the purchase of objects in respect of which export permits have been refused under this Act or for the purchase of cultural property situated outside Canada that is related to the national heritage.

**36. (1) Canadian Heritage Preservation Endowment Account established** — There shall be established in the accounts of Canada a special account to be known as the Canadian Heritage Preservation Endowment Account.

(2) **Amounts to be credited to the Canadian Heritage Preservation Endowment Account** — There shall be credited to the Canadian Heritage Preservation Endowment Account

(a) all moneys received by Her Majesty by gift, bequest or otherwise for the purpose of making grants to institutions and public authorities in Canada for the purchase of objects in respect of which export permits have been refused under this Act, or for the purchase of cultural property situated outside Canada that is related to the national heritage;

(b) all moneys received by Her Majesty as income on or as proceeds from the sale of any securities received by Her Majesty for a purpose referred to in paragraph (a); and

(c) an amount representing interest on the balance from time to time to the credit of the account at such rates and calculated in such manner as the Governor in Council may, on the recommendation of the Minister of Finance, prescribe.

(3) **Amounts that may be charged to the Canadian Heritage Preservation Endowment Account** — There may be charged to the Canadian Heritage Preservation Endowment Account such amounts as the Minister may expend otherwise than under section 35 for grants to institutions and public authorities in Canada for the purchase of objects in respect of which export permits have been refused under this Act or for the purchase of cultural property situated outside Canada that is related to the national heritage.

## FOREIGN CULTURAL PROPERTY

**37. (1) Definitions** — In this section,

"cultural property agreement", in relation to a foreign State, means an agreement between Canada and the foreign State or an international agreement to which Canada and the foreign State are both parties, relating to the prevention of illicit international traffic in cultural property;

"foreign cultural property", in relation to a reciprocating State, means any object that is specifically designated by that State as being of importance for archaeology, prehistory, history, literature, art or science;

"reciprocating State" means a foreign State that is a party to a cultural property agreement.

(2) **Illegal imports** — From and after the coming into force of a cultural property agreement in Canada and a reciprocating State, it is illegal to import into Canada any foreign cultural property that has been illegally exported from that reciprocating State.

(3) **Action for recovery of foreign cultural property** — Where the government of a reciprocating State submits a request in writing to the Minister for the recovery and return of any foreign cultural property that has been imported into Canada illegally by virtue of subsection (2) and that is in Canada in the possession of or under the control of any person, institution or public authority, the Attorney General of Canada may institute an action in the Federal Court or in a

superior court of a province for the recovery of the property by the reciprocating State.

(4) **Notice** — Notice of the commencement of an action under this section shall be served by the Attorney General of Canada on such persons and given in such manner as is provided by the rules of the court in which the action is taken, or, where the rules do not so provide, served on such persons and given in such manner as is directed by a judge of the court.

(5) **Order for recovery of designated property** — A court in which an action has been taken under this section on behalf of a reciprocating State may, after affording all persons that it considers to have an interest in the action a reasonable opportunity to be heard, make an order for the recovery of the property in respect of which the action has been taken or any other order sufficient to ensure the return of the property to the reciprocating State, where the court is satisfied that the property has been illegally imported into Canada by virtue of subsection (2) and that the amount fixed under subsection (6), if any, has been paid to or for the benefit of the person, institution or public authority referred to in that subsection.

(6) **Compensation** — Where any person, institution or public authority establishes to the satisfaction of the court in which an action under this section is being considered that the person, institution or public authority

(a) is a *bona fide* purchaser for value of the property in respect of which the action has been taken and had no knowledge at the time the property was purchased by him or it that the property had been illegally exported from the reciprocating State on whose behalf the action has been taken, or

(b) has a valid title to the property in respect of which the action has been taken and had no knowledge at the time such title was acquired that the property had been illegally exported from the reciprocating State on whose behalf the action has been taken

the court may fix such amount to be paid as compensation by the reciprocating State to that person, institution or public authority as the court considers just in the circumstances.

(7) **Safe-keeping** — The court may, at any time in the course of an action under this section, order that the property in respect of which the action has been taken be turned over to the Minister for safe-keeping and conservation pending final disposition of the action.

(8) **Permit to export** — The Minister shall, on receipt of a copy of an order of a court made under subsection (5), issue a permit authorizing any person authorized by the reciprocating State on behalf of which the action was taken to export the property in respect of which the order was made to that State.

(9) **Limitations inapplicable** — Section 39 of the *Federal Courts Act* does not apply in respect of any action taken under this section.

[S.C. 2002, c. 8, s. 182.]

## DESIGNATION OF CULTURAL PROPERTY

**38. Designation of cultural property** — For the purposes of article 1 of the Convention on the means of prohibiting and preventing the illicit import, export and transfer of ownership of cultural property , any object included in the Control List is hereby designated by Canada as being of importance for archaeology, prehistory, history, literature, art or science.

## REGULATIONS

**39. Regulations** — The Governor in Council, on the recommendation of the Minister and the Minister of Foreign Affairs, may make regulations

(a) prescribing the information, documentation and undertakings to be furnished by applicants for permits and certificates under this Act, the procedures to be followed in applying for and in issuing those permits and certificates, the terms and conditions applicable to them and the duration of the permits;

(b) prescribing the circumstances in which information may be required from persons to whom permits have been issued under this Act and the type of information that may be so required;

(c) prescribing the purposes for which an object may be removed from Canada for a limited period of time for the purpose of paragraph 7(c) and the length of time for which it may be so removed; and

(d) prescribing classes of manuscripts, original documents, archives, photographic positives and negatives, films and sound recordings for the purpose of section 14.

[1995, c. 5, s. 25; 1998, c. 19, s. 261 (in force June 18, 1998).]

## OFFENCES AND PUNISHMENT

**40. Export or attempt to export** — No person shall export or attempt to export from Canada any object included in the Control List except under the authority of and in accordance with a permit issued under this Act.

**41. No transfer of permits** — No person who is authorized under a permit issued under this Act to export an object from Canada shall transfer the permit to or allow it to be used by a person who is not so authorized.

**42. False information** — No person shall wilfully furnish any false or misleading information or knowingly make any misrepresentation

(a) in an application for a permit under this Act;

(b) for the purpose of procuring the issue of a permit under this Act; or

(c) in connection with the use of a permit issued under this Act or the disposition of any object to which such permit relates.

**43. Import or attempt to import foreign cultural property** — No person shall import or attempt to import into Canada any property that it is illegal to import into Canada under subsection 37(2).

**44.** (1) **Export or attempt to export** — No person shall export or attempt to export from Canada any property in respect of which an action has been instituted under subsection 37(3) while the action is being considered.

(2) **Idem** — No person shall export or attempt to export from Canada any property in respect of which an order has been made under subsection 37(5) except under the authority of and in accordance with a permit issued by the Minister under subsection 37(8).

**45.** (1) **Offences and punishment** — Every person who contravenes any of the provisions of sections 40 to 44 is guilty of an offence and liable

(a)   on summary conviction to a fine not exceeding five thousand dollars or to imprisonment for a term not exceeding twelve months or to both; or

(b)   on conviction on indictment to a fine not exceeding twenty-five thousand dollars or to imprisonment for a term not exceeding five years or to both.

(2) **Limitation period** — A prosecution under paragraph (1)(a) may be instituted at any time within but not later than three years after the time when the subject-matter of the complaint arose.

**46. Officers, etc., of corporations** — Where a corporation commits an offence under this Act, any officer, director or agent of the corporation who directed, authorized, assented to, acquiesced in or participated in the commission of the offence is a party to and guilty of the offence and is liable on summary conviction or on conviction on indictment to the punishment provided for the offence whether or not the corporation has been prosecuted or convicted.

**47. Venue** — Any proceedings in respect of an offence under this Act may be instituted, tried or determined at the place in Canada where the offence was committed or at the place in Canada in which the person charged with the offence is, resides or has an office or place of business at the time of institution of the proceedings.

**48.** (1) **Evidence** — The original or a copy of a bill of lading, customs document, commercial invoice or other document (in this section called a "shipping document") is admissible in evidence in any prosecution under this Act in relation to the sending or shipping of an object where it appears from the shipping document that

(a)   the object was sent or shipped from Canada or came into Canada;

(b)   a person, as shipper, consignor or consignee, sent or shipped the object from Canada or brought the object into Canada; or

(c)   the object was sent or shipped to a particular destination or person.

(2) **Proof of the facts** — In the absence of evidence to the contrary, a shipping document that is admissible in evidence under subsection (1) is proof of any of the facts set out in paragraph (1)(a), (b) or (c) that appear from the shipping document.

## GENERAL

**49. Other lawful obligations** — An export permit or other permit to export issued under this Act does not affect the obligation of any person to obtain any licence, permit or certificate to export that may be required under any other law or to pay any tax, duty, toll or other sum required by any law to be paid in respect of the export of any goods.

**50. Customs officers' duties** — An officer, as defined in the *Customs Act*, before permitting the export or import of any object that the officer has reason to suspect is being exported or imported in contravention of any of the provisions of this Act or the regulations, shall satisfy himself that the exporter or importer has not contravened any of the provisions of this Act or the regulations and that all requirements thereof have been complied with in respect of that object.

[R.S., 1985, c. 1 (2nd Supp.), s. 213 (in force November 10, 1986).]

**51. Application of powers under the *Customs Act*** — All officers, as defined in the *Customs Act*, have, with respect to any object to which this Act applies, all the powers they have under the *Customs Act* with respect to the export or import of goods and all the provisions of the *Customs Act* and regulations thereunder respecting search, detention, forfeiture and condemnation apply, with such modifications as the circumstances require,

(a)   to any objects tendered for export or import, exported or imported, or otherwise dealt with contrary to the provisions of this Act and the regulations; and

(b)   to all documents relating to objects described in paragraph (a).

[R.S., 1985, c. 1 (2nd Supp.), s. 213 (in force November 10, 1986).]

**52. Report to Parliament** — As soon as practicable after receiving, pursuant to section 34, the report of the Chairperson of the Review Board, the Minister shall prepare and lay before Parliament a report of the operations under this Act for the fiscal year to which the report of the Chairperson relates and shall include therewith the report of the Chairperson.

[1995, c. 29, s. 22(E) (in force November 1, 1995).]

## RELATED PROVISIONS

1991, c. 49, s. 216(2):

(2) Subsection (1) is applicable after December 11, 1988, except that, in respect of gifts made before February 21, 1990, paragraph 20(c) of the said Act, as enacted by subsection (1), shall be read without reference to the expression "and subsection 118.1(10)".

1991, c. 49, s. 217(2):

(2) Subsection (1) is applicable after February 20, 1990.

1991, c. 49, ss. 218(3), (4):

(3) Subsection (1) is applicable after December 11, 1988, except that, in respect of gifts made before February 21, 1990, subsection 32(1) of the said Act, as

enacted by subsection (1), shall be read without reference to the expression "and a determination by the Review Board of the fair market value of the object".

(4) Subsection (2) is applicable with respect to gifts made after February 20, 1990.

1991, c. 49, s. 219(2):

(2) Subsection 33(1) of the said Act, as enacted by subsection (1), is applicable after February 20, 1990.

1995, c. 38, ss. 8(1) to (3):

**8.** (1) **Transitional** — A person who, before the day on which this section comes into force, has irrevocably disposed of, to a designated institution or public authority, an object, the fair market value of which was determined or redetermined by the Canadian Cultural Property Export Review Board pursuant to section 32 of the *Cultural Property Export and Import Act* between January 1, 1992 and the day on which this section comes into force, may, within six months after the day on which this section comes into force, appeal the determination or redetermination to the Tax Court of Canada.

(2) **Transitional** — A person who, within six months after the day on which this section comes into force, irrevocably disposes of, to a designated institution or public authority, an object, the fair market value of which was determined or redetermined by the Canadian Cultural Property Export Review Board pursuant to section 32 of the *Cultural Property Export and Import Act* between January 1, 1992 and the day on which this section comes into force, may, within six months after the day of the disposition, appeal the determination or redetermination to the Tax Court of Canada.

(3) **Application of certain provisions** — Subsections 33(2) and 33.1(2) and section 33.2 of the *Cultural Property Export and Import Act*, as enacted by section 2 of this Act, apply, with such modifications as the circumstances require, in respect of an appeal under subsection (1) or (2).

# CANADIAN CULTURAL PROPERTY EXPORT CONTROL LIST

(C.R.C., c. 448)

*Short Title*

**1.** This Order may be cited as the Canadian Cultural Property Export Control List.

*Application*

**2.** This Order applies only to an object that is 50 or more years old and was made by a natural person who is no longer living.

[SOR/86-329, s. 1; SOR/2005 – 260, s. 1.]

## GROUP I

### OBJECTS RECOVERED FROM THE SOIL OR WATERS OF CANADA

*Interpretation*

**1.** In this Group,

"Aboriginal peoples of Canada" means, collectively, those persons of Indian or Inuit ancestry, including Métis persons, or persons recognized as being members of an Indian, Inuit or Métis group by the other members of that group, who at any time ordinarily resided in the territory that is now Canada;

"artifact" means an object made or reworked by a person or persons and associated with historic or prehistoric cultures;

"described mineral specimen" means a mineral specimen for which scientific data, illustrations or descriptions appear in a professional publication;

"fossil" means the preserved remains or traces of animals or plants that lived in the geological past but does not include

(a) fossil fuels or fossiliferous rock intended for industrial use, or

(b) a carving or sculpture made by a person or persons from fossiliferous or fossilized matter;

"fossil amber" means fossil resin with or without inclusions;

"invertebrate fossil" means the fossilized remains of an animal that did not possess a backbone;

"meteorite" means any naturally-occurring object of extraterrestrial origin;

"mineral" means an element or chemical compound that occurs naturally in soil or water and includes crystals and naturally occurring metals, and gemstones whether or not polished or facetted by a person or persons. It does not include minerals, ores and concentrates intended for industrial use, or a carving or sculpture made by a person or persons from minerals;

"plant fossil" means the fossilized remains of vegetable matter;

"recovered from the soil", in respect of an object or specimen, means that the object or specimen has originated in or has been excavated from bedrock or sediments, has been retrieved as a find from the surface of bedrock or sediments or has been recovered from snow or ice;

"tektite" means any natural form of silicate glass of non-volcanic origin;

"type fossil specimen" means any fossil specimen or portion thereof of a biological species used in the original scientific study and published description of that species;

"type mineral specimen" means any mineral specimen or portion thereof of a mineral species used in the original scientific study and published description of that species;

"vertebrate fossil" means the fossilized remains of an animal that possessed a backbone;

"vertebrate trace fossil" means the fossilized trace of a vertebrate.

[SOR/97-159, s. 1.]

## Mineralogy

**2.** Mineral specimens, whether composed of a single mineral, a part of a mineral or an aggregate of minerals, recovered from the soil of Canada, the territorial sea of Canada or the inland or other internal waters of Canada, as follows:

(a)   a type mineral specimen or a described mineral specimen of any value;

(b)   a single mineral specimen of a fair market value in Canada of more than $2,000;

(c)   a collection of 10 or more mineral specimens of a fair market value in Canada of more than $5,000 recovered from a specific mine, quarry or locality;

(d)   mineral specimens in bulk, recovered from a specific mineral occurrence, weighing 225 kg (500 pounds) or more of any value; and

(e)   meteorites and tektites of any value.

[SOR/95-170, s. 1; SOR/97-159, s. 2.]

## Palaeontology

**3.** Palaeontological specimens recovered from the soil of Canada, the territorial sea of Canada or the inland or other internal waters of Canada, as follows:

(a)   a type fossil specimen of any value;

(b)   fossil amber of any value;

(c)   a vertebrate fossil specimen of a fair market value in Canada of more than $500;

(d)    an invertebrate fossil specimen of a fair market value in Canada of more than $500;

(e)    specimens in bulk weighing 11.25 kg (25 pounds) or more of vertebrate fossils or vertebrate trace fossils of any value; and

(f)    specimens in bulk weighing 22.5 kg (50 pounds) or more, recovered from a specific outcrop, quarry or locality, that include one or more specimens of any value of the following, namely,

    (i)    invertebrate fossils,

    (ii)   plant fossils, or

    (iii)  fossiliferous rock containing plant fossils or invertebrate fossils.

[SOR/95-170, s. 1; SOR/97-159, s. 3.]

## Archaeology

**4.** (1) An archaeological object of any value recovered from the soil of Canada, the territorial sea of Canada or the inland or other internal waters of Canada not less than 75 years after its burial, concealment or abandonment if the object is an artifact or organic remains, including human remains, associated with or representative of historic or prehistoric cultures.

(2) Without restricting the generality of subitem (1), archaeological objects described in that subitem include

(a)    artifacts that relate to the Aboriginal peoples of Canada, namely,

    (i)    arrow heads, harpoon heads and such other projectile points used as hunting implements,

    (ii)   adzes, axes, awls, celts, chisels and such other tools and agricultural implements,

    (iii)  clubs, tomahawks and such other weapons,

    (iv)   harpoon heads, fish hooks, sinkers, and such other fishing implements,

    (v)    pipes, vessels, potsherds and such other pottery,

    (vi)   effigies, rock drawings, wampum and such other ceremonial and religious articles, and

    (vii)  beads, articles of adornment and such other objects used as trading goods;

(b)    artifacts that relate to the progressive exploration, occupation, defence and development of the territory that is now Canada by non-aboriginal peoples, namely,

    (i)    arms, accoutrements, fragments of uniforms, buckles, badges, buttons, and such other objects related to military activity,

    (ii)   beads, articles of adornment and such other objects used as trading goods associated with the fur trade,

    (iii)  hunting, fishing and trapping implements,

    (iv)   ordnance, ship's gear, anchors and such other objects related to naval activity,

    (v)    religious paraphernalia and such other objects related to missionary activity,

(vi) coins, cargo from shipwrecks or sunken ships and such other objects related to transportation, supply and commerce,

(vii) utensils, implements, tools, weapons, household articles and such other objects related to early settlement and pioneer life, and

(viii) machinery and such other objects related to manufacture and industry; and

(c) organic remains associated with or representative of historic or prehistoric cultures.

[SOR/86-329, s. 2; SOR/97-159, s. 4; SOR/2005, s. 6.]

# GROUP II

## OBJECTS OF ETHNOGRAPHIC MATERIAL CULTURE

### *Interpretation*

**1.** The definitions in this section apply in this Group.

"Aboriginal person of Canada" means a person of Indian or Inuit ancestry, including a Métis person, or a person recognized as being a member of an Indian, Inuit or Métis group by the other members of that group, who at any time ordinarily resided in the territory that is now Canada.

"object of ethnographic material culture" means an object that was made, reworked or adapted for use by a person who is an Aboriginal person of Canada, or an aboriginal person of a country other than Canada, that may

(a) incorporate features reflecting contact with non-aboriginal cultures; and

(b) be a single object or an object together with its component parts that form a single unit.

[SOR/95-170, s. 2; SOR/97-159, s. 5.]

### *Objects of Ethnographic Material Culture*

**2.** An object of ethnographic material culture that

(a) has a fair market value in Canada of more than $3,000 and was made, reworked or adapted for use by an Aboriginal person of Canada;

(b) has a fair market value in Canada of more than $10,000 and was made, reworked or adapted for use by an aboriginal person of the territory that is now
(i) the United States,
(ii) Greenland, or
(iii) the part of the Russian Federation east of 135° longitude; or

(c) has a fair market value in Canada of more than $20,000 and was made, reworked or adapted for use by a person who is an aboriginal person of a territory other than a territory mentioned in paragraph (a) or (b).

[SOR/86-329, ss. 3, 4; SOR/95-170, s. 3; SOR/97-159, s. 5.]

## GROUP III

## MILITARY OBJECTS

### *Interpretation*

**1.** The definitions in this section apply in this Group.

"accoutrement" means a military accessory that is associated with the wearing of or use of a specific hand-carried weapon or piece of ordnance. It includes magazines, loading tools, belts, straps, holsters, mounts, telescopic or other sights, powder horns or flasks, bullet pouches, molds or starters, ramrods or wiping sticks, bayonets, scabbards and carrying cases.

"dress" means an object that is armour, a head-dress, pantaloons, a tunic with trappings, accessories or any other associated articles that form a part of military apparel.

"hand-carried weapon or piece of ordnance" includes

   (a)   a small arm, staff-weapon or an edged weapon; and

   (b)   a cannon or artillery piece that is muzzle-loaded or breech-loaded, whether originally mounted or unmounted, that was used or designed to be used for a warlike purpose.

"military" shall be construed as relating to any warlike force.

[SOR/97-159, s. 6.]

### *Military Objects*

**2.** Military objects made within or out of the territory that is now Canada if they relate to military activities that took place in the territory or if they relate to a person who at any time ordinarily resided in the territory and who participated in military activities that took place out of the territory, namely,

   (a)   an order, decoration, medal, insignia, including a ribbon, collar or sash normally associated with such order, decoration, medal or insignia, that has a fair market value in Canada of more than $3,000;

   (b)   a flag, colour, banner or pennant that has a fair market value in Canada of more than $3,000;

   (c)   dress that has a fair market value in Canada of more than $3,000; and

   (d)   any hand-carried weapon or piece of ordnance, or their associated accoutrements, that has a fair market value in Canada of more than $3,000.

[SOR/86-329, s. 5; SOR/95-170, s. 4; SOR/97-159, s. 7.]

## GROUP IV

## OBJECTS OF APPLIED AND DECORATIVE ART

### *Interpretation*

**1.** In this Group, "object of applied and decorative art" means art in which the principles of design, ornamentation, enrichment and decoration are applied to the production of functional and utilitarian objects or architectural features.
[SOR/97-159, s. 8.]

### *Objects of Applied and Decorative Art*

**2.** (1) Objects of applied and decorative art that are more than 100 years old made in the territory that is now Canada, namely,

(a)  glassware, ceramics, textiles, woodenware and works in base metals that have a fair market value in Canada of more than $1,000; and

(b)  furniture, sculptured works in wood, other than sacred or religious carvings, works in precious metals and other objects of applied and decorative art that have a fair market value in Canada of more than $4,000.

(2) Without restricting the generality of paragraph (1)(a), objects of applied and decorative art described in that paragraph include

(a)  utensils, tools, earthenware and such other household articles;

(b)  costumes, embroidery, lace and such other objects related to dress;

(c)  personal weapons; and

(d)  objects of folk art.

(3) Without restricting the generality of paragraph (1)(b), objects of applied and decorative art described in that paragraph include

(a)  articles made of silver or gold;

(b)  jewellery;

(c)  decorative sculpture;

(d)  architectural features;

(e)  furnishings, including carpets, tapestries and lighting fixtures; and

(f)  objects of folk art.

[SOR/97-159, ss. 9, 10]

**3.** An object of applied and decorative art that was made in the territory that is now Canada, that is not less than 50 years old and that has a fair market value in Canada of more than $3,000, namely, a sacred or religious carving.
[SOR/95-170, s. 5; SOR/97-159, ss. 9, 11.]

**4.** An object of applied and decorative art that is not less than 50 years old, that was made within or outside the territory that is now Canada by a person who at any time ordinarily resided in that territory and that has a fair market value in Canada of more than $6,000.
[SOR/95-170, s. 6; SOR/97-159, ss. 9, 11.]

**5** (1) An object of applied and decorative art that is made outside the territory that is now Canada, that is not less than 50 years old and that has a fair market value in Canada of more than $3,000, namely,

 (a) a Canadian pattern coin;

 (b) a trial strike of a Canadian coin;

 (c) a medal or medallion intended for or awarded to a person who at any time ordinarily resided in the territory that is now Canada; or

 (d) a pre-production proof of a Canadian postage stamp.

(2) An object of applied and decorative art, other than an object described in subsection (1), that is made outside the territory that is now Canada, that is not less than 50 years old, that has a fair market value in Canada of more than $8,000 and that

 (a) was commissioned by a person who at any time ordinarily resided in the territory that is now Canada;

 (b) incorporates a Canadian theme or subject; or

 (c) is identified with a prominent person, institution or memorable event that relates to the art history, history or national life of Canada.

[SOR/86-329, ss. 6 to 9; SOR/97-159, ss. 9, 11.]

**6.** Any object of applied and decorative art, other than an object described in section 5, that was made outside the territory that is now Canada, that is not less than 50 years old and that has a fair market value in Canada of more than $15,000.

[SOR/97-159, ss. 9, 11.]

## GROUP V

## OBJECTS OF FINE ART

### *Interpretation*

**1.** The definitions in this section apply in this Group.

"drawing" means a unique artistic representation or work including calligraphy, usually on paper, parchment or vellum, executed in media such as pen and ink, ink wash, black or colour chalk, pastels, charcoal, graphite, water colour, gouache or metal-point.

"painting" means a unique artistic representation or work executed in oil-base pigments, fresco, collage, tempera, encaustic, synthetic or other media on stretched canvas, mounted paper, cardboard or other manufactured board, metal, glass, wood, silk or other support.

"print" means an artistic representation or work usually on paper or vellum, executed in media such as woodcut, metalcut, wood engraving, engraving, etching, drypoint, mezzotint, aquatint, soft ground, lithography, monotype, cliché-verre or silk screen.

"sculpture" means an artistic representation or work in three dimensions that is carved, modeled or constructed and includes such a representation that has subsequently been cast in plaster, metal or other substance that will take on a rigid form.

[SOR/95-170, s. 7; SOR/97-159, s. 12.]

## Objects of Fine Art

**2.** An object of fine art that is made within or outside the territory that is now Canada by a person who at any time ordinarily resided in the territory that is now Canada and that

  (a)  in the case of drawing or print, has a fair market value in Canada of more than $5,000;

  (b)  in the case of a painting or sculpture, has a fair market value in Canada of more than $15,000; and

  (c)  in the case of works of fine art in media other than those listed in paragraph (a) or (b), or works of art in multi-media, has a fair market value in Canada of more than $5,000.

[SOR/95-170, s. 8(F); SOR/97-159, s. 13.]

**3.** (1) Objects of fine art made within or outside the territory that is now Canada, namely,

  (a)  a drawing or print that has a fair market value in Canada of more than $7,500,

  (b)  a painting or sculpture that has a fair market value in Canada of more than $20,000, and

  (c)  a work of fine art in media other than those listed in paragraph (a) or (b), or works of fine art in multi-media, that has a fair market value in Canada of more than $7,500,

(2) The object referred to in paragraph (1)(a), (b) or (c) must

  (a)  have been commissioned by a person who at any time ordinarily resided in the territory that is now Canada,

  (b)  incorporate a Canadian theme or subject, or

  (c)  be identified with a prominent person, institution or memorable event that relates to the art history, history or national life of Canada.

[SOR/95-170, s. 9; SOR/97-159, s. 13.]

**4.** Objects of fine art, other than the objects described in section 2 or 3, that are made outside the territory that is now Canada, namely,

  (a)  a drawing or print that has a fair market value in Canada of more than $15,000;

  (b)  a painting or sculpture that has a fair market value in Canada of more than $30,000; and

  (c)  a work of fine art in media other than those listed in paragraph (a) or (b), or works of fine art in multi-media, that has a fair market value in Canada of more than $20,000.

[SOR/97-159, s. 13.]

5. For prints executed since 1880, a distinction shall be made between an original print in which the artist has had direct control in the preparation of the printing surface or photomechanical process involved and a reproduction made by only photomechanical means.

[SOR/80-855, s. 1.]

6. The date of a print is established by the date of the execution of the printing surface or the date of the impression from the printing surface.

[SOR/80-855, s. 1; SOR/86-329, ss. 10 to 13.]

7. Photographs are included in Group VII of this List.

[SOR/97-159, s. 14.]

# GROUP VI

## SCIENTIFIC OR TECHNOLOGICAL OBJECTS

### *Interpretation*

**1.** In this Group,

"machine" means a contrivance that is used in the performance of some kind of work or activity and that consists of inter-related parts and uses any source of energy including animal power, manpower, air, water, light, steam, gravity, friction, combustion or electricity, but does not include scrap metal intended for industrial purposes;

"patent model" means the model constructed for the purpose of obtaining a patent for an invention, discovery or process;

"prototype model" means any original working model on which subsequent production was based;

"scale model" means a model reduced in size according to a fixed scale or proportion;

"scientific apparatus" means an assembly of objects forming a unit constructed for the purpose of research in any scientific discipline;

"scientific instrument" means an implement, tool or device used for practical or scientific purposes as an instrument for examining or measuring.

[SOR/97-159, s. 15.]

### *Scientific or Technological Objects*

**2.** An object that was made, designed or invented in the territory that is now Canada, or that was made, designed or invented out of the territory by a person who at any time ordinarily resided in the territory, and that has a fair market value in Canada of more than $3,000, as follows:

(a)    a scientific instrument, other than a scientific instrument that is intended to be used for any scientific or technological purpose;

(b)    an original scientific apparatus; or

(c)    a scale model, patent model or prototype model of a scientific instrument, original scientific apparatus or machine.

[SOR/95-170, s. 10; SOR/97-159, s. 16.]

**3.** A machine, other than a machine that is intended to be used for a manufacturing, industrial or commercial purpose, that was made, designed or invented in the territory that is now Canada or that was made, designed or invented outside that territory by a person who at any time ordinarily resided in that territory, and that has a fair market value in Canada of more than $3,000.

[SOR/95-170, s. 11; SOR/97-159, s. 17.]

**4.** The following objects made out of the territory that is now Canada if they relate to the history of science and the development of technology in Canada, namely,

(a)    a scientific instrument, other than a scientific instrument that is intended to be used for any scientific or technological purpose, that has a fair market value in Canada of more than $5,000; and

(b)    a machine, other than a machine that is intended to be used for a manufacturing, industrial or commercial purpose, that has a fair market value in Canada of more than $5,000.

[SOR/97-159, s. 18.]

**5.** The following objects made out of the territory that is now Canada other than the objects described in item 4, if they are related to the history of science and the development of technology, namely,

(a)    a scientific instrument, other than a scientific instrument that is intended to be used for any scientific or technological purpose, that has a fair market value in Canada of more than $8,000; and

(b)    a machine, other than a machine that is intended to be used for a manufacturing, industrial or commercial purpose, that has a fair market value in Canada of more than $8,000.

[SOR/97-159, s. 19.]

## GROUP VII

## TEXTUAL RECORDS, GRAPHIC RECORDS AND SOUND RECORDINGS

## TEXTUAL RECORDS

### *Interpretation*

**1.** The definitions in this section apply in this section and section 2.

"broadsheet" means a publication that consists of a single sheet printed on both sides, sometimes also referred to as a handbill.

"broadside" means a publication that consists of a single sheet bearing information on one side only that is intended to be affixed to a surface and that is more textual than graphic.

document", "manuscript" or "record" [Repealed, SOR/2005 – 260, s. 15]

"leaflet" means a publication that consists of one or more sheets, printed on both sides, that is folded but not stitched or bound.

"manuscript, record or document" means textual material in holograph or typescript, excluding printed materials and other works intended for public distribution such as printed books, pamphlets, or serials. Nevertheless, objects considered to be a manuscript, record or document include

    (a)    a diary, ledger or letterbook;

    (b)    a literary manuscript;

    (c)    a leaflet, broadsheet, broadside or poster;

    (d)    a letter and enclosures;

    (e)    a cover or sheet that contains postal markings or that incorporates postage or revenue stamps;

    (f)    a memorandum, report or account;

    (g)    sheet music;

    (h)    printed ephemera; and

    (i)    a single newspaper.

"printed book or pamphlet" means a work of at least two pages, exclusive of cover pages, made up of sheets bound, stitched or fastened together so as to form a material whole under an established date of printing. It includes each work in a set issued under a single title.

"serial" means a publication that appears at intervals for an indefinite period.

"serial title" means a run of a serial, irrespective of its continuity.

"textual record" [Repealed SOR/2005-260, s. 15.]

[SOR/97-159, s. 20; SOR/2005-260, s. 15.]

## Textual Records

**2.** (1) Textual records if they were made in the territory that is now Canada, were made outside that territory by a person who at any time ordinarily resided in that territory, or were made outside that territory and relate to the history or national life of Canada, namely,

    (a)    a manuscript, record or document that has a fair market value in Canada of more than $1,000;

    (b)    a collection of associated manuscripts, records or documents that has a fair market value in Canada of more than $2,000;

    (c)    a printed book or pamphlet, a set of printed books or pamphlets under a single title or a serial title, other than a newspaper, that has a fair market value in Canada of more than $3,000; and

    (d)    a collection of associated printed books or pamphlets or serial titles, other than a collection of newspapers, that has a fair market value in Canada of more than $15,000.

(2) Without restricting the generality of subsection (1), examples of paper money considered to be a manuscript, record or document include card money, ordonnances of the French regime, army bills of the years 1813 to 1815 and provincial treasury notes made before the year 1818 for circulation in the territory that is now Canada.

(3) The age of any printed material is determined by the established date of printing for the material.

[SOR/97-159, s. 20.]

## GRAPHIC RECORDS

### *Interpretation*

**3.** The definitions in this section apply in this section and sections 4 to 6.

"cartographic record or document" means

 (a) a collection of cartographic representations composed of manuscript or printed material that is bound, stitched or fastened together to form a unit that has no established date of printing for the unit as a whole;

 (b) a single sheet on which are cartographic representations, irrespective of folding; or

 (c) cartographic material that is

  (i) unattached and issued in a combination other than a printed book, such as boxed maps, irrespective of the date of printing, or

  (ii) in a loose format that clearly forms a single unit of visual information.

"cinematographic film" means positive or negative film, with or without sound, that contains continuous images designed to create the illusion of motion when projected in rapid succession, and includes film issued in any form in a set under a single title that may or may not be part of the film. Cinematographic films issued as a serial are considered to be a collection of associated cinematographic films.

"design" means a preliminary sketch or drawing or an outline sketch, drawing, print or plan of a work of art, an edifice, a machine or any other subject to be constructed or made.

"graphic record" means a book, manuscript, record, document, photographic positive or negative, cinematographic film, map or any designs or material whose primary object is the communication of information in a visual form, other than written or printed language.

"iconographic object" means a graphic representation such as a design, illustration or other document that consists primarily of graphic representations or pictures.

"map" means a document that is a cartographic representation and includes a topographic, hydrographic, military, cadastral, aeronautic or survey map, cartogram, chart or plan.

"photographic record or document" means

(a) a collection of photographs attached or mounted to form a unit, other than a printed book such as a photograph album; or

(b) a collection of loose or unattached photographs that clearly form a single unit of visual information. A photograph may take the form of a daguerrotype, ambrotype, calotype, talbotype, tintype, transparency, cinegraph or hologram.

"pictorial record or document" means

(a) a bound or attached collection of designs such as a sketch book; or

(b) a collection of loose or unattached designs that clearly form a single unit of visual information, such as a set of architectural plans or blueprints.

"printed atlas or cartographic book" means a bound work with an established date of printing and includes each volume of a set of bound works issued under a single title.

"printed book of photographs" or "printed book of pictures or designs" means a bound work with an established date of printing and includes each volume of a set of bound works issued under a single title.

[SOR/95-170, s. 13; SOR/97-159, s. 20.]

## Cartography

**4.** Cartographic objects if they were made in the territory that is now Canada, were made outside that territory by a person who at any time ordinarily resided in that territory or were made outside that territory and relate to the history or national life of Canada, namely,

(a) a map, cartographic record or document that has a fair market value in Canada of more than $1,000;

(b) a collection of associated maps or cartographic records or documents that has a fair market value in Canada of more than $2,000;

(c) a printed atlas or cartographic book or a set of atlases or cartographic books under a single title that has a fair market value in Canada of more than $2,000; and

(d) a collection of associated printed atlases or cartographic books that has a fair market value in Canada of more than $10,000.

[SOR/80-855, s. 3; SOR/95-170, s. 14; SOR/97-159, s. 20.]

## Photography

**5.** Photographic objects if they were made in the territory that is now Canada, were made outside that territory by a person who at any time ordinarily resided in that territory or were made outside that territory and relate to the history or national life of Canada, namely,

(a) a photograph, photographic record or document or a cinematographic film that has a fair market value in Canada of more than $1,000;

(b)   a collection of associated photographs, photographic records or documents or cinematographic films that has a fair market value in Canada of more than $2,000;

(c)   a printed book of photographs or a set of printed books of photographs under a single title that has a fair market value in Canada of more than $2,500; and

(d)   a collection of associated printed books of photographs that has a fair market value in Canada of more than $15,000.

[SOR/95-170, s. 15; SOR/97-159, s. 20.]

## *Iconography*

**6.** Iconographic objects if they were made in the territory that is now Canada, were made outside that territory by a person who at any time ordinarily resided in that territory or were made outside that territory and relate to the history or national life of Canada, namely,

(a)   a design, pictorial record or document that has a fair market value in Canada of more than $1,000;

(b)   a collection of associated designs or pictorial records or documents that has a fair market value in Canada of more than $2,000;

(c)   a printed book of pictures or designs or a set of printed books of pictures or designs under a single title that has a fair market value in Canada of more than $2,000; and

(d)   a collection of associated printed books of pictures or designs that has a fair market value in Canada of more than $10,000.

[SOR/80-855, s. 4; SOR/95-170, s. 16; SOR/97-159, s. 20.]

## SOUND RECORDINGS

### *Interpretation*

**7.** (1) In this section and sections 8 and 9, "sound recording" means

(a)   an object in any medium on which sound has been registered by mechanical or electrical means so that the sound may be reproduced and played back;

(b)   objects of recorded sound issued in a set under a single title, irrespective of the date or dates of recording of the individual units in the set; and

(c)   a collection of physically separated objects of recorded sound where the collection clearly forms a single unit.

(2) A sound recording may take the form of a cylinder, disc, belt, spool, cassette or cartridge.

[SOR/86-329, s. 14; SOR/97-159, s. 20.]

## Sound Recordings

**8.** Sound recordings if they were made in the territory that is now Canada, were made outside that territory by a person who at any time ordinarily resided in that territory or were made outside that territory and relate to the history or national life of Canada, namely,

(a) a sound recording or a document of recorded sound that has a fair market value in Canada of more than $1,000; and

(b) a collection of associated sound recordings or documents of recorded sound that has a fair market value in Canada of more than $2,000.

[SOR/97-159, s. 20.]

## General

**9.** Objects that are made outside the territory that is now Canada, namely,

(a) a graphic or textual object, other than a design or a photograph, that has a fair market value in Canada of more than $10,000;

(b) a collection of associated graphic or textual objects, other than photographs, that has a fair market value in Canada of more than $25,000;

(c) a design that has a fair market value in Canada of more than $3,000;

(d) a photograph that has a fair market value in Canada of more than $2,000; and

(e) a collection of associated photographs that has a fair market value in Canada of more than $10,000.

[SOR/97-159, s. 20.]

# GROUP VIII

# MUSICAL INSTRUMENTS

## Interpretation

**1.** In this Group, "musical instrument" means an object that is a device designed to produce sounds in melodic or harmonic combination.

[SOR/97-159, s. 20.]

## Musical Instruments

**2.** A musical instrument that was made within or outside the territory that is now Canada, that is identified with a prominent person, institution or memorable event that relates to the history or national life of Canada, and that has a fair market value in Canada of more than $3,000.

[SOR/97-159, s. 20.]

**3.** A musical instrument, other than a musical instrument described in section 2, that was made within the territory that is now Canada or made outside that territory by a person who at any time ordinarily resided in that territory and that has a fair market value in Canada of more than $5,000.

[SOR/97-159, s. 20.]

**4.** A musical instrument, other than a musical instrument described in section 2 or 3, that was made outside the territory that is now Canada and that has a fair market value in Canada of more than $50,000.

[SOR/97-159, s. 20.]

# CULTURAL PROPERTY EXPORT REGULATIONS

## (C.R.C., c. 449)

*Short Title*

**1.** These Regulations may be cited as the Cultural Property Export Regulations.

*Interpretation*

**2.** In these Regulations,

"Act" means the *Cultural Property Export and Import Act*;

"object" means any object or class of objects described in subsection 3(2) of the Act that is included in the Canadian Cultural Property Export Control List;

"public record" means any original documentary material made by or received by a public authority or the predecessor in the territory that is now Canada of that public authority that contains information relating to the organization, function, procedure, policy or activity of that public authority.

*Application for an Export Permit*

**3.** An application for an export permit to export any object shall be made in the form set out in Schedule I, signed by the applicant and forwarded to a permit officer.

**4.** The following information shall be furnished and forwarded with an application referred to in section 3 in respect of the object to which the application applies:

(a)  the name, address and telephone number of the applicant;

(b)  where the applicant is not the owner of the object, the name, address and telephone number of the owner;

(c)  the name, address and telephone number of the shipper or consignor;

(d)  the name, address and telephone number of the consignee;

(e)  subject to section 6, a description of the object in sufficient detail to clearly identify it;

(f)  the proposed date of export of the object;

(g)  details in respect of the purpose of exporting the object;

(h)  the fair market value in Canada or, if sold, the selling price of the object;

(i)  any other information required in the application form;

(j)  any information requested by the permit officer to whom the application is made or by any expert examiner to whom the application has been referred or by the Minister where, in his opinion, the information furnished by the applicant requires clarification or the identification of the object is not in sufficient detail; and

(k)    documentary evidence indicating the proposed destination of the object.

**5.** (1) Subject to subsections (3) and (4), there shall be included with an application for an export permit in respect of an object a photograph or, in the case of an object that is a document, a photograph or photostatic copy of the object, satisfactory to the Minister, where the application is in respect of

(a)    an object described in paragraph 2(a), (b) or (e) of Group I of the Control List;

(b)    an object described in paragraph 3(a), (b), (c) or (d) of Group I of the Control List;

(c)    an object or collection of objects described in item 4 of Group I of the Control List;

(d)    an object described in any item in Group II, III, IV, V or VI of the Control List;

(e)    an object described in paragraph 2(a) or (b), 3(a) or (b), 4(a) or (b) or 5(a) or (b) of Group VII of the Control List; and

(f)    an object, other than a printed book, described in item 7 of Group VII of the Control List.

(2) Subject to subsection (4), there shall be included with an application for an export permit in respect of a collection of objects described in paragraph 2(c) of Group I of the Control List a photograph, satisfactory to the Minister, of each specimen in the collection.

(3) For the purposes of subsection (1), where an object described in paragraph (1)(e) or (f) contains more than 12 pages, the application for an export permit for that object need include only photograph or photostatic copies satisfactory to the Minister of 12 pages that are representative of the object as a whole.

(4) Subsections (1) and (2) do not apply to an application for an export permit in respect of the following objects:

(a)    an object referred to in paragraph 6(a) of the Act, where the object was imported into Canada for a temporary purpose, other than resale, if the application includes

    (i)    a permit or document described in subparagraph 6(c)(i),

    (ii)    an ATA Carnet described in subparagraph 6(c)(iii), or

    (iii)    a declaration described in subparagraph 6(c)(iv);

(b)    an object referred to in paragraph 6(b) of the Act if the application includes the reference number used by the institution or public authority to identify or catalogue the object; and

(c)    an object referred to in paragraph 6(c) of the Act, where the object is to be exported by an institution or public authority if the application includes the inventory number, accession number or other reference number used by the institution or public authority to identify or catalogue the object.

**6.** Where an application is being made for an export permit in respect of an object to which section 6 of the Act applies, the object may be identified in the application by setting out

(a)    the name of the object;

  (b)   the name of the maker of the object; and

  (c)   the reference number

      (i)   of

          (A)   the export permit issued by the government of the foreign state where that state authorized the exportation of the object into Canada, or

          (B)   the shipping document covering the entry into Canada of the object that clearly identifies the object

          if a copy of the export permit or shipping document, as the case may be, or a translation thereof in one of the official languages, is forwarded with the application,

     (ii)   issued by an institution or public authority in Canada to identify or catalogue the object,

    (iii)   of an ATA Carnet referred to in the Display Goods Temporary Importation Regulations that was issued in respect of the object on the last occasion the object was imported into Canada, or

    (iv)   of the appropriate import declaration made by the person who imported the object on the last occasion the object was imported into Canada.

**7.** Where an application is being made for an export permit in respect of an object to which paragraph 6(a) of the Act applies, documentary evidence or a signed declaration by the applicant is required to establish that the object in respect of which the application is made was imported into Canada within the 35 years immediately preceding the date of the application and was not exported from Canada under a permit issued under the Act prior to that importation.

**8.** Where a permit officer refers an application for an export permit to an expert examiner for consideration under subsection 7(3) of the Act, the expert examiner may, for the purpose of making a determination under section 8 of the Act, require the applicant to produce the object for his examination.

*Export Permits*

**9.** An export permit shall be issued in the form set out in Part II of Schedule I.

**10.** (1) An export permit shall only be valid for a period equal to 90 days calculated from the day the permit was issued.

(2) Where a person to whom an export permit has been issued requires

  (a)   the reinstatement of the permit where the permit has lapsed or has been suspended or cancelled, or

  (b)   an amendment to the permit,

he shall forward the permit to the Minister with a letter requesting the reinstatement or amendment, as the case may be, and the reasons therefor.

## Terms and Conditions

**11.** Where an export permit has been issued under the Act, the person to whom the permit was issued shall, at the request of the Minister, provide any information that may be necessary to verify any statement made by that person in the application for the export permit and any information to establish

(a) the identity of the consignee referred to in the application;

(b) whether or not the object referred to in the export permit was delivered to the consignee; and

(c) where the object was sold, the selling price of the object.

## Removal of an Object from Canada under Paragraph 6(C) of the Act

**12.** (1) A permit officer shall issue an export permit under paragraph 6(c) of the Act where the applicant for the permit certifies and establishes to that officer's satisfaction that the object is to be removed from Canada for any of the following purposes:

(a) appraisal;

(b) authentication;

(c) conservation;

(d) exhibition;

(e) on loan;

(f) processing;

(g) research;

(h) restoration or repair; or

(i) as personal effects.

(2) The length of time for which an object may be removed from Canada under an export permit issued pursuant to paragraph 6(c) of the Act shall be for a period not exceeding five years.

(3) A person who applies for an export permit to export an object under paragraph 6(c) of the Act shall include in his application for the permit a written undertaking that he will return the object for which the permit was issued to Canada within the time prescribed in the permit.

**13.** Where an object is removed from Canada under an export permit issued under paragraph 6(c) of the Act, the person to whom the permit was issued shall, at any time on the request of the Minister, forward to the Minister the following information:

(a) details in respect of the place where the object is located or has been located during the period it is removed from Canada; and

(b) where the object is damaged, destroyed or lost during the period it is removed from Canada, the details in respect of such damage, destruction or loss.

## Notice of Return of an Object

**14.** (1) Where an object has been removed from Canada under an export permit issued under paragraph 6(c) of the Act, the person to whom the permit was issued shall, within 15 days following the day the object is returned to Canada, forward to the Minister

(a) a Notice of Return in the form set out in Schedule II; and

(b) proof satisfactory to the Minister that the object described in the Notice of Return is the object for which the export permit was issued.

(2) The following information shall be furnished in the Notice of Return referred to in subsection (1):

(a) the exporter's name, address and telephone number;

(b) the reference number of the export permit issued in respect of the object; and

(c) documentary evidence indicating

   (i) the port of entry, and

   (ii) the day of entry,

of the object into Canada.

## Objects Requiring Copies to be Deposited

**15.** The following classes of objects are prescribed for the purposes of section 11 of the Act:

(a) any original archive of national historic interest if it was made in the territory that is now Canada, made out of the territory by a person who at any time normally resided in the territory or made out of the territory and relates to the history or national life of Canada, namely,

   (i) a textual record or document in manuscript form,

   (ii) a map, cartographic record or document in manuscript form,

   (iii) a map, cartographic record or document in printed form made prior to the year 1850,

   (iv) a design, pictorial record or document in manuscript form,

   (v) a design, pictorial record or document in printed form made prior to the year 1880, or

   (vi) a photograph, photographic record or document made prior to the year 1900; and

(b) any original public record made or received by a public authority that is a

   (i) document in graphic or textual form,

   (ii) photograph,

   (iii) cinematographic film, or

   (iv) sound recording.

## Shipping Requirements

**16.** Every exporter of an object or his authorized agent shall, prior to exporting the object described in the export permit issued in respect of that object, give the export permit to the collector of customs at the port of export.

**17.** Where an export permit in respect of an object has been issued and the exporter has indicated that the object is to be sent by means of the Canada Post Office, the exporter shall give the export permit to the postmaster at the time of posting.

## Application for a General Permit

**18.** An application for a general permit referred to in subsection 14(1) of the Act shall be made in the form set out in Schedule III, signed by the applicant and forwarded to the Minister.

**19.** The following information shall be furnished and forwarded with an application referred to in section 18:

(a)    the name, address and telephone number of the applicant;

(b)    the detailed reasons for the application setting out

    (i)    the area of the applicant's business specialization, and

    (ii)    the inconvenience, if any, to obtain an export permit in respect of the individual export of objects;

(c)    a list describing any object exported under an export permit by the applicant during the six-month period preceding the date of the application together with the details in respect of each permit issued during that period;

(d)    the details of any current general permit held by the applicant;

(e)    the volume of the applicant's commercial activities in respect of the purchase and sale of any objects;

(f)    the number of employees of the applicant, the distance between the applicant's place of business and the nearest office of a permit officer;

(g)    any information requested by the Minister where, in his opinion, the information furnished by the applicant requires clarification; and

(h)    any other information required in the application form.

**20.** A general permit referred to in subsection 14(1) of the Act shall be issued in the form set out in Schedule IV.

## Cultural Property General Permit Declaration

**21.** No person shall export any object under a general permit issued to him under subsection 14(1) of the Act unless that person or a person authorized to sign a Cultural Property General Permit Declaration by the general permit under which the object is to be exported, prior to exporting the object, completes a Cultural Property General Permit Declaration in respect of that object.

**22.** (1) A Cultural Property General Permit Declaration referred to in section 21 shall be in the form set out in Schedule V, which form shall be signed by the person referred to in section 21 and shall state that the object intended for export from Canada is an object authorized to be exported from Canada under a general permit and that the conditions set out in that general permit have been complied with.

(2) Where an object is to be exported under a general permit issued under subsection 14(1) of the Act, the declaration referred to in section 21

(a)  shall be given to the postmaster, where the object is to be sent by means of the Canada Post Office; or

(b)  shall be given to the collector of customs at the port of export, where the object is to be sent by means other than the Canada Post Office.

*Lost Permits*

**23.** Where a permit issued under the Act has been lost or destroyed, the person to whom it was issued may request from the Minister a certified true copy of the permit and shall, in so requesting,

(a)  submit a statutory declaration stating whether the permit has been lost or destroyed and an explanation of the lo ss or destruction; and

(b)  in the case of a permit that has been lost, submit an undertaking to return to the Minister, without delay, the original permit, if it is found.

SCHEDULE I                                      Part I

(*ss. 3 and 9*)

Secretary    Secrétariat        APPLICATION FOR CULTURAL
of State     d'État             PROPERTY EXPORT PERMIT

Movable Cultural Property
Ottawa, Canada K1A 0M5

| Applicant's Ref. No. | Date |
| --- | --- |

Applicant (Applicant must be a resident of Canada)

Name _____

Address _____       Telephone _____

Owner (if other than Applicant)

Name _____

Address _____       Telephone _____

Shipper or Consignor

Name _____

Address _____       Telephone _____

Consignee (attach documentary evidence of proposed final destination)

Name _____

Address _____       Telephone _____

Proposed date of export of object _____

EXPORT INFORMATION

TEMPORARY EXPORT

☐ Object is being exported for a temporary purpose such as research, processing, exhibition, restoration, conservation, repair, appraisal or authentication.

Approximate date of return of object to Canada _____

☐ Object is being exported on personal loan or as personal effects of a resident of Canada temporarily residing out of Canada.

Approximate date of return of object to Canada _____

**PERMANENT EXPORT**

☐ Object is being exported after import on a temporary basis as a loan to an institution or public authority in Canada from a non-resident of Canada at the time the loan was made.

Borrower, if other than Applicant

Name _____

_____         _____
Address                                          Telephone

☐ Object is being exported after import on a temporary basis for any other reason.

Explain _____

_____

Object is being exported

☐ as a gift or bequest

☐ on consignment

☐ as a result of a sale or firm offer (attach documentary evidence)

☐ for another reason: Explain _____

_____

Has a prior application for an export permit been refused for the object described in this application?

☐ Yes          ☐ No

If yes give date of Notice of Refusal _____

Was the object which is the subject of this application imported into Canada within the 35 years immediately preceding the date of this application?

☐ Yes          ☐ No

If yes attach a signed declaration to that effect or documentary evidence.

Was the object previously exported from Canada under a permit issued under the Act prior to that importation?

☐ Yes          ☐ No

If yes indicate _____     _____     _____
                Type of permit            Permit No               Date of Issue

I certify that to the best of my knowledge all information given in this application (including my accompanying schedules) is correctly stated. I understand that if an export permit is granted, the permit shall be used solely for the export of an object of which I am the owner or the object of a person named above as owner for whom I am authorized to act in this transaction as the sole responsible representative. I am aware that, if so required by the Minister, I must produce proof within a reasonable time, that the said object was duly delivered at the destination named in this application. Where the permit is granted to export the object for a temporary purpose, I undertake that the object will be returned to Canada within the time specified in the permit.

 

_____<br>Signature

Part II

| | |
|---|---|
| ▮✦ Secretary  Secrétariat<br>of State  d'État | APPLICATION FOR CULTURAL PROPERTY EXPORT<br>PERMIT. THE ORIGINAL BECOMES THE EXPORT<br>PERMIT WHEN APPROVED BY A PERMIT OFFICER |

CULTURAL PROPERTY
EXPORT PERMIT

ORIGINAL

Movable Cultural Property
Ottawa, Canada K1A 0M5

| Applicant's Ref. No. | Date |
|---|---|
| | |

Applicant

Name ————————————————————————

| Address | Telephone |
|---|---|

is authorized to export from any port in Canada, or by mail, within a period of ninety days from the date of issue of this permit, to:

Port and Country

Consignee at final destination

Name ————————————————————————————

| Address | Telephone |
|---|---|

Via (consignor or shipper if other than Applicant)

Name ————————————————————————————

| Address | Telephone |
|---|---|

the object detailed below:

IDENTIFICATION OF OBJECT

| (1) Quantity | (2) Description | (3) Photograph or copy<br>is attached | (4) Total Fair Market<br>Value F.O.B. | (5) Control List<br>Reference |
|---|---|---|---|---|
| 1 | 2<br><br><br>Reference number or identification<br>number where applicable ———— (See Regulations) | | 3  4 | 5 |

(if above space is insufficient continue on a separate sheet in 5 copies)

173

Where an application for permanent export concerns a manuscript, record or document, is it subject to a deposit copy requirement (see Regulations)?

☐ Yes                          ☐ No

Permit: The export of the object described above is subject to the conditions set out in the *Cultural Property Export and Import Act* and the regulations made thereunder.

### FOR PERMIT OFFICER ONLY

☐ Export Permit for Temporary Export issued.
   Valid (if used before expiry date) until

—————  —————  —————
Day          Month          Year

Export Permit for Permanent Export issued

☐ after loan to institution or public
   authority by non-resident of Canada

☐ under paragraph 6 (*a*) of the Act
   (imported within 35 years)

☐ after reference to Control List

☐ on advice of Expert Examiner

☐ on direction of Review Board

Note: Where an application concerns a manuscript, record or document subject to a deposit requirement, has the copy been deposited?

☐ Yes              ☐ No

Date of "Notice of Refusal"    —————

Appeal Deadline    —————

—————————————
Signature of Permit Officer

Permit Number    —————

Date of Issue    —————

Expiry Date    —————
(if unused)

—————————————
Signature of Permit Officer

| Checked for Collector of Customs before forwarding to Movable Cultural Property | | Date Stamp of Port of Validation | |
|---|---|---|---|
| | | | |

Secretary    Secrétariat
of State     d'État

SCHEDULE II
(s. 14)

NOTICE OF RETURN TO CANADA

(to be completed in duplicate by Applicants issued a permit for temporary export)

This is to certify that the object described in export permit No. _____ was returned to Canada on the _____ _____ day of _____ 19____ .

Supporting evidence is attached ☐ or see Customs' stamp, port of entry below ☐.

The undersigned hereby certifies that the information given in this statement and any accompanying documentation is true and correct.

_____     _____
            Signature                              Date

RETURN TO: Movable Cultural Property
Ottawa, Canada K1A 0M5

Where signing authority other than Applicant identified on original application, or if address and telephone changed, add

Name _____

_____
                              Address

_____
      Telephone

| Applicant's Ref. No. | Date | Customs' stamp of port of entry | |
|---|---|---|---|
| | | | _____ |
| | | | For Canada Customs |

**Secretary** **Secrétariat**
**of State** **d'État**

SCHEDULE III / ANNEXE III
*(s./art. 18)*

APPLICATION FOR CULTURAL / DEMANDE DE
PROPERTY GENERAL PERMIT / LICENCE GÉNÉRALE

| Movable Cultural Property | Biens culturels mobiliers | Applicant's Ref. No. | Date |
| Ottawa, Canada K1A 0M5 | Ottawa, Canada K1A 0M5 | N° de référence | |

| Applicant (Applicant must be a resident of Canada) | Name of Business — Nom de l'entreprise |
| Requérant (le requérant doit être un résident du Canada) | |

| Address — Adresse | Tel. — Tél. |

Applicant is owner?   ☐ Yes ☐ No          Le requérant est-il le propriétaire?   ☐ Oui ☐ Non
If answer No, explain:                     Dans la négative, expliquez:

1. This application is in respect of
   (a) the issue of a General Permit under subsection 14(1) of the Act to export the objects described in section 3, or
   (b) the renewal of a current General Permit.
   *Note:* Where the application is in respect of the issue of a General Permit, paragraphs (a) of sections 2 to 7 are required to be completed by the applicant. Where the application is in respect of the renewal of a current General Permit, paragraphs (b) of sections 2 to 7 are required to be completed by the applicant.

1. La présente formule sert à demander
   a) la délivrance d'une licence générale prévue au paragraphe 14(1) de la Loi, en vue d'exporter les objets décrits à l'article 3, ou
   b) le renouvellement d'une licence générale valide.
   *Remarque:* Pour demander la délivrance d'une licence générale, le requérant doit remplir l'alinéa a) des articles 2 à 7. Pour demander le renouvellement d'une licence générale valide, le requérant doit remplir l'alinéa b) des articles 2 à 7.

2. (a) With reference to the export permits you have been issued (if applicable), indicate the number of objects included in the Canadian Cultural Property Export Control List you have exported from Canada over the six month period immediately prior to this application _____ (attach descriptive list of objects).
   (b) Applicant is holder of a valid General Permit

      No. _____

      Issued _____

2. a) Indiquez (le cas échéant) le nombre d'objets compris dans la nomenclature des biens culturels canadiens à exportation contrôlée que vous avez exportés du Canada grâce à une licence d'exportation ordinaire au cours des six mois précédant la présente demande: _____ (joindre une liste descriptive de ces objets).
   b) Le requérant détient une licence générale valide

      N° _____

      Date de délivrance _____

A descriptive list of objects exported under the authority of the General Permit during the eleven month period following the date of its issue is attached (a descriptive list of the balance of objects exported under the permit to be forwarded within 15 days of the expiry date of the permit).

Ci-joint la liste descriptive des objets exportés sous le couvert de cette licence générale au cours des onze mois qui ont suivi la date de sa délivrance. (La liste des objets exportés sous le couvert de la même licence pendant le douzième mois doit être expédiée dans les 15 jours suivant la date d'expiration de la licence).

3. (a) Explain briefly why your present volume of exports following the procedure required for the issue of export permits is causing inconvenience.

3. a) Expliquez brièvement pourquoi le volume actuel de vos exportations pose des problèmes, quand vous avez à demander une licence pour chaque envoi.

_____

_____

_____

_____

(b) Volume of exports has

b) Indiquez si le volume de vos exportations

□ remained constant — est resté le même     □ increased -- a augmenté     □ decreased — a diminué.

4. (a) Describe your area of business specialization and explain briefly how the specialization has been the cause of inconvenience where objects are exported.

4. a) Décrivez votre domaine de spécialisation professionnelle et expliquez brièvement en quoi cette spécialisation pose des problèmes en cas d'exportation d'objets.

_____

_____

_____

_____

(b) Area of specialization is unchanged, □ or is now as follows:

b) Le domaine de spécialisation n'a pas changé □ , est maintenant le suivant:

_____

_____

_____

5. (a) Indicate the number of persons engaged in your business _____

5. a) Nombre de personnes travaillant dans l'entreprise _____

(b) Number of persons engaged in business is unchanged □ , or is now as follows: _____

b) Le nombre de personnes travaillant dans l'entreprise est resté le même □ , est maintenant de: _____

6. (*a*) Where the location of place of business is a factor in obtaining export permits, state the distance from your place of business to the closest Permit Officer authorized to issue export permits and explain why your location is a factor.

6. *a*) Au cas où l'emplacement de l'entreprise rend difficile l'obtention des licences, indiquez la distance entre l'entreprise et le plus proche agent autorisé à délivrer des licences, et expliquez en quoi ce facteur pose des problèmes.

---
---
---
---

(*b*) If location of place of business was a factor, address is unchanged ☐ , or is now as follows:

*b*) Si l'emplacement de l'entreprise était source de difficultés, indiquez si l'adresse de votre entreprise est toujours la même ☐ ; si elle a changé, nouvelle adresse:

---
---
---

7. (*a*) Describe briefly any special circumstances or factors other than the location of your place of business that cause inconvenience in the exportation of objects that would be alleviated by the issue of a General Permit.

7. *a*) Décrivez brièvement toute autre condition ou facteur particulier, emplacement mis à part, qui pose des problèmes pour l'exportation d'objets et que la délivrance d'une licence générale permettrait d'éviter.

---
---
---
---

(*b*) Special circumstances remain unchanged ☐ , or are now as follows:

*b*) Les conditions particulières n'ont pas changé ☐ , sont maintenant les suivantes:

---
---
---

8. Where a General Permit is issued as a result of this application, the following persons whose name, title, and signature are set out hereunder are authorized to act on my behalf to complete a Cultural Property General Permit Declaration.

8. Si, en réponse à la présente demande, j'obtiens une licence générale, j'autorise les personnes dont les nom et prénoms, le titre et la signature figurent ci-dessous, à remplir en mon nom la déclaration d'exportation en vertu d'une licence générale.

Full name – Nom et prénoms     Title – Titre     Signature

| Full name — Nom et prénoms | Title — Titre | Signature |
| --- | --- | --- |
| Full name — Nom et prénoms | Title — Titre | Signature |

9. If, as a result of the present application I am issued a Cultural Property General Permit, I agree to abide by the terms and conditions under which the permit is issued, and in particular, I agree:

(a) to apply, except in the circumstances outlined in section 6 of the Act, for an Export Permit before exporting any object included in the Control List which, in my judgment, might conform to one of the criteria of outstanding significance set out in paragraph 8(3)(a) of the Act and national importance set out in paragraph 8(3)(b) of the Act;

(b) to ensure that a Cultural Property General Permit Declaration accompanies each consignment for export containing objects exported under the authority of the General Permit; and

(c) to provide the Minister within 15 days of the expiry date of the permit a descriptive list of all objects exported under the permit during the 12 month period following its issue.

9. Si, en réponse à la présente demande, j'obtiens une licence générale, je m'engage à respecter les conditions auxquelles est subordonnée la délivrance de cette licence, et en particulier:

a) à demander, sauf dans les conditions énoncées à l'article 6 de la Loi, une licence avant d'exporter un objet compris dans la nomenclature et qui, à mon avis, est susceptible de répondre au critère d'intérêt exceptionnel prévu à l'alinéa 8(3) a) de la Loi ou au critère d'importance nationale prévu à l'alinéa 8(3)b) de la Loi;

b) à vérifier qu'une déclaration d'exportation en vertu d'une licence générale accompagne chaque envoi destiné à l'exportation et contenant des biens culturels visés dans cette licence générale; et

c) à faire parvenir au Ministre, dans les 15 jours qui suivent la date d'expiration de la licence, une liste descriptive de tous les objets exportés sous le couvert de cette licence, au cours des 12 mois suivant sa délivrance.

---

Signature of Applicant — Signature du requérant

Dated at            this            day of

Fait à _____ ce _____ le jour de _____ 19____

| Secretary<br>of State | Secrétariat<br>d'État | SCHEDULE IV / ANNEXE IV<br>(s./art. 20) | |
| --- | --- | --- | --- |
| | | CULTURAL PROPERTY / | BIENS CULTURELS |
| | | GENERAL PERMIT / | LICENCE GÉNÉRALE |
| Movable Cultural Property<br>Ottawa, Canada K1A 0M5 | | Biens culturels mobiliers<br>Ottawa, Canada K1A 0M5 | |

Pursuant to subsection 14(1) of the *Cultural Property Export and Import Act* and the Cultural Property Export Regulations, the Secretary of State hereby issues to

a General Permit to export from Canada objects included in the Canadian Cultural Property Export Control List subject to the terms and conditions set out below.

En vertu du paragraphe 14(1) de la *Loi sur l'exportation et l'importation de biens culturels*, et de son règlement d'application, le Secrétaire d'État délivre par la présente à

une licence générale l'autorisant à exporter du Canada, dans les conditions énoncées ci-après, des objets compris dans la nomenclature des biens culturels canadiens à exportation contrôlée.

---

The following persons who have been authorized by (name of general permit holder) to sign on his behalf may make the declaration required by section 21 of the Regulations

Les personnes suivantes que (nom du détenteur de la licence générale) a autorisées à signer en son nom, sont habilitées à remplir la déclaration visée à l'article 21 du règlement

| Full name – Nom et prénoms | Title – Titre |
| --- | --- |
| Full name – Nom et prénoms | Title – Titre |
| Full name – Nom et prénoms | Title – Titre |
| Full name – Nom et prénoms | Title – Titre |

General Permit No. _____    Licence générale nᵒ _____

Issued at Ottawa this _____ day of _____ 19_____    Délivrée à Ottawa ce _____ ᵉ jour de _____ 19_____

Expiry date _____    Date d'expiration _____

For the Minister – Pour le Ministre

_____

■✹ Secretary   Secrétariat
   of State     d'État

SCHEDULE V / ANNEXE V
*(s./art. 22)*

CULTURAL PROPERTY / DÉCLARATION
GENERAL PERMIT / D'EXPORTATION EN VERTU
DECLARATION / D'UNE LICENCE GÉNÉRALE

Movable Cultural Property          Biens culturels mobiliers
Ottawa, Canada K1A 0M5             Ottawa, Canada K1A 0M5

TO BE COMPLETED ONLY BY A PERSON AU-
THORIZED BY A GENERAL PERMIT TO SIGN A
GENERAL PERMIT DECLARATION.

I declare that the objects described in the attached shipping
documents that are intended for export from Canada are
exported under the authority of General Permit No. _____
and meet all the conditions set out in the Permit.

RÉSERVÉ À LA PERSONNE QU'UNE LICENCE GÉNÉ-
RALE AUTORISE EXPLICITEMENT À SIGNER UNE
TELLE DÉCLARATION.

Je soussigné déclare que les objets décrits dans les documents d'expédition ci-joints et destinés à être exportés hors
du Canada, sont exportés sous le couvert de la licence
générale n⁰ _____ dont ils remplissent toutes les conditions.

Consignee at final destination:

Consignataire à la destination finale:

_____          _____
                    Name – Nom                                        Tel. – Tél.

_____
                    Address – Adresse

General Permit No. – Licence générale n⁰ _____   Date of issue – Date de délivrance _____

Issued in the name of – Délivrée au nom de _____

who is exporting the objects as owner. – qui exporte les objets à titre de propriétaire.

                                        _____
                                        Authorized signature – Fondé de signature

Dated at                this                    day of
Fait à _____  ce _____  le jour de _____ 19_____

PLEASE ATTACH THIS DECLARATION TO SHIPPING DOCUMENTS

JOINDRE LA PRÉSENTE DÉCLARATION AUX DOCUMENTS D'EXPÉDITION

FOR CANADA CUSTOMS – RÉSERVÉ AUX DOUANES CANADIENNES

|  | Date Stamp of Port of Validation. | Timbre dateur du port de validation. |
|---|---|---|
| After customs clearance this Declaration to be returned to:    Après le dédouanement, retourner cette déclaration à l'adresse suivante: | | |
| Secretary of State Movable Cultural Property Ottawa, Canada K1A 0M5    Secrétariat d'État Biens culturels mobiliers Ottawa, Canada K1A 0M5 | | |

QUEEN'S PRINTER FOR CANADA © IMPRIMEUR DE LA REINE POUR LE CANADA
OTTAWA, 1978

# ORDER DESIGNATING THE MINISTER OF COMMUNICATIONS AS MINISTER FOR PURPOSES OF THE ACT

## (SI/93-228)

P.C. 1993-1980 2 December, 1993

His Excellency the Governor General in Council, on the recommendation of the Prime Minister, pursuant to the definition "Minister" in section 2 of the Cultural Property Export and Import Act, is pleased hereby

(a) to revoke Order in Council P.C. 1993-1453 of June 25, 1993*; and

(b) to designate the Minister of Communications, a member of the Queen's Privy Council for Canada, as the Minister for the purposes of that Act.

* SI/93-107, 1993 *Canada Gazette* Part II, p. 3199

# PROPOSED AMENDMENTS TO THE INCOME TAX ACT

[**Note:** the following are excerpts pertaining to Charities law from the Department of Finance document, "**Legislative Proposals Relating to Income Tax**" released July 2005. The document is available online at <http//:www.fin.gc.ca/drleg/ITA05l_e.html>.]

**59. (1) The Act is amended by adding the following after section 38:**

**38.1 Allocation of gain re certain gifts** — If a taxpayer is entitled to an amount of an advantage in respect of a gift of property described in paragraph 38(*a*.1) or (*a*.2),

(*a*) those paragraphs apply only to that proportion of the taxpayer's capital gain in respect of the gift that the eligible amount of the gift is of the taxpayer's proceeds of disposition in respect of the gift; and

(*b*) paragraph 38(*a*) applies to the extent that the taxpayer's capital gain in respect of the gift exceeds the amount of the capital gain to which paragraph 38(*a*.1) or (*a*.2) applies.

**(2) Subsection (1) applies to gifts made after December 20, 2002.**

**60. (1) Paragraph 40(1.01)(*c*) of the Act is replaced by the following:**

(*c*) the amount that the taxpayer claims in prescribed form filed with the taxpayer's return of income for the particular year, not exceeding the eligible amount of the gift, where the taxpayer is not deemed by subsection 118.1(13) to have made a gift of property before the end of the particular year as a consequence of a disposition of the security by the donee or as a consequence of the security ceasing to be a non-qualifying security of the taxpayer before the end of the particular year.

**(2) Paragraph 40(2)(a) of the Act is amended by striking out the word "or" at the end of subparagraph (i), by adding the word "or" at the end of subparagraph (ii) and by adding the following after subparagraph (ii):**

(iii) the purchaser of the property sold is a partnership in which the taxpayer was, immediately after the sale, a majority interest partner;

**61. (1) The portion of subsection 43(2) of the Act before the formula in paragraph (*a*) is replaced by the following:**

(2) **Ecological gifts** — For the purposes of subsection (1) and section 53, where at any time a taxpayer disposes of a covenant or an easement to which land is subject or, in the case of land in the Province of Quebec, a real servitude, in circumstances where subsection 110.1(5) or 118.1(12) applies,

(*a*) the portion of the adjusted cost base to the taxpayer of the land immediately before the disposition that can reasonably be regarded as attributable to the covenant, easement or real servitude, as the case may be, is deemed to be equal to the amount determined by the formula

**(2) Subsection (1) applies to gifts made after December 20, 2002.**

**62. (1) The portion of subsection 43.1(1) of the Act before paragraph (a) is replaced by the following:**

**43.1** (1) **Life estates in real property** — Notwithstanding any other provision of this Act, if at any time a taxpayer disposes of a remainder interest in real property (except as a result of a transaction to which subsection 73(3) would otherwise apply or by way of a gift to a donee described in the definition **"total charitable gifts"**, **"total Crown gifts"** or **"total ecological gifts"** in subsection 118.1(1)) to a person or partnership and retains a life estate or an estate pur autre vie (in this section called the "life estate") in the property, the taxpayer is deemed

**(2) Subsection (1) applies to dispositions that occur after February 27, 1995.**

**65. (2) Subparagraph 53(2)(c)(iii) of the Act is replaced by the following:**

(iii) any amount deemed by subsection 110.1(4) or 118.1(8) to have been the eligible amount of a gift made, or by subsection 127(4.2) to have been an amount contributed, by the taxpayer by reason of the taxpayer's membership in the partnership at the end of a fiscal period of the partnership ending before that time,

**(5) Subsection (2) applies in respect of gifts and contributions made after December 20, 2002.**

**77. (1) Paragraph 69(1)(b) of the English version of the Act is amended by striking out the word "and" at the end of subparagraph (iii).**

**(2) Subsection (2) applies to dispositions that occur after December 23, 1998.**

**88. (4) Paragraph 88(1)(e.6) of the Act is replaced by the following:**

(e.6) if a subsidiary has made a gift in a taxation year (in this section referred to as the "gift year"), for the purposes of computing the amount deductible under section 110.1 by the parent for its taxation years that end after the subsidiary was wound up, the parent is deemed to have made a gift, in each of its taxation years in which a gift year of the subsidiary ended, equal to the amount, if any, by which the total of all amounts, each of which is the amount of a gift or, in the case of a gift made after December 20, 2002, the eligible amount of the gift, made by the subsidiary in the gift year exceeds the total of all amounts deducted under section 110.1 by the subsidiary in respect of those gifts;

**(8) Subsection (4) applies to windings-up that begin after December 20, 2002**

**101. (1) The portion of paragraph 110.1(1)(a) of the Act before subparagraph (i) is replaced by the following:**

(a) **Charitable gifts** — the total of all amounts each of which is the eligible amount of a gift (other than a gift described in paragraph (b), (c) or (d)) made by the corporation in the year or in any of the five preceding taxation years to

**(2) Paragraphs 110.1(1)(a) of the Act is amended by adding the following after subparagraph (iv):**

> (iv.1) a municipal or public body performing a function of government in Canada,

**(3) The description of B in paragraph 110.1(1)(a) of the Act is replaced by the following:**

B is the total of all amounts, each of which is that proportion of the corporation's taxable capital gain for the taxation year in respect of a gift made by the corporation in the taxation year (in respect of which gift an eligible amount is described in this paragraph for the taxation year) that the eligible amount of the gift is of the corporation's proceeds of disposition in respect of the gift,

**(4) Clause (B) in the description of D in paragraph 110.1(1)(a) of the Act is replaced by the following:**

> (B)   the total of all amounts each of which is determined in respect of a disposition that is the making of a gift of property of the class by the corporation in the year (in respect of which gift an eligible amount is described in this paragraph for the taxation year) equal to the lesser of

> (I)   that proportion, of the amount by which the proceeds of disposition of the property exceeds any outlays and expenses, to the extent that they were made or incurred by the corporation for the purpose of making the disposition, that the eligible amount of the gift is of the corporation's proceeds of disposition in respect of the gift, and

> (II)   that proportion, of the capital cost to the corporation of the property, that the eligible amount of the gift is of the corporation's proceeds of disposition in respect of the gift;

**(5) The portion of paragraph 110.1(1)(b) of the Act before subparagraph (i) is replaced by the following:**

> (b)   **Gifts to Her Majesty** — the total of all amounts each of which is the eligible amount of a gift (other than a gift described in paragraph (c) or (d)) made by the corporation to Her Majesty in right of Canada or of a province

**(6) Paragraphs 110.1(1)(c) and (d) of the Act are replaced by the following:**

> (c)   **Gifts to institutions** — the total of all amounts each of which is the eligible amount of a gift (other than a gift described in paragraph (d)) of an object that the Canadian Cultural Property Export Review Board has determined meets the criteria set out in paragraphs 29(3)(b) and (c) of the *Cultural Property Export and Import Act*, which gift was made by the corporation in the year or in any of the five preceding taxation years to an institution or a public authority in Canada that was, at the time the gift was made, designated under subsection 32(2) of that Act either generally or for a specified purpose related to that object; and

(*d*) **Ecological gifts** — the total of all amounts each of which is the eligible amount of a gift of land (including a covenant or an easement to which land is subject or, in the case of land in the Province of Quebec, a real servitude) if

    (i)    the fair market value of the gift is certified by the Minister of the Environment,

    (ii)    the land is certified by that Minister, or by a person designated by that Minister, to be ecologically sensitive land, the conservation and protection of which is, in the opinion of that Minister or that person, important to the preservation of Canada's environmental heritage, and

    (iii)    the gift was made by the corporation in the year or in any of the five preceding taxation years to

        (A)   Her Majesty in right of Canada or of a province,

        (B)   a municipality in Canada,

        (C)   a municipal or public body performing a function of government in Canada, or

        (D)   a registered charity one of the main purposes of which is, in the opinion of that Minister, the conservation and protection of Canada's environmental heritage, and that is approved by that Minister or that person in respect of the gift.

**(7) The portion of subsection 110.1(2) of the Act before paragraph (*a*) is replaced by the following:**

(2) **Proof of gift** — An eligible amount of a gift shall not be included for the purpose of determining a deduction under subsection (1) unless the making of the gift is evidenced by filing with the Minister

**(8) Subsection 110.1(3) of the Act is replaced by the following:**

(2.1) **Where subsection (3) applies** — Subsection (3) applies in circumstances where

    (*a*)    a corporation makes a gift at any time of

        (i)    capital property to a donee described in paragraph (1)(*a*), (*b*) or (*d*), or

        (ii)    in the case of a corporation not resident in Canada, real or immovable property situated in Canada to a prescribed donee who provides an undertaking, in a form satisfactory to the Minister, to the effect that the property will be held for use in the public interest; and

    (*b*)    the fair market value of the property otherwise determined at that time exceeds

        (i)    in the case of depreciable property of a prescribed class, the lesser of the undepreciated capital cost of that class at the end of the taxation year of the corporation that includes that time (determined without reference to the proceeds of disposition designated in respect of the property under subsection (3)) and the adjusted cost base to the corporation of the property immediately before that time, and

(ii) in any other case, the adjusted cost base to the corporation of the property immediately before that time.

(3) **Gifts of capital property** — If this subsection applies in respect of a gift by a corporation of property, and the corporation designates an amount in respect of the gift in its return of income under section 150 for the year in which the gift is made, the amount so designated is deemed to be its proceeds of disposition of the property and, for the purpose of subsection 248(31), the fair market value of the gift, but the amount so designated may not exceed the fair market value of the property otherwise determined and may not be less than the greater of

(a) in the case of a gift made after December 20, 2002, the amount of the advantage, if any, in respect of the gift, and

(b) the amount determined under subparagraph (2.1)(b)(i) or (ii), as the case may be, in respect of the property.

(9) **Subsection 110.1(4) of the Act is replaced by the following:**

(4) **Gifts made by partnership** — If at the end of a fiscal period of a partnership a corporation is a member of the partnership, its share of any amount that would, if the partnership were a person, be the eligible amount of a gift made by the partnership to any donee is, for the purpose of this section, deemed to be the eligible amount of a gift made to that donee by the corporation in its taxation year in which the fiscal period of the partnership ends.

(10) **The portion of paragraph 110.1(5)(b) of the Act before subparagraph (i) is replaced by the following:**

(b) where the gift is a covenant or an easement to which land is subject or, in the case of land in the Province of Quebec, a real servitude, the greater of

(11) **Subsections (1), (3) to (7), (9) and (10) apply to gifts made after December 20, 2002.**

(12) **Subsection Subsection (2) applies to gifts made after May 8, 2000.**

(13) **For gifts made after May 8, 2000 and before December 21, 2002, subparagraph 110.1(1)(d)(i) of the Act is to be read as follows:**

(i) Her Majesty in right of Canada or of a province, a municipality in Canada or a municipal or public body performing a function of government in Canada, or

(14) **Subsection (8) applies to gifts made after 1999 except that, for gifts made after 1999 and on or before December 20, 2002, the reference to "subsection 248(31)" in subsection 110.1(3) of the Act, as enacted by subsection (8), is to be read as a reference to "subsection (1)".**

106. (1) **The definition "total ecological gifts" in subsection 118.1(1) of the Act is replaced by the following:**

"total ecological gifts"
*« total des dons de biens écosensibles »*

"total ecological gifts", in respect of an individual for a taxation year, means the total of all amounts each of which is the eligible amount of a gift (other than a gift described in the definition "total cultural gifts") of land (including a covenant or an easement to which land is subject or, in the case of land in the Province of Quebec, a real servitude) if

(a)   the fair market value of the gift is certified by the Minister of the Environment,

(b)   the land is certified by that Minister, or by a person designated by that Minister, to be ecologically sensitive land, the conservation and protection of which is, in the opinion of that Minister or that person, important to the preservation of Canada's environmental heritage, and

(c)   the gift was made by the individual in the year or in any of the five preceding taxation years to

(i)    Her Majesty in right of Canada or of a province,

(ii)   a municipality in Canada,

(iii)  a municipal or public body performing a function of government in Canada, or

(iv)   a registered charity one of the main purposes of which is, in the opinion of that Minister, the conservation and protection of Canada's environmental heritage, and that is approved by that Minister or that person in respect of the gift,

to the extent that those amounts were not included in determining an amount that was deducted under this section in computing the individual's tax payable under this Part for a preceding taxation year;

**(2) The portion of the definition "total charitable gifts" in subsection 118.1(1) of the Act before paragraph (a) is replaced by the following:**

"total charitable gifts"
  « total des dons de bienfaisance »

"total charitable gifts", in respect of an individual for a taxation year, means the total of all amounts each of which is the eligible amount of a gift (other than a gift described in the definition "total Crown gifts", "total cultural gifts" or "total ecological gifts") made by the individual in the year or in any of the five preceding taxation years (other than in a year for which a deduction under subsection 110(2) was claimed in computing the individual's taxable income) to

**(3) Paragraph (d) of the definition "total charitable gifts" in subsection 118.1(1) of the Act is replaced by the following:**

(d)   a municipality in Canada,

(d.1) a municipal or public body performing a function of government in Canada,

**(4) The portion of the definition "total Crown gifts" in subsection 118.1(1) of the Act before paragraph (a) is replaced by the following:**

"total Crown gifts"
  « total des dons à l'État »

total Crown gifts", in respect of an individual for a taxation year, means the total of all amounts each of which is the eligible amount of a gift (other than a gift described in the definition "total cultural gifts" or "total ecological gifts") made by the individual in the year or in any of the five preceding taxation years to Her Majesty in right of Canada or of a province, to the extent that those amounts were

**(5) The portion of the definition "total cultural gifts" in subsection 118.1(1) of the Act before paragraph (*a*) is replaced by the following:**

"total cultural gifts"

« *total des dons de biens culturels* »

"total cultural gifts", in respect of an individual for a taxation year, means the total of all amounts each of which is the eligible amount of a gift

**(6) The description of B in subparagraph (*a*)(iii) of the definition "total gifts" in subsection 118.1(1) of the Act is replaced by the following:**

B is the total of all amounts, each of which is that proportion of the individual's taxable capital gain for the taxation year in respect of a gift made by the individual in the taxation year (in respect of which gift an eligible amount is included in the individual's total charitable gifts for the taxation year) that the eligible amount of the gift is of the individual's proceeds of disposition in respect of the gift,

**(7) Clause (B) in the description of D in subparagraph (*a*)(iii) of the definition "total gifts" in subsection 118.1(1) of the Act is replaced by the following:**

(B)   the total of all amounts each of which is determined in respect of a disposition that is the making of a gift of property of the class made by the individual in the year (in respect of which gift an eligible amount is included in the individual's total charitable gifts for the taxation year) equal to the lesser of

(I)   that proportion, of the amount by which the proceeds of disposition of the property exceed any outlays and expenses, to the extent that they were made or incurred by the individual for the purpose of making the disposition, that the eligible amount of the gift is of the individual's proceeds of disposition in respect of the gift, and

(II)   that proportion, of the capital cost to the individual of the property, that the eligible amount of the gift is of the individual's proceeds of disposition in respect of the gift, and

**(8) The portion of subsection 118.1(2) of the Act before paragraph (*a*) is replaced by the following:**

(2) **Proof of gift** — An eligible amount of a gift shall not be included in the total charitable gifts, total Crown gifts, total cultural gifts or total ecological gifts of an individual unless the making of the gift is evidenced by filing with the Minister

**(9) Subsection 118.1(6) of the Act is replaced by the following:**

(5.4) **Where subsection (6) applies** — Subsection (6) applies in circumstances where

(*a*) an individual

    (i) makes a gift (by the individual's will or otherwise) at any time of capital property to a donee described in the definition **"total charitable gifts"**, **"total Crown gifts"** or **"total ecological gifts"** in subsection (1), or

    (ii) who is non-resident, makes a gift (by the individual's will or otherwise) at any time of real or immovable property situated in Canada to a prescribed donee who provides an undertaking, in a form satisfactory to the Minister, to the effect that the property will be held for use in the public interest; and

(*b*) the fair market value of the property otherwise determined at that time exceeds

    (i) in the case of depreciable property of a prescribed class, the lesser of the undepreciated capital cost of that class at the end of the taxation year of the individual that includes that time (determined without reference to proceeds of disposition designated in respect of the property under subsection (6)) and the adjusted cost base to the individual of the property immediately before that time, and

    (ii) in any other case, the adjusted cost base to the individual of the property immediately before that time.

(6) **Gifts of capital property** — If this subsection applies in respect of a gift by an individual of property, and the individual or the individual's legal representative designates an amount in respect of the gift in the individual's return of income under section 150 for the year in which the gift is made, the amount so designated is deemed to be the individual's proceeds of disposition of the property and, for the purpose of subsection 248(31), the fair market value of the gift, but the amount so designated may not exceed the fair market value of the property otherwise determined and may not be less than the greater of

(*a*) in the case of a gift made after December 20, 2002, the amount of the advantage, if any, in respect of the gift, and

(*b*) the amount determined under subparagraph (5.4)(*b*)(i) or (ii), as the case may be, in respect of the property.

**(11) Paragraph 118.1(7)(*d*) of the English version of the Act is replaced by the following:**

(*d*) the amount that the individual or the individual's legal representative designates in the individual's return of income under section 150 for the year in which the gift is made is deemed to be the individual's proceeds of disposition of the work of art and, for the purpose of subsection 248(31), the fair market value of the work of art, but the amount so designated may not exceed the fair market value otherwise determined of the work of art and may not be less than the greater of

(i)    the amount of the advantage, if any, in respect of the gift, and

(ii)   the cost amount to the individual of the work of art.

**(13) Paragraph 118.1(7.1)(*d*) of the English version of the Act is replaced by the following:**

(*d*)   the individual is deemed to have received at the particular time proceeds of disposition in respect of the work of art equal to the greater of its cost amount to the individual at that time and the amount of the advantage, if any, in respect of the gift.

**(14) Subsection 118.1(8) of the Act is replaced by the following:**

(8) **Gifts made by partnership** — If at the end of a fiscal period of a partnership an individual is a member of the partnership, the individual's share of any amount that would, if the partnership were a person, be the eligible amount of a gift made by the partnership to any donee is, for the purpose of this section, deemed to be the eligible amount of a gift made to that donee by the individual in the individual's taxation year in which the fiscal period of the partnership ends.

**(15) Paragraphs 118.1(13)(*b*) and (*c*) of the Act are replaced by the following:**

(*b*)   if the security ceases to be a non-qualifying security of the individual at a subsequent time that is within 60 months after the particular time and the donee has not disposed of the security at or before the subsequent time, the individual is deemed to have made a gift to the donee of property at the subsequent time and the fair market value of that property is deemed to be the lesser of the fair market value of the security at the subsequent time and the fair market value of the security at the particular time that would, if this Act were read without reference to this subsection, have been included in calculating the individual's total charitable gifts or total Crown gifts for a taxation year;

(*c*)   if the security is disposed of by the donee within 60 months after the particular time and paragraph (*b*) does not apply to the security, the individual is deemed to have made a gift to the donee of property at the time of the disposition and the fair market value of that property is deemed to be the lesser of the fair market value of any consideration (other than a non-qualifying security of the individual or a property that would be a non-qualifying security of the individual if the individual were alive at that time) received by the donee for the disposition and the fair market value of the security at the particular time that would, if this Act were read without reference to this subsection, have been included in calculating the individual's total charitable gifts or total Crown gifts for a taxation year; and

**(16) Subsections (1), (2), (4) to (8) and (10) to (15) apply to gifts made after December 20, 2002. In addition, for gifts made after May 8, 2000 but on or before December 20, 2002, paragraph (*a*) of the definition "total ecological gifts" in subsection 118.1(1) of the Act is to be read as follows:**

(*a*)    Her Majesty in right of Canada or of a province, a municipality in Canada or a municipal or public body performing a function of government in Canada, or

**(17) Subsection (3) applies to gifts made after May 8, 2000.**

**(18) Subsection (9) applies to gifts made after 1999 except that, for gifts made after 1999 but on or before December 20, 2002, the reference to "subsection 248(31)" in subsection 118.1(6) of the Act, as enacted by subsection (9), shall be read as a reference to "subsection (1)".**

**138. (1) The portion of subsection 143(3.1) of the Act before the description of B in paragraph (*b*) is replaced by the following:**

(3.1) **Election in respect of gifts** — For the purposes of section 118.1, if the eligible amount of a gift made in a taxation year by an *inter vivos* trust referred to in subsection (1) in respect of a congregation would, but for this subsection, be included in the total charitable gifts, total Crown gifts, total cultural gifts or total ecological gifts of the trust for the year and the trust so elects in its return of income under this Part for the year,

(*a*)    the trust is deemed not to have made the gift; and

(*b*)    each participating member of the congregation is deemed to have made, in the year, such a gift the eligible amount of which is the amount determined by the formula

$$A \times B/C$$

where

A    is the eligible amount of the gift made by the trust,

**(2) Subsection (1) applies to gifts made after December 20, 2002.**

**139. (1) The heading before section 143.2 of the Act is replaced by the following:**

*Cost of Tax Shelter Investments and Limited-recourse Debt in Respect of Gifting Arrangements*

**(2) Section 143.2 of the Act is amended by adding the following after subsection (6):**

(6.1) **Limited-recourse debt in respect of a gift or monetary contribution** — The limited-recourse debt in respect of a gift or monetary contribution of a taxpayer, at the time the gift or monetary contribution is made, is the total of

(*a*)    each limited-recourse amount at that time, of the taxpayer and of all other taxpayers not dealing at arm's length with the taxpayer, that can reasonably be considered to relate to the gift or monetary contribution,

(*b*)    each limited-recourse amount at that time, determined under this section when this section is applied to each other taxpayer who deals at arm's length with and holds, directly or indirectly, an interest in the taxpayer, that can reasonably be considered to relate to the gift or monetary contribution, and

(c)   each amount that is the unpaid amount at that time of any other indebtedness, of any taxpayer referred to in paragraph (a) or (b), that can reasonably be considered to relate to the gift or monetary contribution if there is a guarantee, security or similar indemnity or covenant in respect of that or any other indebtedness.

**(3) The portion of subsection 143.2(13) of the Act before paragraph (a) is replaced by the following:**

(13) **Information located outside Canada** — For the purpose of this section, if can reasonably be considered that information relating to indebtedness that relates to a taxpayer's expenditure, gift or monetary contribution is available outside Canada and the Minister is not satisfied that the unpaid principal of the indebtedness is not a limited-recourse amount, the unpaid principal of the indebtedness relating to the taxpayer's expenditure, gift or monetary contribution is deemed to be a limited-recourse amount relating to the expenditure, gift or monetary contribution unless

**(4) Subsections (1) to (3) apply in respect of expenditures, gifts and monetary contributions made after February 18, 2003.**

**148. (2) The portion of the definition "charitable organization" in subsection 149.1(1) of the Act before paragraph (a) is replaced by the following:**

"charitable organization"
    « oeuvre de bienfaisance »

"charitable organization", at any particular time, means an organization, whether or not incorporated,

**(3) Paragraphs (c) and (d) of the definition "charitable organization" in subsection 149.1(1) of the Act are replaced by the following:**

(c)   more than 50% of the directors, trustees, officers or like officials of which deal at arm's length with each other and with

   (i)    each of the other directors, trustees, officers and like officials of the organization,

   (ii)   each person described by subparagraph (d)(i) or (ii), and

   (iii)  each member of a group of persons (other than Her Majesty in right of Canada or of a province, a municipality, another registered charity that is not a private foundation, and any club, society or association described in paragraph 149(1)(l)) who do not deal with each other at arm's length, if the group would, if it were a person, be a person described by subparagraph (d)(i), and

(d)   that is not, at the particular time, and would not at the particular time be, if the organization were a corporation, controlled directly or indirectly in any manner whatever

   (i)    by a person (other than Her Majesty in right of Canada or of a province, a municipality, another registered charity that is not a private foundation, and any club, society or association described in paragraph 149(1)(*l*)),

    (A)  who immediately after the particular time, has contributed to the organization amounts that are, in total, greater than 50% of the capital of the organization immediately after the particular time, and

    (B)  who immediately after the person's last contribution at or before the particular time, had contributed to the organization amounts that were, in total, greater than 50% of the capital of the organization immediately after the making of that last contribution, or

  (ii)  by a person, or by a group of persons that do not deal at arm's length with each other, if the person or any member of the group does not deal at arm's length with a person described in subparagraph (i);

**(4) The portion of the description of A in the definition "disbursement quota" in subsection 149.1(1) of the Act before paragraph (*a*) is replaced by the following:**

A is 80% of the total of all amounts each of which is the eligible amount of a gift for which the foundation issued a receipt described in subsection 110.1(2) or 118.1(2) in its immediately preceding taxation year, other than

**(5) The portion of the description of A.1 in the definition "disbursement quota" in subsection 149.1(1) of the Act before paragraph (*a*) is replaced by the following:**

A.1 is 80% of the total of all amounts each of which is the eligible amount of a gift received in a preceding taxation year, to the extent that the eligible amount

**(6) Paragraph (*d*) of the definition "enduring property" in subsection 149.1(1) in the English version of the Act is replaced by the following:**

  (*d*)  a gift received by the registered charity as a transferee from an original recipient charity or another transferee of a property that was, before that gift was so received, an enduring property of the original recipient charity or of the other transferee because of paragraph (*a*) or (*c*) or this paragraph, or property substituted for the gift, if, in the case of a property that was an enduring property of an original recipient charity because of paragraph (*c*), the gift is subject to the same terms and conditions under the trust or direction as applied to the original recipient charity;

**(7) Subsection 149.1(2) of the Act is amended by striking out the word "or" at the end of paragraph (*a*), by adding the word "or" at the end of paragraph (*b*) and by adding the following after paragraph (*b*):**

  (*c*)  makes a disbursement by way of a gift, other than a gift made

    (i)  in the course of charitable activities carried on by it, or

    (ii)  to a donee that is a qualified donee at the time of the gift.

**(8) Subsection 149.1(3) of the Act is amended by adding the following after paragraph (*b*):**

(*b.1*) makes a disbursement by way of a gift, other than a gift made

    (i)    in the course of charitable activities carried on by it, or

    (ii)   to a donee that is a qualified donee at the time of the gift;

**(9) Subsection 149.1(4) of the Act is amended by adding the following after paragraph (*b*):**

(*b.1*) makes a disbursement by way of a gift, other than a gift made

    (i)    in the course of charitable activities carried on by it, or

    (ii)   to a donee that is a qualified donee at the time of the gift;

**(10) The portion of subsection 149.1(9) of the Act after paragraph (*b*) is replaced by the following:**

is, notwithstanding subsection (8), deemed to be income of the charity for, and the eligible amount of a gift for which it issued a receipt described in subsection 110.1(2) or 118.1(2) in, its taxation year in which the period referred to in paragraph (*a*) expires or the time referred to in paragraph (*b*) occurs, as the case may be.

**(11) Paragraph 149.1(15)(*b*) of the Act is replaced by the following:**

(*b*)   the Minister may make available to the public in any manner that the Minister considers appropriate a listing of all registered, or previously registered, charities and Canadian amateur athletic associations that indicates for each of them

    (i)    its name and address,

    (ii)   its registration number and date of registration, and

    (iii)  the effective date of any revocation, annulment or termination of its registration.

**(12) Subsection (1) applies after 1999 except that, in respect of a foundation that has not been designated before 2000 as a private foundation or a charitable organization under subsection 149.1(6.3) of the Act or under subsection 110(8.1) or (8.2) of the Act, as enacted by chapter 148 of the Revised Statutes of Canada, 1952, and that has not applied after February 15, 1984 for registration under paragraph 110(8)(*c*) of that Act or under the definition "registered charity" in subsection 248(1) of the Act, subparagraph (*a*)(iii) and paragraph (*b*) of the definition "public foundation" in subsection 149.1(1) of the Act, as enacted by subsection (1), are in their application before the earlier of the day, if any, on which the foundation is designated after 1999 as a private foundation or a charitable organization under subsection 149.1(6.3) of the Act and January 1, 2005 to be read**

(*a*)   without reference to "(other than Her Majesty in right of Canada or of a province, a municipality, another registered charity that is not a private foundation, and any club, society or association described in paragraph 149(1)(*l*))"; and (*b*)    as if the reference to "50%" in paragraph (*b*) were a reference to "75%".

**(13) Subsections (2) and (3) apply after 1999 except that, in respect of a charitable organization that has not been designated before 2000 as a private foundation or a public foundation under subsection 149.1(6.3) of the Act or under subsection 110(8.1) or (8.2) of the *Income Tax Act*, as enacted by chapter 148 of the Revised Statutes of Canada, 1952, and that has not applied after February 15, 1984 for registration under paragraph 110(8)(*c*) of that Act or under the definition "registered charity" in subsection 248(1) of the *Income Tax Act*, subparagraphs (*c*)(ii) and (iii) of the definition "charitable organization" in subsection 149.1(1) of the Act, as enacted by subsection (3), apply after the earlier of the day, if any, on which the organization is designated after 1999 as a private foundation or a public foundation under subsection 149.1(6.3) of the Act and December 31, 2004.**

**(14) Subsections (4), (5) and (7) to (9) apply to gifts made after December 20, 2002.**

**(15) Subsection (6) applies to taxation years that begin after March 22, 2004.**

**(16) Subsection (10) applies after December 20, 2002.**

**(17) An application referred to in subsection 149.1(6.3) of the Act, in respect of one or more taxation years after 1999, may be made after 1999 and before the 90th day after this Act is assented to. If a designation referred to in that subsection for any of those taxation years is made in response to the application, the charity is deemed to be registered as a charitable organization, a public foundation or a private foundation, as the case may be, for the taxation years that the Minister of National Revenue specifies.**

**163. (1) Subsections 184(2) to (5) of the Act are replaced by the following:**

(2) **Tax on excessive elections** — If a corporation has elected in accordance with subsection 83(2), 130.1(4) or 131(1) in respect of the full amount of any dividend payable by it on shares of any class of its capital stock (in this section referred to as the "original dividend") and the full amount of the original dividend exceeds the portion of the original dividend deemed by that subsection to be a capital dividend or capital gains dividend, as the case may be, the corporation shall, at the time of the election, pay a tax under this Part equal to 3/5 of the excess.

(3) **Election to treat excess as separate dividend** — If, in respect of an original dividend payable at a particular time, a corporation would, but for this subsection, be required to pay a tax under this Part in respect of an excess referred to in subsection (2), and the corporation elects in prescribed manner on or before the day that is 90 days after the day of mailing of the notice of assessment in respect of the tax that would otherwise be payable under this Part, the following rules apply:

(*a*)    the portion of the original dividend deemed by subsection 83(2), 130.1(4) or 131(1) to be a capital dividend or capital gains dividend, as the case may be, is deemed for the purposes of this Act to be the amount of a separate dividend that became payable at the particular time;

(b)  if the corporation identifies in its election any part of the excess, that part is, for the purposes of any election under subsection 83(2), 130.1(4) or 131(1) in respect of that part, and, where the corporation has so elected, for all purposes of this Act, deemed to be the amount of a separate dividend that became payable immediately after the particular time;

(c)  the amount by which the excess exceeds any portion deemed by paragraph (b) to be a separate dividend for all purposes of this Act is deemed to be a separate taxable dividend that became payable at the particular time; and

(d)  each person who held any of the issued shares of the class of shares of the capital stock of the corporation in respect of which the original dividend was paid is deemed

    (i)  not to have received any portion of the original dividend, and

    (ii)  to have received, at the time that any separate dividend determined under any of paragraphs (a) to (c) became payable, the proportion of that dividend that the number of shares of that class held by the person at the particular time is of the number of shares of that class outstanding at the particular time except that, for the purpose of Part XIII the separate dividend is deemed to be paid on the day that the election in respect of this subsection is made.

(4) **Concurrence with election** — An election under subsection (3) is valid only if

(a)  it is made with the concurrence of the corporation and all its shareholders

    (i)  who received or were entitled to receive all or any portion of the original dividend, and

    (ii)  whose addresses were known to the corporation; and

(b)  either

    (i)  it is made on or before the day that is 30 months after the day on which the original dividend became payable, or

    (ii)  each shareholder described in subparagraph (a)(i) concurs with the election, in which case, notwithstanding subsections 152(4) to (5), any assessment of the tax, interest and penalties payable by each of those shareholders for any taxation year shall be made that is necessary to take the corporation's election into account.

(5) **Exception for non-taxable shareholders** — If each person who, in respect of an election made under subsection (3), is deemed by subsection (3) to have received a dividend at a particular time is also, at the particular time, a person all of whose taxable income is exempt from tax under Part I,

(a)  subsection (4) does not apply to the election; and

(b)  the election is valid only if it is made on or before the day that is 30 months after the day on which the original dividend became payable.

(2) **Subsection (1) applies to original dividends paid by a corporation after its 1999 taxation year except that, for the purpose of subsection 184(5) of the**

Act, as enacted by subsection (1), an election made before the 90th day after this Act is assented to is deemed to have been made in a timely manner.

**172. (1)** Section 207.31 of the Act is replaced by the following:

**207.31 Tax payable by recipient of an ecological gift** — Any charity, municipality or public body performing a function of government in Canada (referred to in this section as the "recipient") that at any time in a taxation year, without the authorization of the Minister of the Environment or a person designated by that Minister, disposes of or changes the use of a property described in paragraph 110.1(1)(*d*) or in the definition **"total ecological gifts"** in subsection 118.1(1) and given to the recipient shall, in respect of the year, pay a tax under this Part equal to 50% of the amount that would be determined for the purposes of section 110.1 or 118.1, if this Act were read without reference to subsections 110.1(3) and 118.1(6), to be the fair market value of the property if the property were given to the recipient immediately before the disposition or change.

**(2)** Subsection (1) applies in respect of dispositions of or changes of use of property after ANNOUNCEMENT DATE.

**183. (1)** Paragraph (*b*) of the definition "gifting arrangement" in subsection 237.1(1) of the Act is replaced by the following:

(*b*)    incur a limited-recourse debt, determined under subsection 143.2(6.1), that can reasonably be considered to relate to a gift to a qualified donee or a monetary contribution referred to in subsection 127(4.1);

**(2)** Subsection (1) applies in respect of gifts and monetary contributions made after 6:00 p.m. (EST) on December 5, 2003.

**185. (14)** Section 248 of the Act is amended by adding the following after subsection (3):

(3.1) **Gift of bare ownership of immovables** — Subsection (3) does not apply in respect of a usufruct or a right of use of an immovable in circumstances where a taxpayer disposes of the bare ownership of the immovable by way of a gift to a donee described in the definition **"total charitable gifts"**, **"total Crown gifts"** or **"total ecological gifts"** in subsection 118.1(1) and retains, for life, the usufruct or the right of use.

**(23)** Section 248 of the Act is amended by adding the following after subsection (29):

(30) **Intention to give** — The existence of an amount of an advantage in respect of a transfer of property does not in and by itself disqualify the transfer from being a gift to a qualified donee if

(*a*)    the amount of the advantage does not exceed 80% of the fair market value of the transferred property; or

(*b*)    the transferor of the property establishes to the satisfaction of the Minister that the transfer was made with the intention to make a gift.

(31) **Eligible amount of gift or monetary contribution** — The eligible amount of a gift or monetary contribution is the amount by which the fair market value of the property that is the subject of the gift or monetary contribution ex-

ceeds the amount of the advantage, if any, in respect of the gift or monetary contribution.

(32) **Amount of advantage** — The amount of the advantage in respect of a gift or monetary contribution by a taxpayer is the total of

(a)   the total of all amounts, other than an amount referred to in paragraph (b), each of which is the value, at the time the gift or monetary contribution is made, of any property, service, compensation, use or other benefit that the taxpayer, or a person or partnership who does not deal at arm's length with the taxpayer, has received, obtained or enjoyed, or is entitled, either immediately or in the future and either absolutely or contingently, to receive, obtain, or enjoy

    (i)   that is consideration for the gift or monetary contribution,

    (ii)   that is in gratitude for the gift or monetary contribution, or

    (iii)   that is in any other way related to the gift or monetary contribution, and

(b)   the limited-recourse debt, determined under subsection 143.2(6.1), in respect of the gift or monetary contribution at the time the gift or monetary contribution is made.

(33) **Cost of property acquired by donor** — The cost to a taxpayer of a property, acquired by the taxpayer in circumstances where subsection (32) applies to include the value of the property in computing the amount of the advantage in respect of a gift or monetary contribution, is equal to the fair market value of the property at the time the gift or monetary contribution is made.

(34) **Repayment of limited-recourse debt** — If at any time in a taxation year a taxpayer has paid an amount (in this subsection referred to as the "repaid amount") on account of the principal amount of an indebtedness which was, before that time, an unpaid principal amount that was a limited-recourse debt referred to in subsection 143.2(6.1) (in this subsection referred to as the "former limited-recourse debt") in respect of a gift or monetary contribution (in this subsection referred to as the "original gift" or "original monetary contribution", respectively, as the case may be) of the taxpayer (otherwise than by way of assignment or transfer of a guarantee, security or similar indemnity or covenant, or by way of a payment in respect of which any taxpayer referred to in subsection 143.2(6.1) has incurred an indebtedness that would be a limited-recourse debt referred to in that subsection if that indebtedness were in respect of a gift or monetary contribution made at the time that that indebtedness was incurred), the following rules apply:

(a)   if the former limited-recourse debt is in respect of the original gift, for the purposes of sections 110.1 and 118.1, the taxpayer is deemed to have made in the taxation year a gift to a qualified donee, the eligible amount of which deemed gift is the amount, if any, by which

    (i)   the amount that would have been the eligible amount of the original gift, if the total of all such repaid amounts paid at or before that time were paid immediately before the original gift was made,

    exceeds

    (ii)  the total of

        (A)  the eligible amount of the original gift, and

        (B)  the eligible amount of all other gifts deemed by this paragraph to have been made before that time in respect of the original gift; and

  (*b*)  if the former limited-recourse debt is in respect of the original monetary contribution, for the purposes of subsection 127(3), the taxpayer is deemed to have made in the taxation year a monetary contribution referred to in that subsection, the eligible amount of which is the amount, if any, by which

    (i)  the amount that would have been the eligible amount of the original monetary contribution, if the total of all such repaid amounts paid at or before that time were paid immediately before the original monetary contribution was made,

exceeds

    (ii)  the total of

        (A)  the eligible amount of the original monetary contribution, and

        (B)  the eligible amount of all other monetary contributions deemed by this paragraph to have been made before that time in respect of the original monetary contribution.

(35) **Deemed fair market value** — For the purposes of subsection (31), paragraph 69(1)(*b*) and subsections 110.1(2.1) and (3) and 118.1(5.4) and (6), the fair market value of a property that is the subject of a gift made by a taxpayer to a qualified donee is deemed to be the lesser of the fair market value of the property otherwise determined and the cost, or in the case of capital property, the adjusted cost base, of the property to the taxpayer immediately before the gift is made if

  (*a*)  the taxpayer acquired the property under a gifting arrangement that is a tax shelter as defined in subsection 237.1(1); or

  (*b*)  except where the gift is made as a consequence of the taxpayer's death,

    (i)  the taxpayer acquired the property less than 3 years before the day that the gift is made, or

    (ii)  the taxpayer acquired the property less than 10 years before the day that the gift is made and it is reasonable to conclude that, at the time the taxpayer acquired the property, one of the main reasons for the acquisition was to make a gift of the property to a qualified donee.

(36) **Non-arm's length transaction** — If a taxpayer acquired a property that is the subject of a gift to which subsection (35) applies because of subparagraph (35)(*b*)(i) or (ii) and the property was, at any time within the 3-year or 10-year period, respectively, that ends when the gift was made, acquired by a person or partnership with whom the taxpayer does not deal at arm's length, for the purpose of applying subsection (35), the cost, or in the case of capital property, the adjusted cost base, of the property to the taxpayer immediately before the gift is

made is deemed to be equal to the lowest amount that is the cost, or in the case of capital property, the adjusted cost base, to the taxpayer or any of those persons or partnerships immediately before the property was disposed of by that person or partnership.

(37) **Non-application of subsection (35)** — Subsection (35) does not apply to a gift

(*a*) of inventory;

(*b*) of real property or an immovable situated in Canada;

(*c*) of an object referred to in subparagraph 39(1)(*a*)(i.1);

(*d*) of property to which paragraph 38(*a.1*) or (*a.2*) would apply, if those paragraphs were read without reference to the expression "other than a private foundation";

(*e*) of a share of the capital stock of a corporation if

    (i) the share was issued by the corporation to the donor,

    (ii) immediately before the gift, the corporation was controlled by the donor, a person related to the donor or a group of persons each of whom is related to the donor, and

    (iii) subsection (35) would not have applied in respect of the consideration for which the share was issued had that consideration been donated by the donor to the qualified donee when the share was so donated; or

(*f*) by a corporation of property if

    (i) the property was acquired by the corporation in circumstances to which subsection 85(1) or (2) applied,

    (ii) immediately before the gift, the shareholder from whom the corporation acquired the property controlled the corporation or was related to a person or each member of a group of persons that controlled the corporation, and

    (iii) subsection (35) would not have applied in respect of the property had the property not been transferred to the corporation and had the shareholder made the gift to the qualified donee when the corporation so made the gift.

(38) **Artificial transactions** — The eligible amount of a particular gift of property by a taxpayer is nil if it can reasonably be concluded that the particular gift relates to a transaction or series of transactions

(*a*) one of the purposes of which is to avoid the application of subsection (35) to a gift of any property; or

(*b*) that would, if this Act were read without reference to this paragraph, result in a tax benefit to which subsection 245(2) applies.

(39) **Substantive gift** — If a taxpayer disposes of a property (in this subsection referred to as the "substantive gift") that is a capital property or an eligible capital property of the taxpayer, to a recipient that is a registered party, a provincial divi-

sion of a registered party, a registered association or a candidate, as those terms are defined in the *Canada Elections Act*, or that is a qualified donee, subsection (35) would have applied in respect of the substantive gift if it had been the subject of a gift by the taxpayer to a qualified donee, and all or a part of the proceeds of disposition of the substantive gift are (or are substituted, directly or indirectly in any manner whatever, for) property that is the subject of a gift or monetary contribution by the taxpayer to the recipient or any person dealing not at arm's length with the recipient, the following rules apply:

    (*a*)    for the purpose of subsection (31), the fair market value of the property that is the subject of the gift or monetary contribution made by the taxpayer is deemed to be that proportion of the lesser of the fair market value of the substantive gift and the cost, or if the substantive gift is capital property of the taxpayer, the adjusted cost base, of the substantive gift to the taxpayer immediately before the disposition to the recipient, that the fair market value otherwise determined of the property that is the subject of the gift or monetary contribution is of the proceeds of disposition of the substantive gift;

    (*b*)    if the substantive gift is capital property of the taxpayer, for the purpose of the definitions **"proceeds of disposition"** of property in subsection 13(21) and section 54, the sale price of the substantive gift is to be reduced by the amount by which the fair market value of the property that is the subject of the gift (determined without reference to this section) exceeds the fair market value determined under paragraph (*a*); and

    (*c*)    if the substantive gift is eligible capital property of the taxpayer, the amount determined under paragraph (*a*) in the description of E in the definition **"cumulative eligible capital"** in subsection 14(5) in respect of the substantive gift is to be reduced by the amount by which the fair market value of the property that is the subject of the gift (determined without reference to this section) exceeds the fair market value determined under paragraph (*a*).

(40) **Reasonable inquiry** — A person shall not issue a receipt referred to in subsection 110.1(2), 118.1(2) or 127(3), with a stated eligible amount in excess of $5,000, unless the person has made reasonable inquiry as to the existence of any circumstances in respect of which subsection (31), (35), (36), (38) or (39) requires that the eligible amount of the gift or monetary contribution be less than the fair market value, determined without reference to subsection (35), and subsections 110.1(3) and 118.1(6), of the property that is the subject of the gift or monetary contribution.

(41) **Information not provided** — Notwithstanding subsection (31), the eligible amount of a gift or monetary contribution made by a taxpayer is nil if the taxpayer does not — before a receipt referred to in subsection 110.1(2), 118.1(2) or 127(3), as the case may be, is issued in respect of the gift or monetary contribution — inform the qualified donee or the recipient, as the case may be, of any circumstances in respect of which subsection (31), (35), (36), (38) or (39) requires that the eligible amount of the gift or monetary contribution be less than the fair

market value, determined without reference to subsection (35) and subsections 110.1(3) and 118.1(6), of the property that is the subject of the gift or monetary contribution.

**(24) Subsection (1) applies in determining whether a person is, for the 2001 and subsequent taxation years, a common-law partner of a taxpayer, except that subsection does not apply to so determine whether a person is a common-law partner of a taxpayer for a taxation year to which a valid election, made under section 144 of the *Modernization of Benefits and Obligations Act*, applied before February 27, 2004. However, on and after February 27, 2004, no such election may be made to affect a current or subsequent taxation year.**

**(34) Subsection (14) applies to dispositions that occur after ANNOUNCEMENT DATE.**

**261. (1) The portion of subsection 188(2) of the English version of the Act before paragraph (*a*) is replaced by the following:**

(2) **Joint and several, or solidary, liability — revocation tax —** A person (other than a qualified donee) who, after the valuation day of a charity, receives an amount from the charity is jointly and severally, or solidarily, liable with the charity for the tax payable under subsection (1) by the charity in an amount not exceeding the amount by which the total of all such amounts so received by the person exceeds the total of all amounts each of which is

**(2) Subsection 188(4) of the English version of the Act is replaced by the following:**

(4) **Joint and several, or solidary, liability — tax transfer —** Where property has been transferred to a charitable organization in circumstances described in subsection (3) and it may reasonably be considered that the organization acted in concert with a charitable foundation for the purpose of reducing the disbursement quota of the foundation, the organization is jointly and severally, or solidarily, liable with the foundation for the tax imposed on the foundation by that subsection in an amount not exceeding the net value of the property.

# INCOME TAX ACT

(R.S.C. 1985, c. 1 (5th Supp.))

[**Note:** Only sections relevant to charitable donations and registered charities are reproduced.] Please also refer to the proposed amendments to the Income Tax Act at p. 185.

## PART I, DIVISION B, SUBDIVISION C
## TAXABLE CAPITAL GAINS AND ALLOWABLE CAPITAL LOSSES

**38. Taxable capital gain and allowable capital loss** — For the purposes of this Act,

(a) subject to paragraph 38(a.1), a taxpayer's taxable capital gain for a taxation year from the disposition of any property is 3/4 of the taxpayer's capital gain for the year from the disposition of the property;

(a.1) a taxpayer's taxable capital gain for a taxation year from the disposition after February 18, 1997 and before 2002 of any property is 3/8 of the taxpayer's capital gain for the year from the disposition of the property where

  (i) the disposition is the making of a gift to a qualified donee (as defined in subsection 149.1(1)), other than a private foundation, of a share, debt obligation or right listed on a prescribed stock exchange, a share of the capital stock of a mutual fund corporation, a unit of a mutual fund trust, an interest in a related segregated fund trust (within the meaning assigned by paragraph 138.1(1)(a)) or a prescribed debt obligation, or

  (ii) the disposition is deemed by section 70 to have occurred and the taxpayer is deemed by subsection 118.1(5) to have made a gift described in subparagraph (i) of the property;

(a.2) a taxpayer's taxable capital gain for a taxation year from the disposition of a property is 1/4 of the taxpayer's capital gain for the year from the disposition of the property where

  (i) the disposition is the making of a gift to a qualified donee (other than a private foundation) of a property described, in respect of the taxpayer, in paragraph 110.1(1)(d) or in the definition "total ecological gifts" in subsection 118.1(1), or

  (ii) the disposition is deemed by section 70 to have occurred and the taxpayer is deemed by subsection 118.1(5) to have made a gift described in subparagraph (i) of the property;

(b) a taxpayer's allowable capital loss for a taxation year from the disposition of any property is 3/4 of the taxpayer's capital loss for the year from the disposition of that property; and

(c)     a taxpayer's allowable business investment loss for a taxation year from
the disposition of any property is 3/4 of the taxpayer's business investment loss for the year from the disposition of that property.

[S.C. 1970-71-72, c. 63, s. 1; S.C. 1977-78, c. 42, s. 2; S.C. 1984, c. 1, s. 12; S.C. 1986, c. 6, s. 16;
S.C. 1988, c. 55, s. 19; S.C. 1998, c. 19, s. 6.]

**39.** (1) **Meaning of capital gain and capital loss** — For the purposes of this Act,

(a)     a taxpayer's capital gain for a taxation year from the disposition of any
property is the taxpayer's gain for the year determined under this subdivision (to the extent of the amount thereof that would not, if section 3 were
read without reference to the expression "other than a taxable capital gain
from the disposition of a property" in paragraph 3(a) and without reference to paragraph 3(b), be included in computing the taxpayer's income
for the year or any other taxation year) from the disposition of any property of the taxpayer other than

. . .

(i.1)   an object that the Canadian Cultural Property Export Review Board
has determined meets the criteria set out in paragraphs 29(3)(b) and
(c) of the *Cultural Property Export and Import Act* and that has
been disposed of,

(A)     in the case of a gift to which subsection 118.1(5) applies,
within the period ending 36 months after the death of the taxpayer or, where written application therefor has been made to
the Minister by the taxpayer's legal representative within that
period, within such longer period as the Minister considers
reasonable in the circumstances, and

(B)     in any other case, at any time,

to an institution or a public authority in Canada that was, at the time
of the disposition, designated under subsection 32(2) of that Act either generally or for a specified purpose related to that object,

**40.** (1.01) **Gift of non-qualifying security** — A taxpayer's gain for a particular taxation year from a disposition of a non-qualifying security of the taxpayer
(as defined in subsection 118.1(18)) that is the making of a gift (other than an
excepted gift, within the meaning assigned by subsection 118.1(19)) to a qualified
donee (as defined in subsection 149.1(1)) is the amount, if any, by which

(a)     where the disposition occurred in the particular year, the amount, if any,
by which the taxpayer's proceeds of disposition exceed the total of the
adjusted cost base to the taxpayer of the security immediately before the
disposition and any outlays and expenses to the extent they were made or
incurred by the taxpayer for the purpose of making the disposition, and

(b)     where the disposition occurred in the 60-month period that ends at the
beginning of the particular year, the amount, if any, deducted under paragraph 40(1.01)(c) in computing the taxpayer's gain for the preceding
taxation year from the disposition of the security

exceeds

(c) the amount that the taxpayer claims in prescribed form filed with the taxpayer's return of income for the particular year, where the taxpayer is not deemed by subsection 118.1(13) to have made a gift of property before the end of the particular year as a consequence of a disposition of the security by the donee or as a consequence of the security ceasing to be a non-qualifying security of the taxpayer before the end of the particular year.

. . .

**43.** (1) **General rule for part dispositions** — For the purpose of computing a taxpayer's gain or loss for a taxation year from the disposition of part of a property, the adjusted cost base to the taxpayer, immediately before the disposition, of that part is the portion of the adjusted cost base to the taxpayer at that time of the whole property that can reasonably be regarded as attributable to that part.

(2) **Ecological gifts** — For the purposes of subsection (1) and section 53, where at any time a taxpayer disposes of a servitude, covenant or easement to which land is subject in circumstances where subsection 110.1(5) or 118.1(12) applies,

(a) the portion of the adjusted cost base to the taxpayer of the land immediately before the disposition that can reasonably be regarded as attributable to the servitude, covenant or easement, as the case may be, is deemed to be equal to the amount determined by the formula

$A \times B/C$

where

A is the adjusted cost base to the taxpayer of the land immediately before the disposition,

B is the amount determined under subsection 110.1(5) or 118.1(12) in respect of the disposition, and

C is the fair market value of the land immediately before the disposition; and

(b) for greater certainty, the cost to the taxpayer of the land shall be reduced at the time of the disposition by the amount determined under paragraph (a).

**43.1.** (1) **Life estates in real property** — Notwithstanding any other provision of this Act, where at any time a taxpayer disposes of a remainder interest in real property (except as a result of a transaction to which subsection 73(3) would otherwise apply or by way of a gift to a donee described in the definition "total charitable gifts" or "total Crown gifts" in subsection 118.1(1)) to a person or partnership and retains a life estate or an estate pur autre vie (in this section called the "estate") in the property, the taxpayer shall be deemed

(a) to have disposed at that time of the life estate in the property for proceeds of disposition equal to its fair market value at that time; and

(b) to have reacquired the life estate immediately after that time at a cost equal to the proceeds of disposition referred to in paragraph 43.1(1)(a).

(2) **Idem** — Where, as a result of an individual's death, a life estate to which subsection 43.1(1) applied is terminated,

(a)    the holder of the life estate immediately before the death shall be deemed to have disposed of the life estate immediately before the death for proceeds of disposition equal to the adjusted cost base to that person of the life estate immediately before the death; and

(b)    where a person who is the holder of the remainder interest in the real property immediately before the death was not dealing at arm's length with the holder of the life estate, there shall, after the death, be added in computing the adjusted cost base to that person of the real property an amount equal to the lesser of

(i)    the adjusted cost base of the life estate in the property immediately before the death, and

(ii)    the amount, if any, by which the fair market value of the real property immediately after the death exceeds the adjusted cost base to that person of the remainder interest immediately before the death.

[S.C. 1994, c. 6, Sch. VIII, s. 13; S.C. 1994, c. 21, s. 16.]

. . .

**46. (5) Excluded property** — For the purpose of this section, "excluded property" of a taxpayer means property acquired by the taxpayer, or by a person with whom the taxpayer does not deal at arm's length, in circumstances in which it is reasonable to conclude that the acquisition of the property relates to an arrangement, plan or scheme that is promoted by another person or partnership and under which it is reasonable to conclude that the property will be the subject of a gift to which subsection 110.1(1), or the definition "total charitable gifts", "total cultural gifts" or "total ecological gifts" in subsection 118.1(1), applies.

[S.C. 2001, c. 17, s. 31 (in force June 14, 2001).]

. . .

## PART I, DIVISION B, SUBDIVISION F
## RULES RELATING TO COMPUTATION OF INCOME

**67.1. (1) Expenses for food, etc.** — For the purposes of this Act, other than sections 62, 63 and 118.2, an amount paid or payable in respect of the human consumption of food or beverages or the enjoyment of entertainment shall be deemed to be 50% of the lesser of

(a)    the amount actually paid or payable in respect thereof, and

(b)    an amount in respect thereof that would be reasonable in the circumstances.

(2) **Exceptions** — Subsection 67.1(1) does not apply to an amount paid or payable by a person in respect of the consumption of food or beverages or the enjoyment of entertainment where the amount

. . .

(b)    relates to a fund-raising event the primary purpose of which is to benefit a registered charity;

. . .

**69.** (1) **Inadequate considerations** — Except as expressly otherwise provided in this Act,

(a)    where a taxpayer has acquired anything from a person with whom the taxpayer was not dealing at arm's length at an amount in excess of the fair market value thereof at the time the taxpayer so acquired it, the taxpayer shall be deemed to have acquired it at that fair market value;

(b)    where a taxpayer has disposed of anything

    (i)    to a person with whom the taxpayer was not dealing at arm's length for no proceeds or for proceeds less than the fair market value thereof at the time the taxpayer so disposed of it, or

    (ii)    to any person by way of gift inter vivos, the taxpayer shall be deemed to have received proceeds of disposition therefor equal to that fair market value; and

(c)    where a taxpayer has acquired property by way of gift, bequest or inheritance, the taxpayer shall be deemed to have acquired the property at its fair market value at the time the taxpayer so acquired it.

. . .

**72.** (1) **Reserves, etc., for year of death** — Where in a taxation year a taxpayer has died,

. . .

(c)    no amount may be claimed under subparagraph 40(1)(a)(iii), paragraph 40(1.01)(c) or subparagraph 44(1)(e)(iii) in computing any gain of the taxpayer for the year;

. . .

## PART I, DIVISION B, SUBDIVISION H
## CORPORATIONS RESIDENT IN CANADA AND THEIR SHAREHOLDERS

**87.** (2) **Rules applicable** — Where there has been an amalgamation of two or more corporations after 1971 the following rules apply

. . .

(m.1)    **Gift of non-qualifying security** — for the purpose of computing the new corporation's gain under subsection 40(1.01) for any taxation year from the disposition of a property, the new corporation is deemed to be the same corporation as, and a continuation of, each predecessor corporation;

. . .

(v)    **Gifts** — for the purposes of section 110.1, the new corporation shall be deemed to be the same corporation as, and a continuation of, each predecessor corporation with respect to gifts;

**88.** (1) **Winding-up** — Where a taxable Canadian corporation (in this subsection referred to as the "subsidiary") has been wound up after May 6, 1974 and not less than 90% of the issued shares of each class of the capital stock of the subsidiary were, immediately before the winding-up, owned by another taxable Canadian corporation (in this subsection referred to as the "parent") and all of the shares of the subsidiary that were not owned by the parent immediately before the winding-up were owned at that time by persons with whom the parent was dealing at arm's length, notwithstanding any other provision of this Act other than subsection 69(11), the following rules apply:

. . .

(e.2) paragraphs 87(2)(c), 87(2)(d.1), 87(2)(e.1), 87(2)(e.3), 87(2)(g) to 87(2)(l), 87(2)(l.3) to 87(2)(u), 87(2)(x), 87(2)(z.1), 87(2)(z.2), 87(2)(aa), 87(2)(cc), 87(2)(ll), 87(2)(nn), 87(2)(pp), 87(2)(rr), 87(2)(tt) and 87(2)(uu), subsection 87(6) and, subject to section 78, subsection 87(7) apply to the winding-up as if the references in those provisions to

  (i)   "amalgamation" were read as "winding-up",

  (ii)  "predecessor corporation" were read as "subsidiary",

  (iii) "new corporation" were read as "parent",

  (iv) "its first taxation year" were read as "its taxation year during which it received the assets of the subsidiary on the winding-up",

  (v)  "its last taxation year" were read as "its taxation year during which its assets were distributed to the parent on the winding-up",

  (vi) "predecessor corporation's gain" were read as "subsidiary's gain",

  (vii) "predecessor corporation's income" were read as "subsidiary's income",

  (viii) "new corporation's income" were read as "parent's income",

  (ix) (Repealed by S.C. 1984, c. 45, s. 28(2).)

  (x)  "any predecessor private corporation" were read as "the subsidiary (if it was a private corporation at the time of the winding-up)",

  (xi) (Repealed by S.C. 1994, c. 7, Sch. II, s. 66(8).)

  (xii) (Repealed by S.C. 1994, c. 7, Sch. II, s. 66(8).)

  (xiii) "two or more corporations" were read as "a subsidiary",

  (xiv) (Repealed by S.C. 1998, c. 19, s. 118(11).)

  (xv) (Repealed by S.C. 1998, c. 19, s. 118(11).)

  (xvi) "the life insurance capital dividend account of any predecessor corporation immediately before the amalgamation" were read as "the life insurance capital dividend account of the subsidiary at the time the subsidiary was wound-up",

  (xvii) "predecessor corporation's refundable Part VII tax on hand" were read as "subsidiary's refundable Part VII tax on hand",

  (xviii) "predecessor corporation's Part VII refund" were read as "subsidiary's Part VII refund",

  (xix) "predecessor corporation's refundable Part VIII tax on hand" were read as "subsidiary's refundable Part VIII tax on hand",

(xx) "predecessor corporation's Part VIII refund" were read as "subsidiary's Part VIII refund", and

(xxi) "predecessor corporation's cumulative offset account" were read as "subsidiary's cumulative offset account";

. . .

(e.6) where a subsidiary has made a gift in a taxation year (in this section referred to as the "gift year"), for the purposes of computing the amount deductible under section 110.1 by the parent for its taxation years ending after the subsidiary was wound up, the parent shall be deemed to have made a gift in each of its taxation years in which a gift year of the subsidiary ended equal to the amount, if any, by which the total of all gifts made by the subsidiary in the gift year exceeds the total of all amounts deducted by the subsidiary under section 110.1 of this Act or paragraph 110(1)(a), (b) or (b.1) of the *Income Tax Act*, chapter 148 of the Revised Statutes of Canada, 1952, in respect of those gifts;

(e.61) the parent is deemed for the purpose of section 110.1 to have made any gift deemed by subsection 118.1(13) to have been made by the subsidiary after the subsidiary ceased to exist;

. . .

## PART I, DIVISION C
## COMPUTATION OF TAXABLE INCOME

**110.** (1) **Deductions permitted** — For the purpose of computing the taxable income of a taxpayer for a taxation year, there may be deducted such of the following amounts as are applicable

. . .

(d.01) **Charitable donation of employee option securities** — subject to subsection (2.1), where the taxpayer disposes of a security acquired in the year by the taxpayer under an agreement referred to in subsection 7(1) by making a gift of the security to a qualified donee (other than a private foundation), an amount in respect of the disposition of the security equal to 1/4 of the lesser of the benefit deemed by paragraph 7(1)(a) to have been received by the taxpayer in the year in respect of the acquisition of the security and the amount that would have been that benefit had the value of the security at the time of its acquisition by the taxpayer been equal to the value of the security at the time of the disposition, if

(i)    the security is a security described in subparagraph 38(a.1)(i),

(ii)   [Repealed, 2002, c. 9, s. 33(1) (in force March 27, 2002)]

(iii)  the gift is made in the year and on or before the day that is 30 days after the day on which the taxpayer acquired the security, and

(iv)   the taxpayer is entitled to a deduction under paragraph (d) in respect of the acquisition of the security;

(2) **Charitable gifts** — Where an individual is, during a taxation year, a member of a religious order and has, as such, taken a vow of perpetual poverty, the
individual may deduct in computing the individual's taxable income for the year
an amount equal to the total of the individual's superannuation or pension benefits
and the individual's earned income for the year (within the meaning assigned by
section 63) if, of the individual's income, that amount is paid in the year to the
order.

(2.1) (Repealed, S.C. 1988, c. 55, s. 77(12).)

**110.1.** (1) **Deductions for gifts** — For the purpose of computing the taxable
income of a corporation for a taxation year, there may be deducted such of the
following amounts as the corporation claims

(a)  **Charitable gifts** — the total of all amounts each of which is the fair
market value of a gift (other than a gift described in paragraph
110.1(1)(b), (c) or (d)) made by the corporation in the year or in any of
the 5 preceding taxation years to

(i)  a registered charity,

(ii)  a registered Canadian amateur athletic association,

(iii)  a corporation resident in Canada and described in paragraph
149(1)(i),

(iv)  a municipality in Canada,

(v)  the United Nations or an agency thereof,

(vi)  a university outside Canada that is prescribed to be a university the
student body of which ordinarily includes students from Canada,

(vii)  a charitable organization outside Canada to which Her Majesty in
right of Canada has made a gift in the year or in the 12-month period preceding the year, or

(viii)  Her Majesty in right of Canada or a province,

not exceeding the lesser of the corporation's income for the year and the amount
determined by the formula

$$0.75A + 0.25(B + C + D)$$

where

A is the corporation's income for the year computed without reference to subsection 137(2),

B is the total of all amounts each of which is a taxable capital gain of the corporation for the year from a disposition that is the making of a gift made by
the corporation in the year and described in this paragraph,

C is the total of all amounts each of which is a taxable capital gain of the corporation for the year, because of subsection 40(1.01), from a disposition of a
property in a preceding taxation year, and

D is the total of all amounts each of which is determined in respect of the corporation's depreciable property of a prescribed class and equal to the lesser of

(A)  the amount included under subsection 13(1) in respect of the class
in computing the corporation's income for the year, and

(B) the total of all amounts each of which is determined in respect of a disposition that is the making of a gift of property of the class made by the corporation in the year that is described in this paragraph and equal to the lesser of

(I) the proceeds of disposition of the property minus any outlays and expenses to the extent that they were made or incurred by the corporation for the purpose of making the disposition, and

(II) the capital cost to the corporation of the property;

(b) **Gifts to Her Majesty** — the total of all amounts each of which is the fair market value of a gift (other than a gift described in paragraph 110.1(1)(c) or (d)) made by the corporation to Her Majesty in right of Canada or a province

(i) in the year or in any of the 5 preceding taxation years, and

(ii) before February 19, 1997 or under a written agreement made before that day;

(c) **Gifts to institutions** — the total of all amounts each of which is the fair market value of a gift (other than a gift described in paragraph 110.1(1)(d)) of an object that the Canadian Cultural Property Export Review Board has determined meets the criteria set out in paragraphs 29(3)(b) and (c) of the *Cultural Property Export and Import Act*, which gift was made by the corporation in the year or in any of the 5 preceding taxation years to an institution or a public authority in Canada that was, at the time the gift was made, designated under subsection 32(2) of that Act either generally or for a specified purpose related to that object; and

(d) **Ecological gifts** — the total of all amounts each of which is the fair market value of a gift of land, including a servitude for the use and benefit of a dominant land, a covenant or an easement, that is certified by the Minister of the Environment, or a person designated by that Minister, to be ecologically sensitive land, the conservation and protection of which is, in the opinion of that Minister, or that person, important to the preservation of Canada's environmental heritage, which gift was made by the corporation in the year or in any of the 5 preceding taxation years to

(i) Her Majesty in right of Canada or a province or a municipality in Canada, or

(ii) a registered charity one of the main purposes of which is, in the opinion of that Minister, the conservation and protection of Canada's environmental heritage, and that is approved by that Minister or that person in respect of the gift.

(1.1) **Limitation on deductibility** — For the purpose of determining the amount deductible under subsection 110.1(1) in computing a corporation's taxable income for a taxation year,

(a) an amount in respect of a gift is deductible only to the extent that it exceeds amounts in respect of the gift deducted under that subsection in computing the corporation's taxable income for preceding taxation years, and

(b)　no amount in respect of a gift made in a particular taxation year is deductible under any of paragraphs 110.1(1)(a) to (d) until amounts deductible under that paragraph in respect of gifts made in taxation years preceding the particular year have been deducted.

(1.2) **Where control acquired** — Notwithstanding paragraph 88(1)(e.6), if control of a particular corporation is acquired at any time by a person or group of persons,

(a)　no amount is deductible under any of paragraphs (1)(a) to (d) in computing any corporation's taxable income for a taxation year that ends on or after that time in respect of a gift made by the particular corporation before that time; and

(b)　no amount is deductible under any of paragraphs (1)(a) to (d) in computing any corporation's taxable income for a taxation year that ends on or after that time in respect of a gift made by any corporation on or after that time if the property that is the subject of the gift was acquired by the particular corporation under an arrangement under which it was expected that control of the particular corporation would be so acquired by a person or group of persons, other than a qualified donee that received the gift, and the gift would be so made.

(2) **Proof of gift** — A gift shall not be included for the purpose of determining a deduction under subsection 110.1(1) unless the making of the gift is proven by filing with the Minister a receipt therefor that contains prescribed information.

(3) **Gifts of capital property** — Where at any time

(a)　a corporation makes a gift of

　(i)　capital property to a donee described in paragraph 110.1(1)(a), (b) or (d), or

　(ii)　in the case of a corporation not resident in Canada, real property situated in Canada to a prescribed donee who provides an undertaking, in a form satisfactory to the Minister, to the effect that the property will be held for use in the public interest, and

(b)　the fair market value of the property at that time exceeds its adjusted cost base to the corporation,

such amount, not greater than the fair market value and not less than the adjusted cost base to the corporation of the property at that time, as the corporation designates in its return of income under section 150 for the year in which the gift is made shall, if the making of the gift is proven by filing with the Minister a receipt containing prescribed information, be deemed to be its proceeds of disposition of the property and, for the purposes of subsection 110.1(1), the fair market value of the gift made by the corporation.

(4) **Gifts made by partnership** — Where a corporation is, at the end of a fiscal period of a partnership, a member of the partnership, its share of any amount that would, if the partnership were a person, be a gift made by the partnership to

any donee shall, for the purposes of this section, be deemed to be a gift made to that donee by the corporation in its taxation year in which the fiscal period of the partnership ends.

(5) **Ecological gifts** — For the purposes of paragraph 110.1(1)(d) and section 207.31, the fair market value of a gift of a servitude, a covenant or an easement to which land is subject is deemed to be the greater of its fair market value otherwise determined and the amount by which the fair market value of the land is reduced as a consequence of the making of the gift.

(6) **Non-qualifying securities** — Subsections 118.1(13), and (14) and (16) to (20) apply to a corporation as if the references in those subsections to an individual were read as references to a corporation and as if a non-qualifying security of a corporation included a share (other than a share listed on a prescribed stock exchange) of the capital stock of the corporation.

(7) **Corporation ceasing to exist** — If, but for this subsection, a corporation (other than a corporation that was a predecessor corporation in an amalgamation to which subsection 87(1) applied or a corporation that was wound up in a winding-up to which subsection 88(1) applied) would be deemed by subsection 118.1(13) to have made a gift after the corporation ceased to exist, for the purpose of this section, the corporation is deemed to have made the gift in its last taxation year, except that the amount of interest payable under any provision of this Act is the amount that it would be if this subsection did not apply to the gift.

[S.C. 1974-75-76, c. 26, s. 70; S.C. 1974-75-76, c. 71, s. 2; S.C. 1976-77, c. 4, s. 44; S.C. 1977-78, c. 1, s. 52; S.C. 1977-78, c. 32, s. 26; S.C. 1979, c. 5, s. 34; S.C. 1980-81-82-83, c. 48, s. 58; S.C. 1980-81-82-83, c. 140, s. 66; S.C. 1984, c. 1, s. 50; S.C. 1986, c. 6, s. 56; S.C. 1988, c. 55, s. 78; S.C. 1994, c. 7, Sch. II, s. 79; S.C. 1994, c. 7, Sch. VIII, s. 46; S.C. 1996, c. 21, s. 20; S.C. 1997, c. 25, s. 22; S.C. 1998, c. 19, s. 20; 2005, c. 19, s. 19]

. . .

## PART I, DIVISION E, SUBDIVISION A
## RULES APPLICABLE TO INDIVIDUALS

**118.1.** (1) **Definitions** — In this section,

"total charitable gifts" of an individual for a taxation year means the total of all amounts each of which is the fair market value of a gift (other than a gift the fair market value of which is included in the total Crown gifts, the total cultural gifts or the total ecological gifts of the individual for the year) made by the individual in the year or in any of the 5 immediately preceding taxation years (other than in a year for which a deduction under subsection 110(2) was claimed in computing the individual's taxable income) to

(a)   a registered charity,
(b)   a registered Canadian amateur athletic association,
(c)   a housing corporation resident in Canada and exempt from tax under this Part because of paragraph 149(1)(i),
(d)   a Canadian municipality,
(e)   the United Nations or an agency thereof,

(f)    a university outside Canada that is prescribed to be a university the student body of which ordinarily includes students from Canada,

(g)    a charitable organization outside Canada to which Her Majesty in right of Canada has made a gift during the individual's taxation year or the 12 months immediately preceding that taxation year, or

(g.1) Her Majesty in right of Canada or a province,

to the extent that those amounts were

(h)    not deducted in computing the individual's taxable income for a taxation year ending before 1988, and

(i)    not included in determining an amount that was deducted under this section in computing the individual's tax payable under this Part for a preceding taxation year;

"total Crown gifts" of an individual for a taxation year means the total of all amounts each of which is the fair market value of a gift (other than a gift the fair market value of which is included in the total cultural gifts or the total ecological gifts of the individual for the year) made by the individual in the year or in any of the 5 immediately preceding taxation years to Her Majesty in right of Canada or a province, to the extent that those amounts were

(a)    not deducted in computing the individual's taxable income for a taxation year ending before 1988,

(b)    not included in determining an amount that was deducted under this section in computing the individual's tax payable under this Part for a preceding taxation year; and

(c)    in respect of gifts made before February 19, 1997 or under agreements in writing made before that day;

"total cultural gifts" of an individual for a taxation year means the total of all amounts each of which is the fair market value of a gift

(a)    of an object that the Canadian Cultural Property Export Review Board has determined meets the criteria set out in paragraphs 29(3)(b) and (c) of the *Cultural Property Export and Import Act*, and

(b)    that was made by the individual in the year or in any of the 5 immediately preceding taxation years to an institution or a public authority in Canada that was, at the time the gift was made, designated under subsection 32(2) of the *Cultural Property Export and Import Act* either generally or for a specified purpose related to that object,

to the extent that those amounts were

(c)    not deducted in computing the individual's taxable income for a taxation year ending before 1988, and

(d)    not included in determining an amount that was deducted under this section in computing the individual's tax payable under this Part for a preceding taxation year;

"total ecological gifts" of an individual for a taxation year means the total of all amounts each of which is the fair market value of a gift (other than a gift the fair market value of which is included in the total cultural gifts of the individual for the year) of land, including a servitude for the use and benefit of a dominant land, a covenant or an easement, that is certified by the Minister of the Environment, or a person designated by that Minister, to be ecologically sensitive land, the conservation and protection of which is, in the opinion of that Minister, or that person, important to the preservation of Canada's environmental heritage, which gift was made by the individual in the year or in any of the 5 immediately preceding taxation years to

(a)  Her Majesty in right of Canada or a province or a municipality in Canada, or

(b)  a registered charity one of the main purposes of which is, in the opinion of the Minister of the Environment, the conservation and protection of Canada's environmental heritage, and that is approved by that Minister, or that person, in respect of that gift,

to the extent that those amounts were not included in determining an amount that was deducted under this section in computing the individual's tax payable under this Part for a preceding taxation year;

"total gifts" of an individual for a taxation year means the total of

(a)  the least of

(i)  the individual's total charitable gifts for the year,

(ii)  the individual's income for the year where the individual dies in the year or in the following taxation year, and

(iii)  in any other case, the lesser of the individual's income for the year and the amount determined by the formula

$$0.75A + 0.25 (B + C + D - E)$$

where

A is the individual's income for the year,

B is the total of all amounts each of which is a taxable capital gain of the individual for the year from a disposition that is the making of a gift made by the individual in the year, which gift is included in the individual's total charitable gifts for the year,

C is the total of all amounts each of which is a taxable capital gain of the individual for the year, because of subsection 40(1.01), from a disposition of a property in a preceding taxation year,

D is the total of all amounts each of which is determined in respect of the individual's depreciable property of a prescribed class and equal to the lesser of

(A) the amount included under subsection 13(1) in respect of the class in computing the individual's income for the year, and

(B) the total of all amounts each of which is determined in respect of a disposition that is the making of a gift of property of the class made by the individual in the year that is included in the individual's total charitable gifts for the year and equal to the lesser of

(I) the proceeds of disposition of the property minus any outlays and expenses to the extent that they were made or incurred by the individual for the purpose of making the disposition, and

(II) the capital cost to the individual of the property, and

E is the total of all amounts each of which is the portion of an amount deducted under section 110.6 in computing the individual's taxable income for the year that can reasonably be considered to be in respect of a gift referred to in the description of B or C,

(b)    the individual's total Crown gifts for the year,

(c)    the individual's total cultural gifts for the year, and

(d)    the individual's total ecological gifts for the year.

(2) **Proof of gift** — A gift shall not be included in the total charitable gifts, total Crown gifts, total cultural gifts or total ecological gifts of an individual unless the making of the gift is proven by filing with the Minister

(a)    a receipt for the gift that contains prescribed information;

(b)    in the case of a gift described in the definition "total cultural gifts" in subsection (1), the certificate issued under subsection 33(1) of the Cultural Property Export and Import Act; and

(c)    in the case of a gift described in the definition "total ecological gifts" in subsection (1), both certificates referred to in that definition.

(2.1) **Ordering** — For the purposes of determining the total charitable gifts, total Crown gifts, total cultural gifts and total ecological gifts of an individual for a taxation year, no amount in respect of a gift described in any of the definitions of those expressions and made in a particular taxation year shall be considered to have been included in determining an amount that was deducted under this section in computing the individual's tax payable under this Part for a taxation year until amounts in respect of such gifts made in taxation years preceding the particular year that can be so considered are so considered.

(3) **Deduction by individuals for gifts** — For the purpose of computing the tax payable under this Part by an individual for a taxation year, there may be deducted such amount as the individual claims not exceeding the amount determined by the formula

$$(A \times B) + [C \times (D - B)]$$

where

A    is the appropriate percentage for the year;

B    is the lesser of $200 and the individual's total gifts for the year;

C    is the highest percentage referred to in subsection 117(2) that applies in determining tax that might be payable under this Part for the year; and

D    is the individual's total gifts for the year.

(4) **Gift in year of death** — Subject to subsection 118.1(13), a gift made by an individual in the particular taxation year in which the individual dies (including, for greater certainty, a gift otherwise deemed by subsection 118.1(5), 118.1(13) or

118.1(15) to have been so made) is deemed, for the purpose of this section other than this subsection, to have been made by the individual in the immediately preceding taxation year, and not in the particular year, to the extent that an amount in respect of the gift is not deducted in computing the individual's tax payable under this Part for the particular year.

(5) **Gift by will** — Subject to subsection 118.1(13), where an individual by the individual's will makes a gift, the gift is, for the purpose of this section, deemed to have been made by the individual immediately before the individual died.

(5.1) **Direct designation – insurance proceeds** — Subsection (5.2) applies to an individual in respect of a life insurance policy where

(a)    the policy is a life insurance policy under which, immediately before the individual's death, the individual's life was insured;

(b)    a transfer of money, or a transfer by means of a negotiable instrument, is made as a consequence of the individual's death and solely because of the obligations under the policy, from an insurer to a qualified donee (other than a transfer the amount of which is not included in computing the income of the individual or the individual's estate for any taxation year but would have been included in computing the income of the individual or the individual's estate for a taxation year if the transfer had been made to the individual's legal representative for the benefit of the individual's estate and this Act were read without reference to subsection 70(3));

(c)    immediately before the individual's death,

(i)    the individual's consent would have been required to change the recipient of the transfer described in paragraph (b), and

(ii)    the donee was neither a policyholder under the policy, nor an assignee of the individual's interest under the policy; and

(d)    the transfer occurs within the 36 month period that begins at the time of the death (or, where written application to extend the period has been made to the Minister by the individual's legal representative, within such longer period as the Minister considers reasonable in the circumstances).

(5.2) **Deemed gift – subsection (5.1)** — Where this subsection applies,

(a)    for the purpose of this section (other than subsection (5.1) and this paragraph) and section 149.1, the transfer described in subsection (5.1) is deemed to be a gift made, immediately before the individual's death, by the individual to the qualified donee referred to in subsection (5.1); and

(b)    the fair market value of the gift is deemed to be the fair market value, at the time of the individual's death, of the right to that transfer (determined without reference to any risk of default with regard to obligations of the insurer).

(5.3) **Direct designation – RRSPs and RRIFs** — Where as a consequence of an individual's death, a transfer of money, or a transfer by means of a negotiable instrument, is made, from a registered retirement savings plan or registered retirement income fund (other than a plan or fund of which a licensed annuities provider is the issuer or carrier, as the case may be) to a qualified donee, solely because of the donee's interest as a beneficiary under the plan or fund, the individual was the annuitant (within the meaning assigned by subsection 146(1) or 146.3(1)) under the plan or fund immediately before the individual's death and the transfer occurs within the 36-month period that begins at the time of the death (or, where written application to extend the period has been made to the Minister by the individual's legal representative, within such longer period as the Minister considers reasonable in the circumstances),

(a)    for the purposes of this section (other than this paragraph) and section 149.1, the transfer is deemed to be a gift made, immediately before the individual's death, by the individual to the donee; and

(b)    the fair market value of the gift is deemed to be the fair market value, at the time of the individual's death, of the right to the transfer (determined without reference to any risk of default with regard to the obligations of the issuer of the plan or the carrier of the fund).

(6) **Gift of capital property** — Where, at any time, whether by the individual's will or otherwise, an individual makes a gift of

(a)    capital property to a donee described in the definition "total charitable gifts", "total Crown gifts" or "total ecological gifts" in subsection 118.1(1), or

(b)    in the case of an individual who is a non-resident person, real property situated in Canada to a prescribed donee who provides an undertaking, in a form satisfactory to the Minister, to the effect that the property will be held for use in the public interest,

and the fair market value of the property at that time exceeds its adjusted cost base to the individual, such amount, not greater than the fair market value and not less than the adjusted cost base to the individual of the property at that time, as the individual or the individual's legal representative designates in the individual's return of income under section 150 for the year in which the gift is made shall, if the making of the gift is proven by filing with the Minister a receipt containing prescribed information, be deemed to be the individual's proceeds of disposition of the property and, for the purposes of subsection 118.1(1), the fair market value of the gift made by the individual.

(7) **Gifts of art** — Except where subsection 118.1(7.1) applies, where at any time, whether by the individual's will or otherwise, an individual makes a gift of a work of art that was created by the individual and that is property in the individual's inventory to a donee described in the definition "total charitable gifts" or "total Crown gifts" in subsection 118.1(1) and at that time the fair market value of the work of art exceeds its cost amount to the individual, such amount, not greater than that fair market value and not less than that cost amount, as is designated in the individual's return of income under section 150 for the year in which the gift is made shall, if the making of the gift is proven by filing with the Minister a receipt containing prescribed information, be deemed to be the individual's

proceeds of disposition of the work of art and, for the purposes of subsection 118.1(1), the fair market value of the gift made by the individual.

(7.1) **Gifts of cultural property** — Where at any time, whether by the individual's will or otherwise, an individual makes a gift described in the definition "total cultural gifts" in subsection 118.1(1) of a work of art that was created by the individual and that is property in the individual's inventory, the individual shall, if the making of the gift is proven by filing with the Minister a receipt containing prescribed information, be deemed to have received proceeds of disposition in respect of the gift at that time equal to its cost amount to the individual at that time.

(8) **Gifts made by partnership** — Where an individual is, at the end of a fiscal period of a partnership, a member of the partnership, the individual's share of any amount that would, if the partnership were a person, be a gift made by the partnership to any donee shall, for the purposes of this section, be deemed to be a gift made by the individual to that donee in the individual's taxation year in which the fiscal period of the partnership ends.

(9) **Commuter's charitable donations** — Where throughout a taxation year an individual resided in Canada near the boundary between Canada and the United States, if

(a) the individual commuted to the individual's principal place of employment or business in the United States, and

(b) the individual's chief source of income for the year was that employment or business,

a gift made by the individual in the year to a religious, charitable, scientific, literary or educational organization created or organized in or under the laws of the United States that would be allowed as a deduction under the United States Internal Revenue Code shall, for the purpose of the definition "total charitable gifts" in subsection 118.1(1), be deemed to have been made to a registered charity.

(10) **Determination of fair market value** — For the purposes of paragraph 110.1(1)(c) and the definition "total cultural gifts" in subsection 118.1(1), the fair market value of an object is deemed to be the fair market value determined by the Canadian Cultural Property Export Review Board.

(10.1) **Determination of fair market value** — For the purposes of subparagraph 69(1)(b)(ii), subsection 70(5), section 110.1 and this section, where at any time the Canadian Cultural Property Export Review Board determines or redetermines an amount to be the fair market value of a property that is the subject of a gift described in paragraph 110.1(1)(a) or in the definition "total charitable gifts" in subsection (1) made by a taxpayer within the two-year period that begins at that time, the last amount so determined or redetermined within the period is deemed to be the fair market value of the property at the time the gift was made and, subject to subsection 110.1(3) and subsections (6) and (7), to be the taxpayer's proceeds of disposition of the property.

(11) **Assessments** — Notwithstanding subsections 152(4) to 152(5), such assessments or reassessments of a taxpayer's tax, interest or penalties payable under

this Act for any taxation year shall be made as are necessary to give effect to a certificate issued under subsection 33(1) of the *Cultural Property Export and Import Act* or to a decision of a court resulting from an appeal made pursuant to section 33.1 of that Act.

(12) **Ecological gifts** — For the purposes of section 207.31 and the definition "total ecological gifts" in subsection 118.1(1), the fair market value of a gift of a servitude, a covenant or an easement to which land is subject is deemed to be the greater of its fair market value otherwise determined and the amount by which the fair market value of the land is reduced as a result of the making of the gift.

(13) **Non-qualifying securities** — For the purpose of this section (other than this subsection), where at any particular time an individual makes a gift (including a gift that, but for this subsection and subsection 118.1(4), would be deemed by subsection 118.1(5) to be made at the particular time) of a non-qualifying security of the individual and the gift is not an excepted gift,

   (a)   except for the purpose of applying subsection 118.1(6) to determine the individual's proceeds of disposition of the security, the gift is deemed not to have been made;

   (b)   if the security ceases to be a non-qualifying security of the individual at a subsequent time that is within 60 months after the particular time and the donee has not disposed of the security at or before the subsequent time, the individual is deemed to have made a gift to the donee of property at the subsequent time and the fair market value of that gift is deemed to be the lesser of the fair market value of the security at the subsequent time and the amount of the gift made at the particular time that would, but for this subsection, have been included in the individual's total charitable gifts or total Crown gifts for a taxation year;

   (c)   if the security is disposed of by the donee within 60 months after the particular time and paragraph 118.1(13)(b) does not apply to the security, the individual is deemed to have made a gift to the donee of property at the time of the disposition and the fair market value of that gift is deemed to be the lesser of the fair market value of any consideration (other than a non-qualifying security of the individual or a property that would be a non-qualifying security of the individual if the individual were alive at that time) received by the donee for the disposition and the amount of the gift made at the particular time that would, but for this subsection, have been included in the individual's total charitable gifts or total Crown gifts for a taxation year; and

   (d)   a designation under subsection 118.1(6) or 110.1(3) in respect of the gift made at the particular time may be made in the individual's return of income for the year that includes the subsequent time referred to in paragraph 118.1(13)(b) or the time of the disposition referred to in paragraph 118.1(13)(c).

(14) **Exchanged security** — Where a share (in this subsection referred to as the "new share") that is a non-qualifying security of an individual has been acquired by a donee referred to in subsection 118.1(13) in exchange for another share (in this subsection referred to as the "original share") that is a non-qualifying security of

the individual by means of a transaction to which section 51, subparagraphs 85.1(1)(a)(i) and 85.1(1)(a)(ii) or section 86 or 87 applies, the new share is deemed for the purposes of this subsection and subsection 118.1(13) to be the same share as the original share.

(15) **Death of donor** — If, but for this subsection, an individual would be deemed by subsection 118.1(13) to have made a gift after the individual's death, for the purpose of this section the individual is deemed to have made the gift in the taxation year in which the individual died, except that the amount of interest payable under any provision of this Act is the amount that it would be if this subsection did not apply to the gift.

(16) **Loanbacks** — For the purpose of this section, where

(a)    at any particular time an individual makes a gift of property,

(b)    if the property is a non-qualifying security of the individual, the gift is an excepted gift, and

(c)    within 60 months after the particular time

     (i)    the donee holds a non-qualifying security of the individual that was acquired by the donee after the time that is 60 months before the particular time, or

     (ii)    where the individual and the donee do not deal at arm's length with each other,

         (A)    the individual or any person or partnership with which the individual does not deal at arm's length uses property of the donee under an agreement that was made or modified after the time that is 60 months before the particular time, and

         (B)    the property was not used in the carrying on of the donee's charitable activities,

the fair market value of the gift is deemed to be that value otherwise determined minus the total of all amounts each of which is the fair market value of the consideration given by the donee to so acquire a non-qualifying security so held or the fair market value of such a property so used, as the case may be.

(17) **Ordering rule** — For the purpose of applying subsection (16) to determine the fair market value of a gift made at any time by a taxpayer, the fair market value of consideration given to acquire property described in subparagraph (16)(c)(i) or of property described in subparagraph (16)(c)(ii) is deemed to be that value otherwise determined minus any portion of it that has been applied under that subsection to reduce the fair market value of another gift made before that time by the taxpayer.

(18) **Non-qualifying security defined** — For the purposes of this section, "non-qualifying security" of an individual at any time means

(a)    an obligation (other than an obligation of a financial institution to repay an amount deposited with the institution or an obligation listed on a prescribed stock exchange) of the individual or the individual's estate or of any person or partnership with which the individual or the estate does not deal at arm's length immediately after that time;

(b)    a share (other than a share listed on a prescribed stock exchange) of the capital stock of a corporation with which the individual or the estate does not deal at arm's length immediately after that time; or

(c)    any other security (other than a security listed on a prescribed stock exchange) issued by the individual or the estate or by any person or partnership with which the individual or the estate does not deal at arm's length immediately after that time.

(19) **Excepted gift** — For the purposes of this section, a gift made by a taxpayer is an excepted gift if

(a)    the security is a share;

(b)    the donee is not a private foundation;

(c)    the taxpayer deals at arm's length with the donee; and

(d)    where the donee is a charitable organization or a public foundation, the taxpayer deals at arm's length with each director, trustee, officer and like official of the donee.

(20) **Financial institution defined** — For the purpose of subsection 118.1(18), "financial institution" means a corporation that is

(a)    a member of the Canadian Payments Association; or

(b)    a credit union that is a shareholder or member of a body corporate or organization that is a central for the purposes of the *Canadian Payments Association Act*.

[S.C. 1988, c. 55, s. 92; S.C. 1994, c. 7, Sch. II, s. 88; S.C. 1994, c. 7, Sch. VIII, s. 53; S.C. 1995, c. 3, s. 34; S.C. 1995, c. 38, s. 3; S.C. 1996, c. 21, s. 23; S.C. 1997, c. 25, s. 26; S.C. 1998, c. 19, s. 22; S.C. 1999, c. 22, s. 32; S.C. 1999, c. 31, s. 136; 2005, c. 19, s. 23.]

# PART I, DIVISION F
## DEFERRED AND OTHER SPECIAL INCOME ARANGEMENTS

*Communal Organizations*

**143.** (1) **Communal organizations** — Where a congregation, or one or more business agencies of the congregation, carries on one or more businesses for purposes that include supporting or sustaining the congregation's members or the members of any other congregation, the following rules apply:

(a)    an *inter vivos* trust is deemed to be created on the day that is the later of

     (i)    December 31, 1976, and

     (ii)    the day the congregation came into existence;

(b)    the trust is deemed to have been continuously in existence from the day determined under paragraph (a);

(c)    the property of the congregation is deemed to be the property of the trust;

(d)    the property of each business agency of the congregation in a calendar year is deemed to be property of the trust throughout the portion of the year throughout which the trust exists;

(e)    where the congregation is a corporation, the corporation is deemed to be the trustee having control of the trust property;

(f)    where the congregation is not a corporation, its council, committee of leaders, executive committee, administrative committee, officers or other group charged with its management are deemed to be the trustees having control of the trust property;

(g)    the congregation is deemed to act and to have always acted as agent for the trust in all matters relating to its businesses and other activities;

(h)    each business agency of the congregation in a calendar year is deemed to have acted as agent for the trust in all matters in the year relating to its businesses and other activities;

(i)    the members of the congregation are deemed to be the beneficiaries under the trust;

(j)    tax under this Part is payable by the trust on its taxable income for each taxation year;

(k)    in computing the income of the trust for any taxation year,

  (i)    subject to paragraph (l), no deduction may be made in respect of salaries, wages or benefits of any kind provided to the members of the congregation, and

  (ii)   no deduction may be made under subsection 104(6), except to the extent that any portion of the trust's income (determined without reference to that subsection) is allocated to the members of the congregation in accordance with subsection (2);

(l)    for the purpose of applying section 20.01 to the trust,

  (i)    each member of the congregation is deemed to be a member of the trust's household, and

  (ii)   section 20.01 shall be read without reference to paragraphs 20.01(2)(b) and (c) and subsection 20.01(3); and

(m)   where the congregation or one of the business agencies is a corporation, section 15.1 shall, except for the purposes of paragraphs 15.1(2)(a) and (c) (other than subparagraphs 15.1(2)(c)(i) and (ii)), apply as if this subsection were read without reference to paragraphs (c), (d), (g) and(h).

(2) **Election in respect of income** — Where the inter vivos trust referred to in subsection (1) in respect of a congregation so elects in respect of a taxation year in writing filed with the Minister on or before the trust's filing-due date for the year and all the congregation's participating members are specified in the election in accordance with subsection (5), the following rules apply:

(a)    for the purposes of subsections 104(6) and (13), the amount payable in the year to a particular participating member of the congregation out of the income of the trust (determined without reference to subsection 104(6)) is the amount determined by the formula

$$0.8 \ (A \ x \ B/C) + D + (0.2A - E)/F$$

where

A is the taxable income of the trust for the year (determined without reference to subsection 104(6) and specified future tax consequences for the year),

B is

(i)    where the particular member is identified in the election as a person to whom this subparagraph applies (in this subsection referred to as a "designated member"), 1, and

(ii)   in any other case, 0.5,

C is the total of

     (i)    the number of designated members of the congregation, and

     (ii)   1/2 of the number of other participating members of the congregation in respect of the year,

D is the amount, if any, that is specified in the election as an additional allocation under this subsection to the particular member,

E is the total of all amounts each of which is an amount specified in the election as an additional allocation under this subsection to a participating member of the congregation in respect of the year, and

F is the number of participating members of the congregation in respect of the year;

(b)    the designated member of each family at the end of the year is deemed to have supported the other members of the family during the year and the other members of the family are deemed to have been wholly dependent on the designated member for support during the year; and

(c)    the taxable income for the year of each member of the congregation shall be computed without reference to subsection 110(2).

(3) **Refusal to accept election** — An election under subsection (2) in respect of a congregation for a particular taxation year is not binding on the Minister unless all taxes, interest and penalties payable under this Part, as a consequence of the application of subsection (2) to the congregation for preceding taxation years, are paid at or before the end of the particular year.

(3.1) **Election in respect of gifts** — For the purposes of section 118.1, where the fair market value of a gift made in a taxation year by an inter vivos trust referred to in subsection (1) in respect of a congregation would, but for this subsection, be included in the total charitable gifts, total Crown gifts, total cultural gifts or total ecological gifts of the trust for the year and the trust so elects in its return of income under this Part for the year,

(a)    the trust is deemed not to have made the gift; and

(b)    each participating member of the congregation is deemed to have made, in the year, such a gift the fair market value of which is the amount determined by the formula

A x B/C

where

A is the fair market value of the gift made by the trust,

B is the amount determined for the year in respect of the member under paragraph(2)(a) as a consequence of an election under subsection (2) by the trust, and

C is the total of all amounts each of which is an amount determined for the year in respect of a participating member of the congregation under paragraph (2)(a) as a consequence of an election under subsection (2) by the trust.

(4) **Definitions** — For the purposes of this section,

"adult" means an individual who, before the time at which the term is applied, has attained the age of eighteen years or is married or in a common-law partnership;

"business agency", of a congregation at any time in a particular calendar year, means a corporation, trust or other person, where the congregation owned all the shares of the capital stock of the corporation (except directors' qualifying shares) or every interest in the trust or other person, as the case may be, throughout the portion of the particular calendar year throughout which both the congregation and the corporation, trust or other person, as the case may be, were in existence;

"congregation" means a community, society or body of individuals, whether or not incorporated,

(a)  the members of which live and work together,

(b)  that adheres to the practices and beliefs of, and operates according to the principles of, the religious organization of which it is a constituent part,

(c)  that does not permit any of its members to own any property in their own right, and

(d)  that requires its members to devote their working lives to the activities of the congregation;

"family" means,

(a)  in the case of an adult who is unmarried and who is not in a common-law partnership, that person and the person's children who are not adults, not married and not in a common-law partnership, and

(b)  in the case of an adult who is married or in a common-law partnership, that person and the person's spouse or common-law partner and the children of either or both of them who are not adults, not married and not in a common-law partnership

but does not include an individual who is included in any other family or who is not a member of the congregation in which the family is included;

"member of a congregation" means

(a)  an adult, living with the members of the congregation, who conforms to the practices of the religious organization of which the congregation is a constituent part whether or not that person has been formally accepted into the organization, and

(b)  a child who is unmarried and not in a common-law partnership, other than an adult, of an adult referred to in paragraph (a), if the child lives with the members of the congregation;

"participating member", of a congregation in respect of a taxation year, means an individual who, at the end of the year, is an adult who is a member of the congregation;

"religious organization" means an organization, other than a registered charity, of which a congregation is a constituent part, that adheres to beliefs, evidenced by the religious and philosophical tenets of the organization, that include a belief in the existence of a supreme being.

"total charitable gifts" has the meaning assigned by subsection 118.1(1);

"total Crown gifts" has the meaning assigned by subsection 118.1(1);

"total cultural gifts" has the meaning assigned by subsection 118.1(1);

"total ecological gifts" has the same meaning as in subsection 118.1(1).

(5) **Specification of family members** — For the purpose of applying subsection (2) to a particular election by the inter vivos trust referred to in subsection (1) in respect of a congregation for a particular taxation year,

(a)    subject to paragraph (b), a participating member of the congregation is considered to have been specified in the particular election in accordance with this subsection only if the member is identified in the particular election and

   (i)    where the member's family includes only one adult at the end of the particular year, the member is identified in the particular election as a person to whom subparagraph (i) of the description of B in subsection (2) (in this subsection referred to as the "relevant subparagraph") applies, and

   (ii)   in any other case, only one of the adults in the member's family is identified in the particular election as a person to whom the relevant subparagraph applies; and

(b)    an individual is considered not to have been specified in the particular election in accordance with this subsection if

   (i)    the individual is one of two individuals who were married to each other, or in a common-law partnership, at the end of a preceding taxation year of the trust and at the end of the particular year,

   (ii)   one of those individuals was

      (A)   where the preceding year ended before 1998, specified in an election under subsection (2) by the trust for the preceding year, and

      (B)   in any other case, identified in an election under subsection (2) by the trust for the preceding year as a person to whom the relevant subparagraph applied, and

   (iii)  the other individual is identified in the particular election as a person to whom the relevant subparagraph applies.

[1970-71-72, c. 63, s. 1; S.C. 1974-75-76, c. 26, s. 97; S.C. 1977-78, c. 1, s. 71; S.C. 1988, c. 55, s. 128; S.C. 1994, c. 7, Sch. II, s. 116; S.C. 1994, c. 21, s. 67; S.C. 2000, c. 19, s. 41; S.C. 2000, c. 12, ss. 134 (Note S.C. 2000, c. 12, s. 134(2)(E) amended by S.C. 2001, c. 17, s. 263(1)(E)), 142; S.C. 2001, c. 17, s. 245.]

**143.2. (1) Definitions** — The definitions in this subsection apply in this section.

"expenditure" means an outlay or expense or the cost or capital cost of a property.

"llllited partner" has the meaning that would be assigned by subsection 96(2.4) if that subsection were read without reference to "if the member's partnership interest is not an exempt interest (within the meaning assigned by subsection 96(2.5)) at that time and".

"limited-recourse amount" means the unpaid principal amount of any indebtedness for which recourse is limited, either immediately or in the future and either absolutely or contingently.

"taxpayer" includes a partnership.

"tax shelter investment" means

(a) a property that is a tax shelter for the purpose of subsection 237.1(1); or

(b) a taxpayer's interest in a partnership where

    (i) an interest in the taxpayer

        (A) is a tax shelter investment, and

        (B) the taxpayer's partnership interest would be a tax shelter investment if

            (I) this Act were read without reference to this paragraph and to the words "having regard to statements or representations made or proposed to be made in connection with the property" in the definition "tax shelter" in subsection 237.1(1),

            (II) the references in that definition to "represented" were read as references to "that can reasonably be expected", and

            (III) the reference in that definition to "is represented" were read as a reference to "can reasonably be expected",

    (ii) another interest in the partnership is a tax shelter investment, or

    (iii) the taxpayer's interest in the partnership entitles the taxpayer, directly or indirectly, to a share of the income or loss of a particular partnership where

        (A) another taxpayer holding a partnership interest is entitled, directly or indirectly, to a share of the income or loss of the particular partnership, and

        (B) that other taxpayer's partnership interest is a tax shelter investment.

(2) **At-risk adjustment** — For the purpose of this section, an at-risk adjustment in respect of an expenditure of a particular taxpayer, other than the cost of a partnership interest to which subsection 96(2.2) applies, means any amount or benefit that the particular taxpayer, or another taxpayer not dealing at arm's length with the particular taxpayer, is entitled, either immediately or in the future and either absolutely or contingently, to receive or to obtain, whether by way of reimbursement, compensation, revenue guarantee, proceeds of disposition, loan or any other form of indebtedness, or in any other form or manner whatever, granted or to be granted for the purpose of reducing the impact, in whole or in part, of any loss that the particular taxpayer may sustain in respect of the expenditure or, where the expenditure is the cost or capital cost of a property, any loss from the holding or disposition of the property.

(3) **Amount or benefit not included** — For the purpose of subsection 143.2(2), an at-risk adjustment in respect of a taxpayer's expenditure does not include an amount or benefit.

    (a)    to the extent that it is included in determining the value of J in the definition "cumulative Canadian exploration expense" in subsection 66.1(6), of M in the definition "cumulative Canadian development expense" in subsection 66.2(5) or of I in the definition "cumulative Canadian oil and gas property expense" in subsection 66.4(5) in respect of the taxpayer; or

    (b)    the entitlement to which arises

        (i)    because of a contract of insurance with an insurance corporation dealing at arm's length with the taxpayer (and, where the expenditure is the cost of an interest in a partnership, with each member of the partnership) under which the taxpayer is insured against any claim arising as a result of a liability incurred in the ordinary course of carrying on the business of the taxpayer or the partnership,

        (ii)    as a consequence of the death of the taxpayer,

        (iii)    in respect of an amount not included in the expenditure, determined without reference to subparagraph 143.2(6)(b)(ii), or

        (iv)    because of an excluded obligation (as defined in subsection 6202.1(5) of the Income Tax Regulations) in relation to a share issued to the taxpayer or, where the expenditure is the cost of an interest in a partnership, to the partnership.

(4) **Amount or benefit** — For the purposes of subsections 143.2(2) and (3), where the amount or benefit to which a taxpayer is entitled at any time is provided by way of an agreement or other arrangement under which the taxpayer has a right, either immediately or in the future and either absolutely or contingently (otherwise than as a consequence of the death of the taxpayer), to acquire property, for greater certainty the amount or benefit to which the taxpayer is entitled under the agreement or arrangement is considered to be not less than the fair market value of the property at that time.

(5) **Amount or benefit** — For the purposes of subsections 143.2(2) and (3), where the amount or benefit to which a taxpayer is entitled at any time is provided by way of a guarantee, security or similar indemnity or covenant in respect of any loan or other obligation of the taxpayer, for greater certainty the amount or benefit to which the taxpayer is entitled under the guarantee or indemnity at any particular time is considered to be not less than the total of the unpaid amount of the loan or obligation at that time and all other amounts outstanding in respect of the loan or obligation at that time.

(6) **Amount of expenditure** — Notwithstanding any other provision of this Act, the amount of any expenditure that is, or is the cost or capital cost of, a taxpayer's tax shelter investment, and the amount of any expenditure of a taxpayer an interest in which is a tax shelter investment, shall be reduced to the amount, if any, by which

    (a)    the amount of the taxpayer's expenditure otherwise determined

exceeds

(b) the total of

(i) the limited-recourse amounts of

(A) the taxpayer, and

(B) all other taxpayers not dealing at arm's length with the taxpayer

that can reasonably be considered to relate to the expenditure,

(ii) the taxpayer's at-risk adjustment in respect of the expenditure, and

(iii) each limited-recourse amount and at-risk adjustment, determined under this section when this section is applied to each other taxpayer who deals at arm's length with and holds, directly or indirectly, an interest in the taxpayer, that can reasonably be considered to relate to the expenditure.

(7) **Repayment of indebtedness** — For the purpose of this section, the unpaid principal of an indebtedness is deemed to be a limited-recourse amount unless

(a) bona fide arrangements, evidenced in writing, were made, at the time the indebtedness arose, for repayment by the debtor of the indebtedness and all interest on the indebtedness within a reasonable period not exceeding 10 years; and

(b) interest is payable at least annually, at a rate equal to or greater than the lesser of

(i) the prescribed rate of interest in effect at the time the indebtedness arose, and

(ii) the prescribed rate of interest applicable from time to time during the term of the indebtedness,

and is paid in respect of the indebtedness by the debtor no later than 60 days after the end of each taxation year of the debtor that ends in the period.

(8) **Limited-recourse amount** — For the purpose of this section, the unpaid principal of an indebtedness is deemed to be a limited-recourse amount of a taxpayer where the taxpayer is a partnership and recourse against any member of the partnership in respect of the indebtedness is limited, either immediately or in the future and either absolutely or contingently.

(9) **Timing** — Where at any time a taxpayer has paid an amount (in this subsection referred to as the "repaid amount") on account of the principal amount of an indebtedness that was, before that time, the unpaid principal amount of a loan or any other form of indebtedness to which subsection 143.2(2) applies (in this subsection referred to as the "former amount or benefit") relating to an expenditure of the taxpayer,

(a) the former amount or benefit is considered to have been an amount or benefit under subsection 143.2(2) in respect of the taxpayer at all times before that time; and

(b)   the expenditure is, subject to subsection 143.2(6), deemed to have been made or incurred at that time to the extent of, and by the payment of, the repaid amount.

(10) **Timing** — Where at any time a taxpayer has paid an amount (in this subsection referred to as the "repaid amount") on account of the principal amount of an indebtedness which was, before that time, an unpaid principal amount that was a limited-recourse amount (in this subsection referred to as the "former limited-recourse indebtedness") relating to an expenditure of the taxpayer,

(a)   the former limited-recourse indebtedness is considered to have been a limited-recourse amount at all times before that time; and

(b)   the expenditure is, subject to subsection 143.2(6), deemed to have been made or incurred at that time to the extent of, and by the amount of, the repaid amount.

(11) **Short-term debt** — Where a taxpayer pays all of the principal of an indebtedness no later than 60 days after that indebtedness arose and the indebtedness would otherwise be considered to be a limited-recourse amount solely because of the application of subsection 143.2(7) or (8), that subsection does not apply to the indebtedness unless

(a)   any portion of the repayment is made with a limited-recourse amount; or

(b)   the repayment can reasonably be considered to be part of a series of loans or other indebtedness and repayments that ends more than 60 days after the indebtedness arose.

(12) **Series of loans or repayments** — For the purpose of paragraph 143.2(7)(a), a debtor is considered not to have made arrangements to repay an indebtedness within 10 years where the debtor's arrangement to repay can reasonably be considered to be part of a series of loans or other indebtedness and repayments that ends more than 10 years after it begins.

(13) **Information located outside Canada** — For the purpose of this section, where it can reasonably be considered that information relating to indebtedness that relates to a taxpayer's expenditure is available outside Canada and the Minister is not satisfied that the unpaid principal of the indebtedness is not a limited-recourse amount, the unpaid principal of the indebtedness relating to the taxpayer's expenditure is deemed to be a limited-recourse amount relating to the expenditure unless

(a)   the information is provided to the Minister; or

(b)   the information is located in a country with which the Government of Canada has entered into a tax convention or agreement that has the force of law in Canada and includes a provision under which the Minister can obtain the information.

(14) **Information located outside Canada** — For the purpose of this section, where it can reasonably be considered that information relating to whether a taxpayer is not dealing at arm's length with another taxpayer is available outside Canada and the Minister is not satisfied that the taxpayer is dealing at arm's

length with the other taxpayer, the taxpayer and the other taxpayer are deemed not to be dealing with each other at arm's length unless

(a) the information is provided to the Minister; or

(b) the information is located in a country with which the Government of Canada has entered into a tax convention or agreement that has the force of law in Canada and includes a provision under which the Minister can obtain the information.

(15) **Assessments** — Notwithstanding subsections 152(4) to (5), such assessments, determinations and redeterminations may be made as are necessary to give effect to this section.

[S.C. 1998, c. 19, s. 168.]

## PART I, DIVISION H
## EXEMPTIONS

### *Miscellaneous Exemptions*

**149.** (1) **Miscellaneous exemptions** — No tax is payable under this Part on the taxable income of a person for a period when that person was

. . .

(f) a registered charity;

### *Charities*

**149.1.** (1) **Definitions** — In this section,

"capital gains pool", of a registered charity for a taxation year, means the amount by which

(a) the total of all amounts, each of which is the amount of a capital gain of the charity from the disposition of an enduring property after March 22, 2004 and before the end of the taxation year (other than a capital gain from a disposition of a bequest or an inheritance received by the charity in a taxation year that included any time before 1994) that is declared by the charity in an information return under subsection (14) for the taxation year during which the disposition occurred,

exceeds

(b) the total of all amounts, each of which is the amount, determined for a preceding taxation year of the charity that began after March 22, 2004, that is the lesser of the amount determined under paragraph (a) of the description of A.1 in the definition "disbursement quota" and the amount claimed by the charity under paragraph (b) of that description;

"charitable foundation" means a corporation or trust that is constituted and operated exclusively for charitable purposes, no part of the income of which is payable to, or is otherwise available for, the personal benefit of any proprietor, member, shareholder, trustee or settlor thereof, and that is not a charitable organization;

"charitable organization" means an organization, whether or not incorporated,

(a)     all the resources of which are devoted to charitable activities carried on by the organization itself,

(b)     no part of the income of which is payable to, or is otherwise available for, the personal benefit of any proprietor, member, shareholder, trustee or settlor thereof,

(c)     more than 50% of the directors, trustees, officers or like officials of which deal with each other and with each of the other directors, trustees, officers or officials at arm's length, and

(d)     where it has been designated as a private foundation or public foundation pursuant to subsection (6.3) of this section or subsection 110(8.1) or (8.2) of the *Income Tax Act*, chapter 148 of the Revised Statutes of Canada, 1952, or has applied after February 15, 1984 for registration under paragraph 110(8)(c) of that Act or under the definition "registered charity" in subsection 248(1), not more than 50% of the capital of which has been contributed or otherwise paid into the organization by one person or members of a group of persons who do not deal with each other at arm's length and, for the purpose of this paragraph, a reference to any person or to members of a group does not include a reference to Her Majesty in right of Canada or a province, a municipality, another registered charity that is not a private foundation, or any club, society or association described in paragraph 149(1)(l);

"charitable purposes" includes the disbursement of funds to qualified donees;

"charity" means a charitable organization or charitable foundation;

"disbursement quota", for a taxation year of a registered charity, means the amount determined by the formula

$$A + A.1 + B + B.1$$

where

A       is 80% of the total of all amounts each of which is the eligible amount of a gift for which the charity issued a receipt described in subsection 110.1(2) or 118.1(2) in its immediately preceding taxation year, other than a gift that is

(a)     an enduring property, or

(b)     received from another registered charity,

A.1    is the amount, if any, by which

(a)     the sum of

(i)      80% of the total of all amounts, each of which is the amount of an enduring property of the charity (other than an enduring property described in subparagraph (ii), an enduring property that was received by the charity as a specified gift, or a bequest or an inheritance received by the charity in a taxation year that included any time before 1994) to the extent that it is expended in the year, and

    (ii)    the total of all amounts, each of which is the fair market value, when transferred, of an enduring property (other than an enduring property that was received by the charity as a specified gift) transferred by the charity in the taxation year by way of gift to a qualified donee

exceeds

(b)    the amount, if any, claimed by the charity, that may not exceed the lesser of

    (i)    3.5% of the amount determined for D, and

    (ii)    the capital gains pool of the charity for the taxation year,

    B    is

(a)    in the case of a private foundation, the total of all amounts each of which is an amount received by it in its immediately preceding taxation year from a registered charity, other than an amount that is a specified gift or an enduring property, or

(b)    in the case of a charitable organization or a public foundation, 80% of the total of all amounts each of which is an amount received by it in its immediately preceding taxation year from a registered charity, other than an amount that is a specified gift or an enduring property, and

    B.1 is the amount determined by the formula C x 0.035 [D - (E + F)]/365

where

    C    is the number of days in the taxation year,

    D    is

(a)    the prescribed amount for the year, in respect of all or a portion of a property (other than a prescribed property) owned by the charity at any time in the 24 months immediately preceding the taxation year that was not used directly in charitable activities or administration, if that amount is greater than $25,000, and

(b)    in any other case, nil,

    E    is the total of the amount determined for subparagraph (a)(ii) of the description of A.1, and 5/4 of the total of the amounts determined for A and subparagraph (a)(i) of the description of A.1, for the year in respect of the charity, and

    F    is the amount equal to

(a)    in the case of a private foundation, the amount determined for B for the year in respect of the charity in accordance with paragraph (a) of the description of B, or

(b)    in the case of a charitable organization or a public foundation, 5/4 of the amount determined for B for the year in respect of the charity in accordance with paragraph (b) of the description of B;

"enduring property" means property of a registered charity that is

(a)    a gift received by the charity by way of bequest or inheritance, including a gift deemed by subsection 118.1(5.2) or (5.3),

(b)    if the registered charity is a charitable organization, a gift from another registered charity (other than a gift described by paragraph (d) or received from another charity in respect of which more than 50% of the members of the board of directors or trustees do not deal at arm's length with each member of the board of directors or trustees of the charitable organization) that is subject to a trust or direction to the effect that the property given, or property substituted for the gift,

(i)　　is to be held by the charitable organization for a period of not more than five years from the date that the gift was received by the charitable organization, and

(ii)　　is to be expended in its entirety over the period referred to in the trust or direction

(A)　　to acquire a tangible capital property of the charitable organization to be used directly in charitable activities or administration,

(B)　　in the course of a program of charitable activities of the charitable organization that could not reasonably be completed before the end of the first taxation year of the charitable organization ending after the taxation year in which the gift was received, or

(C)　　any combination of the uses described in clauses (A) and (B),

(c)　　a gift received by the registered charity (referred to in this definition as the "original recipient charity"), other than a gift received from another registered charity, that is subject to a trust or direction to the effect that the property given, or property substituted for the gift, is to be held by the original recipient charity or by another registered charity (referred to in this definition as a "transferee") for a period of not less than 10 years from the date that the gift was received by the original recipient charity, except that the trust or direction may allow the original recipient charity or the transferee to expend the property before the end of that period to the extent of the amount determined for a taxation year (for the charity or the transferee, as the case may be) by B.1 in the formula in the definition "disbursement quota", or

(d)　　a gift received by the registered charity as a transferee from an original recipient charity or another transferee of a property that was, before that gift was so received, an enduring property of the original recipient charity or of the other transferee because of paragraph (a) or (b) or this paragraph, or property substituted for the gift, if, in the case of a property that was an enduring property of an original recipient charity because of paragraph (b), the gift is subject to the same terms and conditions under the trust or direction as applied to the gift to the original recipient charity;

"non-qualified investment" of a private foundation means

(a)　　a debt (other than a pledge or undertaking to make a gift) owing to the foundation by

(i)　　a person (other than an excluded corporation)

(A)　　who is a member, shareholder, trustee, settlor, officer, official or director of the foundation,

      (B)  who has, or is a member of a group of persons who do not deal with each other at arm's length who have, contributed more than 50% of the capital of the foundation, or

      (C)  who does not deal at arm's length with any person described in clause 149.1(1) "non-qualified investment" (a)(i)(A) or 149.1(1) "non-qualified investment" (a)(i)(B), or

  (ii)  a corporation (other than an excluded corporation) controlled by the foundation, by any person or group of persons referred to in subparagraph 149.1(1) "non-qualified investment" (a)(i), by the foundation and any other private foundation with which it does not deal at arm's length or by any combination thereof,

(b)  a share of a class of the capital stock of a corporation (other than an excluded corporation) referred to in paragraph 149.1(1) "non-qualified investment" (a) held by the foundation (other than a share listed on a prescribed stock exchange or a share that would be a qualifying share within the meaning assigned by subsection 192(6) if that subsection were read without reference to the expression "issued after May 22, 1985 and before 1987"), and

(c)  a right held by the foundation to acquire a share referred to in paragraph 149.1(1) "non-qualified investment" (b),

and for the purpose of this definition, an "excluded corporation" is

(d)  a limited-dividend housing company to which paragraph 149(1)(n) applies,

(e)  a corporation all of the property of which is used by a registered charity in its administration or in carrying on its charitable activities, or

(f)  a corporation all of the issued shares of which are held by the foundation;

"private foundation" means a charitable foundation that is not a public foundation;

"public foundation" means a charitable foundation of which,

(a)  where the foundation has been registered after February 15, 1984 or designated as a charitable organization or private foundation pursuant to subsection 149.1(6.3) or to subsection 110(8.1) or (8.2) of the *Income Tax Act*, chapter 148 of the Revised Statutes of Canada, 1952,

  (i)  more than 50% of the directors, trustees, officers or like officials deal with each other and with each of the other directors, trustees, officers or officials at arm's length, and

  (ii)  not more than 50% of the capital contributed or otherwise paid in to the foundation has been so contributed or otherwise paid in by one person or members of a group of such persons who do not deal with each other at arm's length, or

(b)  in any other case,

  (i)  more than 50% of the directors or trustees deal with each other and with each of the other directors or trustees at arm's length, and

  (ii)  not more than 75% of the capital contributed or otherwise paid in to the foundation has been so contributed or otherwise paid in by one person or by a group of persons who do not deal with each other at arm's length

and for the purpose of subparagraph 149.1(1) "public foundation" (a)(ii), a reference to any person or to members of a group does not include a reference to Her Majesty in right of Canada or a province, a municipality, another registered charity that is not a private foundation, or any club, society or association described in paragraph 149(1)(l);

"qualified donee" means a donee described in any of paragraphs 110.1(1)(a) and 110.1(1)(b) and the definitions "total charitable gifts" and "total Crown gifts" in subsection 118.1(1);

"qualified investment" (Repealed, S.C. 1984, c. 45, s. 57(5).)

"related business", in relation to a charity, includes a business that is unrelated to the objects of the charity if substantially all persons employed by the charity in the carrying on of that business are not remunerated for that employment;

"specified gift" means that portion of a gift, made in a taxation year by a registered charity, that is designated as a specified gift in its information return for the year;

"taxation year" means, in the case of a registered charity, a fiscal period.

(1.1) **Exclusions** — For the purposes of paragraphs 149.1(2)(b), 149.1(3)(b), 149.1(4)(b) and 149.1(21)(a), the following shall be deemed to be neither an amount expended in a taxation year on charitable activities nor a gift made to a qualified donee:

(a)    a specified gift;

(b)    an expenditure on political activities made by a charitable organization or a charitable foundation; and

(c)    a transfer that has, because of paragraph (c) of the description of B in subsection 188(1.1), paragraph 189(6.2)(b) or subsection 189(6.3), reduced the amount of a liability under Part V.

(1.2) **Authority of Minister** — For the purposes of the determination of D in the definition "disbursement quota" in subsection 149.1(1), the Minister may

(a)    authorize a change in the number of periods chosen by a charitable foundation in determining the prescribed amount; and

(b)    accept any method for the determination of the fair market value of property or a portion thereof that may be required in determining the prescribed amount.

(2) **Revocation of registration of charitable organization** — The Minister may, in the manner described in section 168, revoke the registration of a charitable organization for any reason described in subsection 168(1) or where the organization

(a)    carries on a business that is not a related business of that charity; or

(b)    fails to expend in any taxation year, on charitable activities carried on by it and by way of gifts made by it to qualified donees, amounts the total of which is at least equal to the organization's disbursement quota for that year.

(i)    the amount that would be the value of A for the year, and

(ii)    the amount that would be the value of A.1 for the year,

in the definition "disbursement quota" in subsection 149.1(1) in respect of the organization if it were a charitable foundation.

(3) **Revocation of registration of public foundation** — The Minister may, in the manner described in section 168, revoke the registration of a public foundation for any reason described in subsection 168(1) or where the foundation

(a)    carries on a business that is not a related business of that charity;

(b)    fails to expend in any taxation year, on charitable activities carried on by it and by way of gifts made by it to qualified donees, amounts the total of which is at least equal to the foundation's disbursement quota for that year;

(c)    since June 1, 1950, acquired control of any corporation;

(d)    since June 1, 1950, incurred debts, other than debts for current operating expenses, debts incurred in connection with the purchase and sale of investments and debts incurred in the course of administering charitable activities; or

(e)    at any time within the 24 month period preceding the day on which notice is given to the foundation by the Minister pursuant to subsection 168(1) and at a time when the foundation was a private foundation, took any action or failed to expend amounts such that the Minister was entitled, pursuant to subsection 149.1(4), to revoke its registration as a private foundation.

(4) **Revocation of registration of private foundation** — The Minister may, in the manner described in section 168, revoke the registration of a private foundation for any reason described in subsection 168(1) or where the foundation

(a)    carries on any business;

(b)    fails to expend in any taxation year, on charitable activities carried on by it and by way of gifts made by it to qualified donees, amounts the total of which is at least equal to the foundation's disbursement quota for that year;

(c)    since June 1, 1950, acquired control of any corporation; or

(d)    since June 1, 1950, incurred debts, other than debts for current operating expenses, debts incurred in connection with the purchase and sale of investments and debts incurred in the course of administering charitable activities.

(4.1) **Revocation of registration of registered charity** — The Minister may, in the manner described in section 168, revoke the registration

(a)    of a registered charity, if the registered charity has made a gift to another registered charity and it can reasonably be considered that one of the main purposes of making the gift was to unduly delay the expenditure of amounts on charitable activities;

(b)  of the other charity referred to in paragraph (a), if it can reasonably be considered that, by accepting the gift, it acted in concert with the registered charity to which paragraph (a) applies; and

(c)  of a registered charity, if a false statement, within the meaning assigned by subsection 163.2(1), was made in circumstances amounting to culpable conduct, within the meaning assigned by that subsection, in the furnishing of information for the purpose of obtaining registration of the charity.

(5) **Reduction** — The Minister may, on application made to the Minister in prescribed form by a registered charity, specify an amount in respect of the charity for a taxation year and, for the purpose of paragraph 149.1(2)(b), 149.1(3)(b) or 149.1(4)(b), as the case may be, that amount shall be deemed to be an amount expended by the charity in the year on charitable activities carried on by it.

(6) **Devoting resources to charitable activity** — A charitable organization shall be considered to be devoting its resources to charitable activities carried on by it to the extent that

(a)  it carries on a related business;

(b)  in any taxation year, it disburses not more than 50% of its income for that year to qualified donees; or

(c)  it disburses income to a registered charity that the Minister has designated in writing as a charity associated with it.

(6.1) **Charitable purposes** — For the purposes of the definition "charitable foundation" in subsection 149.1(1), where a corporation or trust devotes substantially all of its resources to charitable purposes and

(a)  it devotes part of its resources to political activities,

(b)  those political activities are ancillary and incidental to its charitable purposes, and

(c)  those political activities do not include the direct or indirect support of, or opposition to, any political party or candidate for public office,

the corporation or trust shall be considered to be constituted and operated for charitable purposes to the extent of that part of its resources so devoted.

(6.2) **Charitable activities** — For the purposes of the definition "charitable organization" in subsection 149.1(1), where an organization devotes substantially all of its resources to charitable activities carried on by it and

(a)  it devotes part of its resources to political activities,

(b)  those political activities are ancillary and incidental to its charitable activities, and

(c)  those political activities do not include the direct or indirect support of, or opposition to, any political party or candidate for public office,

the organization shall be considered to be devoting that part of its resources to charitable activities carried on by it.

(6.21) **Marriage for civil purposes** — For greater certainty, subject to subsections (6.1) and (6.2), a registered charity with stated purposes that include the advancement of religion shall not have its registration revoked or be subject to any other penalty under Part V solely because it or any of its members, officials, supporters or adherents exercises, in relation to marriage between persons of the same sex, the freedom of conscience and religion guaranteed under the Canadian Charter of Rights and Freedoms

(6.3) **Designation as public foundation, etc.** — The Minister may, by notice sent by registered mail to a registered charity, on the Minister's own initiative or on application made to the Minister in prescribed form, designate the charity to be a charitable organization, private foundation or public foundation and the charity shall be deemed to be registered as a charitable organization, private foundation or public foundation, as the case may be, for taxation years commencing after the day of mailing of the notice unless and until it is otherwise designated under this subsection or its registration is revoked under subsection 149.1(2), 149.1(3), 149.1(4), 149.1(4.1) or 168(2).

(6.4) **National arts service organizations** — Where an organization that

(a)   has, on written application to the Minister of Canadian Heritage describing all of its objects and activities, been designated by that Minister on approval of those objects and activities to be a national arts service organization,

(b)   has, as its exclusive purpose and its exclusive function, the promotion of arts in Canada on a nation-wide basis,

(c)   is resident in Canada and was formed or created in Canada, and

(d)   complies with prescribed conditions

applies in prescribed form to the Minister of National Revenue for registration, that Minister may register the organization for the purposes of this Act and, where the organization so applies or is so registered, this section, paragraph 38(a.1), sections 110.1, 118.1, 168, 172, 180 and 230 and Part V apply, with such modifications as the circumstances require, to the organization as if it were an applicant for registration as a charitable organization or as if it were a registered charity that is designated as a charitable organization, as the case may be.

(6.5) **Revocation of designation** — The Minister of Canadian Heritage may, at any time, revoke the designation of an organization made for the purpose of subsection 149.1(6.4) where

(a)   an incorrect statement was made in the furnishing of information for the purpose of obtaining the designation, or

(b)   the organization has amended its objects after its last designation was made,

and, where the designation is so revoked, the organization shall be deemed for the purpose of section 168 to have ceased to comply with the requirements of this Act for its registration under this Act.

(7) **Designation of associated charities** — On application made to the Minister in prescribed form, the Minister may, in writing, designate a registered charity as a charity associated with one or more specified registered charities where the Minister is satisfied that the charitable aim or activity of each of the registered charities is substantially the same, and on and after a date specified in such a designation, the

charities to which it relates shall, until such time, if any, as the Minister revokes the designation, be deemed to be associated.

(8) **Accumulation of property** — A registered charity may, with the approval in writing of the Minister, accumulate property for a particular purpose, on terms and conditions, and over such period of time, as the Minister specifies in the approval, and any property accumulated after receipt of such an approval and in accordance therewith, including any income earned in respect of the property so accumulated, shall be deemed

(a)  to have been expended on charitable activities carried on by the charity in the taxation year in which it was so accumulated; and

(b)  not to have been expended in any other year.

(9) **Idem** — Property accumulated by a registered charity as provided in subsection 149.1(8), including any income earned in respect of that property, that is not used for the particular purpose for which it was accumulated either

(a)  before the expiration of any period of time specified by the Minister in the Minister's approval of the accumulation, or

(b)  at an earlier time at which the registered charity decides not to use the property for that purpose

shall, notwithstanding subsection 149.1(8), be deemed to be income of the charity for, and the amount of a gift for which it issued a receipt described in subsection 110.1(2) or 118.1(2) in, its taxation year in which the period referred to in paragraph 149.1(9)(a) expires or the time referred to in paragraph 149.1(9)(b) occurs, as the case may be.

(10) **Deemed charitable activity** — An amount paid by a charitable organization to a qualified donee that is not paid out of the income of the charitable organization shall be deemed to be a devotion of a resource of the charitable organization to a charitable activity carried on by it.

(11) (Repealed, S.C. 1984, c. 45, s. 57(13).)

(12) **Rules** — For the purposes of this section,

(a)  a corporation is controlled by a charitable foundation if more than 50% of the corporation's issued share capital, having full voting rights under all circumstances, belongs to

(i)   the foundation, or

(ii)  the foundation and persons with whom the foundation does not deal at arm's length,

but for the purpose of paragraph 149.1(3)(c) or 149.1(4)(c), as the case may be, a charitable foundation shall be deemed not to have acquired control of a corporation if it has not purchased or otherwise acquired for consideration more than 5% of the issued shares of any class of the capital stock of that corporation;

(b)  there shall be included in computing the income of a charity for a taxation year all gifts received by it in the year including gifts from any other charity but not including

(i)   a specified gift or a gift referred to in paragraph (a) or (b) of the description of A in the definition "disbursement quota" in subsection 149.1(1),

(ii)  any gift or portion of a gift in respect of which it is established that the donor is not a charity and

(A)  has not been allowed a deduction under paragraph 110.1(1)(a) in computing the donor's taxable income or under subsection 118.1(3) in computing the donor's tax payable under this Part, or

(B)  was not taxable under section 2 for the taxation year in which the gift was made, or

(iii) any gift or portion of a gift in respect of which it is established that the donor is a charity and that the gift was not made out of the income of the donor; and

(c)   subsections 104(6) and 104(12) are not applicable in computing the income of a charitable foundation that is a trust.

(13) **Designation of private foundation as public** — On application made to the Minister by a private foundation, the Minister may, on such terms and conditions as the Minister considers appropriate, designate the foundation to be a public foundation, and on and after the date specified in such a designation, the foundation to which it relates shall, until such time, if any, as the Minister revokes the designation, be deemed to be a public foundation.

(14) **Information returns** — Every registered charity shall, within 6 months from the end of each taxation year of the charity, file with the Minister both an information return and a public information return for the year, each in prescribed form and containing prescribed information, without notice or demand therefor.

(15) **Information may be communicated** — Notwithstanding section 241,

(a)   the information contained in a public information return referred to in subsection 149.1(14) shall be communicated or otherwise made available to the public by the Minister in such manner as the Minister deems appropriate; and

(b)   the Minister may make available to the public in such manner as the Minister deems appropriate an annual listing of all registered or previously registered charities indicating for each the name, location, registration number, date of registration and, in the case of a charity the registration of which has been revoked, annulled or terminated, the effective date of the revocation, annulment or termination.

(16) (Repealed, S.C. 1984, c. 45, s. 57(17).)

(17) (Repealed, S.C. 1984, c. 45, s. 57(17).)

(18) (Repealed, S.C. 1984, c. 45, s. 57(17).)

(19) (Repealed, S.C. 1980-81, c. 48, s. 84.1(2).)

(20) **Rule regarding disbursement excess** — Where a registered charity has expended a disbursement excess for a taxation year, the charity may, for the purpose of determining whether it complies with the requirements of paragraph

149.1(2)(b), 149.1(3)(b) or 149.1(4)(b), as the case may be, for the immediately preceding taxation year of the charity and 5 or less of its immediately subsequent taxation years, include in the computation of the amounts expended on charitable activities carried on by it and by way of gifts made by it to qualified donees, such portion of that disbursement excess as was not so included under this subsection for any preceding taxation year.

(21) **Definition of "disbursement excess"** — For the purpose of subsection (20), "disbursement excess", for a taxation year of a charity, means the amount, if any, by which the total of amounts expended in the year by the charity on charitable activities carried on by it and by way of gifts made by it to qualified donees exceeds its disbursement quota for the year.

(22) **Refusal to register** — The Minister may, by registered mail, give notice to a person that the application of the person for registration as a registered charity is refused.

(23) **Annulment of registration** — The Minister may, by registered mail, give notice to a person that the registration of the person as a registered charity is annulled and deemed not to have been so registered, if the person was so registered by the Minister in error or the person has, solely as a result of a change in law, ceased to be a charity.

(24) **Receipts issued before annulment** — An official receipt referred to in Part XXXV of the Income Tax Regulations issued, by a person whose registration has been annulled under subsection (23), before that annulment is, if the receipt would have been valid were the person a registered charity at the time the receipt was issued, deemed to be a valid receipt under that Part.

[**Note:** S.C. 2005, c. 19, s. 35, contains the following provisions:

(7) Subsections (1), (2) and (4) and subsection 149.1(21) of the Act, as enacted by subsection (6), apply to taxation years that begin after March 22, 2004, except that, in the application of subsections (1) and (4) and subsection 149.1(21) of the Act, as enacted by subsection (6), to a taxation year that begins before 2009 of a charitable organization registered by the Minister of National Revenue before March 23, 2004,

(a) the amount claimed by the charitable organization under paragraph (b) of the description of A.1 in the definition "disbursement quota" in subsection 149.1(1) of the Act, as enacted by subsection (1), is deemed to be nil;

(b) paragraph 149.1(2)(b) of the Act, as enacted by subsection (4), is to be read as follows:

(b) fails to expend in any taxation year, on charitable activities carried on by it and by way of gifts made by it to qualified donees, amounts the total of which is at least equal to the total of the amounts determined for A, A.1 and B in the definition "disbursement quota" in subsection (1) for the year in respect of the charity.

(c) subsection 149.1(21) of the Act, as enacted by subsection (6), is to be read as follows:

(21) For the purpose of subsection (20), "disbursement excess" for a taxation year of a charity means the amount, if any, by which

(a)   the total of amounts expended in the year by the charity on charitable activities carried on by it or by way of gifts made by it to qualified donees exceeds

(b)   in the case of a charitable foundation, its disbursement quota for the year, and

(c)   in the case of a charitable organization, the total of the amounts determined for A, A.1 and B in the definition "disbursement quota" in subsection (1) for the year in respect of the charity.

(8) Subsections (3) and (5) and subsections 149.1(22) to (24) of the Act, as enacted by subsection (6), apply in respect of notices issued by the Minister of National Revenue after the day that is 30 days after the day on which this Act is assented to.]

[S.C. 1976-77, c. 4, s. 60; S.C. 1977-78, c. 1, s. 75; S.C. 1979, c. 5, s. 52; S.C. 1980-81-82-83, c. 48, s. 84.1; S.C. 1984, c. 45, s. 57; S.C. 1986, c. 6, s. 85; S.C. 1986, c. 55, s. 58; S.C. 1988, c. 55, s. 134; 1994, c. 7, Sch. II, s. 123; S.C. 1994, c. 21, s. 74; S.C. 1998, c. 19, ss. 41.1, 179; S.C. 2005, c. 19, s. 35; S.C. 2005, c. 33, s. 11.1]

## PART 1, DIVISION I
## RETURNS, ASSESSMENTS, PAYMENT AND APPEALS

### *Returns*

**150. (1) Filing returns of income – general rule** — Subject to subsection (1.1), a return of income that is in prescribed form and that contains prescribed information shall be filed with the Minister, without notice or demand for the return, for each taxation year of a taxpayer.

(a)   **Corporations** — in the case of a corporation, by or on behalf of the corporation within six months after the end of the year if

   (i)   at any time in the year the corporation

     (A)   is resident in Canada,

     (B)   carries on business in Canada, unless the corporation's only revenue from carrying on business in Canada in the year consists of amounts in respect of which tax was payable by the corporation under subsection 212(5.1),

     (C)   has a taxable capital gain, or

     (D)   disposes of a taxable Canadian property, or

   (ii)   tax under this Part is, or but for a tax treaty would be, payable by the corporation for the year;

(1.1) **Exception** — Subsection (1) does not apply to a taxation year of a taxpayer if

(a)   the taxpayer is a corporation that was a registered charity throughout the year; or

. . .

**152.** (6) **Reassessment where certain deductions claimed** — Where a taxpayer has filed for a particular taxation year the return of income required by section 150 and an amount is subsequently claimed by the taxpayer or on the taxpayer's behalf for the year as

. . .

(c)  a deduction under section 118.1 in respect of a gift made in a subsequent taxation year or under section 111 in respect of a loss for a subsequent taxation year,

. . .

**163.2.** (1) **Definitions** — The definitions in this subsection apply in this section.

"culpable conduct" means conduct, whether an act or a failure to act, that

(a)  is tantamount to intentional conduct;
(b)  shows an indifference as to whether this Act is complied with; or
(c)  shows a wilful, reckless or wanton disregard of the law.

"entity" includes an association, a corporation, a fund, a joint venture, an organization, a partnership, a syndicate and a trust.

"excluded activity", in respect of a false statement, means the activity of

(a)  promoting or selling (whether as principal or agent or directly or indirectly) an arrangement, an entity, a plan, a property or a scheme (in this definition referred to as the "arrangement") where it can reasonably be considered that

(i)   subsection 66(12.68) applies to the arrangement,
(ii)  the definition "tax shelter" in subsection 237.1(1) applies to a person's interest in the arrangement, or
(iii) one of the main purposes for a person's participation in the arrangement is to obtain a tax benefit; or

(b)  accepting (whether as principal or agent or directly or indirectly) consideration in respect of the promotion or sale of an arrangement.

"false statement" includes a statement that is misleading because of an omission from the statement.

"gross compensation" of a particular person at any time, in respect of a false statement that could be used by or on behalf of another person, means all amounts to which the particular person, or any person not dealing at arm's length with the particular person, is entitled, either before or after that time and either absolutely or contingently, to receive or obtain in respect of the statement.

"gross entitlements" of a person at any time, in respect of a planning activity or a valuation activity of the person, means all amounts to which the person, or another person not dealing at arm's length with the person, is entitled, either before or after that time and either absolutely or contingently, to receive or obtain in respect of the activity.

"participate" includes

(a)  to cause a subordinate to act or to omit information; and

(b) to know of, and to not make a reasonable attempt to prevent, the participation by a subordinate in an act or an omission of information.

"person" includes a partnership.

"planning activity" includes

(a) organizing or creating, or assisting in the organization or creation of, an arrangement, an entity, a plan or a scheme; and

(b) participating, directly or indirectly, in the selling of an interest in, or the promotion of, an arrangement, an entity, a plan, a property or a scheme.

"subordinate", in respect of a particular person, includes any other person over whose activities the particular person has direction, supervision or control whether or not the other person is an employee of the particular person or of another person, except that, if the particular person is a member of a partnership, the other person is not a subordinate of the particular person solely because the particular person is a member of the partnership.

"tax benefit" means a reduction, avoidance or deferral of tax or other amount payable under this Act or an increase in a refund of tax or other amount under this Act.

"valuation activity" of a person means anything done by the person in determining the value of a property or a service.

(2) **Penalty for misrepresentations in tax planning arrangements** — Every person who makes or furnishes, participates in the making of or causes another person to make or furnish a statement that the person knows, or would reasonably be expected to know but for circumstances amounting to culpable conduct, is a false statement that could be used by another person (in subsections (6) and (15) referred to as the "other person") for a purpose of this Act is liable to a penalty in respect of the false statement.

(3) **Amount of penalty** — The penalty to which a person is liable under subsection (2) in respect of a false statement is

(a) where the statement is made in the course of a planning activity or a valuation activity, the greater of $1,000 and the total of the person's gross entitlements, at the time at which the notice of assessment of the penalty is sent to the person, in respect of the planning activity and the valuation activity; and

(b) in any other case, $1,000.

(4) **Penalty for participating in a misrepresentation** — Every person who makes, or participates in, assents to or acquiesces in the making of, a statement to, or by or on behalf of, another person (in this subsection, subsections (5) and (6), paragraph (12)(c) and subsection (15) referred to as the "other person") that the person knows, or would reasonably be expected to know but for circumstances amounting to culpable conduct, is a false statement that could be used by or on behalf of the other person for a purpose of this Act is liable to a penalty in respect of the false statement.

(5) **Amount of penalty** —The penalty to which a person is liable under subsection (4) in respect of a false statement is the greater of

(a) $1,000, and

(b) the lesser of

    (i) the penalty to which the other person would be liable under subsection 163(2) if the other person made the statement in a return filed for the purposes of this Act and knew that the statement was false, and

    (ii) the total of $100,000 and the person's gross compensation, at the time at which the notice of assessment of the penalty is sent to the person, in respect of the false statement that could be used by or on behalf of the other person.

(6) **Reliance in good faith** —For the purposes of subsections (2) and (4), a person (in this subsection and in subsection (7) referred to as the "advisor") who acts on behalf of the other person is not c onsidered to have acted in circumstances amounting to culpable conduct in respect of the false statement referred to in subsection (2) or (4) solely because the advisor relied, in good faith, on information provided to the advisor by or on behalf of the other person or, because of such reliance, failed to verify, investigate or correct the information.

(7) **Non-application of subsection (6)** — Subsection (6) does not apply in respect of a statement that an advisor makes (or participates in, assents to or acquiesces in the making of) in the course of an excluded activity.

(8) **False statements in respect of a particular arrangement** — For the purpose of applying this section (other than subsections (4) and (5)),

(a) where a person makes or furnishes, participates in the making of or causes another person to make or furnish two or more false statements, the false statements are deemed to be one false statement if the statements are made or furnished in the course of

    (i) one or more planning activities that are in respect of a particular arrangement, entity, plan, property or scheme, or

    (ii) a valuation activity that is in respect of a particular property or service; and

(b) for greater certainty, a particular arrangement, entity, plan, property or scheme includes an arrangement, an entity, a plan, a property or a scheme in respect of which

    (i) an interest is required to have, or has, an identification number issued under section 237.1 that is the same number as the number that applies to each other interest in the property,

    (ii) a selling instrument in respect of flow-through shares is required to be filed with the Minister because of subsection 66(12.68), or

    (iii) one of the main purposes for a person's participation in the arrangement, entity, plan or scheme, or a person's acquisition of the property, is to obtain a tax benefit.

(9) **Clerical services** — For the purposes of this section, a person is not considered to have made or furnished, or participated in, assented to or acquiesced in the making of, a false statement solely because the person provided clerical services (other than bookkeeping services) or secretarial services with respect to the statement.

(10) **Valuations** — Notwithstanding subsections (6) and 163(3), a statement as to the value of a property or a service (which value is in this subsection referred to as the "stated value"), made by the person who opined on the stated value or by a person in the course of an excluded activity is deemed to be a statement that the person would reasonably be expected to know, but for circumstances amounting to culpable conduct, is a false statement if the stated value is

(a)    less than the product obtained when the prescribed percentage for the property or service is multiplied by the fair market value of the property or service; or

(b)    greater than the product obtained when the prescribed percentage for the property or service is multiplied by the fair market value of the property or service.

(11) **Exception** — Subsection (10) does not apply to a person in respect of a statement as to the value of a property or a service if the person establishes that the stated value was reasonable in the circumstances and that the statement was made in good faith and, where applicable, was not based on one or more assumptions that the person knew or would reasonably be expected to know, but for circumstances amounting to culpable conduct, were unreasonable or misleading in the circumstances.

(12) **Special rules** — For the purpose of applying this section,

(a)    where a person is assessed a penalty that is referred to in subsection (2) the amount of which is based on the person's gross entitlements at any time in respect of a planning activity or a valuation activity and another assessment of the penalty is made at a later time,

    (i)    if the person's gross entitlements in respect of the activity are greater at that later time, the assessment of the penalty made at that later time is deemed to be an assessment of a separate penalty, and

    (ii)    in any other case, the notice of assessment of the penalty sent before that later time is deemed not to have been sent;

(b)    a person's gross entitlements at any time in respect of a planning activity or a valuation activity, in the course of which the person makes or furnishes, participates in the making of or causes another person to make or furnish a false statement, shall exclude the total of all amounts each of which is the amount of a penalty (other than a penalty the assessment of which is void because of subsection (13)) determined under paragraph (3)(a) in respect of the false statement for which notice of the assessment was sent to the person before that time; and

(c)    where a person is assessed a penalty that is referred to in subsection (4), the person's gross compensation at any time in respect of the false statement that could be used by or on behalf of the other person shall exclude the total of all amounts each of which is the amount of a penalty (other than a penalty the assessment of which is void because of subsection (13)) determined under subsection (5) to the extent that the false statement was used by or on behalf of that other person and for which notice of the assessment was sent to the person before that time.

(13) **Assessment void** — For the purposes of this Act, if an assessment of a penalty that is referred to in subsection (2) or (4) is vacated, the assessment is deemed to be void.

(14) **Maximum penalty** — A person who is liable at any time to a penalty under both subsections (2) and (4) in respect of the same false statement is liable to pay a penalty that is not more than the greater of

(a)    the total amount of the penalties to which the person is liable at that time under subsection (2) in respect of the statement, and

(b)    the total amount of the penalties to which the person is liable at that time under subsection (4) in respect of the statement.

(15) **Employees** — Where an employee (other than a specified employee or an employee engaged in an excluded activity) is employed by the other person referred to in subsections (2) and (4),

(a)    subsections (2) to (5) do not apply to the employee to the extent that the false statement could be used by or on behalf of the other person for a purpose of this Act; and

(b)    the conduct of the employee is deemed to be that of the other person for the purposes of applying subsection 163(2) to the other person.

. . .

## REVOCATION OF REGISTRATION OF CERTAIN ORGANIZATIONS AND ASSOCIATIONS

**168.** (1) **Notice of intention to revoke registration** — Where a registered charity or a registered Canadian amateur athletic association

(a)    applies to the Minister in writing for revocation of its registration,

(b)    ceases to comply with the requirements of this Act for its registration as such,

(c)    fails to file an information return as and when required under this Act or a regulation,

(d)    issues a receipt for a gift or donation otherwise than in accordance with this Act and the regulations or that contains false information,

(e)    fails to comply with or contravenes any of sections 230 to 231.5, or

(f)    in the case of a registered Canadian amateur athletic association, accepts a gift or donation the granting of which was expressly or impliedly conditional on the association making a gift or donation to another person, club, society or association,

the Minister may, by registered mail, give notice to the registered charity or registered Canadian amateur athletic association that the Minister proposes to revoke its registration.

(2) **Revocation of registration** — Where the Minister gives notice under subsection 168(1) to a registered charity or to a registered Canadian amateur athletic association,

(a) if the charity or association has applied to the Minister in writing for the revocation of its registration, the Minister shall, forthwith after the mailing of the notice, publish a copy of the notice in the *Canada Gazette*, and

(b) in any other case, the Minister may, after the expiration of 30 days from the day of mailing of the notice, or after the expiration of such extended period from the day of mailing of the notice as the Federal Court of Appeal or a judge of that Court, on application made at any time before the determination of any appeal pursuant to subsection 172(3) from the giving of the notice, may fix or allow, publish a copy of the notice in the *Canada Gazette*,

and on that publication of a copy of the notice, the registration of the charity or association is revoked.

(3) *Charities Registration (Security Information) Act* — Notwithstanding subsections (1), (2) and (4), if a registered charity is the subject of a certificate that is determined to be reasonable under subsection 7(1) of the *Charities Registration (Security Information) Act*, the registration of the charity is revoked as of the making of that determination.

(4) **Objection to proposal or designation** — A person that is or was registered as a registered charity or is an applicant for registration as a registered charity that objects to a notice under subsection (1) or any of subsections 149.1(2) to (4.1), (6.3), (22) and (23) may, on or before the day that is 90 days after the day on which the notice was mailed, serve on the Minister a written notice of objection in the manner authorized by the Minister, setting out the reasons for the objection and all the relevant facts, and the provisions of subsections 165(1), (1.1) and (3) to (7) and sections 166, 166.1 and 166.2 apply, with any modifications that the circumstances require, as if the notice were a notice of assessment made under section 152.

[S.C. 1970-71-72, c. 63, s. 1; S.C. 1976-77, c. 4, s. 87; S.C. 1984, c. 45, s. 69; S.C. 1986, c. 6, s. 91; S.C. 2001, c. 41, s. 127; S.C. 2005, c. 19, s. 38]

PART I, DIVISION J
APPEALS TO THE TAX COURT
OF CANADA AND THE FEDERAL COURT

**169.** (1.1) **Ecological gifts** — Where at any particular time a taxpayer has disposed of a property, the fair market value of which has been confirmed or redetermined by the Minister of the Environment under subsection 118.1(10.4), the taxpayer may, within 90 days after the day on which that Minister has issued a certificate under subsection 118.1(10.5), appeal the confirmation or redetermination to the Tax Court of Canada.

. . .

**171.** (1.1) **Ecological gifts** — On an appeal under subsection 169(1.1), the Tax Court of Canada may confirm or vary the amount determined to be the fair market value of a property and the value determined by the Court is deemed to be the fair market value of the property determined by the Minister of the Environment.

**172.** (1) (Repealed, S.C. 1988, c. 61, s. 18(1).)

(2) (Repealed, S.C. 1988, c. 61, s. 18(1).)

(3) **Appeal from refusal to register, revocation of registration, etc.** — Where the Minister

    (a)   refuses to register an applicant for registration as a Canadian amateur athletic association,

    (a.1) confirms a proposal, decision or designation in respect of which a notice was issued by the Minister to a person that is or was registered as a registered charity, or is an applicant for registration as a registered charity, under any of subsections 149.1(2) to (4.1), (6.3), (22) and (23) and 168(1), or does not confirm or vacate that proposal, decision or designation within 90 days after service of a notice of objection by the person under subsection 168(4) in respect of that proposal, decision or designation,(b)  refuses to accept for registration for the purposes of this Act any retirement savings plan,

    (c)   refuses to accept for registration for the purposes of this Act any profit sharing plan or revokes the registration of such a plan,

    (d)   refuses to issue a certificate of exemption under subsection 212(14),

    (e)   refuses to accept for registration for the purposes of this Act an education savings plan,

    (e.1) sends notice under subsection 146.1(12.1) to a promoter that the Minister proposes to revoke the registration of an education savings plan,

    (f)   refuses to register for the purposes of this Act any pension plan or gives notice under subsection 147.1(11) to the administrator of a registered pension plan that the Minister proposes to revoke its registration,

    (f.1) refuses to accept an amendment to a registered pension plan, or

    (g)   refuses to accept for registration for the purposes of this Act any retirement income fund,

the applicant or the organization, foundation, association or registered charity, as the case may be, in a case described in paragraph 172(3)(a) or 172(3)(a.1), the applicant in a case described in paragraph 172(3)(b), 172(3)(d), 172(3)(e) or 172(3)(g), a trustee under the plan or an employer of employees who are beneficiaries under the plan, in a case described in paragraph 172(3)(c), the promoter in a case described in paragraph 172(3)(e.1), or the administrator of the plan or an employer who participates in the plan, in a case described in paragraph 172(3)(f) or 172(3)(f.1), may appeal from the Minister's decision, or from the giving of the notice by the Minister, to the Federal Court of Appeal.

(4) **Deemed refusal to register** — For the purposes of subsection 172(3), the Minister shall be deemed to have refused

(a)   to register an applicant for registration as a Canadian amateur athletic association,

(b)   to accept for registration for the purposes of this Act any retirement savings plan or profit sharing plan,

(c)   to issue a certificate of exemption under subsection 212(14),

(d)   to accept for registration for the purposes of this Act any education savings plan, or

(e)   (Repealed by S.C. 1986, c. 6, s. 92(3).)

(f)   to accept for registration for the purposes of this Act any retirement income fund,

where the Minister has not notified the applicant of the disposition of the application within 180 days after the filing of the application with the Minister, and, in any such case, an appeal from the refusal to the Federal Court of Appeal pursuant to subsection 172(3) may, notwithstanding anything in subsection 180(1), be instituted under section 180 at any time by filing a notice of appeal in the Court.

(5) **Idem** — For the purposes of subsection 172(3), the Minister shall be deemed to have refused

(a)   to register for the purposes of this Act any pension plan, or

(b)   to accept an amendment to a registered pension plan

where the Minister has not notified the applicant of the Minister's disposition of the application within 1 year after the filing of the application with the Minister, and, in any such case, an appeal from the refusal to the Federal Court of Appeal pursuant to subsection 172(3) may, notwithstanding anything in subsection 180(1), be instituted under section 180 at any time by filing a notice of appeal in the Court.

(6) **Application of s. 149.1(1)** — The definitions in subsection 149.1(1) apply to this section.

[S.C. 1970-71-72, c. 63, s. 1; S.C. 1974-75-76, c. 26, s. 108; S.C. 1976-77, c. 4, s. 87; S.C. 1977-78, c. 1, s. 79; S.C. 1977-78, c. 32, s. 41; S.C. 1980-81-82-83, c. 158, s. 58; S.C. 1984, c. 45, ss. 57, 72; S.C. 1986, c. 6, s. 92; S.C. 1988, c. 55, s. 147; S.C. 1988, c. 61, s. 18; S.C. 1990, c. 35, s. 18; S.C. 1994, c. 7, Sch. II, s. 141; S.C. 1998, c. 19, s. 46; S.C. 2005, c. 19, s. 39]

## PART I.3, TAX ON LARGE CORPORATIONS

**181.1.** (3) **Where tax not payable** — No tax is payable under this Part for a taxation year by a corporation

. . .

(c)   that was throughout the year exempt from tax under section 149 on all of its taxable income.

## PART V, TAX AND PENALTIES IN RESPECT OF REGISTERED CHARITIES

**187.7. Application of s. 149.1(1)** — The definitions in subsection 149.1(1) apply to this Part.

[S.C. 1984, c. 45, s. 57.]

**188.** (1) **Deemed year-end on notice of revocation** — If on a particular day the Minister issues a notice of intention to revoke the registration of a taxpayer as a registered charity under any of subsections 149.1(2) to (4.1) and 168(1) or it is determined, under subsection 7(1) of the Charities Registration (Security Information) Act, that a certificate served in respect of the charity under subsection 5(1) of that Act is reasonable on the basis of information and evidence available,

(a) the taxation year of the charity that would otherwise have included that day is deemed to end at the end of that day;

(b) a new taxation year of the charity is deemed to begin immediately after that day; and

(c) for the purpose of determining the charity's fiscal period after that day, the charity is deemed not to have established a fiscal period before that day.

(1.1) **Revocation tax** — A charity referred to in subsection (1) is liable to a tax, for its taxation year that is deemed to have ended, equal to the amount determined by the formula

$$A - B$$

where

A    is the total of all amounts, each of which is

(a) the fair market value of a property of the charity at the end of that taxation year,

(b) the amount of an appropriation (within the meaning assigned by subsection (2)) in respect of a property transferred to another person in the 120-day period that ended at the end of that taxation year, or

(c) the income of the charity for its winding-up period, including gifts received by the charity in that period from any source and any income that would be computed under section 3 as if that period were a taxation year; and

B    is the total of all amounts (other than the amount of an expenditure in respect of which a deduction has been made in computing income for the winding-up period under paragraph (c) of the description of A), each of which is

(a) a debt of the charity that is outstanding at the end of that taxation year,

(b) an expenditure made by the charity during the winding-up period on charitable activities carried on by it, or

(c) an amount in respect of a property transferred by the charity during the winding-up period and not later than the latter of one year from the end of the taxation year and the day, if any, referred to in paragraph (1.2)(c), to a person that was at the time of the transfer an eligible donee in respect of the charity, equal to the amount, if any, by which the fair market value of the property, when transferred, exceeds the consideration given by the person for the transfer.

(1.2) **Winding-up period** — In this Part, the winding-up period of a charity is the period that begins immediately after the day on which the Minister issues a notice of intention to revoke the registration of a taxpayer as a registered charity under any of subsections 149.1(2) to (4.1) and 168(1) (or, if earlier, immediately after the day on which it is determined, under subsection 7(1) of the Charities Registration (Security Information) Act, that a certificate served in respect of the charity under subsection 5(1) of that Act is reasonable on the basis of information and evidence available), and that ends on the day that is the latest of

(a) the day, if any, on which the charity files a return under subsection 189(6.1) for the taxation year deemed by subsection (1) to have ended, but not later than the day on which the charity is required to file that return,

(b) the day on which the Minister last issues a notice of assessment of tax payable under subsection (1.1) for that taxation year by the charity, and

(c) if the charity has filed a notice of objection or appeal in respect of that assessment, the day on which the Minister may take a collection action under section 225.1 in respect of that tax payable.

(1.3) **Eligible donee** — In this Part, an eligible donee in respect of a particular charity is a registered charity

(a) of which more than 50% of the members of the board of directors or trustees of the registered charity deal at arm's length with each member of the board of directors or trustees of the particular charity;

(b) that is not the subject of a suspension under subsection 188.2(1);

(c) that has no unpaid liabilities under this Act or under the Excise Tax Act;

(d) that has filed all information returns required by subsection 149.1(14); and

(e) that is not the subject of a certificate under subsection 5(1) of the Charities Registration (Security Information) Act or, if it is the subject of such a certificate, the certificate has been determined under subsection 7(1) of that Act not to be reasonable.

(2) **Shared liability – revocation tax** — A person who, after the time that is 120 days before the end of the taxation year of a charity that is deemed by subsection (1) to have ended, receives property from the charity, is jointly and severally, or solidarily, liable with the charity for the tax payable under subsection (1.1) by the charity for that taxation year for an amount not exceeding the total of all appropriations, each of which is the amount by which the fair market value of such a property at the time it was so received by the person exceeds the consideration given by the person in respect of the property.

(2.1) **Non-application of revocation tax** — Subsections (1) and (1.1) do not apply to a charity in respect of a notice of intention to revoke given under any of subsections 149.1(2) to (4.1) and 168(1) if the Minister abandons the intention and so notifies the charity or if

(a) within the one-year period that begins immediately after the taxation year of the charity otherwise deemed by subsection (1) to have ended, the Minister has registered the charity as a charitable organization, private foundation or public foundation; and

(b) the charity has, before the time that the Minister has so registered the charity,

(i) paid all amounts, each of which is an amount for which the charity is liable under this Act (other than subsection (1.1)) or the Excise Tax Act in respect of taxes, penalties and interest, and

(ii) filed all information returns required by or under this Act to be filed on or before that time.

(3) **Transfer of property tax** — Where, as a result of a transaction or series of transactions, property owned by a registered charity that is a charitable foundation and having a net value greater than 50% of the net asset amount of the charitable foundation immediately before the transaction or series of transactions, as the case may be, is transferred before the end of a taxation year, directly or indirectly, to one or more charitable organizations and it may reasonably be considered that the main purpose of the transfer is to effect a reduction in the disbursement quota of the foundation, the foundation shall pay a tax under this Part for the year equal to the amount by which 25% of the net value of that property determined as of the day of its transfer exceeds the total of all amounts each of which is its tax payable under this subsection for a preceding taxation year in respect of the transaction or series of transactions.

(3.1) **Non-application of subsection (3)** — Subsection (3) does not apply to a transfer that is a gift to which subsection 188.1(11) applies.

(4) **Idem** — Where property has been transferred to a charitable organization in circumstances described in subsection 188(3) and it may reasonably be considered that the organization acted in concert with a charitable foundation for the purpose of reducing the disbursement quota of the foundation, the organization is jointly and severally liable with the foundation for the tax imposed on the foundation by that subsection in an amount not exceeding the net value of the property.

(5) **Definitions** — In this section,

"net asset amount" of a charitable foundation at any time means the amount determined by the formula

$$A - B$$

where

A is the fair market value at that time of all the property owned by the foundation at that time, and

B is the total of all amounts each of which is the amount of a debt owing by or any other obligation of the foundation at that time;

"net value" of property owned by a charitable foundation, as of the day of its transfer, means the amount determined by the formula

$$A - B$$

where

A is the fair market value of the property on that day, and

B is the amount of any consideration given to the foundation for the transfer.

[S.C. 1970-71-72, c. 63, s. 1; S.C. 1973-74, c. 14, s. 60; S.C. 1984, c. 45, s. 78; S.C. 1988, c. 55, s. 153; S.C. 1994, c. 7, Sch. II, s. 155; S.C. 1994, c. 21, s. 84; S.C. 2005, c. 19, s. 43]

**188.1.** (1) **Penalties for charities – carrying on business** — Subject to subsection (2), a registered charity is liable to a penalty under this Part equal to 5% of its gross revenue for a taxation year from any business that it carries on in the taxation year, if the registered charity

(a)   is a private foundation; or

(b)   is not a private foundation and the business is not a related business in relation to the charity.

(2) **Increased penalty for subsequent assessment** — A registered charity that, less than five years before a particular time, was assessed a liability under subsection (1) or this subsection, for a taxation year, is liable to a penalty under this Part equal to its gross revenue for a subsequent taxation year from any business that, after that assessment and in the subsequent taxation year, it carries on at the particular time if the registered charity

(a)   is a private foundation; or

(b)   is not a private foundation and the business is not a related business in relation to the charity.

(3)   **Control of corporation by a charitable foundation** — If at a particular time a charitable foundation has acquired control (within the meaning of subsection 149.1(12)) of a particular corporation, the foundation is liable to a penalty under this Part for a taxation year equal to

(a)   5% of the total of all amounts, each of which is a dividend received by the foundation from the particular corporation in the taxation year and at a time when the foundation so controlled the particular corporation, except if the foundation is liable under paragraph (b) for a penalty in respect of the dividend; or

(b)   if the Minister has, less than five years before the particular time, assessed a liability under paragraph (A) or this paragraph for a preceding taxation year of the foundation in respect of a dividend received from any corporation, the total of all amounts, each of which is a dividend received, after the particular time, by the foundation, from the particular corporation, in the taxation year and at a time when the foundation so controlled the particular corporation.

(4) **Undue benefits** — A registered charity that, at a particular time in a taxation year, confers on a person an undue benefit is liable to a penalty under this Part for the taxation year equal to

   (a)    105% of the amount of the benefit, except if the charity is liable under paragraph (b) for a penalty in respect of the benefit; or

   (b)    if the Minister has, less than five years before the particular time, assessed a liability under paragraph (A) or this paragraph for a preceding taxation year of the charity and the undue benefit was conferred after that assessment, 110% of the amount of the benefit.

(5) **Meaning of undue benefits** — For the purposes of this Part, an undue benefit conferred on a person (referred to in this Part as the "beneficiary") by a registered charity includes a disbursement by way of a gift or the amount of any part of the income, rights, property or resources of the charity that is paid, payable, assigned or otherwise made available for the personal benefit of any person who is a proprietor, member, shareholder, trustee or settlor of the charity, who has contributed or otherwise paid into the charity more than 50% of the capital of the charity, or who deals not at arm's length with such a person or with the charity, as well as any benefit conferred on a beneficiary by another person, at the direction or with the consent of the charity, that would, if it were not conferred on the beneficiary, be an amount in respect of which the charity would have a right, but does not include a disbursement or benefit to the extent that it is

   (a)    an amount that is reasonable consideration or remuneration for property acquired by or services rendered to the charity;

   (b)    a gift made, or a benefit conferred, in the course of a charitable act in the ordinary course of the charitable activities carried on by the charity, unless it can reasonably be considered that the eligibility of the beneficiary for the benefit relates solely to the relationship of the beneficiary to the charity; or

   (c)    a gift to a qualified donee.

(6) **Failure to file information returns** — Every registered charity that fails to file a return for a taxation year as and when required by subsection 149.1(14) is liable to a penalty equal to $500.

(7) **Incorrect information** — Except where subsection (8) or (9) applies, every registered charity that issues, in a taxation year, a receipt for a gift otherwise than in accordance with this Act and the regulations is liable for the taxation year to a penalty equal to 5% of the amount reported on the receipt as representing the amount in respect of which a taxpayer may claim a deduction under subsection 110.1(1) or a credit under subsection 118.1(3).

(8) **Increased penalty for subsequent assessment** — Except where subsection (9) applies, if the Minister has, less than five years before a particular time, assessed a penalty under subsection (7) or this subsection for a taxation year of a registered charity and, after that assessment and in a subsequent taxation year, the charity issues, at the particular time, a receipt for a gift otherwise than in accordance with this Act and the regulations, the charity is liable for the subsequent

taxation year to a penalty equal to 10% of the amount reported on the receipt as representing the amount in respect of which a taxpayer may claim a deduction under subsection 110.1(1) or a credit under subsection 118.1(3).

(9) **False information** — If at any time a person makes or furnishes, participates in the making of or causes another person to make or furnish a statement that the person knows, or would reasonably be expected to know but for circumstances amounting to culpable conduct (within the meaning assigned by subsection 163.2(1)), is a false statement (within the meaning assigned by subsection 163.2(1)) on a receipt issued by, on behalf of or in the name of another person for the purposes of subsection 110.1(2) or 118.1(2), the person (or, where the person is an officer, employee, official or agent of a registered charity, the registered charity) is liable for their taxation year that includes that time to a penalty equal to 125% of the amount reported on the receipt as representing the amount in respect of which a taxpayer may claim a deduction under subsection 110.1(1) or a credit under subsection 118.1(3).

(10) **Maximum amount** — A person who is liable at any time to penalties under both section 163.2 and subsection (9) in respect of the same false statement is liable to pay only the greater of those penalties.

(11) **Delay of expenditure** — If, in a taxation year, a registered charity has made a gift of property to another registered charity and it may reasonably be considered that one of the main purposes for the making of the gift was to unduly delay the expenditure of amounts on charitable activities, each of those charities is jointly and severally, or solidarily, liable to a penalty under this Act for its respective taxation year equal to 110% of the fair market value of the property.

[**Note:** S.C. 2005, c. 19, s. 44 contains the following provision:

(2) Subsection (1) applies to taxation years that begin after March 22, 2004.]

**188.2.** (1) **Notice of suspension with assessment** — The Minister shall, with an assessment referred to in this subsection, give notice by registered mail to a registered charity that the authority of the charity to issue an official receipt referred to in Part XXXV of the Income Tax Regulations is suspended for one year from the day that is seven days after the notice is mailed, if the Minister has assessed the charity for a taxation year for

(a) a penalty under subsection 188.1(2);

(b) a penalty under paragraph 188.1(4)(b) in respect of an undue benefit, other than an undue benefit conferred by the charity by way of a gift; or

(c) a penalty under subsection 188.1(9) if the total of all such penalties for the taxation year exceeds $25,000.

(2) **Notice of suspension – general** — The Minister may give notice by registered mail to a registered charity that the authority of the charity to issue an official receipt referred to in Part XXXV of the Income Tax Regulations is suspended for one year from the day that is seven days after the notice is mailed

(a) if the charity contravenes any of sections 230 to 231.5; or

(b)  if it may reasonably be considered that the charity has acted, in concert with another charity that is the subject of a suspension under this section, to accept a gift or transfer of property on behalf of that other charity.

(3) **Effect of suspension** — If the Minister has issued a notice to a registered charity under subsection (1) or (2), subject to subsection (4),

(a)  the charity is deemed, in respect of gifts made and property transferred to the charity within the one-year period that begins on the day that is seven days after the notice is mailed, not to be a donee, described in paragraph 110.1(1)(A) or in the definition "total charitable gifts" in subsection 118.1(1), for the purposes of

  (i)  subsections 110.1(1) and 118.1(1),

  (ii)  the definitions "qualified donee" and "registered charity" in subsection 248(1), and

  (iii)  Part XXXV of the Income Tax Regulations; and

(b)  if the charity is, during that period, offered a gift from any person, the charity shall, before accepting the gift, inform that person that

  (i)  it has received the notice,

  (ii)  no deduction under subsection 110.1(1) or credit under subsection 118.1(3) may be claimed in respect of a gift made to it in the period, and

  (iii)  a gift made in the period is not a gift to a qualified donee.

(4) **Application for postponement** — If a notice of objection to a suspension under subsection (1) or (2) has been filed by a registered charity, the charity may file an application to the Tax Court of Canada for a postponement of that portion of the period of suspension that has not elapsed until the time determined by the Court.

(5) **Grounds for postponement** — The Tax Court of Canada may grant an application for postponement only if it would be just and equitable to do so.

[**Note:** S.C. 2005, c. 19, s. 44, contains the following provision:

(2) Subsection (1) applies to taxation years that begin after March 22, 2004.]

[S.C. 2005, c. 19, s. 44.]

. . .

**189.** (1) **Tax regarding non-qualified investment** — Where at any particular time in a taxation year a debt (other than a debt in respect of which subsection 80.4(1) applies or would apply but for subsection 80.4(3)) is owing by a taxpayer to a registered charity that is a private foundation and at that time the debt was a non-qualified investment of the foundation, the taxpayer shall pay a tax under this Part for the year equal to the amount, if any, by which

(a)  the amount that would be payable as interest on that debt for the period in the year during which it was outstanding and was a non-qualified investment of the foundation if the interest were payable at such prescribed rates as are in effect from time to time during the period

exceeds

(b)  the amount of interest for the year paid on that debt by the taxpayer not later than 30 days after the end of the year.

(2) **Computation of interest on debt** — For the purpose of paragraph 189(1)(a), where a debt in respect of which subsection 189(1) applies (other than a share or right that is deemed by subsection 189(3) to be a debt) is owing by a taxpayer to a private foundation, interest on that debt for the period referred to in that paragraph shall be computed at the least of

(a)  such prescribed rates as are in effect from time to time during the period,

(b)  the rate per annum of interest on that debt that, having regard to all the circumstances (including the terms and conditions of the debt), would have been agreed on, at the time the debt was incurred, had the taxpayer and the foundation been dealing with each other at arm's length and had the ordinary business of the foundation been the lending of money, and

(c)  where that debt was incurred before April 22, 1982, a rate per annum equal to 6% plus 2% for each calendar year after 1982 and before the taxation year referred to in subsection 189(1).

(3) **Share deemed to be debt** — For the purpose of subsection 189(1), where a share, or a right to acquire a share, of the capital stock of a corporation held by a private foundation at any particular time during the corporation's taxation year was at that time a non-qualified investment of the foundation, the share or right shall be deemed to be a debt owing at that time by the corporation to the foundation

(a)  the amount of which was equal to,

(i)   in the case of a share or right last acquired before April 22, 1982, the greater of its fair market value on April 21, 1982 and its cost amount to the foundation at the particular time, or

(ii)  in any other case, its cost amount to the foundation at the particular time,

(b)  that was outstanding throughout the period for which the share or right was held by the foundation during the year, and

(c)  in respect of which the amount of interest paid in the year is equal to the total of all amounts each of which is the amount of a dividend received on the share by the foundation in the year,

and the reference in paragraph 189(1)(a) to "such prescribed rates as are in effect from time to time during the period" shall be read as a reference to "2/3 of such prescribed rates as are in effect from time to time during the period".

(4) **Computation of interest with respect to a share** — For the purposes of subsection 189(3), where a share or right in respect of which that subsection applies was last acquired before April 22, 1982, the reference therein to "2/3 of such

prescribed rates as are in effect from time to time during the period" shall be read as a reference to "the lesser of

(a)　a rate per annum equal to 4% plus 1% for each 5 calendar years contained in the period commencing after 1982 and ending before the particular time, and

(b)　a rate per annum equal to 2/3 of such prescribed rates as are in effect from time to time during the year".

(5) **Share substitution** — For the purpose of subsection 189(3), where a share or right is acquired by a charity in exchange for another share or right in a transaction after April 21, 1982 to which section 51, 85, 85.1, 86 or 87 applies, it shall be deemed to be the same share or right as the one for which it was substituted.

(6) **Taxpayer to file return and pay tax** — Every taxpayer who is liable to pay tax under this Part (except a charity that is liable to pay tax under section 188(1)) for a taxation year shall, on or before the day on or before which the taxpayer is, or would be if tax were payable by the taxpayer under Part I for the year, required to file a return of income or an information return under Part I for the year,

(a)　file with the Minister a return for the year in prescribed form and containing prescribed information, without notice or demand therefor;

(b)　estimate in the return the amount of tax payable by the taxpayer under this Part for the year; and

(c)　pay to the Receiver General the amount of tax payable by the taxpayer under this Part for the year.

(6.1) **Revoked charity to file returns** — Every taxpayer who is liable to pay tax under subsection 188(1.1) for a taxation year shall, on or before the day that is one year from the end of the taxation year, and without notice or demand,

(a)　file with the Minister

(i)　a return for the taxation year, in prescribed form and containing prescribed information, and

(ii)　both an information return and a public information return for the taxation year, each in the form prescribed for the purpose of subsection 149.1(14); and

(b)　estimate in the return referred to in subparagraph (a)(i) the amount of tax payable by the taxpayer under subsection 188(1.1) for the taxation year; and

(c)　pay to the Receiver General the amount of tax payable by the taxpayer under subsection 188(1.1) for the taxation year.

(6.2) **Reduction of revocation tax liability** — If the Minister has, during the one-year period beginning immediately after the end of a taxation year of a person, assessed the person in respect of the person's liability for tax under subsection 188(1.1) for that taxation year, has not after that period reassessed the tax liability of the person, and that liability exceeds $1,000, that liability is, at any particular time, reduced by the total of

(a)   the amount, if any, by which

    (i)   the total of all amounts, each of which is an expenditure made by the charity, on charitable activities carried on by it, before the particular time and during the period (referred to in this subsection as the "post-assessment period") that begins immediately after a notice of the latest such assessment was mailed and ends at the end of the one-year period

exceeds

    (ii)   the income of the charity for the post-assessment period, including gifts received by the charity in that period from any source and any income that would be computed under section 3 if that period were a taxation year, and

(b)   all amounts, each of which is an amount, in respect of a property transferred by the charity before the particular time and during the post-assessment period to a person that was at the time of the transfer an eligible donee in respect of the charity, equal to the amount, if any, by which the fair market value of the property, when transferred, exceeds the consideration given by the person for the transfer.

(6.3) **Reduction of liability for penalties** — If the Minister has assessed a registered charity in respect of the charity's liability for penalties under section 188.1 for a taxation year, and that liability exceeds $1,000, that liability is, at any particular time, reduced by the total of all amounts, each of which is an amount, in respect of a property transferred by the charity after the day on which the Minister first assessed that liability and before the particular time to a person that was at the time of the transfer an eligible donee in respect of the charity, equal to the amount, if any, by which the fair market value of the property, when transferred, exceeds the total of

(a)   the consideration given by the person for the transfer, and

(b)   the part of the amount in respect of the transfer that has resulted in a reduction of an amount otherwise payable under subsection 188(1.1).

(7) **Minister may assess** — Without limiting the authority of the Minister to revoke the registration of a registered charity, the Minister may also at any time assess a taxpayer in respect of any amount that a taxpayer is liable to pay under this Part.

(8) **Provisions applicable to Part** — Subsections 150(2) and (3), sections 152 and 158, subsection 161(11), sections 162 to 167 and Division J of Part I apply in respect of an amount assessed under this Part and of a notice of suspension under subsection 188.2(1) or (2) as if the notice were a notice of assessment made under section 152, with any modifications that the circumstances require including, for greater certainty, that a notice of suspension that is reconsidered or reassessed may be confirmed or vacated, but not varied, except that

(a)   section 162 does not apply in respect of a return required to be filed under paragraph (6.1)(a); and

   (b)   the reference in each of subsections 165(2) and 166.1(3) to the expression "Chief of Appeals in a District Office or a Taxation Centre" is to be read as a reference to the expression "Assistant Commissioner, Appeals Branch".

**(8.1) Clarification re objections under subsection 168(4)** — For greater certainty, in applying the provisions referred to in subsection (8), with any modifications that the circumstances require,

   (a)   a notice of objection referred to in subsection 168(4) does not constitute a notice of objection to a tax assessed under subsection 188(1.1); and

   (b)   an issue that could have been the subject of a notice of objection referred to in subsection 168(4) may not be appealed to the Tax Court of Canada under subsection 169(1).

**(9) Interest** — Subsection 161(11) does not apply to a liability of a taxpayer for a taxation year

   (a)   under subsection 188(1.1) to the extent that the liability is reduced by subsection (6.2), or paid, before the end of the one-year period that begins immediately after the end of the taxation year deemed to have ended by paragraph 188(1)(a); or

   (b)   under section 188.1 to the extent that the liability is reduced by subsection (6.3), or paid, before the end of the one-year period that begins immediately after the liability was first assessed.

[S.C. 1970-71-72, c. 63, s. 1; S.C. 1973-74, c. 14, s. 60; S.C. 1984, c. 45, s. 78; S.C. 1985, c. 45, s. 102; S.C. 1986, c. 6, s. 99; S.C. 1994, c. 21, s. 85; S.C. 2005, c. 19, s. 45]

. . .

## PART XI.2, TAX IN RESPECT OF DISPOSITIONS OF CERTAIN PROPERTIES

**207.3 Tax payable by institution or public authority** — Every institution or public authority that, at any time in a year, disposes of an object within 10 years after the object became an object described in subparagraph 39(1)(a)(i.1) shall pay a tax under this Part, in respect of the year, equal to 30% of the object's fair market value at that time, unless the disposition was made to another institution or public authority that was, at that time, designated under subsection 32(2) of the *Cultural Property Export and Import Act* either generally or for a specified purpose related to that object.

[S.C. 1974-75-76, c. 50, s. 51; S.C. 1994, c. 7, Sch. II, s. 168; S.C. 1999, c. 22, s. 74.]

**207.31 Tax payable by recipient of an ecological gift** — Any charity or municipality that, at any time in a taxation year, without the authorization of the Minister of the Environment, or a person designated by that Minister, disposes or changes the use of a property described in paragraph 110.1(1)(d) or in the definition "total ecological gifts" in subsection 118.1(1) and given to the charity or municipality after February 27, 1995 shall, in respect of the year pay a tax under this Part equal to 50% of the fair market value of the property at the time of the disposition or change.

[S.C. 1996, c. 21, s. 53.]

**207.4.** (1) **Return and payment of tax** — Any institution, public authority, charity or municipality that is liable to pay a tax under subsection 207.3 or 207.31 in respect of a year shall, within 90 days after the end of the year,

(a) file with the Minister a return for the year under this Part in prescribed form and containing prescribed information without notice or demand therefor;

(b) estimate in the return the amount of tax payable by it under this Part in respect of the year; and

(c) pay to the Receiver General the amount of tax payable by it under this Part in respect of the year.

(2) **Provisions applicable to Part** — Subsections 150(2) and 150(3), sections 152 and 158, subsections 161(1) and 161(11), sections 162 to 167 and Division J of Part I are applicable to this Part with such modifications as the circumstances require.

[S.C. 1974-75-76, c. 50, s. 51; S.C. 1986, c. 6, s. 114; S.C. 1996, c. 21, s. 54.]

## PART XII.2, TAX ON DESIGNATED INCOME
## OF CERTAIN TRUSTS

**210.1 Application of Part** —This Part does not apply in a taxation year to a trust that was throughout the year

. . .

(c) a trust that was exempt from tax under Part I by reason of subsection 149(1);

. . .

## PART XIII, TAX ON INCOME FROM CANADA
## OF NON-RESIDENT PERSONS

**212.** (1) **Tax** — Every non-resident person shall pay an income tax of 25% on every amount that a person resident in Canada pays or credits, or is deemed by Part I to pay or credit, to the non-resident person as, on account or in lieu of payment of, or in satisfaction of,

. . .

(b) **Interest** — interest except

. . .

(iv) interest payable on any bond, debenture or similar obligation to a person with whom the payer is dealing at arm's length and to whom a certificate of exemption that is in force on the day the amount is paid or credited was issued under subsection 212(14),

. . .

(14) **Certificate of exemption** — The Minister may, on application, issue a certificate of exemption to any non-resident person who establishes to the satisfaction of the Minister that

(a) an income tax is imposed under the laws of the country of which the non-resident person is a resident;

(b) the non-resident person is exempt under the laws referred to in paragraph 212(14)(a) from the payment of income tax to the government of the country of which the non-resident person is a resident; and

(c) the non-resident person is

(i) a person who is or would be, if the non-resident person were resident in Canada, exempt from tax under section 149,

(ii) a trust or corporation that is operated exclusively to administer or provide superannuation, pension, retirement or employee benefits, or

(iii) a trust, corporation or other organization constituted and operated exclusively for charitable purposes, no part of the income of which is payable to, or is otherwise available for, the personal benefit of any proprietor, member, shareholder, trustee or settlor thereof.

. . .

**217.** (1) **Alternative re Canadian benefits** — In this section, a non-resident person's "Canadian benefits" for a taxation year is the total of all each of which is an amount paid or credited in the year and in respect of which tax under this Part would, but for this section, be payable by the person because of any of paragraphs 212(1)(h), 212(1)(j) to 212(1)(m) and 212(1)(q).

(2) **Part I return** — No tax is payable under this Part in respect of a non-resident person's Canadian benefits for a taxation year if the person

(a) files with the Minister, within 6 months after the end of the year, a return of income under Part I for the year; and

(b) elects in the return to have this section apply for the year.

(3) **Taxable income earned in Canada** — Where a non-resident person elects under paragraph (2)(b) for a taxation year, for the purposes of Part I

(a) the person is deemed to have been employed in Canada in the year; and

(b) the person's taxable income earned in Canada for the year is deemed to be the greater of

(i) the amount that would, but for subparagraph 217(3)(b)(ii), be the person's taxable income earned in Canada for the year if

(A) paragraph 115(1)(A) included the following subparagraph after subparagraph 217(3)(b)(i):

(i.1) the non-resident person's Canadian benefits for the year, within the meaning assigned by subsection 217(1), and

(B) paragraph 115(1)(f) were read as follows:

115(1)(f) such of the other deductions permitted for the purpose of computing taxable income as can reasonably be considered wholly applicable to the described in subparagraphs 115(1)(a)(i) to 115(1)(a)(vi)."; and

(ii) the person's income (computed without reference to subsection 56(8)) for the year minus the total of such of the deductions permitted for the purpose of computing taxable income as can reasonably be considered wholly applicable to the described in subparagraphs 115(1)(a)(i) to 115(1)(a)(vi).

(4) **Tax credits – limitation** — Sections 118 to 118.91 and 118.94 do not apply in computing the tax payable under Part I for a taxation year by a non-resident person who elects under paragraph 217(2)(b) for the year, unless

(a) where section 114 applies to the person for the year, all or substantially all of the person's income for the year is included in computing the person's taxable income for the year; or

(b) in any other case, all or substantially all of the person's income for the year is included in computing the amount determined under subparagraph 217(3)(b)(i) in respect of the person for the year.

(5) **Tax credits allowed** — In computing the tax payable under Part I for a taxation year by a non-resident person to whom neither paragraph 217(4)(A) nor paragraph 217(4)(b) applies for the year there may, notwithstanding section 118.94 and subsection 217(4), be deducted the lesser of

(a) the total of

(i) such of the that would have been deductible under any of section 118.2, subsections 118.3(2) and 118.3(3) and sections 118.6, 118.8 and 118.9 in computing the person's tax payable under Part I for the year if the person had been resident in Canada throughout the year, as can reasonably be considered wholly applicable, and

(ii) the that would have been deductible under any of sections 118 and 118.1, subsection 118.3(1) and sections 118.5 and 118.7 in computing the person's tax payable under Part I for the year if the person had been resident in Canada throughout the year, and

(b) the appropriate percentage for the year of the person's Canadian benefits for the year.

(6) **Special credit** — In computing the tax payable under Part I for a taxation year by a non-resident who elects under paragraph 217(2)(b) for the year, there may be deducted the amount determined by the formula

$$A \times [(B - C) / B]$$

where

A    is the amount of tax under Part I that would, but for this subsection, be payable by the person for the year;

B    is the amount determined under subparagraph 217(3)(b)(ii) in respect of the person for the year; and

C    is the amount determined under subparagraph 217(3)(b)(i) in respect of the person for the year.

[S.C. 1970-71-72, c. 63, s. 1"217"; S.C. 1974-75-76, c. 26, s. 122; S.C. 1976-77, c. 4, s. 73; S.C. 1977-78, c. 32, s. 51; S.C. 1980-81-82-83, c. 140, s. 119; S.C. 1988, c. 55, s. 165; S.C. 1994, c. 7, Sch. II, s. 179; S.C. 1996, c. 21, s. 56; S.C. 1997, c. 25, s. 64; S.C. 1998, c. 19, s. 64.]

## PART XIV, ADDITIONAL TAX ON NON-RESIDENT CORPORATIONS

. . .

**219.** (2) **Exempt corporations** — No tax is payable under this Part for a taxation year by a corporation that was, throughout the year,

. . .

(c)    a corporation exempt from tax under section 149.

. . .

## PART XV, ADMINISTRATION AND ENFORCEMENT

### *General*

**230.** (2) **Records and books** — Every registered charity and registered Canadian amateur athletic association shall keep records and books of account at an address in Canada recorded with the Minister or designated by the Minister containing

(a)    information in such form as will enable the Minister to determine whether there are any grounds for the revocation of its registration under this Act;

(b)    a duplicate of each receipt containing prescribed information for a donation received by it; and

(c)    other information in such form as will enable the Minister to verify the donations to it for which a deduction or tax credit is available under this Act.

. . .

**237.1.** (1) **Definitions** — In this section,

"gifting arrangement" means any arrangement under which it may reasonably be considered, having regard to statements or representations made or proposed to be made in connection with the arrangement, that if a person were to enter into the arrangement, the person would

(a)    make a gift to a qualified donee, or a contribution referred to in subsection 127(4.1), of property acquired by the person under the arrangement; or

(b)    incur a limited-recourse amount that can reasonably be considered to relate to a gift to a qualified donee or a contribution referred to in subsection 127(4.1).

"person" includes a partnership;

"promoter" in respect of a tax shelter means a person who in the course of a business

(a)  sells or issues, or promotes the sale, issuance or acquisition of, the tax shelter,

(b)  acts as an agent or adviser in respect of the sale or issuance, or the promotion of the sale, issuance or acquisition, of the tax shelter, or

(c)  accepts, whether as a principal or agent, consideration in respect of the tax shelter,

and more than one person may be a tax shelter promoter in respect of the same tax shelter;

"tax shelter" means

(a)  a gifting arrangement described by paragraph (b) of the definition "gifting arrangement"; and

(b)  a gifting arrangement described by paragraph (A) of the definition "gifting arrangement", or a property (including any right to income) other than a flow-through share or a prescribed property, in respect of which it can reasonably be considered, having regard to statements or representations made or proposed to be made in connection with the gifting arrangement or the property, that, if a person were to enter into the gifting arrangement or acquire an interest in the property, at the end of a particular taxation year that ends within four years after the day on which the gifting arrangement is entered into or the interest is acquired,

(i)  the total of all amounts each of which is

(A)  an amount, or a loss in the case of a partnership interest, represented to be deductible in computing the person's income for the particular year or any preceding taxation year in respect of the gifting arrangement or the interest in the property (including, if the property is a right to income, an amount or loss in respect of that right that is stated or represented to be so deductible), or

(B)  any other amount stated or represented to be deemed under this Act to be paid on account of the person's tax payable, or to be deductible in computing the person's income, taxable income or tax payable under this Act, for the particular year or any preceding taxation year in respect of the gifting arrangement or the interest in the property, other than an amount so stated or represented that is included in computing a loss described in clause (A),

would equal or exceed

(ii)  the amount, if any, by which

(A)  the cost to the person of the property acquired under the gifting arrangement, or of the interest in the property at the end of the particular year, determined without reference to section 143.2, would exceed

(B)  the total of all amounts each of which is the amount of any prescribed benefit that is expected to be received or enjoyed, directly or indirectly, in respect of the property acquired under the gifting arrangement, or of the interest in the property, by the person or another person with whom the person does not deal at arm's length.

(2) **Application** — A promoter in respect of a tax shelter shall apply to the Minister in prescribed form for an identification number for the tax shelter unless an identification number therefor has previously been applied for.

(3) **Identification** — On receipt of an application under subsection 237.1(2) for an identification number for a tax shelter, together with prescribed information and an undertaking satisfactory to the Minister that books and records in respect of the tax shelter will be kept and retained at a place in Canada that is satisfactory to the Minister, the Minister shall issue an identification number for the tax shelter.

(4) **Sales prohibited** — No person shall, whether as a principal or an agent, sell or issue, or accept consideration in respect of, a tax shelter before the Minister has issued an identification number for the tax shelter.

(5) **Providing tax shelter number** — Every promoter in respect of a tax shelter shall

(a)  make reasonable efforts to ensure that all persons who acquire or otherwise invest in the tax shelter are provided with the identification number issued by the Minister for the tax shelter;

(b)  prominently display on the upper right-hand corner of any statement of earnings prepared by or on behalf of the promoter in respect of the tax shelter the identification number issued for the tax shelter; and

(c)  on every written statement made after 1995 by the promoter that refers either directly or indirectly and either expressly or impliedly to the issuance by the Canada Customs and Revenue Agency of an identification number for the tax shelter, as well as on the copies of the portion of the information return to be forwarded pursuant to subsection 237.1(7.3), prominently display

(i)  where the statement or return is wholly or partly in English, the following:

"The identification number issued for this tax shelter shall be included in any income tax return filed by the investor. Issuance of the identification number is for administrative purposes only and does not in any way confirm the entitlement of an investor to claim any tax benefits associated with the tax shelter."

(ii)  where the statement or return is wholly or partly in French, the following:

"Le numéro d'inscription attribué à cet abri fiscal doit figurer dans toute déclaration d'impôt sur le revenu produite par l'investisseur. L'attribution de ce numéro n'est qu'une formalité administrative et ne confirme aucunement le droit de l'investisseur aux avantages fiscaux découlant de cet abri fiscal."

and

(iii) where the statement includes neither English nor French, the following:

"The identification number issued for this tax shelter shall be included in any income tax return filed by the investor. Issuance of the identification number is for administrative purposes only and does not in any way confirm the entitlement of an investor to claim any tax benefits associated with the tax shelter."

"Le numéro d'inscription attribué à cet abri fiscal doit figurer dans toute déclaration d'impôt sur le revenu produite par l'investisseur. L'attribution de ce numéro n'est qu'une formalité administrative et ne confirme aucunement le droit de l'investisseur aux avantages fiscaux découlant de cet abri fiscal."

(6) **Deductions and claims disallowed** — No amount may be deducted or claimed by a person in respect of a tax shelter unless the person files with the Minister a prescribed form containing prescribed information, including the identification number for the tax shelter.

(6.1) **Deductions and claims disallowed** — No amount may be deducted or claimed by any person for any taxation year in respect of a tax shelter of the person where any person is liable to a penalty under subsection 237.1(7.4) or 162(9) in respect of the tax shelter or interest on the penalty and

(a) the penalty or interest has not been paid; or

(b) the penalty and interest have been paid, but an amount on account of the penalty or interest has been repaid under subsection 164(1.1) or applied under subsection 164(2).

(6.2) **Assessments** — Notwithstanding subsections 152(4) to 152(5), such assessments, determinations and redeterminations may be made as are necessary to give effect to subsection 237.1(6.1).

(7) **Information return** — Every promoter in respect of a tax shelter who accepts consideration in respect of the tax shelter or who acts as a principal or agent in respect of the tax shelter in a calendar year shall, in prescribed form and manner, file an information return for the year containing

(a) the name, address and either the Social Insurance Number or business number of each person who so acquires or otherwise invests in the tax shelter in the year,

(b) the amount paid by each of those persons in respect of the tax shelter, and

(c) such other information as is required by the prescribed form unless an information return in respect of the tax shelter has previously been filed.

(7.1) **Time for filing return** — An information return required under subsection 237.1(7) to be filed in respect of the acquisition of an interest in a tax shelter in a calendar year shall be filed with the Minister on or before the last day of February of the following calendar year.

(7.2) **Time for filing – special case** — Notwithstanding subsection 237.1(7.1), where a person is required under subsection 237.1(7) to file an information return in respect of a business or activity and the person discontinues that business or activity, the return shall be filed on or before the earlier of

(a)  the day referred to in subsection 237.1(7.1); and

(b)  the day that is 30 days after the day of the discontinuance.

(7.3) **Copies to be provided** — Every person required to file a return under subsection 237.1(7) shall, on or before the day on or before which the return is required to be filed with the Minister, forward to each person to whom the return relates 2 copies of the portion of the return relating to that person.

(7.4) **Penalty** — Every person who files false or misleading information with the Minister in respect of an application under subsection 237.1(2) or, whether as a principal or as an agent, sells, issues or accepts consideration in respect of a tax shelter before the Minister has issued an identification number for the tax shelter is liable to a penalty equal to the greater of

(a)  $500, and

(b)  25% of the total of all amounts each of which is the consideration received or receivable from a person in respect of the tax shelter before the correct information is filed with the Minister or the identification number is issued, as the case may be.

(8) **Application of ss. 231 to 231.3** — Without restricting the generality of sections 231 to 231.3, where an application under subsection 237.1(2) with respect to a tax shelter has been made, notwithstanding that a return of income has not been filed by any taxpayer under section 150 for the taxation year of the taxpayer in which an amount is claimed as a deduction in respect of the tax shelter, sections 231 to 231.3 apply, with such modifications as the circumstances require, for the purpose of permitting the Minister to verify or ascertain any information in respect of the tax shelter.

[**Note:** S.C. 2003, c. 15, s. 87 contains the following provisions:

(3)  The portion of the definition "tax shelter" in subsection 237.1(1) of the Act before paragraph (a), as enacted by subsection (1), and the portion of the definition "gifting arrangement" in subsection 237.1(1) of the Act before paragraph (a), as enacted by subsection (2), apply after February 18, 2003.

(4)  Paragraph (a) of the definition "tax shelter" in subsection 237.1(1) of the Act, as enacted by subsection (1), and paragraph (b) of the definition "gifting arrangement" in subsection 237.1(1) of the Act, as enacted by

subsection (2) apply in respect of property acquired, and gifts, contributions, statements and representations made, after February 18, 2003.

(5)   Paragraph (b) of the definition "tax shelter" in subsection 237.1(1) of the Act, as enacted by subsection (1), and paragraph (A) of the definition "gifting arrangement" in subsection 237.1(1) of the Act, as enacted by subsection (2), apply in respect of property acquired, and statements and representations made, after February 18, 2003.]

[S.C. 1988, c. 55, s. 180; S.C. 1994, c. 7, Sch. II, s. 188; S.C. 1998, c. 19, s. 234; S.C. 1999, c. 17, par. 169(d); S.C. 2003, c. 15, s. 87.]

**237.2. Application of s. 237.1** — Section 237.1 is applicable with respect to interests acquired after August 31, 1989.

[S.C. 1988, c. 55, s. 180.]

. . .

## Offences and Punishment

**241.** (1) **Provision of information** — Except as authorized by this section, no official shall

(a)   knowingly provide, or knowingly allow to be provided, to any person any taxpayer information;

(b)   knowingly allow any person to have access to any taxpayer information; or

(c)   knowingly use any taxpayer information otherwise than in the course of the administration or enforcement of this Act, the *Canada Pension Plan*, the *Unemployment Insurance Act* or the *Employment Insurance Act* or for the purpose for which it was provided under this section.

. . .

(3.2) **Registered charities** — An official may provide to any person the following taxpayer information relating to a charity that at any time was a registered charity:

(a)   a copy of the charity's governing documents, including its statement of purpose;

(b)   any information provided in prescribed form to the Minister by the charity on applying for registration under this Act;

(c)   the names of the persons who at any time were the charity's directors and the periods during which they were its directors;

(d)   a copy of the notification of the charity's registration, including any conditions and warnings;

(e)   if the registration of the charity has been revoked or annulled, a copy of the entirety of or any part of any letter sent by or on behalf of the Minister to the charity relating to the grounds for the revocation or annulment;

(f)   financial statements required to be filed with an information return referred to in subsection 149.1(14);

(g)   a copy of the entirety of or any part of any letter or notice by the Minister to the charity relating to a suspension under section 188.2 or an assessment of tax or penalty under this Act (other than the amount of a liability under subsection 188(1.1)); and

(h)    an application by the charity, and information filed in support of the application, for a designation, determination or decision by the Minister under subsection 149.1(6.3), (7), (8) or (13).

(4) **Where taxpayer information may be disclosed** — An official may

. . .

(f.1)   provide taxpayer information to an official solely for the purposes of the administration and enforcement of the *Charities Registration (Security Information) Act*;

[S.C. 2005, c. 19, s. 51]

## PART XVII, INTERPRETATION

**248.** (1) **Definitions** — In this Act,

. . .

"private foundation" has the meaning assigned by section 149.1;

"public foundation" has the meaning assigned by section 149.1;

"qualified donee" has the meaning assigned by subsection 149.1(1);

"registered charity" at any time means

(a)    a charitable organization, private foundation or public foundation, within the meanings assigned by subsection 149.1(1), that is resident in Canada and was either created or established in Canada, or

(b)    a branch, section, parish, congregation or other division of an organization or foundation described in paragraph 248(1) "registered charity" (a), that is resident in Canada and was either created or established in Canada and that receives donations on its own behalf,

that has applied to the Minister in prescribed form for registration and that is at that time registered as a charitable organization, private foundation or public foundation;

# INCOME TAX REGULATIONS

(C.R.C., c. 945)

[Note: Only regulations relevant to charitable donations and registered charities are reproduced]

## PART II

### INFORMATION RETURNS

*Estates and Trusts*

**204.** (1) Every person having the control of, or receiving income, gains or profits in a fiduciary capacity, or in a capacity analogous to a fiduciary capacity, shall make a return in prescribed form in respect thereof.

. . .

(3) Subsection (1) does not require a trust to make a return for a taxation year at the end of which it is

. . .

(c) a registered charity;

## PART XXXV

### RECEIPTS FOR DONATIONS AND GIFTS

*Interpretation*

**3500.** In this Part,

"employees' charity trust" means a registered charity that is organized for the purpose of remitting, to other registered charities, donations that are collected from employees by an employer;

"official receipt" means a receipt for the purposes of subsection 110.1(2) or (3) or 118.1(2), (6) or (7) of the Act, containing information as required by section 3501 or 3502;

"official receipt form" means any printed form that a registered organization or other recipient of a gift has that is capable of being completed, or that originally was intended to be completed, as an official receipt by it;

"other recipient of a gift" means a person, to whom a gift is made by a taxpayer, referred to in any of subparagraphs 110.1(1)(a)(iii) to (vii), paragraphs 110.1(1)(b) and (c), subparagraph 110.1(3)(a)(ii), paragraphs (c) to (g) of the definition "total charitable gifts" in subsection 118.1(1), the definition "total Crown gifts" in subsection 118.1(1), paragraph (b) of the definition "total cultural gifts" in subsection 118.1(1) and paragraph 118.1(6)(b) of the Act;

"registered organization" means a registered charity, a registered Canadian amateur athletic association or a registered national arts service organization.

[SOR/81-269, s. 2; SOR/86-488, s. 5; SOR/88-165, s. 18; SOR/94-140, s. 8; SOR/94-686, s. 51(F).]

### *Contents of Receipts*

**3501.** (1) Every official receipt issued by a registered organization shall contain a statement that it is an official receipt for income tax purposes and shall show clearly in such a manner that it cannot readily be altered,

  (a)  the name and address in Canada of the organization as recorded with the Minister;
  (b)  the registration number assigned by the Minister to the organization;
  (c)  the serial number of the receipt;
  (d)  the place or locality where the receipt was issued;
  (e)  where the donation is a cash donation, the day on which or the year during which the donation was received;
  (e.1) where the donation is a gift of property other than cash

      (i)   the day on which the donation was received,
      (ii)  a brief description of the property, and
      (iii) the name and address of the appraiser of the property if an appraisal is done;

  (f)  the day on which the receipt was issued where that day differs from the day referred to in paragraph (e) or (e.1);
  (g)  the name and address of the donor including, in the case of an individual, his first name and initial;
  (h)  the amount that is

      (i)   the amount of a cash donation, or
      (ii)  where the donation is a gift of property other than cash, the amount that is the fair market value of the property at the time that the gift was made; and

  (i)  the signature, as provided in subsection (2) or (3), of a responsible individual who has been authorized by the organization to acknowledge donations.

(1.1) Every official receipt issued by another recipient of a gift shall contain a statement that it is an official receipt for income tax purposes and shall show clearly in such a manner that it cannot readily be altered,

  (a)  the name and address of the other recipient of the gift;
  (b)  the serial number of the receipt;
  (c)  the place or locality where the receipt was issued;
  (d)  where the donation is a cash donation, the day on which or the year during which the donation was received;

(e) where the donation is a gift of property other than cash,

  (i) the day on which the donation was received,
  (ii) a brief description of the property, and
  (iii) the name and address of the appraiser of the property if an appraisal is done;

(f) the day on which the receipt was issued where that day differs from the day referred to in paragraph (d) or (e);

(g) the name and address of the donor including, in the case of an individual, his first name and initial;

(h) the amount that is

  (i) the amount of a cash donation, or
  (ii) where the donation is a gift of property other than cash, the amount that is the fair market value of the property at the time that the gift was made; and

(i) the signature, as provided in subsection (2) or (3.1), of a responsible individual who has been authorized by the other recipient of the gift to acknowledge donations.

(2) Except as provided in subsection (3) or (3.1), every official receipt shall be signed personally by an individual referred to in paragraph (1)(i) or (1.1)(i).

(3) Where all official receipt forms of a registered organization are

(a) distinctively imprinted with the name, address in Canada and registration number of the organization,

(b) serially numbered by a printing press or numbering machine, and

(c) kept at the place referred to in subsection 230(2) of the Act until completed as an official receipt,

the official receipts may bear a facsimile signature.

(3.1) Where all official receipt forms of another recipient of the gift are

(a) distinctively imprinted with the name and address of the other recipient of the gift,

(b) serially numbered by a printing press or numbering machine, and

(c) if applicable, kept at a place referred to in subsection 230(1) of the Act until completed as an official receipt,

the official receipts may bear a facsimile signature.

(4) An official receipt issued to replace an official receipt previously issued shall show clearly that it replaces the original receipt and, in addition to its own serial number, shall show the serial number of the receipt originally issued.

(5) A spoiled official receipt form shall be marked "cancelled" and such form, together with the duplicate thereof, shall be retained by the registered organization or the other recipient of a gift as part of its records.

(6) Every official receipt form on which

(a) the day on which the donation was received,

(b) the year during which the donation was received, or

(c)    the amount of the donation,

was incorrectly or illegibly entered shall be regarded as spoiled.

[SOR/81-269, s. 3.]

## Employees' Charity Trusts

**3502.** Where

(a)    a registered organization

     (i)    is an employees' charity trust, or

     (ii)    has appointed an employer as agent for the purpose of remitting, to that registered organization, donations that are collected by the employer from the employer's employees, and

(b)    each copy of the return required by section 200 to be filed for a year by an employer of employees who donated to the registered organization in that year shows

     (i)    the amount of each employee's donations to the registered organization for the year collected by the employer, and

     (ii)    the registration number assigned by the Minister to the registered organization,

section 3501 shall not apply and the copy of the portion of the return, relating to each employee who made a donation to the registered organization in that year, that is required by section 209 to be distributed to the employee for filing with the employee's income tax return shall be an official receipt.

[SOR/94-140, s. 10; SOR/94-686, s. 51(F).]

## Universities Outside Canada

**3503.** For the purposes of subparagraph 110.1(1)(a)(vi) and paragraph (f) of the definition "total charitable gifts" in subsection 118.1(1) of the Act, the universities outside Canada named in Schedule VIII are hereby prescribed to be universities the student body of which ordinarily includes students from Canada.

[SOR/90-411, s. 1; SOR/94-686, s. 51(F).]

## Prescribed Donees

**3504.** For the purposes of subparagraph 110.1(3)(a)(ii) and paragraph 118.1(6)(b) of the Act, The Nature Conservancy, a charity established in the United States, is a prescribed donee.

[SOR/86-488, s. 6; SOR/94-140, s. 11; SOR/94-686, s. 51(F).]

# PART XXXVII

## CHARITABLE FOUNDATIONS

### *Interpretation*

**3700.** In this Part,

"charitable foundation" has the meaning assigned by paragraph 149.1(1)(a) of the Act;

"limited-dividend housing company" means a limited-dividend housing company described in paragraph 149(1)(n) of the Act;

"non-qualified investment" has the meaning assigned by paragraph 149.1(1)(e.1) of the Act;

"prescribed stock exchange" means a stock exchange referred to in Part XXXII;

"taxation year" has the meaning assigned by paragraph 149.1(1)(l) of the Act.

[SOR/87-632, s. 1; SOR/94-686, ss. 51(F), 73(F).]

### *Disbursement Quota*

**3701.** (1) For the purposes of clause 149.1(1)(e)(iv)(A) of the Act, the prescribed amount referred to therein for a taxation year of a charitable foundation shall be determined in accordance with the following rules:

(a)   choose a number, not less than two and not more than eight, of equal and consecutive periods that total twenty-four months and that end immediately before the beginning of the year;

(b)   aggregate for each period chosen under paragraph (a) all amounts, each of which is the value, determined in accordance with section 3702, of property or a portion thereof owned by the foundation, and not used directly in charitable activities or administration, on the last day of the period;

(c)   aggregate all amounts, each of which is the aggregate of values determined for each period under paragraph (b); and

(d)   divide the aggregate amount determined under paragraph (*c*) by the number of periods chosen under paragraph (a).

(2) For the purposes of subsection (1) and subject to subsection (3),

(a)   the number of periods chosen by a charitable foundation under paragraph (1)(*a*) shall, unless otherwise authorized by the Minister, be used for the taxation year and for all subsequent taxation years; and

(b)   a charitable foundation shall be deemed to have existed on the last day of each of the periods chosen by it.

(3) The number of periods chosen under paragraph (1)(a) may be changed by the foundation for its first taxation year commencing after 1986 and the new number shall, unless otherwise authorized by the Minister, be used for that taxation year and all subsequent taxation years.

[SOR/87-632, s. 1; SOR/94-686, s. 51(F).]

*Determination of Value*

**3702.** (1) For the purposes of subsection 3701(1), the value of property or a portion thereof owned by a charitable foundation, and not used directly in charitable activities or administration, on the last day of a period shall be determined as of that day and shall be

(a)　in the case of a non-qualified investment, the greater of its fair market value on that day and its cost amount to the foundation;

(b)　subject to paragraph (c), in the case of property other than a non-qualified investment that is

(i)　a share of a corporation that is listed on a prescribed stock exchange, the closing price or the average of the bid and asked prices of that share on that day or, if there is no closing price or bid and asked prices on that day, on the last preceding day for which there was a closing price or bid and asked prices,

(ii)　a share of a corporation that is not listed on a prescribed stock exchange, the fair market value of that share on that day,

(iii)　an interest in real property, the fair market value on that day of the interest less the amount of any debt of the foundation incurred in respect of the acquisition of the interest and secured by the real property or the interest therein, where the debt bears a reasonable rate of interest,

(iv)　a contribution that is the subject of a pledge, nil,

(v)　an interest in property where the foundation does not have the present use or enjoyment of the interest, nil,

(vi)　a life insurance policy, other than an annuity contract, that has not matured, nil, and

(vii)　a property not described in any of subparagraphs (i) to (vi), the fair market value of the property on that day; and

(c)　in the case of any property described in paragraph (*b*)

(i)　that is owned in connection with the charitable activities of the foundation and is a share of a limited-dividend housing company or a loan,

(ii)　that has ceased to be used for charitable purposes and is being held pending disposition or for use in charitable activities, or

(iii)　that has been acquired for use in charitable activities,

the lesser of the fair market value of the property on that day and an amount determined by the formula

$$\frac{A}{.045} \times \frac{12}{B}$$

where

"A" is the income earned on the property in the period, and

"B" is the number of months in the period.

(2) For the purposes of subsection (1), a method that the Minister may accept for the determination of the fair market value of property or a portion thereof on the last day of a period is an independent appraisal made

(a) in the case of property described in subparagraph (1)(b)(ii) or (iii), not more than three years before that day; and

(b) in the case of property described in paragraph (1)(a), subparagraph (1)(b)(vii) or paragraph (1)(c), not more than one year before that day.

[SOR/87-632, s. 1; SOR/94-686, ss. 22(F), 51(F), 73(F), 79(F).]

# PART LXII

## PRESCRIBED SECURITIES, SHARES AND DEBT OBLIGATIONS

*Prescribed Securities*

**6210**. For the purposes of paragraph 38(a.1) of the Act, a prescribed debt obligation is a bond, debenture, note, mortgage or similar obligation

(a) of or guaranteed by the Government of Canada; or

(b) of the government of a province or an agent of that government.

[SOR/2001-187, s. 6.]

RELATED PROVISION:

SOR/2001-187

**7.** (5) Sections 5 and 6 apply after February 18, 1997.

# SCHEDULE VIII

(s. 3503)

## UNIVERSITIES OUTSIDE CANADA

1. The universities situated in the United States that are prescribed by section 3503 are the following:

Abilene Christian University, Abilene, Texas
Adams State College, Alamosa, Colorado
Academy of the New Church, The, Bryn Athyn, Pennsylvania
Alfred University, Alfred, New York
American Film Institute Center for Advanced Film and Television Studies, Los Angeles, California
American Graduate School of International Management, Glendale, Arizona
American International College, Springfield, Massachusetts
American University, The, Washington, District of Columbia

American University in Cairo, The, New York, New York
Amherst College, Amherst, Massachusetts
Anderson College, Anderson, South Carolina
Andover Newton Theological School, Newton Centre, Massachusetts
Andrews University, Berrien Springs, Michigan
Antioch College, Yellow Springs, Ohio
Arizona State University, Tempe, Arizona
Asbury Theological Seminary, Wilmore, Kentucky
Associated Mennonite Biblical Seminary, Elkhart, Indiana
Atlantic Union College, South Lancaster, Massachusetts
Augsburg College, Minneapolis, Minnesota
Aurora University, Aurora, Illinois
Azusa Pacific College, Azusa, California
Babson College, Babson Park, Massachusetts
Bard College, Annandale-On-Hudson, New York
Barnard College, New York, New York
Bastyr University, Seattle, Washington
Bates College, Lewiston, Maine
Baylor College of Medicine, Houston, Texas
Baylor University, Waco, Texas
Beloit College, Beloit, Wisconsin
Bennington College, Bennington, Vermont
Bentley College, Waltham, Massachusetts
Beth Medrash Govoha, Lakewood, New Jersey
Bethel College, Mishawaka, Indiana
Bethel College, North Newton, Kansas
Bethel College and Seminary, St. Paul, Minnesota
Biola University, La Mirada, California
Bob Jones University, Greenville, South Carolina
Boston College, Chestnut Hill, Massachusetts
Boston University, Boston, Massachusetts
Bowdoin College, Brunswick, Maine
Bowling Green State University, Bowling Green, Ohio
Brandeis University, Waltham, Massachusetts
Brigham Young University–Hawaii Campus, Laie, Hawaii
Brigham Young University, Provo, Utah
Brown University, Providence, Rhode Island
Bryn Mawr College, Bryn Mawr, Pennsylvania
Bucknell University, Lewisburg, Pennsylvania
California Institute of Technology, Pasadena, California
California Lutheran University, Thousand Oaks, California
Calvin College, Grand Rapids, Michigan
Calvin Theological Seminary, Grand Rapids, Michigan
Canisius College, Buffalo, New York
Carleton College, Northfield, Minnesota
Carnegie-Mellon University, Pittsburgh, Pennsylvania
Carroll College, Helena, Montana

Case Western Reserve University, Cleveland, Ohio
Catholic University of America, The, Washington, District of Columbia
Cedarville College, Cedarville, Ohio
Central Michigan University, Mount Pleasant, Michigan
Central Yeshiva Tomchei Tmimim-Lubavitch, Brooklyn, New York
City University, Bellevue, Washington
Claremont McKenna College, Claremont, California
Clark University, Worcester, Massachusetts
Clarkson University, Potsdam, New York
Colby College, Waterville, Maine
Colby-Sawyer College, New London, New Hampshire
Colgate – Rochester Divinity School, The, Rochester, New York
Colgate University, Hamilton, New York
College of William and Mary, Williamsburg, Virginia
Colorado College, The, Colorado Springs, Colorado
Colorado School of Mines, Golden, Colorado
Colorado State University, Fort Collins, Colorado
Columbia International University, Columbia, South Carolina
Columbia Union College, Takoma Park, Maryland
Columbia University in the City of New York, New York, New York
Concordia College, Moorhead, Minnesota
Connecticut College, New London, Connecticut
Conway School of Landscape Design, Conway, Massachusetts
Cornell University, Ithaca, New York
Cornerstone College and Grand Rapids Baptist Seminary, Grand Rapids,
    Michigan
Covenant College, Lookout Mountain, Tennessee
Creighton University, Omaha, Nebraska
Curtis Institute of Music, The, Philadelphia, Pennsylvania
Dallas Theological Seminary, Dallas, Texas
Dartmouth College, Hanover, New Hampshire
Denison University, Granville, Ohio
De Paul University, Chicago, Illinois
Dordt College, Sioux Center, Iowa
Drake University, Des Moines, Iowa
Drew University, Madison, New Jersey
Drury College, Springfield, Missouri
Duke University, Durham, North Carolina
Duquesne University, Pittsburgh, Pennsylvania
Eastern College, St. Davids, Pennsylvania
Eastern Mennonite University, Harrisonburg, Virginia
Eastern Washington University, Cheney, Washington
Eckerd College, St. Petersburg, Florida
Ecumenical Theological Center, Detroit, Michigan
Elmira College, Elmira, New York
Emerson College, Boston, Massachusetts
Emmanuel School of Religion, Johnson City, Tennessee

Emmaus Bible College, Dubuque, Iowa
Emory University, Atlanta, Georgia
Emporia State University, Emporia, Kansas
Ferris State University, Big Rapids, Michigan
Florida Atlantic University, Boca Raton, Florida
Florida Gulf Coast University, Fort Myers, Florida
Florida State University, Tallahassee, Florida
Fordham University, New York, New York
Franciscan University of Steubenville, Steubenville, Ohio
Fresno Pacific College, Fresno, California
Fuller Theological Seminary, Pasadena, California
Gallaudet College, Washington, District of Columbia
Geneva College, Beaver Falls, Pennsylvania
George Washington University, The, Washington, District of Columbia
Georgia Institute of Technology, Atlanta, Georgia
Goddard College, Plainfield, Vermont
God's Bible School and College, Cincinnati, Ohio
Gonzaga University, Spokane, Washington
Gordon College, Wenham, Massachusetts
Gordon-Conwell Theological Seminary, South Hamilton, Massachusetts
Goshen College, Goshen, Indiana
Graceland College, Lamoni, Iowa
Grace University, Omaha, Nebraska
Greenville College, Greenville, Illinois
Grinnell College, Grinnell, Iowa
Hamilton College, Clinton, New York
Hampshire College, Amherst, Massachusetts
Harvard University, Cambridge, Massachusetts
Hebrew Union College — Jewish Institute of Religion, Cincinnati, Ohio
Hillsdale College, Hillsdale, Michigan
Holy Trinity Orthodox Seminary, The, Jordanville, New York
Hope College, Holland, Michigan
Houghton College, Houghton, New York
Huntington College, Huntington, Indiana
Illinois Institute of Technology, Chicago, Illinois
Indiana University, Bloomington, Indiana
Iowa State University of Science and Technology, Ames, Iowa
Ithaca College, Ithaca, New York
Jamestown College, Jamestown, North Dakota
Jewish Theological Seminary of America, The, New York, New York
Johns Hopkins University, The, Baltimore, Maryland
Juilliard School, The, New York, New York
Kansas State University, Manhattan, Kansas
Kenyon College, Gambier, Ohio
Kettering University, Flint, Michigan
Lafayette College, Easton, Pennsylvania
Lake Superior State University, Sault Ste. Marie, Michigan

Lawrence Technological University, Southfield, Michigan
Lehigh University, Bethlehem, Pennsylvania
Leland Stanford Junior University (Stanford University), Stanford, California
Le Moyne College, Syracuse, New York
LeTourneau College, Longview, Texas
Liberty University, Lynchburg, Virginia
Life Chiropractic College-West, San Lorenzo, California
Life University, Marietta, Georgia
Logan College of Chiropractic, St. Louis, Missouri
Loma Linda University, Loma Linda, California
Louisiana State University and Agricultural and Mechanical College, Baton
 Rouge, Louisiana
Loyola University, Chicago, Illinois
Macalester College, St. Paul, Minnesota
Magdalen College, Warner, New Hampshire
Maharishi University of Management, Fairfield, Iowa
Manhattanville College, Purchase, New York
Mankato State University, Mankato, Minnesota
Maranatha Baptist Bible College, Watertown, Wisconsin
Marquette University, Milwaukee, Wisconsin
Massachusetts Institute of Technology, Cambridge, Massachusetts
Mayo Foundation, Rochester, Minnesota
Mayo Graduate School of Medicine, Rochester, Minnesota
Meadville-Lombard Theological School, Chicago, Illinois
Medaille College, Buffalo, New York
Medical University of South Carolina, Charleston, South Carolina
Medical College of Ohio, Toledo, Ohio
Mercyhurst College, Erie, Pennsylvania
Mesivta Yeshiva Rabbi Chaim Berlin, Brooklyn, New York
Messiah College, Grantham, Pennsylvania
Miami University, Oxford, Ohio
Michigan State University, Detroit College of Law, East Lansing, Michigan
Michigan State University, East Lansing, Michigan
Michigan Technological University, Houghton, Michigan
Middlebury College, Middlebury, Vermont
Minot State University, Minot, North Dakota
Mirrer Yeshiva Central Institute, Brooklyn, New York
Montana State University, Bozeman, Montana
Montana Tech of the University of Montana, Butte, Montana
Moody Bible Institute, Chicago, Illinois
Moravian College, Bethlehem, Pennsylvania
Mount Holyoke College, South Hadley, Massachusetts
Mount Ida College, Newton Centre, Massachusetts
Multnomah Bible College, Portland, Oregon
Naropa Institute, The, Boulder, Colorado
National College of Chiropractic, The, Lombard, Illinois
Nazarene Theological Seminary, Kansas City, Missouri

Ner Israel Rabbinical College, Baltimore, Maryland
New England College, Henniker, New Hampshire
New School University, New York, New York
New York University, New York, New York
Niagara University, Niagara University, New York
North American Baptist Seminary, Sioux Falls, South Dakota
North Carolina State University at Raleigh, Raleigh, North Carolina
North Central College, Naperville, Illinois
North Dakota State University of Agriculture and Applied Science, Fargo, North Dakota
Northeastern University, Boston, Massachusetts
Northern Michigan University, Marquette, Michigan
Northwest College of The Assemblies of God, Kirkland, Washington
Northwestern College, Orange City, Iowa
Northwestern College, St. Paul, Minnesota
Northwestern University, Evanston, Illinois
Northwood University, Midland, Michigan
Nova Southeastern University, Fort Lauderdale, Florida
Nyack College, Nyack, New York
Oakland University, Rochester, Michigan
Oakwood College, Huntsville, Alabama
Oberlin College, Oberlin, Ohio
Ohio College of Podiatric Medicine, Cleveland, Ohio
Ohio State University, The, Columbus, Ohio
Ohio University, Athens, Ohio
Old Dominion University, Norfolk, Virginia
Oral Roberts University, Tulsa, Oklahoma
Oregon State University, Corvallis, Oregon
Pace University, New York, New York
Pacific Graduate School of Psychology, Menlo Park, California
Pacific Lutheran University, Tacoma, Washington
Pacific Union College, Angwin, California
Pacific University, Forest Grove, Oregon
Palm Beach Atlantic College, West Palm Beach, Florida
Palmer College of Chiropractic, Davenport, Iowa
Palmer College of Chiropractic-West, Sunnyvale, California
Park College, Kansas City, Missouri
Pennsylvania College of Podiatric Medicine, Philadelphia, Pennsylvania
Pennsylvania State University, The, University Park, Pennsylvania
Philadelphia College of Bible, Langhorne, Pennsylvania
Philadelphia University, Philadelphia, Pennsylvania
Pine Manor College, Chestnut Hill, Massachusetts
Pomona College, Claremont, California
Princeton Theological Seminary, Princeton, New Jersey
Princeton University, Princeton, New Jersey
Principia College, The, Elsah, Illinois
Providence College, Providence, Rhode Island

Purdue University, Lafayette, Indiana
Rabbinical College of America, Morristown, New Jersey
Rabbinical College of Long Island, Long Beach, New York
Rabbinical Seminary of America, Forest Hills, New York
Reconstructionist Rabbinical College, Wyncote, Pennsylvania
Reed College, Portland, Oregon
Reformed Bible College, Grand Rapids, Michigan
Reformed Theological Seminary, Jackson, Mississippi
Rensselaer Polytechnic Institute, Troy, New York
Rice University, Houston, Texas
Roberts Wesleyan College, North Chili, New York
Rochester Institute of Technology, Rochester, New York
Rockefeller University, New York, New York
Rush University, Chicago, Illinois
Rutgers — The State University, New Brunswick, New Jersey
St. Bonaventure University, St. Bonaventure, New York
St. John's College, Annapolis, Maryland
St. John's College, Santa Fe, New Mexico
St. John's University, Jamaica, New York
St. Lawrence University, Canton, New York
Saint John's University, Collegeville, Minnesota
Saint Louis University, St. Louis, Missouri
St. Mary's University of San Antonio, San Antonio, Texas
Saint Olaf College, Northfield, Minnesota
St. Vladimir's Orthodox Theological Seminary, Crestwood, New York
San Francisco State College, San Francisco, California
San José State University, San José, California
Santa Clara University, Santa Clara, California
Sarah Lawrence College, Bonxville, New York
Scripps College, Claremont, California
Scripps Research Institute, The, La Jolla, California
Seattle Pacific College, Seattle, Washington
Seattle Pacific University, Seattle, Washington
Sherman College of Straight Chiropractic, Spartonburq, South Carolina
Simmons College, Boston, Massachusetts
Simpson College, Indianola, Iowa
Simpson College, Redding, California
Skidmore College, Saratoga Springs, New York
Smith College, The, Northampton, Massachusetts
South Dakota School of Mines and Technology, Rapid City, South Dakota
Southern Adventist University, Collegedale, Tennessee
Southern Illinois University of Carbondale, Carbondale, Illinois
Southern Methodist University, Dallas, Texas
Southwestern Adventist College, Keene, Texas
Spring Arbor College, Spring Arbor, Michigan
Springfield College, Springfield, Massachusetts
State University College at Oswego, Oswego, New York

State University College at Potsdam, Potsdam, New York
State University of New York at Binghamton, Binghamton, New York
State University of New York at Buffalo, Buffalo, New York
State University of New York at Stony Brook, Stony Brook, New York
State University of New York College of Arts and Science at Plattsburgh, Plattsburgh, New York
Stephens College, Columbia, Missouri
Stevens Institute of Technology, Hoboken, New Jersey
Sunbridge College, Chestnut Ridge, New York
Swarthmore College, Swarthmore, Pennsylvania
Syracuse University, Syracuse, New York
Tabor College, Hillsboro, Kansas
Talmudic College of Florida, Miami Beach, Florida
Talmudical Yeshiva of Philadelphia, Philadelphia, Pennsylvania
Taylor University, Upland, Indiana
Teachers College, Columbia University, New York, New York
Telshe Yeshiva Rabbinical College of Telshe, Inc., Wickcliffe, Ohio
Telshe Yeshiva-Chicago, Rabbinical College of Telshe-Chicago, Inc., Chicago, Illinois
Temple University, Philadelphia, Pennsylvania
Texas A&M University, College Station, Texas
Texas Chiropractic College, Pasadena, Texas
Texas Woman's University, Denton, Texas
The Herman M. Finch University of Health Sciences/The Chicago Medical School, North Chicago, Illinois
Thomas Aquinas College, Santa Paula, California
Touro College, New York, New York
Trinity Bible College, Ellendale, North Dakota
Trinity Christian College, Palos Heights, Illinois
Trinity College, Hartford, Connecticut
Trinity Episcopal School for Ministry, Ambridge, Pennsylvania
Trinity Evangelical Divinity School, Deerfield, Illinois
Trinity Lutheran College, Issaquah, Washington
Trinity University, San Antonio, Texas
Tufts University, Medford, Massachusetts
Tulane University, New Orleans, Louisiana
Union College, Lincoln, Nebraska
Union College, Schenectady, New York
Union Institute, The, Cincinnati, Ohio
Union Theological Seminary, New York, New York
University of Akron, The, Akron, Ohio
University of Alabama at Birmingham, The, Birmingham, Alabama
University of Arizona, The, Tucson, Arizona
University of Arkansas at Little Rock, Little Rock, Arkansas
University of California, Berkeley, California
University of California, Davis, California
University of California, Irvine, California

University of California, Los Angeles, California
University of California, Riverside, California
University of California, San Diego, California
University of California, Santa Barbara, California
University of California, Santa Cruz, California
University of California, San Francisco, California
University of Central Florida, Orlando, Florida
University of Chicago, The, Chicago, Illinois
University of Cincinnati, Cincinnati, Ohio
University of Colorado, Boulder, Colorado
University of Delaware, Newark, Delaware
University of Denver, Denver, Colorado
University of Detroit Mercy, Detroit, Michigan
University of Florida, Gainesville, Florida
University of Georgia, The, Athens, Georgia
University of Hawaii, Honolulu, Hawaii
University of Houston, Houston, Texas
University of Idaho, Moscow, Idaho
University of Illinois, Urbana, Illinois
University of Iowa, Iowa City, Iowa
University of Judaism, Los Angeles, California
University of Kansas, Lawrence, Kansas
University of Kentucky, Lexington, Kentucky
University of Maine, Orono, Maine
University of Maryland, College Park, Maryland
University of Massachusetts at Amherst, Amherst, Massachusetts
University of Miami, Coral Gables, Florida
University of Michigan, The, Ann Arbor, Michigan
University of Minnesota, Minneapolis, Minnesota
University of Missouri, Columbia, Missouri
University of Missouri, St. Louis, Missouri
University of Montana-Missoula, The, Missoula, Montana
University of Nebraska, The, Lincoln, Nebraska
University of Nevada-Reno, Reno, Nevada
University of North Carolina at Chapel Hill, Chapel Hill, North Carolina
University of North Dakota, Grand Forks, North Dakota
University of North Texas, Denton, Texas
University of Notre Dame du Lac, Notre Dame, Indiana
University of Oklahoma, Norman, Oklahoma
University of Oregon, Eugene, Oregon
University of Pennsylvania, Philadelphia, Pennsylvania
University of Pittsburgh, Pittsburgh, Pennsylvania
University of Portland, Portland, Oregon
University of Rhode Island, Kingston, Rhode Island
University of Rochester, Rochester, New York
University of San Diego, San Diego, California
University of Southern California, Los Angeles, California

University of Southern Mississippi, The, Hattiesburg, Mississippi
University of Texas, Austin, Texas
University of Texas Southwestern Medical Center at Dallas, The, Dallas, Texas
University of the Pacific, Stockton, California
University of Tulsa, Tulsa, Oklahoma
University of Utah, Salt Lake City, Utah
University of Vermont, Burlington, Vermont
University of Virginia, Charlottesville, Virginia
University of Washington, Seattle, Washington
University of Wisconsin, Madison, Wisconsin
University of Wyoming, The, Laramie, Wyoming
Utah State University of Agriculture and Applied Science, Logan, Utah
Valparaiso University, Valparaiso, Indiana
Vanderbilt University, Nashville, Tennessee
Vassar College, Poughkeepsie, New York
Villanova University, Villanova, Pennsylvania
Wake Forest University, Winston-Salem, North Carolina
Walla Walla College, College Place, Washington
Washington and Lee University, Lexington, Virginia
Washington Bible College, Lanham, Maryland
Washington State University, Pullman, Washington
Washington University, St. Louis, Missouri
Wayne State University, Detroit, Michigan
Wellesley College, Wellesley, Massachusetts
Wesleyan University, Middletown, Connecticut
Western Baptist College, Salem, Oregon
Western Conservative Baptist Seminary, Portland, Oregon
Western Michigan University, Kalamazoo, Michigan
Western States Chiropractic College, Portland, Oregon
Western University of Health Sciences, Pomona, California
Western Washington University, Bellingham, Washington
Westfield State College, Westfield, Massachusetts
Westminster Theological Seminary in California, Escondido, California
Westminster Theological Seminary, Philadelphia, Pennsylvania
West Virginia University, Morgantown, West Virginia
Wheaton College, Norton, Massachusetts
Wheaton College, Wheaton, Illinois
Wheelock College, Boston, Massachusetts
Whitman College, Walla Walla, Washington
Whittier College, Whittier, California
Whitworth College, Spokane, Washington
William Tyndale College, Farmington Hills, Michigan
Williams College, Willamstown, Massachusetts
Wittenberg University, Springfield, Ohio
Wright State University, Dayton, Ohio
Yale University, New Haven, Connecticut

Yeshiva Ohr Elchonon Chabad/West Coast Talmudic Seminary, Los Angeles, California
Yeshiva University, New York, New York

2. The universities situated in the United Kingdom of Great Britain and Northern Ireland that are prescribed by section 3503 are the following:

Aston University, Birmingham, England
Cranfield University, Bedfordshire, England
Gateshead Talmudical College, Gateshead, England
Imperial College of Science, Technology and Medicine, London, England
King's College London, London, England
London Business School, London, England
Loughborough University, Leicestershire, England
Queen's University of Belfast, The, Belfast, Northern Ireland
University of Aberdeen, Aberdeen, Scotland
University of Bath, The, Bath, England
University of Birmingham, Birmingham, England
University of Bradford, Bradford, England
University of Bristol, Bristol, England
University of Cambridge, Cambridge, England
University College London, London, England
University of Dundee, The, Dundee, Scotland
University of Durham, Durham, England
University of Edinburgh, Edinburgh, Scotland
University of Exeter, Exeter, England
University of Glasgow, Glasgow, Scotland
University of Leeds, Leeds, England
University of Liverpool, Liverpool, England
University of London, London, England
University of Manchester, The, Manchester, England
University of Newcastle, The, Newcastle upon Tyne, England
University of North London, London, England
University of Nottingham, The, Nottingham, England
University of Oxford, Oxford, England
University of Reading, Reading, England
University of St. Andrews, St. Andrews, Scotland
University of Sheffield, Sheffield, England
University of Southampton, Southampton, England
University of Strathclyde, Glasgow, Scotland
University of Surrey, Guildford, Surrey, England
University of Sussex, Brighton, England
University of Wales, Cardiff, Wales

3. The universities situated in France that are prescribed by section 3503 are the following:

American University in Paris, Paris
Catholic Faculties of Lyon, Lyon
Catholic Institute of Paris, Paris

Catholic University of Lille, The, Lille
École Nationale des Ponts et Chaussées, Paris
European Institute of Business Administration (INSEAD), Fontainebleau
Hautes Études Commerciales, Paris
Paris Graduate School of Management, Paris

4. The universities situated in Austria that are prescribed by section 3503 are the following:

University of Vienna, Vienna

5. The universities situated in Belgium that are prescribed by section 3503 are the following:

Catholic University of Louvain, Louvain

6. The universities situated in Switzerland that are prescribed by section 3503 are the following:

Franklin College of Switzerland, Sorengo (Lugano)
University of Geneva, Geneva
University of Lausanne, Lausanne

7. The universities situated in Vatican City that are prescribed by section 3503 are the following:

Pontifical Gregorian University

8. The universities situated in Israel that are prescribed by section 3503 are the following:

Bar-Ilan University, Ramat-Gan
Ben Gurion University of the Negev, Beersheba, Jerusalem College for Women, Bayit-Vegan, Jerusalem
École biblique et archéologique française, Jerusalem
Hebrew University of Jerusalem, The, Jerusalem
Jerusalem College of Technology, Jerusalem
Technion-Israel Institute of Technology, Haifa
Tel-Aviv University, Tel-Aviv
University of Haifa, Haifa
Weizmann Institute of Science, Rehovot
Yeshivat Aish Hatorah, Jerusalem

9. The universities situated in Lebanon that are prescribed by section 3503 are the following:

St. Joseph University, Beirut

10. The universities situated in Ireland that are prescribed by section 3503 are the following:

National University of Ireland, Dublin
Royal College of Surgeons in Ireland, Dublin
University of Dublin, Dublin

11. The universities situated in the Federal Republic of Germany that are prescribed by section 3503 are the following:

Ruprecht-Karls-Universität Heidenberg, Heidenberg

Ukrainian Free University, Munich

12. The universities situated in Poland that are prescribed by section 3503 are the following:

Catholic University of Lublin, Lublin

Jagiellonian University, Krakow

13. The universities situated in Spain that are prescribed by section 3503 are the following:

University of Navarra, Pamplona

14. The universities situated in the People's Republic of China that are prescribed by section 3503 are the following:

Nanjing University, Nanjing

15. The universities situated in Jamaica that are prescribed for the purposes of section 3503 are the following:

University of the West Indies, Mona Campus, Kingston

16. [Repealed, SOR/2001-172, s. 7]

17. The universities situated in Australia that are prescribed by section 3503 are the following:

Adelaide University, Adelaide

Queensland University of Technology, Brisbane

University of Melbourne, The, Parkville

University of Queensland, The, Brisbane

University of Sydney, The, Sydney

University of Tasmania, Hobart

18. The university situated in the Republic of Croatia that is prescribed by section 3503 is the following:

University of Zagreb, Zagreb

19. The universities situated in South Africa that are prescribed by section 3503 are the following:

University of Natal, Durban

University of the Witwatersrand, The, Johannesburg

20. For the purposes of section 3503 the universities situated in the Netherlands are the following:

Leiden University, Leiden

Nyenrode University, Breukelen

University of Groningen, Groningen

21. For the purposes of section 3503 the universities situated in Hong Kong are the following:

Hong Kong University of Science and Technology, The,

Kowloon University of Hong Kong, The, Hong Kong

22. The universities situated in New Zealand that are prescribed by section 3503 are the following:

University of Otago, Dunedin

Victoria University of Wellington, Wellington

23. The university situated in Hungary that is prescribed by section 3503 is the following:

Central European University, Budapest

24. The university situated in India that is prescribed by section 3503 is the following:

Panjab University, Chandigarh

[SOR/78-256, s. 1; SOR/79-336, s. 1; SOR/80-321, ss. 1 to 4; SOR/81-234, s. 1; SOR/82-408, s. 1; SOR/83-359, ss. 1 to 3; SOR/84-222, ss. 1, 2; SOR/85-332, ss. 1, 2; SOR/86-382, ss. 1 to 3; SOR/87-472, ss. 1, 2; SOR/88-209, ss. 1 to 3; SOR/89-233, ss. 1 to 3; SOR/90-411, ss. 2 to 4; SOR/91-198, ss. 1 to 3; SOR/92-332, ss. 1 to 4; SOR/93-229, ss. 1, 2; SOR/94-395, ss. 1 to 6; SOR/95-184, ss. 1, 2; SOR/96-250, ss. 1 to 6; SOR/97-385, s. 1; SOR/2000-191, ss. 1 to 9; SOR/2001-172, ss. 1 to 10; SOR/2003-5, ss. 15 to19; SOR/2005-123; SOR/2005-185, s. 5]

## RELATED PROVISIONS

SOR/96-250:

**7.** Sections 1 to 6 apply after December 31, 1994.

SOR/97-385:

**2.** Section 1 applies to the 1996 and subsequent taxation years.

SOR/2000-191:

**10.** (1) Subsections 1(1) and (5), 2(1) and (4), sections 3 to 5, and subsection 7(1) apply as of the day on which these Regulations are published in the *Canada Gazette*.

(2) Subsections 1(2), 2(2) and 7(2) apply as of January 1, 1997.

(3) Subsections 1(3), 2(3) and sections 6 and 8 apply as of January 1, 1998.

(4) Subsection 1(4) and section 9 apply as of January 1, 1999.

SOR/2001-172:

**11.** (1) Subsections 1(1), 2(1), sections 3 to 5, subsection 6(1) and section 7 apply as of the day on which these Regulations are published in the *Canada Gazette*.

(2) Subsections 1(2), 2(2), 6(2), section 8 and subsection 10(1) apply as of January 1, 1999.

(3) Subsections 1(3), 2(3), section 9 and subsection 10(2) apply as of January 1, 2000.

# ACCUMULATIONS ACT

(R.S.O. 1990, c. A.5)

**1.** (1) **Maximum accumulation periods** — No disposition of any real or personal property shall direct the income thereof to be wholly or partially accumulated for any longer than one of the following terms:

1. The life of the grantor.

2. Twenty-one years from the date of making an *inter vivos* disposition.

3. The duration of the minority or respective minorities of any person or persons living or conceived but not born at the date of making an *inter vivos* disposition.

4. Twenty-one years from the death of the grantor, settlor or testator.

5. The duration of the minority or respective minorities of any person or persons living or conceived but not born at the death of the grantor, settlor or testator.

6. The duration of the minority or respective minorities of any person or persons who, under the instrument directing the accumulations, would, for the time being, if of full age, be entitled to the income directed to be accumulated.

(2) **Application of subs. (1) restrictions** — The restrictions imposed by subsection (1) apply in relation to a power to accumulate income whether or not there is a duty to exercise that power, and such restrictions also apply whether or not the power to accumulate extends to income produced by the investment of income previously accumulated.

(3) **Idem** — The restrictions imposed by subsection (1) apply to every disposition of real or personal property, whether made before or after its enactment.

(4) **Previous acts, etc., not affected** — Nothing in subsection (1) affects,

(a) the validity of any act done; or

(b) any right acquired or obligation incurred,

under this Act before the 6th day of September, 1966.

(5) **Accumulations for the purchase of land** — No accumulation for the purchase of land shall be directed for any longer period than permitted under subsection (1).

[1993, c. 27, Sched.]

(6) **Application of invalid accumulations** — Where an accumulation is directed contrary to this Act, such direction is null and void, and the rents, issues, profits and produce of the property so directed to be accumulated shall, so long as they are directed to be accumulated contrary to this Act, go to and be received by

such person as would have been entitled thereto if such accumulation had not been so directed.

**2. Saving as to debts or portions for children** — Nothing in this Act extends to any provision for payment of debts of a grantor, settlor, devisor or other person, or to any provision for raising portions for a child of a grantor, settlor or devisor, or for a child of a person taking an interest under any such conveyance, settlement or devise, or to any direction touching the produce of timber or wood upon any lands or tenements, but all such provisions and directions may be made and given as if this Act had not been passed.

[2005, c. 5, s. 2.]

**3. (1) Rules as to accumulations not applicable to employee benefit trusts** — The rules of law and statutory enactments relating to accumulations do not apply and shall be deemed never to have applied to the trusts of a plan, trust or fund established for the purpose of providing pensions, retirement allowances, annuities, or sickness, death or other benefits to employees or to their surviving spouses, dependants or other beneficiaries.

(2) **Definition** — In this section,

"spouse" means,

(a)   a spouse as defined in section 1 of the *Family Law Act*, or

(b)   either of two persons who live together in a conjugal relationship outside marriage.

[2005, c. 5, s. 2.]

# ASSESSMENT ACT

(R.S.O. 1990, c. A.31)

[**Note:** Only sections pertaining to Charities are reproduced.]

. . .

**2.** (2) **Regulations by the Minister** — The Minister may make regulations,

. . .

(b)    defining "conservation land" for the purposes of paragraph 25 of subsection 3 (1);

(c)    defining "conservation land" and "managed forest land" for the purposes of subsection 19 (5.2);

. . .

(d.1) providing for a procedure to determine whether land is conservation land for the purposes of paragraph 25 of subsection 3 (1) and, without limiting the generality of the foregoing, the regulations may,

    (i)    provide for the determination of any matter to be made by a person or body identified in the regulations,

    (ii)    provide for a process of appealing such determinations,

    (iii)    adopt documents by reference as those documents are amended from time to time, including amendments made after the regulation was made;

. . .

(d.3) providing for different procedures than the procedures provided in sections 39.1 and 40 for resolving issues as to whether land is in the farm property class or managed forests property class or whether land is conservation land for the purposes of paragraph 25 of subsection 3 (1) and, without limiting the generality of the foregoing, the regulations may,

    (i)    provide for the functions of the assessment corporation or an assessor under section 39.1 to be carried out by a person or body identified in the regulations,

    provide for the functions of the Assessment Review Board under sections 39.1 and 40 to be carried out by a body or official identified in the regulations;

(d.4) for the purposes of regulations made under clause (d.3),

    (i)    varying the application of section 39.1 or 40 or any other provisions of this Act,

    (ii)   prescribing provisions to operate in place of section 39.1 or 40 or any other provisions of this Act,

    (iii)  prescribing provisions to operate in addition to section 39.1 or 40 or any other provisions of this Act;

(d.5) in relation to public hospitals that close,

    (i)    continuing the tax exemption under section 3 with respect to land that was used and occupied by the hospital,

    (ii)   continuing the application of section 323 of the *Municipal Act, 2001* with respect to the hospital and prescribing a limit on the annual amount levied under that section that is different from the limit under subsection (3) of that section;

**3. (1) Property assessable and taxable, exemptions** — All real property in Ontario is liable to assessment and taxation, subject to the following exemptions from taxation:

. . .

2.    **Cemeteries, burial sites** — A cemetery for which a consent has been issued under the *Cemeteries Act (Revised)* and a burial site as defined in that Act so long as the cemetery or burial site is actually being used for the interment of the dead.

**Note:** paragraph 2 is repealed by, 2002, c. 33, s. 141 and the following substituted:

(2)    Cemeteries, burial sites — A cemetery and a burial site, as those terms are defined in the *Funeral, Burial and Cremation Services Act, 2002*, so long as the land is actually being used for the interment of the dead or any ancillary purpose prescribed by the Minister, and not including any portion of the land used for any other purpose.

(2.1)  Crematoriums — Land on which is located a crematorium, as defined in the *Funeral, Burial and Cremation Services Act, 2002* and which is part of a cemetery or burial site, as those terms are defined in the *Funeral, Burial and Cremation Services Act, 2002*, if,

    (i)    the Registrar under the Cemeteries Act (Revised) consented to the establishment of the crematorium on or before January 1, 2002,

    (ii)   the ownership of the land has not changed since January 1, 2002, and

    (iii)  the taxation year is a taxation year that is no more than five years after the taxation year in which the *Funeral, Burial and Cremation Services Act, 2002* comes into force.

[2002, c. 33, s. 141, not in force].

3.   **Churches, etc.** — Land that is owned by a church or religious organization or leased to it by another church or religious organization and that is,

   (i)   a place of worship and the land used in connection with it,

   (ii)  a churchyard, cemetery or burying ground, or

**Note:** subparagraph ii is repealed by, 2002, c. 33, s. 141 and the following substituted:

   (ii)  a churchyard,

   (ii.1) a burying ground so long as the land is actually being used for the interment of the dead or any ancillary purpose prescribed by the Minister, and not including any portion of the land used for any other purpose, or

     [2002, c. 33, s. 141, not in force.]

   (iii) 50 per cent of the assessment of the principal residence and land used in connection with it of the member of the clergy who officiates at the place of worship referred to in subparagraph i, so long as the residence is located at the site of the place of worship.

This paragraph applies to the 2001 and subsequent taxation years.

4.   **Public educational institutions** — Land owned, used and occupied solely by a university, college, community college or school as defined in the *Education Act* or land leased and occupied by any of them if the land would be exempt from taxation if it was occupied by the owner.

5.   **Philanthropic organizations, etc.** — Land owned, used and occupied solely by a non-profit philanthropic, religious or educational seminary of learning or land leased and occupied by any of them if the land would be exempt from taxation if it was occupied by the owner. This paragraph applies only to buildings and up to 50 acres of land.

6.   **Public hospitals** — Land used and occupied by a public hospital that receives provincial aid under the *Public Hospitals Act* but not any portion of the land occupied by a tenant of the hospital.

        . . .

10.   **Boy Scouts and Girl Guides** — Property owned, occupied and used solely and only by The Boy Scouts Association or The Canadian Girl Guides Association or by any provincial or local association or other local group in Ontario that is a member of either Association or is otherwise chartered or officially recognized by it.

11.   **House of refuge, etc.**— Land owned, used and occupied by a non-profit philanthropic corporation for the purpose of a house of refuge, the reformation of offenders, the care of children or a similar purpose but excluding land used for the purpose of a day care centre.

12.   **Charitable institutions** — Land owned, used and occupied by,

   (i)   The Canadian Red Cross Society,

   (ii)  The St. John Ambulance Association, or

    (iii)  any charitable, non-profit philanthropic corporation organized for the relief of the poor if the corporation is supported in part by public funds.

13.  **Children's aid societies** — The property of a children's aid society discharging the functions of a children's aid society under the *Child and Family Services Act*, whether held in the name of the society or in the name of a trustee or otherwise, if used exclusively for the purposes of and in connection with the society.

14.  **Scientific or literary institutions, etc.** — The property of every public library and other public institution, literary or scientific, and of every agricultural or horticultural society or association, to the extent of the actual occupation of the property for the purposes of the institution or society.

    (a)  For the purposes of this paragraph, an agricultural society under the *Agricultural and Horticultural Organizations Act* shall be deemed to be in actual occupation where the property of the society is rented and the rent is applied solely for the purposes of the society.

15.  **Battle sites** — Land acquired by a society or association by reason of its being the site of any battle fought in any war, and maintained, preserved and kept open to the public in order to promote the spirit of patriotism.

16.  **Exhibition buildings of companies** — The land of every company formed for the erection of exhibition buildings to the extent to which the council of the municipality in which the land is situate consents that it shall be exempt.

. . .

25.  **Conservation land** — Land that is conservation land as defined in the regulations.

26.  **Small theatres** — Land used as a theatre that contains fewer than 1,000 seats and that, when it is used in the taxation year, is used predominantly to present live performances of drama, comedy, music or dance. This paragraph does not apply to land used as a dinner theatre, nightclub, tavern, cocktail lounge, bar, striptease club or similar establishment. This paragraph does not apply to a building that was converted to a theatre unless the conversion involved modifications to the building.

    **(1.1) Non-application: special exemptions** — Despite any provision in any Act of special or general application, an exemption from assessment or taxation under such an Act for burial sites, burying grounds or cemeteries shall, on and after the day section 141 of the *Funeral, Burial and Cremation Services Act, 2002* comes into force, no longer apply.

[2002, c. 33, s. 141, not in force.]

. . .

    **4. Exemption of religious institutions** — The council of any local municipality may pass by-laws exempting from taxes, other than school taxes and local improvement rates, the land of any religious institution named in the by-law, provided that the land is owned by the institution and occupied and used solely for recreational purposes, on such conditions as may be set out in the by-law. R.S.O. 1990, c. A.31, s. 4.

. . .

**6. Exemption of Navy League** — The council of any local municipality may pass by-laws exempting from taxes, other than school taxes and local improvement rates, the land belonging to and vested in the Navy League of Canada under the conditions that may be set out in the by-law, so long as the land is occupied and used solely for the purposes of carrying out the activities of the Ontario division of the Navy League. R.S.O. 1990, c. A.31, s. 6.

. . .

**17.** (1) **Land assessed against owner** — Subject to section 18, land shall be assessed against the owner.

(2) **Land held by trustees, etc.** — Land held by a person as a trustee, guardian, executor or administrator shall be assessed against the person as owner in the same manner as if the person did not hold the land in a representative capacity, but the fact that the person is a trustee, guardian, executor or administrator shall, if known, be stated in the roll, and the person is only personally liable when and to the extent that the person has property as trustee, guardian, executor or administrator, available for payment of the taxes.
[1997, c. 29, s. 7.]

**17.1** (1) **Land to be assessed against owner and tenant for certain Education Act purposes** — For the purposes of rates levied under Division C of Part IX of the *Education Act*, land shall, subject to section 18, be assessed against the owner of it and against the tenant of it to the extent of the assessed value of the portion of the land occupied by the tenant.

(2) **Land held by trustees, etc.** — For the purposes of rates levied under Division C of Part IX of the *Education Act*, land held by a person as trustee, guardian, executor or administrator shall be assessed against the person as owner or tenant of the land, as the case may require, in the same manner as if the person did not hold the land in a representative capacity.

(3) **Same** — The fact that the person is a trustee, guardian, executor or administrator shall, if known, be stated in the roll.

(4) **Same** — The person is only personally liable when and to the extent that the person has property as trustee, guardian, executor or administrator, available for payment of the taxes.
[1997, c. 31, s. 143.]

. . .

**19.** (5.2) **Conservation land, managed forest land** — The current value of land that is conservation land or managed forests land as defined in the regulations shall be based only on the current use of the land and not other uses to which the land could be put.

[1997, c. 5, s. 12.]

. . .

**25.** (10) **Liability to taxation of pipe line on exempt property** — Where a pipe line is located on, in, under, along or across any highway or any lands, other than lands held in trust for a band or body of Indians, exempt from taxation under this or any special or general Act, the pipe line is nevertheless liable to assessment and taxation in accordance with this section.

(11) **Tax liability** — Despite the other provisions of this Act or any other special or general Act, a pipe line liable for assessment and taxation under this section is not liable for assessment and taxation in any other manner for municipal purposes, including local improvements, but all other land and buildings of the pipe line company liable for assessment and taxation under this or any other special or general Act continue to be so liable. R.S.O. 1990, c. A.31, s. 25 (11); 1997, c. 5, s. 16 (2).

. . .

**27.1.** (1) **Large commercial theatres, Toronto** — In this section,

"large commercial theatre" means, in respect of a taxation year, land or any portion of land that is used as a theatre, if,

   (a)   the theatre contains 1,000 or more seats,

   (b)   the theatre is used, other than by a charitable or non-profit organization, on a total of at least 183 days in the taxation year to present live performances with the intention of generating a profit, and

   (c)   when the theatre is used, other than by a charitable or non-profit organization, to present live performances with the intention of generating a profit, no food or beverages may be consumed in the area in which people view the performances and any food or beverage service provided by the theatre is restricted to lobby areas.

(2) **Large commercial theatres in Toronto** — For each taxation year, the owner of a large commercial theatre that is located in the City of Toronto and that is not liable to taxation shall pay the City of Toronto the amount calculated in accordance with the following formula:

$$P = (T \times F) - S$$

where,

      P =   the amount of the payment,

      T =   the taxes for municipal purposes that would be payable if the theatre were liable to taxation,

      F =   the fraction that represents the proportion of the taxation year during which the theatre is used, other than by a charitable or non-profit organization, to present live performances of productions presented with the intention of generating a profit,

S =   any amount that a by-law under subsection (3) permits the owner to deduct from the payment.

(3) **Subsidy** — The council of the City of Toronto may, by by-law, permit an owner to deduct from a payment under subsection (2) an amount determined in accordance with the by-law that represents all or a portion of the revenue from the use of the theatre, other than by a charitable or non-profit organization, to present live performances of productions presented with the intention of generating a profit, that is used to fund or financially support not-for-profit activities that take place on the same parcel of land or on another parcel of land in Ontario owned by the owner.

(4) **City must pass a by-law** — The council of the City of Toronto shall pass a by-law under subsection (3).

(5) **When payable** — Payments required under this section in respect of a taxation year shall be made not later than March 31 in the year following the taxation year.

(6) **Collection of payments** — The provisions of this Act and the *Municipal Act* with respect to the collection of taxes apply with necessary modifications to payments required under this section.

[1997, c. 29, s. 12.]

. . .

**32.** (3) **Change in tax liability** — If, as a result of an amendment to this Act or the regulations, a property becomes exempt from taxation for a year or for part or all of the preceding year,

(a)   the assessor shall make any assessment necessary to change the tax liability for the property;

(b)   the clerk of the municipality, on receiving notice of the change in tax liability, shall alter the tax roll; and

(c)   the municipality shall refund or credit to the owner the amount of any overpayment of taxes and any interest paid by the owner on the amount of the overpayment. 2004, c. 31, Sched. 3, s. 10 (2).

. . .

(5) **Transitional** — For the purposes of subsections (3) and (4), a reference to the preceding year includes a reference to a year ending before, on or after the day subsections (3) and (4) come into force. 2004, c. 31, Sched. 3, s. 10 (2).

. . .

**33.** (3) **Property incorrectly described as exempt from taxation** — If any land that is liable to taxation has been entered on the tax roll for the current year or for any part or all of either or both of the next two preceding years as exempt from taxation, and no taxes have been levied on that land, the assessor shall make any assessment necessary to correct the omission and the clerk of the municipality upon notification thereof shall enter that land as liable to taxation on the tax roll and the taxes that would have been payable if that land had been entered in the tax roll as property liable to tax shall be levied and collected, but no such amendment shall be made where that land has been held by any court or assessment tribunal not to be liable to taxation.

(4) **Managed forests, conservation land** — Subsection (5) applies with respect to,

(a)    land in the managed forests property class;

(b)    land that is conservation land for the purposes of paragraph 25 of subsection 3 (1);

(c)    land in respect of which subsection 19 (5.2) applies.

(5) **Re-assessment, etc.** — If land described in subsection (4) ceases to be such land, the assessor shall make any assessment and classification necessary as a result of the land ceasing to be such land and the following apply with respect to that assessment and classification:

1.    The assessment and classification shall not affect a taxation year that ends more than four years before the assessment and classification is made.

2.    The assessor shall notify the clerk of the municipality and the clerk shall enter the assessment and classification on the tax roll and the taxes that would have been paid for the years affected shall be levied and collected.

(6) **Changes to next assessment roll** — If an assessor makes an assessment or classification under this section, the appropriate changes shall be made on the assessment roll for the next year, even if the day as of which land is valued for the next year is the same as for the current year.

[1997, c. 29, s. 17; 1998, c. 3, s. 7; 2002, c. 17, Sched. F, Table.]

**34.** (1) **Supplementary assessments to be added to tax roll** — If, after notices of assessment have been given under section 31 and before the last day of the taxation year for which taxes are levied on the assessment referred to in the notices,

(a)    an increase in value occurs which results from the erection, alteration, enlargement or improvement of any building, structure, machinery, equipment or fixture or any portion thereof that commences to be used for any purpose;

(b)    land or a portion of land ceases,

(i)    to be exempt from taxation,

(ii)    to be farm lands the current value of which is determined in accordance with subsection 19 (5),

(iii)    to be conservation land or managed forests land the current value of which is based on current use under subsection 19 (5.2),

    (iv)   to be land the current value of which is based on current use under regulations made under subsection 19 (2), or

    (v)   to be classified in a subclass of real property;

  (c)   [Repealed: 1997, c. 5, s. 22.]

  (d)   a pipeline increases in value because it ceases to be entitled to the reduction provided for in subsection 25 (9),

the assessor may make the further assessment that may be necessary to reflect the change, and the clerk of the municipality upon notification thereof shall enter a supplementary assessment on the tax roll and the amount of taxes to be levied thereon shall be the amount of taxes that would have been levied for the portion of the taxation year left remaining after the change occurred if the assessment had been made in the usual way.

[1997, c. 5, s. 22; 1997, c. 29, s. 18; 1998, c. 3, s. 8; 2002, c. 17, Sched. F, Table.]

. . .

**55. By-laws and agreements fixing assessment or granting exemption from taxation not affected** — This Act does not affect the terms of any agreement made with a municipal corporation, or any by-law heretofore or hereafter passed by a municipal council under any other Act for fixing the assessment of any property, or for commuting or otherwise relating to municipal taxation, but whenever in any Act of the Legislature or by any proclamation of the Lieutenant Governor in Council or by any valid by-law of a municipality heretofore passed or by any valid agreement heretofore entered into the assessment of the real and personal property of any person in a municipality is fixed at a certain amount for a period of years, unexpired at the time of the coming into force of this Act, or the taxes payable annually by any person in respect of the real and personal property are fixed at a stated amount during any such period, or the real and personal property of any person or any part thereof is exempt from municipal taxation in whole or in part for any such period, the fixed assessment or commutation of taxes or exemption shall be deemed to include any other assessment and any taxes thereon in respect of the property or business mentioned in such Act, proclamation, by-law or agreement to which the person or the property of the person would otherwise be liable under this Act.

[1997, c. 5, s. 37.]

# GENERAL

(O. Reg. 282/98)

## Part IV
## Exempt Conservation Land

*Determination of Conservation Land*

**24.** For the purposes of paragraph 25 of subsection 3 (1) of the Act,

"conservation land" means land that is eligible conservation land under section 26 of this Regulation.

[O. Reg. 388/04, s. 1.]

**25.** (1) Land, excluding any portion of the land that has a building or other improvement on it, is eligible to be classified as eligible conservation land if,

(a)  it satisfies the requirements of subsection (2) or (3); and

(b)  it is maintained in a manner that contributes to the natural heritage and the biodiversity objectives for conserving the land.

(2) For the purposes of clause (1) (a), the land satisfies the requirements of this subsection if it satisfies one of the following conditions:

1.  The land is identified by the Minister of Natural Resources as provincially significant wetland on the basis of the wetland evaluation system set out in the Ministry of Natural Resources document entitled "Ontario Wetland Evaluation System Southern Manual" (3rd edition), dated March, 1993, as revised in May, 1994 and December, 2002, or in the Ministry of Natural Resources document titled "Ontario Wetland Evaluation System Northern Manual" (1st edition), dated March, 1993, as revised in May, 1994 and December, 2002.

2.  The land is identified by the Minister of Natural Resources as a provincially significant area of natural and scientific interest using the criteria set out in the Ministry of Natural Resources document entitled "A Framework for the Conservation of Ontario's Biological Heritage", dated May, 1980, or in the Ministry of Natural Resources document titled "A Framework for the Conservation of Ontario's Earth Science Features", dated October, 1981.

3.  The land is identified by the Minister of Natural Resources as a habitat of the endangered species listed in Regulation 328 of the Revised Regulations of Ontario, 1990 (Endangered Species) made under the *Endangered Species Act*, using the criteria set out in the Ministry of

Natural Resources document entitled "Guidelines for Mapping Endangered Species Habitats under the Conservation Land Tax Incentive Program", as it may be amended from time to time and set out in a Decision Notice posted on the environmental registry under the *Environmental Bill of Rights, 1993*.

4.    The land is designated as an escarpment natural area in the Niagara Escarpment Plan under the *Niagara Escarpment Planning and Development Act*.

(3) For the purposes of clause (1) (a), the land satisfies the requirements of this subsection if the land is owned by a registered charity, within the meaning of subsection 248 (1) of the *Income Tax Act* (Canada), one of whose primary objectives is natural heritage conservation or by a conservation authority established under the *Conservation Authorities Act* and the land satisfies one of the following conditions:

1.    It is designated as an escarpment protection area in the Niagara Escarpment Plan under the *Niagara Escarpment Planning and Development Act*.

2.    It is located within a Featured Area and contributes to the natural heritage protection objectives established for the Featured Area as set out in the "Ontario Living Legacy Land Use Strategy, July 1999", published by the Queen's Printer.

3.    It is a natural heritage feature or area that meets the criteria of the natural heritage provisions of the Provincial Policy Statement as issued and re-issued under section 3 of the *Planning Act*.

4.    It is identified by the Minister of Natural Resources as a regionally significant area of natural and scientific interest using the criteria set out in the Ministry of Natural Resources document entitled "A Framework for the Conservation of Ontario's Biological Heritage", dated May, 1980, or in the Ministry of Natural Resources document entitled "A Framework for the Conservation of Ontario's Earth Science Features", dated October, 1981.

5.    It is a habitat of species of special concern, as designated by the Ministry of Natural Resources, based on the criteria in the "Categories and Criteria for Status Assessment" of the Committee on the Status of Species at Risk in Ontario.

6.    It is identified as having species occurrences or ecological communities with an S-Rank designation of S1-S3, as determined by the Natural Heritage Information Centre of the Ministry of Natural Resources.

7.    It is designated as a natural core area, natural linkage area or countryside in the Oak Ridges Moraine Conservation Plan under the *Oak Ridges Moraine Conservation Act, 2001*.

8.    It is a natural heritage area identified within a regional or watershed plan or strategy developed by a conservation authority under the *Conservation*

*Authorities Act* or by another public agency under another provincial or federal statute.

9.   It is designated as an environmentally sensitive area, environmentally significant area, environmental protection area, natural heritage system or another area with an equivalent designation within a municipal official plan or zoning by-law under the *Planning Act*.

10.  It is within, abuts or abuts a road allowance that abuts a provincial park, national park, conservation reserve or provincial wildlife area and contributes significantly to the natural heritage objectives of the park, reserve or wildlife area.

11.  It is an area identified under the Great Lakes Wetlands Conservation Action Plan described in the "Great Lakes Wetlands Conservation Action Plan Highlights Report (2000-2003)", published by Environment Canada.

(4) Despite paragraph 10 of subsection (3), no part of the land that is more than 1,000 metres from the boundary of the park, reserve or wildlife area is eligible to be classified as eligible conservation land.

[O. Reg. 388/04, s. 1.]

**26.** Land is eligible conservation land for a taxation year if the following requirements are met:

1.   The land is eligible under section 25 to be classified as eligible conservation land for the taxation year.

2.   The owner submits a completed application to the Minister of Natural Resources for designation of the land under this section for the taxation year and the application is submitted,

   (i)   on or before February 28, 2005, if the land is described in subsection 25 (3) and the application relates to the 2005 taxation year, or

   (ii)  on or before July 31 of the previous year, in any other case.

3.   In the application, the owner undertakes,

   (i)   not to engage in activities during the taxation year that are inconsistent with the natural heritage and biodiversity objectives for conserving the land,

   (ii)  to allow a person selected by the Minister of Natural Resources to inspect the land, and

   (iii) to co-operate with the person described in subparagraph ii in the course of the inspection.

4.   The Minister of Natural Resources designates the land for the taxation year for the purposes of this section.

5.   The owner does not breach any undertaking given in the application.

[O. Reg. 388/04, s. 1.]

*Application of Part*

**27.** This Part applies with respect to the 1999 and subsequent taxation years.
[O. Reg. 46/99, s. 1.]

. . .

# Part VII
## Disputes Relating to Conservation Land

*Definitions*

**37.** In this Part,

"Administrator" means the Minister of Natural Resources or the employee of the Ministry of Natural Resources to whom the Minister has delegated his or her powers under this Part;

"Commissioner" means the Mining and Lands Commissioner appointed under the *Ministry of Natural Resources Act*.

*Requests for Reconsideration under Section 39.1 of the Act*

**38.** (1) A person who has received a notice of assessment under the Act in respect of land may request, under subsection 39.1 (1) of the Act, a reconsideration as to whether the land is conservation land but such a request must be made to the Administrator and not the assessment commissioner.

(2) A request may not be made under subsection (1) after the expiry of the time limit for making a complaint to the Assessment Review Board under subsection 40 (2) of the Act.

(3) Section 39.1 of the Act applies with respect to a request described in subsection (1) with the following modifications:

1. References to the assessment commissioner or the assessor shall be deemed to be references to the Administrator.

2. If the Administrator is required to give notice of a settlement to the Assessment Review Board under subsection 39.1 (5) of the Act, the Administrator shall also give notice of the settlement to the assessment commissioner.

3. Section 39 applies, with necessary modifications, with respect to the application of section 40 of the Act under subsection 39.1 (8) of the Act.

4. If a settlement is agreed to that the land is conservation land, the person who requested the settlement shall be deemed to have requested the assessment commissioner, under section 39.1 of the Act, to re-determine

the current value of the land in accordance with subsection 19 (5.2) of the Act.

### Complaints under Section 40 of the Act

**39.** Any person, including a municipality or school board, may make a complaint under subsection 40 (1) of the Act that land is or is not conservation land and the following apply with respect to such a complaint:

1. The Assessment Review Board shall refer the issue as to whether the land is conservation land to the Commissioner.

2. The Commissioner shall hold a hearing to determine whether the land is conservation land. Upon determining the issue, the Commissioner shall give the parties and the Assessment Review Board a copy of its decision.

3. The parties to the hearing by the Commissioner are as provided under subsection 40 (5) of the Act except that the Administrator is a party instead of the assessment commissioner. Subsection 40 (7) of the Act applies to the Commissioner but a party added by the Commissioner is a party only to the hearing by the Commissioner.

4. The procedure that applies under the following provisions of the *Mining Act* with respect to matters under that Act shall apply, with necessary modifications, with respect to the hearing by the Commissioner under paragraph 2,

    (i)    subsections 114 (2), (3) and (4),

    (ii)   sections 115, 116, 118 to 122 and 125 to 128, and

    (iii)  subsection 129 (1).

5. The Assessment Review Board shall determine any remaining issues in accordance with section 40 of the Act including any redetermination of the current value of the land necessary as a result of subsection 19 (5.2) of the Act becoming or ceasing to be applicable as a result of the determination as to whether or not the land is conservation land.

6. The decision of the Commissioner shall be deemed to be a decision of the Assessment Review Board for the purposes of subsection 40 (12) of the Act.

7. Subsection 40 (13) of the Act applies with respect to the Commissioner.

8. The Commissioner may state a case under section 43 of the Act with respect to issues referred to it.

9. Section 43.1 of the Act applies with respect to decisions of the Commissioner. O. Reg. 282/98, s. 39.

*Special Consideration if Deadline Missed*

**40.** (1) The Administrator, on a request described in subsection 38 (1), shall agree to a settlement determining that the land is conservation land if,

    (a)   the requirements for the land to be conservation land have been complied with except that the deadline for submitting an application for designation of the land as conservation land was missed;

    (b)   the land would have been conservation land if the deadline had not been missed; and

    (c)   in the Administrator's opinion, there are mitigating circumstances explaining why the deadline was missed.

(2) The Commissioner, on a complaint described in section 39, shall make a determination that the land is conservation land if,

    (a)   clauses (1) (a) and (b) are satisfied; and

    (b)   in the Commissioner's opinion, there are mitigating circumstances explaining why the deadline was missed.

[O. Reg. 46/99, s. 2.]

. . .

**46.** (1) For the purposes of subsection 19 (5.2) of the Act,

"conservation land" means land that is conservation land, as defined in section 24 of this Regulation, for the taxation year for which current value is determined under subsection 19 (5.2) of the Act;

"managed forest land" means land in the managed forests property class for the taxation year for which current value is determined under subsection 19 (5.2) of the Act.

(2) This section applies with respect to the 1998 and subsequent taxation years.

# CHARITABLE GIFTS ACT

## (R.S.O. 1990, c. C.8)

**1. Definition** — In this Act,

"person" includes a corporation and the heirs, executors, administrators or other legal representatives of a person to whom the context can apply according to law.

**2.** (1) **Where interest to be disposed of** — Despite any general or special Act, letters patent, by-law, will, codicil, trust deed, agreement or other instrument, wherever an interest in a business that is carried on for gain or profit is given to or vested in a person in any capacity for any religious, charitable, educational or public purpose, such person has power to dispose of and shall dispose of such portion thereof that represents more than a 10 per cent interest in such business.

(2) **Exception** — Subsection (1) does not apply to an interest in a business given to or vested in any organization of any religious denomination.

(3) **Life interests, etc.** — Where an interest to which subsection (1) applies is subject to a life interest, life annuity or income for life, so much of the interest as is necessary to provide such life interest, life annuity or income for life shall be deemed to be given or vested when such life interest, life annuity or income for life ceases to exist.

(4) **Meaning of "interest in a business"** — For the purposes of this Act, a person shall be deemed to have an interest in a business,

(a) if the person is a part owner of the business;

(b) if the person holds or controls, directly or indirectly through a combination or series of two or more persons, one or more shares in a corporation that owns or controls or partly owns or controls the business; or

(c) if the person holds or controls, directly or indirectly through a combination or series of two or more persons, one or more bonds, debentures, mortgages or other securities upon any asset of the business.

(5) **Idem** — For the purposes of this Act but subject to subsection (3), an interest in a business shall be deemed to be given to or vested in a person for a religious, charitable, educational or public purpose so long as the interest or the proceeds thereof or the income therefrom is to be used for any such purpose at any time and even though before any such use is made thereof the interest or the proceeds thereof or the income therefrom is to pass into or through the hands of one or more persons or is subject to a life or other intermediary interest.

**3.** (1) **Where interest to be disposed of, wills** — Where an interest to which section 2 applies was given or vested pursuant to a will or other testamentary instrument, section 2 shall be complied with within seven years after the death of the testator.

(2) **Idem, trust deeds, etc.** — Where an interest to which section 2 applies was given or vested pursuant to an instrument other than a will or other testamentary instrument, section 2 shall be complied with within seven years after the date of the instrument.

(3) **Extension of time** — A judge of the Ontario Court (General Division) may from time to time extend the period mentioned in subsection (1) or (2) for such further period as he or she considers proper, if the judge is satisfied that the extension will benefit the religious, educational, charitable or public purpose concerned.

(Note: The name of the Ontario Court (General Division) was renamed the Superior Court of Justice – S.O. 1996, c. 25, s. 8, effective April 19, 1999)

**4.** (1) **Determination of profits** — Where and so long as an interest to which section 2 applies represents more than a 50 per cent interest in the business, the person to whom it is given or in whom it is vested and the person having control of the management of the business or the person's nominee and the Public Trustee shall on or before the 30th day of June in each year determine jointly the amount of the profits earned by the business in its fiscal year ending in the calendar year next preceding.

(2) **Distribution of profits** — The business shall pay to the person to whom the interest is given or in whom it is vested the person's share of the then undistributed profits of the business in the amounts and on the dates determined jointly by the persons mentioned in subsection (1).

(3) **Annual return** — For the purposes of this section, the person to whom the interest is given or in whom it is vested shall on or before the 31st day of March in each such year deliver to the Public Trustee a return with respect to its fiscal year ending in the calendar year next preceding showing,

(a)    the assets and liabilities of the business;
(b)    all accounts of profit and loss of the business;
(c)    the particulars of any fee paid to any director; and
(d)    where the amount of salary and other remuneration paid to any person is $8,000 or more, the particulars thereof,

and the return shall be verified by the certificate of an officer or the auditor of the business that the statements therein are true.

(4) **Examination of accounts, etc.** — For the purposes of this section, the Public Trustee may require of any person such further or other information and may make such examination of the accounts and records of the business as he or she considers necessary.

(5) **Determination by court** — If the persons mentioned in subsection (1) fail to determine jointly any matter mentioned in subsection (1) or (2), the matter shall be determined by a judge of the Ontario Court (General Division), and in determining the amount of the profits of the business the judge may disallow in whole or in part any deduction, expenditure, expense, reserve, allowance or other sum that he or she considers to be unnecessary, excessive or improper having regard to the nature of the business and its financial position.

(Note: The name of the Ontario Court (General Division) was renamed the Superior Court of Justice – S.O. 1996, c. 25, s. 8, effective April 19, 1999)

**5. Rights of acquisition** — Where an interest in a business is being disposed of pursuant to section 2, any person acquiring any portion of such interest for other than religious, charitable, educational or public purposes may, subject to the approval of a judge of the Ontario Court (General Division) as to the consideration for and the terms and conditions of the acquisition, so acquire such portion although the person is the person disposing of such interest or is an officer, director, agent or employee of such person.

(Note: The name of the Ontario Court (General Division) was renamed the Superior Court of Justice – S.O. 1996, c. 25, s. 8, effective April 19, 1999)

**6. Investment of proceeds** — The proceeds of any disposition pursuant to section 2 may be invested only in investments authorized by the *Insurance Act* for the investment of the funds of joint stock insurance companies, but no such investment shall be made that results in the person making the investment holding more than a 10 per cent interest in any one business.

**7.** (1) **Investigation** — The Treasurer of Ontario may appoint any person to make an investigation for any purpose related to the administration or enforcement of this Act respecting any interest in any business that has been given to or vested in any person for any religious, charitable, educational or public purpose or respecting any person to or in whom any such interest has been given or vested.

(2) **Powers** — Every person appointed under subsection (1) to make an investigation has the powers of a commission under Part II of the *Public Inquiries Act*, which Part applies to the investigation as if it were an inquiry under that Act.

**8. Powers of court** — Upon the application of the Attorney General or any person interested, a judge of the Ontario Court (General Division) may make such orders as he or she considers proper to carry out the intent of this Act or to determine any matter arising under it.

(Note: The name of the Ontario Court (General Division) was renamed the Superior Court of Justice – S.O. 1996, c. 25, s. 8, effective April 19, 1999)

**9. Offence** — Every person who contravenes this Act is guilty of an offence and on conviction is liable to a fine of not more than $10,000 or to imprisonment for a term of not more than one year, or to both.

**10. *Charities Accounting Act* unaffected** — Nothing in this Act affects the operation of the *Charities Accounting Act*.

# CHARITIES ACCOUNTING ACT

(R.S.O. 1990, c. C.10)

**Amended by:** 1993, c. 27, Sched.; 1996, c. 25, s. 2; 1997, c. 23, s. 3; 1999, c. 12, Sched. B, s. 1; 2000, c. 26, Sched. A, s. 2; 2001, c. 9, Sched. B, s. 3; 2002, c. 17, Sched. F, Table; 2002, c. 18, Sched. A, s. 2.

**1.** (1) **Notice of donation to be given to Public Guardian and Trustee** — Where, under the terms of a will or other instrument in writing, real or personal property or any right or interest in it or proceeds from it are given to or vested in a person as executor or trustee for a religious, educational, charitable or public purpose, or are to be applied by the person for any such purpose, the person shall give written notice to,

(a) the person, if any, designated in the will or other instrument as the beneficiary or as the person to receive the gift from the executor or trustee; and

(b) the Public Guardian and Trustee, in the case of an instrument other than a will.

(2) **Charitable corporations, etc., brought within Act** — Any corporation incorporated for a religious, educational, charitable or public purpose shall be deemed to be a trustee within the meaning of this Act, its instrument of incorporation shall be deemed to be an instrument in writing within the meaning of this Act, and any real or personal property acquired by it shall be deemed to be property within the meaning of this Act.

(3) **Time for giving notice** — The notice shall be given, in the case of an instrument other than a will, within one month after it has been executed, and, in the case of a will, within the same period after the death of the testator.

(4) **Where notice not necessary** — No notice is necessary where the trust was completely executed before the 31st day of March, 1914, but the remaining sections of this Act nevertheless apply to every such trust.

(5) **Contents of notice** — The notice shall state the nature of the property coming into the possession or under the control of the executor or trustee.

(6) **Copy of instrument** — The notice shall be accompanied by a copy of the will or other instrument; in the case of a notice under clause (1) (b), the Public Guardian and Trustee may require a notarial copy.

[1997, c. 23, s. 3 (in force November 28, 1997); 2000, c. 26, Sched. A, s. 2 (in force December 6, 2000).]

**1.1 Delegation of investment functions to agent** — Sections 27 to 31 of the *Trustee Act* apply to,

(a) an executor or trustee referred to in subsection 1 (1); and

(b)    a corporation that is deemed to be a trustee under subsection 1 (2).

[2001, c. 9, Sched. B, s. 3 (in force June 29, 2001); 2002, c. 18, Sched. A, s. 2 (in force June 29, 2001).]

**2. (1) Executor or trustee to furnish information to Public Guardian and Trustee** — Every such executor or trustee shall, from time to time upon request, furnish to the Public Guardian and Trustee particulars in writing of,

    (a)    the condition, disposition or such other particulars as are required of the property devised, bequeathed or given or which has come into the hands of the executor or trustee;

    (b)    the names and addresses of the executors or trustees; and

    (c)    the administration or management of the estate or trust.

**(2) Corporation to furnish information to Public Guardian and Trustee** — Where such executor or trustee, either directly or indirectly through any person on the executor's or trustee's behalf or through any corporation or through a series or combination of such persons, corporations or persons and corporations, controls a corporation or the election of the directors thereof through the holding of a majority of the shares thereof or a sufficient number of shares or any class of shares thereof to enable the executor or trustee to exercise such control in fact, or in any other manner whatsoever, the corporation, the officers and manager of such corporation or any of them shall from time to time furnish to the Public Guardian and Trustee in writing such information concerning the corporation, its operation, assets, profits or losses, and finances as the Public Guardian and Trustee requests.

**(3) Application to court where corporation involved** — A judge of the Superior Court of Justice, upon the application of the Public Guardian and Trustee and upon notice to the corporation concerned and to such other person or persons as a judge of the Superior Court of Justice directs, shall inquire into and determine any question relating to the failure to furnish information to the Public Guardian and Trustee pursuant to subsection (2), and shall inquire into and determine the control of the election of directors or the ownership, control or management of, or any matter affecting, any corporation mentioned in subsection (2), or its operation, assets, profits or losses, and finances and may make such order as is considered necessary or proper to,

    (a)    compel the giving of information to the Public Guardian and Trustee;

    (b)    determine who controls the corporation;

    (c)    determine who controls the election of the directors of the corporation;

    (d)    protect or preserve the assets or financial stability of the corporation and the assets held by such executor or trustee relating to the corporation; and

    (e)    ensure the proper operation and management of the corporation and its assets.

[1999, c. 12, Sched. B, s. 1 (in force December 22, 1999); 2000, c. 26, Sched. A, s. 2 (in force December 6, 2000).]

**3. Auditing accounts as to charitable legacies or grants** — Whenever required so to do by the Public Guardian and Trustee, an executor or trustee shall submit the accounts of dealings with the property coming into the hands or under the control of the executor or trustee under the terms of the bequest or gift, to be passed and examined and audited by a judge of the Superior Court of Justice.

[1999, c. 12, Sched. B, s. 1 (in force December 22, 1999); 2000, c. 26, Sched. A, s. 2 (in force December 6, 2000).]

**4. Application to court where executor or trustee in default** — If any such executor or trustee,

(a) refuses or neglects to comply with section 1, 2 or 3, or with any of the regulations made under this Act;

(b) is found to have misapplied or misappropriated any property or fund coming into the executor's or trustee's hands;

(c) has made any improper or unauthorized investment of any money forming part of the proceeds of any such property or fund; or

(d) is not applying any property, fund or money in the manner directed by the will or instrument,

a judge of the Superior Court of Justice upon the application of the Public Guardian and Trustee, may make an order,

(e) directing the executor or trustee to do forthwith or within the time stated in the order anything that the executor or trustee has refused or neglected to do in compliance with section 1, 2 or 3, or with the regulations made under this Act;

(f) requiring the executor or trustee to pay into court any funds in the executor's or trustee's hands and to assign and transfer to the Accountant of the Superior Court of Justice, or to a new trustee appointed under clause (g), any property or securities in the hands or under the control of the executor or trustee;

(g) removing such executor or trustee and appointing some other person to act in the executor's or trustee's stead;

(h) directing the issue of an attachment against the executor or trustee to the amount of any property or funds as to which the executor or trustee is in default;

(i) fixing the costs of the application and directing how and by whom they shall be payable;

(j) giving such directions as to the future investment, disposition and application of any such property, funds or money as the judge considers just and best calculated to carry out the intentions of the testator or donor;

(k) imposing a penalty by way of fine or imprisonment not exceeding twelve months upon the executor or trustee for any such default or misconduct or for disobedience to any order made under this section;

(l) appointing an executor or trustee in place of an executor or trustee who has died, or has ceased to act, or has been removed, or has gone out of Ontario, even if the will or other instrument creating the trust confers the power to make such an appointment upon another executor or trustee or upon any other person.

[1999, c. 12, Sched. B, s. 1 (in force December 22, 1999); 2000, c. 26, Sched. A, s. 2 (in force December 22, 1999); 2000, c. 26, Sch. A, s. 2 (in force December 6, 2000).]

**5.** (1) **Regulations** — The Attorney General, on the advice of the Public Guardian and Trustee, may make regulations,

(a) prescribing forms of notices and returns to be made under this Act;

(b) respecting the practice and procedure upon passing the accounts of an executor or trustee under this Act and the tariff of fees and costs to be applicable thereto;

(c) requiring returns to be made by any such executor or trustee to any ministry of the Government and the form of such returns;

(d) regulating the practice and procedure upon applications under section 4.

(2) **Practice** — Except as otherwise provided by the regulations, the practice and procedure of the Superior Court of Justice apply to proceedings under this Act.

(3) Repealed: 1997, c. 23, s. 3 (3).

(4) **Notice of action to set aside will to be served on Public Guardian and Trustee** — Where an action or other proceeding is brought to set aside, vary or construe any such will or other instrument, written notice thereof shall be served upon the Public Guardian and Trustee, and if no one appears as representing the religious, educational, charitable or public institution, or if there is no named beneficiary, or a discretion is given to the executor or trustee as to a choice of beneficiaries, the Public Guardian and Trustee may intervene in the action or other proceeding and has the right to object or consent and to be heard upon any argument as a party to the action or other proceeding.

[1996, c. 25, s. 2 (in force October 31, 1996); 1997, c. 23, s. 3 (in force November 28, 1997); 1999, c. 12, Sch. B, s. 1 (in force December 22, 1999); 2000, c. 26, Sch. A, s. 2 (in force December 6, 2000)]

**5.1** (1) **Regulations** — The Attorney General, on the advice of the Public Guardian and Trustee, may make regulations,

(a) providing that acts or omissions that would otherwise require the approval of the Superior Court of Justice in the exercise of its inherent jurisdiction in charitable matters shall be treated, for all purposes, as though they had been so approved;

(b) requiring the making and keeping of records relating to charitable property and respecting the making, keeping, transfer and disposal of such records.

(2) **Limitation** — Regulations under clause (1) (a) may be made only in relation to,

(a) the giving of benefits from charitable property to,

(i) executors and trustees referred to in subsection 1 (1),

(ii) corporations deemed by subsection 1 (2) to be trustees within the meaning of this Act,

(iii) directors of corporations described in subclause (ii) or of persons described in subclause (i) who are corporations, or

(iv) persons who, because of their relationship or connection to a person, corporation or director described in subclause (i), (ii) or (iii), cannot be given such benefits without court approval; and

(b)  the administration and management of charitable property that is held for restricted or special purposes.

(3) **Governing instrument** — Regulations made under clause (1) (a) do not apply to an act or omission that conflicts with the will or instrument referred to in subsection 1 (1) or with the instrument deemed by subsection 1 (2) to be an instrument in writing under this Act.

(4) **General or particular** — Regulations made under this section may be general or particular in their application and, without limiting the generality of the foregoing, may be subject to the conditions set out in the regulations.

(5) **Definition** — In this section,

"charitable property" means property that is within the inherent jurisdiction of the court in charitable matters.

[1996, c. 25, s. 2 (in force October 31, 1996); 1999, c. 12, Sch. B, s. 1 (in force December 22, 1999); 2000, c. 26, Sch. A, s. 2 (in force December 6, 2000).]

**6.** (1) **Collection of funds from the public, right of complaint** — Any person may complain as to the manner in which a person or organization has solicited or procured funds by way of contribution or gift from the public for any purpose, or as to the manner in which any such funds have been dealt with or disposed of.

(2) **Form of complaint** — Every such complaint shall be in writing and delivered by the complainant to a judge of the Superior Court of Justice.

(3) **Order for investigation** — Wherever the judge is of opinion that the public interest can be served by an investigation of the matter complained of, he or she may make an order directing the Public Guardian and Trustee to make such investigation as the Public Guardian and Trustee considers proper in the circumstances.

(4) **Powers of Public Guardian and Trustee** — In making an investigation directed under subsection (3), the Public Guardian and Trustee has and may exercise any of the powers conferred on him or her by this Act and any of the powers of a commission under Part II of the Public Inquiries Act, which Part applies to the investigation as if it were an inquiry under that Act.

(5) **Cost of investigation** — The cost of any such investigation, when approved by the Attorney General, forms part of the expenses of the administration of justice in Ontario.

(6) **Report of investigation** — As soon as the Public Guardian and Trustee has completed the investigation, he or she shall report in writing thereon to the Attorney General and to the judge who ordered the investigation.

(7) **Order for audit** — Upon receipt of the report, the judge may order a passing of the accounts in question, in which case section 23 of the *Trustee Act* applies, and the judge may make such order as to the costs of the Public Guardian and Trustee thereon as he or she considers proper.

(8) **Where section not to apply** — Nothing in this section applies to any religious or fraternal organization or to any person who solicited or procured any funds of any religious or fraternal organization.

[1999, c. 12, Sch. B, s. 1 (in force December 22, 1999); 2000, c. 26, Sch. A, s. 2 (in force December 6, 2000).]

**7. Definitions** — In sections 8, 9 and 10,

"charitable purpose" means,

    (a)   the relief of poverty,

    (b)   education,

    (c)   the advancement of religion, and

    (d)   any purpose beneficial to the community, not falling under clause (a), (b) or (c);

"land" includes an interest in land other than an interest in land held as security for a debt.

**8.** (1) **Actual use or occupation of land for charitable purpose** — A person who holds land for a charitable purpose shall hold the land only for the purpose of actual use or occupation of the land for the charitable purpose.

(2) **Vesting in Public Guardian and Trustee** — Where in the opinion of the Public Guardian and Trustee, land held for a charitable purpose,

    (a)   has not been actually used or occupied for the charitable purpose for a period of three years;

    (b)   is not required for actual use or occupation for the charitable purpose; and

    (c)   will not be required for actual use or occupation for the charitable purpose in the immediate future,

the Public Guardian and Trustee may vest the land in himself or herself by registering a notice in the land registry office to that effect and stating that the Public Guardian and Trustee intends to sell the land, and shall, where practicable, deliver a copy of the notice to the person who held the land for the charitable purpose.

(3) **Sale by Public Guardian and Trustee** — Where land vests in the Public Guardian and Trustee under subsection (2), the Public Guardian and Trustee shall cause the land to be sold with all reasonable speed and shall apply the proceeds of sale, less his or her reasonable expenses in respect of the sale, to the charitable purpose.

(4) **Computation of time** — Where land has been granted or devised in reversion or remainder for a charitable purpose, the three-year period referred to in clause (2) (a) shall be calculated from the date on which the interest of the person to whom the land had been so devised or granted becomes an interest in possession.

(5) **Order to revest and sanctioning retention for period** — If, upon application to the Superior Court of Justice by any person having an interest, the court is satisfied that the land,

    (a)   has been actually used or occupied for the charitable purpose within the preceding three years;

    (b)   is required for actual use or occupation for the charitable purpose; or

    (c)   will be required for actual use or occupation for the charitable purpose in the immediate future, the court may make an order revesting in a charity land that has vested in the Public Guardian and Trustee under subsection (2) and sanctioning retention of the land by the charity for a period that is specified in the order.

(6) **Renewal of period** — Where in an application under subsection (5), the court finds that land is not required for actual use or occupation for the charitable purpose but will be required for actual use or occupation in the immediate future, the period specified in the order under subsection (5) shall not exceed three years, but on application by any person having an interest, the court may make an order extending the period for a further period not exceeding three years.

(7) **Effect of sanction of retention** — The Public Guardian and Trustee shall not cause the land to vest in himself or herself under subsection (2) during any period for which the retention is sanctioned by an order under subsection (5) or (6).

[1999, c. 12, Sch. B, s. 1 (in force December 22, 1999); 2000, c. 26, Sch. A, s. 2 (in force December 6, 2000)]

**9.** (1) **Authority for certain public bodies to receive property for charitable purposes** — Subject to section 8, a municipal corporation or local board thereof, a university or a public hospital may receive, hold and enjoy real or personal property devised, bequeathed or granted to it for a charitable purpose, upon the terms expressed in the devise, bequest or grant.

(2) **Agreement re administration** — A municipal corporation or local board thereof, university or public hospital holding property under subsection (1) may enter into an agreement with the person devising, bequeathing or granting the property for the holding, management, administration or disposition of the property.

(3) **Application of section** — This section applies even if the devise, bequest or grant was made before it was authorized by this section.

(4) **Definition** — In this section,

"local board" includes a school board and a conservation authority.

[2002, c. 17, Sched. F, Table (in force January 1, 2003).]

**10.** (1) **Application for order re carrying out trust** — Where any two or more persons allege a breach of a trust created for a charitable purpose or seek the direction of the court for the administration of a trust for a charitable purpose, they may apply to the Superior Court of Justice and the court may hear the application and make such order as it considers just for the carrying out of the trust under the law.

(2) **Notice to Public Guardian and Trustee** — An application under subsection (1) shall be upon notice to the Public Guardian and Trustee who may appear and be represented by counsel at the hearing.

(3) **Investigation by Public Guardian and Trustee** — Where the court is of the opinion that the public interest can be served by an investigation of the matter alleged in the application, the court may make an order directing the Public Guardian and Trustee to make such investigation as the Public Guardian and Trustee considers proper in the circumstances and report in writing thereon to the court and the Attorney General.

(4) **Powers of Public Guardian and Trustee** — In making an investigation directed under subsection (3), the Public Guardian and Trustee has and may exercise any of the powers conferred on him or her by this Act and any of the powers of a commission under Part II of the *Public Inquiries Act*, which Part applies to the investigation as if it were an inquiry under that Act.

[1999, c. 12, Sch. B, s. 1 (in force December 22, 1999); 2000, c. 26, Sch. A, s. 2 (in force December 6, 2000).]

**11. Application of Act** — This Act applies despite any provision in any will or other instrument excluding its application or giving to an executor or trustee any discretion as to the application of property, funds or the proceeds thereof to religious, educational, charitable or public purposes. R.S.O. 1990, c. C.10, s. 11.

**12. Other rights and remedies not affected** — This Act does not apply to or affect or in any way interfere with any right or remedy that any person may have under any other Act or in equity or at common law or otherwise. R.S.O. 1990, c. C.10, s. 12.

**13.** (1) **Consent orders and judgments in charitable matters** — A draft order or judgment that could have been made by the Superior Court of Justice under this Act, under any other Act dealing with charitable matters, or in the exercise of its inherent jurisdiction in charitable matters, shall be deemed to be an order or judgment of that court if the following persons give a written consent to its terms:

1. The Public Guardian and Trustee.
2. Every other person who would have been required to be served in a proceeding to obtain the order or judgment.

(2) **PGT's seal** — In the case of the Public Guardian and Trustee, the consent shall be sealed. 1997, c. 23, s. 3 (4).

(3) **Effective date** — The terms of the draft order or judgment take effect when it is filed with the Superior Court of Justice.

[1997, c. 23, s. 3 (in force November 28, 1997); 1999, c. 12, Sch. B, s. 1 (in force December 22, 1999).]

# APPROVED ACTS OF EXECUTORS AND TRUSTEES

## (O. Reg. 4/01)

### *Approval of Specified Acts*

**1.** (1) The acts authorized by this Regulation that would otherwise require the approval of the Superior Court of Justice in the exercise of its inherent jurisdiction in charitable matters shall be treated, for all purposes, as though they had been so approved.

(2) Subsection (1) does not constitute authorization of an act that conflicts with one of the following in a particular case:

1.   The will or the instrument in writing relating to the property.
2.   A court order relating to the will or instrument or relating to the property.

(3) An executor or trustee must maintain records demonstrating that he, she or it has complied with the requirements of this Regulation when engaging in an act that is authorized under subsection (1).

(4) An executor or trustee is not required by virtue of this Regulation to give any indemnity or to make any payment.

### *Authorization to Indemnify*

**2.** (1) In the circumstances and subject to the restrictions set out in this section, an executor or trustee and, if the executor or trustee is a corporation, each director or officer of the corporation may be indemnified for personal liability arising from their acts or omissions in performing their duties as executor, trustee, director or officer.

(2) An executor, trustee, director or officer cannot be indemnified for liability that relates to their failure to act honestly and in good faith in performing their duties.

(3) In the circumstances and subject to the restrictions set out in this section, insurance may be purchased to indemnify the executor, trustee, director or officer for the personal liability described in subsection (1).

(4) The terms of the indemnity or insurance policy must not impair a person's right to bring an action against the executor, trustee, director or officer.

(5) The executor or trustee or, if the executor or trustee is a corporation, the board of directors of the corporation shall consider the following factors before giving an indemnity or purchasing insurance:

1.   The degree of risk to which the executor, trustee, director or officer is or may be exposed.

2.      Whether, in practice, the risk cannot be eliminated or significantly re-duced by means other than the indemnity or insurance.

3.      Whether the amount or cost of the insurance is reasonable in relation to the risk.

4.      Whether the cost of the insurance is reasonable in relation to the revenue available to the executor or trustee.

5.      Whether it advances the administration and management of the property to give the indemnity or purchase the insurance.

(6) The purchase of insurance must not, at the time of the purchase, unduly impair the carrying out of the religious, educational, charitable or public purpose for which the executor or trustee holds the property.

(7) No indemnity shall be paid or insurance purchased if doing so would result in the amount of the debts and liabilities exceeding the value of the property or, if the executor or trustee is a corporation, render the corporation insolvent.

(8) The indemnity may be paid or the insurance purchased from the property to which the personal liability relates and not from any other charitable property.

(9) If the executor, trustee, director or officer is deceased, the indemnity or the proceeds of the insurance may be paid to his or her estate.

### Combining Property Held for Restricted or Special Purposes

**3.** (1) In this section,

"contributed property" means, in respect of an individual property, additional prop-erty that is added to, and forms part of, a pre-existing individual property.

(2) In the circumstances and subject to the restrictions described in this section, an executor or trustee may combine property received by the executor or trustee for a restricted or special purpose with other property received by the executor or trus-tee for another restricted or special purpose and may hold the combined property in one account in a financial institution or invest it as if it were a single property.

(3) The property may be combined only if it advances the administration and management of each of the individual properties to do so.

(4) All gains, losses, income and expenses must be allocated rateably, on a fair and reasonable basis, to the individual properties in accordance with generally accepted accounting principles.

(5) The executor or trustee must maintain the following records for each of the individual properties, in addition to such other records as may be required by law:

1.      The value of the individual property immediately before it becomes part of the combined property, and the date on which it becomes part of the combined property.

2.      The value of any portion of the individual property that does not become part of the combined property.

3.      The source and the value of contributed property relating to an individual property, and the date on which the contributed property is received.

4.   The value of the contributed property immediately before it becomes part of the combined property, and the date on which it becomes part of the combined property.

5.   The amount of the revenue received by the combined property that is allocated to the individual property, and the date of each allocation.

6.   The amount of the expenses paid from the combined property that are allocated to the individual property, and the date of each allocation.

7.   The value of all distributions from the combined property made for the purposes of the individual property, and the purpose and date of each distribution.

(6) The executor or trustee must maintain the following records for the combined property, in addition to such other records as may be required by law:

1.   The value of each individual property that becomes part of the combined property, and the date on which it becomes part of the combined property.

2.   The value of contributed property that becomes part of the combined property, the date on which it becomes part of the combined property, and details of the individual property to which the contributed property relates.

3.   The amount of the revenue received by the combined property, the amount allocated to each individual property and the date of each allocation.

4.   The amount of the expenses paid from the combined property, the amount allocated to each individual property and the date of each allocation.

5.   The value of all distributions from the combined property made for the purposes of an individual property and the purpose and date of each distribution.

# CORPORATIONS ACT

(R.S.O. 1990, c. C.38)

[Note: Only sections pertaining to non-share capital charitable corporations are reproduced]

**Amended by:** 1992, c. 32, s. 6; 1993, c. 16, s. 3; 1993, c. 27, Sched.; 1994, c. 11, s. 384; 1994, c. 17, s. 31; 1994, c. 27, s. 78; 1997, c. 19, s. 31; 1997, c. 28, ss. 50, 51; 1998, c. 18, Sched. E, ss. 59-82; 1999, c. 6, s. 16; 1999, c. 12, Sched. F, ss. 21, 22; 2000, c. 26, Sched. B, s. 9; 2001, c. 9, Sched. D, s. 5; 2002, c. 17, Sched. F, Table; 2002, c. 24, Sched. B, ss. 25, 31; 2004, c. 19, s. 10.

**1. Definitions** — In this Act,

"books" includes loose-leaf books where reasonable precautions are taken against the misuse of them;

"Commission" means the Ontario Securities Commission;

"company" means a corporation with share capital;

"corporation" means a corporation with or without share capital, but in Part III "corporation" means a corporation without share capital;

"court" means the Superior Court of Justice;

"Minister" means the member of the Executive Council to whom the administration of this Act is assigned by the Lieutenant Governor in Council;

"officer" means president, chair of the board of directors, vice-president, secretary, assistant secretary, treasurer, assistant treasurer, manager or any other person designated an officer by by-law of the corporation;

"private company" means a company as to which by its special Act, letters patent or supplementary letters patent,

(a)   the right to transfer its shares is restricted,

(b)   the number of its shareholders, exclusive of persons who are in the employment of the company, is limited to fifty, two or more persons holding one or more shares jointly being counted as a single shareholder, and

(c)   any invitation to the public to subscribe for its shares or securities is prohibited;

"public company" means a company that is not a private company;

"registers" includes loose-leaf registers where reasonable precautions are taken against the misuse of them;

"securities" means the bonds, debentures, debenture stock or other like liabilities of a corporation whether constituting a charge on its property or not;

"special resolution" means a resolution passed by the directors and confirmed with or without variation by at least two-thirds of the votes cast at a general meeting of the shareholders or members of the corporation duly called for that purpose, or, in lieu of such confirmation, by the consent in writing of all the shareholders or members entitled to vote at such meeting.

[2001, c. 9, Sched. D, s. 5.]

**2. Non-application of Act** — This Act does not apply to a company to which the *Business Corporations Act* or the *Co-operative Corporations Act* applies.

# PART I

## CORPORATIONS, INCORPORATION AND NAME

**3. Application of Part** — This Part, except where it is otherwise expressly provided, applies,

(a) to every corporation incorporated by or under a general or special Act of the Parliament of the late Province of Upper Canada;

(b) to every corporation incorporated by or under a general or special Act of the Parliament of the late Province of Canada that has its head office and carries on business in Ontario and that was incorporated with objects to which the authority of the Legislature extends; and

(c) to every corporation incorporated by or under a general or special Act of the Legislature,

but this Part does not apply to a corporation incorporated for the construction and working of a railway, an incline railway or a street railway, or to a corporation within the meaning of the *Loan and Trust Corporations Act* except as provided by that Act.

**4. (1) Incorporation by letters patent** — The Lieutenant Governor may in his or her discretion, by letters patent, issue a charter to any number of persons, not fewer than three, of eighteen or more years of age, who apply therefor, constituting them and any others who become shareholders or members of the corporation thereby created a corporation for any of the objects to which the authority of the Legislature extends, except those of railway and incline railway and street railway corporations and corporations within the meaning of the *Loan and Trust Corporations Act*.

(2) [Repealed: 1994, c. 27, s. 78.]

(3) **Incorporation of private company with limited objects** — Despite subsection (1), a private company may be incorporated under this Act with power to lend and invest money on mortgage of real estate or otherwise, or with power to accept and execute the office of liquidator, receiver, assignee, trustee in bankruptcy or trustee for the benefit of creditors and to accept the duty of and to act generally in the winding up of corporations, partnerships and estates, other than estates of deceased persons, and shall not by reason thereof be deemed to be a corporation within the meaning of the *Loan and Trust Corporations Act*, but the number of its shareholders, exclusive of persons who are in the employment of the company, shall be limited by its letters patent or supplementary letters patent

to five, two or more persons holding one or more shares jointly being counted as a single shareholder, and no such company shall issue securities except to its shareholders, or borrow money on the security of its property except from its shareholders, or receive money on deposit.

**5.** (1) **Supplementary letters patent** — The Lieutenant Governor may in his or her discretion issue supplementary letters patent to any corporation that applies therefor amending or otherwise altering or modifying its letters patent or prior supplementary letters patent.

(2) **No supplementary letters patent if corporation in default** — Despite subsection (1), the Lieutenant Governor shall not issue supplementary letters patent to a corporation that is in default of a filing requirement under the *Corporations Information Act* or that has any unpaid fees or penalties outstanding.

(3) **Commencement** — Subsection (2) comes into force on a day to be named by proclamation of the Lieutenant Governor.

**6. Powers of Minister** — The Minister may in his or her discretion and under the seal of his or her office have, use, exercise and enjoy any power, right or authority conferred by this Act on the Lieutenant Governor, but not those conferred on the Lieutenant Governor in Council.

**7. Sufficiency of material to be established** — An applicant under this Act shall establish to the satisfaction of the Minister the sufficiency of the application and all documents filed therewith and shall furnish such evidence regarding the application as the Minister considers proper.

**8. Proof under oath** — The Minister or any person in his or her ministry to whom an application is referred may take evidence under oath with respect thereto.

**9. Variation of terms of application** — On an application for letters patent, supplementary letters patent or an order, the Lieutenant Governor may give the corporation a name different from its proposed or existing name, may vary the objects or other provisions of the application and may impose such conditions as he or she considers proper.

**10. Defects in form not to invalidate letters patent** — The provisions of this Act relating to matters preliminary to the issue of letters patent or supplementary letters patent or an order are directory only, and no letters patent or supplementary letters patent or order are void or voidable on account of any irregularity or insufficiency in any matter preliminary to the issue thereof.

**11.** [Repealed: 1994, c. 27, s. 78.]

**12.** (1) **Commencement of existence** — A corporation comes into existence on the date of the letters patent incorporating it.

(2) **Effective date of letters patent, etc.** — Letters patent of incorporation, letters patent of continuation, letters patent of amalgamation and supplementary letters patent, issued under this Act or any predecessor thereof, take effect on the date set forth therein.

**13.** (1) **Corporate name** — A corporation shall not be given a name,

  (a)    that is the same as or similar to the name of a known corporation, association, partnership, individual or business if its use would be likely to deceive, except where the corporation, association, partnership, individual or person consents in writing that its, his or her name in whole or in part be granted, and, if required by the Minister,

      (i)    in the case of a corporation, undertakes to dissolve or change its name within six months after the incorporation of the new corporation, or

      (ii)    in the case of an association, partnership or individual, undertakes to cease to carry on its, his or her business or activities, or change its, his or her name, within six months after the incorporation of the new corporation;

  (b)    that suggests or implies a connection with the Crown or any member of the Royal Family or the Government of Canada or the government of any province of Canada or any department, branch, bureau, service, agency or activity of any such government without the consent in writing of the appropriate authority;

  (c)    that, when the objects applied for are of a political nature, suggests or implies a connection with a political party or a leader of a political party;

  (d)    that is objectionable on any public grounds.

(2) **Change of name** — If a corporation, through inadvertence or otherwise, has acquired a name that is objectionable, the Minister may, after giving the corporation an opportunity to be heard, issue supplementary letters patent changing the name of the corporation to the name specified in the supplementary letters patent.

(2.1) **Written hearing** — A hearing under subsection (2) shall be in writing in accordance with rules made by the Minister under the *Statutory Powers Procedure Act*.

(3) **Reference to court** — A person who feels aggrieved as a result of the giving of a name under subsection (1) or the changing or refusing to change a name under subsection (2) may, upon at least seven days notice to the Minister and to such other persons as the court directs, apply to the court for a review of the matter, and the court may make an order changing the name of the corporation to such name as it considers proper or may dismiss the application.

(4) **Filing** — A copy of an order made under subsection (3), certified under the seal of the court, shall be filed with the Minister by the corporation within ten days after it is made.

(5) **Offence** — A corporation that fails to comply with subsection (4) is guilty of an offence and on conviction is liable to a fine of not more than $200, and every director or officer of the corporation who authorizes, permits or acquiesces in any such failure is guilty of an offence and on conviction is liable to a like fine.
[1998, c. 18, Sch. E, s. 59.]

**14. Change not to affect rights, etc.** — A change in the name of a corporation does not affect its rights or obligations.

**15. Unauthorized use of "Limited", etc.** — A person, partnership or association that trades or carries on a business or undertaking under a name in which "Limited", "Limitée", "Incorporated", "Incorporée", or "Corporation" or any abbreviation thereof is used, unless incorporated, is guilty of an offence and on conviction is liable to a fine of not more than $200.

**16.** (1) **Corrected letters patent, etc.** — If letters patent or supplementary letters patent issued under this Act or a predecessor of this Act contain an error, the directors or members of the corporation may apply to the Minister for corrected letters patent or corrected supplementary letters patent.

(2) **Same** — The Minister, on his or her own initiative or on an application under subsection (1), may issue corrected letters patent or corrected supplementary letters patent.

(3) **Surrender of documents** — The corporation shall surrender the letters patent or supplementary letters patent which are being corrected,

(a)  at the time of making an application under subsection (1); or

(b)  forthwith upon the request of the Minister if he or she is issuing the correcting documents on his or her own initiative.

(4) **Conditions** — The Minister may issue the corrected letters patent or supplementary letters patent subject to such conditions as he or she may impose.

(5) **Date of corrections** — Corrected letters patent or supplementary letters patent may bear the date of the letters patent or supplementary letters patent which are being replaced.

[1994, c. 27, s. 78 (3).]

. . .

# PART II

## COMPANIES

**22. Use of name** — Despite subsection 20 (1) and section 21, a company may use its name in such form and in such language as the letters patent or supplementary letters patent provide.

**23.** (1) **Incidental powers** — A company possesses, as incidental and ancillary to the objects set out in the letters patent or supplementary letters patent, power,

(a)  to carry on any other business capable of being conveniently carried on in connection with its business or likely to enhance the value of or make profitable any of its property or rights;

(b)  to acquire or undertake the whole or any part of the business, property and liabilities of any person carrying on any business that the company is authorized to carry on;

(c)  to apply for, register, purchase, lease, acquire, hold, use, control, license, sell, assign or dispose of patents, patent rights, copyrights, trade marks, formulae, licences, inventions, processes, distinctive marks and similar rights;

(d) to enter into partnership or into any arrangement for sharing of profits, union of interests, co-operation, joint adventure, reciprocal concession or otherwise with any person or company carrying on or engaged in or about to carry on or engage in any business or transaction that the company is authorized to carry on or engage in or any business or transaction capable of being conducted so as to benefit the company, and to lend money to, guarantee the contracts of, or otherwise assist any such person or company, and to take or otherwise acquire shares and securities of any such company, and to sell, hold, reissue, with or without guarantee, or otherwise deal with the same;

(e) to take or otherwise acquire and hold shares in any other company having objects altogether or in part similar to those of the company or carrying on any business capable of being conducted so as to benefit the company;

(f) to enter into arrangements with any public authority that seem conducive to the company's objects and obtain from any such authority any rights, privileges or concessions;

(g) to establish and support or aid in the establishment and support of associations, institutions, funds or trusts for the benefit of employees or former employees of the company or its predecessors, or the dependants or connections of such employees or former employees, and grant pensions and allowances, and make payments towards insurance or for any object similar to those set forth in this clause, and subscribe or guarantee money for charitable, benevolent, educational or religious objects or for any exhibition or for any public, general or useful objects;

(h) to promote any company for the purpose of acquiring or taking over any of the property and liabilities of the company, or for any other purpose that may benefit the company;

(i) to purchase, lease or take in exchange, hire or otherwise acquire any personal property and any rights or privileges that the company may think necessary or convenient for the purposes of its business;

(j) to construct, improve, maintain, work, manage, carry out or control any roads, ways, tramways, branches, sidings, bridges, reservoirs, watercourses, wharves, factories, warehouses, electric works, shops, stores and other works and conveniences that may advance the company's interests, and to contribute to, subsidize or otherwise assist or take part in the construction, improvement, maintenance, working, management, carrying out or control thereof;

(k) to raise and assist in raising money for, and to aid by way of bonus, loan, promise, endorsement, guarantee or otherwise, any person or company with whom the company may have business relations or any of whose shares, securities or other obligations are held by the company and to guarantee the performance or fulfilment of any contracts or obligations of any such person or company, and in particular to guarantee the payment of the principal of and interest on securities, mortgages and liabilities of any such person or company;

(l)  to draw, make, accept, endorse, discount, execute and issue bills of exchange, promissory notes, bills of lading, warrants and other negotiable or transferable instruments;

(m)  to sell, lease, exchange or dispose of the undertaking of the company or any part thereof as an entirety or substantially as an entirety for such consideration as the company thinks fit, and in particular for shares or securities of any other company having objects altogether or in part similar to those of the company, if authorized so to do by a special resolution;

(n)  to sell, improve, manage, develop, exchange, lease, dispose of, turn to account or otherwise deal with the property of the company in the ordinary course of its business;

(o)  to adopt such means of making known the products of the company as seems expedient, and in particular by advertising in the press, by circulars, by purchase and exhibition of works of art or interest, by publication of books and periodicals or by granting prizes and rewards or making donations;

(p)  to cause the company to be registered and recognized in any foreign country or province or territory of Canada, and to designate persons therein according to the laws of such foreign country or province or territory to represent the company and to accept service for and on behalf of the company of any process or suit;

. . .

(s)  to pay all costs and expenses of or incidental to the incorporation and organization of the company;

(t)  to invest and deal with the money of the company not immediately required for its objects in such manner as may be determined;

(u)  to do any of the above things and all things authorized by the letters patent and supplementary letters patent as principals, agents, contractors, trustees or otherwise, and either alone or in conjunction with others;

(v)  to do all such other things as are incidental or conducive to the attainment of the above objects and of the objects set out in the letters patent and supplementary letters patent.

(2) **Powers may be withheld** — Any of the powers set out in subsection (1) may be withheld or limited by the letters patent or supplementary letters patent.

. . .

**59.** (1) **Borrowing powers** — The directors may pass by-laws,

(a)  for borrowing money on the credit of the company;

(b)  for issuing, selling or pledging securities of the company; or

(c)  for charging, mortgaging, hypothecating or pledging all or any of the property of the company, including book debts and unpaid calls, rights, powers, franchises and undertaking, to secure any securities or any money borrowed, or other debt, or any other obligation or liability of the company.

(2) **Definition** — The expression "property of the company" in subsection (1) and in every predecessor thereof includes and has included always both present and future property of the company.

(3) **Borrowing by-laws to be confirmed** — No by-law passed under subsection (1) is effective until it has been confirmed by at least two-thirds of the votes cast at a general meeting of shareholders duly called for considering it.

**60. Irredeemable securities** — A condition contained in a security or in a deed for securing a security is not invalid by reason only that the security is thereby made irredeemable or redeemable only on the happening of a contingency, however remote, or on the expiration of a period, however long.

**61.** (1) **Duplicate to be filed** — A duplicate original, or a copy certified under the seal of the company, of any charge, mortgage or other instrument of hypothecation or pledge made by the company to secure its securities shall be filed forthwith in the office of the Minister.

(2) **Exception** — Subsection (1) does not apply to a charge or mortgage filed with the Minister under any other Act.

. . .

**67.** (1) **Idem** — Where the letters patent, supplementary letters patent or by-laws of a company do not provide for cumulative voting under section 65, the letters patent, supplementary letters patent or by-laws may provide that the shareholders may, by a resolution passed by at least two-thirds of the votes cast at a general meeting of which notice specifying the intention to pass such resolution has been given, remove any director before the expiration of his or her term of office, and may, by a majority of the votes cast at that meeting, elect any person in his or her stead for the remainder of the term.

(2) **Exception** — Subsection (1) does not affect the operation of any provision respecting the removal of directors in the letters patent or supplementary letters patent of a company issued before the 30th day of April, 1954.

. . .

**69. Payment of president and directors** — No by-law for the payment of the president as president or of any director as a director is effective until it has been confirmed at a general meeting of the shareholders duly called for that purpose.

**70.** (1) **Executive committee** — Where the number of directors on the board of directors of a company is more than six, the directors may pass a by-law authorizing them to elect from among their number an executive committee consisting of not fewer than three and to delegate to the executive committee any powers of the board, subject to the restrictions, if any, contained in the by-law or imposed from time to time by the directors.

(2) **Confirmation** — The by-law is not effective until it has been confirmed by at least two-thirds of the votes cast at a general meeting of the shareholders duly called for that purpose.

(3) **Quorum** — An executive committee may fix its quorum at not less than a majority of its members.

**71.** (1) **Disclosure by directors of interests in contracts** — Every director of a company who is in any way directly or indirectly interested in a proposed contract or a contract with the company shall declare his or her interest at a meeting of the directors of the company.

(2) **Time of declaration** — In the case of a proposed contract, the declaration required by this section shall be made at the meeting of the directors at which the question of entering into the contract is first taken into consideration or, if the director is not at the date of that meeting interested in the proposed contract, at the next meeting of the directors held after he or she becomes so interested, and, in a case where the director becomes interested in a contract after it is made, the declaration shall be made at the first meeting of the directors held after he or she becomes so interested.

(3) **General notice** — For the purposes of this section, a general notice given to the directors of a company by a director to the effect that he or she is a shareholder of or otherwise interested in any other company, or is a member of a specified firm and is to be regarded as interested in any contract made with such other company or firm, shall be deemed to be a sufficient declaration of interest in relation to a contract so made, but no such notice is effective unless it is given at a meeting of the directors or the director takes reasonable steps to ensure that it is brought up and read at the next meeting of the directors after it is given.

(4) **Effect of declaration** — If a director has made a declaration of his or her interest in a proposed contract or contract in compliance with this section and has not voted in respect of the contract, the director is not accountable to the company or to any of its shareholders or creditors for any profit realized from the contract, and the contract is not voidable by reason only of the director holding that office or of the fiduciary relationship established thereby.

(5) **Confirmation by shareholders** — Despite anything in this section, a director is not accountable to the company or to any of its shareholders or creditors for any profit realized from such contract and the contract is not by reason only of the director's interest therein voidable if it is confirmed by a majority of the votes cast at a general meeting of the shareholders duly called for that purpose and if the director's interest in the contract is declared in the notice calling the meeting.

(6) **Offence** — If a director is liable in respect of profit realized from any such contract and the contract is by reason only of his or her interest therein voidable, the director is guilty of an offence and on conviction is liable to a fine of not more than $200.

. . .

**80. Director indemnified in suits respecting execution of office** — Every director and officer of a company, and his or her heirs, executors and administrators, and estate and effects, respectively, may, with the consent of the company, given at any meeting of the shareholders, from time to time and at all times, be indemnified and saved harmless out of the funds of the company, from and against,

(a)    all costs, charges and expenses whatsoever that he, she or it sustains or incurs in or about any action, suit or proceeding that is brought, commenced or prosecuted against him, her or it, for or in respect of any act, deed, matter or thing whatsoever, made, done or permitted by him, her or it, in or about the execution of the duties of his, her or its office; and

(b)    all other costs, charges and expenses that he, she or it sustains or incurs in or about or in relation to the affairs thereof, except such costs, charges or expenses as are occasioned by his, her or its own wilful neglect or default.

[1998, c. 18, Sch. E, s. 62 (in force March 1, 1999).]

**81.** (1) **Liability of directors for wages** — The directors of a company are jointly and severally liable to the employees, apprentices and other wage earners thereof for all debts due while they are directors for services performed for the company, not exceeding six months wages, and for the vacation pay accrued for not more than twelve months under the *Employment Standards Act* or any predecessor thereof and the regulations thereunder or under any collective agreement made by the company.

(2) **Limitation of liability** — A director is not liable under subsection (1),

(a)    unless the company has been sued for the debt within six months after it has become due and execution has been returned unsatisfied in whole or in part, or the company has within that period gone into liquidation or has been ordered to be wound up or has made an authorized assignment under the *Bankruptcy Act* (Canada), or a receiving order under the *Bankruptcy Act* (Canada) has been made against it and the claim on the debt has been fully filed and proved; and

(b)    unless he or she is sued for the debt while a director or within six months after he or she ceases to be a director.

(3) **Idem** — After execution has been so returned against the company, the amount recoverable against the director is the amount remaining unsatisfied on the execution.

(4) **Rights of director who pays the debt** — If the claim for the debt has been proved in liquidation or winding-up proceedings or under the *Bankruptcy Act (Canada)*, a director who pays the debt is entitled to any preference that the creditor paid would have been entitled to or, if a judgment has been recovered for the debt, the director is entitled to an assignment of the judgment.

(5) **Director holding shares in fiduciary capacity** — No director holding shares as executor, administrator, guardian or trustee who is registered on the books of the company as a shareholder and therein described as representing in any such capacity a named estate, person or trust is personally liable under this section, but the estate, person or trust is subject to all the liabilities imposed by this section.

[1992, c. 32, s. 6 (in force April 3, 1995).]

**82.** (1) **Place of meetings** — Subject to subsections (2) and (3), the meetings of the shareholders, the board of directors and the executive committee shall be held at the place where the head office of the company is situate.

(2) **Exception** — Where the by-laws of the company so provide, the meetings of the board of directors and of the executive committee may be held at any place in or outside Ontario and the meetings of the shareholders may be held at any place in Ontario.

(3) **Exception** — Where the letters patent or supplementary letters patent of the company so provide, the meetings of the shareholders may be held at one or more places outside Ontario designated therein.

(4) **Where section not to apply** — This section does not affect the operation of any provision in the letters patent or supplementary letters patent of a company issued before the 30th day of April, 1954, respecting the holding of the meetings of the shareholders at any place outside Ontario.

. . .

**84.** (1) **Proxies** — Every shareholder, including a shareholder that is a corporation, entitled to vote at a meeting of shareholders may by means of a proxy appoint a person, who need not be a shareholder, as the shareholder's nominee to attend and act at the meeting in the manner, to the extent and with the power conferred by the proxy.

(2) **Execution and termination** — A proxy shall be executed by the shareholder or the shareholder's attorney authorized in writing or, if the shareholder is a corporation, under its corporate seal or by an officer or attorney thereof duly authorized, and ceases to be valid one year from its date.

(3) **Contents** — In addition to the requirements, where applicable, of section 88, a proxy shall contain the date thereof and the appointment and name of the nominee and may contain a revocation of a former proxy and restrictions, limitations or instructions as to the manner in which the shares in respect of which the proxy is given are to be voted or that may be necessary to comply with the laws of any jurisdiction in which the shares of the company are listed on a stock exchange or a restriction or limitation as to the number of shares in respect of which the proxy is given.

(4) **Revocation** — In addition to revocation in any other manner permitted by law, a proxy may be revoked by instrument in writing executed by the shareholder or by the shareholder's attorney authorized in writing or, if the shareholder is a corporation, under its corporate seal or by an officer or attorney thereof duly authorized, and deposited either at the head office of the company at any time up to and including the last business day preceding the day of the meeting, or any adjournment thereof, at which the proxy is to be used or with the chair of such meeting on the day of the meeting, or adjournment thereof, and upon either of such deposits the proxy is revoked.

(5) **Time limit for deposit** — The directors may by resolution fix a time not exceeding forty-eight hours, excluding Saturdays and holidays, preceding any meeting or adjourned meeting of shareholders before which time proxies to be used at that meeting must be deposited with the company or an agent thereof, and any period of time so fixed shall be specified in the notice calling the meeting or in the information circular relating thereto.

. . .

**93.** (1) **Shareholders' meetings** — Subject to subsection (2) and in the absence of other provisions in that behalf in the by-laws of the company,

(a)   notice of the time and place for holding a meeting of the shareholders shall, unless all the shareholders entitled to notice of the meeting have waived in writing the notice, be given by sending it to each shareholder entitled to notice of the meeting by prepaid mail ten days or more before the date of the meeting to the shareholder's last address as shown on the books of the company;

(b)   no shareholder in arrear in respect of any call is entitled to vote at a meeting;

(c)   all questions proposed for the consideration of the shareholders at a meeting of shareholders shall be determined by the majority of the votes cast and the chair presiding at the meeting has a second or casting vote in case of an equality of votes;

(d)   the chair presiding at a meeting of shareholders may, with the consent of the meeting and subject to such conditions as the meeting decides, adjourn the meeting from time to time and from place to place;

(e)   the president or, in his or her absence, a vice-president who is a director shall preside as chair at a meeting of shareholders, but, if there is no president or such a vice-president or if at a meeting neither of them is present within fifteen minutes after the time appointed for the holding of the meeting, the shareholders present shall choose a person from their number to be the chair;

(f)   unless a poll is demanded, an entry in the minutes of a meeting of shareholders to the effect that the chair declared a motion to be carried is admissible in evidence as proof of the fact, in the absence of evidence to the contrary, without proof of the number or proportion of votes recorded in favour of or against the motion.

(2) **Notice** — The by-laws of the company shall not provide for fewer than ten days notice of meetings of shareholders and shall not provide that notice may be given otherwise than individually.

(3) **Poll** — If a poll is demanded, it shall be taken in such manner as the by-laws prescribe, and, if the by-laws make no provision therefor, then as the chair directs.

**94.** (1) **Auditors** — The shareholders of a company at their first general meeting shall appoint one or more auditors to hold office until the first annual meeting and, if the shareholders fail to do so, the directors shall forthwith make such appointment or appointments.

(2) **Idem** — The shareholders shall at each annual meeting appoint one or more auditors to hold office until the next annual meeting and, if an appointment is not so made, the auditor in office shall continue in office until a successor is appointed.

(3) **Casual vacancy** — The directors may fill any casual vacancy in the office of auditor, but, while such vacancy continues, the surviving or continuing auditor, if any, may act.

(4) **Removal** — The shareholders may, by resolution passed by at least two-thirds of the votes cast at a general meeting of which notice of intention to pass the resolution has been given, remove any auditor before the expiration of the auditor's term of office, and shall by a majority of the votes cast at that meeting appoint another auditor in the auditor's stead for the remainder of the term.

(5) **Remuneration** — The remuneration of an auditor appointed by the shareholders shall be fixed by the shareholders, or by the directors if they are authorized so to do by the shareholders, and the remuneration of an auditor appointed by the directors shall be fixed by the directors.

(6) **Appointment by Minister** — If for any reason no auditor is appointed, the Minister may, on the application of a shareholder, appoint one or more auditors for that year and fix the remuneration to be paid by the company for the services of the auditor or auditors.

(7) **Notice** — Notice of the appointment of an auditor shall be given in writing to the auditor forthwith after the appointment is made.

**95.** (1) **Qualification of auditor** — Except as provided in subsection (2), no person shall be appointed as auditor of a company who is a director, officer or employee of that company or an affiliated company or who is a partner, employer or employee of any such director, officer or employee.

. . .

**96.** (1) **Annual audit** — The auditor shall make such examination as will enable the auditor to report to the shareholders as required under subsection (2).

(2) **Auditor's report** — The auditor shall make a report to the shareholders on the financial statement, other than the part thereof that relates to the period referred to in subclause 97 (1) (b) (ii), to be laid before the company at any annual meeting during the auditor's term of office and shall state in the report whether in the auditor's opinion the financial statement referred to therein presents fairly the financial position of the company and the results of its operations for the period under review in accordance with generally accepted accounting principles applied on a basis consistent with that of the preceding period.

(3) **Idem** — If the financial statement contains a statement of source and application of funds or a statement of changes in net assets, the auditor shall include in the auditor's report a statement whether in the auditor's opinion, in effect, the statement of source and application of funds or the statement of changes in net assets presents fairly the information shown therein.

(4) **Idem** — The auditor in the auditor's report shall make such statements as the auditor considers necessary,

    (a)   if the company's financial statement is not in agreement with its accounting records;

(b)   if the company's financial statement is not in accordance with the requirements of this Act;

(c)   if the auditor has not received all the information and explanations that the auditor has required; or

(d)   if proper accounting records have not been kept, so far as appears from the auditor's examination.

(5) **Right of access, etc.** — The auditor of a company has right of access at all times to all records, documents, books, accounts and vouchers of the company and is entitled to require from the directors and officers of the company such information and explanation as in the auditor's opinion are necessary to enable the auditor to report as required by subsection (2).

(6) **Auditor may attend shareholders' meetings** — The auditor of a company is entitled to attend any meeting of shareholders of the company and to receive all notices and other communications relating to any such meeting that a shareholder is entitled to receive and to be heard at any such meeting that the auditor attends on any part of the business of the meeting that concerns the auditor as auditor.

**96.1. Exemption from annual audit** — In respect of a financial year of a company, the company is exempt from the requirements of this Part regarding the appointment and duties of an auditor if,

(a)   the company is not a public company;

(b)   the annual income of the company is less than $10,000; and

(c)   all of the shareholders consent, in writing, to the exemption in respect of the year.

[1998, c. 18, Sch. E, s. 63 (in force March 1, 1999).]

**97.** (1) **Information to be laid before annual meeting** — The directors shall lay before each annual meeting of shareholders,

(a)   in the case of a private company, a financial statement for the period that commenced on the date of incorporation and ended not more than six months before such annual meeting or, if the company has completed a financial year, that commenced immediately after the end of the last completed financial year and ended not more than six months before such annual meeting, as the case may be, made up of,

(i)    a statement of profit and loss for such period,

(ii)   a statement of surplus for such period, and

(iii)  a balance sheet as at the end of such period;

. . .

(c)   the report of the auditor to the shareholders;

(d)   such further information respecting the financial position of the company as the letters patent, supplementary letters patent or by-laws of the company require.

. . .

(3) **Auditor's report to be read** — The report of the auditor to the shareholders shall be read at the annual meeting and shall be open to inspection by any shareholder.

. . .

**113.** (1) **Amalgamation** — Any two or more companies, including a holding and subsidiary company, having the same or similar objects may amalgamate and continue as one company.

(2) **Agreement** — The companies proposing to amalgamate may enter into an agreement for the amalgamation prescribing the terms and conditions of the amalgamation, the mode of carrying the amalgamation into effect and stating the name of the amalgamated company, the names and address for service of each of the first directors of the company and how and when the subsequent directors are to be elected with such other details as may be necessary to perfect the amalgamation and to provide for the subsequent management and working of the amalgamated company, the authorized capital of the amalgamated company and the manner of converting the authorized capital of each of the companies into that of the amalgamated company.

(3) **Adoption by shareholders** — The agreement shall be submitted to the shareholders of each of the amalgamating companies at general meetings thereof called for the purpose of considering the agreement, and, if two-thirds of the votes cast at each such meeting are in favour of the adoption of the agreement, that fact shall be certified upon the agreement by the secretary of each of the amalgamating companies.

(4) **Joint application for letters patent** — If the agreement is adopted in accordance with subsection (3), the amalgamating companies may apply jointly to the Lieutenant Governor for letters patent confirming the agreement and amalgamating the companies so applying, and on and from the date of the letters patent such companies are amalgamated and are continued as one company by the name in the letters patent provided, and the amalgamated company possesses all the property, rights, privileges and franchises and is subject to all liabilities, contracts, disabilities and debts of each of the amalgamating companies.

[1998, c. 18, Sch. E, s. 46 (in force March 1, 1999); 2001, c. 9, Sch. D, s. 5 (in force June 29, 2001).]

. . .

# PART III

## CORPORATIONS WITHOUT SHARE CAPITAL

**117. Application of Part** — This Part, except where it is otherwise expressly provided, applies,

(a)   to every corporation incorporated by or under a general or special Act of the Parliament of the late Province of Upper Canada;

(b)   to every corporation incorporated by or under a general or special Act of the Parliament of the late Province of Canada that has its head office and carries on business in Ontario and that was incorporated with objects to which the authority of the Legislature extends; and

(c)   to every corporation incorporated by or under a general or special Act of the Legislature,

but this Part does not apply to a corporation incorporated for the construction and working of a railway, incline railway or street railway.

**118. Incorporation** — A corporation may be incorporated to which Part V applies or that has objects that are within the jurisdiction of the Province of Ontario.

[1994, c. 27, s. 78 (in force March 1, 1995).]

**119.** (1) **Application for incorporation** — The applicants for the incorporation of a corporation shall file with the Lieutenant Governor an application showing:

1.   The names in full and the address for service of each of the applicants.
2.   The name of the corporation to be incorporated.
3.   The objects for which the corporation is to be incorporated.
4.   The place in Ontario where the head office of the corporation is to be situate.
5.   The names of the applicants who are to be the first directors of the corporation.
6.   Any other matters that the applicants desire to have embodied in the letters patent.

(2) **Idem** — The applicants may ask to have embodied in the letters patent any provision that may be made the subject of a by-law of the corporation.

(3) **Exception** — Subsection (2) does not apply to a provision providing for the election and retirement of directors in accordance with subsection 287 (2) or (5).

[1998, c. 18, Sch. E, s. 65 (in force March 1, 1999); 2001, c. 9, Sch. D, s. 5 (in force June 29, 2001).]

**120. Classes of membership** — The letters patent, supplementary letters patent or by-laws of a corporation may provide for more than one class of membership and in that case shall set forth the designation of and the terms and conditions attaching to each class.

**121. Applicants become members** — Upon incorporation of a corporation, each applicant becomes a member thereof.

**122. Members not liable** — A member shall not, as such, be held answerable or responsible for any act, default, obligation or liability of the corporation or for any engagement, claim, payment, loss, injury, transaction, matter or thing relating to or connected with the corporation.

**123. Number of members** — Unless the letters patent, supplementary letters patent or by-laws of a corporation otherwise provide, there is no limit on the number of members of the corporation.

**124.** (1) **Admission to membership** — Subject to subsection (2), a person or unincorporated association may be admitted to membership in a corporation by resolution of the board of directors, but the letters patent, supplementary letters patent or by-laws may provide that such resolution is not effective until it has been confirmed by the members in general meeting.

(2) **Idem** — The letters patent, supplementary letters patent or by-laws of a corporation may provide for the admission of members by virtue of their office.

[1994, c. 27, s. 78 (in force March 1, 1995)]

**125. Voting powers of members** — Each member of each class of members of a corporation has one vote, unless the letters patent, supplementary letters patent or by-laws of the corporation provide that each such member has more than one vote or has no vote.

**126.** (1) **Not to be carried on for gain** — A corporation, except a corporation to which Part V applies, shall be carried on without the purpose of gain for its members and any profits or other accretions to the corporation shall be used in promoting its objects and the letters patent shall so provide, and, where a company is converted into a corporation, the supplementary letters patent shall so provide.

(2) **Exception** — Nothing in subsection (1) prohibits a director from receiving reasonable remuneration and expenses for his or her services to the corporation as a director or prohibits a director or member from receiving reasonable remuneration and expenses for his or her services to the corporation in any other capacity, unless the letters patent, supplementary letters patent or by-laws otherwise provide.

**127. Directors by virtue of their office** — Subject to section 286, the letters patent, supplementary letters patent or by-laws of a corporation may provide for persons becoming directors by virtue of their office, in lieu of election.

**128.** (1) **Memberships not transferable, termination** — Unless the letters patent or supplementary letters patent otherwise provide, the interest of a member in a corporation is not transferable and lapses and ceases to exist upon the member's death or when the member ceases to be a member by resignation or otherwise in accordance with the by-laws of the corporation.

(2) **Where transferable** — Where the letters patent or supplementary letters patent provide that the interest of a member in the corporation is transferable, the by-laws shall not restrict the transfer of such interest.

**129.** (1) **By-laws** — The directors of a corporation may pass by-laws not contrary to this Act or to the letters patent or supplementary letters patent to regulate,

(a) the admission of persons and unincorporated associations as members and as members by virtue of their office and the qualification of and the conditions of membership;
(b) the fees and dues of members;
(c) the issue of membership cards and certificates;
(d) the suspension and termination of memberships by the corporation and by the member;
(e) the transfer of memberships;

(f)    the qualification of and the remuneration of the directors and the directors by virtue of their office, if any;

(g)    the time for and the manner of election of directors;

(h)    the appointment, remuneration, functions, duties and removal of agents, officers and employees of the corporation and the security, if any, to be given by them to it;

(i)    the time and place and the notice to be given for the holding of meetings of the members and of the board of directors, the quorum at meetings of members, the requirement as to proxies, and the procedure in all things at members' meetings and at meetings of the board of directors;

(j)    the conduct in all other particulars of the affairs of the corporation.

(2) **Confirmation** — A by-law passed under subsection (1) and a repeal, amendment or re-enactment thereof, unless in the meantime confirmed at a general meeting of the members duly called for that purpose, is effective only until the next annual meeting of the members unless confirmed thereat, and, in default of confirmation thereat, ceases to have effect at and from that time, and in that case no new by-law of the same or like substance has any effect until confirmed at a general meeting of the members.

(3) **Rejection** — The members may at the general meeting or the annual meeting mentioned in subsection (2) confirm, reject, amend or otherwise deal with any by-law passed by the directors and submitted to the meeting for confirmation, but no act done or right acquired under any such by-law is prejudicially affected by any such rejection, amendment or other dealing.

**130.** (1) **By-laws respecting delegates** — The directors of a corporation may pass by-laws providing for,

(a)    the division of its members into groups that are composed of territorial groups, common interest groups or both territorial and common interest groups;

(b)    the election of some or all of its directors,

     (i)    by such groups on the basis of the number of members in each group, or

     (ii)    for the groups in a defined geographical area, by the delegates of such groups meeting together;

(c)    the election of delegates and alternative delegates to represent each group on the basis of the number of members in each group;

(d)    the number and method of electing delegates;

(e)    the holding of meetings of delegates;

(f)    the authority of delegates at meetings or providing that a meeting of delegates shall for all purposes be deemed to be and to have all the powers of a meeting of the members;

(g)    the holding of meetings of members or delegates territorially or on the basis of common interest.

(2) **Confirmation** — No by-law passed under subsection (1) is effective until it has been confirmed by at least two-thirds of the votes cast at a general meeting of the members duly called for considering the by-law.

(3) **Voting** — A delegate has only one vote and shall not vote by proxy.

(4) **Qualification of delegates** — No person shall be elected a delegate who is not a member of the corporation.

(5) **Saving** — No such by-law shall prohibit members from attending meetings of delegates and participating in the discussions at such meetings.

[1998, c. 18, Sch. E, s. 66 (in force March 1, 1999).]

**131.** (1) **Supplementary letters patent** — A corporation may apply to the Lieutenant Governor for the issue of supplementary letters patent,

(a) extending, limiting or otherwise varying its objects;

(b) changing its name;

(c) varying any provision in its letters patent or prior supplementary letters patent;

(d) providing for any matter or thing in respect of which provision may be made in letters patent under this Act;

(e) converting it into a company;

(f) converting it into a corporation, with or without share capital.

(2) **Authorization** — An application under subsection (1) shall be authorized by a special resolution.

(3) [Repealed: 1999, c. 12, Sch. F, s. 21.]

(4) **Contents of application for conversion into company** — If the application is under clause (1) (e) or (f) and the corporation is to become a company, the application shall set forth the authorized capital, the classes of shares, if any, into which it is to be divided, the number of shares of each class, the par value of each share or, where the shares are to be without par value, the consideration, if any, exceeding which each share or the aggregate consideration, if any, exceeding which all the shares of each class may not be issued, and, where there are to be preference shares, the preferences, rights, conditions, restrictions, limitations or prohibitions attaching to them or each class of them, and the terms and conditions on which the members will become shareholders.

(5) [Repealed: 1998, c. 18, Sch. E, s. 67.]

(6) **Special Act corporations excepted** — This section does not apply to a corporation incorporated by special Act, except that a corporation incorporated by special Act may apply under this section for the issue of supplementary letters patent changing its name.

[1998, c. 18, Sch. E, s. 67 (in force March 1, 1999); 1999, c. 12, Sch. F, s. 21 (in force March 27, 2000).]

**132.** (1) **Disposition of property on dissolution** — A corporation may pass by-laws providing that, upon its dissolution and after payment of all of its debts and liabilities, its remaining property or a part of that property shall be distributed or disposed of to the Crown in right of Ontario or its agents, the Crown in right of Canada or its agents, municipal corporations, charitable organizations or organizations whose objects are beneficial to the community.

(2) **Confirmation** — Such a by-law is not effective until it has been confirmed by two-thirds of the votes cast at a general meeting of the members duly called for that purpose.

(3), (4) [Repealed: 1998, c. 18, Sch. E, s. 68.]

(5) **Where no by-law** — In the absence of such by-law and upon the dissolution of the corporation, the whole of its remaining property shall be distributed equally among the members or, if the letters patent, supplementary letters patent or by-laws so provide, among the members of a class or classes of members.

[1998, c. 18, Sch. E, s. 68; 2004, c. 19, s. 10]

**133.** (1) **Application of Part II provisions to Part III corporations** — Section 22, clauses 23 (1) (a) to (p) and (s) to (v), subsection 23 (2), sections 59 to 61, 67, 69 to 71, 80 to 82, 84, 93 and 94, subsection 95 (1), sections 96 and 96.1, clauses 97 (1) (a), (c) and (d), subsection 97 (3) and section 113 apply with necessary modifications to corporations to which this Part applies, and in so applying them the words "company" and "private company" mean "corporation" and the word "shareholder" means "member".

(2) **Charitable corporation** — Despite subsection (1), in the case of a corporation to which this Part applies, the objects of which are exclusively for charitable purposes, it is sufficient notice of any meeting of the members of the corporation if notice is given by publication at least once a week for two consecutive weeks next preceding the meeting in a newspaper or newspapers circulated in the municipality or municipalities in which the majority of the members of the corporation reside as shown by their addresses on the books of the corporation.

(2.1) **Exemption** — Despite subsection (1), section 96.1 does not apply to a corporation referred to in subsection 1 (2) of the *Charities Accounting Act*.

(2.2) **Conditions for indemnification** — Despite subsection (1), a corporation referred to in subsection 1 (2) of the *Charities Accounting Act* cannot provide the indemnification referred to in section 80 unless,

    (a)    the corporation complies with the *Charities Accounting Act* or a regulation made under that Act that permits the provision of an indemnification; or

    (b)    the corporation or a director or officer of the corporation obtains a court order authorizing the indemnification.

(3) **Insurers** — Clauses 97 (1) (a), (c) and (d), subsections 97 (2) and (3), subsection 98 (1), except clause (a) thereof, subsection 98 (2), sections 99, 101, 102, 107 and 108 and subsections 109 (1) and (3) apply with necessary modifications to corporations to which Part V applies, and in so applying them the words "company" and "private company" mean "corporation" and the word "shareholder" means "member".

[1994, c. 27, s. 78 (in force March 1, 1995); 1998, c. 18, Sch. E, s. 69 (in force March 1, 1999); 2000, c. 26, Sch. B, s. 9 (in force March 1, 1999).]

. . .

# PART VI

## WINDING UP

**228. "contributory" defined** — In this Part,

"contributory" means a person who is liable to contribute to the property of a corporation in the event of the corporation being wound up under this Part.

**229. Application** — Subject to section 2, this Part applies,

(a) to every corporation incorporated by or under a general or special Act of the Parliament of the late Province of Upper Canada;

(b) to every corporation incorporated by or under a general or special Act of the Parliament of the late Province of Canada that has its head office and carries on business in Ontario and that was incorporated with objects to which the authority of the Legislature extends;

(c) to every corporation incorporated by or under a general or special Act of the Legislature;

(d) to every insurer within the meaning of Part V that is incorporated under or subject to this Act except where inconsistent with Part V,

but this Part does not apply to a corporation incorporated for the construction and working of a railway, incline railway or street railway, or to a corporation within the meaning of the *Loan and Trust Corporations Act* except as provided by that Act.

**230.** (1) **Voluntary winding up** — Where the shareholders or members of a corporation by a majority of the votes cast at a general meeting called for that purpose pass a resolution requiring the corporation to be wound up, the corporation may be wound up voluntarily.

(2) **Appointment of liquidator** — At such meeting, the shareholders or members shall appoint one or more persons, who may be directors, officers or employees of the corporation, as liquidator of the estate and effects of the corporation for the purpose of winding up its affairs and distributing its property, and may at that or any subsequent general meeting fix the liquidator's remuneration and the costs, charges and expenses of the winding up.

**231.** (1) **Publication of notice of winding up** — Notice of a resolution requiring the voluntary winding up of a corporation shall be filed with the Minister and be published in *The Ontario Gazette* by the corporation within fourteen days after the resolution has been passed.

(2) **Offence** — A corporation that fails to comply with subsection (1) is guilty of an offence and on conviction is liable to a fine of not more than $200 and every director or officer who authorizes, permits or acquiesces in such failure is guilty of an offence and on conviction is liable to a like fine.

**232. Inspectors** — A corporation being wound up voluntarily may, in general meeting, by resolution, delegate to any committee of its shareholders or members, contributories or creditors hereinafter referred to as inspectors, the power of appointing the liquidator and filling any vacancy in the office of liquidator, or may by a like resolution enter into any arrangement with its creditors with respect to the powers to be exercised by the liquidator and the manner in which they are to be exercised.

**233. Vacancy in office of liquidator** — If in a voluntary winding up a vacancy occurs in the office of liquidator by death, resignation or otherwise, the shareholders or members in general meeting may, subject to any arrangement the corporation may have entered into with its creditors upon the appointment of inspectors, fill such vacancy, and a general meeting for that purpose may be convened by the continuing liquidator, if any, or by any contributory, and shall be deemed to have been duly held if called in the manner prescribed by the by-laws of the corporation, or, in default thereof, in the manner prescribed by this Act for calling general meetings of the shareholders or members of the corporation.

**234. Removal of liquidator** — The shareholders or members of the corporation may, by a majority of the votes cast at a general meeting called for that purpose, remove a liquidator appointed under section 230 or 232, and in such case shall appoint another liquidator.

**235. Commencement of winding up** — A voluntary winding up commences at the time of the passing of the resolution requiring the winding up.

**236. Corporation to cease business** — Where a corporation is being wound up voluntarily, it shall, from the date of the commencement of its winding up, cease to carry on its undertaking, except in so far as may be required for the beneficial winding up thereof, and all transfers of shares, except transfers made to or with the sanction of the liquidator, or alterations in the status of the shareholders or members of the corporation, taking place after the commencement of its winding up, are void, but its corporate existence and all its corporate powers, even if it is otherwise provided by its instrument of incorporation or by-laws, continue until its affairs are wound up.

**237. No proceedings against corporation after voluntary winding up except by leave** — After the commencement of a voluntary winding up,

(a) no action or other proceeding shall be commenced against the corporation; and

(b) no attachment, sequestration, distress or execution shall be put in force against the estate or effects of the corporation,

except by leave of the court and subject to such terms as the court may impose.

**238. (1) Settlement of list of contributories** — Upon a voluntary winding up, the liquidator shall settle the list of contributories, and any list so settled is proof, in the absence of evidence to the contrary, of the liability of the persons named therein to be contributories.

**(2) Payment from contributories** — Upon a voluntary winding up, the liquidator may, before having ascertained the sufficiency of the property of the corporation, call on all or any of the contributories for the time being settled on the list of contributories to the extent of their liability to pay any sum that the liquidator considers necessary to satisfy the liabilities of the corporation and the costs, charges and expenses of winding up, and for the adjustment of the rights of the contributories among themselves, and the liquidator may, in making a call, take into consideration the probability that some of the contributories upon whom the call is made may partly or wholly fail to pay their respective portions of the call.

**239.** (1) **Meetings of corporation during winding up** — The liquidator may, during the continuance of the voluntary winding up, call general meetings of the shareholders or members of the corporation for the purpose of obtaining its sanction by resolution, or for any other purpose the liquidator thinks fit.

(2) **Where winding up continues more than one year** — In the event of a voluntary winding up continuing for more than one year, the liquidator shall call a general meeting of the shareholders or members of the corporation at the end of the first year and of each succeeding year from the commencement of the winding up, and shall lay before the meeting an account showing the liquidator's acts and dealings and the manner in which the winding up has been conducted during the preceding year.

**240. Arrangements with creditors may be authorized** — The liquidator, with the sanction of a resolution of the shareholders or members of the corporation passed in general meeting or of the inspectors, may make such compromise or other arrangement as the liquidator considers expedient with any creditor or person claiming to be a creditor or having or alleging to have a claim, present or future, certain or contingent, ascertained or sounding only in damages, against the corporation or whereby the corporation may be rendered liable.

**241. Power to compromise with debtors and contributories** — The liquidator may, with the like sanction, compromise all calls and liabilities to call, debts and liabilities capable of resulting in debts, and all claims, whether present or future, certain or contingent, ascertained or sounding only in damages, subsisting or supposed to subsist between the corporation and any contributory, alleged contributory or other debtor or person apprehending liability to the corporation and all questions in any way relating to or affecting the property of the corporation, or the winding up of the corporation, upon the receipt of such sums payable at such times and generally upon such terms as are agreed upon, and the liquidator may take any security for the discharge of such calls, debts or liabilities and give a complete discharge in respect thereof.

**242.** (1) **Power to accept shares, etc., as consideration for sale of property to another company** — Where a corporation is proposed to be or is in the course of being wound up voluntarily and the whole or a portion of its business or property is proposed to be transferred or sold to another corporation, the liquidator of the first-mentioned corporation, with the sanction of a resolution of the shareholders or members passed in general meeting of the corporation by which the liquidator was appointed conferring either a general authority on the liquidator or an authority in respect of any particular arrangement, may receive, in compensation or in part compensation for such transfer or sale, cash or shares or other like interest in the purchasing corporation for the purpose of distribution among the shareholders or members of the corporation that is being wound up in the manner set forth in the arrangement, or may, in lieu of receiving cash or shares or other like interest, or in addition thereto, participate in the profits of or receive any other benefit from the purchasing corporation.

(2) **Confirmation of sale or arrangement** — A sale made or arrangement entered into by the liquidator under this section is binding on the shareholders or members of the corporation that is being wound up voluntarily if,

(a)  in the case of a company, the shareholders or classes of shareholders, as the case may be, at a general meeting duly called for the purpose, by votes representing at least three-fourths of the shares or of each class of shares represented at the meeting; or

(b)  in the case of a corporation without share capital, the members or classes of members, as the case may be, at a general meeting duly called for the purpose, by votes representing at least three-fourths of the members or of each class of members represented at the meeting,

approve the sale or arrangement and if the sale or arrangement is approved by an order made by the court on the application of the corporation.

(3) **Where resolution not invalid** — No resolution shall be deemed invalid for the purposes of this section because it was passed before or concurrently with a resolution for winding up the corporation or for appointing the liquidator.

**243. Winding up by court** — A corporation may be wound up by order of the court,

(a)  where the shareholders or members by a majority of the votes cast at a general meeting called for that purpose pass a resolution authorizing an application to be made to the court to wind up the corporation;

(b)  where proceedings have been begun to wind up voluntarily and it appears to the court that it is in the interest of contributories and creditors that the proceedings should be continued under the supervision of the court;

(c)  where it is proved to the satisfaction of the court that the corporation, though it may be solvent, cannot by reason of its liabilities continue its business and that it is advisable to wind it up; or

(d)  where in the opinion of the court it is just and equitable for some reason, other than the bankruptcy or insolvency of the corporation, that it should be wound up.

**244. (1) Who may apply** — The winding-up order may be made upon the application of the corporation or of a shareholder or of a member or, where the corporation is being wound up voluntarily, of the liquidator or of a contributory or of a creditor having a claim of $200 or more.

(2) **Notice** — Except where the application is made by the corporation, four days notice of the application shall be given to the corporation before the making of the application.

**245. Power of court** — The court may make the order applied for, may dismiss the application with or without costs, may adjourn the hearing conditionally or unconditionally or may make any interim or other order as is considered just, and upon the making of the order may, according to its practice and procedure, refer the proceeding for the winding up and may also delegate any powers of the court conferred by this Act to any officer of the court.

**246.** (1) **Appointment of liquidator** — The court in making the winding-up order may appoint one or more persons as liquidator of the estate and effects of the corporation for the purpose of winding up its affairs and distributing its property.

(2) **Remuneration** — The court may at any time fix the remuneration of the liquidator.

(3) **Vacancy** — If a liquidator appointed by the court dies or resigns or the office becomes vacant for any reason, the court may by order fill the vacancy.

(4) **Removal of liquidator** — The court may by order remove for cause a liquidator appointed by it, and in such case shall appoint another liquidator.

**247. Costs and expenses** — The costs, charges and expenses of a winding up by order of the court shall be assessed by an assessment officer.

**248. Commencement of winding up** — Where a winding-up order is made by the court without prior voluntary winding-up proceedings, the winding up shall be deemed to commence at the time of service of notice of the application, and, where the application is made by the corporation, at the time the application is made.

**249. Winding up after order** — Where a winding-up order has been made by the court, the winding up of the corporation shall be conducted in the same manner and with the like consequences as provided for a voluntary winding up, except that the list of contributories shall be settled by the court unless it has been settled by the liquidator prior to the winding-up order, in which case the list is subject to review by the court, and except that all steps in the winding up are subject to the order and direction of the court.

**250.** (1) **Meeting of members of company may be ordered** — Where a winding-up order has been made by the court, the court may direct meetings of the shareholders or members of the corporation to be called, held and conducted in such manner as the court deems fit for the purpose of ascertaining their wishes, and may appoint a person to act as chair of any such meeting and to report the result of it to the court.

(2) **Order for delivery by contributories and others of property, etc.** — Where a winding-up order has been made by the court, the court may require any contributory for the time being settled on the list of contributories, or any trustee, receiver, banker or agent or officer of the corporation to pay, deliver, convey, surrender or transfer forthwith, or within such time as the court directs, to the liquidator any sum or balance, books, papers, estate or effects that are in the person's hands and to which the corporation appears to be entitled.

(3) **Inspection of books** — Where a winding-up order has been made by the court, the court may make an order for the inspection of the books and papers of the corporation by its creditors and contributories, and any books and papers in the possession of the corporation may be inspected in conformity with such order.

**251. No proceedings against corporation after court winding up except by leave** — After the commencement of a winding up by order of the court,

(a) no action or other proceeding shall be proceeded with or commenced against the corporation; and

(b) no attachment, sequestration, distress or execution shall be put in force against the estate or effects of the corporation,

except by leave of the court and subject to such terms as the court may impose.

**252. Application of ss. 253 to 265, 268** — Sections 253 to 265 and 268 apply to corporations being wound up voluntarily or by order of the court.

**253.** (1) **Where no liquidator** — If from any cause there is no liquidator, the court may by order on the application of a shareholder or member of the corporation appoint one or more persons as liquidator.

(2) **Idem** — Where there is no liquidator, the estate and effects of the corporation shall be under the control of the court until the appointment of a liquidator.

**254.** (1) **Consequences of winding up** — Upon a winding up,

(a) the liquidator shall apply the property of the corporation in satisfaction of all its liabilities proportionately and, subject thereto, shall distribute the property rateably among the shareholders or members according to their rights and interests in the corporation;

(b) in distributing the property of the corporation, the wages of all employees, apprentices and other wage earners in the employment of the corporation due at the date of the commencement of the winding up or within one month before, not exceeding three months wages and for vacation pay accrued for not more than twelve months under the *Employment Standards Act* and the regulations thereunder or under a collective agreement made by the corporation, shall be paid in priority to the claims of the ordinary creditors, and such persons are entitled to rank as ordinary creditors for the residue of their claims;

(c) all the powers of the directors cease upon the appointment of a liquidator, except in so far as the liquidator may sanction the continuance of such powers.

[1993, c. 27, Sched.]

(2) **Distribution of property** — Section 53 of the *Trustee Act* applies with necessary modifications to liquidators.

**255. Payment of costs and expenses** — The costs, charges and expenses of a winding up, including the remuneration of the liquidator, are payable out of the property of the corporation in priority to all other claims.

**256.** (1) **Powers of liquidators** — The liquidator may,

(a) bring or defend any action, suit or prosecution, or other legal proceedings, civil or criminal, in the name and on behalf of the corporation;

(b) carry on the business of the corporation so far as is necessary for the beneficial winding up of the corporation;

(c) sell in whole or in parcels the real and personal property, effects and things in action of the corporation by public auction or private sale;

(d)    do all acts and execute, in the name and on behalf of the corporation, all deeds, receipts and other documents, and for that purpose use the seal of the corporation;

(e)    draw, accept, make and endorse any bill of exchange or promissory note in the name and on behalf of the corporation;

(f)    raise upon the security of the property of the corporation any requisite money;

(g)    take out in the liquidator's official name letters of administration to the estate of any deceased contributory and do in the liquidator's official name any other act that is necessary for obtaining payment of any money due from a contributory or from a contributory's estate and which act cannot be done conveniently in the name of the corporation;

(h)    do and execute all such other things as are necessary for winding up the affairs of the corporation and distributing its property.

(2) **Bills of exchange, etc., to be deemed drawn in due course** — The drawing, accepting, making or endorsing of a bill of exchange or promissory note by the liquidator on behalf of the corporation has the same effect with respect to the liability of the corporation as if such bill or note had been drawn, accepted, made or endorsed by or on behalf of the corporation in the course of carrying on its business.

(3) **Where money deemed to be due to liquidator** — Where the liquidator takes out letters of administration or otherwise uses the liquidator's official name for obtaining payment of any money due from a contributory, such money shall be deemed, for the purpose of enabling the liquidator to take out such letters or recover such money, to be due to the liquidator personally.

**257. Nature of liability of contributory** — The liability of a contributory creates a debt accruing due from the contributory at the time the liability commenced, but payable at the time or respective times when calls are made for enforcing such liability.

**258. Who liable in case of death** — If a contributory dies before or after he or she has been placed on the list of contributories, the contributory's legal representatives are liable in due course of administration to contribute to the property of the corporation in discharge of the liability of such deceased contributory and shall be contributories accordingly.

**259.** (1) **Deposit in bank by liquidator** — The liquidator shall deposit in Ontario in a bank listed in Schedule I or II of the *Bank Act* (Canada) all sums of money that the liquidator has belonging to the corporation if such sums amount to $100 or more.

(2) **Approval of bank by inspectors** — If inspectors have been appointed, the bank shall be one approved by them.

(3) **Separate deposit account to be kept; withdrawal from account** — Such deposit shall not be made in the name of the liquidator individually, but a separate deposit account shall be kept of the money belonging to the corporation in the liquidator's name as liquidator of the corporation and in the name of the inspectors, if

any, and such money shall be withdrawn only on the joint cheque of the liquidator and one of the inspectors, if any.

(4) **Liquidators to produce bank pass-book** — At every meeting of the shareholders or members of the corporation the liquidator shall produce a pass-book or statement of account showing the amount of the deposits, the dates at which they were made, the amounts withdrawn and the dates of withdrawal, and mention of such production shall be made in the minutes of the meeting, and the absence of such mention is admissible in evidence as proof, in the absence of evidence to the contrary, that the pass-book or statement of account was not produced at the meeting.

(5) **Idem** — The liquidator shall also produce the pass-book or statement of account whenever so ordered by the court upon the application of the inspectors, if any, or of a shareholder or member of the corporation.

**260. Proving claim** — For the purpose of proving claims, sections 25, 26 and 27 of the *Assignments and Preferences Act* apply with necessary modifications, except that, where the word "judge" is used therein, the word "court" as used in this Act shall be substituted.

**261. Application or motion for direction** — Upon the application or motion of the liquidator or of the inspectors, if any, or of any creditors, the court, after hearing such parties as it directs to be notified or after such steps as it prescribes have been taken, may by order give its direction in any matter arising in the winding up.

**262.** (1) **Examination of persons as to estate** — The court may at any time after the commencement of the winding up summon to appear before the court or liquidator any director or officer of the corporation or any other person known or suspected to possess any of the estate or effects of the corporation, or alleged to be indebted to it, or any person whom the court considers capable of giving information concerning its trade, dealings, estate or effects.

(2) **Damages against delinquent directors, etc.** — Where in the course of the winding up it appears that a person who has taken part in the formation or promotion of the corporation or that a past or present director or officer, employee, liquidator or receiver of the corporation has misapplied or retained in the person's own hands, or become liable or accountable for, money of the corporation, or has committed any misfeasance or breach of trust in relation to it, the court may, on the application or motion of the liquidator or of any creditor or contributory, examine into the conduct of such person and order the person to repay the money so misapplied or retained, or for which the person has become liable or accountable, together with interest at such rate as the court considers just, or to contribute such sum to the property of the corporation by way of compensation in respect of such misapplication, retention, misfeasance or breach of trust as the court considers just.

**263.** (1) **Proceedings by shareholders** — If a shareholder or member of the corporation desires to cause any proceeding to be taken that, in the shareholder's or member's opinion, would be for the benefit of the corporation, and the liquidator, under the authority of the shareholders or members, or of the inspectors, if any, refuses or neglects to take such proceeding after being required so to do, the shareholder or member may obtain an order of the court authorizing the shareholder or member to take such proceeding in the name of the liquidator or corporation, but at the shareholder's or member's own expense and risk, upon such terms and conditions as to indemnity to the liquidator or corporation as the court prescribes.

(2) **Benefits, when for shareholders** — Thereupon any benefit derived from such proceeding belongs exclusively to the shareholder or member instituting the proceeding for that person's benefit and that of any other shareholder or member who has joined the shareholder or member in causing the institution of the proceeding.

(3) **When for corporation** — If before such order is granted, the liquidator signifies to the court the liquidator's readiness to institute such proceeding for the benefit of the corporation, an order shall be made prescribing the time within which the liquidator is to do so, and in that case the advantage derived from the proceeding, if instituted within such time, belongs to the corporation.

**264. Rights conferred by Act to be in addition to other powers** — The rights conferred by this Act are in addition to any other right of instituting proceedings against any contributory, or against any debtor of the corporation, for the recovery of any call or other sum due from such contributory or debtor or such person's estate.

**265. Stay of winding-up proceedings** — At any time during a winding up, the court, upon the application or motion of a shareholder or member or creditor or contributory and upon proof to its satisfaction that all proceedings in relation to the winding up ought to be stayed, may make an order staying the proceedings altogether or for a limited time on such terms and subject to such conditions as the court considers fit.

**266. (1) Account of voluntary winding up to be made by liquidator to a general meeting** — Where the affairs of the corporation have been fully wound up voluntarily, the liquidator shall make up an account showing the manner in which the winding up has been conducted, and the property of the corporation disposed of, and thereupon shall call a general meeting of the shareholders or members of the corporation for the purpose of having the account laid before them and hearing any explanation that may be given by the liquidator, and the meeting shall be called in the manner provided by the by-laws for calling general meetings.

(2) **Notice of holding of meeting** — The liquidator shall within ten days after the holding of the meeting file a notice with the Minister stating that the meeting was held and the date thereof.

(3) **Dissolution** — On the expiration of three months from the date of the filing of the notice, the corporation is dissolved.

(4) **Extension** — At any time during the three-month period mentioned in subsection (3), the court may, on the application of the liquidator or any other person interested, make an order deferring the date on which the dissolution of

the corporation is to take effect to a date fixed in the order, and in such event the corporation is dissolved on the date so fixed.

**(5) Copy of extension order to be filed** — The person on whose application the order was made shall within ten days after it was made file with the Minister a copy of it certified under the seal of the court.

**(6) Offence** — A person who fails to comply with any requirement of this section is guilty of an offence and on conviction is liable to a fine of not more than $200.

**267. (1) Order for dissolution** — Despite section 266, in the case of a voluntary winding up or in the case of a winding up by order of the court, the court at any time after the affairs of the corporation have been fully wound up may, upon the application or motion of the liquidator or any other person interested, make an order dissolving it, and it is dissolved at and from the date of the order.

**(2) Copy of dissolution order to be filed** — The person on whose application the order was made shall within ten days after it was made file with the Minister a copy of it certified under the seal of the court.

**(3) Offence** — A person who fails to comply with any requirement of this section is guilty of an offence and on conviction is liable to a fine of not more than $200.

**268. (1) Where shareholder unknown** — Where the liquidator is unable to distribute rateably the property of the corporation among the shareholders or members because a shareholder or member is unknown or the person's whereabouts is unknown, the share of the property of the corporation of such shareholder or member may, by agreement with the Public Trustee, be delivered or conveyed by the liquidator to the Public Trustee to be held in trust for the shareholder or member, and thereupon subsections 319 (5) and (6) apply thereto.

**(2) Idem** — A delivery or conveyance under subsection (1) shall be deemed to be a rateable distribution among the shareholders or members for the purposes of clause 254 (1) (a).

**(3) Where creditor unknown** — Where the liquidator is unable to pay all the debts of the corporation because a creditor is unknown or the creditor's whereabouts is unknown, the liquidator may, by agreement with the Public Trustee, pay to the Public Trustee an amount equal to the amount of the debt due to the creditor to be held in trust for the creditor and thereupon subsections 319 (5) and (6) apply thereto.

**(4) Idem** — A payment under subsection (3) shall be deemed to be in satisfaction of the debt for the purposes of clause 254 (1) (a).

**269. (1) Disposal of books, etc., after winding up** — Where a corporation has been wound up under this Act and is about to be dissolved, its books, accounts and documents and those of the liquidator may be disposed of as it by resolution directs in case of voluntary winding up, or as the court directs in case of winding up under order.

**(2) Where responsibility as to custody of books, etc., to cease** — After the lapse of five years from the date of the dissolution of the corporation, no responsibility rests on it or the liquidator, or anyone to whom the custody of such books, accounts and documents has been committed by reason that the same or any of them are not forthcoming to any person claiming to be interested therein.

**270.** (1) **Provision for discharge of liquidator and distribution by the court** — Where a corporation is being wound up under an order of the court and the realization and distribution of its property has proceeded so far that in the opinion of the court it is expedient that the liquidator should be discharged and that the property of the corporation remaining in the liquidator's hands can be better realized and distributed by the court, the court may make an order discharging the liquidator and for payment, delivery and transfer into court, or to such officer or person as the court may direct, of such property, and it shall be realized and distributed by or under the direction of the court among the persons entitled thereto in the same way as nearly as may be as if the distribution were being made by the liquidator.

(2) **Disposal of books and documents** — In such case, the court may make an order directing how the books, accounts and documents of the corporation and of the liquidator are to be disposed of, and may order that they be deposited in court or otherwise dealt with as it thinks fit.

**271. Rules of procedure** — The Lieutenant Governor in Council may make rules for the due carrying out of this Part, and, except as otherwise provided by this Act or by such rules, the practice and procedure in a winding up under the *Winding-up Act* (Canada) apply.

# PART VII

## CORPORATIONS, GENERAL

**272. Application of Part** — Subject to section 2, this Part, except where it is otherwise expressly provided, applies,

(a)  to every corporation incorporated by or under a general or special Act of the Parliament of the late Province of Upper Canada;

(b)  to every corporation incorporated by or under a general or special Act of the Parliament of the late Province of Canada that has its head office and carries on business in Ontario and that was incorporated with objects to which the authority of the Legislature extends; and

(c)  to every corporation incorporated by or under a general or special Act of the Legislature,

but this Part does not apply to a corporation incorporated for the construction and working of a railway, incline railway or street railway, or to a corporation within the meaning of the *Loan and Trust Corporations Act* except as provided by that Act.

**273. Incorporation subject to trusts** — A corporation is, upon its incorporation, invested with all the property and rights, real and personal, theretofore held by or for it under any trust created with a view to its incorporation.

**274. General corporate powers** — A corporation, unless otherwise expressly provided in the Act or instrument creating it, has and shall be deemed to have had from its creation the capacity of a natural person and may exercise its powers beyond the boundaries of Ontario to the extent to which the laws in force where the powers are sought to be exercised permit, and may accept extra-provincial powers and rights.

**275. Incidental powers** — A corporation has power,

(a)   to construct, maintain and alter any buildings or works necessary or convenient for its objects;

(b)   to acquire by purchase, lease or otherwise and to hold any land or interest therein.

[1994, c. 27, s. 78 (in force March 1, 1995).]

**276.** [Repealed, 1994, c. 27, s. 78.]

**277. (1) Head office** — Subject to subsection (2), a corporation shall at all times have its head office in the place in Ontario where the letters patent provide that the head office is to be situate.

**(2) Change of head office** — A corporation may by special resolution change the location of its head office to another place in Ontario.

**(3) Where municipality annexed or amalgamated** — Where the location of the head office of a corporation is changed by reason only of the annexation or amalgamation of the place in which the head office is situate to or with another municipality, such change does not constitute and has never constituted a change within the meaning of subsection (2).

(4) Repealed: 1998, c. 18, Sch. E, s. 72.

(5) Repealed: 1998, c. 18, Sch. E, s. 72.

[1998, c. 18, Sch. E, s. 72 (in force March 1, 1999).]

**278.** [Repealed, 1994, c. 27, s. 78]

**279. Seal** — A corporation may, but need not, have a corporate seal.

[1998, c. 18, Sch. E, s. 73 (in force March 1, 1999).]

**280. (1) Contracts in writing under seal** — A contract that if made between individual persons would be by law required to be in writing and under seal may be made on behalf of a corporation in writing under the seal of the corporation.

**(2) Contracts in writing not under seal** — A contract that if made between individual persons would be by law required to be in writing signed by the parties to be charged therewith may be made on behalf of a corporation in writing signed by any person acting under its authority, express or implied.

**(3) Parol contracts** — A contract that if made between individual persons would be by law valid although made by parol only and not reduced into writing may be made by parol on behalf of a corporation by any person acting under its authority, express or implied.

**281. Power of attorney by corporation** — A corporation may, by writing under seal, empower any person, either generally or in respect of any specified matters, as its attorney to execute on its behalf deeds to which it is a party in any capacity in any place situate in or outside Ontario, and every deed signed by such attorney on behalf of the corporation and under the attorney's seal binds the corporation and has the same effect as if it were under the seal of the corporation.

**282. Authentication of documents, etc.** — A document requiring authentication by a corporation may be signed by any director or by any authorized person and need not be under seal.

**283.** (1) **Directors** — The affairs of every corporation shall be managed by a board of directors howsoever designated.

(2) **Number** — The board of directors of a corporation shall consist of a fixed number of directors not fewer than three.

(3) **Conduct of business** — Subject to subsection 298 (1) and subsection (3.1), no business of a corporation shall be transacted by its directors except at a meeting of directors at which a quorum of the board is present.

(3.1) **Means of meetings** — Unless the by-laws otherwise provide, if all the directors of a corporation present at or participating in the meeting consent, a meeting of directors or of a committee of directors may be held by such telephone, electronic or other communication facilities as permit all persons participating in the meeting to communicate with each other simultaneously and instantaneously, and a director participating in the meeting by those means is deemed for the purposes of this Act to be present at the meeting.

(4) **Idem** — Where there is a vacancy or vacancies in the board of directors, the remaining directors may exercise all the powers of the board so long as a quorum of the board remains in office.

(5) **Purchase of liability insurance** — Subject to subsection (6), a corporation may purchase and maintain insurance for a director or officer of the corporation against any liability incurred by the director or officer, in the capacity as a director or officer of the corporation, except where the liability relates to the person's failure to act honestly and in good faith with a view to the best interests of the corporation.

(6) **Charitable corporation** — A corporation referred to in subsection 1 (2) of the *Charities Accounting Act* may not purchase insurance described in subsection (5) unless,

   (a)   the corporation complies with the *Charities Accounting Act* or a regulation made under that Act that permits the purchase; or

   (b)   the corporation or a director or officer of the corporation obtains a court order authorizing the purchase.

[1998, c. 18, Sch. E, s. 74 (in force March 1, 1999).]

**284.** (1) **First directors** — The persons named as first directors in the Act or instrument creating the corporation are the directors of the corporation until replaced by the same number of others duly elected or appointed in their stead.

(2) **Idem** — The first directors of the corporation have all the powers and duties and are subject to all the liabilities of directors.

(3) **Definition** — In the case of corporations incorporated before the 30th day of April, 1954, "first directors" in this section means provisional directors.

**285.** (1) **Change in number of directors** — A corporation may by special resolution increase or decrease the number of its directors.

(2) Repealed: 1998, c. 18, Sch. E, s. 75.

(3) Repealed: 1998, c. 18, Sch. E, s. 75.

[1998, c. 18, Sch. E, s. 75 (in force March 1, 1999).]

**286.** (1) **Qualification of directors, must be shareholders** — Subject to subsections (2) and (3), no person shall be a director of a corporation unless he or she is a shareholder or member of the corporation, and, if the person ceases to be a shareholder or member, he or she thereupon ceases to be a director.

(2) **Exception** — A person may be a director of a corporation if he or she becomes a shareholder or member of the corporation within ten days after his or her election or appointment as a director, but, if the person fails to become a shareholder or member within such ten days, the person thereupon ceases to be a director and shall not be re-elected or reappointed unless he or she is a shareholder or member of the corporation.

(3) **Exception, hospitals and stock exchanges** — A corporation,

(a)　operating a hospital within the meaning of the *Public Hospitals Act*; or

(b)　operating a recognized stock exchange,

may by by-law provide that a person may, with his or her consent in writing, be a director of the corporation even though the person is not a shareholder or member of the corporation.

(4) **Age** — A director shall be eighteen or more years of age.

(5) **Bankrupts** — No undischarged bankrupt shall be a director, and, if a director becomes a bankrupt, he or she thereupon ceases to be a director.

**287.** (1) **Election of directors** — The directors shall be elected by the shareholders or members in general meeting and the election shall be by ballot or in such other manner as the by-laws of the corporation prescribe.

(2) **Idem** — Unless the by-laws otherwise provide, the election of directors shall take place yearly and all the directors then in office shall retire, but, if qualified, are eligible for re-election.

(3) **Exception** — Subsection (2) does not affect the operation of any by-law passed before the 30th day of April, 1954, that provides that the election of directors shall take place otherwise than yearly.

(4) **Continuance in office** — If an election of directors is not held at the proper time, the directors continue in office until their successors are elected.

(5) **Rotation of directors** — The by-laws may provide for the election and retirement of directors in rotation, but in that case no director shall be elected for a term of more than five years and at least three directors shall retire from office in each year.

[1998, c. 18, Sch. E, s. 76 (in force March 1, 1999).]

**288.** (1) **Quorum of directors** — Unless the letters patent, supplementary letters patent or a special resolution otherwise provides, a majority of the board of directors constitutes a quorum, but in no case shall a quorum be less than two-fifths of the board of directors.

(2) **Vacancies** — As long as there is a quorum of directors in office, any vacancy occurring in the board of directors may be filled for the remainder of the term by the directors then in office.

(3) **Idem** — Whenever there is not a quorum of directors in office, the director or directors then in office shall forthwith call a general meeting of the shareholders or members to fill the vacancies, and, in default or if there are no directors then in office, the meeting may be called by any shareholder or member.

**289.** (1) **Officers, president** — The directors shall elect a president from among themselves.

(2) **Other officers** — The directors shall appoint a secretary and may appoint one or more vice-presidents and other officers.

(3) **Corporations without share capital** — Despite subsections (1) and (2), in the case of a corporation without share capital, if the letters patent, supplementary letters patent or by-laws so provide, the officers of the corporation or any of them may be elected or appointed at a general meeting of the members duly called for that purpose.

(4) **Acting secretary** — If the office of secretary is vacant or if for any reason the secretary is unable to act, anything required or authorized to be done by the secretary may be done by an assistant secretary or, if there is no assistant secretary able to act, by any other officer of the corporation authorized generally or specifically in that behalf by the directors.

**290. Chair of the board** — A corporation may by special resolution provide for the election by the directors from among themselves of a chair of the board of directors and define his or her duties, and may assign to the chair of the board of directors any or all of the duties of the president or other officer of the corporation, and in that case the special resolution shall fix and prescribe the duties of the president.

**291.** (1) **Qualification of officers** — Except in the case of the president and the chair of the board of directors, no officer of the corporation need be a director or a shareholder or member of the corporation unless the by-laws so provide.

(2) **Application of subs. (1)** — Subsection (1) does not apply to a corporation operating a recognized stock exchange.

**292. Validity of acts of directors, etc.** — The acts of a director or of an officer are valid despite any defect that may afterwards be discovered in his or her appointment or qualification.

**293. Annual meetings** — A corporation shall hold an annual meeting of its shareholders or members not later than eighteen months after its incorporation and subsequently not more than fifteen months after the holding of the last preceding annual meeting.

**294. General meetings** — The directors may at any time call a general meeting of the shareholders or members for the transaction of any business, the general nature of which is specified in the notice calling the meeting.

**295.** (1) **Requisition for meeting** — Shareholders of a company holding not less than one-tenth of the issued shares of the company that carry the right to vote at the meeting proposed to be held, or not less than one-tenth of the members of a corporation without share capital entitled to vote at the meeting proposed to be held, as the case may be, may request the directors to call a general meeting of the shareholders or members for any purpose connected with the affairs of the corporation that is not inconsistent with this Act.

(2) **Requisition** — The requisition shall state the general nature of the business to be presented at the meeting and shall be signed by the requisitionists and deposited at the head office of the corporation and may consist of several documents in like form signed by one or more requisitionists.

(3) **Duty of directors to call meeting** — Upon deposit of the requisition, the directors shall call forthwith a general meeting of the shareholders or members for the transaction of the business stated in the requisition.

(4) **Where requisitionists may call meeting** — If the directors do not within twenty-one days from the date of the deposit of the requisition call and hold such meeting, any of the requisitionists may call such meeting which shall be held within sixty days from the date of the deposit of the requisition.

(5) **Calling of meeting** — A meeting called under this section shall be called as nearly as possible in the same manner as meetings of shareholders or members are called under the by-laws, but, if the by-laws provide for more than twenty-one days notice of meetings, twenty-one days notice is sufficient for the calling of such meeting.

(6) **Repayment of expenses** — Any reasonable expenses incurred by the requisitionists by reason of the failure of the directors to call such meeting shall be repaid to the requisitionists by the corporation and any amount so repaid shall be retained by the corporation out of any money due or to become due from the corporation by way of fees or other remuneration in respect of their services to such of the directors as were in default, unless at such meeting the shareholders or members by a majority of the votes cast reject the repayment to the requisitionists.

**296.** (1) **Circulation of shareholders' resolutions, etc.** — On the requisition in writing of shareholders of a company holding not less than one-twentieth of the issued shares of the company that carry the right to vote at the meeting to which the requisition relates or not less than one-twentieth of the members of a corporation without share capital entitled to vote at the meeting to which the requisition relates, as the case may be, the directors shall,

(a)   give to the shareholders or members entitled to notice of the next meeting of shareholders or members notice of any resolution that may properly be moved and is intended to be moved at that meeting; or

(b)   circulate to the shareholders or members entitled to vote at the next meeting of shareholders or members a statement of not more than 1,000 words with respect to the matter referred to in any proposed resolution or with respect to the business to be dealt with at that meeting.

(2) **Notice** — The notice or statement or both, as the case may be, shall be given or circulated by sending a copy thereof to each shareholder or member entitled thereto in the same manner and at the same time as that prescribed by this Act for the sending of notice of meetings of shareholders or members.

(3) **Idem** — Where it is not practicable to send the notice or statement or both at the same time as the notice of the meeting is sent, the notice or statement or both shall be sent as soon as practicable thereafter.

(4) **Deposit of requisition, etc.** — The directors are not bound under this section to give notice of any resolution or to circulate any statement unless,

(a)    the requisition, signed by the requisitionists, is deposited at the head office of the corporation,

    (i)    in the case of a requisition requiring notice of a resolution to be given, not less than ten days before the meeting,

    (ii)   in the case of a requisition requiring a statement to be circulated, not less than seven days before the meeting; and

(b)    there is deposited with the requisition a sum reasonably sufficient to meet the corporation's expenses in giving effect thereto.

(5) **Where directors not bound to circulate statement** — The directors are not bound under this section to circulate any statement if, on the application of the corporation or any other person who claims to be aggrieved, the court is satisfied that the rights conferred by this section are being abused to secure needless publicity for defamatory matter, and on any such application the court may order the costs of the corporation to be paid in whole or in part by the requisitionists even though they are not parties to the application.

(6) **Where no liability** — A corporation and a director, officer, employee or person acting on its behalf, except a requisitionist, is not liable in damages or otherwise by reason only of the circulation of a notice or statement or both in compliance with this section.

(7) **Duty to deal with requisitioned matter** — Despite anything in the by-laws of the corporation, where the requisitionists have complied with this section, the resolution, if any, mentioned in the requisition shall be dealt with at the meeting to which the requisition relates.

(8) **Repayment of expenses** — The sum deposited under clause (4) (b) shall be repaid to the requisitionists by the corporation unless at the meeting to which the requisition relates the shareholders or members by a majority of the votes cast reject the repayment to the requisitionists.

(9) **Offence** — A director of a corporation who authorizes, permits or acquiesces in any contravention of any requirement of this section is guilty of an offence and on conviction is liable to a fine of not more than $200

**297. Court may direct method of holding meetings** — If for any reason it is impracticable to call a meeting of shareholders or members of the corporation in any manner in which meetings of shareholders or members may be called or to conduct the meeting in the manner prescribed by this Act, the letters patent, supplementary letters patent or by-laws, the court may, on the application of a director or a shareholder or member who would be entitled to vote at the meeting, order a meeting to be called, held and conducted in such manner as the court thinks fit, and any meeting called, held and conducted in accordance with such an order shall for all purposes be deemed to be a meeting of shareholders or members of the corporation duly called, held and conducted.

**298.** (1) **By-laws and resolutions** — Any by-law or resolution signed by all the directors is as valid and effective as if passed at a meeting of the directors duly called, constituted and held for that purpose.

(2) **Idem** — Any resolution signed by all the shareholders or members is as valid and effective as if passed at a meeting of the shareholders or members duly called, constituted and held for that purpose.

(3) **Alternative method of confirming by-laws** — Any by-law passed at any time during a corporation's existence may, in lieu of confirmation at a general meeting, be confirmed in writing by all the shareholders or members entitled to vote at such meeting.

(4) **Evidentiary value of signatures** — Where a by-law or resolution purports to have been passed or confirmed under this section by the signatures of all the directors, shareholders or members, as the case may be, of the corporation, the signatures to such by-law or resolution are admissible in evidence as proof, in the absence of evidence to the contrary, of the signatures of all the directors, shareholders or members, as the case may be, and are admissible in evidence as proof, in the absence of evidence to the contrary, that the signatories to the by-law or resolution were all the directors, shareholders or members, as the case may be, at the date that the by-law or resolution purports so to have been passed or confirmed.

[1998, c. 18, Sch. E, s. 77 (in force March 1, 1999).]

**299.** (1) **Minute books** — A corporation shall cause minutes of all proceedings at meetings of the shareholders or members and of the directors and of any executive committee to be entered in books kept for that purpose.

(2) **Evidence** — Any such minutes, if purporting to be signed by the chair of the meeting at which the proceedings were had or by the chair of the next succeeding meeting, are admissible in evidence as proof, in the absence of evidence to the contrary, of the proceedings.

(3) **Validity** — Where minutes in accordance with this section have been made of the proceedings of a meeting of the shareholders or members or of the directors or any executive committee, then, until the contrary is proved, the meeting shall be deemed to have been duly called, constituted and held and all proceedings had thereat to have been duly had and all appointments of directors, officers or liquidators made thereat shall be deemed to have been duly made.

**300. Documents and registers** — A corporation shall cause the following documents and registers to be kept:

1. A copy of the letters patent and of any supplementary letters patent issued to the corporation and of the memorandum of agreement, if any, or, if incorporated by special Act, a copy of the Act.
2. All by-laws and special resolutions of the corporation.
3. A register of shareholders or members in which are set out the names alphabetically arranged of all persons who are shareholders or members or have been within ten years shareholders or members of the corporation and the address of every such person while a shareholder or member and, in the case of a company, in which are set out also the number and class of shares held by each shareholder and the amounts paid up and remaining unpaid on their respective shares.
4. A register of directors in which are set out the names and addresses of all persons who are or have been directors of the corporation with the several dates on which each became or ceased to be a director.

[2004, c. 19, s. 10]

**301. Documents evidence** — The documents and registers mentioned in sections 41 and 300 are admissible in evidence as proof, in the absence of evidence to the contrary, before and after dissolution of the corporation, of all facts purporting to be stated therein.

**302. Books of account** — A corporation shall cause to be kept proper books of account and accounting records with respect to all financial and other transactions of the corporation and, without derogating from the generality of the foregoing, records of,

    (a) all sums of money received and disbursed by the corporation and the matters with respect to which receipt and disbursement took place;

    (b) all sales and purchases of the corporation;

    (c) the assets and liabilities of the corporation; and

    (d) all other transactions affecting the financial position of the corporation.

**303. Untrue entries** — A director, officer or employee of a corporation who makes or assists in making any entry in the minutes of proceedings mentioned in section 299, in the documents and registers mentioned in sections 41 and 300 or in the books of account or accounting records mentioned in section 302, knowing it to be untrue, is guilty of an offence and on conviction is liable to a fine of not more than $1,000 or to imprisonment for a term of not more than three months, or both.

**304.** (1) **Records to be kept at head office** — The minutes of proceedings mentioned in section 299, the documents and registers mentioned in sections 41 and 300 and the books of account and accounting records mentioned in section 302 shall, during the normal business hours of the corporation, be open to inspection by any director and shall, except as provided in section 43 and in subsections (2) and (3) of this section, be kept at the head office of the corporation.

(2) **Records of account at branch** — A corporation may keep at any place where it carries on business such parts of the accounting records as relate to the

operations and assets and liabilities thereof or to such business of the corporation as was carried on or supervised or accounted for at such place, but there shall be kept at the head office of the corporation or such other place as is authorized under subsection (3) such records as will enable the directors to ascertain quarterly with reasonable accuracy the financial position of the corporation

(3) **Exemption** — A corporation may keep any of the records mentioned in subsection (1) at a place other than the head office of the corporation if the records are available for inspection during regular office hours at the head office by means of a computer terminal or other electronic technology.

(4) **Offence** — A director, officer or employee of a corporation who contravenes subsection (1) is guilty of an offence and on conviction is liable to a fine of not more than $200.

(5) **Rescission of orders made under subs. (3)** — The Minister may by order upon such terms as the Minister sees fit rescind any order made under subsection (3) or any order made by the Lieutenant Governor in Council under a predecessor of that subsection.

[1998, c. 18, Sch. E., s. 78 (in force March 1, 1999).]

**305. (1) Records to be open for inspection** — The minutes of proceedings at meetings of shareholders or members mentioned in section 299 and the documents and registers mentioned in sections 41 and 300, during the normal business hours of the corporation, shall, at the place or places where they are kept, be open to inspection by the shareholders or members and creditors of the corporation or their agents or legal representatives, and any of them may make extracts therefrom.

(2) **Offence** — Every person who refuses to permit a person entitled thereto to inspect such minutes, documents or registers, or to make extracts therefrom, is guilty of an offence and on conviction is liable to a fine of not more than $200.

**306. (1) List of shareholders** — No shareholder or member or creditor or the agent or legal representative of any of them shall make or cause to be made a list of all or any of the shareholders or members of the corporation, unless the person has filed with the corporation or its agent an affidavit of such shareholder, member or creditor in the following form in English or French, and, where the shareholder, member or creditor is a corporation, the affidavit shall be made by the president or other officer authorized by resolution of the board of directors of such corporation:

Form of Affidavit

Province of Ontario In the matter of

County of (Insert name of corporation)

I, ........................ of the ................ of ..................... in the ................................. of ........................................

make oath and say (or affirm):

1.　　I am a shareholder (or member or creditor) of the above-named corporation.

(Where the shareholder, member or creditor is a corporation, indicate office and authority of deponent in paragraph 1.)

2. I am applying to make a list of the shareholders (or members) of the above-named corporation.

3. I require the list of shareholders (or members) only for purposes connected with the above-named corporation.

4. The list of shareholders (or members) and the information contained therein will be used only for purposes connected with the above-named corporation.

Sworn, etc.

(2) **Offence** — Every person, other than a corporation or its agent, who uses a list of all or any of the shareholders or members of the corporation for the purpose of delivering or sending to all or any of such shareholders or members advertising or other printed matter relating to shares or securities, other than the shares or securities of the corporation, or for purposes not connected with the corporation is guilty of an offence and on conviction is liable to a fine of not more than $1,000.

(3) **Purposes connected with the corporation, defined** — Purposes connected with the corporation include any effort to influence the voting of shareholders or members at any meeting of the corporation and include the acquisition or offering of shares to acquire control or to effect an amalgamation or reorganization and any other purpose approved by the Minister.

**307.** (1) **Where list of shareholders to be furnished** — Any person, upon payment of a reasonable charge therefor and upon filing with the corporation or its agent the affidavit referred to in subsection (2), may require a corporation, other than a private company, or its transfer agent to furnish within ten days from the filing of such affidavit a list setting out the names alphabetically arranged of all persons who are shareholders or members of the corporation, the number of shares owned by each such person and the address of each such person as shown on the books of the corporation made up to a date not more than ten days prior to the date of filing the affidavit.

(2) **Affidavit** — The affidavit referred to in subsection (1) shall be made by the applicant and shall be in the following form in English or French:

Form of Affidavit

Province of Ontario In the matter of

County of (Insert name of corporation)

I, ........................ of the ................. of ..................... in the ...................

of .....................................

make oath and say (or affirm):

(Where the applicant is a corporation, indicate office and authority of deponent.)

1. I hereby apply for a list of the shareholders (or members) of the above-named corporation.

2. I require the list of shareholders (or members) only for purposes connected with the above-named corporation.

3.    The list of shareholders (or members) and the information contained therein will be used only for purposes connected with the above-named corporation.

Sworn, etc.

(3) **Idem, where applicant a corporation** — Where the applicant is a corporation, the affidavit shall be made by the president or other officer authorized by resolution of the board of directors of such corporation.

(4) **Offence** — Every person who uses a list of shareholders or members of a corporation obtained under this section,

(a)    for the purpose of delivering or sending to all or any of such shareholders or members advertising or other printed matter relating to shares or securities other than the shares or securities of the corporation; or

(b)    for any purpose not connected with the corporation,

is guilty of an offence and on conviction is liable to a fine of not more than $1,000.

(5) **Offence** — Every corporation or transfer agent that fails to furnish a list in accordance with subsection (1) when so required is guilty of an offence and on conviction is liable to a fine of not more than $1,000, and every director or officer of such corporation or transfer agent who authorized, permitted or acquiesced in such offence is also guilty of an offence and on conviction is liable to a like fine.

(6) **Interpretation** — Purposes connected with the corporation include any effort to influence the voting of shareholders or members at any meeting of the corporation, any offer to acquire shares in the corporation or any effort to effect an amalgamation or reorganization and any other purpose approved by the Minister.

**308. Offence** — Every person who offers for sale or sells or purchases or otherwise traffics in a list or a copy of a list of all or any of the shareholders or members of a corporation is guilty of an offence and on conviction is liable to a fine of not more than $1,000, and, where such person is a corporation, every director or officer of such corporation who authorized, permitted or acquiesced in such offence is also guilty of an offence and on conviction is liable to a like fine.

**309. (1) Power of court to correct** — If the name of a person is, without sufficient cause, entered in or omitted from the minutes of proceedings mentioned in section 299 or from the documents or registers mentioned in sections 41 and 300, or if default is made or unnecessary delay takes place in entering therein the fact of any person having ceased to be a shareholder or member of the corporation, the person or shareholder or member aggrieved, or any shareholder or member of the corporation, or the corporation itself, may apply to the court for an order that the minutes, documents or registers be rectified, and the court may dismiss such application or make an order for the rectification of the minutes, documents or registers, and may direct the corporation to compensate the party aggrieved for any damage the party has sustained.

(2) **Decision as to title** — The court may, in any proceeding under this section, decide any question relating to the entitlement of a person who is a party to such proceeding to have the person's name entered in or omitted from such minutes,

documents or registers, whether such question arises between two or more share-holders or members or alleged shareholders or members, or between any share-holder or member or alleged shareholder or member and the corporation.

(3) **Trial of issue** — The court may direct an issue to be tried.

(4) **Appeal** — An appeal lies from the decision of the court as if it had been given in an action.

(5) **Jurisdiction of courts not affected** — This section does not deprive any court of any jurisdiction it otherwise has.

(6) **Costs** — The costs of any proceeding under this section are in the discretion of the court.

**310.** (1) **Investigations and audits** — Upon an application by the shareholders of a company holding shares representing not less than one-tenth of the issued capital of the company, or upon an application of at least one-tenth of the members of a corporation without share capital, the court may appoint an inspector to investigate the affairs and management of the corporation or may appoint a person to audit its books.

(2) **Evidence** — The application shall be supported by such evidence as the court requires for the purpose of showing that the applicants have good reason for requiring the investigation or audit, as the case may be.

(3) **Security for costs** — The court may require the applicants to give security to cover the probable cost of the investigation or audit and may make rules and prescribe the manner in which and the extent to which the investigation or audit is to be conducted.

(4) **Report on and expense of investigation or audit** — Such inspector or auditor shall report thereon to the court and the expense of the investigation shall, in the discretion of the court, be defrayed by the corporation or by the applicants or partly by the corporation and partly by the applicants.

(5) **Corporation may appoint inspector for same purpose** — A corporation may, by resolution passed at an annual meeting or at a general meeting called for that purpose, appoint an inspector to investigate its affairs and management.

(6) **Powers and duties of inspector** — The inspector appointed under subsection (5) has the same powers and shall perform the same duties as an inspector appointed under subsection (1) and the inspector shall make his or her report in such manner and to such persons as the corporation by resolution directs.

(7) **Production of books and documents** — All officers and agents of the corporation shall produce for the examination of any inspector or auditor appointed under this section all books and records in their custody or power.

(8) **Examination on oath** — Any such inspector or auditor may examine upon oath the officers, agents and employees of the corporation in relation to its affairs and management.

(9) **Offence** — Every officer or agent who refuses to produce any book or record referred to in subsection (7) and every person so examined who refuses to

answer any question relating to the affairs and management of the corporation is guilty of an offence and on conviction is liable to a fine of not more than $200.

(10) **Report admissible in proceedings** — A copy of the report of the inspector or auditor, as the case may be, authenticated by the court or under the seal of the corporation whose affairs and management the inspector or auditor has investigated, is admissible in any legal proceeding as evidence of the opinion of the inspector or auditor in relation to any matter contained in the report.

**311.** (1) **Corporation with fewer than three shareholders or members exercising corporate powers** — If a corporation exercises its corporate powers when its shareholders or members are fewer than three for a period of more than six months after the number has been so reduced, every person who was a shareholder or member of the corporation during the time that it so exercised its corporate powers after such period of six months and is aware of the fact that it so exercised its corporate powers is severally liable for the payment of the whole of the debts of the corporation contracted during such time and may be sued for the debts without the joinder in the action of the corporation or of any other shareholder or member.

(2) **Shareholder or member may avoid liability** — A shareholder or member who has become aware that the corporation is so exercising its corporate powers may serve a protest in writing on the corporation and may by registered letter notify the Minister of such protest having been served and of the facts upon which it is based, and such shareholder or member may thereby and not otherwise, from the date of the protest and notification, exonerate himself, herself or itself from liability.

(3) **Revocation of charter** — If after notice from the Minister the corporation refuses or neglects to bring the number of its shareholders or members up to three, such refusal or neglect may be regarded by the Lieutenant Governor as sufficient cause for the making of an order under subsection 317 (1).

**312.** (1) **Bringing corporations under this Act** — A corporation incorporated otherwise than by letters patent and being at the time of its application a subsisting corporation may apply for letters patent under this Act, and the Lieutenant Governor may issue letters patent continuing it as if it had been incorporated under this Act.

(2) **Change of powers, etc.** — Where a corporation applies for the issue of letters patent under subsection (1), the Lieutenant Governor may, by the letters patent, limit or extend the powers of the corporation, name its directors and change its corporate name, as the applicant desires.

(3) **Transfer of foreign corporations** — A corporation incorporated under the laws of any jurisdiction other than Ontario may, if it appears to the Lieutenant Governor to be thereunto authorized by the laws of the jurisdiction in which it was incorporated, apply to the Lieutenant Governor for letters patent continuing it as if it had been incorporated under this Act, and the Lieutenant Governor may issue such letters patent on application supported by such material as appears satisfactory and such letters patent may be issued on such terms and subject to such

limitations and conditions and contain such provisions as appear to the Lieutenant Governor to be fit and proper.

**313.** (1) **Transfer of Ontario corporations** — A corporation incorporated under the laws of Ontario other than an insurance company may, if authorized by a special resolution, by the Minister and by the laws of any other jurisdiction in Canada, apply to the proper officer of that other jurisdiction for an instrument of continuation continuing the corporation as if it had been incorporated under the laws of that other jurisdiction.

(1.1) **Same, insurance company** — An insurance company incorporated under this Act may, if authorized by special resolution, by the Superintendent of Financial Services appointed under section 5 of the *Financial Services Commission of Ontario Act, 1997* and by the laws of any other jurisdiction in Canada, apply to the proper officer of that other jurisdiction for an instrument of continuation continuing the insurance company as if it had been incorporated under the laws of that other jurisdiction.

(2) **Notice** — The corporation shall file with the Minister a notice of the issue of the instrument of continuation and on and after the date of the filing of such instrument this Act ceases to apply to that corporation.

(3) Repealed: 1999, c. 12, Sch. F, s. 22 (3).

[1999, c. 12, Sch. F, s. 22 (in force March 27, 2000),]

**313.1** (1) **Continuance as co-operative corporation** — A corporation incorporated under this Act may, if authorized by a special resolution and by the Minister, apply under the *Co-operative Corporations Act* to be continued as a co-operative corporation.

(2) **Certificate to be filed with Minister** — The corporation must file with the Minister a copy of the certificate of continuance issued under the *Co-operative Corporations Act* within 60 days after the date of issuance.

(3) **Act ceases to apply** — This Act ceases to apply to the corporation on the date upon which the corporation is continued under the *Co-operative Corporations Act*.

[1994, c. 17, s. 31 (in force June 23, 1994).]

**314. Rights of creditors preserved** — All rights of creditors against the property, rights and assets of a corporation amalgamated under section 113 or continued under section 312, and all liens upon its property, rights and assets are unimpaired by such amalgamation or continuation, and all debts, contracts, liabilities and duties of the corporation thenceforth attach to the amalgamated or continued corporation and may be enforced against it.

**315.** (1) **Forfeiture for non-user** — If a corporation incorporated by letters patent does not go into actual operation within two years after incorporation or for any two consecutive years does not use its corporate powers, the Lieutenant Governor, after having given the corporation such notice as he or she considers proper, may by order declare such powers forfeited, except so far as is necessary for the winding up of the corporation.

(2) **Rights of creditors not affected** — No such forfeiture affects prejudicially the rights of creditors as they exist at the date of the forfeiture.

(3) **Revival** — Where the powers of a corporation have been forfeited under subsection (1) or a predecessor of subsection (1), the Lieutenant Governor on the application of the corporation may by order, on such terms and conditions as he or she sees fit to impose, revive the corporate powers.

**316. Social clubs cause for cancellation** — Despite anything to the contrary in any Act, in any letters patent or in any supplementary letters patent, if it is made to appear to the satisfaction of the Minister that a corporation that has objects in whole or in part of a social nature,

(a)   occupies and uses a house, room or place as a club that, except for paragraph 197 (2) (a) of the *Criminal Code* (Canada), would be a common gaming house as defined in subsection (1) thereof; or

(b)   occupies premises that are equipped, guarded, constructed or operated so as to hinder or prevent lawful access to and inspection by police or fire officers, or are found fitted or provided with any means or contrivance for playing any game of chance or any mixed game of chance and skill, gaming or betting or with any device for concealing, removing or destroying such means or contrivance,

the Lieutenant Governor may make an order under subsection 317 (1).

**317.** (1) **Termination of existence for cause** — Where sufficient cause is shown, the Lieutenant Governor may by order, upon such terms and conditions as he or she considers fit,

(a)   cancel the letters patent of a corporation and declare it to be dissolved on such date as the order may fix;

(b)   declare the corporate existence of a corporation incorporated otherwise than by letters patent to be terminated and the corporation to be dissolved on such date as the order may fix; or

(c)   cancel any supplementary letters patent issued to a corporation.

(2) **Inquiry** — The Minister, under such circumstances and at any time as the Minister in his or her discretion thinks advisable, may authorize any officer of the Ministry of the Minister to conduct an inquiry for the purpose of determining whether or not there is sufficient cause for the making of an order under subsection (1).

(3) **Powers of inquiring officer** — Every officer so authorized has the power to summon any person to appear before him or her as a witness in such inquiry and to require such person to give evidence on oath, touching any matter relevant to the purpose of the inquiry, and to produce such documents and things as such officer considers requisite for that purpose.

(4) **Witnesses** — Every such officer has the same power to enforce the attendance of witnesses and to compel them to give evidence and to produce documents and things as is vested in any court in civil cases.

(5) **Witness may be required to answer** — Section 9 of the *Evidence Act* applies to any witness and to the evidence given by him or her before any such officer in any such inquiry.

(6) **Appeal** — An appeal lies from an order made under subsection (1) to the Divisional Court upon a question of law only.

(7) **Minister to be heard** — The Minister is entitled to be heard, by counsel or otherwise, upon the argument of any such appeal.

(8) **No costs** — No costs are payable by or to any person by reason of or in respect of any such appeal.

(9) **Order for dissolution** — Where it appears that a corporation is in default of a filing requirement under the *Corporations Information Act* and that notice of such default has been sent in accordance with section 324 to the corporation or has been published once in *The Ontario Gazette*, the Lieutenant Governor may by order, after ninety days after the notice has been sent or published,

    (a)    cancel the letters patent of the corporation and declare it to be dissolved on such date as the order may fix; or

    (b)    declare the corporate existence of the corporation, if it was incorporated otherwise than by letters patent, to be terminated and the corporation to be dissolved on such date as the order may fix.

(10) **Revival** — Where a corporation has been dissolved under subsection (9) or any predecessor thereof, the Lieutenant Governor, on the application of any interested person, may in his or her discretion by order, on such terms and conditions as he or she sees fit to impose, revive the corporation, and thereupon the corporation shall, subject to the terms and conditions of the order and to any rights acquired by any person after its dissolution, be restored to its legal position, including all its property, rights, privileges and franchises, and be subject to all its liabilities, contracts, disabilities and debts, as at the date of its dissolution, in the same manner and to the same extent as if it had not been dissolved.

[1993, c. 16, s. 3 (in force March 1, 1995); 1994, c. 27, s. 78 (in force March 1, 1995).]

**318.** (1) **Continuation of existence for particular purpose** — Despite the dissolution of a corporation under this Act,

    (a)    a civil, criminal or administrative action or proceeding commenced by or against the corporation before its dissolution may be continued as if the corporation had not been dissolved;

    (b)    a civil, criminal or administrative action or proceeding may be brought against the corporation as if the corporation had not been dissolved;

    (c)    any property that would have been available to satisfy any judgment or order if the corporation had not been dissolved remains available for such purpose; and

    (d)    title to land belonging to the corporation immediately before its dissolution remains available to be sold in power of sale proceedings.

(2) **Interpretation** — In this section and section 322,

"proceeding" includes a power of sale proceeding relating to land commenced pursuant to a mortgage.

(3) **Service of process** — For the purposes of this section, the service of any process on a corporation after its dissolution shall be deemed to be sufficiently made if it is made upon any person shown on the records of the Ministry as being a director or officer of the corporation immediately before the dissolution.

(4) **Notice of action** — A person who commences an action, suit or proceeding against a corporation after its dissolution, shall serve the writ or other document commencing the action, suit or proceeding, on the Public Guardian and Trustee in accordance with the rules that apply generally to service on a party to an action, suit or proceeding.

(5) **Notice of power of sale proceeding** — A person who commences a power of sale proceeding relating to land against a corporation after its dissolution shall serve a notice of the proceeding on the Public Guardian and Trustee in accordance with the notice requirements in the *Mortgages Act* that apply with respect to a person with an interest in the land recorded in the records of the appropriate land registry office.

[1998, c. 18, Sch. E, s. 79 (in force March 1, 1999).]

**319.** (1) **Surrender of charter** — The charter of a corporation incorporated by letters patent may be surrendered if the corporation proves to the satisfaction of the Lieutenant Governor,

   (a)   that the surrender of its charter has been authorized,

      (i)   by a majority of the votes cast at a meeting of its shareholders or members duly called for that purpose or by such other vote as the letters patent or supplementary letters patent of the corporation provide, or

      (ii)   by the consent in writing of all the shareholders or members entitled to vote at such meeting;

   (b)   that it has parted with its property by distributing it rateably among its shareholders or members according to their rights and interests in the corporation;

   (c)   that it has no debts, obligations or liabilities or its debts, obligations or liabilities have been duly provided for or protected or its creditors or other persons having interests in its debts, obligations or liabilities consent; and

   (d)   that there are no proceedings pending in any court against it.

(2) **Acceptance of surrender and dissolution of corporation** — The Lieutenant Governor, upon due compliance with this section, may by order accept the surrender of the charter and declare the corporation to be dissolved on such date as the order may fix.

(3) **Where shareholder unknown** — When a corporation surrenders its charter and a shareholder or member is unknown or the whereabouts of a shareholder or member is unknown, it may, by agreement with the Public Trustee, deliver or convey the person's share of the property to the Public Trustee to be held in trust for the person, and such delivery or conveyance shall be deemed to be a rateable distribution among the shareholders or members for the purposes of clause (1) (b).

(4) **Where creditor unknown** — When a corporation surrenders its charter and a creditor is unknown or the whereabouts of a creditor is unknown, it may, by agreement with the Public Trustee, pay to the Public Trustee an amount equal to the amount of the debt due to the creditor to be held in trust for the creditor, and such payment shall be deemed to be due protection of the debt for the purposes of clause (1) (c).

(5) **Power to convert** — If the share of the property so delivered or conveyed to the Public Trustee under subsection (3) is in a form other than money, the Public Trustee may at any time, and within ten years after such delivery or conveyance shall, convert it into money.

(6) **Payment to person entitled** — If the share of the property delivered or conveyed under subsection (3) or its equivalent in money, or the amount paid under subsection (4), as the case may be, is claimed by the person beneficially entitled thereto within ten years after it was so delivered, conveyed or paid, it shall be delivered, conveyed or paid to the person, but, if not so claimed, it vests in the Public Trustee for the use of Ontario, and, if the person beneficially entitled thereto at any time thereafter establishes the person's right thereto to the satisfaction of the Lieutenant Governor in Council, an amount equal to the amount so vested in the Public Trustee shall be paid to the person.

(7) **Property now held by Public Trustee** — Where an order has been made before the 30th day of April, 1954, accepting the surrender of the charter of a corporation and the Public Trustee is holding property of the corporation in trust for its shareholders, members or creditors, subsections (5) and (6) apply to the property so held, except that the ten-year period mentioned in subsection (6) commences on the 30th day of April, 1954.

[1994, c. 27, s. 78 (in force March 1, 1995).]

**320. Termination of existence of corporation not incorporated by letters patent** — The corporate existence of a corporation incorporated otherwise than by letters patent may be terminated by order of the Lieutenant Governor upon application therefor by such corporation under like circumstances, in like manner and with like effect as a corporation incorporated by letters patent may surrender its charter.

**321. (1) Liability of shareholders to creditors** — Despite the dissolution of a corporation, the shareholders or members among whom its property has been distributed remain liable to its creditors to the amount received by them respectively upon such distribution, and an action may be brought within one year from the date of such dissolution in a court of competent jurisdiction to enforce such liability.

(2) **Action against one shareholder as representing class** — Where there are numerous shareholders or members, such court may permit an action to be brought against one or more shareholders or members as representatives of the class and, if the plaintiff establishes the plaintiff's claim as creditor, may make an order of reference and add as parties on the reference all such shareholders or members as are found and the referee shall determine the amount that each should

contribute towards the plaintiff's claim and may direct payment of the sums so determined.

**322.** (1) **Forfeiture of undisposed property** — Any property of a corporation that has not been disposed of at the date of its dissolution is immediately on the dissolution forfeit to and vests in the Crown.

(2) **Exception** — Despite subsection (1), if a judgment is given or an order or decision is made or land is sold in an action, suit or proceeding commenced in accordance with section 318 and the judgment, order, decision or sale affects property belonging to the corporation before its dissolution, unless the plaintiff, applicant or mortgagee has not complied with subsection 318 (4) or (5),

    (a)    the property shall be available to satisfy the judgment, order or other decision; and

    (b)    title to the land shall be transferred to a purchaser free of the Crown's interest, in the case of a power of sale proceeding.

(3) **No notice** — Despite clause (2) (b), a person who commences a power of sale proceeding relating to land before the dissolution of a corporation but the sale of the land was not completed until after the dissolution, is not required to serve the notice mentioned in subsection 318 (5) and title to the land may be transferred to a purchaser free of the Crown's interest.

[1998, c. 18, Sch. E, s. 80 (in force March 1, 1999).]

**323. Evidence of by-laws** — A copy of any by-law of a corporation under its seal and purporting to be signed by an officer of the corporation, or a certificate similarly authenticated to the effect that a person is a shareholder or member of the corporation and that dues or other sums payable are due and have not been paid, or that a call or assessment that has been made is due and has not been paid, shall be received in all courts as proof, in the absence of evidence to the contrary, of the by-law or of the statements contained in such certificate.

**324.** (1) **Service of notice** — Subject to the letters patent, supplementary letters patent or by-laws, a notice or demand to be served or made by a corporation upon a shareholder or member may be served or made personally or sent by registered letter addressed to the shareholder or member at the person's last address as shown on the books of the corporation.

(2) **Time of service** — Subject to the letters patent, supplementary letters patent or by-laws, a notice or other document served by mail by a corporation on a shareholder or member shall be deemed to be served at the time when it would be delivered in the ordinary course of mail.

(3) **Delivery of notices, etc.** — A notice or other document that is required or permitted by this Act or the regulations to be sent by the Lieutenant Governor or the Minister may be sent by ordinary mail or by any method, including registered mail, certified mail or prepaid courier, where there is a record by the person who has delivered it that the notice or document has been sent.

(4) **Same** — A notice or other document referred to in subsection (3) may be sent by telephone transmission of a facsimile of the notice or other document or

by another form of electronic transmission where there is a record that the notice or other document has been sent.

(5) **Deemed delivery** — A notice or other document sent by mail by the Lieutenant Governor or Minister shall be deemed to have been received by the intended recipient on the earlier of,

(a) the day the intended recipient actually receives it; or

(b) the fifth business day after the day it is mailed.

(6) **Same** — A notice or other document sent by a method referred to in subsection (4) shall be deemed to have been received by the intended recipient on the earlier of,

(a) the day the intended recipient actually receives it; or

(b) the first business day after the day the transmission is sent by the Lieutenant Governor or Minister.

[1994, c. 27, s. 78 (in force March 1, 1995).]

**325. Proof of matters under this Act** — Proof of any matter that is necessary to be made under this Act may be made by certificate.

**326. Reciprocal insurance** — A corporation that insures property with or insures the property of other persons, where such insurance is reciprocal and for protection only and not for profit, shall not be deemed to be an insurer or an insurance corporation within the meaning of this Act.

**326.1 (1) Powers of Minister** — The Minister may make regulations prescribing the form and content of letters patent, supplementary letters patent, or other documents or notices that this Act requires to be filed.

(2) **Fees** — The Minister may by order require the payment of fees and approve the amount of the fees to be paid under this Act for,

(a) the filing of letters patent, supplementary letters patent and other documents or other services; and

(b) search reports, copies of documents and information, or other services.

[1998, c. 18, Sch. E, s. 81 (in force March 1, 1999).]

**327. Regulations** — The Lieutenant Governor in Council may make regulations,

(a) Repealed: 1998, c. 18, Sch. E, s. 82.

Note: Despite the repeal of clause (a) (1998, c. 18, Sch. E, subs. 82 (1)), regulations made under clause (a), as that clause read immediately before March 1, 1999, continue until the Minister makes an order under subsection 326.1 (2), as enacted by s. 81, that is inconsistent with those regulations.

Note: Despite the repeal of clause (a) (1998, c. 18, Sch. E, subs. 82 (1), the Lieutenant Governor in Council may by regulation revoke regulations made under clause (a), as that clause read immediately before March 1, 1999, if the Minister makes an order under subs. 326.1 (2), as enacted by s. 81, that is inconsistent with those regulations.

(b) respecting any matter that the Lieutenant Governor in Council considers requisite for carrying out the objects of this Act, and, without limiting the generality of the foregoing, respecting names of corporations or classes thereof, objects of corporations, authorized capital of companies, the preferences, rights, conditions, restrictions, limitations or prohibitions attaching to shares or classes of shares of companies, or any other matter pertaining to letters patent, supplementary letters patent or orders or the applications therefor.

[1998, c. 18, Sch. E, s. 82 (in force March 1, 1999).]

**328. Fees to be paid in advance** — No letters patent and no supplementary letters patent shall be issued and no order shall be made and no document shall be accepted for filing under this Act until all fees therefor have been paid.

**329. Appeal** — An appeal lies to the Divisional Court from any order made by a court under this Act.

**330.** (1) **Untrue statements** — Every person who makes or assists in making a statement in any return, certificate, financial statement or other document required by or for the purposes of this Act or the regulations made under this Act, knowing it to be untrue, is guilty of an offence and on conviction is liable to a fine of not more than $1,000 or to imprisonment for a term of not more than three months, or to both.

(2) **Limitation of action** — No prosecution under subsection (1) shall be commenced more than one year after the facts upon which the prosecution is based first came to the personal knowledge of the Minister or Deputy Minister.

**331. General penalty** — Every corporation that, and every person who, being a director or officer of the corporation, or acting on its behalf, commits any act contrary to this Act, or fails or neglects to comply with any such provision, is guilty of an offence and on conviction, if no penalty for such act, failure or neglect is expressly provided by this Act, is liable to a fine of not more than $200.

**332. Aggrieved shareholders** — Where a shareholder or member or creditor of a corporation is aggrieved by the failure of the corporation or a director, officer or employee of the corporation to perform any duty imposed by this Act, the shareholder, member or creditor, despite the imposition of any penalty and in addition to any other rights that he, she or it may have, may apply to the court for an order directing the corporation, director, officer or employee, as the case may be, to perform such duty, and upon such application the court may make such order or such other order as the court thinks fit.

**333.** (1) **Order for compliance** — Where it appears to the Commission that any person or company to which section 73, subsection 85 (1) or subsection 86 (1) applies has failed to comply with or is contravening any such provision, despite the imposition of any penalty in respect of such non-compliance or contravention, the Commission may apply to the court for an order directing such person or company to comply with such provision or for an order restraining such person or company from contravening such provision, and upon the application, the court may make such order or such other order as the court thinks fit.

(2) **Appeal** — An appeal lies to the Divisional Court from an order made under subsection (1).

# GENERAL

(R.R.O. 1990, Reg. 181)

## NAMES

**1.** (1) The following documents shall accompany any application for letters patent, supplementary letters patent, an extra-provincial licence or an amended extra-provincial licence containing a proposed name for a corporation or a change of corporate name:

1. An original Ontario biased or weighted computer printed search report for the same name as the proposed name from the new updated automated name search system (NUANS) owned by the Department of Consumer and Corporate Affairs, Canada, dated not more than ninety days before the submission of the application.

2. Any consent or consent and undertaking required by the Act or by the Minister.

[O. Reg. 638/94, s. 1.]

(2) A computer printed search report referred to in subsection (1) shall accompany an application for revival under section 317 of the Act if the application changes the name of the corporation or at least ten years have elapsed since the corporation was dissolved.

[O. Reg. 402/95, s. 1; O. Reg. 248/05]

(3) The computer printed search report referred to in subsection (1) is not required where the application is for letters patent, supplementary letters patent, reservation of a name or revival for a corporation incorporated under Part III of the Act if incorporation is required by a government authority as a condition to the awarding of financial assistance under a government program.

[O. Reg. 625/93, s. 1 (2).]

**2.** (1) [Repealed, O. Reg. 625/93, s. 2 (1).]

(2) No name that is identified in a computer printed search report as proposed in Ontario shall be used as a corporate name by a person other than the one who proposed the name unless a consent in writing has been obtained from the person who first proposed the name.

[O. Reg. 625/93, s. 2 (2).]

**3.** (1) The following words and expressions shall not be used in a corporate name:

1. "Amalgamated", "fusionné" or any other related word or expression in French, unless the corporation is an amalgamated corporation resulting from the amalgamation of two or more corporations.

2. [Repealed, O. Reg. 625/93, s. 3 (2).]

3.   "College", "collège", "institute", "institut", "university" or "université", except with a consent in writing on behalf of the Ministry of Education and Training.

4.   "Engineer", "ingénieur", "engineering", "génie" or "ingénierie" or any variation thereof, except with the consent in writing of the Association of Professional Engineers of Ontario

5.   [Repealed, O. Reg. 248/05]

6.   "Royal", where used as an adjective, unless the consent of the Crown has been obtained through the Secretary of State.

7.   Numerals indicating the year of incorporation, unless the proposed corporation is the successor to a corporation the name of which is the same as or similar to the proposed corporation, or the year is the year of amalgamation of the corporation.

8.   Any word or expression that would lead to an inference that the corporation is a business corporation.

[O. Reg. 625/93, s. 3 (1-3) O. Reg. 248/05]

(2) The name of a fraternal society incorporated under section 176 of the Act shall include the words "fraternal society" or "société fraternelle".

[O. Reg. 625/93, s. 3 (4).]

(3) The name of a pension fund or employees' mutual benefit society incorporated under section 185 of the Act shall include the words "pension fund society", "employees' mutual benefit society", "caisse de retraite" or "société de secours mutuel d'employés", as the case may be, and the name in whole or in part of the parent corporation.

[O. Reg. 625/93, s. 3 (4).]

(4) If the name of a corporation includes the word "veteran", "ancien combattant" or any abbreviation or derivation of those words, the letters patent of the corporation shall provide that at all times at least 95 per cent of the members of the corporation shall be composed of war veterans, their spouses or children, unless the name has been in continuous use for at least 20 years.

[O. Reg. 43/00, s. 1 (1); O. Reg. 301/05]

(5) In subsection (4),

"spouse" means,

(a)   a spouse as defined in section 1 of the *Family Law Act*, or

(b)   either of two persons who live together in a conjugal relationship outside marriage;

"war veteran" means a person who served in the armed forces of any country while that country was in a state of war.

[O. Reg. 43/00, s. 1 (2); O. Reg. 301/05]

**4.** The name of a corporation formed by the amalgamation of two or more corporations may be the same as the name of one of the amalgamating corporations, if the name is not a number name.

[O. Reg. 625/93, s. 4.]

**5.** Unless the proposed corporate name has been in continuous use for at least twenty years before the date of filing the application, or unless the proposed corporate name has through use acquired a meaning that renders the name distinctive, a corporate name shall not be,

(a)   too general;

(b)   primarily or only a given name or surname used alone of an individual who is living or has died within thirty years preceding the date of filing an application for letters patent or supplementary letters containing the name;

(c)   primarily or only a geographic name used alone.

**6.** (1) A corporate name shall not contain a word or expression, an element of which is the family name of a particular individual, who is living or who has died within the previous thirty years whether or not preceded by a given name or initials, unless the individual, his or her heir, executor, administrator, assigns or guardian consents in writing to the use of the name.

(2) Subsection (1) does not apply where the corporation that will use the proposed name is the successor or affiliate of another corporation that has, as an element of its name, the family name, if,

(a)   the other corporation consents in writing to the use of the name; and

(b)   where the proposed name would contravene clause 13 (1) (a) of the Act, the other corporation undertakes in writing to dissolve itself or to change its name to a name that complies with clause 13 (1) (a) of the Act within six months after the incorporation of the new corporation.

(3) Subsection (1) does not apply where,

(a)   the required consent cannot be obtained; and

(b)   the family name is of historic or patriotic significance and has a connection with the objects of the corporation.

**7.** A corporate name shall not contain any word or expression in any language that describes in a misleading manner the activities or services in association with which the corporate name is proposed to be used.

**8.** (1) Only letters from the Roman alphabet or Arabic numerals or a combination thereof, and punctuation marks and other marks set out in subsection (2), may form part of the name of a corporation.

(2) The following punctuation marks and other marks are permitted as part of a corporation name:

! " " « » # $ % & ' ( ) * + , - . / \ : ; < = > ? [ ] ' □ _ _ ， ´ ` ^ ¨ @

[O. Reg. 625/93, s. 5; O. Reg. 248/05]

(3) A corporate name shall not consist only or primarily of a combination of marks set out in subsection (2) and at least the first three characters of the corporate name shall be letters from the Roman alphabet or Arabic numerals or a combination thereof.

**9.** (1) The name of a corporation shall not exceed 120 characters in length, including punctuation marks and spaces.

(2) The name of a corporation shall be set out in an application filed under the Act in block capital letters and with only one space between each word.

[O. Reg. 248/05]

## CAPITAL

**10.** Where preference shares of a class have attached thereto conditions, restrictions, limitations or prohibitions on the right to vote, the preferences, rights, conditions, restrictions, limitations or prohibitions attaching to that class of preference shares shall provide that the holders of that class are entitled to notice of any meeting of shareholders called for the purpose of authorizing the dissolution of the company or the sale of its undertaking or a substantial part thereof.

## OBJECTS

**11.** [Repealed, O. Reg. 625/93, s. 6.]

**12.** (1) Where the proposed objects of a corporation include horse racing, the application for letters patent or supplementary letters patent shall be accompanied by the consent in writing of the Ontario Racing Commission.

(2) The proposed objects of a corporation shall not include dog racing, but may include the breeding of racing dogs.

## MISCELLANEOUS

**13.** Where the letters patent or supplementary letters patent of a corporation provide that the directors of the corporation shall be elected for a term of more than one year, the term shall be an integral number of years, not exceeding five.

**14.** The letters patent or supplementary letters patent of a private company may provide that an application for an order accepting the surrender of the charter of the company may be authorized at a general meeting of its shareholders duly called for that purpose by a majority of the votes cast at the meeting or by at least 50 per cent of the votes of all shareholders entitled to vote at the meeting.

**15.** (1) [Repealed, O. Reg. 192/99, s. 1 (1).]

(2) A notice of resolution requiring the voluntary winding up of a corporation required to be filed with the Minister under subsection 231 (1) of the Act shall be signed manually by a director or officer of the corporation or by the liquidator.

(3) A notice required to be filed by a liquidator with the Minister under subsection 266 (2) of the Act shall be signed manually by the liquidator.

(4) [Repealed, O. Reg. 192/99, s. 1 (2).]

(5) A notice signed by an agent or attorney on behalf of a director or officer of a corporation or a liquidator is not a notice signed manually by the director, officer or liquidator.

## FORM OF DOCUMENTS

**16.** (1) All documents delivered to or filed with the Minister including all affidavits, applications, assurances, balance sheets, by-laws, consents, dissents, notices and statements shall be printed, typewritten or reproduced legibly, in a manner suitable for photographing on microfilm, on one side of good quality white paper that is,

    (a)   210 millimetres by 297 millimetres with a margin of 30 millimetres on the left-hand side; or

    (b)   8½ inches by 11 inches, with a margin of 1¼ inches on the left-hand side.

(2) A document consisting of two or more pages shall have no backing or binding and shall be stapled in the upper left-hand corner and each page shall be numbered consecutively.

(3) Where a form is provided by the Minister, the form or a facsimile of the form reproduced on good quality white paper of the size set out in subsection (1) shall be used.

**16.1** If a corporation has a seal, it may set out the seal on any form prescribed by this Regulation.

[O. Reg. 189/99, s. 1.]

## FORMS

**17.** [Repealed, O. Reg. 248/05]

**18.** [Repealed, O. Reg. 248/05]

**19.** (1) [Repealed, O. Reg. 248/05]

(2) Where an application for supplementary letters patent is made under clause 34 (1) (b) of the Act or under clause 131 (1) (b) of the Act, the application shall contain a statement that the corporation is not insolvent within the meaning of subsection (4).

(3) Where the application is one to which section 35 of the Act applies, the application shall contain a statement that the corporation is not insolvent and, after the issue of the supplementary letters patent, will not be insolvent within the meaning of subsection (4).

(4) For the purposes of this section, a corporation is insolvent if its liabilities exceed the realizable value of its assets or if the corporation is unable to pay its debts as they become due.

**20.** [Repealed, O. Reg. 402/95, s. 2.]

**21.** [Repealed, O. Reg. 192/99, s. 2.]

**22.** [Repealed, O. Reg. 248/05]

**23.** (1) An application for an order accepting the surrender of a charter of a corporation under subsection 319 (1) of the Act or for an order terminating the existence of a corporation under section 320 of the Act shall be accompanied by,

    (a)   in the case of a company, a consent from the Corporations Tax Branch of the Ministry of Finance; and

    (b)   in the case of a company that is a reporting issuer under the *Securities Act*, a consent from the Ontario Securities Commission.

(2) [Repealed, O. Reg. 248/05]

(3) Where a shareholder or member is unknown or the shareholder's or member's whereabouts is unknown and the corporation has delivered or conveyed the shareholder's or member's share of the property to the Public Guardian and Trustee to be held in trust for the shareholder or member or where a creditor is unknown or his, her or its whereabouts is unknown and the corporation has paid to the Public Guardian and Trustee an amount equal to the amount of the debt due to the creditor to be held in trust for the creditor, the application shall set out a statement to that effect.

[O. Reg. 248/05]

**24.** The Minister may require that an application for an order to revive a dissolved corporation under subsection 317 (10) of the Act be accompanied by,

    (a)   a statement in writing by the Public Guardian and Trustee that he or she has no objection to the revival of the corporation; and

    (b)   in the case of a company, a consent from the Corporations Tax Branch of the Ministry of Finance to the revival of the corporation.

[O. Reg. 638/94, s. 2; O. Reg. 248/05]

**25.** [Repealed, O. Reg. 248/05]

## CONTINUATION

**26.** [Repealed, O. Reg. 248/05]

**27.** (1) An application for authorization to transfer to another jurisdiction under section 313 of the Act shall be in Form 13 in duplicate.

(2) Except in the case of continuance under the laws of another Canadian jurisdiction, the application for authorization to be continued as a corporation under the laws of another jurisdiction shall be accompanied by a legal opinion stating that the laws of the other jurisdiction provide that,

    (a)   the corporation's property continues as its property;

    (b)   the corporation continues to be liable for its obligations;

    (c)   an existing cause of action, claim or liability to prosecution is unaffected;

    (d)   the corporation may continue to prosecute a civil, criminal or administrative action or proceeding being prosecuted by or against it;

(e)  a conviction, ruling, order or judgment against the corporation may be enforced against it and a ruling, order or judgment in favour of the corporation may be enforced by it.

[Reg. 177/94, s. 3; O. Reg. 189/99, s. 2.]

**27.1** [Repealed, O. Reg. 248/05]

## INSIDER REPORTING

**28.** A report required to be filed by an insider under subsections 73 (1) and (2) of the Act shall be prepared in accordance with Form 14.

**29.** A report of subsequent changes required to be filed by an insider under subsection 73 (3) of the Act shall be prepared in accordance with Form 15.

## INFORMATION CIRCULAR

**30.** (1) An information circular shall be prepared in accordance with Form 16.

(2) The information required by Form 16 shall be given as of a date specified in the circular, which date shall be a date occurring not more than thirty days before the date on which the information circular is first sent to any shareholders of the corporation.

(3) The information contained in an information circular shall be clearly presented and the statements contained therein shall be divided into groups according to subject-matter and each group of statements shall be preceded by an appropriate heading.

(4) The order of items set out in Form 16 need not be followed.

(5) Where practicable and appropriate, the information required by Form 16 shall be presented in tabular form.

(6) All amounts required by Form 16 shall be stated in figures.

(7) Information required to be set out under more than one item in Form 16 need only be set out under one of the items.

(8) No statement need be made in an information circular that an item is inapplicable and answers to items that are inapplicable may be omitted.

(9) Information that is not known by or is unavailable to the person on whose behalf an information circular is prepared and that is not reasonably within the power of that person to ascertain or obtain may be omitted from the information circular if a brief statement is made in the information circular indicating the reasons why the information is not known or is unavailable.

(10) An information circular prepared for a meeting need not contain any information contained in any other information circular, notice of meeting or form of proxy sent to a person whose proxies are being solicited for the same meeting if reference is made in the information circular to the document that contains the information.

**31.** Every person who sends or delivers to shareholders an information circular or proxy to which sections 83 to 89 of the Act apply in respect of a meeting of shareholders of a company shall forthwith file with the Ontario Securities Commission a copy of the information circular, proxy and all other material sent or delivered by the person in connection with the meeting.

## BENEFICIAL OWNERSHIP OF SHARES

**32.** (1) For the purposes of section 73 of the Act, a report filed by a company that includes a statement of capital securities beneficially owned or deemed to be beneficially owned by a subsidiary of the company under clause 72 (2) (c) of the Act or that includes a statement of changes in the subsidiary's beneficial ownership of capital securities shall be deemed to be a report filed by the subsidiary and the subsidiary need not file a separate report.

(2) For the purposes of section 73 of the Act, a report filed by an individual that includes a statement of capital securities beneficially owned or deemed to be beneficially owned under clause 72 (2) (b) of the Act by a company controlled by the individual or by an affiliate, if any, of the controlled company or that includes a statement of changes in the beneficial ownership of the capital securities of the controlled company or affiliate shall be deemed to be a report filed by the controlled company or by the affiliate and the controlled company and the affiliate need not file a separate report.

## SEARCHES

**33.** If a required fee is paid for a search requested in person, the Minister may produce for examination the original documents on file, if any, in which case no microfiche or microfiche copy of the documents will be supplied.

[O. Reg. 192/99, s. 3.]

# CORPORATIONS TAX ACT

(R.S.O. 1990, c. C.40)

[**Note:** Only sections pertaining to Charities are reproduced.]

## Part I — General

*Liability for Taxes*

**2.** (1) **Taxes payable** — Every corporation that is incorporated under the laws of Canada or a province thereof and that has a permanent establishment in Ontario shall for every taxation year of the corporation pay to Her Majesty for the uses of Ontario the taxes imposed by this Act at the time and in the manner provided in this Act.

(2) **Idem** — Every corporation that is incorporated under the laws of a jurisdiction outside Canada and that at any time in the taxation year or a previous taxation year,

    (a)   had a permanent establishment in Ontario within the meaning of section 4; or

    (b)   owned real property, timber resource property or a timber limit in Ontario the income from which arose from the sale or rental thereof or is a royalty or timber royalty; or

    (c)   disposed of taxable Canadian property, within the meaning given to that expression by subsection 248 (1) of the *Income Tax Act* (Canada) if the reference in that definition to section 2 of that Act were a reference to this section, that was property situated in Ontario as prescribed by regulation,

shall for every taxation year of the corporation pay to Her Majesty for the uses of Ontario the taxes imposed by this Act at the time and in the manner provided in this Act.

[2004, c. 16, s. 2.]

. . .

## Part II — Income Tax

### DIVISION C — COMPUTATION OF TAXABLE INCOME

**34.** (1) *Income Tax Act* **(Canada), Part I (C), applicable** — Except as hereinafter in this Division provided, in computing the taxable income of a corporation for a taxation year, Division C of Part I of the *Income Tax Act* (Canada) is applicable for the purposes of this Act in so far as the said Division applies to additions and deductions permitted to corporations.

(1.1) **Gifts to Her Majesty in right of Ontario** — The amount of a deduction for a taxation year under subsection 110.1 (1) of the *Income Tax Act* (Canada) in respect of gifts made to Her Majesty in right of Ontario, to a Crown agency within the meaning of the *Crown Agency Act* or to a foundation established under the *Crown Foundations Act, 1996* is the lesser of "A" and "B",

where,

"A"   is the amount by which the income of the corporation for the taxation year exceeds the total of all other amounts, if any, deducted by the corporation under this Act for the taxation year,

(a)   under paragraph 110.1 (1) (b) of the *Income Tax Act* (Canada), as it applies for the purposes of this Act in respect of gifts to Her Majesty in right of Canada or to a province other than Ontario, or

(b)   under paragraph 110.1 (1) (A) of the *Income Tax Act* (Canada) as it applies for the purposes of this Act in respect of other gifts, and

"B"   is the amount that is the lesser of,

(a)   the income of the corporation for the taxation year, and

(b)   the amount of gifts made in the taxation year or in any of the five preceding taxation years to Her Majesty in right of Ontario, a Crown agency within the meaning of the *Crown Agency Act* or a foundation established under the *Crown Foundations Act, 1996* that was not deducted in the year or in a previous taxation year.

(2) **Receipts for gifts to charities, etc.** — In the application of subsections 110.1 (2) and (3) of the *Income Tax Act* (Canada) for the purposes of this Act, a "receipt" includes a photostatic reproduction of the receipt.

(3) **Interpretation** — In the application of the definition of "registered Canadian amateur athletic association" and "registered charity" in subsection 248 (1) of the *Income Tax Act* (Canada) for the purposes of this Act, the references therein to "Minister" shall be read as references to the Minister of National Revenue.

[1998, c. 34, s. 36; 2004, c. 16, s. 2]

. . .

# DIVISION F — SPECIAL RULES APPLICABLE IN CERTAIN CIRCUMSTANCES

**44.1 (1) Rules applicable to specified tax credits** — Despite any other provision of this Act, a corporation that is exempt from tax under this Act for a taxation year by virtue of section 57 shall not deduct or claim an amount in respect of a specified tax credit under this Act for the taxation year.

[1996, c. 24, s. 27; 2004, c. 16, s. 2.]

. . .

**56. Application of *Income Tax Act* (Canada) s. 143** — Section 143 of the *Income Tax Act* (Canada) is, in so far as it applies to corporations, applicable for the purposes of this Act.

[2004, c. 16, s. 2.]

DIVISION G — EXEMPTIONS

**57. (1) Exemptions** — Except as hereinafter provided, no tax is payable under this Part upon the taxable income of a corporation for a period when that corporation was,

(a)    **Charities and other corporations** — a corporation referred to in any of paragraphs 149 (1) (c), (d), (d.1), (d.2), (d.3), (d.4), (d.5), (d.6), (e), (f), (h.1), (i), (j), (k), (m), (n), (o.1), (o.2), (o.3) and (t) of the *Income Tax Act* (Canada); or

(b)    **Non-profit organizations** — a club, society or association that, in the opinion of the Minister, was not a charity within the meaning given to that expression by subsection 149.1 (1) of the *Income Tax Act* (Canada) and that was organized and operated exclusively for social welfare, civic improvement, pleasure or recreation or for any other purpose except profit, which has not in the taxation year or in any previous taxation year distributed any part of its income to any proprietor, member or shareholder thereof, or appropriated any of its funds or property in any manner whatever to or for the benefit of any proprietor, member or shareholder thereof, unless the proprietor, member or shareholder was a club, society or association, the primary purpose and function of which was the promotion of amateur athletics in Canada.

**(2) Tax payable where distribution made to members or shareholders** — Where a corporation described in clause (1) (b),

(a)    has in the taxation year distributed any part of its income or distributed or otherwise appropriated any of its funds or property in any manner whatever to or for the benefit of any proprietor, member or shareholder thereof, such corporation shall be liable to the taxes imposed under this Act for the taxation year in which the distribution is made and for subsequent taxation years, and in computing its income for the taxation year in which the distribution is made, it shall include the aggregate of its income of all previous taxation years; or

(b)    has distributed any of its income or distributed or otherwise appropriated any of its funds or property in any manner whatever to or for the benefit of any proprietor, member or shareholder thereof on the winding up or discontinuance of its business, the corporation shall be deemed to have received income in that taxation year equal to the amount, if any, by which the amount of the funds and the value of the property distributed or appropriated, as the case may be, exceeds the aggregate of,

     (i)    amounts paid in by proprietors, members or shareholders on account of capital, and

393

    (ii)   that part of the corporation's surplus that is attributed to income that was exempt under this section other than taxable capital gains,
and the corporation shall be liable for the taxes imposed under this Act for the taxation year in which the distribution is made.

(3) **Income not to include taxable capital gains** — For the purposes of clause (1) (b), in computing the part, if any, of any income that was distributed or otherwise appropriated for the benefit of any person, the amount of such income shall be deemed to be the amount thereof otherwise determined less the amount of any taxable capital gains included therein.

(4) **Application of rules in *Income Tax Act* (Canada), s. 149** — The rules in subsections 149 (1.1), (1.2), (1.3), (2), (3), (4), (4.1), (4.2), (4.3), (6), (8), (9), (10) and (11) of the *Income Tax Act* (Canada) apply for the purposes of this section.

(5) **Idem** — In the application of paragraph 149 (1) (t) and subsection 149 (4.1) of the *Income Tax Act* (Canada), references to the Superintendent of Financial Institutions shall be read as references to the Superintendent of Financial Institutions for Canada.

(6) **Idem** — In the application of subsection 149 (2) of the *Income Tax Act* (Canada) for the purposes of this Act, the said subsection shall be read without the reference therein to paragraph (l).

(6.1) **Idem** — In the application of subsection 149 (4.3) of the *Income Tax Act* (Canada) for the purposes of this Act, the reference to "this Part" shall be read as a reference to Part II of this Act and the reference to paragraph 20 (1) (a) of that Act shall be read as a reference to clause 11 (10) (a) of this Act.

(7) **Application of *Income Tax Act* (Canada), subs. 149 (10)** — In the application of subsection 149 (10) of the *Income Tax Act* (Canada) for the purposes of this Act, the reference to "this Part" shall be read as a reference to Part II of this Act.

[1994, c. 14, s. 20; 1998, c. 34, s. 47; 1999, c. 9, s. 83; 2004, c. 16, s. 2]

. . .

# Part II.1 — Corporate Minimum Tax

**57.11 Exemption** — No tax is payable under this Part by a corporation for a taxation year if,

    (a)   no tax under Part II is payable by the corporation for the taxation year by reason of section 57;

. . .

# Part III — Capital Tax

## DIVISION D — COMPUTATION OF CAPITAL TAX PAYABLE

**71.** (1) **Liability for tax under this Part** — Except as provided in subsections (3), 11 (15) and 66 (6), none of the following corporations are required to pay any tax otherwise payable under this Part:

1.    A corporation referred to in subsection 57 (1), other than a corporation subject to the rules in subsection 149 (10) of the *Income Tax Act* (Canada) as made applicable by subsection 57 (7) of this Act.

. . .

**73. Part-year exemption** — Where the exemption under section 57 applies to a part of a taxation year only, subsection 71 (1) does not apply, and in any such case the tax otherwise payable under this Part shall be in the proportion thereof that the number of days of the taxation year for which the exemption under subsection 57 (1) does not apply bears to 365. R.S.O. 1990, c. C.40, s. 73; 1999, c. 9, s. 94 (1); 2004, c. 16, s. 2 (2).

. . .

# Part V — Returns, Payments, Assessments and Appeals

## DIVISION A — RETURNS

**75.** (1) **Tax return** — Every corporation, other than a corporation which is exempt from tax under sections 57 and 71, shall deliver a return for each taxation year to the Minister on or before the last day of the sixth month after the end of the taxation year.

[1994, c. 14, s. 33; 2004, c. 16, s. 2.]

# SMALL BUSINESS INVESTMENT TAX CREDIT FOR BANKS

(O. Reg. 318/97)

## Part II — Investments Through a Small Business Investment Fund

*Interpretation*

**11.** (1) In this Part,

"small business investment fund" means a corporation, fund, association or similar organization that satisfies the following conditions:

1.  The primary objective and activity of the corporation, fund, association or organization is the investment of capital in small businesses carried on in Ontario.
2.  The corporation, fund, association or organization carries out its activities or business through a permanent establishment in Ontario.
3.  All or substantially all of the investments made by the corporation, fund, association or organization are eligible investments in qualifying small business corporations or qualifying small businesses that satisfy the following conditions:
    i.   Neither the total assets nor the gross revenue of the qualifying small business corporation or qualifying small business exceeds $5,000,000.
    ii.  If the qualifying small business corporation or qualifying small business is a member of a corporate group or associated group, neither the total assets nor the gross revenue of the group exceeds $5,000,000.

(2) Despite subsection (1), a corporation, fund, association or organization is not a small business investment fund if it is a registered charity.

# DONATION OF FOOD ACT, 1994

## (S.O. 1994, CHAPTER 19)

**1.** (1) **Liability of donor** — A person who donates food or who distributes donated food to another person is not liable for damages resulting from injuries or death caused by the consumption of the food unless,

(a) the food was adulterated, rotten or otherwise unfit for human consumption; and

(b) in donating or distributing the food, the person intended to injure or to cause the death of the recipient of the food or acted with reckless disregard for the safety of others.

(2) **Liability of director, agent, etc.** — The director, agent, employee or volunteer of a corporation that donates food or that distributes donated food is not personally liable for any damages resulting from injuries or death caused by the consumption of the food unless,

(a) the food was adulterated, rotten or otherwise unfit for human consumption; and

(b) in donating or distributing the food, the director, agent, employee or volunteer,

(i) did not act in good faith,

(ii) acted beyond the scope of his or her role as director, agent, employee or volunteer, and

(iii) intended to injure or to cause the death of the recipient of the food or acted with reckless disregard for the safety of others.

**2. Non-application** — This Act does not apply to a person who distributes donated food for profit.

**3. Commencement** — This Act comes into force on the day it receives Royal Assent.

**4. Short title** — The short title of this Act is the *Donation of Food Act, 1994.*

# EDUCATION ACT

(R.S.O. 1990, c. E.2)

## Part IX — Finance

### DIVISION A — GENERAL

*Miscellaneous*

**257.2.1** (1) **Tax relief, etc., in unorganized territory** — The Minister of Finance may make regulations to limit the changes in taxes for school purposes from the taxes for school purposes in 1997 or to give relief from taxes for school purposes in territory without municipal organization.

(1.1) **Limiting changes in taxes** — The Minister of Finance may make regulations to limit the changes in taxes for school purposes from the taxes for school purposes in 2000 or in any subsequent year or to give relief from taxes for school purposes in territory without municipal organization.

(2) **Exception** — This section does not apply with respect to territory without municipal organization that is deemed to be attached to a municipality for the purposes of taxation.

(3) **What regulations can provide for, etc.** — The following apply with respect to regulations under subsections (1) and (1.1):

1.  Without limiting what a regulation may provide for, the regulations may provide for any matter provided under sections 318, 319, 361, 362 and 367 and Part IX of the *Municipal Act, 2001*.

2.  A regulation may require rebates to be paid by boards.

3.  A regulation made in 2001 or a later year may relate to the entire year in which it is made.

4.  A regulation may delegate anything to boards or other persons or bodies and may attach conditions to such delegations.

5.  A regulation may be general or specific in its application.

[**Note:** The amendments made by S.O. 1998, c. 33 apply, except where the context otherwise requires, with respect to the entire 1998 taxation year not just that portion of it that follows December 18, 1998.]

(4) **Conflicts** — In the case of a conflict between a regulation and this Act or the *Provincial Land Tax Act*, the regulation prevails.

[1998, c. 3, s. 34; c. 33, s. 40; 2000, c. 25, s. 45; 2002, c. 8, Sched. A, s. 1; c. 17, Sched. F, Table]

# TAX RELIEF IN UNORGANIZED TERRITORY FOR 2001 AND SUBSEQUENT YEARS

(O. Reg. 3/02)

## Part I — Interpretation

**1. Application** — This Regulation applies with respect to taxes for 2001 and later years for school purposes in territory without municipal organization that is not deemed to be attached to a municipality for the purposes of taxation.

. . .

## Part IV — Rebates to Charities — Commercial and Industrial Property Classes

**7.** (1) **Rebate to eligible charity** — An eligible charity is entitled to a rebate of taxes for school purposes for the 2001 and subsequent taxation years on property the charity occupies if,

(a) the property is in the commercial property class or the industrial property class; and

(b) a written application for the rebate, together with sufficient documentation to establish eligibility for the rebate, is given to the secretary of the levying board,

    (i) for the 2001 taxation year, on or before March 31, 2002, or

    (ii) for the 2002 or a subsequent taxation year, on or before June 1 of the taxation year.

(2) In this Part,

"eligible charity" means a registered charity as defined in subsection 248 (1) of the *Income Tax Act* (Canada) that has a valid registration number issued by the Canada Customs and Revenue Agency.

(3) The amount of the rebate to which an eligible charity is entitled for a year under this section is,

(a) the total of all amounts paid by the eligible charity for the year under section 444.1 of the *Municipal Act*, as made applicable by section 8, if the charity is required to pay an amount under that section; or

(b) 40 per cent of the taxes paid for school purposes for the year by the eligible charity on the property it occupies, if clause (a) does not apply to the charity for the year.

(4) The following rules apply with respect to a rebate under this section:

1.  The levying board shall pay one-half of the rebate for a taxation year to the eligible charity within 60 days after receipt of the charity's application for the rebate and shall pay the balance of the rebate within 120 days after receipt of the application.

2.  As a condition of receiving a rebate for a year, a charity shall repay all amounts, if any, by which the rebates the charity received for the year from other levying boards or municipalities exceed the rebates from the other levying boards or municipalities to which the charity is entitled for the year.

3.  The costs of a rebate of taxes on property shall be shared by the levying boards and all other school boards that share in the revenue from the taxes for school purposes on the property in the same proportion as the levying boards and school boards share in the revenue.

4.  The levying board shall pay interest, at the rate determined under subsection 257.11 (4) of the *Education Act*, on the amount of the rebate to which an eligible charity is entitled under this section, if the levying board fails to rebate or credit the amount within the time specified in paragraph 1.

5.  No fee may be charged by the levying board to process an application under this section.

## Part V — Gross Leases

**8. Application of *Municipal Act*, s. 444.1** — Section 444.1 of the *Municipal Act* applies, with necessary modifications, as though it formed part of this Regulation, with respect to property in territory described in section 1 with the following modifications:

1.  A reference to a municipality in subsection 444.1 (10) of the *Municipal Act* shall be read as a reference to the territory described in section 1 that is within the jurisdiction of the levying board.

2.  A reference to a local municipality in subsection 444.1 (13) of the *Municipal Act* shall be read as a reference to the levying board.

3.  A reference to property taxes shall be read as a reference to taxes for school purposes.

# ESTATES ACT

(R.S.O. 1990, c. E. 21)

**49**. (8) **Notice of taking accounts to be served on Public Trustee** — Where by the terms of a will or other instrument in writing under which such an executor, administrator or trustee acts, real or personal property or any right or interest therein, or proceeds therefrom have heretofore been given, or are hereafter to be vested in any person, executor, administrator or trustee for any religious, educational, charitable or other purpose, or are to be applied by them to or for any such purpose, notice of taking the accounts shall be served upon the Public Trustee.

# HOSPITALS AND CHARITABLE INSTITUTIONS INQUIRIES ACT

(R.S.O. 1990, c. H.15)

**1. Inquiry** — Whenever the Lieutenant Governor in Council considers it expedient to cause inquiry to be made concerning any matter connected with or affecting a hospital, sanatorium, charitable institution or other organization that is granted aid out of money appropriated by the Legislature, the Lieutenant Governor in Council may, by commission, appoint one or more persons to conduct such inquiry, and every person so appointed has for that purpose the powers of a commission under Part II of the *Public Inquiries Act*, which Part applies to such inquiry as if it were an inquiry under that Act.

# INCOME TAX ACT

### (R.S.O. 1990, c. I.2)

[**Note:** Only sections pertaining to charitable donations and registered charities are reproduced.]

## Part I — Interpretation

**1.** (1) **Interpretation** — In this Act,

. . .

"individual" means a person other than a corporation and includes a trust referred to in subdivision k of Division B of Part I of the Federal Act;

. . .

(3) The tax payable by a taxpayer under this Act or under Part I of the Federal Act means the tax payable by the taxpayer as fixed by assessment or reassessment subject to variation on objection or on appeal, if any, in accordance with this Act or Part I of the Federal Act, as the case may be.

(4) **Idem** — For the purposes of this Act, except where they are at variance with the definitions contained in this section, the definitions and interpretations contained in or made by regulation under the Federal Act apply.

(5) **Idem** — In any case of doubt, the provisions of this Act shall be applied and interpreted in a manner consistent with similar provisions of the Federal Act.

(6) **Modification of Federal provisions** — Where a provision (in this subsection referred to as "that section") of the Federal Act or the Federal Regulations is made applicable for the purposes of this Act, that section, as amended from time to time heretofore or hereafter, applies with such modifications as the circumstances require for the purposes of this Act as though it had been enacted as a provision of this Act and, in applying that section for the purposes of this Act, in addition to any other modifications required by the circumstances,

   (a)   a reference in that section to tax under Part I of the Federal Act shall be read as a reference to tax under this Act;

   (b)   where that section contains a reference to tax under any of Parts I.1 to XIV of the Federal Act, that section shall be read without reference therein to tax under any of those Parts and without reference to any portion of that section which applies only to or in respect of tax under any of those Parts;

   (c)   a reference in that section to a particular provision of the Federal Act that is the same as or similar to a provision of this Act shall be read as a reference to the provision of this Act;

(d)    a reference in that section to a particular provision of the Federal Act that applies for the purposes of this Act shall be read as a reference to the particular provision as it applies for the purposes of this Act;

(e)    where that section contains a reference to any of Parts I.1 to XIV of the Federal Act or to a provision in any of those Parts, that section shall be read without reference therein to that Part or without reference to that provision, as the case may be, and without reference to any portion of that section that applies only because of the application of any of those Parts or the application of a provision in any of those Parts;

(f)    where that section contains a reference to the *Bankruptcy and Insolvency Act* (Canada), that section shall be read without reference therein to the *Bankruptcy and Insolvency Act* (Canada);

(g)    a reference in that section to a Federal regulation that applies for the purposes of this Act shall be read as a reference to the regulation as it applies for the purposes of this Act;

(h)    a reference in that section to a word or expression set out in Column 1 of the following Table shall be read as a reference to the word or expression set out opposite thereto in Column 2 of the following Table:

| Table | |
|---|---|
| Column 1 | Column 2 |
| Her Majesty | Her Majesty in right of Ontario |
| Canada | Ontario |
| Canada Customs and Revenue Agency | Ontario Ministry of Finance |
| Commissioner of Customs and Revenue | Deputy Head |
| Minister | Provincial Minister |
| Deputy Attorney General of Canada | Deputy Attorney General of Ontario |
| Tax Court of Canada | Superior Court of Justice |
| Tax Court of Canada Act | Courts of Justice Act |
| Federal Court of Canada | Superior Court of Justice |
| Federal Court Act | Courts of Justice Act |
| Registrar of the Tax Court of Canada | local registrar of the Superior Court of Justice |
| in the Registry of the Federal Court | in the Superior Court of Justice |

     (7) **Application of s. 257, Federal Act** — Section 257 of the Federal Act applies for the purposes of this Act.

[1993, c. 29, s. 1 (7); 1996, c. 24, s. 11 (2); 1999, c. 9, s. 115 (2); 2001, c. 23, s. 126; 2004, c. 16, s. 3.]

# Part II
# Income Tax

## DIVISION A — LIABILITY FOR TAX

**2. Income tax on individuals** — An income tax shall be paid as hereinafter required for each taxation year by every individual,

(a)   who was resident in Ontario on the last day of the taxation year; or

(b)   who, not being resident in Ontario on the last day of the taxation year, had income earned in the taxation year in Ontario as defined in section 4.

[2004, c. 16, s. 3.]

. . .

## DIVISION B — COMPUTATION OF TAX

**4. (3.1) Non-refundable credits** — Subject to the rules in subsection (3.2), an individual may deduct from the amount of tax payable under paragraph 1, 2, 3 or 4 of subsection (3) for a taxation year ending after December 31, 1999 any of the following credits to which the individual is entitled for the taxation year in the amount determined for the year under section 4.0.1:

. . .

18. A credit for charitable and other gifts if the individual is entitled to a deduction under subsection 118.1 (3) of the Federal Act for the year.

. . .

**(3.2) Non-refundable credits** — The following rules apply in determining the amount, if any, deductible by an individual under subsection (3.1) for a taxation year:

1.   In calculating the total amount an individual may deduct under subsection (3.1), the individual shall deduct the credits to which he or she is entitled in the order in which the credits are listed in that subsection.

2.   The total amount of the tax credits an individual may deduct under subsection (3.1) must not exceed the amount of tax payable by him or her under paragraph 1, 2, 3 or 4 of subsection (3) for the taxation year.

. . .

5.   An individual who becomes bankrupt in a calendar year is entitled to deduct only the credits described in the following subparagraphs in computing his or her tax payable for a taxation year that ends in the calendar year:

     i.   the credits the individual otherwise would be entitled to deduct under paragraphs 8, 9, 13, 14, 17, 18 and 19 of subsection (3.1) for the taxation year that reasonably can be considered wholly applicable to the taxation year, and

    ii.    the part of the credits the individual otherwise would be entitled to deduct under paragraphs 1 to 7, 10, 11, 15 and 16 of subsection (3.1) for the taxation year that reasonably can be considered applicable to the taxation year.

6.    The total of all credits deductible under paragraph 5 for all taxation years of an individual ending in a calendar year must not exceed the total amount that would have been deductible for the calendar year if the individual had not been bankrupt.

7.    An individual who is resident in Canada only part of a taxation year is entitled to deduct only the following credits for the taxation year:

    i.    the credits the individual otherwise would be entitled to deduct under paragraphs 8, 9, 13, 14, 17, 18 and 19 of subsection (3.1) for the taxation year that reasonably can be considered wholly applicable to any period during the year in which the individual was resident in Canada, computed as if that period were the whole taxation year, and

    ii.    the part of any credits the individual otherwise would be entitled to deduct under paragraphs 1 to 7, 10, 11, 15 and 16 of subsection (3.1) for the taxation year that reasonably can be considered applicable to any period in the year in which the individual was resident in Canada, computed as though the period were the whole taxation year.

8.    The total of all amounts deductible under paragraph 7 for the taxation year shall not exceed the total amount that would have been deductible for the taxation year if the individual had been resident in Canada throughout the year.

. . .

10.    If a separate return of income with respect to an individual is filed under subsection 70 (2), 104 (23) or 150 (4) of the Federal Act, as it applies for the purposes of this Act, for a particular period and another return of income with respect to the individual is filed under this Act for a period ending in the calendar year in which the particular period ends, the total of all credits under paragraphs 8 to 15 and 17 to 19 of subsection (3.1) claimed in the returns must not exceed the total that could be deducted under those paragraphs for the year with respect to the individual if no separate returns were filed.

11.    No amount may be deducted under subsection (3.1), other than a credit under paragraph 18 of that subsection, in determining the amount of tax payable by a trust.

. . .

**4.0.1** (1) **Non-refundable credits** — The amounts of the non-refundable credits for a taxation year, if any, that may be deducted by an individual under subsection 4 (3.1) are the amounts determined under this section after any adjustments required for the year by section 4.0.2.

. . .

(24) **Credit, charitable gifts, etc.** — The amount of an individual's credit for charitable and other gifts for a taxation year is the amount calculated using the formula,

$$(A \times G) + [H \times (J - G)]$$

in which,

"A"  is the lowest tax rate for the year,

"G"  is the lesser of $200 and the amount of the individual's total gifts for the year under section 118.1 of the Federal Act,

"H"  is the highest tax rate for the year, and

"J"   is the amount of the individual's total gifts for the year under section 118.1 of the Federal Act.

[2000, c. 42, s. 51; 2004, c. 16, s. 3.]

. . .

# DIVISION C — SPECIAL CASES

**6. Tax exemption** — An individual who is exempt from tax under Part I of the Federal Act in respect of a period of time, by virtue of subsection 149 (1) of the Federal Act, shall be exempt for the same period from tax payable under this Act, other than tax payable under section 2.1.

[1996, c. 1, Sched. C, s. 6; 2004, c. 16, s. 3.]

. . .

**8.** (1) **Definitions** — In this section,

"housing unit" includes,

(a)  subject to clauses (b) and (c), any premises that an individual ordinarily occupies and inhabits as the individual's residence in the taxation year,

but does not include,

(b)  premises that are part of a chronic care facility or other similar institution that is prescribed, or that are part of any charitable institution, home for special care, home for the aged, public nursing home or private nursing home, or

(c)  premises, except any students' residence that is designated by the Provincial Minister for the taxation year under subsection (8), during such time in a taxation year as,

(i)  such premises are exempt from the payment of taxes levied under the *Provincial Land Tax Act*, the *Local Roads Boards Act* or taxes for municipal and school purposes levied in respect of real property in Ontario that is assessed as residential or multi-residential property, or

    (ii)    the owner does not pay a grant equal to the full amount of the taxes described in subclause (i) that would, if such premises were not exempt, be payable or a grant equal to an amount prescribed by the Minister in respect of such premises or class of premises,

except when such excluded premises are occupied and inhabited by an individual of a class prescribed for the purpose of this definition;

"income" of a person for a taxation year means the amount equal to the sum of the person's taxable income for the taxation year and all amounts deducted by the person under Division C of Part I of the Federal Act in determining such taxable income, less any amounts added under Division C of Part I of the Federal Act in determining such taxable income;

"individual" means a person, other than,

    (a)    a corporation,

    (b)    a trust or estate referred to in subdivision k of Division B of Part I of the Federal Act,

    (c)    except for the purposes of subsections (8.1), (8.3), (8.4), (9), (15), (15.1), (15.2), (15.3), (15.4), (15.5), (15.6), (16) and (16.1), a person who died in the taxation year or a person who is, on December 31 in the taxation year,

        (i)    under the age of sixteen years,

        (ii)    except for the purposes of subsection (4), under the age of nineteen years who was at any time in the taxation year a qualified dependant and who at the end of the taxation year is residing in the principal residence of a person who received, or whose cohabiting spouse or common-law partner received, an amount during the taxation year in respect of the person under section 122.6 of the Federal Act,

        (iii)    a person referred to in paragraph 149 (1) (a) or (b) of the Federal Act,

        (iv)    a person, or a member of the family of a person, who is on active military service as a member of the armed forces of a country other than Canada and is not a Canadian citizen, or

        (v)    a person who, by virtue of an agreement, convention or tax treaty entered into by Canada and another country, is not required to pay tax under the Federal Act with respect to the taxation year, or

    (d)    a qualifying environmental trust;

"municipal tax" means,

    (a)    taxes for municipal and school purposes levied in respect of real property in Ontario that is assessed as residential or multi-residential property,

    (b)    taxes levied for local improvements to real property in Ontario,

    (c)    taxes levied under the *Provincial Land Tax Act* or the *Local Roads Boards Act*, and

    (d)    such other taxes or special rates as are prescribed in the regulations;

"occupancy cost", in respect of a taxation year, means,

(a) municipal tax paid in the taxation year in respect of a principal residence of the individual or of a person who is the cohabiting spouse or common-law partner of the individual, to the extent that the principal residence is beneficially owned by them or either of them or is held in trust for the use and occupation of them or either of them as a principal residence, or

(b) 20 per cent of,

    (i) municipal tax paid in the taxation year in respect of a principal residence that is not beneficially owned by the individual and the individual's cohabiting spouse or common-law partner or by either of them or is not held in trust for them or either of them, but only to the extent that the municipal tax is included by the owner of the residence in computing the owner's taxable income under the Federal Act for the taxation year, and

    (ii) rent paid in the taxation year for occupation of a principal residence of the individual, if the rent is paid by or on behalf of the individual or the individual's cohabiting spouse or common-law partner and is calculated to exclude all payments on account of meals or board;

"Ontario home ownership savings plan" means an Ontario home ownership savings plan under the *Ontario Home Ownership Savings Plan Act*;

"principal residence", in respect of an individual, means a housing unit in Ontario that was occupied by the individual during the taxation year as his or her primary place of residence and that is designated by the individual in the prescribed manner as the individual's principal residence for the taxation year;

"qualifying contribution" made by an individual to an Ontario home ownership savings plan means a contribution that is a qualifying contribution under the *Ontario Home Ownership Savings Plan Act* and in respect of which a receipt in the prescribed form has been issued by the depositary of the plan and has been filed by the individual with the Minister;

"recorded agent" means a person on record with the Chief Election Officer as being authorized to accept contributions on behalf of a political party, constituency association or candidate registered under the *Election Finances Act*;

"senior" means an individual who has attained the age of sixty-five years on or before the 31st day of December in the taxation year;

"tax payable" and "tax otherwise payable" mean the amount of tax that would be payable under this Act, other than the Ontario Health Premium, if the tax were calculated without reference to section 120.1 of the Federal Act and without reference to this section and subsections 4 (3.4) and (3.5) of this Act.

[1992, c. 18, s. 55 ; 1992, c. 25, s. 3 ; 1993, c. 29, s. 6; 1996, c. 1, Sched. C, s. 8; 1996, c. 29, s. 9; 1997, c. 19, s. 9; 1997, c. 43, Sched. B, s. 4; 1998, c. 9, s. 81; 1998, c. 34, s. 69; 2000, c. 42, s. 55; 2001, c. 23, s. 131; 2002, s. 22, s. 108; 2004, c. 16, s. 3; 2004, c. 29, s. 7; 2004, c. 31, Sched. 19, s. 5; 2005, c. 5, s. 33.]

. . .

## DIVISION C.1 — TAX OVERPAYMENTS

**8.7** (1) **Ontario research employee stock option tax over-payment** — An individual other than a trust shall be deemed to have made an overpayment on account of tax payable under this Act for a taxation year ending before January 1, 2010 in the amount of his or her Ontario research employee stock option tax overpayment, if any, for the year if the following conditions are satisfied:

. . .

5. The individual deducted an amount under paragraph 110 (1) (d), (d.01) or (d.1) of the Federal Act in respect of a benefit relating to the eligible stock option agreement in computing his or her income for the taxation year or a prior taxation year.

. . .

## DIVISION D — RETURNS, ASSESSMENTS, PAYMENT AND APPEALS

**10.** (1) **Assessment and withholdings** — The following provisions of the Federal Act apply for the purposes of this Act and, in their application, any reference in them to section 150 or subsection 150 (1) of the Federal Act shall be read to include a reference to subsection 9 (1) of this Act:

. . .

2.      Subsections 152 (1), (1.11), (1.12), (2), (3), (3.1), (4), (4.01), (4.1), (4.2), (4.3), (4.4), (5), (6), (7), (8) and (9).

[1997, c.10, s. 4; 1999, c. 9, s. 123; 2004, c. 16, s. 3]

# LAND TRANSFER TAX ACT

(R.S.O. 1990, c. L. 6)

**1.1 Exemptions under other Acts** — No person otherwise subject to tax under this Act is exempt therefrom by reason of an exemption granted to the person, or to or in respect of the personal or real property of the person, by or under any other Act, unless the other Act expressly mentions this Act.

[2001, c. 23, s. 142.]

**2.** (1) **Tax** — Every person who tenders for registration in Ontario a conveyance by which any land is conveyed to or in trust for a transferee shall pay when the conveyance is tendered for registration or before it is tendered for registration,

(a) a tax computed at the rate of,

    (i) one-half of 1 per cent of the value of the consideration for the conveyance up to and including $55,000,

    (ii) 1 per cent of the value of the consideration which exceeds $55,000 up to and including $250,000, and

    (iii) 1.5 per cent of the value of the consideration which exceeds $250,000; and

(b) if the value of the consideration for the conveyance exceeds $400,000 and the conveyance is a conveyance of land that contains at least one and not more than two single family residences, an additional tax of one-half of 1 per cent of the amount by which the value of the consideration exceeds $400,000.

[1997, c. 10, s. 9; 2004, c. 31, Sched. 21, s. 2.]

. . .

**22.** (2) **Regulations** — The Lieutenant Governor in Council may make regulations,

(a) exempting from tax any person tendering or submitting for registration any class of conveyance to which it is determined that this Act was not intended to apply, or any conveyance to persons prescribed for the purpose of this clause;

(b) exempting from tax arising under section 3 prescribed dispositions or prescribed beneficial interests in land to which it is determined that section 3 was not intended to apply, or exempting from such tax prescribed dispositions of beneficial interests in land to persons prescribed for the purposes of this clause;

. . .

# EXEMPTION(S) — FOR CERTAIN LIFE LEASE INTERESTS

(O. Reg. 88/04)

**1. Definitions** — In this Regulation,

"life lease development" means land with self-contained units, organized as what is commonly known as a life lease project, where the right to occupy a unit is solely for the lifetime of an individual or for a term of at least 20 years;

"life lease interest" means the exclusive right to occupy a unit in a life lease development;

"non-profit organization" means a non-profit organization within the meaning of paragraph 149(1)(l) of the *Income Tax Act* (Canada) and includes a municipality;

"registered charity" means a charitable organization registered under subsection 248 (1) of the *Income Tax Act* (Canada).

[O. Reg. 321/05, s. 1.]

**2. Exemption, acquisition of a life lease interest** — The Act does not apply to the acquisition after July 18, 1989 by one or more individuals of a life lease interest where sufficient information is provided to enable the Minister or any collector to determine that the following conditions are met:

1.    The owner of the life lease development is a non-profit organization or a registered charity.

2.    Each individual acquired the life lease interest in order to use the unit as his or her principal residence or as the principal residence of the individual's parent or spouse.

[O. Reg. 321/05, s. 2.]

**3. Exemption, reversion of a life lease interest** — The Act does not apply to the reversion after July 18, 1989 of a life lease interest in a unit in a life lease development to the owner of the life lease development where sufficient information is provided to enable the Minister or any collector to determine that the following conditions are met:

1.    The owner of the life lease development is a non-profit organization or a registered charity.

2.    The reversion occurs pursuant to the terms of the agreement under which the life lease interest in the unit was originally acquired.

3.    The reversion occurs for the purpose of enabling the owner of the life lease development to sell the life lease interest to another purchaser.

**4. (1) Refunds** — If a payment of tax was made after July 18, 1989 but before March 28, 2003 under the Act in respect to the purchase of a life-lease interest, the Minister may, upon receipt of satisfactory evidence that the amount was paid, refund such amount.

(2) Subsection (1) applies only in respect of transactions which, if section 2 or 3 had been in force on the date of the payment of the tax, would have been exempt under those sections.

(3) A refund under this section may only be paid if an application for the refund has been received by the Minister before March 28, 2007.

# EXEMPTION - HOSPITAL RESTRUCTURING

(O. Reg. 676/98)

**1.** No tax is payable under the Act in respect of a conveyance of land or a disposition of a beneficial interest in land to a hospital approved as a public hospital under the *Public Hospitals Act* or a hospital established or approved as a community psychiatric hospital under the *Community Psychiatric Hospitals Act*,

(a)   if the conveyance or disposition is from another hospital; and

(b)   if the conveyance or disposition takes place in the course of or as a result of an amalgamation of hospitals, the closure of hospital programs or the transfer of a hospital program to the transferee hospital.

# MINISTRY OF COMMUNITY AND SOCIAL SERVICES ACT

(R.S.O. 1990, c. M. 20)

. . .

**13.** (1) **Regulations governing occupation and operation of institutions** — Where any institution or organization is operated or managed for charitable objects or purposes and where,

    (a)   the persons operating and managing the institution so request; or

    (b)   the institution or organization procures funds for its operation from the public and the Lieutenant Governor in Council considers it necessary to ensure proper application of such funds; or

    (c)   any approval, licence or registration for the operation of the institution or organization required by any Act administered by the Minister, has been refused or revoked; or

    (d)   the Lieutenant Governor in Council considers it necessary in the best interests of those residing in or relying on the services of such institution or organization and for their immediate protection,

the Lieutenant Governor in Council may make regulations,

    (e)   designating such institution or organization to be subject to the control of the Minister;

    (f)   governing the operation and activities of any institution or organization designated under clause (e) and the procuring of funds from the public and the application thereof by such institution or organization;

    (g)   authorizing the Minister to operate and manage any such institution or organization designated under clause (e) and for that purpose, despite sections 25 and 39 of the *Expropriations Act*, authorizing the Minister to immediately occupy and operate, or arrange for the occupation and operation by a person or organization designated by him or her, any premises occupied or used by such institution or organization, but the rights of the owner under that Act, except the right to possession, shall not be affected thereby.

(2) **Warrant for entry and occupation** — Where the Minister has been authorized under this section to occupy any premises, if the persons in occupation refuse to permit the Minister or persons authorized by him or her for that purpose to enter upon and occupy the premises or resist such entry, the Minister may apply without notice to a judge of the Ontario Court (General Division) for a warrant directing the sheriff to put the Minister or persons authorized by him or her in occupation of the premises and the judge, upon being satisfied that the Minister is so authorized to occupy the premises and of such refusal or resistance, may issue

such warrant and the sheriff shall forthwith execute the warrant and make a return to the judge of the execution thereof.

(3) **Period of occupation** — Except with the consent of the person operating and managing an institution, the Minister shall not occupy and operate or arrange for the occupation and operation of the premises of an institution under subsection (1) for a period longer than a year, but the Lieutenant Governor in Council may from time to time extend such period.

**14. Establishment of charitable institutions by Minister** — The Minister, with the approval of the Lieutenant Governor in Council, may establish, with property acquired by Her Majesty by way of gift or donation, any institution that may be operated or managed for charitable objects or purposes under any Act administered by the Minister, and the Minister may by way of lease or agreement provide for the management and operation on a non-profit basis of the institution by any person or organization with authority therefor under such Act subject to such Act and the regulations thereunder and upon such terms and conditions as may be agreed upon.

# CONTROL OF ORGANIZATION BY MINISTER

(O. Reg. 191/04)

**1.** The Apartments for Living for Physically Handicapped Association is designated to be subject to the control of the Minister.

**2.** The Minister is authorized to operate and manage the Apartments for Living for Physically Handicapped Association and for that purpose the Minister is authorized to immediately occupy and operate, or arrange for the occupation and operation by a person or organization designated by the Minister of, any premises occupied or used by the Apartments for Living for Physically Handicapped Association.

# MUNICIPAL ACT, 2001

(S.O. 2001, c. 25)

## Part X — Tax Collection

**361.** (1) **Rebates for charities** — Every municipality, other than a lower-tier municipality, shall have a tax rebate program for eligible charities for the purposes of giving them relief from taxes or amounts paid on account of taxes on eligible property they occupy.

(2) **Eligible charities, property** — For the purposes of this section,

(a)   a charity is eligible if it is a registered charity as defined in subsection 248 (1) of the *Income Tax Act* (Canada) that has a registration number issued by the Canada Customs and Revenue Agency;

(b)   a property is eligible if it is in one of the commercial classes or industrial classes, within the meaning of subsection 308(1).

(3) **Program requirements** — A tax rebate program under this section is subject to the following requirements:

1.   The program must provide for a rebate for an eligible charity that pays taxes or amounts on account of taxes on eligible property it occupies.

2.   The amount of a rebate required under paragraph 1 must be at least 40 per cent, or such other percentage as the Minister of Finance may prescribe, of the taxes or amounts on account of taxes paid by the eligible charity on the property it occupies. If the eligible charity is required to pay an amount under section 367 or 368, the amount of the rebate shall be the total of the amounts paid by the eligible charity under those sections.

3.   The program must provide that payment of one-half of the rebate must be made within 60 days after the receipt by the municipality of the application of the eligible charity for the rebate for the taxation year and the balance of the rebate must be paid within 120 days of the receipt of the application.

4.   The program must permit the eligible charity to make an application for a rebate for a taxation year based on an estimate of the taxes or amounts on account of taxes payable by the eligible charity on the property it occupies.

5.   The program must provide for final adjustments, to be made after the taxes or amounts on account of taxes paid by the charity can be determined, in respect of differences between the estimated rebate paid by the municipality and the rebate to which the charity is entitled.

6.   The program must require, as a condition of receiving a rebate for a year, that a charity repay any other municipality amounts by which the rebates

the charity received for the year from that other municipality exceed the rebates from that other municipality to which the charity is entitled for the year.

7.      An application for a taxation year must be made after January 1 of the year and no later than the last day of February of the following year.

(4) **Program options** — The following apply with respect to what a tax rebate program under this section may provide but is not required to provide:

1.      The program may provide for rebates to organizations that are similar to eligible charities or a class of such organizations defined by the municipality.

2.      The program may provide for rebates to eligible charities or similar organizations for taxes or amounts on account of taxes on property that is in any class of real property prescribed under the *Assessment Act*.

3.      The program may provide for rebates that are greater than those required under subsection (3) and may provide for different rebate amounts for different eligible charities or similar organizations up to 100 per cent of the taxes paid by the eligible charity or similar organization.

4.      The program may provide for adjustments in respect of the rebates for a year to be deducted from amounts payable in the next year for the next year's rebates.

(5) **Procedural requirements** — The program may include procedural requirements that must be satisfied for an eligible charity to be entitled to a rebate required under subsection (3).

(6) **Who gives rebates** — Rebates under a program of a municipality under this section shall be given by the municipality unless the municipality is an upper-tier municipality, in which case the rebates shall be given by the lower-tier municipalities.

(7) **Sharing amounts of rebates** — The amount of a rebate paid under this section on a property shall be shared by the municipalities and school boards that share in the revenue from the taxes on the property in the same proportion as the municipalities and school boards share in those revenues.

(8) **Statement of costs shared by school boards** — The municipality that gives a rebate to a charity or similar organization shall also give the charity or similar organization a written statement of the proportion of the costs of the rebate that is shared by school boards.

(9) **Interest** — The municipality shall pay interest, at the same rate of interest that applies under subsection 257.11 (4) of the *Education Act*, on the amount of any rebate to which the eligible charity is entitled under this section if the municipality fails to rebate or credit the amount within the time specified in paragraph 3 of subsection (3) or within such other time as the Minister of Finance may prescribe.

(10) **No fee** — Despite this Act, no fee may be charged by the municipality to process an application under this section.

(10.1) **Change of assessment** — The following apply if the assessment of an eligible property for a year changes as a result of a request under section 39.1 of the *Assessment Act*, a complaint under section 40 of that Act or an application under section 46 of that Act:

1.   A rebate under subsection (3) with respect to the year shall be redetermined using the new taxes on property for the year based on the new assessment.

2.   If, as a result of a redetermination under paragraph 1, the amount of the rebate is increased, the increased amount shall be paid to the eligible charity in accordance with this section.

3.   If, as a result of a redetermination under paragraph 1, the amount of the rebate is decreased and amounts paid on account of the rebate exceed the redetermined amount of the rebate, the excess payments are a debt due to the municipality which gave the rebate but the municipality shall not take any action to collect the debt, including the imposition of interest, until 120 days after providing the eligible charity with notice of the debt.

(11) **Regulations** — The Minister of Finance may make regulations,

(a)   governing programs under this section including prescribing additional requirements for the programs;

(b)   governing procedural requirements the programs must include;

(c)   prescribing a percentage for the purpose of paragraph 2 of subsection (3);

(d)   prescribing a time period for the purpose of subsection (9).

(12) **Interpretation** — In this section, "tax" includes charges under section 208.

[2002. c. 17, Sched. A, s. 64; c. 22, s. 159]

# PERPETUITIES ACT

(R.S.O. 1990, c. P.9)

**1. Definitions** — In this Act,

"court" means the Ontario Court (General Division);

"in being" means living or conceived;

"limitation" includes any provision whereby property or any interest in property, or any right, power or authority over property, is disposed of, created or conferred.

**2. Rule against perpetuities to continue; saving** — Except as provided by this Act, the rule of law known as the rule against perpetuities continues to have full effect.

**3. Possibility of vesting beyond period** — No limitation creating a contingent interest in property shall be treated as or declared to be invalid as violating the rule against perpetuities by reason only of the fact that there is a possibility of such interest vesting beyond the perpetuity period.

**4.** (1) **Presumption of validity and "Wait and See"** — Every contingent interest in property that is capable of vesting within or beyond the perpetuity period is presumptively valid until actual events establish,

(a)   that the interest is incapable of vesting within the perpetuity period, in which case the interest, unless validated by the application of section 8 or 9, shall be treated as void or declared to be void; or

(b)   that the interest is incapable of vesting beyond the perpetuity period, in which case the interest shall be treated as valid or declared to be valid.

(2) **General power of appointment** — A limitation conferring a general power of appointment, which but for this section would have been void on the ground that it might become exercisable beyond the perpetuity period, is presumptively valid until such time, if any, as it becomes established by actual events that the power cannot be exercised within the perpetuity period.

(3) **Special power of appointment, etc.** — A limitation conferring any power, option or other right, other than a general power of appointment, which but for this section would have been void on the ground that it might be exercised beyond the perpetuity period, is presumptively valid, and shall be declared or treated as void for remoteness only if, and so far as, the right is not fully exercised within the perpetuity period.

**5.** (1) **Applications to determine validity** — An executor or a trustee of any property or any person interested under, or on the validity or invalidity of, an interest in such property may at any time apply to the court for a declaration as to the validity or invalidity with respect to the rule against perpetuities of an interest in that property, and the court may on such application make an order as to validity or invalidity of an interest based on the facts existing and the events that have occurred at the time of the application and having regard to sections 8 and 9.

(2) **Interim income** — Pending the treatment or declaration of a presumptively valid interest within the meaning of subsection 4 (1) as valid or invalid, the income arising from such interest and not otherwise disposed of shall be treated as income arising from a valid contingent interest, and any uncertainty whether the limitation will ultimately prove to be void for remoteness shall be disregarded.

**6.** (1) **Measurement of perpetuity period** — Except as provided in section 9, subsection 13 (3) and subsections 15 (2) and (3), the perpetuity period shall be measured in the same way as if this Act had not been passed, but, in measuring that period by including a life in being when the interest was created, no life shall be included other than that of any person whose life, at the time the interest was created, limits or is a relevant factor that limits in some way the period within which the conditions for vesting of the interest may occur.

(2) **Idem** — A life that is a relevant factor in limiting the time for vesting of any part of a gift to a class shall be a relevant life in relation to the entire class.

(3) **Idem** — Where there is no life satisfying the conditions of subsection (1), the perpetuity period is twenty-one years.

**7.** (1) **Presumptions and evidence as to future parenthood** — Where, in any proceeding respecting the rule against perpetuities, a question arises that turns on the ability of a person to have a child at some future time, then,

    (a)    it shall be presumed,

          (i)    that a male is able to have a child at the age of fourteen years or over, but not under that age, and

          (ii)    that a female is able to have a child at the age of twelve years or over, but not under that age or over the age of fifty-five years; but

    (b)    in the case of a living person, evidence may be given to show that he or she will or will not be able to have a child at the time in question.

(2) **Idem** — Subject to subsection (3), where any question is decided in relation to a limitation of interest by treating a person as able or unable to have a child at a particular time, then he or she shall be so treated for the purpose of any question that arises concerning the rule against perpetuities in relation to the same limitation or interest despite the fact that the evidence on which the finding of ability or inability to have a child at a particular time is proved by subsequent events to have been erroneous.

(3) **Idem** — Where a question is decided by treating a person as unable to have a child at a particular time and such person subsequently has a child or children at that time, the court may make such order as it sees fit to protect the right that such child or children would have had in the property concerned as if such question had not been decided and as if such child or children would, apart from such decision, have been entitled to a right in the property not in itself invalid by the application of the rule against perpetuities as modified by this Act.

(4) **Idem** — The possibility that a person may at any time have a child by adoption or by means other than by procreating or giving birth to a child shall not be considered in deciding any question that turns on the ability of a person to have

a child at some particular time, but, if a person does subsequently have a child or children by such means, then subsection (3) applies to such child or children.

**8.** (1) **Reduction of age** — Where a limitation creates an interest in property by reference to the attainment by any person or persons of a specified age exceeding twenty-one years, and actual events existing at the time the interest was created or at any subsequent time establish,

    (a)    that the interest, would, but for this section, be void as incapable of vesting within the perpetuity period; but

    (b)    that it would not be void if the specified age had been twenty-one years,

the limitation shall be read as if, instead of referring to the age specified, it had referred to the age nearest the age specified that would, if specified instead, have prevented the interest from being so void.

(2) **Exclusion of class members to avoid remoteness** — Where the inclusion of any persons, being potential members of a class or unborn persons who at birth would become members or potential members of the class, prevents subsection (1) from operating to save a limitation creating an interest in favour of a class of persons from being void for remoteness, such persons shall be excluded from the class for all purposes of the limitation, and the limitation takes effect accordingly.

(3) **Idem** — Where a limitation creates an interest in favour of a class to which subsection (2) does not apply and actual events at the time of the creation of the interest or at any subsequent time establish that, but for this subsection, the inclusion of any persons, being potential members of a class or unborn persons who at birth would become members or potential members of the class, would cause the limitation to the class to be void for remoteness, such persons shall be excluded from the class for all purposes of the limitation, and the limitation takes effect accordingly.

(4) **Interpretation** — For the purposes of this section, a person shall be treated as a member of a class if in the person's case all the conditions identifying a member of the class are satisfied, and a person shall be treated as a potential member if in the person's case some only of those conditions are satisfied but there is a possibility that the remainder will in time be satisfied.

**9.** (1) **Spouses** — Where any disposition is made in favour of any spouse of a person in being at the commencement of the perpetuity period, or where a limitation creates an interest in property by reference to the time of the death of the survivor of a person in being at the commencement of the perpetuity period and any spouse of that person, for the purpose of validating any such disposition or limitation, that but for this section would be void as offending the rule against perpetuities as modified by this Act, the spouse of such person shall be deemed to be a life in being at the commencement of the perpetuity period even though such spouse was not born until after that time.

(2) **Definition** — For the purposes of subsection (1),

"spouse" means a person,

    (a)    to whom the person is married, or

    (b)   with whom the person is living in a conjugal relationship outside marriage, if the two persons,

        (i)   have cohabited for at least a year,

        (ii)   are together the parents of a child, or

        (iii)   have together entered into a cohabitation agreement under section 53 of the *Family Law Act.*

[1999, c. 6, s. 54; 2005, c. 5. s. 57.]

**10.** (1) **Saving** — A limitation that, if it stood alone, would be valid under the rule against perpetuities is not invalidated by reason only that it is preceded by one or more limitations that are invalid under the rule against perpetuities, whether or not such limitation expressly or by implication takes effect after, or is subject to, or is ulterior to and dependent upon, any such invalid limitation.

(2) **Acceleration of expectant interests** — Where a limitation is invalid under the rule against perpetuities, any subsequent interest that, if it stood alone, would be valid shall not be prevented from being accelerated by reason only of the invalidity of the prior interest.

**11.** (1) **Powers of appointment** — For the purpose of the rule against perpetuities, a power of appointment shall be treated as a special power unless,

    (a)   in the instrument creating the power it is expressed to be exercisable by one person only; and

    (b)   it could, at all times during its currency when that person is of full age and capacity, be exercised by the person so as immediately to transfer to the person the whole of the interest governed by the power without the consent of any other person or compliance with any other condition, not being a formal condition relating only to the mode of exercise of the power.

(2) **Idem** — A power that satisfies the conditions of clauses (1) (a) and (b) shall, for the purpose of the rule against perpetuities, be treated as a general power.

(3) **Idem** — For the purpose of determining whether an appointment made under a power of appointment exercisable by will only is void for remoteness, the power shall be treated as a general power where it would have been so treated if exercisable by deed.

**12.** (1) **Administrative powers of trustees** — The rule against perpetuities does not invalidate a power conferred on trustees or other persons to sell, lease, exchange or otherwise dispose of any property, or to do any other act in the administration (as opposed to the distribution) of any property including, where authorized, payment to trustees or other persons of reasonable remuneration for their services.

(2) **Application of subs. (1)** — Subsection (1) applies for the purpose of enabling a power to be exercised at any time after this Act comes into force, despite the fact that the power is conferred by an instrument that took effect before that time.

**13.** (1) **Options to acquire reversionary interests** — The rule against perpetuities does not apply to an option to acquire for valuable consideration an interest reversionary on the term of a lease,

(a)   if the option is exercisable only by the lessee or the lessee's successors in title; and

(b)   if it ceases to be exercisable at or before the expiration of one year following the determination of the lease.

(2) **Application of subs. (1)** — Subsection (1) applies to an agreement for a lease as it applies to a lease, and "lessee" shall be construed accordingly.

(3) **Other options** — In the case of all other options to acquire for valuable consideration any interest in land, the perpetuity period under the rule against perpetuities is twenty-one years, and any such option that according to its terms is exercisable at a date more than twenty-one years from the date of its creation is void on the expiry of twenty-one years from the date of its creation as between the person by whom it was made and the person to whom or in whose favour it was made and all persons claiming through either or both of them, and no remedy lies for giving effect to it or making restitution for its lack of effect.

(4) **Options to renew leases** — The rule against perpetuities does not apply, nor do the provisions of subsection (3) apply, to options to renew a lease.

**14. Easements, *profits à prendre*, etc.—** In the case of an easement, *profit à prendre* or other similar interest to which the rule against perpetuities may be applicable, the perpetuity period is forty years from the time of the creation of such easement, *profit à prendre* or other similar interest, and the validity or invalidity of such easement, *profit à prendre* or other similar interest, so far as remoteness is concerned, shall be determined by actual events within such forty-year period, and the easement, *profit à prendre* or other similar interest is void only for remoteness if, and to the extent that, it fails to acquire the characteristics of a present exercisable right in the servient land within the forty-year period.

**15.** (1) **Determinable interests** — In the case of,

(a)   a possibility of reverter on the determination of a determinable fee simple; or

(b)   a possibility of a resulting trust on the determination of any determinable interest in property,

the rule against perpetuities as modified by this Act applies in relation to the provision causing the interest to be determinable as it would apply if that provision were expressed in the form of a condition subsequent giving rise on its breach to a right of re-entry or an equivalent right in the case of personal property, and, where the event that determines the determinable interest does not occur within the perpetuity period, the provision shall be treated as void for remoteness and the determinable interest becomes an absolute interest.

(2) **Idem** — In the case of a possibility of reverter on the determination of a determinable fee simple, or in the case of a possibility of a resulting trust on the determination of any determinable interest in any property, or in the case of a

right of re-entry following on a condition subsequent, or in the case of an equiva
lent right in personal property, the perpetuity period shall be measured as if the
event determining the prior interest were a condition to the vesting of the subsequent interest, and failing any life in being at the time the interests were created
that limits or is a relevant factor that limits in some way the period within which
that event may take place, the perpetuity period is twenty-one years from the time
when the interests were created.

(3) **Idem** — Even though some life or lives in being may be relevant in determining the perpetuity period under subsection (2), the perpetuity period for the
purposes of this section shall not exceed a period of forty years from the time
when the interests were created and shall be the lesser of a period of forty years
and a period composed of the relevant life or lives in being and twenty-one years.

**16.** (1) **Specific non-charitable trusts** — A trust for a specific non-charitable
purpose that creates no enforceable equitable interest in a specific person shall be
construed as a power to appoint the income or the capital, as the case may be, and,
unless the trust is created for an illegal purpose or a purpose contrary to public
policy, the trust is valid so long as and to the extent that it is exercised either by
the original trustee or the trustee's successor, within a period of twenty-one years,
despite the fact that the limitation creating the trust manifested an intention, either
expressly or by implication, that the trust should or might continue for a period in
excess of that period, but, in the case of such a trust that is expressed to be of perpetual duration, the court may declare the limitation to be void if the court is of
opinion that by so doing the result would more closely approximate the intention
of the creator of the trust than the period of validity provided by this section.

(2) **Idem** — To the extent that the income or capital of a trust for a specific
non-charitable purpose is not fully expended within a period of twenty-one years,
or within any annual or other recurring period within which the limitation creating
the trust provided for the expenditure of all or a specified portion of the income or
the capital, the person or persons, or the person or person's successors, who
would have been entitled to the property comprised in the trust if the trust had
been invalid from the time of its creation, are entitled to such unexpended income
or capital.

**17.** (1) **Rule in** *Whitby vs. Mitchell* **abolished** — The rule of law prohibiting
the limitation, after a life interest to an unborn person, of an interest in land to any
unborn issue of an unborn person is abolished, but without affecting any other
rule relating to perpetuities.

(2) **Definition** — For the purposes of subsection (1),

"issue" means issue of a person, whether born within or outside marriage, subject to
sections 158 and 159 of the *Child and Family Services Act.*

**18.** (1) **Rules as to perpetuities not applicable to employee-benefit trusts** —
The rules of law and statutory enactments relating to perpetuities do not apply and
shall be deemed never to have applied to the trusts of a plan, trust or fund established for the purpose of providing pensions, retirement allowances, annuities, or
sickness, death or other benefits, to employees or to their surviving spouses, dependants or other beneficiaries.

(2) **Definition** — In this section,

"spouse" means,

(a)   a spouse as defined in section 1 of the *Family Law Act*, or

(b)   either of two persons who live together in a conjugal relationship outside marriage.

[2005, c. 5, s. 57.]

**19. Application of Act** — Except as provided in subsection 12 (2) and in section 18, this Act applies only to instruments that take effect on or after the 6th day of September, 1966, and such instruments include an instrument made in the exercise of a general or special power of appointment on or after that date even though the instrument creating the power took effect before that date.

# PROVINCIAL LAND TAX ACT

(R.S.O. 1990, c. P. 32)

. . .

*Liability to Tax, Exemption*

**3.** (1) **Land assessable and taxable, exemptions** — All land situate in territory without municipal organization is liable to assessment and taxation under this Act, subject to the following exemptions from taxation:

3. **Churches, etc.** — Every place of worship and land used in connection therewith, every churchyard, and every cemetery or burying ground that is enclosed and actually required, used and occupied for the interment of the dead, but not land rented or leased to a church or religious organization by a person other than another church or religious organization.

**Note: paragraph 3 is repealed by 2002, c. 33, subsection 147 (1) and the following substituted:**

3. **Churches, etc.** — Every place of worship and land used in connection therewith, every churchyard, and every cemetery or burying ground that is enclosed and actually required, used and occupied for the interment of the dead or for any ancillary purpose prescribed by the Minister, but not including any portion of the land used for any other purpose nor land rented or leased to a church or religious organization by a person other than another church or religious organization.

[2002, c. 33, s. 147, not in force].

4. **Public educational institutions** — The buildings and grounds of and attached to or otherwise actually used in connection with and for the purpose of a university, high school, public or separate school or other educational institution supported in whole or in part by Provincial money, whether vested in a trustee or otherwise, only so long as such buildings and grounds are actually used and occupied by such institution.

5. **Philanthropic or religious seminaries** — The buildings and grounds of and attached to or otherwise actually used in connection with and for the purposes of a seminary of learning maintained for philanthropic or religious purposes, the whole profits from which are devoted or applied to such purposes, only so long as such buildings and grounds are actually used and occupied by such seminary.

6. **Educational seminaries** — The buildings and grounds not exceeding in the whole fifty acres of and attached to or otherwise actually used in connection with and for the purposes of a seminary of learning maintained for educational purposes, the whole profits from which are devoted or applied to such purposes, only so long as such buildings and grounds are actually used and occupied by such seminary, but such exemption does not extend to include any part of the land

of such a seminary that is used for farming or agricultural pursuits and is worked on shares with any other person, or if the annual or other crops, or any part thereof, from such land are sold.

7. **Boy Scouts and Girl Guides** — Land owned, occupied and used exclusively by The Boy Scouts Association or the Canadian Girl Guides Association or by any provincial or local association or other local group in Ontario that is a member of either of such associations or is otherwise chartered or officially recognized by either of them.

8. **Charitable institutions** — Land owned, occupied and used exclusively by an incorporated charitable institution organized for the relief of the poor, The Canadian Red Cross Society, St. John Ambulance Association, or any similar incorporated institution conducted on philanthropic principles and not for the purpose of profit or gain, that is supported, in part at least, by public money.

9. **Agricultural societies** — Land owned by an agricultural society under the *Agricultural and Horticultural Organizations Act*.

. . .

15. **Further exemptions** — Land of a designated class that is declared by the Lieutenant Governor in Council to be exempt wholly or partially from taxation under this Act.

16. **Community centres** — The buildings and grounds of an athletics field, an outdoor swimming pool, an outdoor skating rink or a community hall owned by a board as defined in the *Education Act* and having jurisdiction only in territory without municipal organization and in respect of which a grant has been made under the *Community Recreation Centres Act*.

. . .

18. **Public hospitals** — Buildings and grounds of and attached to or otherwise actually used in connection with and for the purposes of a public hospital receiving aid under the *Public Hospitals Act*, and all land owned and used by such a public hospital for farming purposes, but no land is exempt from assessment and taxation by virtue of this paragraph when occupied by any tenant or lessee who is liable to taxation under this Act.

. . .

20. **Conservation land** — Land that is conservation land as defined in the regulations under the *Assessment Act* for the purposes of paragraph 25 of section 3 of that Act.

. . .

[**Note:** The Act is amended by adding subsection (1.1), 2002, c. 33, s. 147, not in force.]

(1.1) **Non-application: special exemptions** — Despite any provision in any Act of special or general application, an exemption from assessment or taxation under such an Act for burial sites, burying grounds or cemeteries shall, on and after the day section 147 of the *Funeral, Burial and Cremation Services Act, 2002* comes into force, no longer apply.

. . .

*Pipe Lines*

**10**. (6) **Liability to tax on pipe line on exempt land** — Where a pipe line is located on, in, under, along or across a highway or any lands, other than lands held in trust for a band or body of Indians, exempt from taxation under this or any special or general Act, the pipe line is nevertheless liable to assessment and taxation in accordance with this section.

. . .

[**Note:** The Act is amended by adding s. 21.2, 2002, c. 33, s. 148, not in force]

**21.2** (1) **Tax cancellation, reduction or refund re: cemeteries** — The purpose of this section is to provide tax relief to a cemetery owner if the cemetery's care and maintenance fund is not adequately funded.

(2) **Application for cancellation, reduction, refund** — If a cemetery is located in unorganized territory and the cemetery owner has a deficiency in one or more of its care and maintenance funds as prescribed, the cemetery owner may apply to the collector for the cancellation, reduction or refund of all or part of the taxes assessed or levied against the part of the land that is eligible land in the year in respect of which the application is made.

(3) **Timing of application** — An application under subsection (2) shall be delivered to the collector on or before February 28 of the year following the taxation year in respect of which the notice is given or such later date as the Minister of Finance may prescribe.

(4) **Registrar's notice** — The application under subsection (2) shall include a notice from the registrar prepared under section 54 of the *Funeral, Burial and Cremation Services Act, 2002*, which notice shall,

  (a)  confirm whether the owner has a deficiency in its care and maintenance fund; and

  (b)  direct the collector to cancel the taxes assessed or levied on the eligible land or to reduce or refund the taxes by the amount specified in the notice.

(5) **Decision by registrar** — The decision made by the registrar as to whether the taxes assessed or levied against the eligible land should be cancelled, reduced or refunded and as to the amount of any reduction or refund of the taxes assessed or levied against the eligible land shall be made in accordance with the regulations, but in no case shall the amount of a refund exceed the amount of the taxes assessed or levied in respect of the eligible land in the taxation year in respect of which the application is made.

(6) **Compliance by collector** — Upon receipt of a notice under subsection (4), the collector shall carry out the direction contained in the notice.

(7) **Same** — The collector shall issue any refund to which a cemetery owner is entitled under this Act within 120 days after the last day on which the owner is entitled to make an application under subsection (3).

(8) **Regulations** — The Minister of Finance may make regulations,

(a)  defining deficiency for the purposes of this section;

(b)  prescribing the cemetery that has a deficiency in its care and mainte-nance fund for the purposes of subsection (2) and respecting the manner in which the owner of one or more cemeteries may calculate deficiencies in his or her care and maintenance funds;

(c)  prescribing a date for the purposes of subsection (3);

(d)  governing the decision made by the registrar as to whether to cancel the taxes assessed or levied against the eligible land or as to the amount of the reduction or refund of the taxes assessed or levied against the eligible land and respecting the determination as to the amount of the reduction or refund.

(9) **Definitions** — In this section,

"care and maintenance fund" and "cemetery" have the same meaning as they have in the *Funeral, Burial and Cremation Services Act, 2002*;

"commercial cemetery" means a cemetery operated for the purpose of making a profit for the owner;

"crematorium", "funeral establishment", "licensed services" and "licensed supplies" have the same meaning as they have in the *Funeral, Burial and Cremation Services Act, 2002*;

"deficiency" means a deficiency as defined by regulation;

"eligible land" means land located on a cemetery other than a commercial cemetery that is liable to assessment and taxation in respect of the operation of a crematorium, funeral establishment, transfer service or other business related to the provision of licensed supplies or licensed services;

"registrar" means the registrar appointed with respect to cemeteries under the *Funeral, Burial and Cremation Services Act, 2002*;

"transfer service" means a transfer service as defined in the *Funeral, Burial and Cremation Services Act, 2002*.

. . .

*Regulations*

**38.** (1) **Regulations** — The Lieutenant Governor in Council may make regula-tions,

. . .

(b)  designating classes of land and declaring the same to be exempt, wholly or partially, from taxation under this Act;

# PUBLIC GUARDIAN AND TRUSTEE ACT

(R.S.O. 1990, c. P.51)

. . .

**12. Charitable and public trusts** — The Public Guardian and Trustee may accept and administer any charitable or public trust.

[1992, c. 32, s. 25.]

# RELIGIOUS ORGANIZATIONS' LANDS ACT

## (R.S.O. 1990, c. R.23)

**1.** (1) **Definitions** — In this Act,

"meeting" means a meeting of the members of a religious organization that has been called by notice in accordance with section 18;

"religious organization" means an association of persons,

(a)  that is charitable according to the law of Ontario,

(b)  that is organized for the advancement of religion and for the conduct of religious worship, services or rites, and

(c)  that is permanently established both as to the continuity of its existence and as to its religious beliefs, rituals and practices,

and includes an association of persons that is charitable according to the law of Ontario and that is organized for the advancement of and for the conduct of worship, services or rites of the Buddhist, Christian, Hindu, Islamic, Jewish, Baha'i, Longhouse Indian, Sikh, Unitarian or Zoroastrian faith, or a subdivision or denomination thereof;

"trustees" means the trustees appointed by a religious organization to acquire, hold and possess land for its benefit, and includes their successors.

(2) **Idem** — In interpreting clause (a) of the definition of "religious organization" in subsection (1), an organization does not cease to be charitable for the reason only that activities that are not charitable but are merely ancillary to a charitable purpose are carried on in conjunction with a charitable purpose.

(3) **Derivative organizations** — Where a separate religious organization is formed out of an existing religious organization, whether voluntarily or otherwise, and the new organization meets the requirements of clauses (a) and (b) of the definition of "religious organization" in subsection (1), it shall nevertheless be considered to be a religious organization for the purposes of this Act.

**2. Acquisition and holding of land** — A religious organization may acquire and hold land for the purpose of,

(a)  a place of worship;

(b)  a residence for its religious leader;

(c)  a burial or cremation ground;

(d)  a bookstore or a printing or publishing office;

(e)  a theological seminary or similar institution of religious instruction;

(f)  a religious camp, retreat or training centre; or

(g)  any other religious purpose,

in the name of trustees, individually or by collective designation, and their successors in perpetual succession for the benefit of the religious organization.

**3.** (1) **Appointment and tenure of trustees** — A religious organization may by resolution adopted at a meeting of the organization,

(a)  appoint trustees and fill any vacancy in the office of trustee;

(b)  provide for the retirement or removal of trustees and for the appointment of their successors;

(c)  remove any trustee from office;

(d)  decrease or increase the number of trustees;

(e)  confer upon trustees the power to acquire, hold and possess land for one or more of the purposes set out in section 2.

(2) **Termination of office** — Unless the constitution or a resolution of the religious organization otherwise provides, a trustee holds office until he or she dies, resigns or ceases to be a member of the organization.

(3) **Powers of trustees where vacancy** — Where a vacancy occurs in the number of the trustees of a religious organization, until the vacancy is filled, the remaining trustees then in office have all the estate in and title to the land of the organization and have all the powers conferred by this Act with respect thereto as were originally vested in the whole number.

(4) **Powers of successor trustees** — A trustee appointed to fill a vacancy together with the trustees originally appointed or subsequently appointed and who remain in office have all the estate, title and powers vested in the original trustees.

(5) **Vesting of land in successor trustees** — Where no trustees of a religious organization remain in office, the land to which the organization is entitled vests automatically in trustees subsequently appointed by the organization and their successors without the necessity of any conveyance.

(6) **Where successor trustees not provided for** — Where a religious organization is entitled to land and the manner of appointing trustees or their successors is not set out in the instrument granting or devising the land, it vests automatically in the trustees appointed under subsection (1) and their successors to be held in trust for the organization without the necessity of any conveyance.

**4. Property vested in one person** — Where, under the constitution, customs or practices of a religious organization, its property is vested in one person, the person shall be deemed to be a trustee and has the powers and duties of trustees under this Act.

**5. (1) Joint trustees** — Each of two or more religious organizations may by resolution appoint joint trustees and provide for the appointment of their successors and may enter into agreements respecting the holding of land for their joint benefit by such joint trustees for any of the purposes enumerated in section 2 and all the provisions of this Act apply with necessary modifications to such joint trustees.

(2) **Conveyance to joint trustees** — Where land referred to in subsection (1) was, before the agreement, held by different bodies of trustees, the religious organizations may direct them in the agreement or otherwise to convey or transfer the land to the joint trustees appointed in accordance with subsection (1) and their successors.

**6. (1) Authorization required to exercise of powers** — The trustees of a religious organization shall not exercise any of the powers conferred upon them by this Act until they are authorized to do so by resolution of the organization, and the organization may attach such terms or conditions to any such authorization as it considers expedient.

(2) **Authorization in case of joint trustees** — In the case of joint trustees for two or more religious organizations, the authorization shall be obtained by resolutions adopted by each religious organization for whose benefit land is or is to be held.

**7. Power to enter into agreements to purchase land** — The trustees of a religious organization may enter into agreements to purchase land for the benefit of the organization for any of the purposes of this Act.

**8. Power to conduct actions** — The trustees of a religious organization may, individually or by collective designation, maintain and defend actions for the protection of the land and of the interest of the religious organization therein.

**9.** (1) **Power to mortgage land** — The trustees of a religious organization may secure any debt contracted for the acquisition or improvement of land under this Act, or for the building, repairing, extending or improving of any buildings thereon, by a mortgage or charge on all or any part of the land of the organization.

(2) Power to release equity of redemption — If a mortgage or charge on land held by the trustees of a religious organization for the benefit of the organization is in arrears as to principal or interest, or both, the trustees may release, transfer or convey to the mortgagee or chargee or the assigns of the mortagee or chargee the equity of redemption in the land, or any part thereof, in satisfaction of the whole or any part of the debt.

**10.** (1) **Power to lease** — The trustees of a religious organization may lease, for one term of forty years or for more than one term of not more than forty years in all, any land held by them for the benefit of the organization which is no longer required by it for any of the purposes enumerated in section 2, at such rent and upon such terms and conditions as they consider expedient.

(2) **Power to agree to renewal terms** — In any such lease, the trustees,

(a)    may, subject to the forty year maximum period specified in subsection (1), agree for the renewal thereof at the expiration of any or every term of years for a further term or terms at such rent and on such terms and conditions as may be agreed; or

(b)    may agree to pay to the lessee, the lessee's heirs, executors, administrators, successors or assigns a sum equal to the value of any buildings or other improvements that may at the expiration of any term be on the demised land.

(3) **Method of ascertaining rent** — The method of ascertaining the amount of the rent during any renewal term or the value of the buildings or other improvements to be paid at the end of any term may be specified in the original or in any subsequent lease.

(4) **Recovery of rent and the land** — The trustees may take all proceedings for the recovery of rent or arrears of rent and of the demised land that landlords are entitled by law to take.

(5) **Power to enter into short term leases** — A religious organization may by resolution give its trustees a general authorization to lease any land held by them for terms not exceeding three years per term and when so authorized the trustees may, without further authorization, lease the land from time to time for a term or terms not exceeding three years per term.

**11. Easements and covenants** — The trustees of a religious organization may, upon such terms and conditions as the organization may by resolution approve, grant easements or enter into covenants in respect of land held by them.

**12.** (1) **Power to sell** — The trustees of a religious organization may, upon such terms and conditions as the organization may by resolution approve, sell or exchange at any time land held by them if the organization has by resolution determined that the land is no longer necessary for its purposes.

(2) **Surplus land subject to *Charities Accounting Act*** — When land of a religious organization is not required for its actual occupation for a purpose set out in section 2 and is not leased under section 10, the *Charities Accounting Act* applies in the same manner as if the land were then assured to the religious organization for charitable purposes.

(3) **Special powers not affected** — Subsection (1) does not affect any special powers or trusts for sale contained in any instrument inconsistent therewith.

**13. Conveyance to trustees of new religious organization** — The trustees of a religious organization out of which a separate religious organization is formed may convey or transfer to the trustees of the separate organization such part of the land held by them as is appropriate.

**14. Conveyance where religious organizations unite** — Where a religious organization desires to unite with another religious organization, the trustees of either organization may convey or transfer any land held by them to the trustees of the other religious organization or to the trustees of the united religious organization.

**15. Conveyance to denominational board or trustees** — The trustees of a religious organization may convey or transfer any land held by them for the benefit of the organization to an incorporated board or to trustees of the denomination or subdivision thereof of which the organization forms a part.

**16. Duty to account** — The trustees of a religious organization selling or leasing land under the authority of this Act shall on the first Monday in June in each year have ready and open for the inspection of the members of the organization a detailed statement showing the rents that accrued during the preceding year and all sums in their hands for the use and benefit of the organization that were in any manner derived from land under their control or subject to their management, and also showing the application of any portion of the money that has been expended on behalf of the organization.

**17. Resolutions** — A resolution respecting any of the purposes of this Act is adopted if the majority of those present at the meeting called for that purpose and entitled to vote thereat vote in favour of the resolution.

**18.** (1) **Notice of meeting** — A notice calling a meeting of a religious organization for any of the purposes of this Act,

(a)    shall specify the purpose of the meeting; and

(b)    shall be given in accordance with the constitution, practice or custom of the religious organization.

(2) **Idem** — Where the constitution, practice or custom of a religious organization has no provision for the giving of notice calling a meeting, at least two weeks notice shall be given personally or by mail, or notice may be given by announcement at an open service at least once in each of the two weeks immediately preceding the week in which the meeting is proposed to be held.

**19.** (1) **Keeping of records** — A copy of a resolution adopted under this Act shall be signed by the chair and the secretary of the meeting at which it was adopted and shall be entered in the minute book or other record kept for that purpose.

(2) **Evidence** — A copy of a resolution adopted under this Act, certified as being a true copy by an officer of the organization, is proof, in the absence of evidence to the contrary, of the matters therein stated.

(3) **Omissions** — Failure to comply with subsection (1) does not invalidate the resolution or anything done under it.

**20. Instruments made pursuant to Act** — Any instrument affecting land made by or to trustees under this Act shall be expressed to be made under this Act, but failure to do so does not render the instrument void.

**21.** (1) **Former conveyance** — Where letters patent from the Crown or a grant, conveyance or devise made before the 14th day of June, 1979 is made to persons described as trustees for a religious organization and to their successors, this Act applies to them and to the religious organization in the same manner as if the persons were duly appointed as trustees under this Act.

(2) **Use of several names** — Where more than one letters patent from the Crown, grant, conveyance or devise have been made for the benefit of a religious organization under different names, the organization may at a meeting by resolution adopt one of the names or another name as the name in which its trustees shall hold the land thereafter.

**22. Change of name** — A change in the name of a religious organization or manner in which the trustees are described does not affect the title to land held by the organization or its trustees in the former name.

**23.** (1) **Application to court for directions where religious organization has ceased to exist** — Where a religious organization has ceased to exist, or where the authorization required under section 6 cannot be obtained for any reason other than a dispute among the members of the organization concerning the organization's property, the persons in whom the land of the organization is vested as trustees or, upon their failure to do so or where no trustees remain in office, any interested person or the Public Trustee may apply to the Ontario Court (General Division) for directions, and the court may authorize the trustees or may appoint and authorize any other person to exercise any of the powers conferred by this Act.

(2) **Power of court to direct sale** — Upon such an application, the court may direct that the land or any part thereof be disposed of or that it or the proceeds of sale thereof be distributed in such manner as it considers proper, and the court may make such vesting orders as are expedient in the circumstances.

**24.** (1) **Applications to court as to applicability of Act** — Any organization or other body that wishes to have determined whether or not it is entitled to acquire, hold and possess land under this Act may at any time apply to the Ontario Court (General Division), and the court may determine the matter.

(2) **Applications to court by Public Trustee** — In like manner, the Public Trustee may apply to have determined whether any organization or other body that purports to hold and possess or that intends to acquire, hold and possess land under this Act is entitled to do so.

**25.** (1) **Notice to Public Trustee** — Notice of an application under subsection 23 (1) or subsection 24 (1) shall be given by the applicant to the Public Trustee.

(2) **Idem** — In any other proceeding in which the application of this Act is in issue, the court may direct that notice be given to the Public Trustee.

**26.** (1) **Subject to special Acts** — This Act is subject to any special Act applying to a religious organization.

(2) **Subject to trust instruments** — This Act is subject to any trusts or powers of trustees in any deed, conveyance or other instrument.

# RETAIL SALES TAX ACT

(R.S.O. 1990, c. R. 31)

[**Note:** Only selected sections have been reproduced.]

. . .

**1.1 Exemptions under other Acts** — No person otherwise subject to tax under this Act is exempt therefrom by reason of an exemption granted to the person, or to or in respect of the personal or real property of the person, by or under any other Act, unless the other Act expressly mentions this Act.

[2001, c. 23, s. 189.]

. . .

**2.** (20) **Tax on merchandise tendered in trade** — Where tangible personal property is accepted at the time of sale by a person or a vendor on account of the price of other tangible personal property sold, the purchaser shall pay a tax at the rate provided in subsection (1) calculated on the difference between the fair value of the property sold and the credit allowed for the tangible personal property accepted on account of the purchase price in trade.

[1993, c. 12, s. 2.]

(20.1) **Exception** — Subsection (20) does not apply if any purchaser could acquire the tangible personal property exempt from tax imposed by this Act at the time it is so accepted.

[1993, c. 12, s. 2.]

(21) **Where exempt property put to taxable use** — Where tangible personal property has been purchased exempt from the tax imposed by this Act, and the tangible personal property is subsequently put to a taxable use, the purchaser shall pay the tax imposed by this Act on the fair value of the tangible personal property at the time of change of use.

. . .

**4.2** (1) **Tax on used motor vehicles** — Despite section 2, every purchaser of a used motor vehicle shall pay to Her Majesty in right of Ontario a tax in respect of the consumption or use thereof, computed at the rate of 8 per cent of the fair market value thereof.

[1993, c. 12, s. 5.]

. . .

(4) **Exemptions** — Subsection (1) does not apply in respect of a used motor vehicle that is,

. . .

(c)    acquired by a person by bequest;

. . .

(d.1) acquired by a school, college or university as a gift;

. . .

(f)    acquired through a transaction prescribed by the Minister.

[1993, c. 12, s. 5; 1994, c. 13, s. 6; 1999, c. 6, s. 59; 2000, c. 10, s. 27; 2005, c. 5, s. 62.]

**7.** (1) **Exemptions** — The purchaser of the following classes of tangible personal property and taxable services is exempt from the tax imposed by section 2:

. . .

2. Taxable services that are described in clause (c) or (d) of the definition of "taxable services" in subsection 1 (1) and that are,

    i.    provided to repair, adjust, restore or maintain real property,

    ii.    provided to install tangible personal property that will become real property upon installation,

    iii.    provided to maintain, restore or repair tangible personal property where the repairs or repair parts used in the maintenance, restoration or repair may be purchased exempt from tax,

    iv.    provided to repair or recondition tangible personal property purchased for resale by a vendor,

    v.    provided by a person for the person's own consumption or use, or

    vi.    provided to install tangible personal property that may be purchased exempt from tax under this subsection.

    vii.    [Repealed: 2000, c. 10, s. 28.]

    viii    [Repealed: 2002, c. 22, s. 172.]

[1994, c. 13, s. 9; 1997, c. 10, s. 32; 2000, c. 10, s. 28; 2002, c. 22, s. 172.]

. . .

18. Equipment purchased by the governing body of a university that is designed for use, and used exclusively, in research or investigation, and repair parts therefor, but the exemption conferred by this paragraph does not apply to any equipment, or repair parts therefor, or labour to install such parts or equipment, where that equipment is used in the instruction of students, or to any type or class of equipment that is prescribed by the Minister to be excluded from this paragraph, or repair parts for such equipment, or the labour to install such equipment or repair parts.

. . .

20. Used clothing or used footwear or a combination thereof sold by a religious, charitable, benevolent or non-profit organization in one transaction the total consideration for which does not exceed $50.

. . .

23. Fire fighting vehicles, as defined by the Minister, when purchased at a price of more than $1,000 per vehicle for the exclusive use of a municipality, university, public hospital, local services board or volunteer group, and repair parts for such vehicles.

. . .

38. Equipment, as defined by the Minister, that is purchased for use exclusively by one of the following, and repairs made to such equipment:

    i.    The Ontario Cancer Treatment and Research Foundation,

    ii.    a hospital approved as a public hospital under the *Public Hospitals Act*,

    iii.    a hospital approved or established as a community psychiatric hospital under the *Community Psychiatric Hospitals Act*,

    iv.    a facility approved or established as a psychiatric facility under the *Mental Health Act*.

[1998, c. 5, s. 45.]

. . .

44. Publications, as defined by the Minister, purchased by a school, school board, community college or university or by a public library established under the *Public Libraries Act*.

[2000, c. 42, s. 93.]

. . .

50. Works of art purchased by a museum or art gallery more than 50 per cent of the revenue of which is provided by public donations and grants by public bodies.

. . .

53. Equipment, as defined by the Minister, that is to be used by a religious institution exclusively in that part of its premises where religious worship or sabbath school is regularly conducted, and repairs to such equipment, but not including any equipment acquired for resale by a religious institution.

. . .

55. Publications, as defined by the Minister, of a religious, charitable or benevolent organization. R.S.O. 1990, c. R.31, s. 7 (1), par. 55.

63. Equipment (and repair parts for the equipment) to be used exclusively for research or investigation, if the equipment is purchased by a non-profit institution that conducts medical research, as prescribed by the Minister, as its only function.
[1997, c. 10, s. 32.]

64. A gift to a school, college or university.
[2000, c. 10, s. 28.]

. . .

66. Audio books, as defined by the Minister. However, the exemption applies only in the circumstances prescribed by the Minister.
[2001, c. 23, s. 192.]

67. Admissions to a place of amusement that are donated to a registered charity, as defined in subsection 248 (1) of the *Income Tax Act* (Canada), by an owner or operator of the place of amusement.
[2002, c. 8, Sched. J, s. 2.]

. . .

**9.** (2) **Exemption from tax on entertainment, etc.** — The tax imposed by subsection 2 (5) is not payable in respect of the price of admission to any entertainment, event, dance, performance or exhibition staged or held where no performer taking part in that entertainment, event, dance, performance or exhibition receives, or will receive, either directly or indirectly, any remuneration or any other consideration for the performance or where 90 per cent of the performers who regularly participate in the cast of a theatrical or musical performance staged or held in a place of amusement are persons who are Canadian citizens resident in Canada or who are permanent residents in Canada as defined in the *Immigration Act* (Canada) or to any entertainment, event, dance, performance or exhibition that is staged or held in a place of amusement by, or under the auspices or sponsorship of,

(a) a registered Canadian amateur athletic association, as defined by subsection 248 (1) of the *Income Tax Act* (Canada), including a branch or affiliate association to which the registration under that Act of the Canadian amateur association of which it is a branch or affiliate has been extended;

(b) a registered charity, as defined by subsection 248 (1) of the *Income Tax Act* (Canada);

(c) a labour organization or society, or a benevolent or fraternal benefit society or order;

(d) an agricultural society constituted under the *Agricultural and Horticultural Organizations Act*, during any agricultural fair held by the agricultural society except where the entertainment, event, performance or exhibition is a sporting event;

(e) an educational institution; or

(f) an organization that is substantially assisted or supported financially from public funds of the Province of Ontario and that is prescribed by the Minister for the purpose of this subsection.

(3) **Exemption from tax, hospital restructuring** — The tax imposed by subsection 2 (1) or section 4.2 is not payable by any of the following hospitals or facilities on its acquisition of tangible personal property from another such hospital or facility as a result of an amalgamation or closure of the hospital or facility or on the transfer of a program from another such hospital or facility:

1. A hospital approved as a public hospital under the *Public Hospitals Act*.

2. A hospital approved or established as a community psychiatric hospital under the *Community Psychiatric Hospitals Act*.

3. A facility approved or established as a psychiatric facility under the *Mental Health Act*.

[1992, c. 13, s. 5; 1996, c. 29 s. 27; 1998, c. 5, s. 46; 2004, c. 16, Sched. D, Table.]

. . .

## Regulations

**48.** (1) **Lieutenant Governor in Council regulations** — For the purpose of carrying into effect the provisions of this Act according to their true intent and of supplying any deficiency therein, the Lieutenant Governor in Council may make such regulations as are considered necessary and advisable.

(2) **Idem** — Without limiting the generality of subsection (1), the Lieutenant Governor in Council may make regulations,

. . .

(d) providing for the rebate of the tax in whole or in part to the governing body of any religious, charitable or benevolent organization in respect of tangible personal property entering into capital investment by such organization and prescribing the terms and conditions under which such rebates may be made;

. . .

(j) prescribing circumstances or situations in which the purchaser of an admission to an entertainment, event, dance, performance or exhibition is excluded from the exemption from tax on the price of admission contained in subsection 9 (2);

. . .

(3) **Minister's regulations** — The Minister may make regulations,

. . .

(c) providing for the use of purchase exemption certificates and other documents where purchasers or classes of purchasers are exempt from tax under this Act;

# DEFINITIONS, EXEMPTIONS AND REBATES

## (R.R.O. 1990, Reg. 1012)

[**Note:** Only selected sections have been reproduced.]

**1.** (1) The following expressions used in subsection 7 (1) of the Act are defined by the Minister:Subsection 1(3)

. . .

"audio book" means an audio recording in which all or substantially all of the content is a spoken reading of a book;

"books" means books that are printed and bound and that are published solely for educational, technical, cultural or literary purposes and that contain no advertising, including pages that are printed for insertion in such books, but not directories, price lists, time tables, rate books, catalogues, reports, fashion books, albums, books ruled for accounting or bookkeeping purposes, blank exercise, drawing or work books or any similar books and loose leaf sheets or pages that are printed for insertion in such books;

. . .

"equipment", as used in paragraph 38 of subsection 7 (1) of the Act, means any patient care item or supply used in a patient room or any other area where the medical or surgical treatment of patients normally occurs, and laboratory research and diagnostic equipment, but does not include,

(a) accounting and bookkeeping equipment and office furniture and all similar office and administrative equipment,

(b) brooms, floor polishers, laundry carts, vacuum cleaners, and all similar housekeeping equipment,

(c) cutlery, dishes, glassware, kitchen utensils and all similar kitchen and dietary supplies,

(d) lawn mowers, maintenance staff uniforms, electrical tools, ladders, small tools, lathes, saws and all similar maintenance equipment,

(e) motion picture equipment, games, television sets and radios and all similar recreational equipment,

(f) motor vehicles,

(g) carpets, coat racks, chairs and any other furniture or furnishings that are not used in a part of the hospital where patients normally receive medical or surgical treatment, or

(h) any other piece of equipment that is not used directly in the medical or surgical treatment of patients;

"equipment", as used in paragraph 54 of subsection 7 (1) of the Act, means fish nets, fur stretchers, snares and snare wire, skinning knives, snow shoes and steel traps of all makes;

"equipment", as used in paragraph 53 of subsection 7 (1) of the Act, means,

altars, altar cloths and linens,

altar desks,

baptismal bowls, fonts and shells,

chairs, pews, stools and tables,

chimes and bells,

choir stalls,

collection plates,

communion ware,

confessionals and confessional counters,

draperies and carpets,

kneelers and prie-dieux lecterns and lectern cloths,

mass linen,

memorial plaques and tablets,

monuments and statues,

organs and pianos,

public address systems,

pulpits and pulpit cloths,

special lighting apparatus,

stained glass windows,

and similar equipment used exclusively in religious worship or Sabbath school, but does not include clothing or vestments;

. . .

"fire fighting vehicles" means motor vehicles specially designed and equipped at the time of purchase for use primarily in fire fighting, rescue and emergency response and includes pumpers, initial attack fire apparatus, mobile water supply apparatus, wildland fire apparatus, aerial ladder apparatus, aerial ladder platform or other types of platform apparatus, light, medium and heavy rescue vehicles, hazardous materials apparatus, mobile command post units and other similar vehicles, but does not include fire chief's vehicles;

. . .

"medical research" means,

(a) basic biomedical research to explore the fundamental biological processes underlying health and disease in humans, or

(b) applied clinical research to develop new technologies for disease prevention, diagnosis, treatment and rehabilitation, but does not include,

    (c)   epidemiological population-based studies, the analysis of health care systems or the instruction of students;

. . .

"publications of a religious, charitable or benevolent organization" means,

    (a)   church calendars, hymn and mass cards, photographs, paintings, drawings, mottoes and similar artwork produced solely for the promotion of religion including any plates made to produce printed materials,

    (b)   bibles, scriptures, missals, prayer books, hymn books, pamphlets, booklets and similar printed matter published solely for the promotion of religion,

    (c)   printed instructional materials purchased for use and not resale by a religious, charitable or benevolent organization, and

    (d)   films, filmstrips, video tapes and video discs purchased by a religious, charitable or benevolent organization and used to promote the objects of the religious, charitable or benevolent organization, and not for commercial exhibition or for profit,

but does not include directories, price lists, time tables, rate books, catalogues, stationery, forms or any similar printed matter;

. . .

(3) The following are publications for the purposes of paragraph 44 of subsection 7 (1) of the Act if they are of an educational nature and not for commercial exhibition for profit:

    1.   Films and filmstrips.

    2.   Audio tapes and audio discs.

    3.   Video tapes and video discs.

    4.   Compact discs — read-only memory (CD-ROMs) that are not primarily computer programs.

(4) The following are not publications for the purposes of paragraph 44 of subsection 7 (1) of the Act:

    1.   Any written material.

    2.   Microfilm or microfiche.

    3.   Equipment to play or show material specified in paragraphs 1 to 4 of subsection (3).

Under subsection 2 (9) of the Act, it is hereby determined that the fair value of property that is stage props, sets and costumes, manufactured by a person that is a religious, charitable, benevolent or non-profit organization for use by that person in its staging of a live theatrical or musical performance does not include the cost of labour and manufacturing overhead incurred in the manufacture of such property.

[O. Reg. 1/97, s. 1; O. Reg. 383/99, s. 1; O. Reg. 266/01, s. 1; O. Reg. 118/02, s. 1.]

. . .

**6.** (1) In this section,

"blanket purchase exemption certificate" means a purchase exemption certificate provided by a person to a vendor that applies to one or more sales to the person by the vendor or to one or more premium payments to the vendor until the person revokes the certificate or the Minister cancels the certificate;

"single purchase exemption certificate" means a purchase exemption certificate provided by a person to a vendor that applies to only one sale, contract of insurance or benefits plan.

(2) In each of the following circumstances, a person may provide a valid purchase exemption certificate to a vendor instead of paying to the vendor the amount of tax that would otherwise be levied and collected by the vendor under the Act:

1. On a sale of tangible personal property to the person if,

    i. the person alleges he or she is exempt from tax under the Act, or

    ii. the person alleges he or she is purchasing the property for the purposes of resale and, if the person is not resident in Ontario, he or she has a vendor permit under the Act and provides the number to the vendor.

2. On a sale to the person of a taxable service described in clause (a), (c), (c.1), (d) or (d.1) of the definition of "taxable service" in subsection 1 (1) of the Act if,

    i. the person alleges that he or she is purchasing the service for the purposes of resale and, if the person is not resident in Ontario, he or she has a vendor permit under the Act and provides the number to the vendor, or

    ii. the taxable service is supplied in respect of taxable tangible personal property with respect to which the person alleges he or she is exempt from tax under the Act.

(3) Instead of providing a purchase exemption certificate to a vendor under subsection (2), a person who satisfies one of the following paragraphs may present to the vendor the identity card described in that paragraph:

. . .

4. An identity card issued by the Canadian National Institute for the Blind on the sale of audio books, if the person is exempt from tax in respect of the sale by reason of paragraph 66 of subsection 7 (1) of the Act.

(4) A purchase exemption certificate provided by a person under subsection (2) may be either a single purchase exemption certificate or blanket purchase exemption certificate and is valid only if it includes,

(a)   the name of the person or name under which the person transacts business;

(b)   the address of the person or the address at which the person carries on business;

(c)   the name of the person who is authorized to acquire the tangible personal property or taxable service or enter into the contract of insurance or benefits plan;

(d)   the reason for claiming the exemption from payment of tax;

(e)   the person's vendor permit number under the Act if the person is a vendor under the Act;

(f)   the carrier account number issued by the Ministry of Transportation if the person is a registrant; and

(g)   the date the person provided the purchase exemption certificate.

(5) A person who provides a valid blanket purchase exemption certificate to a vendor is not required to supply any additional purchase exemption certificates on individual sales or premium payments until the blanket purchase exemption certificate is revoked or cancelled.

(6) Every person who provides a blanket purchase exemption certificate shall promptly revoke the certificate if any information required to be included in the certificate was omitted or is not currently correct, but the person may provide a replacement certificate with the correct information, if the person is entitled under subsection (2) to use a valid blanket purchase exemption certificate.

[O. Reg. 449/05, s. 1.]

**10.** (1) In this section,

"bus" means a motor vehicle, excluding a van or a motorized mobile home within the meaning of Regulation 628 of the Revised Regulations of Ontario, 1990 (Vehicle Permits), designed to carry,

(a)   ten or more persons who are not confined to wheelchairs and that is used to provide transportation, or

(b)   three or more persons who are confined to wheelchairs and that is used to provide transportation for persons with physical disabilities;

. . .

"long-term lease" means a lease of a vehicle for a term of twelve months or longer;

. . .

"motor vehicle" means a motor vehicle for which a permit is required under section 7 of the *Highway Traffic Act* but does not include a motorcycle, a motor assisted bicycle, a motorized mobile home within the meaning of Regulation 628 of the

Revised Regulations of Ontario, 1990 (Vehicle Permits) or a dune buggy within the meaning of Regulation 863 of the Revised Regulations of Ontario, 1990 (General);

"person with a permanent physical disability" means a person ordinarily resident in Ontario,

(a) who is permanently deprived of the use of an arm or leg,

(b) whose mobility within the usual surroundings that he or she lives or works in is permanently restricted to the use of a wheelchair, crutches, braces or other device designed to assist mobility,

(c) whose permanent visual acuity in both eyes with proper refractive lenses is 20/200 or less, or

(d) whose greatest diameter of field of vision is permanently less than 20 degrees;

. . .

"purchaser of a motor vehicle" means a purchaser who acquires ownership of the vehicle or a purchaser who leases the vehicle under a long-term lease;

. . .

"van" means a motor vehicle having a body type described as "VN" on a permit issued under section 7 or the *Highway Traffice Act*.

(2) In order to determine visual acuity for the purpose of clause (c) of the definition of "person with a permanent physical disability", measurements shall be taken using a Snellen chart or a chart that is equivalent to a Snellen chart.

(3) Subject to the limits set out in subsection (4), the Minister may, upon receipt of a written application, rebate to the purchaser of a motor vehicle the tax paid under section 2 or 4.2 of the Act by the purchaser if the Minister is satisfied that the purchaser is, at the time of the application, and was, at the time of the purchase, one of the following:

. . .

3. A religious, charitable or non-profit organization, other than a municipality or local board, that purchased the vehicle for use, principally, to transport persons with a permanent physical disability.

(4) The Minister may rebate the tax paid under,

(a) section 2 of the Act on modifications made to a motor vehicle purchased on or after June 1, 1989 if the modifications were solely to assist a person with a permanent physical disability; and

(b) section 2 or 4.2 of the Act on the purchase of a motor vehicle, before the modifications, if any, referred to in clause (a) were made, to a maximum of,

(i) $1,600, in respect of a motor vehicle that is not a van or a bus,

   (ii)   $2,400, in respect of a van, or

   (iii)   the tax paid, in respect of a bus.

(5) A rebate shall not be made under this section in respect of,

(a)   an application submitted to the Minister more than four years after the tax was paid;

(b)   a motor vehicle that will be used for profit or as part of an undertaking carried on for gain;

(c)   a motor vehicle if, thirty days after the purchase or lease of that motor vehicle, the same purchaser or a member of the family of the purchaser or the person with a permanent physical disability or a member of the family of that person or the principal care giver owned or leased, under a long-term lease, another motor vehicle with respect to which a rebate has been made under this section, section 12 of Regulation 903 of the Revised Regulations of Ontario, 1980, as it existed on the 28th day of February, 1981 or section 32 of Regulation 904 of the Revised Regulations of Ontario, 1980, as it existed on the 31st day of May, 1989; or

(d)   a motor vehicle that is,

   (i)   ordered from a vendor or purchased after May 18, 2004, or

   (ii)   ordered from a vendor or purchased before May 19, 2004 but not delivered before August 1, 2004.

(6) Clause (5) (c) does not apply to a religious, charitable or non-profit organization.

. . .

(9) An application for a rebate under this section must be accompanied by the following:

1.   A copy of the purchase or long-term lease contract for the motor vehicle in respect of which a rebate is claimed setting out the purchase price or lease payments and the tax paid by the applicant.

. . .

4.   If the applicant is a religious, charitable or non-profit organization, a statement certifying that the motor vehicle was purchased to be used principally to transport persons with permanent physical disabilities and that the applicant is a religious, charitable or non-profit organization other than a municipality or local board.

. . .

(10) No more than one rebate may be made under this section in a twelve-month period to a purchaser leasing a motor vehicle under a long-term lease and the total amount of the rebates made under this section shall not exceed the amounts specified in subsection (4).

(11) A rebate under this section may be made only to a purchaser of a motor vehicle who applies for it.

(12) No tax imposed under section 4 of the Act is refundable under this section.

[O. Reg. 35/91, s. 2; O. Reg. 8/94, s. 2; O. Reg. 383/99, s. 4; O. Reg. 107/00, s. 1; O. Reg. 325/05, s. 1; O. Reg. 364/05, s. 1.]

. . .

**12.** The following persons or classes of persons are exempt from tax with respect to their consumption of prepared food products where the prepared food products are provided by them to others without specific charge:

1.  Hospitals.

2.  Nursing homes and homes for the aged.

3.  Penal or correctional institutions.

4.  Religious, charitable or benevolent organizations.

5.  Employers where the prepared food products are provided to their employees in eating establishments operated by or on behalf of the employer.

6.  Schools and universities where the prepared food products are provided to a student in an eating establishment operated by or on behalf of the school or university.

. . .

**14.3** (1) A purchaser of an audio book is exempt under paragraph 66 of subsection 7 (1) of the Act from tax,

(a) if he or she is legally blind and the audio book is purchased for his or her own use; or

(b) if he or she purchases the audio book on behalf of a person who is legally blind for that person's own use.

(2) For the purposes of subsection (1), a person is legally blind if his or her permanent visual acuity in both eyes with proper refractive lenses is 20/200 or less, when measured using a Snellen chart or a chart that is equivalent to a Snellen chart, or whose greatest diameter of field of vision is permanently less than 20 degrees.

[O. Reg. 118/02, s. 2.]

**17.** For the purpose of clause 9 (2) (f) of the Act, the organizations named in the Schedule are prescribed.

. . .

**28.** (4) A person claiming exemption from tax under clause 4.2 (4) (c), (d) or (e) of the Act shall complete the form provided by the Minister and provide to the person authorized by the Minister,

(a)    a copy of the will under which the bequest was made;

(b)    a document that evidences the making of the gift; or

. . .

(5) Instead of providing the documents referred to in subsection (4), the person may provide an affidavit verifying that the vehicle was acquired in the circumstances described in clause 4.2 (4) (c), (d) or (e) of the Act.

. . .

(7) For the purposes of clause 4.2 (4) (f) of the Act, the following transactions are prescribed:Schedule 1

5. The transfer of a vehicle donated to a religious, charitable or benevolent organization if the donor has paid the applicable tax under the Act and the organization,

      i.    provides to the person authorized by the Minister an affidavit stating that the transfer is a gift and that the tax was paid upon the purchase of the vehicle, and

      ii.    completes the form provided by the Minister.

[O. Reg. 8/94, s. 6; O. Reg. 379/01, s. 7.]

## SCHEDULE 1
### ORGANIZATIONS SUBSTANTIALLY ASSISTED OR SUPPORTED FINANCIALLY FROM PUBLIC FUNDS OF THE PROVINCE OF ONTARIO PRESCRIBED BY THE MINISTER FOR THE PURPOSE OF CLAUSE 9 (2) (F) OF THE ACT

| Item Number | Organization |
| --- | --- |
| 1. | Art Gallery of Ontario |
| 2. | Board of Governors of an Ontario College of Applied Arts and Technology |
| 3. | Board of Governors of the Ontario College of Art |
| 4. | Board of Governors of an Ontario University and Ryerson Polytechnical Institute |
| 5. | CJRT-FM Inc. |
| 6. | College of Agricultural Technology (Alfred) |
| 7. | College of Agricultural Technology (Centralia) |
| 8. | College of Agricultural Technology (Kemptville) |
| 9. | College of Agricultural Technology (New Liskeard) |
| 10. | College of Agricultural Technology (Ridgetown) |
| 11. | Huronia Historical Advisory Council |
| 12. | McMichael Canadian Art Collection |

| 13. | Old Fort William Advisory Committee |
|-----|-------------------------------------|
| 14. | Ontario Agricultural Museum |
| 15. | Ontario Heritage Foundation |
| 16. | Ontario Institute for Studies in Education |
| 17. | Ontario Place Corporation |
| 18. | Ontario Science Centre |
| 19. | Provincial Parks Council |
| 20. | Royal Botanical Gardens |
| 21. | Royal Ontario Museum |
| 22. | St. Lawrence Parks Commission |
| 23. | Science North |
| 24. | Thunder Bay Ski Jumps Limited |

# GENERAL

## (R.R.O. 1990, Reg. 1013)

[**Note:** Only selected sections have been reproduced.]

**1.** In the Act and this Regulation,

. . .

"capital investment" means, in respect of a religious, charitable or benevolent organization, the result of any construction project that, when complete, is real property, including real property that is leasehold property;

. . .

"community college" means a college of applied arts and technology that offers programs of instruction in day or evening courses for full-time or part-time students in one or more fields of vocational, technological, general and recreational education and training;

. . .

"educational institution" means a school or university;

. . .

"food products" includes poultry or other livestock purchased for human consumption, insulin, vitamins, artificial sweeteners and any dietary supplement or adjunct that is not a drug or medicine, but does not include liquor, beer, wine, chewing gum, lozenges, cat, dog, bird or other animal foods, root beer extracts, malt and malt extracts;

. . .

"non-profit organization" means a club, society, association or any group organized and operated exclusively for social welfare, civic improvement, pleasure or recreation or for any other purpose except profit, no part of the income of which is payable to or otherwise available for the personal benefit of any organizer, trustee, officer or member thereof, except reasonable compensation paid to such persons, employees, performers or others for work and services actually performed by them, but does not include a registered charity within the meaning of the *Income Tax Act* (Canada);

. . .

"prepared food products" means meals, lunches, food products sold hot, individual portions of prepackaged snack cake or pastry and other arrangements of food purchased from an eating establishment for consumption on or off the premises where the food is sold and includes non-alcoholic beverages sold with or without other prepared food products and soft drinks sold with prepared food products as part of a single transaction at a total price that exceeds $4;

. . .

"religious", "charitable" or "benevolent organization" means any organization defined as a "registered charity" by subsection 248 (1) of the *Income Tax Act* (Canada) and that holds a registration number issued by the Department of National Revenue;

"school" means,

    (a)   a public school, separate school or secondary school under the jurisdiction of a school board,

    (b)   the body of pupils enrolled in any of the elementary or secondary school courses of study in an educational institution operated by the Government of Ontario,

    (c)   a nursing assistant's school, and

    (d)   a private school as defined in the *Education Act* that is operated by a religious, charitable or benevolent organization;

. . .

"university" means a post-secondary educational institution that is, by an Act of the Assembly, authorized to grant degrees and any affiliated college or institution, a community college and a college of agricultural technology;

"vendor" includes a person who has no fixed place of business in Ontario, or an agent who makes sales on behalf of a principal, and where used in subsection 2 (20) of the Act includes any seller, but does not include a person engaged in the business of farming while that person is not engaged in any other activity but the business of farming;

. . .

"volunteer group" means a group of citizens resident in an unorganized township who perform functions on behalf of, and in the public interest of, the community in that township in or near which they reside, provided that such group is organized and operated for any purpose except profit and that no part of the income from the organization or operation of the group is available for the personal benefit of any member of the group.

[O. Reg. 150/91, s. 1; O. Reg. 624/92, s. 1; O. Reg. 131/93, s. 1; O. Reg. 62/94, s. 1; O. Reg. 375/94, s. 1; O. Reg. 201/95, s. 1; O. Reg. 314/97, s. 1; O. Reg. 444/99, s. 1; O. Reg. 237/00, s. 1; O. Reg. 247/03, s. 1.]

. . .

## RESPONSIBILITIES OF VENDORS

**3.** (1) In this section,

. . .

"valid purchase exemption certificate" means, in respect of a sale of tangible personal property or a taxable service to a person or in respect of a contract of insurance or a benefits plan, a purchase exemption certificate,

(a)  that the person is authorized to use under section 6 of Regulation 1012 of the Revised Regulations of Ontario, 1990 (Definitions, Exemptions and Rebates) made under the Act, and

(b)  that contains all of the information required under subsection 6 (4) of that regulation.

(2) Every vendor shall collect tax from a purchaser on the sale of tangible personal property or a taxable service in respect of which tax is otherwise payable under the Act unless the person provides a valid purchase exemption certificate to the vendor or presents a valid identity card to the vendor.

. . .

(4) If a person provides a purchase exemption certificate to a vendor that does not contain the information required under subsection 6 (4) of Regulation 1012 of the Revised Regulations of Ontario, 1990 (Definitions, Exemptions and Rebates) made under the Act, the vendor shall levy and collect the tax, if any, that would otherwise be payable under the Act on the sale of the tangible personal property or the taxable service to the person or on the payment by the person of the premium under the contract of insurance or benefits plan, as the case may be.

[O. Reg. 448/05, s. 1.]

## REBATE OF TAX

**14.** (1) The Minister may rebate to the governing body of a religious, charitable or benevolent organization an amount as calculated under subsection (3) or (4), in respect of tangible personal property incorporated into a building or structure,

(a)  owned by the organization; or

(b)  leased to the organization for a period of not less than twenty years.

(2) Subsection (1) does not apply with respect to a building or structure that,

(a)  is a university that receives financial assistance directly or indirectly from the province;

(b)  is a school, as defined in clause (a), (b) or (c) of the definition of "school" in section 1;

(c)  is a hospital or nurses' residence; or

(d)    is, or on completion will be, owned by or leased to a municipality or local board.

(2.1) A religious, charitable or benevolent organization is not eligible for a rebate unless it is a registered charity under the *Income Tax Act* (Canada) at the time of applying for the rebate.

(2.2) Subject to subsection (2.2.1), a religious, charitable or benevolent organization is not eligible for a rebate in respect of the purchase, lease or acquisition of a building or structure.

(2.2.1) A religious, charitable or benevolent organization is eligible for a rebate in respect of the lease of a building or structure if,

(a)    the lease is for a period of not less than 20 years;

(b)    under the terms of the lease, possession of the building or structure is to be transferred to the organization immediately following substantial completion of the building or structure; and

(c)    the organization has the right to acquire the building or structure for nil or nominal consideration after the period described in clause (a).

(2.3) A religious, charitable or benevolent organization that leases a building or structure described in subsection (1) is not eligible for a rebate unless, at the time of applying for the rebate, the remaining term of the lease is at least ten years from,

(a)    the date on which it purchased the tangible personal property in respect of which it applies for the rebate; or

(b)    the date on which it entered into a written construction contract under subsection (4).

(3) If the religious, charitable or benevolent organization or the lessor purchases the tangible personal property in respect of which it applies for a rebate, the amount of the rebate comprises the tax paid on the tangible personal property.

(4) If the religious, charitable or benevolent organization or the lessor enters into a written construction contract for the supply and incorporation into a building or structure of the tangible personal property in respect of which the organization applies for a rebate, the amount of the rebate is determined by applying the following percentages to the payments made in satisfaction of the total contract price, which price shall include the price of construction and the architect's fees:

1.    If the payments made in satisfaction of a contract price are subject to the tax imposed by Part IX of the *Excise Tax Act* (Canada), 3.0 per cent of the payments and the tax imposed by Part IX of the *Excise Tax Act* (Canada).

2.    In all situations other than those set out in paragraph 1, 3.4 per cent.

(4.1) If a construction contract pursuant to an arrangement described in subsection (2.2.1) was entered into before March 28, 2003, the amount of the rebate to the governing body of the religious, charitable or benevolent organization shall be determined under subsection (4) using as a total contract price the amount of the total contract price, as otherwise determined, that is paid on or after that date.

(5) No rebate shall be made under subsection (4) with respect to that portion of the contract price that is attributable to,

(a) land or land improvement costs;

(b) the value of performance bonds;

(c) equipment rental charges;

(d) charges for temporary facilities;

(e) building permit fees;

(f) the cost of tangible personal property that does not become a fixture after installation;

(g) demolition charges;

(h) the cost of making, installing or repairing stained glass windows; or

(i) charges for development or project consulting services.

(6) Where a construction contract requires progress payments on account of the contract price to be made by the religious, charitable or benevolent organization or the lessor, the amount to be paid under subsection (1) may be made by instalments equal to the appropriate percentage referred to in subsection (4) of the progress payments required to be made.

(7) An application for a rebate under this section shall be made in writing, and shall set out such information as the Minister may require to determine the eligibility of the applicant for the rebate claimed.

(8) No rebate shall be made under subsection (3) unless the application is made,

(a) within three years after the payment of the tax in respect of which the rebate is claimed if the materials are purchased before the 1st day of January, 1991; or

(b) within four years after the payment of the tax in respect of which the rebate is claimed if the materials are purchased on or after the 1st day of January, 1991.

(9) No rebate shall be made under subsection (4) unless the application is made,

(a) within three years after the last payment has been made under the contract in respect of which the rebate is claimed if the contract is entered into before the 1st day of January, 1991; or

(b) within four years after the last payment has been made under the contract in respect of which the rebate is claimed if the contract is entered into on or after the 1st day of January, 1991.

(10) A religious, charitable or benevolent organization is not eligible for a rebate unless it provides an undertaking, in a form satisfactory to the Minister,

that all of the rebate will be used solely for the religious, charitable or benevolent purposes of the organization.

(11) In this section,

"lessor" means the lessor under a lease of a building or structure in respect of which a religious, charitable or benevolent organization is eligible for a rebate under this section by reason of subsection (2.2.1).

[O. Reg. 150/91, s. 3; O. Reg. 624/92, s. 2; O. Reg. 375/94, s. 2; O. Reg. 247/03, s. 2.]

. . .

**22.** (1) Subject to subsection (2), where a religious, charitable, benevolent or non-profit organization holds, stages or operates in any year, fundraising events including bazaars or rummage sales, the purchaser is exempt from the payment and the organization is exempt from the collection of the tax imposed by subsection 2 (1) of the Act in respect of the tangible personal property sold by that organization at those fundraising events if,

(a) the events are not scheduled on a weekly, monthly or other regularly scheduled basis; and

(b) the organization has paid to the Minister of Finance an amount equal to the amount of any tax in respect of the tangible personal property sold by the organization at the events that would have been payable by the organization if the tangible personal property that the organization purchased for sale at such events had been purchased by the organization for its own consumption and use.

(2) Despite subsection (1), the purchaser shall pay, and the religious, charitable, benevolent or non-profit organization shall collect, tax on prepared food products, where the prepared food products are,

(a) sold by the organization at an occasion or event sponsored or arranged by another organization or person who contracts with the religious, charitable, benevolent or non-profit organization for catering; or

(b) sold on a site or as part of an event where persons in the business of selling prepared food products are selling prepared food products.

(3) A person who purchases prepared food products that are sold as part of a program, whereby the prepared food products are provided at nominal charge to persons who are disabled, disadvantaged or underprivileged or who because of age or an infirmity require support, is exempt from the tax imposed in the Act with respect to the purchase of the prepared food products.

(4) [Repealed, O. Reg. 427/95, s. 1.]

**22.1** (1) A student who receives prepared food products under a meal plan is exempt from the tax imposed by the Act with respect to the prepared food products.

(2) In subsection (1),

"meal plan" means an arrangement whereby a student enrolled at an educational institution is entitled to acquire at least 40 meals consisting of prepared food products over a period of not less than four weeks at a total non-refundable cost to the student of not less than $120 where,

(a)   the meals are acquired from an eating establishment located on the premises of the educational institution and operated by or on behalf of the educational institution, and

(b)   the student pays a single comprehensive price or deposits an amount of money in an account with the educational institution from which the price of the meals acquired by the student is deducted;

"student" means an individual who is enrolled in at least one credit course at an educational institution in Ontario that is a university, a community college or a school that provides residential facilities to the individuals enrolled in courses at the school.

[O. Reg. 427/95, s. 2.]

. . .

**26.** (1) A purchaser is excluded from the exemption from tax that would otherwise be available under subsection 9 (2) of the Act in respect of the price of admission to a professional sporting event in Ontario that is held under the auspices or sponsorship of a sponsor, except in the circumstances described in subsection (2).

(2) Subsection (1) does not apply to a purchaser referred to in that subsection if,

(a)   the sponsor actively participates in planning and managing the professional sporting event;

(b)   the organizer of the event can reasonably anticipate that there will be net proceeds from the event; and

(c)   the sponsor is entitled, under the sponsorship agreement, to receive at least 90 per cent of the net proceeds from the event and intends to use those proceeds solely for the purposes of the sponsor.

(3) In this section,

"direct expenses", with respect to a professional sporting event, do not include travel expenses or expenses relating to the remuneration of players;

"home game" means, in respect of a sports team, a game played by the team in the location where it ordinarily plays games against a team that ordinarily plays its games in another location;

"net proceeds" means, with respect to a professional sporting event, the amount by which the sum of the gate receipts and the broadcasting, parking and concession revenues from the event exceeds the direct expenses of the organizers for the event;

"organizer" means a person who enters into a sponsorship agreement with a sponsor;

"professional league" means Major League Baseball, the Canadian Football League, the National Basketball Association, the National Hockey League, the

National Lacrosse League, United Soccer League or any other league of sports teams in which the players on a team are ordinarily paid salary or other remuneration by the team that is not just a reimbursement of expenses incurred by the players;

"professional sporting event" means a game,

(a) that is played in Ontario as a home game by a sports team that belongs to a professional league, and

(b) that is played during the regular season of the professional league to which the sports team belongs;

"sponsor" means, with respect to a professional sporting event, a person described in clause 9 (2) (a), (b), (c), (e) or (f) of the Act;

"sponsorship agreement" means an agreement between a sponsor and a person under which the sponsor agrees to sponsor one or more professional sporting events.

[O. Reg. 319/01, s. 3.]

# SUBSTITUTE DECISIONS ACT, 1992,

(S.O. 1992, c. 30)

## Part I — Property

*Property Management*

. . .

**37.** (1) **Required expenditures** — A guardian of property shall make the following expenditures from the incapable person's property:

1. The expenditures that are reasonably necessary for the person's support, education and care.

2. The expenditures that are reasonably necessary for the support, education and care of the person's dependants.

3. The expenditures that are necessary to satisfy the person's other legal obligations.

(2) **Guiding principles** — The following rules apply to expenditures under subsection (1):

1. The value of the property, the accustomed standard of living of the incapable person and his or her dependants and the nature of other legal obligations shall be taken into account.

2. Expenditures under paragraph 2 may be made only if the property is and will remain sufficient to provide for expenditures under paragraph 1.

3. Expenditures under paragraph 3 may be made only if the property is and will remain sufficient to provide for expenditures under paragraphs 1 and 2.

(3) **Optional expenditures** — The guardian may make the following expenditures from the incapable person's property:

1. Gifts or loans to the person's friends and relatives.

2. Charitable gifts.

(4) **Guiding principles** — The following rules apply to expenditures under subsection (3):

1. They may be made only if the property is and will remain sufficient to satisfy the requirements of subsection (1).

2. Gifts or loans to the incapable person's friends or relatives may be made only if there is reason to believe, based on intentions the person expressed before becoming incapable, that he or she would make them if capable.

3. Charitable gifts may be made only if,

    i.    the incapable person authorized the making of charitable gifts in a power of attorney executed before becoming incapable, or

    ii.   there is evidence that the person made similar expenditures when capable.

4.    If a power of attorney executed by the incapable person before becoming incapable contained instructions with respect to the making of gifts or loans to friends or relatives or the making of charitable gifts, the instructions shall be followed, subject to paragraphs 1, 5 and 6.

5.    A gift or loan to a friend or relative or a charitable gift shall not be made if the incapable person expresses a wish to the contrary.

6.    The total amount or value of charitable gifts shall not exceed the lesser of,

    i.    20 per cent of the income of the property in the year in which the gifts are made, and

    ii.   the maximum amount or value of charitable gifts provided for in a power of attorney executed by the incapable person before becoming incapable.

(5) **Increase, charitable gifts** — The court may authorize the guardian to make a charitable gift that does not comply with paragraph 6 of subsection (4),

(a)    on motion by the guardian in the proceeding in which the guardian was appointed, if the guardian was appointed under section 22 or 27; or

(b)    on application, if the guardian is the statutory guardian of property.

(6) **Expenditures for person's benefit** — Expenditures made under this section shall be deemed to be for the incapable person's benefit.

[1996, c. 2, s. 24]

# TRUSTEE ACT

(R.S.O. 1990, c. T.23)

**Amended by:** 1992, c. 32, s. 27; 1993, c. 27, Sched.; 1994, c. 27, s. 43 (2); 1998, c. 18, Sched. B, s. 16; 2000, c. 26, Sched. A, s. 15; 2001, c. 9, Sched. B, s. 13; 2002, c. 24, Sched. B, s. 47; 2005, c. 5, s. 71.]

**1. Definitions** — In this Act,

"assign" means the execution and performance by a person of every necessary or suitable deed or act for assigning, surrendering, or otherwise transferring land of which such person is possessed, either for the whole estate of the person so possessed or for any less estate, and "assignment" has a corresponding meaning;

"contingent right" as applied to land includes a contingent and executory interest, and a possibility coupled with an interest, whether the object of the gift or limitation of such interest or possibility is or is not ascertained, and also a right of entry whether immediate or future, vested or contingent;

"convey" applied to a person means the execution and delivery by such person of every necessary or suitable assurance for conveying or disposing to another land whereof such person is seized, or wherein the person is entitled to a contingent right, either for the whole estate or for any less estate, together with the performance of all formalities required by law to the validity of such conveyance, and "conveyance" has a corresponding meaning;

"devisee" includes the heir of a devisee, and the devisee of an heir, and any person who may claim right by devolution of title of a similar description;

"instrument" includes a deed, a will and a written document and an Act of the Legislature, but not a judgment or order of a court;

"land" includes messuages, and all other hereditaments, whether corporeal or incorporeal, chattels and other personal property transmissible to heirs, money to be laid out in the purchase of land, and any share of the same hereditaments and properties, or any of them, and any estate of inheritance, or estate for any life or lives, or other estate transmissible to heirs, and any possibility, right or title of entry or action, and any other interest capable of being inherited, whether the same estates, possibilities, rights, titles and interests, or any of them, are in possession, reversion, remainder or contingency;

"mental incompetent" or "mentally incompetent person" means any person who has been declared a mentally incompetent person;

"mortgage" is applicable to every estate, interest or property, in land or personal estate, that is merely a security for money, and "mortgagee" has a corresponding meaning and includes every person deriving title under the original mortgagee;

"person of unsound mind" means any person, not a minor, who, not having been declared a mentally incompetent person, is incapable, from infirmity of mind, to manage his or her own affairs;

"personal estate" includes leasehold estates and other chattels real, and also money, shares of government and other funds, securities for money (not being real estate), debts, choses in action, rights, credits, goods, and all other property, except real estate, which by law devolves upon the executor or administrator, and any share or interest therein;

"personal representative" means an executor, an administrator, and an administrator with the will annexed;

"possessed" is applicable to any vested estate less than a life estate, legal or equitable, in possession or in expectancy, in any land;

"securities" includes stocks, funds and shares;

"seized" is applicable to any vested interest for life, or of a greater description, and extends to estates, legal and equitable, in possession, or in futurity, in any land;

"stock" includes fully paid-up shares, and any fund, annuity, or security transferable in books kept by any incorporated bank, company or society, or by instrument of transfer, either alone or accompanied by other formalities, and any share or interest therein;

"transfer", in relation to stock, includes the performance and execution of every deed, power of attorney, act or thing, on the part of the transferor to effect and complete the title in the transferee;

"trust" does not mean the duties incident to an estate conveyed by way of mortgage but, with this exception, includes implied and constructive trusts and cases where the trustee has some beneficial estate or interest in the subject of the trust, and extends to and includes the duties incident to the office of personal representative of a deceased person, and "trustee" has a corresponding meaning and includes a trustee however appointed and several joint trustees;

"will" includes,

   (a)    a testament,

   (b)    a codicil,

   (c)    an appointment by will or by writing in the nature of a will in exercise of a power, and

   (d)    any other testamentary disposition.

## RETIREMENT OF TRUSTEES

**2.** (1) **Retirement of trustees** — Where there are more than two trustees, if one of them by deed declares a desire to be discharged from the trust, and if the co-trustees and such other person, if any, as is empowered to appoint trustees, consent by deed to the discharge of the trustee, and to the vesting in the co-trustees alone of the trust property, then the trustee who desires to be discharged shall be deemed to have retired from the trust, and is, by the deed, discharged therefrom under this Act without any new trustee being appointed.

(2) **Application of section** — This section does not apply to executors or administrators.

## APPOINTMENT OF NEW TRUSTEES

**3.** (1) **Power of appointing new trustees** — Where a trustee dies or remains out of Ontario for more than twelve months, or desires to be discharged from all or any of the trusts or powers reposed in or conferred on the trustee, or refuses or is unfit to act therein, or is incapable of acting therein, or has been convicted of an indictable offence or is bankrupt or insolvent, the person nominated for the purpose of appointing new trustees by the instrument, if any, creating the trust, or if there is no such person, or no such person able and willing to act, the surviving or continuing trustees or trustee for the time being, or the personal representatives of the last surviving or continuing trustee, may by writing appoint another person or other persons (whether or not being the persons exercising the power) to be a trustee or trustees in the place of the trustee dying, remaining out of Ontario, desiring to be discharged, refusing or being unfit or incapable.

(2) **Survivorship** — Until the appointment of new trustees, the personal representatives or representative for the time being of a sole trustee, or where there were two or more trustees, of the last surviving or continuing trustee, are or is capable of exercising or performing any power or trust that was given to or capable of being exercised by the sole or last surviving trustee

**4. Authority of surviving trustee to appoint successor by will** — Subject to the terms of any instrument creating a trust, the sole trustee or the last surviving or continuing trustee appointed for the administration of the trust may appoint by will another person or other persons to be a trustee or trustees in the place of the sole or surviving or continuing trustee after his or her death.

**5.** (1) **Power of court to appoint new trustees** — The Superior Court of Justice may make an order for the appointment of a new trustee or new trustees, either in substitution for or in addition to any existing trustee or trustees, or although there is no existing trustee.

(2) **Limitation of effect of order** — An order under this section and any consequential vesting order or conveyance does not operate as a discharge from liability for the acts or omissions of the former or continuing trustees.

[2000, c. 26, Sched. A, s. 15.]

**6. What may be done** — On the appointment of a new trustee for the whole or any part of trust property,

 (a) **increase in number** — the number of trustees may be increased; and

 (b) **separate trustees for distinct trusts** — a separate set of trustees may be appointed for any part of the trust property held on trusts distinct from those relating to any other part or parts of the trust property, even though no new trustees or trustee are or is to be appointed for other parts of the trust property, and any existing trustee may be appointed or remain one of such separate set of trustees or, if only one trustee was originally appointed, then one separate trustee may be so appointed for the first-mentioned part; and

(c) **where not less than two to be appointed** — it is not obligatory to appoint more than one new trustee where only one trustee was originally appointed or to fill up the original number of trustees where more than two trustees were originally appointed but, except where only one trustee was originally appointed, a trustee shall not be discharged under section 3 from the trust unless there will be a trust corporation or at least two individuals as trustees to perform the trust; and

(d) **execution and performance of requisite deeds and acts** — any assurance or thing requisite for vesting the trust property, or any part thereof, in the person who is the trustee, or jointly in the persons who are the trustees, shall be executed or done.

**7. Powers of new trustee** — Every new trustee so appointed, as well before as after all the trust property becomes by law or by assurance or otherwise vested in the trustee, has the same powers, authorities and discretions, and may in all respects act as if the trustee had been originally appointed a trustee by the instrument, if any, creating the trust.

[1993, c. 27, Sched.]

**8. Nominated trustee dying before testator** — The provisions of this Act relative to the appointment of new trustees apply to the case of a person nominated trustee in a will but dying before the testator.

## VESTING INSTRUMENTS

**9. (1) Vesting of trust property in new or continuing trustees without conveyance** — Where an instrument, executed after the 1st day of July, 1886, by which a new trustee is appointed to perform any trust, contains a declaration by the appointor to the effect that any estate or interest in any land subject to the trust, or in any personal estate so subject, shall vest in the person or persons who, by virtue of such instrument, shall become and be the trustee or trustees for performing the trust, that declaration shall, without any conveyance or assignment, operate to vest in the trustee, or in the trustees as joint tenants, and for the purposes of the trust, that estate, interest or right.

**(2) On retirement of a trustee** — Where such an instrument, by which a retiring trustee is discharged under this Act, contains such a declaration as is in this section mentioned by the retiring and continuing trustees, and by the other person, if any, empowered to appoint trustees, that declaration shall, without any conveyance or assignment, operate to vest in the continuing trustees alone as joint tenants, and for the purposes of the trust, the estate, interest or right to which the declaration relates.

**(3) Application to mortgages, stocks, shares, etc.** — This section does not extend to land conveyed by way of mortgage for securing money subject to the trust, or to any share, stock, annuity, or property transferable only in books kept by a company or other body, or in a manner prescribed by or under an Act of the Parliament of Canada or of the Legislature.

(4) **Interpretation for registration purposes** — For the purpose of registration the persons making the declaration shall be deemed the conveying parties, and the conveyance shall be deemed to be made by them under a power conferred by this Act.

## VESTING ORDERS, ORDERS RELEASING CONTINGENT RIGHTS, ETC.

**10.** (1) **Vesting orders** — In any of the following cases,

(a)  where the Superior Court of Justice appoints or has appointed a new trustee; or

(b)  where a trustee entitled to or possessed of any land, or entitled to a contingent right therein, either solely or jointly with any other person is a minor, or is out of Ontario, or cannot be found; or

(c)  where it is uncertain who was the survivor of two or more trustees jointly entitled to or possessed of any land; or

(d)  where it is uncertain whether the last trustee known to have been entitled to or possessed of any land is living or dead; or

(e)  where there is no heir or personal representative of a trustee who was entitled to or possessed of land and has died intestate as to that land, or where it is uncertain who is the heir or personal representative or devisee of a trustee who was entitled to or possessed of land and is dead; or

(f)  where a trustee jointly or solely entitled to or possessed of any land, or entitled to a contingent right therein, has been required by or on behalf of a person entitled to require a conveyance of the land or a release of the right, to convey the land or to release the right, and has wilfully refused or neglected to convey the land or release the right for fourteen days after the date of the requirement,

the Superior Court of Justice may make an order, vesting the land in any such person in any such manner, and for any such estate, as the court may direct, or releasing, or disposing of the contingent right to such person as the court may direct.

(2) **Vesting of estate** — Where the order is consequential on the appointment of a new trustee, the land shall be vested for such estate as the court may direct in the persons who, on the appointment, are the trustees.

(3) **Where trustee out of Ontario** — Where the order relates to a trustee entitled jointly with another person, and such trustee is out of Ontario or cannot be found, the land or right shall be vested in such other person, either alone or with some other person.

[2000, c. 26, Sched. A, s. 15.]

**11. Orders as to contingent rights of unborn persons** — Where any land is subject to a contingent right in an unborn person, or a class of unborn persons, who, on coming into existence, would, in respect thereof, become entitled to or possessed of the land on any trust, the Superior Court of Justice may make an order releasing the land from the contingent right, or may make an order vesting in any person the estate to or of which the unborn person, or class of unborn persons, would, on coming into existence, be entitled or possessed in the land.

[2000, c. 26, Sched. A, s. 15.]

**12. Vesting order in place of conveyance by minor mortgagee** — Where any person entitled to or possessed of land, or entitled to any contingent right in land, by way of security for money, is a minor, the Superior Court of Justice may make an order vesting or releasing or disposing of the land or right in like manner as in the case of a minor trustee.

[2000, c. 26, Sched. A, s. 15.]

**13. (1) Vesting orders as to stock and choses in action** — In any of the following cases,

(a) where the Superior Court of Justice appoints, or has appointed, a new trustee; or

(b) where a trustee entitled alone, or jointly with another person, to stock or to a chose in action,

    (i) is a minor, or

    (ii) is out of Ontario, or

    (iii) cannot be found, or

    (iv) neglects or refuses to transfer stock, or receive the dividends or income thereof, or to sue for or recover a chose in action, according to the direction of the person absolutely entitled thereto, for fourteen days next after a request in writing has been made to the trustee by the person so entitled, or

    (v) neglects or refuses to transfer stock, or receive the dividends or income thereof, or to sue for or recover a chose in action for fourteen days next after an order of the Superior Court of Justice for that purpose has been served on the trustee; or

(c) where it is uncertain whether a trustee entitled, alone or jointly with another person, to stock or to a chose in action is alive or dead,

the Superior Court of Justice may make an order vesting the right to transfer, or call for a transfer of stock, or to receive the dividends or income thereof, or to sue for or recover a chose in action, in any such person as the court may appoint.

(2) **Vesting in new trustee** — Where the order is consequential on the appointment by the court of a new trustee, the right shall be vested in the persons who, on the appointment, are the trustees.

(3) **Vesting in person having joint interest** — Where the person whose right is dealt with by the order was entitled jointly with another person, the right shall be vested in that last-mentioned person either alone, or jointly with any other person whom the court may appoint.

(4) **Appointment of person to transfer** — Where a vesting order may be made under this section, the court may, if it is more convenient, appoint some proper person to make, or join in making, the transfer.

(5) **Transfer, how to be made** — The person in whom the right to transfer or call for the transfer of any stock is vested by an order of the court under this Act

may transfer the stock to himself, herself or itself, or any other person, according to the order, and all incorporated banks and all companies shall obey every order made under this section.

(6) **After notice of order, no transfer to be made contrary thereto** — After notice in writing of an order under this section, it is not lawful for any incorporated bank or any company to transfer any stock to which the order relates, or to pay any dividends thereon except in accordance with the order.

(7) **Court may make declaration** — The Superior Court of Justice may make declarations and give directions concerning the manner in which the right to any stock or chose in action, vested under this Act, is to be exercised.

(8) **Ships, shares in** — The provisions of this Act as to vesting orders apply to shares in ships registered under the Acts relating to merchant shipping as if they were stock.

[2000, c. 26, Sched. A, s. 15.]

## TRUSTEES FOR CHARITIES

**14. Exercise of powers in favour of charities, etc.** — The Superior Court of Justice may exercise the powers herein conferred for the purpose of vesting any land or personal estate in the trustee of any charity or society over which the court would have jurisdiction upon action duly instituted.

[2000, c. 26, Sched. A, s. 15.]

**15. (1) Power to order a sale in proper cases** — Where land is held by trustees for a charitable purpose and it is made to appear that the land can be no longer advantageously used for such charitable purpose or that for any other reason the land ought to be sold, a judge of the Superior Court of Justice may make an order authorizing the sale thereof and may give such directions in relation thereto and for securing the due investment and application of the money arising from the sale as may be considered proper.

(2) **Notice to Public** — No such order shall be made unless notice of the application has been given to the Public Trustee.

[2000, c. 26, Sched. A, s. 15.]

## WHO MAY APPLY

**16. (1) Who may apply for appointment of new trustee, or vesting order, etc.** — An order under this Act for the appointment of a new trustee, or concerning any land or personal estate, subject to a trust, may be made upon the application of any person beneficially interested therein, whether under disability or not, or upon the application of any person duly appointed as a trustee thereof.

(2) **In case of mortgaged property** — An order concerning any land or personal estate subject to a mortgage may be made on the application of any person beneficially interested in the equity of redemption, whether under disability or not, or of any person interested in the money secured by the mortgagee.

## CERTAIN POWERS AND RIGHTS OF TRUSTEES

**17. Power and discretion of trustee for sale** — Subject to the *Estates Administration Act*, where a trust for sale or a power of sale of land or personal estate is vested in a trustee, the trustee may sell or concur with any other person in selling all or any part of the property, either subject to prior charges or not, and either together or in lots, by public auction or by private contract subject to such conditions respecting title or evidence of title or other matter as the trustee thinks fit, with power to vary any contract for sale, and to buy in at any auction, or to rescind any contract for sale and to resell, without being answerable for any loss.

**18.** (1) **Sales by trustees not impeachable on certain grounds** — A sale made by a trustee shall not be impeached by any beneficiary upon the ground that any of the conditions subject to which the sale was made were unnecessarily depreciatory, unless it also appears that the consideration for the sale was thereby rendered inadequate.

(2) **Collusion between purchaser and trustee** — Such sale shall not, after the execution of the conveyance, be impeached as against the purchaser upon the ground that any of the conditions subject to which the sale was made were unnecessarily depreciatory, unless it appears that the purchaser was acting in collusion with the trustee at the time when the contract for the sale was made.

**19. Dedication or sale of land by trustee for municipal highway** — With the approval of the Ontario Municipal Board or of a judge of the Superior Court of Justice, a person who holds land or a charge or claim against it or has control of the legal title, upon any trust or for a specified or particular purpose, may, to the extent of the estate or interest, dedicate or sell, or join in dedicating or selling, to the corporation of the municipality within which it is situate, any portion of the land required by the corporation for the work of establishing, extending, widening or diverting a street, and the Board or the judge may approve thereof if it appears that it will not have the effect of defeating or seriously affecting the substantial objects or intent of the trust or purpose but the approval is not necessary if such dedication or sale is otherwise within such person's powers.

[2000, c. 26, Sched. A, s. 15.]

## POWER TO AUTHORIZE RECEIPT OF MONEY

**20.** (1) **By solicitor** — A trustee may appoint a solicitor as agent to receive and give a discharge for any money or valuable consideration or property receivable by the trustee under the trust.

(2) **By banker** — A trustee may appoint a manager or a branch manager of a bank listed in Schedule I or II to the *Bank Act* (Canada) or a solicitor to be the trustee's agent to receive and give a discharge for any money payable to the trustee under or by virtue of a policy of assurance or otherwise.

(3) **Appointment not a breach of trust** — A trustee shall not be charged with a breach of trust by reason only of having made or concurred in making any such appointment.

(4) **Liability of trustee, in certain cases, not affected** — Nothing in this section exempts a trustee from any liability that would have been incurred if this Act had not been passed, in case the trustee permits any money, valuable consideration, or property to remain in the hands or under the control of the banker or solicitor for a period longer than is reasonably necessary to enable the banker or solicitor to pay or transfer the same to the trustee.

**21.** (1) **Power to insure buildings** — A trustee may insure against loss or damage by fire, tempest or other casualty, any building or other insurable property to any amount, including the amount of any insurance already on foot, not exceeding three-fourths of the value of such building or property, and pay the premiums for such insurance out of the income thereof or out of the income of any other property subject to the same trusts, without obtaining the consent of any person who may be entitled wholly or partly to such income.

(2) **Exception** — This section does not apply to any building or property that a trustee is bound forthwith to convey absolutely to any beneficiary upon being requested to do so.

**22.** (1) **Power of trustees of renewable leaseholds to renew** — A trustee of any leaseholds for lives or years that are renewable from time to time may, if the trustee thinks fit, and shall, if thereto required by any person having any beneficial interest, present or future or contingent, in the leaseholds, use the trustee's best endeavours to obtain from time to time a renewed lease of the same land on reasonable terms, and for that purpose may from time to time make or concur in making a surrender of the lease for the time being subsisting, and do all such other acts as are requisite; but where, by the terms of the settlement or will, the person in possession for life or other limited interest is entitled to enjoy the same without any obligation to renew or to contribute to the expense of renewal, this section does not apply unless the consent in writing of that person is obtained to the renewal on the part of the trustee.

(2) **To raise money for the purpose** — If money is required to pay for the renewal, the trustee effecting the renewal may pay the same out of any money then held in trust for the persons beneficially interested in the land to be comprised in the renewed lease, and, if the trustee does not hold sufficient money for the purpose, the trustee may raise the money required by mortgage of the land to be comprised in the renewed lease, or of any other land for the time being subject to the uses or trusts to which that land is subject, and no person advancing money upon a mortgage purporting to be made under this power is bound to see that the money is wanted, or that no more is raised than is wanted for the purpose or to see to the due application of the money.

**23.** (1) **Filing of accounts** — A trustee desiring to pass the accounts of dealings with the trust estate may file the accounts in the office of the Superior Court of Justice, and the proceedings and practice upon the passing of such accounts shall be the same and have the like effect as the passing of executors' or administrators' accounts in the court.

(2) **Fixing compensation of trustee** — Where the compensation payable to a trustee has not been fixed by the instrument creating the trust or otherwise, the

judge upon the passing of the accounts of the trustee has power to fix the amount of compensation payable to the trustee and the trustee is thereupon entitled to retain out of any money held the amount so determined.

[2000, c. 26, Sched. A, s. 15.]

**23.1** (1) **Expenses of trustees** — A trustee who is of the opinion that an expense would be properly incurred in carrying out the trust may,

(a)　pay the expense directly from the trust property; or

(b)　pay the expense personally and recover a corresponding amount from the trust property.

(2) **Later disallowance by court** — The Superior Court of Justice may afterwards disallow the payment or recovery if it is of the opinion that the expense was not properly incurred in carrying out the trust.

[2001, c. 9, Sched. B, s. 13.]

**24. Receipts of trustees to be effectual discharges** — The payment of any money to and the receipt thereof by any person to whom the same is payable upon any trust, or for any limited purpose, and such payment to and receipt by the survivors of two or more mortgagees or holders or the executors or administrators of such survivors or their assigns, effectually discharges the person paying the same from seeing to the application or being answerable for the misapplication thereof.

**25. Powers of two or more trustees** — Where a power or trust is given to or vested in two or more trustees jointly it may be exercised or performed by the survivor or survivors of them for the time being.

## INVESTMENTS

**26. Investments authorized by other Acts or regulations** — If a provision of another Act or the regulations under another Act authorizes money or other property to be invested in property in which a trustee is authorized to invest and the provision came into force before section 16 of Schedule B of the *Red Tape Reduction Act, 1998*, the provision shall be deemed to authorize investment in the property in which a trustee could invest immediately before the coming into force of section 16 of Schedule B of the *Red Tape Reduction Act, 1998*.

[1998, c. 18, Sched. B, s. 16.]

**27.** (1) **Investment standards** — In investing trust property, a trustee must exercise the care, skill, diligence and judgment that a prudent investor would exercise in making investments.

(2) **Authorized investments** — A trustee may invest trust property in any form of property in which a prudent investor might invest.

(3) **Mutual, pooled and segregated funds** — Any rule of law that prohibits a trustee from delegating powers or duties does not prevent the trustee from investing in mutual funds, pooled funds or segregated funds under variable insurance contracts, and sections 27.1 and 27.2 do not apply to the purchase of such funds.

(4) **Common trust funds** — If trust property is held by co-trustees and one of the co-trustees is a trust corporation as defined in the *Loan and Trust Corpora-*

*tions Act*, any rule of law that prohibits a trustee from delegating powers or duties does not prevent the co-trustees from investing in a common trust fund, as defined in that Act, that is maintained by the trust corporation and sections 27.1 and 27.2 do not apply.

(5) **Criteria** — A trustee must consider the following criteria in planning the investment of trust property, in addition to any others that are relevant to the circumstances:

1. General economic conditions.
2. The possible effect of inflation or deflation.
3. The expected tax consequences of investment decisions or strategies.
4. The role that each investment or course of action plays within the overall trust portfolio.
5. The expected total return from income and the appreciation of capital.
6. Needs for liquidity, regularity of income and preservation or appreciation of capital.
7. An asset's special relationship or special value, if any, to the purposes of the trust or to one or more of the beneficiaries.

(6) **Diversification** — A trustee must diversify the investment of trust property to an extent that is appropriate to,

(a) the requirements of the trust; and
(b) general economic and investment market conditions.

(7) **Investment advice** — A trustee may obtain advice in relation to the investment of trust property.

(8) **Reliance on advice** — It is not a breach of trust for a trustee to rely on advice obtained under subsection (7) if a prudent investor would rely on the advice under comparable circumstances.

(9) **Terms of trust** — This section and section 27.1 do not authorize or require a trustee to act in a manner that is inconsistent with the terms of the trust.

(10) **Same** — For the purposes of subsection (9), the constating documents of a corporation that is deemed to be a trustee under subsection 1 (2) of the *Charities Accounting Act* form part of the terms of the trust.

[1998, c. 18, Sched. B, s. 16; 2001, c. 9, Sched. B, s. 13.]

**27.1** (1) **Trustee may delegate functions to agent** — Subject to subsections (2) to (5), a trustee may authorize an agent to exercise any of the trustee's functions relating to investment of trust property to the same extent that a prudent investor, acting in accordance with ordinary investment practice, would authorize an agent to exercise any investment function.

(2) **Investment plan or strategy** — A trustee may not authorize an agent to exercise functions on the trustee's behalf unless the trustee has prepared a written plan or strategy that,

(a) complies with section 28; and
(b) is intended to ensure that the functions will be exercised in the best interests of the beneficiaries of the trust.

(3) **Agreement** — A trustee may not authorize an agent to exercise functions on the trustee's behalf unless a written agreement between the trustee and the agent is in effect and includes,

(a)   a requirement that the agent comply with the plan or strategy in place from time to time; and

(b)   a requirement that the agent report to the trustee at regular stated intervals.

(4) **Trustee's duty** — A trustee is required to exercise prudence in selecting an agent, in establishing the terms of the agent's authority and in monitoring the agent's performance to ensure compliance with those terms.

(5) **Same** — For the purpose of subsection (4),

(a)   prudence in selecting an agent includes compliance with any regulation made under section 30; and

(b)   prudence in monitoring an agent's performance includes,

(i)   reviewing the agent's reports,

(ii)   regularly reviewing the agreement between the trustee and the agent and how it is being put into effect, including considering whether the plan or strategy of investment should be revised or replaced, replacing the plan or strategy if the trustee considers it appropriate to do so, and assessing whether the plan or strategy is being complied with,

(iii)   considering whether directions should be provided to the agent or whether the agent's appointment should be revoked, and

(iv)   providing directions to the agent or revoking the appointment if the trustee considers it appropriate to do so.

[2001, c. 9, Sched. B, s. 13.]

**27.2** (1) **Duty of agent** — An agent who is authorized to exercise a trustee's functions relating to investment of trust property has a duty to do so,

(a)   with the standard of care expected of a person carrying on the business of investing the money of others;

(b)   in accordance with the agreement between the trustee and the agent; and

(c)   in accordance with the plan or strategy of investment.

(2) **No further delegation** — An agent who is authorized to exercise a trustee's functions relating to investment of trust property shall not delegate that authority to another person.

(3) **Proceeding against agent** — If an agent is authorized to exercise a trustee's functions relating to investment of trust property and the trust suffers a loss because of the agent's breach of the duty owed under subsection (1) or (2), a proceeding against the agent may be commenced by,

(a)   the trustee; or

(b)   a beneficiary, if the trustee does not commence a proceeding within a reasonable time after acquiring knowledge of the breach.

[2001, c. 9, Sched. B, s. 13.]

**28. Protection from liability** — A trustee is not liable for a loss to the trust arising from the investment of trust property if the conduct of the trustee that led to the loss conformed to a plan or strategy for the investment of the trust property, comprising reasonable assessments of risk and return, that a prudent investor could adopt under comparable circumstances.

[1998, c. 18, Sched. B, s. 16.]

**29. Assessment of damages** — If a trustee is liable for a loss to the trust arising from the investment of trust property, a court assessing the damages payable by the trustee may take into account the overall performance of the investments.

[1998, c. 18, Sched. B, s. 16.]

**30. Regulations, agents** — The Attorney General may make regulations governing or restricting the classes of persons or the qualifications of persons who are eligible to be agents under section 27.1 and establishing conditions for eligibility.

[2001, c. 9, Sched. B, s. 13.]

**31. Application, ss. 27-30** — Sections 27 to 30 apply to a trust whether it is created before or after the date section 13 of Schedule B to the *Government Efficiency Act, 2001* comes into force.

[2001, c. 9, Sched. B, s. 13.]

**32.** Repealed: 1998, c. 18, Sched. B, s. 16.

**33.** Repealed: 1998, c. 18, Sched. B, s. 16.

**34.** Repealed: 1998, c. 18, Sched. B, s. 16.

## TECHNICAL BREACHES OF TRUST

**35. (1) Relief of trustees committing technical breach of trust** — If in any proceeding affecting a trustee or trust property it appears to the court that a trustee, or that any person who may be held to be fiduciarily responsible as a trustee, is or may be personally liable for any breach of trust whenever the transaction alleged or found to be a breach of trust occurred, but has acted honestly and reasonably, and ought fairly to be excused for the breach of trust, and for omitting to obtain the directions of the court in the matter in which the trustee committed the breach, the court may relieve the trustee either wholly or partly from personal liability for the same.

(2) **Exception, investment loss** — Subsection (1) does not apply to liability for a loss to the trust arising from the investment of trust property.

[1998, c. 18, Sched. B, s. 16.]

## PAYMENT INTO COURT

**36. (1) Payment into court by trustees of trust funds or securities by order of court** — Where any money belonging to a trust is in the hands or under the control of or is vested in a sole trustee or several trustees and it is the desire of the trustee, or of the majority of the trustees, to pay the money into court, the Superior Court of Justice may order the payment into court to be made by the sole trustee, or by the majority of the trustees, without the concurrence of the other or others if the concurrence cannot be obtained.

(2) **Payment or delivery to Accountant of court** — Where any such money is deposited with a banker or broker or other depository, the court may order payment thereof to the Accountant of the Superior Court of Justice, and payment made under the order is valid and takes effect as if it had been made on the authority or by the act of all the persons entitled to the money paid.

(3) **Payment into court by persons holding trust money for trustee** — Where the trustee has been absent from Ontario for a year and is not likely to return at an early date, or in the event of the trustee's death, or where the trustee in Ontario cannot give an acquittance of the money, any person with whom trust money has been deposited or to whose hands trust money has come may make an application similar to that authorized by subsection (1).

(4) **Money found to be due minor, etc., on final passing of accounts to be paid into court** — Where, on the passing of the final accounts of a personal representative, guardian or trustee by a judge of the Superior Court of Justice, there is found to be in the hands of such personal representative, guardian or trustee any money belonging to a minor or to a mentally incapable person, or to a person whose address is unknown, it is the duty of such personal representative, guardian or trustee to pay the money into the Superior Court of Justice to the credit of the person who is entitled to it.

(5) **Accountant to be furnished with copy of order, etc.** — A certified copy of the order or report of the judge shall be left with the Accountant when the money is paid in, and the person paying it in is entitled to deduct $5 for costs.

(6) **Payment into court of money to which minor or mentally incapable person entitled** — If a minor or mentally incapable person is entitled to any money, the person by whom the money is payable may pay it into court to the credit of the minor or mentally incapable person.

(6.1) **Same** — The payment shall be made to the Accountant of the Superior Court of Justice.

(6.2) **Accompanying affidavit, minor** — If the person entitled to the money is a minor, the person by whom it is payable shall deliver an affidavit containing the following to the Accountant at the time of the payment into court:

1.  A statement that the money is being paid into court under subsection (6).
2.  A statement of the facts entitling the minor to the money.
3.  If the affidavit deals with more than one minor beneficiary's entitlement, the amount of each individual entitlement.
4.  If the amount being paid into court differs from an amount specified in a document that establishes the minor's entitlement, an explanation of the difference.
5.  The minor's date of birth.
6.  The full name and postal address of,
    i.   the minor,
    ii.  the minor's parents, or the parent with lawful custody if it is known that only one parent has lawful custody,

    iii.   any person, if known, who has lawful custody of the minor but is not his or her parent, and

    iv.   any guardian of property, if known, appointed under section 47 of the *Children's Law Reform Act.*

(6.3) **Accompanying affidavit, mentally incapable person** — If the person entitled to the money is a mentally incapable person, the person by whom it is payable shall deliver an affidavit containing the following to the Accountant at the time of the payment into court:

1.    A statement that the money is being paid into court under subsection (6).
2.    A statement of the facts entitling the mentally incapable person to the money.
3.    The mentally incapable person's date of birth.
4.    The full name and postal address of,

    i.   the mentally incapable person,

    ii.   the mentally incapable person's guardian of property, if any, under the *Substitute Decisions Act, 1992,*

    iii.   the person, if known, who holds a continuing power of attorney for property for the mentally incapable person.

(6.4) **Copy of document** — An affidavit under subsection (6.2) or (6.3) shall have attached to it, as a schedule, a copy of any document that establishes,

(a)    the person's entitlement to the money;

(b)    the amount to which the person is entitled;

(c)    any conditions to be met before the person is entitled to receive the money, including, in the case of a minor, the attainment of a specified age.

(6.5) **Discharge** — Payment into court in accordance with subsection (6), (6.2) or (6.3), as the case may be, and with subsection (6.4) is a sufficient discharge for the money paid into court.

(7) **Transfer of trust** — Where a trustee desires to be relieved from the trust, the court may order all property held for the trust to be transferred to the Public Trustee.

(8) **Disposition** — Money paid into court is subject to the order of the court.

(9) **P.G.T.** — Where, however, the Public Guardian and Trustee is the guardian of property of the person to whom money is due, as mentioned in subsections (4) and (6), the money shall be paid to the Public Guardian and Trustee.

[1992, c. 32, s. 27; 2000, c. 26, Sched. A, s. 15.]

## PERSONAL REPRESENTATIVES AND DEVISEES IN TRUST

**37. Removal of personal representatives** — (1) The Superior Court of Justice may remove a personal representative upon any ground upon which the court may remove any other trustee, and may appoint some other proper person or persons to act in the place of the executor or administrator so removed.

**(2) Security by person appointed** — Every person so appointed shall, unless the court otherwise orders, give such security as would be required to be given if letters of administration were granted to the person under the *Estates Act*.

**(3) Who may apply** — The order may be made upon the application of any executor or administrator desiring to be relieved from the duties of the office, or of any executor or administrator complaining of the conduct of a co-executor or co-administrator, or of any person interested in the estate of the deceased.

**(4) When new appointment unnecessary** — Where the executor or adminis trator removed is not a sole executor or administrator, the court need not, unless it sees fit, appoint any person to act in the place of the person removed, and if no such appointment is made the rights and estate of the executor or administrator removed passes to the remaining executor or administrator as if the person so removed had died.

**(5) Chain of representation** — The executor of any person appointed an executor under this section shall not by virtue of such executorship be an executor of the estate of which his or her testator was appointed executor under this section, whether such person acted alone or was the last survivor of several executors.

**(6) Copy of order to be filed** — A certified copy of the order of removal shall be filed with the Estate Registrar for Ontario and another copy with the local registrar of the Superior Court of Justice, and such officers shall, at or upon the entry of the grant in the registers of their respective offices, make in red ink a short note giving the date and effect of the order, and shall also make a reference thereto in the index of the register at the place where the grant is indexed.

**(7) Endorsement** — The date of the grant shall be endorsed on the copy of the order filed with the Estate Registrar for Ontario.

[2000, c. 26, Sched. A, s. 15.]

## RIGHTS AND LIABILITIES OF PERSONAL REPRESENTATIVES

### Actions for torts

**38. (1) Actions by executors and administrators for torts** — Except in cases of libel and slander, the executor or administrator of any deceased person may maintain an action for all torts or injuries to the person or to the property of the deceased in the same manner and with the same rights and remedies as the deceased would, if living, have been entitled to do, and the damages when recovered shall form part of the personal estate of the deceased; but, if death results from such injuries, no damages shall be allowed for the death or for the loss of the expectation of life, but this proviso is not in derogation of any rights conferred by Part V of the *Family Law Act*.

**(2) Actions against executors and administrators for torts** — Except in cases of libel and slander, if a deceased person committed or is by law liable for a wrong to another in respect of his or her person or to another person's property, the person wronged may maintain an action against the executor or administrator of the person who committed or is by law liable for the wrong.

(3) **Limitation of actions** — An action under this section shall not be brought after the expiration of two years from the death of the deceased.

**39. Action of account** — A personal representative has an action of account as the testator or intestate might have had if he or she had lived.

**40. Powers of executor to whom probate granted** — An administrator with the will annexed or an executor to whom probate is granted has all the power conferred by the testator upon the executor named in his or her will and may in all respects act as effectually as though the administrator or executor alone had been named by the testator as the sole executor.

**41. Power of executor to convey land** — Where there is in a will a direction, express or implied, to sell, dispose of, appoint, mortgage, encumber or lease any land, and no person is by the will or otherwise by the testator appointed to execute and carry the same into effect, the executor, if any, named in the will may execute and carry into effect every such direction in respect of such land and any estate or interest therein in the same manner and with the same effect as if appointed by the testator for that purpose.

**42. Power of administrator with will annexed to convey land** — Where from any cause a court of competent jurisdiction has committed to a person, who has given security to the satisfaction of such court for any dealing with such land and its proceeds, letters of administration with a will annexed which contains an express or implied power to sell, dispose of, appoint, mortgage, encumber or lease any land, whether such power is conferred on an executor named in the will or the testator has not by the will or otherwise appointed a person to execute it, the administrator may exercise the power in respect of such land in the same manner and with the same effect as if appointed by the testator for that purpose.

**43. Conveyance by personal representative in pursuance of a contract by deceased** — Where a person has entered into a contract in writing for the sale and conveyance of land and has died intestate or without providing by will for the conveyance of such land to the person entitled or to become entitled to such conveyance, and where the deceased would be bound, were he or she alive, to execute a conveyance, his or her personal representative shall make and give to the person entitled to the same a good and sufficient conveyance of such land, of such nature as the deceased, if living, would be liable to give, but without covenants, except as against the acts of the grantor, and the conveyance is as valid and effectual as if the deceased were alive at the time of the making thereof, and had executed the same, but does not have any further validity or effect.

**44. (1) Power to raise money by sale or mortgage to satisfy charges** — Where by any will coming into operation after the 18th day of September, 1865, a testator charges land, or any specific part thereof, with the payment of debts or with the payment of any legacy or other specific sum of money, and devises the land so charged to executors or to a trustee without any express provision for the raising of such debt, legacy or sum of money out of such land, the devisee may raise such debt, legacy or money by a sale of such land or any part thereof, or by a mortgage of the same.

(2) **Purchaser's position** — Purchasers or mortgagees are not bound to inquire whether the powers conferred by this section, or any of them, have been duly and correctly exercised by the person acting in virtue thereof.

**45. Duties and liabilities of an executor and administrator acting under the powers in this Act** — Every personal representative, as respects the additional powers vested by this Act, and any money or assets received in consequence of the exercise of such powers, is subject to all the liabilities, and compellable to discharge all the duties which, as respects the acts to be done under such powers, would have been imposed upon a person appointed by the testator, or would have been imposed by law upon any person appointed by law, or by any court of competent jurisdiction to execute such power.

**46.** (1) **Survivorship** — Where there are several personal representatives and one or more of them dies, the powers conferred upon them shall vest in the survivor or survivors, unless there is some provision to the contrary in the will.

(2) **Idem** — Until the appointment of new personal representatives, the personal representatives or representative for the time being of a sole personal representative, or, where there were two or more personal representatives, of the last surviving or continuing personal representative, may exercise or perform any power or trust that was given to, or capable of being exercised by the sole or last surviving personal representative.

## EFFECT OF REVOCATION OF AN ERRONEOUS GRANT

### Revocation of erroneous grant

**47.** (1) **Validity of prior acts** — Where a court of competent jurisdiction has admitted a will to probate, or has appointed an administrator, even though the grant of probate or the appointment may be subsequently revoked as having been erroneously made, all acts done under the authority of the probate or appointment, including all payments made in good faith to or by the personal representative, are as valid and effectual as if the same had been rightly granted or made, but upon revocation of the probate or appointment, in cases of an erroneous presumption of death, the supposed decedent, and in other cases the new personal representative may, subject to subsections (2) and (3), recover from the person who acted under the revoked grant or appointment any part of the estate remaining in the person's hands undistributed and, subject to the *Limitations Act, 2002*, from any person who erroneously received any part of the estate as a devisee, legatee or one of the next of kin, or as a spouse of the decedent or supposed decedent, the part so received or the value thereof.

(2) **Expenses** — The person acting under the revoked probate or appointment may retain out of any part of the estate remaining undistributed the proper costs and expenses incurred in the administration.

(3) **Fraud** — Nothing in this section protects any person acting as personal representative where the person has been party or privy to any fraud whereby the grant or appointment has been obtained, or after becoming aware of any fact by reason of which revocation thereof is ordered unless, in the latter case, the person acts under a contract for valuable consideration and otherwise binding made before the person becomes aware of the fact.

(4) **Definition** In this section,

"spouse" means a spouse as defined in section 1 of the *Family Law Act*.

[2002, c. 24, Sched. B, s. 47; 2005, c. 5, s. 71]

## ADMINISTRATION OF ESTATES

**48.** (1) **Payment of debts** — A personal representative may pay or allow any debt or claim on any evidence that the representative thinks sufficient.

(2) **Security and settlement** — A personal representative, or two or more trustees acting together, or a sole acting trustee, where, by the instrument, if any, creating the trust, a sole trustee is authorized to execute the trusts and powers thereof may, if and as they may think fit, accept any composition or any security, real or personal, for any debt or for any property, real or personal, claimed, and may allow any time for payment for any debt, and may compromise, compound, abandon, submit to arbitration or otherwise settle any debt, account, claim or thing whatever relating to the testator's or intestate's estate or to the trust, and for any of these purposes may enter into, give, execute, and do such agreements, instruments of composition or arrangement, releases, and other things as seem expedient without being responsible for any loss occasioned by any act or thing done in good faith.

**49.** (1) **Application of income of estate of deceased person** — Unless a contrary intention appears from the will,

(a) the personal representative of a deceased person, in paying the debts, funeral and testamentary expenses, estate, legacy, succession and inheritance taxes or duties, legacies or other similar disbursements, shall not apply or be deemed to have applied any income of the estate in or towards the payment of any part of the capital of any such disbursements or of any part of the interest, if any, due thereon at the date of death of such person;

(b) until the payment of the debts, funeral and testamentary expenses, estate, legacy, succession and inheritance taxes or duties, legacies, or other similar disbursements mentioned in clause (a), the income from the property required for the payment thereof, with the exception of any part of such income applied in the payment of any interest accruing due thereon after the date of death of the deceased, shall be treated and applied as income of the residuary estate,

but, in any case where the assets of the estate are not sufficient to pay the disbursements in full, the income shall be applied in making up such deficiency.

(2) **Idem** — Subsection (1) shall be deemed always to have been part of the law of Ontario.

(3) **Part application of other rules validated** — Despite subsections (1) and (2), in any case in which the personal representative has before the 30th day of May, 1961 applied any rule of law or of administration different from the provisions of subsection (1), such application is valid and effective.

**50.** (1) **In case of deficiency of assets, debts to rank proportionately** — On the administration of the estate of a deceased person, in the case of a deficiency of assets, debts due to the Crown and to the personal representative of the deceased person, and debts to others, including therein debts by judgment or order, and other debts of record, debts by specialty, simple contract debts and such claims for damages as are payable in like order of administration as simple contract debts shall be paid proportionately and without any preference or priority of debts of one rank or nature over those of another but nothing herein prejudices any lien existing during the lifetime of the debtor on any of the debtor's property.

(2) **Overpayment to creditor** — Where a personal representative pays more to a creditor or claimant than the entitlement under subsection (1), the overpayment does not entitle any other creditor or claimant to recover more than the amount to which the creditor or claimant would be entitled if the overpayment had not been made.

(3) **Relief from personal liability** — Where a personal representative pays more to a creditor or claimant than the entitlement under subsection (1), the court may relieve the personal representative either wholly or partly from personal liability if it is satisfied that the personal representative has acted honestly and reasonably and for the protection or conservation of the assets of the estate.

**51.** (1) **Liability of executor or administrator in respect of covenants, etc., in leases** — Where a personal representative, liable as such to the rents, or upon the covenants or agreements contained in a lease or agreement for a lease granted or assigned to the testator or intestate, has satisfied all liabilities under the lease or agreement for a lease, which accrued due and were claimed up to the time of the assignment hereinafter mentioned, and has set apart a sufficient fund to answer any future claim that may be made in respect of any fixed and ascertained sum covenanted or agreed by the lessee to be laid out on the property demised, or agreed to be demised, although the period for laying out the same may not have arrived, and has assigned the lease, or agreement for lease, to a purchaser thereof, the personal representative may distribute the residuary estate of the deceased to and among the parties entitled thereto, without appropriating any part or any further part thereof, as the case may be, to meet any future liability under the lease or agreement for lease.

(2) **No personal liability for subsequent claim** — The personal representative so distributing the residuary estate is not personally liable in respect of any subsequent claim under the lease or agreement for lease.

(3) **Right to follow assets not affected** — Nothing in this section prejudices the right of the lessor, or those claiming under the lessor, to follow the assets of

the deceased into the hands of the person or persons to or among whom they have been distributed.

**52.** (1) **Liability of personal representative in respect of rents, etc., in conveyances on rent-charge, etc.** — Where a personal representative, liable as such to the rent or upon the covenants or agreements contained in any conveyance on chief rent or rent-charge, whether any such rent is by limitation of use, grant or reservation, or agreement for such conveyance, granted or assigned to or made and entered into with the testator or intestate, has satisfied all liabilities under the conveyance, or agreement for a conveyance, which accrued due and were claimed up to the time of the conveyance hereinafter mentioned, and has set apart a sufficient fund to answer any future claim that may be made in respect of any fixed and ascertained sum covenanted or agreed by the grantee to be laid out on the property conveyed, or agreed to be conveyed, although the period for laying out the same may not have arrived, and has conveyed such property, or assigned such agreement for conveyance to a purchaser thereof, the personal representative may distribute the residuary estate of the deceased to and among the persons entitled thereto, without appropriating any part or any further part thereof, as the case may be, to meet any further liability under the conveyance or agreement for conveyance.

(2) **No personal liability for any subsequent claim** — A personal representative so distributing the residuary estate is not personally liable in respect of any subsequent claim under the conveyance or agreement for conveyance.

(3) **Right of grantor, etc., to follow assets not affected** — Nothing in this section prejudices the right of the grantor, or those claiming under the grantor, to follow the assets of the deceased into the hands of the person or persons to or among whom they have been distributed.

**53.** (1) **Distribution of assets under trust deeds for benefit of creditors, or of the assets of intestate** — A trustee or assignee acting under the trusts of a deed or assignment for the benefit of creditors generally, or of a particular class or classes of creditors, where the creditors are not designated by name therein, or a personal representative who has given such or the like notices as, in the opinion of the court in which such trustee, assignee or personal representative is sought to be charged, would have been directed to be given by the Superior Court of Justice in an action for the execution of the trusts of such deed or assignment, or in an administration suit, for creditors and others to send in to such trustee, assignee or personal representative, their claims against the person for the benefit of whose creditors such deed or assignment is made, or against the estate of the testator or intestate, as the case may be, at the expiration of the time named in the notices, or the last of the notices, for sending in such claims, may distribute the proceeds of the trust estate, or the assets of the testator or intestate, as the case may be, or any part thereof among the persons entitled thereto, having regard to the claims of which the trustee, assignee or representative has then notice, and is not liable for the proceeds of the trust estate, or assets, or any part thereof so distributed to any person of whose claim there was no notice at the time of the distribution.

(2) **Right of creditor to follow assets not affected** Nothing in this section prejudices the right of any creditor or claimant to follow the proceeds of the trust estate, or assets, or any part thereof into the hands of persons who have received the same.

(3) **Subs. (1) not to apply to heirs, etc.** — Subsection (1) does not apply to heirs, next of kin, devisees or legatees claiming as such.

[2000, c. 26, Sched. A, s. 15]

**54. Exercise of general power by will, effect of** — Property over which a deceased person had a general power of appointment, which he or she might have exercised for his or her own benefit without the assent of any other person, shall be assets for the payment of his or her debts where the same is appointed by will, and, under an execution against the personal representatives of such deceased person, such assets may be seized and sold after the deceased person's own property has been exhausted.

**55. Rights and liabilities of executors of executors** — Executors of executors have the same actions for the debts and property of the first testator as he or she would have had if in life, and are answerable for such of the debts and property of the first testator as they recover as the first executors would be if they had recovered the same.

**56. Liability of personal representative of one who commits waste** — The personal representative of any person who, acting with or without authority as executor or administrator, wastes or converts to his or her own use any part of the estate of any deceased person is liable and chargeable in the same manner as the testator or intestate would have been if he or she had been living.

**57. (1) Deficiency of assets** — On the administration of the estate of a deceased person, in case of a deficiency of assets, every creditor holding security on the estate of the deceased debtor or on the estate of a third person for whom the estate of the deceased debtor is only indirectly or secondarily liable, shall place a value on such security and the creditor shall rank upon the distribution of assets only upon the unsecured portion of the claim after deducting the value of the security, unless the personal representative elects to take over the security as hereinafter provided.

(2) **Where personal representative requires creditor to prove claim** — The personal representative of a deceased person who is of the opinion that there may be a deficiency of assets may require any creditor to prove the claim and to state whether security is held for it or any part thereof, and to give full particulars of the same and if such security is on the estate of the deceased debtor or on the estate of a third person for whom the estate of the deceased debtor is only indirectly or secondarily liable, to place a specified value on such security and the personal representative may either consent to the creditor ranking for the amount of the claim after deducting such valuation or may require from the creditor an assignment of the security at an advance of 10 per cent upon the specified value to be paid out of the estate as soon as the personal representative has realized upon such security or is in a position to make payment out of the assets of the estate and in either case the difference between the value at which the security is retained or

taken, as the case may be, and the amount of the claim of the creditor, shall be the amount for which the creditor ranks upon the estate of the deceased debtor.

(3) **Inspectors, directing of; remuneration of** — Where inspectors have been appointed as hereinafter provided or where the estate is being administered under the direction of or by a court, the personal representative in making an election shall act under the direction of the inspectors or of the court, as the case may be, and the remuneration of the inspectors shall be determined by the judge on the passing of accounts.

(4) **Where claim based on negotiable instruments** — If the claim of the creditor is based upon a negotiable instrument upon which the estate of the deceased debtor is only indirectly or secondarily liable and which is not mature or exigible, the creditor shall be considered to hold security within the meaning of this section and shall put a value on the liability of the person primarily liable thereon as the security for the payment thereof, but after the maturity of such liability and its non-payment the creditor is entitled to amend and revalue the claim.

**58. When creditor holding security fails to value same** — Where a creditor fails to value any security held by the creditor which under this Act the creditor is called upon to value, the personal representative may apply to the Superior Court of Justice for an order that unless a specified value is placed on such security and notified in writing to the personal representative, within a time to be limited by the order, such claimant, in respect of the claim or the part thereof for which security is held, is wholly barred of any right to share in the proceeds of the estate unless the judge upon the application of the creditor extends the time for the valuation of the security.

[2000, c. 26, Sched. A, s. 15.]

**59.** (1) **Calling meeting of creditors where there is a deficiency of assets** — Where in the administration of the estate of a deceased person the personal representative fears that there may be a deficiency of assets or that all the creditors will not be paid in full, the personal representative may call a meeting of creditors and lay before them the situation of the estate and at such meeting inspectors may be appointed by the creditors to assist the personal representative in the administration of the estate and to advise with respect thereto.

(2) **Creditors' request for meeting** — In any such case the personal representative shall call a meeting of creditors for the purpose aforesaid at the request in writing of creditors holding 10 per cent of the amount of claims filed against the estate.

(3) **Appointment of creditor as an inspector** — In cases where no meeting of creditors has been held, the personal representative may appoint a creditor or creditors as inspector or inspectors to assist in the realizing and management of the estate but in such case the appointment shall be approved by the judge before the inspectors accept office.

## APPLICATIONS TO COURT FOR ADVICE

**60.** (1) **Trustee, etc., may apply for advice in management of trust property** — A trustee, guardian or personal representative may, without the institution of an action, apply to the Superior Court of Justice for the opinion, advice or direction of the court on any question respecting the management or administration of the trust property or the assets of a ward or a testator or intestate.
[2000, c. 26, Sched. A, s. 15.]

(2) **Indemnity of trustee, etc., acting as advised** — The trustee, guardian or personal representative acting upon the opinion, advice or direction given shall be deemed, so far as regards that person's responsibility, to have discharged that person's duty as such trustee, guardian or personal representative, in the subject-matter of the application, unless that person has been guilty of some fraud, wilful concealment or misrepresentation in obtaining such opinion, advice or direction.

## ALLOWANCE TO TRUSTEES AND PERSONAL REPRESENTATIVES

**61.** (1) **Allowance to trustees, etc.** — A trustee, guardian or personal representative is entitled to such fair and reasonable allowance for the care, pains and trouble, and the time expended in and about the estate, as may be allowed by a judge of the Superior Court of Justice.

(2) **Though estate not before the court** — The amount of such compensation may be settled although the estate is not before the court in an action.

(3) **Allowance to personal representative for services** — The judge, in passing the accounts of a trustee or of a personal representative or guardian, may from time to time allow a fair and reasonable allowance for care, pains and trouble, and time expended in or about the estate.

(4) **Allowance to barrister or solicitor trustee for professional services** — Where a barrister or solicitor is a trustee, guardian or personal representative, and has rendered necessary professional services to the estate, regard may be had in making the allowance to such circumstance, and the allowance shall be increased by such amount as may be considered fair and reasonable in respect of such services.

(5) **Where allowance fixed by the instrument** — Nothing in this section applies where the allowance is fixed by the instrument creating the trust.
[2000, c. 26, Sched. A, s. 15.]

## MISCELLANEOUS

**62. Trustees buying or selling** — A trustee who is either a vendor or a purchaser may sell or buy without excluding the application of section 1 of the *Vendors and Purchasers Act*.

**63. Indemnity** — This Act or an order purporting to be made under it is a complete indemnity to all persons for any acts done under the Act or order, as the case may be.

**64. Costs may be ordered to be paid out of estate** — The Superior Court of Justice may order the costs of and incidental to any application, order, direction, conveyance, assignment or transfer under this Act to be paid or raised out of the property in respect of which it is made, or out of the income thereof, or to be borne and paid in such manner and by such persons as the court considers proper.

[2000, c. 26, Sched. A, s. 15.]

**65. Application of *Perpetuities Act*** — Where in the administration of any trust, estate or fund any question relating to the disposition, transmission or devolution of any property arises, including the right of any person to terminate a trust or an accumulation directed under a trust or other disposition, and it becomes relevant to inquire whether any person is or at a relevant date was or will be capable of procreating or giving birth to a child, section 7 of the *Perpetuities Act* applies to any such question as it applies to questions concerning the rule against perpetuities.

**66. Application of Act** — Subject to section 67, unless otherwise expressed therein, this Act applies to all trusts whenever created and to all trustees whenever appointed.

**67. Powers, etc. under Act and trust instrument** — The powers, rights and immunities conferred by this Act are in addition to those conferred by the instrument creating the trust, and have effect subject to the terms thereof.

**68. Express terms of trust instrument to prevail** — Nothing in this Act authorizes a trustee to do anything that the trustee is in express terms forbidden to do, or to omit to do anything that the trustee is in express terms directed to do by the instrument creating the trust.

# UNIVERSITY FOUNDATIONS ACT, 1992

## (S.O. 1992, c. 22)

**Amended by:** 1993, c. 1, s. 21; O. Reg. 731/93; 2002, c. 8, Sched. P, s. 7; 2004, c. 17, s. 32.

**1. Establishment of foundations** — A foundation is established for each university prescribed by the regulations made under this Act.

**2. Objects** — The objects of each foundation are to solicit, receive, manage and distribute money and other property to support education and research at the university for which the foundation is established.

**3. Crown agency** — Each foundation is a Crown agency within the meaning of the *Crown Agency Act*.

**4.** (1) **Corporation** — Each foundation is a corporation without share capital.

(2) **Composition** — Each foundation is composed of the members of its board of directors.

(3) **Capacity and powers** — A foundation has all the capacity and powers of a natural person for the purpose of carrying out the foundation's objects.

(4) **Use of money received** — A foundation may use money and other property that is received by the foundation for the purpose of carrying out the foundation's objects, subject to any terms under which the money or property was given to the foundation.

(5) **Collection of personal information** — A foundation may collect personal information within the meaning of section 38 of the *Freedom of Information and Protection of Privacy Act* for the purpose of carrying out the foundation's objects.

(6) **Application of *Corporations Act*** — The *Corporations Act* does not apply to a foundation, except as provided by the regulations made under this Act.

(7) **Application of *Corporations Information Act*** — The *Corporations Information Act* does not apply to a foundation.

**5.** (1) **Board of directors** — The affairs of each foundation are under the control and management of the foundation's board of directors.

(2) **Composition** — The board of directors shall be composed of not less than five and not more than eleven members.

(3) **Appointment** — The Lieutenant Governor in Council shall appoint the members of the board.

(4) **Term of office** — The members of the board shall be appointed to hold office for terms not exceeding three years and may be reappointed.

(5) **Remuneration** — The members of the board shall not receive any remuneration, but the foundation may reimburse members of the board for their reasonable expenses.

(6) **Chair** — The Minister shall designate one of the members of the board as the chair of the board and may designate another member as the vice-chair of the board.

(7) **Duty of chair** — The chair shall preside over all meetings of the board.

(8) **Acting chair** — If the chair is absent or unable to act or if the office is vacant, the vice-chair shall exercise and perform the powers and duties of the chair.

(9) **Quorum** — A majority of the members of the board constitutes a quorum.

(10) **By-laws** — The board may pass by-laws regulating its proceedings, specifying the powers and duties of the officers and employees of the foundation and generally for the control and management of the affairs of the foundation.

**6.** (1) **Policy directives** — The Minister of Colleges and Universities may issue policy directives that have been approved by the Lieutenant Governor in Council on matters relating to a foundation's exercise of its powers and duties.

(2) **Consultation** — Before issuing a policy directive, the Minister shall consult with the board of directors of the foundation with respect to the content and effect of the directive on the foundation.

(3) **Best interests** — Compliance with a policy directive shall be deemed to be in the best interests of the foundation.

(4) **Power** — The foundation may do such things as in its opinion are necessary, usual or incidental to the furtherance of the objectives set out in a policy directive.

(5) **Directors** — The members of the board of directors shall ensure that policy directives are implemented promptly and efficiently.

(6) **Notice** — If a policy directive is issued under subsection (1), the Minister shall cause it to be published in *The Ontario Gazette* and shall give or cause to be given notice of the directive to all members of the Assembly.

**7. Indemnification** — A foundation shall indemnify a director or officer of the foundation or a former director or officer of the foundation for any obligation arising from an act done in good faith in the execution of the person's duties or from any neglect or default in the execution in good faith of the person's duties.

**8. Fiscal year** — The fiscal year of each foundation begins on the 1st day of April in each year and ends on the 31st day of March of the following year.

**9.** (1) **Auditor** — The board of directors of each foundation shall appoint one or more auditors licensed under the *Public Accountancy Act* to audit the accounts and transactions of the foundation.

(2) **Auditor General** — The Auditor General may also audit the accounts and transactions of a foundation.

[2004, c. 17, s. 32]

**10.** (1) **Annual report** — Each foundation shall, after the close of each fiscal year, deliver to the Minister of Colleges and Universities an annual report on the affairs of the foundation, including an audited financial statement.

(2) **Tabling** — The Minister shall submit the annual report to the Lieutenant Governor in Council and shall then table the report in the Assembly.

(3) **Other reports** — The Minister may require a foundation to submit such other reports as the Minister requires on the affairs of the foundation.

**11.** (1) **Regulations** — The Lieutenant Governor in Council may make regulations,

(a) prescribing an institution mentioned in the Schedule as a university for which a foundation shall be established by this Act;

(b) prescribing the name of a foundation established by this Act;

(c) authorizing personal information within the meaning of section 38 of the *Freedom of Information and Protection of Privacy Act* to be collected by a foundation established by this Act in a manner other than directly from the individual to whom the information relates, and regulating the manner in which the information is collected;

(d) making a provision of the *Corporations Act* applicable to a foundation;

(e) adding a post-secondary educational institution to the Schedule.

(2) **Revocation** — If a regulation prescribing an institution under clause (1) (a) is revoked, the foundation established by this Act ceases to exist and the assets and liabilities of the foundation become assets and liabilities of the institution.

**12. Commencement** — This Act comes into force on the day it receives Royal Assent.

**13. Short title** — The short title of this Act is the *University Foundations Act, 1992*.

## SCHEDULE

Brock University
Carleton University
Lakehead University
Laurentian University of Sudbury
McMaster University
Nipissing University
Ontario College of Art & Design
Queen's University at Kingston
Ryerson University
The University of Western Ontario
Trent University
University of Guelph
University of Ottawa/Université d'Ottawa
University of Toronto
University of Waterloo
University of Windsor
Wilfrid Laurier University
York University

[1993, c. 1, s. 21; 2002, c. 8, Sched. P, s. 7; O. Reg. 731/93; s. 2.]

# GENERAL

(O. Reg. 731/93)

## PRESCRIBED INSTITUTIONS

**1.** (1) Each institution listed in Column 1 of the Table is prescribed as a university for which a foundation shall be established by the Act.

(2) The name listed in Column 2 of the Table opposite an institution listed in Column 1 is prescribed as the name of the foundation established by the Act for that institution.

. . .

TABLE

PRESCRIBED INSTITUTIONS

| COLUMN 1 | COLUMN 2 |
|---|---|
| 1. Brock University | Brock University Foundation |
| 2. Carleton University | Carleton University Foundation |
| 3. Lakehead University | Lakehead University Foundation |
| 3.1 McMaster University | McMaster University Foundation |
| 4. Queen's University at Kingston | Foundation at Queen's University at Kingston |
| 5. Trent University | Trent University Foundation |
| 6. University of Guelph | University of Guelph Foundation |
| 6.1 University of Ottawa/Université d'Ottawa | University of Ottawa Foundation/ Fondation de l'Université d'Ottawa |
| 7. [Repealed O. Reg. 324/03] | |
| 8. [Repealed O. Reg. 324/03] | |
| 8.1 University of Windsor | University of Windsor Foundation |
| 9. [Repealed O. Reg. 324/03] | |
| 10. [Repealed O. Reg. 324/03] | |

[O. Reg. 781/93, s. 1; O. Reg. 309/94, s. 1; O. Reg. 51/95, s. 1; O. Reg. 324/03]

# Index

*Note: All numerical references are to section and subsection numbers for the Acts and Regulations.*

The following abbreviations are used in this Index:

AA – Accumulations Act, R.S.O. c. A.5
ASA – Assessment Act, R.S.O. c. A.31
AAET – Approved Acts of Executors and Trustees, O. Reg. 4/01
CA – Corporations Act, R.S.O. 1990, c. C.38
CAA – Charities Accounting Act, R.S.O. 1990, c. C.10
CC – Criminal Code, R.S.C. 1985, c. C-46
CCA – Canada Corporations Act, R.S.C. 1970, c. C-32
CCPECL – Canadian Cultural Property Export Control List, C.R.C., c. 448
CCR – Canada Corporations Regulations, C.R.C., c. 424
CGA – Charitable Gifts Act, R.S.O. 1990, c. C.8
CMA – Civil Marriage Act
CPEIA – Cultural Property Export and Import Act (R.S.C. 1985, c. C-51)
CPER – Cultural Property Export Regulations, C.R.C., c. 449
CR-G – Corporations Regulation – General, R.R.O. 1990, Reg. 181
CR(SI)A – Charities Registration (Security Information) Act, S.C. 2001, c. 41, s. 113
CTA – Corporations Tax Act, R.S.O. 1990, c. C.40
C-USTCA – Canada-United States Tax Convention Act, 1984, S.C. 1984, c. 20
DFA – Donation of Food Act, 1994, S.O. 1994, c.19
EA – Education Act, R.S.O. 1990, c. E.2
ESA – Estates Act, R.S.O. 1990, c. E.21
HCIIA – Hospitals and Charitable Institutions Inquiries Act, R.S.O. 1990, c. H.15
ITA – Income Tax Act, R.S.C. 1985, c.1 (5th Supp.)
ITR – Income Tax Regulations, C.R.C., c. 945
LTA – Land Transfer Act, R.S.O. 1990, c. L.6
MCA – Ministry of Community and Social Services Act, R.S.O. c. M.20
MUA – Municipal Act, 2001, S.O. 2001, c. 25
PA – Perpetuities Act, R.S.O. 1990, c. P.9
PLA – Provincial Land Tax Act, R.S.O. 1990, c. P. 32
PGA – Public Guardian and Trustee Act, R.S.O. 1990, c. P.51
ROLA – Religious Organizations' Lands Act, R.S.O. 1990, c. R.23
RSA – Retail Sales Tax Act, R.S.O. c. R.31
SA – Substitute Decisions Act, 1992, S.O. 1992, c.30
TA – Trustee Act, R.S.O. 1990, c. T.23
UFA – University Foundations Act, 1992, S.O. 1992, c. 22
UFR-G – University Foundations Regulation – General, O. Reg. 731/9

## ACCUMULATIONS ACT

CHILDREN, SAVING RE DEBTS OR
  PORTIONS FOR, AA 2
EMPLOYEE BENEFIT TRUSTS, AA 3
INVALID ACCUMULATIONS, AA 1(6)
MAXIMUM ACCUMULATIONS PERIODS,
  AA 1(1)-(3)
PREVIOUS ACTS, AA 1(4)
PURCHASE OF LAND, ACCUMULATIONS

FOR, AA 1(5)

## APPROVED ACTS OF EXECUTORS AND TRUSTEES (under CAA)

APPROVAL OF SPECIFIED ACTS, AAET 1
AUTHORIZATION TO INDEMNIFY, AAET 2
COMBINING PROPERTY HELD FOR
  RESTRICTED OR SPECIAL PURPOSES,
  AAET 3

## ASSESSMENT ACT

AGREEMENTS, ASA 55

CHANGES IN TAX LIABILITY, ASA 32(3), (5)

CONSERVATION/MANAGED FOREST
LAND, ASA 19(5.2)

EXEMPTIONS, ASA 3, 4, 6
- conservation land ASA O. Reg. 282/98, ss. 24-46
- errors re, ASA 33(3)-(6)

LAND ASSESSED AGAINST OWNER, ASA
17, 17.1

LARGE COMMERCIAL THEATRES
(TORONTO), ASA 27.1

PIPELINE ON EXEMPT PROPERTY, ASA
25(10), (11)

REGULATIONS, POWER TO MAKE, ASA
2(2)

SUPPLEMENTARY ASSESSMENTS, ASA
34(1)

## CANADA CORPORATIONS ACT

ACCOUNT AND ACCOUNTING RECORDS,
CCA 117

ACTION BETWEEN COMPANY AND
SHAREHOLDERS, CCA 147

AUDIT
- annual audit, CCA 132(1)
- auditor's report, CCA 132(2)

AUDITOR
- access to records, CCA 132(4)
- appointment, CCA 130, CCA 130(7)
- attendance at meetings, CCA 132(5)
- disqualification for appointment, CCA 131
- notice of appointment, CCA 130(8)
- notice of intention to nominate, CCA 130(3)
- removal, CCA 130(5)
- remuneration, CCA 130(6)
- report of, CCA 132(2)
- required attendance, CCA 132(6)
- statement of auditor's position, CCA 131(3)
- statements, CCA 132(3)
- vacancy, CCA 130(4)

BANKRUPTCY
- notice, CCA 133(12)

BOOKS
- account and accounting records, CCA 117
- contents, CCA 109
- evidence, CCA 138
- neglect to keep books, CCA 113
- rectification, CCA 218(4), CCA 218(5)
- refusal to produce books, CCA 115(3)

- registrations and transfers, CCA 218(2), CCA
  218(3)
- shareholder list, CCA 111.1

BORROWING POWERS
- debentures
- • perpetual debenture, CCA 66
- • reissue, CCA 67
- delegation of powers, CCA 65(2)
- generally, CCA 65(1)
- limitation, CCA 65(3)

BY-LAWS
- change of provisions, CCA 20(4)
- companies without share capital, CCA 155(2),
  CCA 155(3)
- evidence, CCA 139

CAPACITY, CCA 218(1)

CHARGES
- acquisition of property, CCA 68(4)
- copies, CCA 68(11)
- delivery of prescribed particulars,
  CCA 68(1)–(3)
- failure to comply, CCA 68(9)
- information, CCA 68–73
- inspection, CCA 72–73
- particulars, CCA 68(6)
- register
- company's, CCA 71
- • inspection, CCA 73
- • Minister's, CCA 68(5), CCA 68(10), CCA 70

CHARTER
- forfeiture, CCA 31
- revival, CCA 31(3)
- surrender, CCA 32–33

COMPANIES WITH SHARE CAPITAL
- accounts, CCA 117–133
- audits, CCA 117–133
- books, CCA 109–116
- borrowing powers, CCA 65–67
- change of provisions of letters patent, CCA 20
- charter
- • forfeiture, CCA 31
- • revival, CCA 31(3)
- surrender, CCA 32–33
- contracts, CCA 21–23
- directors, CCA 93–99
- evidence, CCA 138–143
- fees, CCA 151
- formation of new companies, CCA 5.6–12
- general powers and duties, CCA 15–16
- head office, CCA 24
- interpretation, CCA 3

CANADA CORPORATIONS REGULATIONS
— *Cont'd*
INTERPRETATION, CCR 2, CCR 12, CCR 32
NAMES. *See* CORPORATE NAMES
NOTICE
• directors' circular, CCR 51
• dissident's proxy circular, CCR 39
• management proxy circular, CCR 34
OFFICERS
• statement of remuneration, CCR Sched. I
  Form 4
PROXIES AND PROXY SOLICITATION
• date of proxy circular information, CCR 40
• dissident's proxy circular
• • accompanying statement, CCR 39
• • contents, CCR 36–39
• • dissident, defined, CCR 35
• financial statements, CCR 41
• interpretation, CCR 32
• management proxy circular
• • accompanying statement, CCR 34
• • contents, CCR 33
SHORT TITLE, CCR 1
STATUTORY DECLARATION, CCR Sched. I
  Form 6
TAKE-OVER BIDS
• amendment, CCR 49
• certificate required, CCR 48
• directors' approval, CCR 46
• directors' circular
• • certificate required, CCR 55
• • contents, CCR 50
• • directors' approval, CCR 53
• • experts' consent, CCR 54
• • notice, CCR 51
• • report to accompany financial statements,
  CCR 52
• experts' consent, CCR 47
• offeror has effective control, CCR 45
• take-over bid circular under ss.135.6(2), CCR 42
• take-over bid circular under ss.135.92, CCR
  43–44

### CANADA-UNITED STATES TAX CONVENTION ACT, 1984

EXEMPT ORGANIZATIONS, C–USTCA
  Sched. I

### CANADIAN CULTURAL PROPERTY EXPORT CONTROL LIST (under CPEIA)

APPLIED AND DECORATIVE ART
  OBJECTS, 1–6, CCPECL Group IV
ARCHAEOLOGY, 4, CCPECL Group I
CARTOGRAPHY, 4, CCPECL Group VII
ETHNOGRAPHIC MATERIAL CULTURE, 1–
  2, CCPECL Group II
FINE ART, 1–7, CCPECL Group V
GRAPHIC RECORDS
• cartography, 4, CCPECL Group VII
• general, 9, CCPECL Group VII
• iconography, 6, CCPECL Group VII
• interpretation, 3, CCPECL Group VII
• photography, 5, CCPECL Group VII
ICONOGRAPHY, 6, CCPECL Group VII
INTERPRETATION, CCPECL 2
MILITARY OBJECTS, 1–2, CCPECL Group III
MINERALOGY, 2, CCPECL Group I
MUSICAL INSTRUMENTS, 1–4, CCPECL
  Group VIII
OBJECT
• applied and decorative art
• • described, 2–6, CCPECL Group IV
• • interpretation, 1, CCPECL Group IV
• defined, CCPECL 2
• ethnographic material culture
• • defined, 2, CCPECL Group II
• • interpretation, 1, CCPECL Group II
• fine art
• • described, 2–7, CCPECL Group V
• • interpretation, 1, CCPECL Group V
• military objects, 1–2, CCPECL Group III
• recovered from Canadian soil or waters
• • archaeology, 4, CCPECL Group I
• • interpretation, 1, CCPECL Group I
• • mineralogy, 2, CCPECL Group I
• • palaeontology, 3, CCPECL Group I
• scientific or technological objects
• • described, 2–5, CCPECL Group VI
• • interpretation, 1, CCPECL Group VI
PALAEONTOLOGY, 3, CCPECL Group I
PHOTOGRAPHY, 5, CCPECL Group VII
SCIENTIFIC OR TECHNOLOGICAL
  OBJECTS, 1–5, CCPECL Group VI
SHORT TITLE, CCPECL 1
SOUND RECORDINGS, 7–8, 9, CCPECL Group
  VII
TEXTUAL RECORDS, 1–2, 9, CCPECL Group
  VII

# EDUCATION ACT

# ESTATES ACT

# HOSPITALS AND CHARITABLE INSTITUTIONS INQUIRIES ACT

# INCOME TAX ACT

## UNIVERSITY FOUNDATIONS REGULATION - GENERAL (under UFA)